THE
CIVIL WAR

CLASSIC CONFLICTS

THE
CIVIL WAR

A HISTORICAL ACCOUNT OF AMERICA'S WAR OF SECESSION

WILLIAM C. DAVIS

SMITHMARK

A SALAMANDER BOOK

This edition published in 1996 by SMITHMARK Publishers,
a division of U.S. Media Holdings, Inc.,
16 East 32nd Street,
New York, NY 10016

1 3 5 7 9 8 6 4 2

SMITHMARK books are available for bulk purchase for sales
promotion and premium use. For details write or call the manager
of special sales, SMITHMARK Publishers Inc.,
16 East 32nd Street,
New York, NY 10016;
(212) 532-6600

ISBN 0-8317-7416-9

All correspondence concerning the content of this book should be
addressed to Salamander Books Ltd,
129–137 York Way,
London N7 9LG,
England

CREDITS

Designed by DW Design, London
Filmset by SX Composing
Printed in the United States of America

This book was originally published in three illustrated volumes:
Fighting Men of the Civil War, Commanders of the Civil War and
Battlefields of the Civil War.

CONTENTS

INTRODUCTION

When North and South lost their sense, their inhibitions, and their tempers, and went to war against each other, none could say with certainty how it all would end, though every man who stepped forward to enlist thought, at that instant, that he knew. Ironically, there was one man, already long dead when the first shots were fired in 1861, who had known.

William Jenks wrote what must unquestionably be the very first history of the American Civil War. It was a tiny tome – more of a long pamphlet, really – and with the ungainly title *A Memoir of the Northern Kingdom.* Yet in it Jenks captured the very essence of the conflict. He told how generations of agitation over slavery and the nature of the national compact finally brought the sections to blows. He told of the role of the press and the pulpit in exciting passions sufficiently to sever the bonds of blood and brotherhood. He told of the rise of a Republican Party, and of how one Republican from Illinois dominated the conflict.

In its pages, *A Memoir of the Northern Kingdom* detailed the recurring campaigns and the bloody battles, conflicts that turned Virginia especially into a blood-sodden dominion. Jenks wrote of the four years the war lasted, and of how, finally, exhausted and overwhelmed, the South yielded to the North and the country was reunited, now to be forever more not the *Union* but the *United States.* There was nothing new in Jenks' narration, no surprises, no great insights. It was in broad outline, much the same story as every one of the thousands of Civil War histories that would follow.

Only Jenks wrote his account in 1808 – fifty-three years *before* the Civil War began. He wrote it as a political tract in opposition to the administration of President James Madison. And yet his fictional predictions were almost uncannily correct. When Jenks wrote of Illinois Republicans, he was speaking of the rising power of what were then called Westerners in national affairs. Yet just a year after the pamphlet appeared, Abraham Lincoln was born, and one day to be forever identified with Illinois, and the Republicans. Jenks only serious misprediction was in saying that the war would come in 1856 instead of 1861. But then, in that earlier year a South Carolina Congressman attacked a Massachusetts Senator in the

Capitol and beat him senseless, and out in Kansas pro- and anti-slavery forces were already killing each other. Certainly some could see in those acts the first *real* blows of the Civil War.

Jenks' work was long forgotten and he dead when Confederate guns opened fire on Fort Sumter on April 12, 1861, and the shooting war finally commenced for real. He should have been remembered, for he had been able to see half a century ahead of its coming what all of them should have seen, and many did fear. Already by 1808 the divisions and the issues that would disunite the states were at their insidious work. The seemingly insoluble sore of slavery tore at American vitals in 1808 just as it would decades later. Even then the questions of nationalism versus regionalism made men take sides against each other. It was all there for them to see, if only they had been able to see beyond their temporal prejudices and ambitions and fears.

But they did not see it, momentous as it was, until it was too late and the catastrophe that Jenks predicted engulfed them. Indeed, some affairs in the lives of men and the histories of nations may be so great, so tangled, and so deep-rooted, that compromise alone cannot settle them. Perhaps America needed a war to purge itself and to come to an understanding of itself. If so, it paid surely the heaviest price ever exacted of a free people in the act of defining freedom.

In the four years ahead of them all that dark dawn in April, they would meet each other on 10,000 battlefields of that war. More than two and one-half million of their men would go to war, and at least 620,000 of them would never return. Massive armies clashed at country crossroads destined to be forever remembered. Indeed, so great were these forces of North and South that when the Army of the Potomac and the Army of Northern Virginia met in battle at Fredericksburg, Virginia, in December 1862, they constituted between their populations, enough men to form the fifth largest city on the continent, larger even than Boston or New Orleans. That was the scale of this war.

Moreover, wherever they went, they left a landscape scarred, cities blighted, and a civilian population traumatized by the unholy mess of it all. Richmond, Charleston, Atlanta, Columbia, and more, were nearly destroyed. Scarcely a single ante-bellum building survives in Atlanta today thanks to the fires of 1864. A whole section of Richmond is still known as "the Burnt District," even to people who have no idea where the name comes from. In some rural communities, virtually the entire military age male population went to war and did not come home. Families ceased to be. Men changed the course of rivers as mighty as the James and the Mississippi. Whole industries like railroading mushroomed overnight, while others like whaling disappeared forever, casualties of the war. The shots fired in America echoed around the world, as its war with itself suddenly thrust the country onto the world stage and made the resultant reunited states a major global power for the first time.

Yet first and last, and most of all, the conflict happened here, to us, and by us. Those young men who went off to war, gaily at first, filled with enthusiasm and cheer and high hopes, and later grudgingly, impelled by grim determination or fatalism rather than élan, were the mercury of their generation. As the heat of the conflict rose, so did their determination and their sacrifice. And miraculously, when the guns stopped and the battlefields cooled, so did their tempers and their bitterness. No people in history ever went to war with each other so explosively, to return to peace so completely and with so little bitterness. It could only have happened because of the nature of Johnny Reb and Billy Yank. For all the willingness with which they maimed and killed each other, somehow they never came to hate each other. If anything, four years of being adversaries taught them instead just how much they had in common. Fighting bred not rancor, but respect.

And through it all they retained their distinctive character as young Americans. In their compassion they were remarkable. On innumerable fields soldiers held their fire rather than bring down a foeman who had shown particular bravery. At Fredericksburg there was Richard Kirkland, who had done his best to kill the Yankees charging up Marye's Heights toward him, but who then collected canteens and went over the stone wall between the lines to take water to the enemy wounded and dying. Elsewhere their humor and sense of irony sustained them in the darkest hours, like the Yankee on the Virginia Peninsula in 1862 who had a bad tooth pulled, and then eased the pain in his jaw by ramming the tooth down his rifle barrel and firing it across the lines at the Confederates. Theirs was an irrepressible sense of fun, and if they were all too often behaving badly, it was not out of maliciousness, but rather from the inventive spirit of rambunctious youth with time on its hands.

Even more surprising is how many of these young men, with no background at war and no training as soldiers, emerged to become leaders. The youngest generals in American history won their stars in the Civil War. George Armstrong Custer remains to date the youngest major general in our past. One Confederate boy became a brigadier just after his twenty-first birthday, while the Pennsylvanian Galusha Pennypacker overcame his dreadful name to become a general when he was not yet old enough to vote for the president who signed his commission.

Leadership was a vital component in this war, and there were many kinds. At its most elemental, leadership was the company corporal, and even more so the sergeant, who drilled the men and bullied and mothered them in camp and on the march, and who stood shoulder to shoulder with them in the time of trial on the battlefield. Not a few men who began the war as boy privates, grew to company noncommissioned rank, then on through the commissioned ranks even to become colonels commanding regiments. They had learned leadership from the ground up in the school of the soldier, and had learned as well to earn the respect of the men they expected to follow their example and their orders.

Of course, best known of all the leaders are the 1,000 or more men who became generals Blue and Gray. Some were destined to command from birth, like Robert E. Lee. Others' destiny in infancy would seem to have been poverty and obscurity, as with Nathan Bedford Forrest, but the chances of war propelled them to the very heights of glory. Men in this war expected their leaders to lead from the front, which did wonders for inspiration and example, but cost a high price in the death of outstanding officers who fell while needlessly exposing themselves. It is no wonder then that the best died first, and as the war dragged on, the quality of leadership at many levels deteriorated, just as did the quality of the soldiers in the ranks. But still they persevered, and out of the conflict came immortal names never to be forgotten here or around the world – Lee, Grant, Sherman, Jackson, Stuart, Forrest, and a host of others. Indeed, for the next several generations to follow Appomattox, the American military would continue to define leadership by the example of these daring, gallant, and often inspiring commanders.

Inevitably it was on the battlefield that the spirit and patriotism of the men in the ranks, and the ability of their leaders, came together to try to decide the issue. The Civil War was a war on a host of fronts, economic, civil, diplomatic, industrial, and more. But first and foremost it was a *war*, and *battles* decide wars. For one thing, it was to be a global war for many Americans, for the navies North and South plied every sea on the planet, the Confederates in their dread raiders like the *Alabama* and the *Shenandoah* preying mercilessly on Yankee shipping, and the great Yankee cruisers trying vigilantly to hunt them down. The men on those ships fought a special kind of war, one of simultaneously greater and lesser freedom than that of their comrades in the armies. They ate better and saw much of the world, but for them the tedium of a soldier's camp life was compressed to the confines of a deck for months at a time.

On those other battlefields, the ones that sowed the fields of Virginia and Tennessee and Missouri with iron and lead, more than two million men strove to settle the issue, and then for the rest of time they and their descendants would argue over which battle was the one, the *decisive* fight that turned the tide. The truth, of course, is that *none* of them was decisive, and *all* of them were. A battle might decide the result of a campaign, and the result of a campaign might settle the course of a whole season, even a whole year, but no battle turned the issue of the entire war. As late as the fall of 1864, a different outcome in the Atlanta Campaign might very possibly have changed the course of the rest of the conflict, and with it the Union. The fact is that every event of that war was contingent on what came before. No battle stood alone; they were all a part of a fabric that, like a banner in the wind, fluttered this way then that in response to changes in the breeze. In the end, of course, it was an irresistible North wind that brought down the Confederacy, yet forever more people will argue and ask "what if?"

What we can say of the battles is that they show men at their worst and their best, they reveal the working of men's minds and hearts on the greatest game board of all amid a sort of bloody chess in which all of them, from general to private, are pawns caught up in events they did not cause, but forced by rules as old as time to fight the wars that politicians make.

None of them could know that as Charleston spun toward the sun that April morning in 1861. Many expected there to be no fight, much less any war. A sensible few like Jefferson Davis and William T. Sherman, expected a long and bloody war, and sensed that the continent would be changed by its outcome. A garrison of hardly 100 shivering and hungry Yankees in a brick fort surrounded by an ersatz assemblage of rustics and dandies in the batteries ringing Charleston harbor, hardly seemed the sort of fulcrum on which the course of nations – perhaps even a world – would pivot. But with that first signal shell that exploded over the harbor at 4:30 in the morning, the lever began to move. Fort Sumter was not enough to stop its ardent Confederate besiegers, but it was more than enough to start a war. In its wake, the millions who would leave home to become soldiers, the thousands of them who would stand or fail the test of leadership, and the endless miles of innocent America that they would turn into battlegrounds, all awaited the coming dawn to learn what history had in store for them. And as they confidently and hopefully marched into that brutal enlightenment, they left behind them a record that will capture men's imaginations as long as we continue to thrill at bravery or weep at sacrifice. In a conflict that swept up every one on the continent, and in which even the earth itself became a participant, no one then or ever afterward could escape those thrilling, terrible years. "And the war came," said Lincoln, and so it did, and once it came, it would never leave. In the American heart and conscience and imagination, it came to stay.

William C. Davis,
November 1995

PART 1
BATTLEFIELDS

I

FIRST MANASSAS (FIRST BULL RUN)

General Irvin McDowell won only one battle in his career, and that was with a watermelon. Certainly he was brave enough. A graduate of the United States Military Academy at West Point, he served with distinction in the 1846-8 war with Mexico, and won promotion and favorable mention in reports. After the Battle of Buena Vista he took a permanent place on General Winfield Scott's staff for the balance of the war, and became so close to Scott personally that he continued in the general-in-chief's military family for more than a decade afterward. Yet they shared little in common. Scott was outgoing, in the main popular with his subordinates, a man with an agile mind that helped compensate for his excessive pride and occasional petulance when challenged.

One thing McDowell did share with his mentor, however, was a Homeric appetite. He was, in fact, an unquestioned glutton. One of his own later staff members recalled that "at dinner he was such a Gargantuan feeder and so absorbed in the dishes before him that he had but little time for conversation." That may have been just as well, for McDowell made a poor social companion at best. Consistently unable to remember names and faces, he possessed little charm or personality. He lost his temper too easily, listened only carelessly to others, and often sat lost within his own thoughts, meeting almost everyone with what one of his closest supporters had to confess was a "rough indifference." It did not help that he capped his substantial obesity by wearing a ridiculous bowl-shaped straw hat that gave him more the appearance of an incongruously over-weight Chinese coolie than the general of the first army of the Union. Perhaps his seeming distraction and aloofness stemmed from his constant concern for his next meal. He touched neither wine nor spirits but "fairly gobbled the larger part of every dish within reach," recalled his adjutant Captain James B. Fry.

And when done with that, he launched a culinary campaign against an entire water-melon, which he defeated and consumed single-handedly, afterward pronouncing his vanquished foe to be "monstrous fine."

In the weeks immediately following the fall of Fort Sumter, Northern authorities belatedly commenced the task of raising volunteers in order to expand its pitiably small 16,000-man Regular Army. The new Confederacy, by contrast, had been the recipient of newly raised and equipped volunteer regiments from the seceded states even before the convention in Montgomery, Alabama, adopted its constitution. Lincoln issued a call for 75,000 volunteers from the states remaining in the Union, and even while the youth of the North flocked to the recruiting stations, Washington wrestled with the question of who should take command.

One thing was immediately clear. None of Lincoln's existing few generals would do for this active field command. Scott and John E. Wool were each over 70. Edwin V. Sumner was approaching 64, and the only other field grade general, David E. Twiggs, had gone over to the Confederates. It required a younger, more vigorous man to take over molding the new army being formed in and around Washington, espe-cially since it was this army, and not others being raised in Ohio and the West, that everyone expected to put down the rebellion and win the war. Washington lay but a scant 100 miles from Richmond, Virginia, which in May became the Confederate capital. Thus North and South alike took it for granted that the fate of America as one nation or two would be decided on the rolling, iron-red soil of the Old Dominion. The man who commanded Lincoln's army in Washington would be expected to march into Virginia, meet and defeat the Rebels in his front, and march on to Richmond, and triumph.

No wonder, then, that even before McDowell received his new command, there were other men south of the Potomac, themselves new generals and amateurs at the business of command, hurriedly preparing to meet his inevitable advance. Jefferson Davis faced the same problem confronted by Lincoln when it came to command of his armies, but at least he could meet the issue with a few advantages. While Old Twiggs was too aged to be considered for command of the Confederates in Virginia, Davis did have at hand Joseph E. Johnston, himself a Virginian, and a battle-seasoned veteran of Mexico. He left the United States Army with the staff rank of brigadier which, by Davis' promotion policy, automatically entitled him to a generalcy. Johnston was an obvious choice to command in Virginia. Furthermore, in Beauregard, Davis had the war's first authentic popular hero. Even though a child could have taken Fort Sumter, still Beauregard's success demanded that he be made a high-ranking general as well, and with the scene of operations quickly shifting to Virginia, good sense dictated that the Creole be sent there as well.

Happily, Davis required not one but two armies in Virginia. Geography dictated such. One, the principal force, needed to position itself between Richmond and Washington, and as close to the Potomac as possible in order to protect northern

Virginia. But barely 100 miles to the west there was another Virginia, the Shenandoah Valley. Mountains made it, the Alleghenies on the west, and the less imposing but still significant Blue Ridge on the east. The Valley ran roughly northeast to southwest, from the Potomac down deep into the Virginia heartland. It presented a natural pathway of invasion to the Federals, for by marching south into the Valley, they could cross the Blue Ridge at one of the few gaps available, and emerge deep in the rear of any Confederates in northern Virginia. Thus Davis had to hold the Shenandoah, a task he gave to Johnston, while eventually he assigned Beauregard command of the newly designated Army of the Potomac being formed in and around Manassas Junction, about 25 miles southwest of Washington.

There was something special about Manassas. From the junction, the Manassas Gap Railroad led straight west, through Manassas Gap, to the Shenandoah, providing the northernmost east-west link between the two sides of the Blue Ridge. Immediately Davis and his generals saw the opportunity this offered. By maintaining control of that gap and by using the railroad, they could with relative speed shift troops from one side of the mountains to the other, allowing a concentration of forces back and forth to meet any threat. Only by meeting and pinning down both Johnston and Beauregard simultaneously, or by seizing the gap or breaking the railroad, could the Yankees prevent such a tactic from being employed. To the Confederates it presented a chance to hold Virginia with a minimum of its precious regiments. Moreover, since Davis and his generals hoped to more than merely defend in a coming engagement, it gave them a weapon with which they might be able to combine two numerically inferior Rebel armies in order to meet and overwhelm a Union force that neither of them could otherwise hope to meet successfully.

Since the map looked just the same to men in Washington, Lincoln and Scott saw the same possibility. Consequently, their strategy for the advance into Virginia called from the first for simultaneous movements. McDowell was to move against Manassas Junction, while another, smaller, volunteer force commanded by General Robert Patterson, was to cross the Potomac and take Harpers Ferry at the northern end of the Shenandoah, and then move south, keeping Johnston fully engaged and, if possible, driving him away from the Manassas Gap line.

First they had to raise their army. The young men of the North responded with heartening alacrity to the call for volunteers. Throughout May and June the regiments poured into Washington. Even as they arrived, the newly appointed McDowell moved across the Potomac to occupy Arlington and Alexandria, giving Lincoln a foothold in Virginia and somewhat lessening the psychological trauma of having Confederate flags flying just across the river from the Capital. Meanwhile the new general built his army. From New York, Massachusetts, Ohio, Pennsylvania, Michigan, Rhode Island, Maine, Connecticut, and more, came the raw young regiments. By the middle part of July there were more than 30,000 men under arms and awaiting combat in and around Washington. Most of them were poorly trained, and their enthusiasm was expected to make up for their general lack of preparation and readiness.

At least McDowell managed to put them under leaders who did have some experience. He divided his army into five divisions, commanded respectively by Daniel Tyler, David Hunter, Samuel P. Heintzelman, Theodore Runyan, and Dixon S. Miles. Tyler enjoyed an excellent reputation in the Old Army. Heintzelman was a veteran of the Mexican and Indian conflicts with a record for bravery. Hunter had spent forty years in uniform, though seeing no action. In the 1830s one of his closest Army friends had been Lieutenant Jefferson Davis. Runyan was a cypher, a militia general from New Jersey with no more experience than his small division. Miles had more experience than all the rest, but also a reputation for losing battles with the bottle.[1]

Among the brigade commanders in those divisions some soon-to-be distinguished names could be found, including future army commanders William T. Sherman, Ambrose Burnside, and Oliver O. Howard. But for now they were all almost uniformly men unheard-of outside the small confines of the old Regular Army, and many of them had already returned to civilian life when the war broke out. None of them was prepared for the demands of this war. Not one had ever led more than a company of 70 or 80 men in action before. Now they were called upon to lead thousands.

Most inexperienced of all, of course, was the man who had to lead them all, Irvin McDowell. Lincoln and Scott placed almost constant pressure upon him for a plan of campaign, even as his army was still forming. Repeatedly McDowell protested that his men were untried, untrained, "green" as he put it. Scott only replied, "you are green, it is true; but they are green, also; you are all green alike."[2]

McDowell insisted that Manassas provided the key to northern Virginia, as indeed it did. To drive Beauregard away and seize the junction, he proposed to drive first for Centreville, about four miles northeast of Manassas. If successful that far, his move would force the Rebels back to their next natural line of defense, a stream two miles above Manassas, and running roughly northwest to south east. McDowell knew that it would only be crossable at a stone bridge on the Warrenton Turnpike and at a handful of fords, all of which he could expect to be heavily fortified and guarded. Instead of attacking there, he proposed merely to keep Beauregard occupied with demonstrations in his front, while he pushed a column far down the stream, crossing below the Confederate right flank. Once across, he could then drive straight west toward Manassas, putting himself in Beauregard's rear, cutting his rail communications both with Johnston in the Shenandoah and with Richmond as well. The Rebels would have no choice but to abandon their positions with little or no fight, and McDowell would find the road to the enemy capital open to him.

The Army of Northeastern Virginia marched out of its camps along the Potomac on July 16, unaware that the time and direction of its movement was such an ill-kept secret that word came to Beauregard almost at exactly the same time that the order finally reached the Yankee troops. The Creole had been building up his army just as frantically and just as energetically as his adversary, and against obstacles nearly as great.[3]

Beauregard took command in and around a little stream called Bull Run on June 1, to find only 6,000 soldiers to hand, and a great deal of work needed to defend the several fords and the bridge over the stream. Immediately Richmond began forwarding new volunteer regiments to him as soon as they became available, but the infant bureaucracy proved woefully inadequate to the needs of supply, and the general found his men ill-equipped and inadequately fed and clothed. By late June, however, he could see his army grown to the point that he could give it some formal organization, and he had in hand a number of officers, many with Mexican and Indian War experience, to whom he could turn for command.

The First Brigade, South Carolinians, went to Milledge L. Bonham. The Second Brigade went to the newly commissioned Brigadier General Richard S. Ewell. David R. Jones was to lead the Third Brigade. Colonel George Terrett led the Fourth Brigade for only two weeks before being superseded by another new brigadier, James Longstreet. The Fifth Brigade belonged to the hapless Colonel Philip Cocke. It was he who first anticipated the defensive possibilities of northern Virginia, and it was he who began the building of the army that Beauregard came to command. Yet the credit would elude him. His health ravaged, he would take his own life before the year was out. The Sixth Brigade went to the stuttering new Virginia colonel Jubal A. Early. By June Beauregard could count some 15,000 men in his ranks, arranged in a cumbersome organization that would better have seen all those brigades formed into two or three divisions, as McDowell had done. Then Beauregard would have to issue orders to two or three subordinates, instead of to all six brigade commanders, a situation that doubled the paperwork necessary, and with it the possibility for confusion.[4]

At the far right of the Confederate line sat Union Mills Ford which, though Beauregard did not know it, was the one where McDowell actually hoped to cross his army. Beauregard feared for little there, in fact, since it required the enemy to make the longest march possible to reach Manassas. A mile and one-half upstream, however, sat McLean's Ford, a mile above it lay Blackburn's Ford, and less than a mile above that came Mitchell's Ford. All three were closer to the center of Beauregard's line, and could be threatened by the enemy. Happily they sat on a convex bend of the stream, so that all three lay within easy reach of a centrally placed force of two or three brigades, allowing Beauregard to use a minimum of his small command to defend along the interior line. A minor ford of no probable use to either side lay upstream of Mitchell's, but then came Ball's Ford, to which two good roads from Centreville led, and then above it sat Lewis' Ford. Not much farther along came the stone bridge on the turnpike from Centreville to Warrenton. It offered the best and easiest crossing of Bull Run available, served by the best road through that countryside. Obviously McDowell would make some attempt to take it if he advanced against the left half of Beauregard's line. Happily, after the road crossed the bridge, it was flanked on either side by hills, the gentler Matthews Hill on the north, and the more substantial Henry Hill on the south. The latter had an excellent view of the bridge, the road, and of the crossroad that led off northward to the ford at Sudley Springs, a mile and one-half northward, and the last of the crossings. By placing men on Henry Hill, Beauregard could impede passage toward Manassas from both the ford and the bridge.

Beauregard may have been a pompous blowhard at times, but he had an excellent eye for terrain, and looking at the positions along Bull Run he instantly recognized that he could defend all of the major crossing points with just two concentrations of his forces, one around Henry Hill and the stone bridge, and the other around McLean's Ford. But he was not to be satisfied with defense. In spite of having had more than one proposed offensive refused by President Davis, Beauregard moved several of his brigades in advance of Bull Run, and even beyond Centreville. With only 18,000 men in his army now, he implored Davis to order Johnston to come and join him in a concentration against McDowell, as if Johnston did not have a foe of his own to contend with in the Valley. And whereas Beauregard somehow believed that Johnston had more than 22,000 men with him in the Shenandoah, in fact barely half that number faced Patterson. Finally, only the arrival of a message on July 16 that McDowell would march that afternoon brought Beauregard up against hard reality. Heavily outnumbered, he had no choice but to withdraw toward Bull Run.[5]

The Federals gave him plenty of time. McDowell's advance was a halting affair. The fact was, no one knew anything about moving tens of thousands of soldiers in their long, serpentine columns, over farm lanes and country roads. Then, too, the Yankees suffered from an exaggerated fear of hidden batteries and other deadly obstructions before them, when in fact they met but little resistance from Confederate outposts. Still after the regiments left their camps around 2 p.m. on July 16, they covered barely more than ten miles before stopping and bivouacking for the night. The next day's march proved more stirring, as the Rebels before them evacuated Fairfax Court House without a fight, and only the fatigue of his men from a full day's march in the heat, dust, and humidity, prevented McDowell from ordering them on to Centreville that evening. Instead he gave Tyler orders to attack Centreville the next morning, and then set out himself to reconnoiter toward Union Mills and his hoped-for crossing place that would put him behind Beauregard's positions and thus win the battle.

What the general found upset all his plans at the last minute. The country leading toward Union Mills proved to be all but impassable for a large army. He would have to abandon his original intention. Thinking quickly, he simply reversed his plan and decided to send his main power in a flank march around the enemy's other flank by crossing at Sudley Ford, meanwhile continuing with his original concept of a feinted show of force at the fords in Beauregard's center in hopes of deceiving him into believing that an attack would be made there. Thus McDowell amended his orders. While Heintzelman and Hunter's divisions marched to be ready to turn northwest toward

Sudley, Miles would occupy Centreville as a reserve after Tyler had taken it, while Tyler himself was now to advance beyond the town toward Bull Run. He was to make a show of force to confuse Beauregard, but McDowell made his wishes emphatically clear: "Do not bring on an engagement."[6]

That same evening Beauregard frantically tried to augment his forces, calling to Richmond for more reinforcements, including the Hampton Legion from South Carolina, and pleading once again for Johnston to be ordered to him. With all of his forces withdrawn behind Bull Run at last, his line now stretched almost six miles, from Ewell at Union Mills, to Jones at McLean's Ford, Longstreet and Bonham at Blackburn's and Mitchell's, Cocke watching Island, Ball's, and Lewis' Fords, and a newly-arrived half-brigade of two small regiments at the stone bridge. Still expecting that McDowell would advance against his center at Mitchell's Ford, Beauregard placed half of his cavalry and almost half of his artillery in support of Bonham. Thus he stood arrayed at dawn on July 18. Then came news that should have been cheering. Richmond had ordered Johnston to move east of the Blue Ridge to join him. Beauregard met the telegram with disgust, throwing it down with the exclamation that "It is too late." Johnston could never arrive in time to keep them from being overwhelmed by the enemy's superior numbers. Just the same, one of his aides volunteered to ride to the west toward Johnston's last known position at Winchester, more than fifty miles distant. Beauregard almost thought it a fool's errand, but allowed Colonel Alexander Chisolm to go anyway. At almost the same time came word that Tyler was advancing through Centreville toward Bull Run.[7]

Tyler himself rode down toward Blackburn's Ford to learn what he could. He saw little other than enemy pickets and a few cannon, the balance of Beauregard's men being concealed. He should have known better, but despite his many years in the army, Tyler had never seen actual combat. Believing his eyes, he concluded that he could cross Bull Run at that point, almost unopposed, brush aside the few Rebels he saw, and march directly for Manassas. At once he opened a tentative artillery fire, and then sent his skirmishers forward, men from Massachusetts dressed in gray militia uniforms. For the first time, though not the last along Bull Run, men found themselves confused by uniform colors. "Who *are* you?" the Yankees called out when they encountered gray-clad Confederate pickets. "Who are *you?*" came the confused reply. The confusion ended when a lieutenant from the Bay State replied, "Massachusetts men." An instant later a Rebel volley rang out, the lieutenant lay dead, and the unplanned and unwanted Battle of Blackburn's Ford began.[8]

It was a muddled affair. Following almost an hour of skirmishing, Tyler decided to send in more regiments, despite McDowell's order not to bring on a general engagement. Even though aides told him that he had done enough, that he had felt out the foe's strength and himself made a show of force, Tyler would not be dissuaded. He sent a whole brigade off toward the ford. Unfortunately, when finally he decided that he had gone too far and that the enemy was in too greater strength in front of him to push his way through to Manassas, he found his brigade too hotly engaged to extricate it right away. Some regiments broke and ran under the heavy Rebel fire, others stood their ground, pinned down by Confederate fire and unsupported. Others, out of the line of fire and left standing idle, broke ranks to pick blackberries. Only well into the late afternoon, when McDowell himself arrived and peremptorily ordered Tyler to disengage, did the so-called Battle of Blackburn's Ford conclude.

By standards soon to be established elsewhere along Bull Run, it was nothing more than a skirmish, Tyler's losses being a mere 83 killed, wounded, and missing. But it proved clearly to be a repulse, leaving Tyler's men dejected as they tramped back to Centreville for the night. By contrast, the Rebels, commanded chiefly by Longstreet and Early, lost only 70, most of them wounded. The only substantive damage that might have come out of the affair was when a Federal artillery projectile flew way over the Confederates and struck a house far in the rear, just when Beauregard and his staff were about to sit for a late midday meal, "very near destroying some of us," wrote an aide, "and our dinner spoiled."[9]

If Beauregard felt aggrieved over the loss of his lunch, still he experienced nothing but elation at the sight of Tyler's columns retreating toward Centreville that evening. And surely that was as nothing compared to his emotion the next morning when, at 6 a.m., Colonel Chisolm leaped from a panting horse and ran into his headquarters. He had found Johnston. After an exhausting thirty-three-mile ride, Chisolm had reached Piedmont Station on the Manassas Gap Railroad, and there found the forward elements of Johnston's army. That general had achieved a signal success against the hopelessly timid and inept Patterson. After more than a month of feint and maneuver, Johnston issued orders to his men early on July 18 to prepare their rations and pack their baggage. Silently they simply marched away from the unsuspecting foe, moving first to Winchester, then turning eastward toward the Blue Ridge. Only when his army was well along in the day's march did Johnston issue an order informing them that they were on their way to join Beauregard at Bull Run.

Johnston himself rode ahead of the army, arriving first at Piedmont Station that evening. When he met Chisolm, he sent the colonel back into the night with the word that Johnston would start boarding his brigades as soon as they reached the station, and that his army should begin to arrive at Manassas Junction late on July 19 or the next morning. If McDowell did not initiate the battle before then, the concentration would be completed. Literally at the eleventh hour, it appeared that the Confederates might be able to make a revolutionary new use of modern transportation technology, and perhaps wrest a victory from what appeared until that moment to be almost certain defeat. At the very least, Johnston's command merged with Beauregard's would give them almost equal odds.[10]

The first of Johnston's brigades arrived late in the afternoon on July 19. They were all Virginians, led by the oddest Virginian of them all, Brigadier General Thomas J.

Jackson – hypochondriac, religious fanatic, disciplinary martinet, and, some thought, lunatic. He sucked on lemons, eschewed pepper, seldom laughed, and when he did merely opened his mouth without emitting a sound. In former days at Lexington's Virginia Military Institute, one aggrieved student had challenged him to a duel, and another tried to assassinate him. His men did not love him – yet.

Portions of Colonel Francis Bartow's Second Brigade arrived next, shortly after dawn July 20. A much-liked Georgian, Bartow had no real military experience, but represented the trend for prominent civilians who raised regiments of volunteers being given commissions to command. Soon after noon, another train arrived, this one bearing most of the Third Brigade, commanded by Brigadier General Bernard E. Bee of South Carolina, a career officer of high regard. Once more the train sped off to the west, this time picking up the Fourth Brigade, normally commanded by Colonel Arnold Elzey. However, Brigadier General Edmund Kirby Smith of Florida, commanding the Fifth Brigade, feared that the coming battle would be over before his command could reach Bull Run, and so he accompanied Elzey's brigade, and being senior, took command. Johnston, meanwhile, sent his artillery and his cavalry, commanded by Colonel J.E.B. Stuart, overland toward Bull Run. Both arrived on July 20, to find that Richmond had also augmented Beauregard's command from other sources, sending scattered regiments and the Hampton Legion, which only arrived at 2 a.m. on July 21. When Elzey and Smith arrived later that morning, Johnston and Beauregard combined would total about 35,000, compared to the nearly 37,000 under McDowell's overall command. It was a wonderfully near thing, this concentration. Indeed, when the train bearing the Fourth Brigade and its two commanders finally chugged within earshot of Manassas Junction, Smith and Elzey could already hear the sound firing in the distance toward Bull Run. The battle had begun.[11]

With a delicious irony, army commanders on both sides of Bull Run on July 20 planned almost exactly the same battle for the morrow. McDowell continued in his determination to send his main force off to his right, crossing at Sudley Ford, and then sweeping down on the Confederate left. This would uncover the stone bridge, allowing more Federals to cross in mass and then drive directly along the Warrenton turnpike to Gainesville, on the Manassas Gap Railroad. Unaware that Johnston was even then arriving at Manassas, McDowell believed that cutting the rail line at Gainesville would prevent troops from the Shenandoah from reinforcing Beauregard. That done, he could then turn on the Confederate army and drive it back from Manassas Junction itself. Some of McDowell's subordinates argued their belief that Johnston had already arrived. After all, they could hear the whistles of the locomotives arriving from Piedmont station, but their commander refused to countenance such thoughts. He had been assured that Patterson still had Johnston pinned down in the Valley.

In fact, of course, thanks to being senior in grade, Joseph E. Johnston was even then assuming command of all the Confederates massed on the other side of Bull Run. Arriving so late, and with no personal knowledge of the ground, he readily accepted a plan of attack presented to him by Beauregard, even though its planning was faulty, and the wording of the battle orders themselves was positively incomprehensible. It placed nine of their combined brigades on the right half of the six-mile long line, from Mitchell's Ford down to Union Mills, but only one and one-half brigades were to hold the three miles to the left, including the stone bridge, reflecting Beauregard's unshakable conviction that the enemy would try to strike his center again as at Blackburn's Ford. But he intended to launch an attack himself, striking across at the enemy center with two brigades driving straight toward Centreville, while the bulk of his command swept around the Federal left to take his flank and cut him off from retreat to Washington. It was almost a mirror image of McDowell's strategy, which meant that the advantage, if any, could well go to the general who struck first.[12]

That was McDowell. At 2 a.m., July 21, while the Confederates still slept, he put his columns in motion. Miles would remain at Centreville. Hunter was to take the lead and find his way to Sudley Ford, cross, and push the foe back to uncover the next crossing near the stone bridge. This done, Heintzelman was to cross here. Then they would continue until they uncovered the stone bridge, where Tyler would cross after making demonstrations intended to pin down Rebels on the enemy left. The night march proved to be dreadful. Tyler slowed everyone as he moved forward, and did not reach the slope leading down to the stone bridge and Bull Run until 5 a.m. or later. Sporadic rifle and artillery fire broke out from either side of the stream, but the man commanding the spare brigade and one-half on the Confederate side soon guessed that this was only a demonstration, and that Tyler would not attack. For nearly two hours he remained unsure of the foe's intentions until a message reached him revealing that Yankees had been seen crossing Bull Run at Sudley's Ford. "Look out on your left," it said, "you are turned."

That was Hunter. His had been a miserable march in the darkness, his men often having to hack their way through a virtual forest of trees and undergrowth on the so-called "road" they traveled to Sudley's. Worse, a local guide took Hunter on a "short cut" that in fact added three miles to the route. Consequently, it was 9 a.m. or later before the leading elements of Burnside's brigade finally soaked their cuffs in Bull Run and crossed unopposed to the Confederate side. Quickly they turned to their left and rushed toward the Warrenton road, barely more than a mile away, with nothing between them and a clear route to the railroad except a regiment from South Carolina, a battalion from Louisiana, and one incredible man.

Colonel Nathan G. Evans brought West Point and Old Army experience to his command of this half-brigade, but more to the point, he brought instincts as a rough-and-tumble brawler. His staff thought him the most accomplished braggart in the Confederacy. There was no question of his being among the most intemperate drinkers. He even kept a special orderly with him whose chief duty was to carry a small keg of whiskey and keep it near to hand at all times. But woe to the man who tanged with "Shanks" Evans, as his friends called him. Outflanked and outnumbered, and far from any supporting troops, his immediate instinct was to attack. When Tyler appeared in his front at the stone bridge, Evans quickly saw through the demonstration, and now with word of Hunter's approach, he immediately led most of his tiny command off to meet the threat, leaving a mere four companies concealed from view above the bridge to face Tyler's entire division, fewer than 400 men holding down almost 10,000.[13]

In the next couple of hours, Evans and his brave little command saved Beauregard and Johnston from disaster. Indeed, even as "Shanks" rushed his men and his keg toward Hunter, the Creole had almost entirely lost control of the battle even before it began. McDowell's seizing the initiative before him virtually negated his own offensive plans, and during the hours immediately after dawn and Tyler's appearance at the stone bridge, Beauregard repeatedly adopted and then abandoned a succession of extravagant new plans, sometimes so confused and contradictory that in one instance one of his orders literally directed Jones and his brigade to attack Ewell. Johnston, meanwhile, showed a peculiar reluctance to interfere with his subordinate's conduct probably because of his own ignorance of the ground, as well as a fear of responsibility that he would manifest throughout the war ahead. Only after word of Hunter's crossing reached Beauregard did he finally abandon his own notion of attacking, and start rushing reinforcements toward Evans. He ordered Bee, Bartow, and Jackson to move without delay.[14]

Evans, of course, did not wait for help. He rushed his men to the crest of Matthews Hill, north of the Warrenton road, and there emplaced them on the forward crest. As soon as Hunter's leading regiments from Burnside's brigade emerged from the trees in the distance, Evans opened fire. Even though Hunter sent forward an advance to drive the Confederates away, Evans held his ground, soon deceiving the Yankees into thinking they faced far more than a few hundred Rebels and one resolute colonel. Before long, Hunter himself fell with a painful wound in his neck, the lead from an unknown Confederate being probably the first gift received on this, his birthday. Burnside assumed command of the division, and soon believed that he faced two full brigades posted on Matthews Hill. He brought Hunter's other brigade, under Colonel Andrew Porter, up in support, but still Evans held them in check.

And then the cocky Confederate launched an attack of his own, sending the 1st Louisiana Battalion, later known as the Louisiana Tigers, straight toward the center of Burnside's line. They were the sweepings of New Orleans' gutters, men of a dozen nationalities, drunkards, brawlers, criminals, who waved their gruesome bowie knives in the air as they charged. Their numbers were too few to drive the Yankees back, but they stopped Burnside's advance in its track, exchanging lives for time. Minutes later, as Evans was about to withdraw from the hill to avoid being overwhelmed by the lengthening enemy line that now extended far beyond both his flanks, he saw Bee's brigade rushing up from the rear, with Bartow not far behind. All their forces combined totaled not more than 4,500, barely half the number of Yankees now facing them, but Bee, now senior officer on the scene, immediately took his cue from Evans and prepared to attack once more. They must continue to gain time for Jackson and other reinforcements to arrive.

With Evans on the left, Bee in the center, and Bartow on the right, the Rebel line swept forward. Down the slope of the hill they sped, hurling themselves into Burnside's lines on the edge of a wood. Immediately the fighting became intense, though not hand to hand. Rather, the Confederates took cover in thickets or else simply stood out in the open, trading volleys with the Federals. None could say with certainty how long they stood the fire. Some said fifteen minutes, other thought it more like ninety. Whatever the time, its toll was terrible. First Evans was forced to withdraw, then Bartow, leaving Bee's men alone as the enemy stretched his lines and moved forward to overlap and envelop them. In some companies, more than a third of the men were hit. Officers, trying to inspire the men by example, exposed themselves heroically, and paid a dear cost. Finally Bee, too, had to withdraw to avoid being overwhelmed, and joined Bartow and Evans, already establishing a new defensive line on the south bank of Young's Branch, a stream several hundred yards in the rear, south of Matthews Hill, and roughly parallel to and in advance of the Warrenton pike. Within minutes the Yankees began to pursue.[15]

Suddenly, after a frustrating morning, everything seemed to be going McDowell's way. Despite losing Hunter early in the action, the Federal advance was going according to program, though behind schedule. Then, just as Bee's attack lost its force and the Confederates started to pull back, McDowell ordered Tyler to attack across Bull Run. Sherman had found an unguarded shallow spot above the bridge earlier that morning, and now he led his 3,400-man brigade across just in time to come up on the right flank of Bee's line and add impetus to the Confederate withdrawal. As Sherman moved his brigade to join with Burnside's and Heintzelman's, an elated McDowell rode along the lines waving his hat and joyfully shouting "Victory! Victory! The day is ours!" And so it appeared. Tyler was sending more men across after Sherman, Heintzelman's freshly arriving troops constantly streamed into the line, and Burnside's brigades, though badly mauled by the morning's fighting, still had strength. Half the Yankee army was across Bull Run and ready to hammer down Beauregard and Johnston's flank.[16]

The Confederate generals had not been idle all morning, yet neither had they really taken control of their destinies as yet. Beauregard continued to expect his brigades on his far right to cross the stream and move against Centreville, a threat that must certainly force McDowell to pull back his own attacking divisions. Only Beauregard had issued so many orders in the past 24 hours, and such conflicting ones, that he had forgotten what he said to whom. Some of his brigade commanders never even got their orders to advance. At last Johnston started to act decisively. After diplomatically suggesting repeatedly that they should send everything available to their endangered left, he finally announced to Beauregard that "The battle is there. I am going." As Johnston rode off, Beauregard finally woke up to the state of affairs, perhaps because Johnston's own decision now signaled that he was assuming active command. Immediately the Creole began ordering most of the rest of his unoccupied brigades to hasten to the left.[17]

By noon McDowell still appeared to hold the advantage. His line north of Young's Branch was poised, ready to continue its advance, and he still heavily outnumbered the Confederates, who had pulled back to the better ground on the northern slope of Henry Hill. More reinforcements sporadically reached them. Hampton arrived and helped stabilize the line when Bee and the others retreated south of Young's Branch. Then, even as the lines were reforming, he looked off to his left and saw a fresh brigade come into view on the crest of Henry Hill. It was Jackson. That morning he had not waited for orders from Beauregard. Hearing the increasingly heavy firing off to the left, he led his brigade in that direction on his own initiative. By 11:30 he watched his men tramp up the back slope of Henry Hill, but that was as far as he went. He had his men take cover by laying down, and resolved to await either further orders or the enemy's attack.

Bee, meanwhile, had retired with one of his regiments, the 4th Alabama. Though the musketry was hot, the Yankees had not resumed their advance as yet, so Bee rode over to see Jackson. "General, they are beating us back," he said. Jackson only replied that "We'll give them the bayonet." Apparently without further discussion, Bee rode to the 4th Alabama and asked if the men had it in them to follow him back into the fight. Jackson had said nothing about launching an assault, and made no preparations in his own command to do so. Either Bee interpreted the bayonet remark to mean that Jackson intended that they should charge, or else he felt disgusted that Jackson seemed inclined to stay put on the crest behind his bayonets, and therefore decided to attack again on his own.

In either case, before he led the Alabamians back toward Young's Branch and the Yankee line, Bee uttered some last words to his men. No one who heard them left an immediately contemporaneous record of what Bee said, but four days later a reporter with the army repeated what someone present told him. "There is Jackson standing like a stone wall," cried Bee. "Let us determine to die here, and we will conquer. Follow me." Many have thought it a tribute to Jackson, yet at the time the Virginian was doing nothing, his men resting on their arms atop the hill in relative safety. A few believed otherwise, and a major on Jackson's own staff later claimed that Bee soon complained to him of Jackson standing still "like a stone wall" while his Alabamians and some of Bartow's Georgians went back into the fight.[18]

They did not conquer, as Bee had promised, but they did die there, being almost shattered by Yankee artillery. Bee himself took a mortal wound, and died within hours. Beauregard and Johnston reached the crest of Henry Hill just in time to see the survivors come streaming back up the forward slope. At once they agreed that the former would remain on the battle line to direct the placement of the troops, while the latter rode to the rear and, in his capacity as overall commander, saw to the coordination of the reinforcements rushing toward the battle-line, sending them where most needed. It was a good arrangement. Then, even as Johnston rode off, Beauregard sent Bartow and his remaining Georgians around to extend Jackson's left flank, and in moments a bullet killed the beloved colonel almost instantly.

In the next hour, more and more regiments and fragments of regiments came on the scene, and Beauregard used them to extend his flanks, both of which were still in danger of being overlapped. By 1 p.m. his line stood almost complete, with nine full regiments and bits of others in place, perhaps 8,000 men in all. He was still heavily outnumbered, but he had thirteen cannon on the field, too, and from their elevation on the hill they could do good work in repulsing a Yankee attack. They soon got their chance, for McDowell decided now to resume his offensive. Strangely, he chose to do it by sending two of his own batteries out in advance of his infantry, across Young's Branch, and up the forward slope of Henry Hill, almost under the guns of Jackson's infantry. It seemed an absurd move, exposing the artillerymen to a withering rifle fire, but McDowell no doubt trusted that the current and widespread fear of artillery fire would demoralize the Confederates before they could do damage to his cannoneers. He also promised to send forward infantry supports.

Nearly another hour passed before the eleven guns went forward, and the whole movement proved to be a shambles. The promised infantry support almost collapsed when it got just past the guns, and Jackson's line gave them a first volley. Then as the Yankees tried to rally, "Jeb" Stuart and his cavalry came on the field, by accident, at exactly the right time and place. They emerged from a wood beyond Beauregard's left, and one of the first things they saw was the exposed flank of the infantry support as it staggered under Jackson's volleys. Stuart immediately ordered a charge, and put much of the Federal infantry to rout. What remained was pushed back when the 33d Virginia of Jackson's brigade advanced without orders. The Yankees did not see where the Virginians came from. Further, this regiment wore blue uniforms, as many Confederate outfits did at the beginning of the war. Consequently, the commanders lost fatal time arguing among themselves about whether the advancing Virginians were the enemy, or another friendly support regiment. The Rebels' first volley settled the argument, but too late for the Federals to turn their guns against them. Almost all of the artillery horses were killed on the spot, and from the two batteries, only one cannon was successfully withdrawn, The Virginians swarmed over the rest and happily found them loaded, turning and firing them against the fleeing Yankees. Now Jackson ordered the rest of his brigade forward to pursue the retreat, and Beauregard sent other regiments into the advance as well, to capitalize on the enemy's repulse.[19]

From now until 4 p.m. or later, the battle raged on without a clear advantage to either side, McDowell benefitting from his superiority of numbers, and the Confederates from their good position atop Henry Hill. Charge followed upon charge. Colonel Wade Hampton went down with a wound, and the Federal cannon were retaken, then taken again, before they could be hauled out of the no-man's-land between the armies. Both army commanders made the mistake of sending forward single regiments at a time, as if afraid to risk too much at a single assault. The result, of course, was that units were used up savagely by such piecemeal actions. Only Jackson made full brigade strength assaults, and they proved devastating. When McDowell sent his own men against Jackson in counter-assault, the Virginian fully earned his infant nickname of "Stonewall," and this time there could be no mistake that it was a tribute to the general and his men, who would soon thereafter be known to posterity as the Stonewall Brigade.

The continuous fighting on the hot July afternoon took a heavy toll on both sides, but as the Confederates stubbornly held their ground, and as more and more of McDowell's regiments were repulsed, the sight of Union soldiers retreating, and the disorganized flight of many of them back through the lines, exerted a demoralizing effect upon the fresh regiments still arriving, as well as on the men still in the lines. Ever so gradually it became McDowell's turn to lose control of the battle as, in seeming exasperation, he could think of little to do but keep sending forth more small assaults. Then Heintzelman fell with a painful, though not fatal, wound, and he had to leave the field. Just as he went to the rear, he met the fresh brigade of Colonel Oliver O. Howard, just arrived. At once McDowell ordered Howard off to the far right, to charge up Henry Hill immediately. The Confederates stopped first one of his regiments, then another, and within minutes Howard's brigade was streaming back toward Young's Branch in near panic. Meanwhile, the Rebels had sufficiently mauled Sherman's brigade over on their own far right, that this portion of the line was now relatively secure. The arrival of more regiments sent forward by Johnston extended and stabilized the extreme left, and Jackson, of course, anchored the center.

Just as McDowell's strength waned, Beauregard's grew, and chance and coincidence now combined to give the Confederates even better news. Another train had arrived near Manassas Junction – Smith and Elzey at last. Still it took them three hours or more to march to the front. Along the way, Smith encountered Johnston at his headquarters. Asking for orders, Smith was told simply to "Go where the fire is hottest." He led his men first toward Jackson's right, but then learned that it was the far left that needed support. Before he could move, Smith fell from his saddle with a Yankee bullet in his chest, and Elzey took command once more. He moved his brigade in a wide arc around to the left, moving in part through the cover of a wood in the left rear of the line. As a result, when he emerged, he discovered that he had gotten somewhat beyond the left flank, and in advance, and right there before him sat the exposed flank of Howard's already demoralized command.

He charged, and blasted into Howard with a force that carried him all the way to

Young's Branch. Howard simply crumpled before him. Within minutes, Early's brigade, which had been marching almost all day, finally arrived and joined Elzey, along with some of Stuart's cavalry and a few field pieces. They all drove forward, and faced with these fresh brigades, Howard's men melted, running in panic for their lives, and spreading their demoralization to the other Federal units through which they passed. Seeing Early and Elzey advancing almost without resistance, Beauregard now ordered his whole line to charge the remainder of McDowell's line. The battle was won.[20]

In fact, McDowell's army already felt shaky before Howard arrived on the scene. Its commander, and most of his subordinates, were exhausted from their long night march, and then spent themselves in their ill-advised piecemeal assaults that sacrificed the initial advantage of numbers, all the while allowing Johnston and Beauregard to speed more reinforcements to Henry Hill to even the odds. Then when Howard retreated so spectacularly, the willpower of the rest simply gave way. Well before McDowell gave the order for a general retreat, the men had made the decision for themselves and a disorderly scramble for the rear commenced. McDowell did manage to get a few units to stand their ground as a rearguard to cover the withdrawal, but for the rest, there was little semblance of anything other than terror. "The retreat soon became a rout," McDowell would report, "and this soon degenerated still further into a panic." The Confederates sent Early and Stuart and a few other fresh units in pursuit, but they were for the most part too exhausted themselves to mount an effective chase. Only some of Beauregard's artillery made a significant contribution to the enemy rout when its shells upturned a wagon on the bridge over Cub Run, a stream some distance toward Centreville. The result further demoralized the Federals who needed to use that bridge to retreat, and all remaining semblance of order vanished. Intermixed now with the fleeing bluecoats were a good number of civilians from Washington, including several politicians, who had come along with the army to picnic during the battle and watch the fun as McDowell presumably walked right over the Rebel upstarts. They, too, scrambled for safety.[21]

It did not help that when McDowell finally reached Centreville that evening, he found Miles drunk. Immediately he relieved him of command, and personally assigned Miles' brigades and the few others not battered in the day's fight to establish a defensive line between Centreville and the victorious Confederates. But though Johnston and Beauregard tried to organize a substantial pursuit, urged on by President Davis who arrived on the field just as the fighting concluded, it simply could not be done. They had suffered at least 387 killed, and 1,582 wounded, with a few more missing, and all-told casualties probably reached 2,000, about twelve percent of the 17,000 or more who bore the brunt of the fighting. One regiment lost fully one-third of its numbers. But still they had the victory, and with it the spoils. McDowell's losses totaled 460 in killed, another 1,124 wounded, and a staggering 1,312 in missing, most of whom would soon be in Southern prisons. Moreover, in the wake of their hasty retreat, the Federals left cannon, wagons, supplies, and at least one Congressman.[22]

Following so soon after the victory at Fort Sumter, the Confederate triumph gave the Southern cause an indescribable boost of morale and confidence. "Joy ruled the hour," wrote a clerk in Richmond. Many believed that the war was already over, though more mature heads thought otherwise.

REFERENCES

1 US War Department, *War of the Rebellion: Official Records of the Union and Confederate Armies* (Washington, 1880-1901), Series I, Volume 2, p.761; I, 51, Part 1, pp.411, 413-4 (hereinafter cited as *O.R.*)

2 US Committee on the Conduct of the War, *Report of the Joint Committee on the Conduct of the War* (Washington, 1863), Part 2, p.38.

3 *O.R.*, I, pt.2, pp.718-21.5.

4 *Ibid.*, pp.943-44.

5 *Ibid.*, pp.447-48; Alfred Roman, *The Military Operations of General Beauregard in the War Between the States* (New York, 1884), I, pp.77, 89; Rose Greenhow, *My Imprisonment and the First Year of Abolition Rule at Washington* (London, 1863), p.16.

6 *Report of the Joint Committee*, p.39.

7 *O.R.* I, 51, pt.2, p.177; A.R. Chisolm, Notes on Blackburn's Ford, Chisolm to George P. Smith, April 15, 1901, Alexander R. Chisolm Papers, New-York Historical Society.

8 Warren H. Cudworth, *History of the First Regiment Massachusetts Infantry* (Boston, 1866), p.42.

9 John C. Gregg to "Friend Heber," July 25, 1861, Peter Schmitt Collection, Western Michigan University, Kalamazoo; *O.R.*, I, 2, pp.306-307, 314; John L. Manning to his wife, July 18, 1861, Williams-Chesnut-Manning Papers, South Caroliniana Library, University of South Carolina, Columbia.

10 Chisolm, Notes on Blackburn's Ford.

11 William C. Davis, *Battle at Bull Run* (New York, 1977), pp.136-43.

12 *O.R.*, I, 2, pp.779-80; *Report of the Joint Committee*, p.207.

13 E.P. Alexander, *Military Memoirs of a Confederate* (New York, 1907), p.30; Thomas Pelot to Lalla Pelot, September 15, 1861, Lalla Pelot Papers, Duke University Library, Durham, North Carolina.

14 *O.R.*, I, 2, pp.489, 518.

15 *O.R.*, I, 2, pp.384, 390; Thomas Goldsby, "Report," M.J. Solomons Scrapbook, Duke University Library.

16 William Todd, *The Seventy-Ninth Highlanders* (Albany, N.Y., 1886), p.34.

17 Alexander, *Military Memoirs*, pp.32-34.

18 Charleston, *Mercury*, July 25, 1861.

19 *Report of the Joint Committee*, pp.169, 216; *O.R.*, I, 2, pp.394, 407, 495.

20 Bradley T. Johnson, "Memoir of the First Maryland Regiment," *Southern Historical Society Papers*, IX (1881), p.482.

21 *O.R.*, I, 2, p.320; Davis, *Bull Run*, p.239.

22 *O.R.*, I, 2, pp.568, 570, I, 51, pt. 1, pp.17-19; *Report of the Joint Committee*, p.41.

II

SHILOH (PITTSBURG LANDING)

William T. Sherman produced probably more memorable quotations than any other general of the Civil War. "Hold the fort," he said, and if legend may be believed, perhaps he did years later declare that "War is hell." But certainly there is one memorable expression that he would have preferred everyone forget he ever uttered, and that was his confident assurance to his commander U.S. Grant on the morning of April 5, 1862, from his riverside position at Pittsburg Landing, Tennessee. "I have no doubt that nothing will occur today," he declared, and in words that would return to haunt him later, he added that, "I do not apprehend anything like an attack on our position." He was only half right. Nothing did happen that day. But the next morning he would be fighting for his life in the bloodiest battle ever yet seen in the hemisphere.[1]

Direct, unsubtle, apparently guileless, Ulysses S. Grant presented the proverbial "face in the crowd." Other than his horsemanship, nothing about him before the war commanded notice or admiration. His lackluster performance at West Point, followed by a noteworthy but all-too-brief spate of glory in the Mexican War, repeated itself in a post-war peacetime service from which he resigned in 1854 under suspicion of more than the customary intemperance. He unwittingly summarized his own utter lack of sophistication when he reportedly commented on his musical tastes. He only knew two songs, he said. One was "Yankee Doodle" . . . and the other one wasn't. Only the desperation of Illinois' governor for experienced officers to train his new volunteer regiments in 1861, brought about Grant's return to uniform to organize and command the 21st Illinois. No one was more surprised than Grant when soon thereafter Washington created four new volunteer brigadiers for Illinois and, almost by default, one of the stars fell on his shoulder. Soon he attracted notice, however, with an unsuccessful attack on Belmont, Missouri, which, though it failed, still gained him wide notoriety in the Union. Soon thereafter he began urging that an attack be made on the center of the Confederates' long extended Western line, reaching from Cumberland Gap clear across Kentucky to Columbus on the Mississippi River.

Many in the North, including Grant's immediate superior, Major General Henry W. Halleck, and even President Lincoln himself, believed that the weak spot in that line lay where the Tennessee and Cumberland Rivers cut across it as they flowed north to south through western Kentucky and into Tennessee. It fell to Grant to prove them right, when he took Fort Henry on the Tennessee River and Fort Donelson on the Cumberland in February 1862. Doing so gave him access to both streams, providing pathways straight into the rear of the Rebel line. The foe had no choice but to abandon all of Kentucky and almost all of central and western Tennessee. It was a major triumph that, for a time, made Grant a hero eclipsing all others in the North. Indeed, so formidable was his popularity that when a jealous Halleck removed him from command just three weeks after Fort Donelson on erroneous charges, Lincoln himself intervened, and Halleck returned Grant to command of his army on March 17.

As vital as Forts Henry and Donelson were to keeping Grant the lifelong failure in command, so did their fall severely threaten the tenure of the man who came to this war riding such a crest of success and fame. General Albert Sidney Johnston won acclaim wherever he went, from an exemplary performance at West Point in the 1820s, to service in the Black Hawk War a decade later, before he resigned and went to Texas where he became a general and later Secretary of War in the infant republic. Then came the Mexican War, in which he led a volunteer regiment with distinction, later a return to the Regular Army, and in 1855 he received a commission as colonel in command of the elite new 2nd US Cavalry, his subordinates including the likes of George H. Thomas and Robert E. Lee. By 1860 he was a brevet brigadier general in command of the Department of the Pacific, but when his adopted Texas seceded in 1861, he resigned his commission, at first resolved not to fight for either side.

Yet both sides wanted him, and in the end his Southern birth and sympathies won out. Friendship may have helped, too. Confederate President Jefferson Davis had been a cadet at the Military Academy at the same time as Johnston, though two years behind. For some reason Johnston, to whom all the young men looked up, adopted Davis as one of his friends. As a result, the younger cadet idolized his comrade with an unquestioning hero-worship so compelling that to the end of his life Davis could not or would not admit of any fault or failing in Johnston. Even when chosen president of the new Southern nation, Davis still stood in awe in his old friend, and immediately sought to woo him into Confederate gray. Even without being able to communicate with Johnston, who was still on the west coast, Davis commissioned him a full grade general, in seniority second only to Adjutant General Samuel Cooper, who was too old to do active service. This meant that Johnston would be the senior field general in the entire Confederate Army, with everyone else – Joseph E. Johnston, Lee, Beauregard, and more – his subordinates. Yet still Davis heard nothing from Sidney Johnston, who was believed to be making his dangerous way clear across the continent. Early in September 1861, Davis lay ill in his sickroom on the second floor of the Executive Mansion in Richmond, his staff under orders not to disturb him. But one day he heard the muffled sounds of a caller downstairs, and a distinctly familiar boot tread in the entrance foyer. "That is Sidney Johnston's step," he cried joyfully. "Bring him up." Within days General Johnston was on his way west to take command of Department No. 2, embracing almost all of the Confederacy between the Appalachians and the Mississippi as well as parts of the territory further west.[2]

Then his troubles began. His command was too large, his resources too few, and his own apprehension of Yankee intentions let him down. When Grant moved in February, 1862, the forts on the rivers were unfinished and ill-prepared. Fort Henry fell without a fight, and though the struggle for Donelson was tough and sanguinary, still the outcome was almost never in doubt. Disasters elsewhere along the line in eastern Kentucky only added to Johnston's problems, and the loss of so much territory, especially the transportation and supply center at Nashville, was a severe emotional blow to the Confederacy. At once, many who had hailed Johnston as a genius before, now called for his censure, even replacement. Only the unwavering support of Davis kept him in command. Meanwhile, Beauregard, who continued to be the most popular Southern military hero, had made himself an increasing nuisance in Virginia after the victory at Bull Run. He fretted over his rank and started to feud with Davis over credit for the Manassas victory, all the while chaffing at being under Joseph E. Johnston's continued command. Even before the loss of the forts, Davis had reassigned Beauregard to serve as second-in-command to Sidney Johnston, thus ridding himself of a problem. After Henry and Donelson, Beauregard's prestige would actually work in favor of restoring confidence in Johnston and his army.

Even while retreating into northern Mississippi, Johnston himself was already planning a restoration of his own. There were two Yankee armies that posed threats to him. One was Grant's, and by far the smaller at about 30,000. The other was the Army of the Ohio, commanded by Major General Don C. Buell, numbering about 50,000. Originally posted in Kentucky, Buell moved forward to Nashville immediately after Johnston's withdrawal. Johnston immediately feared that the two armies would link to form one massive force against which he could hardly hope to contend, for even by the end of March after receiving heavy reinforcements, he still could not muster more than 45,000 of all arms. Indeed, this is exactly what Halleck hoped to do, but even after Washington officially expanded his command to include Buell, the Army of the Ohio's slow and recalcitrant general persistently dragged his feet and delayed. He feared that Johnston would try to get into his own rear if he moved too far from his base. Unspoken was the inner fear and suspicion he almost certainly felt that if he joined with Grant, he would become merely a subordinate to him and that Grant, being senior major general, even though by only a few days, would reap all future glory for himself, of which some thought he had already taken more than his fair share.

Johnston's one hope of preventing any such combination (given his unawareness that Buell was his unwitting ally on this point) lay in meeting and defeating the separate forces in detail before they could merge. Once all of his scattered forces withdrew from Tennessee, he concentrated them in and around Corinth, Mississippi, so that by March 23 his army was nearly complete, and now he reorganized it into the newly designated Army of the Mississippi. It proved an odd and unbalanced organization, devised in fact by Beauregard, to whom Johnston delegated far too much responsibility, the same mistake made by another General Johnston during the Battle of Bull Run. Beauregard created four corps, the I Corps commanded by General Leonidas Polk.

Polk was everyone's mistake, from Davis on down. A West Pointer, he resigned immediately after graduation, and never did a day of active military service. Yet he, too, enjoyed an intimate friendship with Davis, having been a part of the Johnston clique at the Military Academy. He bore much of the responsibility for the failure to have the river forts properly completed, and for the rest of the war he would be a liability to a succession of commanders, especially the man leading the II Corps, General Braxton Bragg. He, at least, had battlefield experience from Mexico and elsewhere, though combined with one of the most irascible and unstable temperaments in the Old Army. Though not a favorite of Davis before the Civil War, he would become one very quickly. Inexplicably, while Polk's corps numbered 9,400, Bragg's totaled a staggering 16,200, and both seriously outnumbered the III Corps assigned to the best trained and skilled soldier of the lot, General William J. Hardee. He led barely more than 6,700, yet every professional soldier on the continent knew him at least by name thanks to his authorship of the favored drill manual then in use by both sides, commonly called simply *Hardee's Tactics*. Finally Beauregard created a Reserve Corps numbering some 7,200, and gave it first to General George B. Crittenden, who soon found himself relieved of command for drunkenness. In his place Johnston assigned Brigadier General John C. Breckinridge, a man with no battlefield experience at all. Yet he was a Kentuckian, and the Confederates needed to woo Kentucky into seceding and joining the Confederacy, and supporting Southern forces when again they entered the state, as Johnston confidently expected he would before long. Having been a senator and vice president of the United States just before the war, Breckinridge brought political benefits that might outweigh his lack of experience.

All the while that Johnston and Beauregard reorganized and struggled to arm and equip the army, they watched Yankee movements in Tennessee, taking some heart from what appeared to be indecision and sloth. Grant sent occasional reconnaissances and probes out of his bases on the Tennessee at Savannah and Pittsburg Landing, but there was no further advance. Obviously he was waiting for Buell, and that general, though finally moving from Nashville, was doing so in such a dilatory fashion that it took him two weeks just to cross the Duck River, less than halfway between Nashville and Grant's divisions. Within two or three days of his arrival at Corinth, Johnston decided to take advantage of the opportunity this presented by moving against Pittsburg Landing as soon as possible. On April 1 he put his troops on notice to prepare for active campaigning. The next day, receiving intelligence that Buell was across the Duck and moving toward Grant, Johnston resolved to delay no more. Orders went to the corps commanders to be ready to march at 3 a.m. on April 3. Pittsburg Landing lay a scant twenty-five miles from Corinth. Despite the recent heavy rains that had all rivers and streams swollen, and most roads turned into mires, the Confederates could hope to reach and strike the enemy in two or three days at the most.

Unfortunately it started to go wrong from the first. Confusion and badly worded orders resulted in the troops being a full twelve hours late in starting the march. Meanwhile, the peculiarly detached Johnston allowed Beauregard to devise the actual battle plan, as he had at Manassas, and just as happened there, the final drafts of the orders were complicated, contradictory, and ill-conceived. Units took wrong routes, others bogged down in the muddy tracks that passed for roads, and by nightfall on April 4 all of the corps were miles short of where Johnston expected them to be. Still that afternoon the commanding general issued attack orders for the next morning, but late that night a torrential storm blew through that soaked the army and the already dismal roads. All movement had to be postponed until the rain stopped. Johnston began to lose his customary calm, yet by late afternoon of April 5 not all of his troops were yet in position. The fear that Yankee scouts, encountered from time to time during the day, would have alerted Grant and ruined a hoped-for surprise attack tormented him. Moreover, some of his units, like Breckinridge and his Reserve Corps, had not been able to leave their original camps until that morning, and had slogged more than twenty miles that day, arriving wet, muddy, and exhausted.

Almost within earshot of the uneasy Confederates as they tried to sleep that night, lay another army, incredibly still unsuspecting what dawn would bring. Five of Grant's six divisions made their camps here. It was Sherman who had selected the spot originally. Despite the loss at Bull Run, Sherman had performed well and won promotion to brigadier. Almost immediately Washington sent him west, where he soon commanded the Department of the Cumberland, only to lose the command when nervous exhaustion, seemingly erratic behavior, and newspaper sensationalism all combined to create a rumor that he had lost his mind. A much-needed rest at home restored his health, but his reputation as "crazy Sherman" would take longer to heal. Still, Grant instinctively saw something in him to trust, the beginning of one of the most successful commander-subordinate relationships in military history. Hoping to launch a speedy offensive against Johnston, Grant allowed Sherman to select Pittsburg Landing as a likely meeting place for the expected link-up with Buell, should he ever arrive. Meanwhile, it served as a good spot on the Tennessee to maintain supply and communications with their base at Cairo, Illinois.

Sherman had actually moved his own and the other divisions with him a mile or two inland from the landing, to the vicinity of Shiloh Church, and it was a sound move. The Tennessee here ran north-south for a stretch. Roughly parallel and about four miles to the west flowed Owl Creek. Thus the two streams afforded excellent protection to both of his flanks. In between Sherman posted his own division on the right, almost extending to the banks of the creek. On his left sat the division of Benjamin Prentiss, a new general who, like Breckinridge, owed his commission to political, not military, experience. His men were new and barely trained, and perhaps it was because of this, in part, that Sherman sandwiched them in the line between two of his own brigades on the right, and a third far to the left. Because of the wooded and often tangled terrain, and the route of the roads necessary for movement and communication, Prentiss and his two brigades stood at a slight angle in the Yankee line, and a bit in advance of the units on either side. Some distance behind Sherman camped the division commanded by another politico, Major General John McClernand, a ruthlessly ambitious wire-puller and consummate egotist already disliked by both Sherman and Grant. Off to McClernand's left, some distance in rear of Prentiss, sat the division of Brigadier General Stephen Hurlbut, yet another political appointee with no military experience. And completing the forces immediately present was Brigadier General W.H.L. Wallace's division. Characteristically, he, too, owed his stars to politics. Sherman had placed him far in the rear, and not far from Pittsburg Landing itself.

In fact, of the five generals commanding divisions here, only Sherman possessed either West Point training or practical experience in command, and even he never experienced action until Bull Run. Grant had one other division, commanded by yet another amateur, Brigadier General Lew Wallace, stationed a few miles down the Tennessee at Crump's Landing, and though he might have had good reason to feel a bit uneasy with such an overwhelming preponderance of amateurism in his high command, thanks to Lincoln's penchant for giving important positions to men of political influence, still Grant had confidence in Sherman and little or no apprehension that the position around Shiloh stood in any peril. As for his own plans, he was only waiting for Buell to arrive before launching a drive of his own against Corinth and Johnston. To be sure, reports of enemy activity on the roads south of Sherman did come in during the first days of the month of April, but incredibly no one seems to have spotted more than Confederate outposts, or else no one credited that such contacts might presage a major enemy movement. Reportedly Lew Wallace received one report that indicated Johnston's whole army was on the move, but if such news did reach him, when he passed it on to Grant it was simply not believed. Wallace himself later admitted that it was just too incredible to believe that more than 40,000 Confederates could have gotten that close and not been spotted long before. And thus on the morning of April 5 Sherman could assure Grant that no danger whatsoever existed of an attack, even as Hardee's men spent the entire day no more than two miles from Shiloh.[3]

It was shortly prior to dawn on April 6 when Federal cavalrymen out on patrol rather more than a mile south of Shiloh Church suddenly saw Confederate horsemen in the distance ahead of them. Shots were fired, and hastily they withdrew, but not before Mississippians from Hardee's corps exchanged volleys at long range with men of Prentiss' First Brigade. The battle had begun.

Johnston's plan for the battle came almost entirely from Beauregard, superseding one of his own that he abandoned sometime on April 5. Instead of advancing with his corps lined up abreast of one another, with Breckinridge held in reserve, Johnston would now launch his attack with the corps lined up one behind another along the front, a plan that sacrificed all the advantages of the numbers Johnston had concentrated for the attack, just as the Creole's battle plan for Bull Run would have done. Only McDowell taking the initiative first prevented Beauregard's plans from going into motion in that battle, thereby saving the general from his own folly.

The skirmishing continued for more than half an hour and grew in intensity, yet for the time being no one in the Federal camps around Shiloh Church seemed to appreciate what faced them. Many continued to believe that this was nothing more than a reconnaissance, albeit a large one. But then Prentiss' advance parties saw something that made their hearts stop. Suddenly from out of the wood in the distance they saw an endless line of gray and butternut clad soldiers, with a seeming sea of fluttering red and white flags waving above them. It was Hardee's corps, augmented by a brigade from Bragg, and nearly 9,000 strong. Moving like what Beauregard called "an Alpine avalanche," they surged forward shortly before 7:00 a.m. Some distance in their rear, General Johnston heard the sounds of increased firing, swallowed the last of his morning coffee, and mounted his steed "Fire Eater." Wheeling in his saddle before dashing off to the front, he confidently told his staff that "Tonight we will water our horses in the Tennessee River."[4]

Hastily, even as realization of what faced him slowly dawned, Prentiss roused more and more of his units from their morning meals and rushed them toward the sounds of the firing, though he had not yet himself seen the enemy. In fact, subordinates actually gave what little management there was on the firing line, and made the actual dispositions of the troops that the general sent forward. With Hardee rapidly overlapping both flanks of the heavily outnumbered advance, the Yankees worked to set up a stiffer line of defense on a crest overlooking a wooded ravine several hundred yards behind the firing. By about 7:30 two regiments stood atop the crest when they saw swarming over the hilltop on the opposite side of the ravine seemingly uncountable thousands of the enemy. At once they fired the first volley, briefly halting the foe, and then the two sides commenced trading blast after blast at each other across the tree-tops between them.

A few Confederate units broke and ran at this, their first taste of fire, and the confusion they caused slowed Hardee's advance for precious minutes. But soon after 8 a.m. the Southerners recovered and pushed forward in an assault, bayonets glistening at the muzzles of their rifles. They almost overwhelmed the Yankees before Prentiss' men pulled back in some confusion, withdrawing right into their camps. Here the general hoped to establish a better defense, and fresh regiments awaited the coming of the foe. But then they saw Rebels advancing through the woods in their front, while they could hear the growing sound of advancing enemy fire on their right. Fire briefly stalled the Rebel juggernaut, but not for long. Making matters worse, some of the Yankees took their places in line woefully unprepared. In the rush that morning, the 15th Michigan actually marched off without any ammunition for its rifles, an oversight only discovered now that they stood in line with the enemy advancing. "We stood at order arms and looked at them as they shot," one enlisted man recalled. There was nothing else they could do.[5]

Still Prentiss' resistance did credit to his division, and they inflicted some grievous casualties on the foe, including Brigadier General Addley Gladden, leading Bragg's single brigade attached to Hardee. A Yankee artillery shell practically ripped off his left arm. He would die within a week. The loss of Gladden and the by now heavy fire coming from Prentiss succeeded in slowing Hardee's advance. At least an hour before, the general sent word to Hurlbut, advising that this was no mere reconnaissance, and pleading for assistance, but none was yet forthcoming. Meanwhile, more and more of his inexperienced volunteers were either falling to Rebel bullets or losing their nerve and racing for Pittsburg Landing. A situation that started out bad was rapidly becoming critical. One of his brigades, the first to be engaged that morning, lay dispersed and battered, with only isolated pockets of men now holding out in and around their camps, and then a Rebel bullet killed its commander. The line collapsed and the remnant of his men abandoned their camps and raced for the rear. Prentiss once more ordered his remaining troops to fall back in hopes of linking with reinforcements, should they ever come. A renewed enemy attack put one of his regiments completely to rout. From his entire division the general now had barely two regiments that had retained any organization, and almost his entire command was in retreat toward the Tennessee. Johnston might indeed be drinking from the river before nightfall.

Over on Prentiss' right, Sherman, too, had been taken by surprise, though Hardee struck Prentiss first and the sounds of firing there gave the others at least some warning. Still as late as 7 a.m. some of his regiments remained around their breakfast fires, even though they could hear the sound of guns to their left. Uncertain of the extent of the Rebel advance, Sherman himself rode to his front to see what he could, narrowly missing death when an enemy skirmishing party suddenly appeared not fifty yards distant and sent a volley at him that killed men around him and slightly injured his hand. He had seen enough, and hastily rode back to rush forward reinforcements. The battle he thought so unlikely had come to find him.

Thanks to a better position, a little more warning, and at least some previous experience at Fort Donelson, Sherman's division reacted more quickly and successfully than Prentiss'. Despite the momentum of Hardee's attack in their front, these Federals managed first to slow him substantially, and then to stop him cold, sending some of his own regiments back in disorder and confusion. Moreover, Sherman outnumbered the single brigade of Rebels facing him, led by General Patrick R. Cleburne, and now held him in check as Cleburne impatiently awaited support from the second Confederate wave, Bragg's corps, more than a mile to the rear, and probably at least half an hour from arrival. The folly of Beauregard's battle plan was already becoming apparent as it launched the attack with its smallest corps, with real strength and support too far behind to capitalize on an advantage.

For the next two hours the intensity of the combat on Sherman's front steadily increased as more and more of Bragg's units finally reached the battleline. Gradually the Confederates extended their flanks on either side. Prentiss' withdrawal left Sherman's left terribly vulnerable, and soon some of Hardee's units turned to their own left to join with Bragg in driving against Sherman. Meanwhile, as several brigades struggled along the center of the lines, one of Bragg's units had a clear path to get around Sherman's right as well. Only its dilatory advance prevented an opportunity to get into the Yankee rear and perhaps overwhelm Sherman. Even then, as more and more of his units came into the fight only to be sent reeling in confusion from well-placed Rebel artillery fire and the incredible show of force, Sherman began to see that he could not control the battle in his front. His own performance was exemplary, however. Under the heaviest fire, with repeated near escapes from enemy bullets, he remained calm and inspiring, chewing a cigar and showing himself seemingly everywhere to try to inspirit the men.

It proved to be of no avail. Before very long his own camps lay in imminent danger of being overrun. First his left gave way entirely under the combined pressure of Hardee and Bragg, and this only further jeopardized his right, though it held on stubbornly, sustained by the fortitude of the men in the ranks, and the delays and mistakes plaguing the foe in that sector. It was all buying vital time, for Sherman had earlier sent urgent messages to McClernand, Hurlbut, and W.H.L. Wallace, advising them that this was no reconnaissance in their front, but a full-scale Confederate attack that endangered their position, Pittsburg Landing, and the whole army.

The first reinforcements to reach Sherman were Colonel Julius Raith's brigade from McClernand, though they arrived just in time to become a portion of the left flank that Hardee and Bragg chewed up and crumpled back. Shortly after 10 a.m. Sherman had been forced to withdraw from the area of Shiloh Church. An hour later the whole line was clearly a shambles. Sherman himself had two horses killed under him in the heavy fire, and was now riding a commandeered artillery horse, only to have it shot down within a few minutes. His men could hold no more. Rallying those whom he could inspire to stand firm, Sherman saw the rest of his division melt into the woods to the rear. Now it would be McClernand's turn.[6]

By now Grant had reached the scene and was trying to ascertain just what had happened and how bad the damage was. He first learned of the attack around 7:30 when a messenger arrived at his headquarters. Stepping outside, the general could hear for himself the sound of distant artillery, and though uncertain as yet of the extent of the engagement, he took it for granted that this was a serious attack. He sent word off to Buell to rush toward Pittsburg Landing. Then he boarded the transport *Tigress* and steamed upriver, stopping first at Crump's Landing to meet with Lew Wallace and order him to have his division ready to move in any direction ordered whenever Grant sent further instructions. Then the *Tigress* steamed off again, reaching Pittsburg Landing around 9 o'clock. As soon as he got there and spoke with men on the scene, he realized that the Confederates intended to contest his hold on the landing itself, and he immediately sent word back downriver to Wallace to come on right away, though he did not specify what road he should take from Crump's Landing.[7]

Immediately Grant rode forward to the scene of action to meet with Sherman and McClernand, and there he saw with his own eyes the deplorable state of affairs. He had been forewarned by the sight of hundreds of demoralized soldiers huddled under the sheltering banks of the Tennessee when he reached the landing. Now at the front he saw even worse. Never an excitable man in the face of the enemy, Granted stayed calm now, though in estimating Johnston's forces at 100,000 or more, and in sending repeated appeals to Buell to rush to join with him, he betrayed the anxiety he felt for his army. He knew he was in serious trouble.

Fortunately, a gathering pocket of stiff Federal resistance began to cluster in the vicinity of a peach orchard well to the left, where parts of General John McArthur's brigade of W.H.L. Wallace's division had come forward. Meanwhile, off to their left the brigade of Brigadier General David Stuart had come up. In fact, when first spotted, Stuart's command was mistaken for an attacking party of Yankees seeking to turn the Confederate right, for here, again, Beauregard's plan worked against them. Even without the disorganization caused by the rough terrain and the morning's fighting, Hardee's, and then Bragg's lines simply could not stretch themselves sufficiently to cover all the ground between Owl Creek and the Tennessee. As a result, and thanks to the unfolding of the fighting on their left against Sherman, the Southerners' right lay "in the air," largely unprotected. As they advanced, they encountered Stuart in the distance, and mistaking his purely defensive posture as a threat, halted their advance in that sector. Word went back to Johnston, who now saw his plan to drive the enemy away from Pittsburg Landing seriously jeopardized. He was pushing the Yankees back, to be sure, but if he continued as he was, he would wind up driving them back to the landing instead of away from it. Now this appearance of Stuart only emphasized the need to shift the pressure of his attack from the left and center to his right. With Hardee and Bragg already fully committed, and with Polk's corps inadvertently wandering piecemeal into places in the line without directions, he had only Breckinridge's Reserve Corps available. At once Johnston ordered the Kentuckian to take his two brigades to their right. They must dislodge Stuart and any other resistance near that peach orchard, and do it quickly, so that the balance of the attack could be pressed as planned.[8]

Even before Breckinridge arrived, another brigade struck Stuart and put all but a few hundred of his men to flight, thus clearing the Yankee left flank and opening what could be a clear path along the Tennessee to the landing. But then the Confederates who routed Stuart failed to press forward; they were out of ammunition. This plus McArthur's timely arrival brought precious stability to the Yankee left at a crucial moment. Yet the few men that Stuart rallied, added to McArthur, posed no match for any serious renewal of the Rebel pressure. There could not have been a better time for Hurlbut and two of his brigades to come rushing forward at last. Hurlbut brought them straight forward, past McArthur, through the peach trees and slightly beyond. Here he posted one brigade facing south, and the other on its right facing slightly west. McArthur took position on Hurlbut's left, and somewhat behind him, while recently arrived units of W.H.L. Wallace's prolonged Hurlbut's right. He may not have intended it, but Hurlbut's two brigades formed a considerable salient projecting dangerously in advance of the rest of the newly established line. His exposed position soon became evident, and before long he pulled his men back to the orchard itself, and the cover of the trees and some fences. Attacking Confederates would have to come at them over open ground with little or no cover.

No one on either side in the battle could have foretold that this peaceful orchard and rustic road were about to become the scene of the most intense fighting ever seen. Near about noon, with Breckinridge not yet on the scene and the rest of the Confederate corps hopelessly intermingled and confused, Bragg simply told Hardee to take command of the left, Polk the center, and he would direct affairs on the right. One of his first acts was to send a fresh brigade forward toward the sunken road, not knowing what awaited them. The first volleys from Prentiss were devastating, inaugurating what would be more than five hours of vicious combat. Immediately after that first repulse Grant himself arrived at the road, took in the vital importance of the position, and made it clear to Prentiss that the fate of the army could depend on his holding out "at all hazards." Prentiss would do his best.[9]

In a short while he did better than that. Aided by his position, and the fact that the curve of the road allowed for a concentration of fire, his men and their artillery shattered the Confederate attackers. By 3 p.m., at least four successive assaults against the position had suffered a bloody repulse, and perhaps already Rebs and Yanks alike thought they could hear in the constant buzzing of the bullets a distinct similarity to the sound of hornets. Ever after, that small piece of ground so vital to Grant would be known as the Hornets' Nest.

By this time the advance elements of Breckinridge's corps finally arrived on the scene, just as broken by the rough terrain as the units that preceded them. Their commander immediately began sending them into the assaults aimed at pushing back

Prentiss and Hurlbut, and he, too, found himself unable to break through. Johnston himself rode to the peach orchard early in the afternoon to see firsthand the resistance that was stalling his advance, and one point a frustrated Breckinridge rode up to him with the complaint that he could not get one of his Tennessee regiments to fight. Governor Isham Harris of Tennessee happened to be with Johnston, heard the remark, and himself went to rally his native sons. That done, Breckinridge tried to get his Third Brigade to go forward in a bayonet charge personally ordered by Johnston. The men balked. They had seen too much death already in the Hornets' Nest.

Again frustrated, Breckinridge came to Johnston, and the commanding general returned with him. His presence and calm and collected manner soon fortified the wavering soldiers' resolve, and with Johnston, Breckinridge, and Harris, in the lead, the brigade advanced with a yell at about 2 p.m. They almost devastated the defenders, pushing back Hurlbut's left dangerously, taking much of the ground near the peach orchard, and only stopping when they came up against stouter defenses at the northern edge of the orchard. The hail of fire had been terrific. At least two spent bullets struck Johnston, causing nothing more than bruises. A third hit the sole of his left boot, narrowly missing his foot. Johnston was rather more elated than concerned about the danger, and that plus the excitement of the assault that had definitely gained good ground probably made him entirely oblivious to a fourth rifle bullet, one that did not harmlessly bound off or tickle his foot. This one came from behind, quite possibly fired by a Confederate whose aim was wild in the confusion, and it buried itself in his right leg behind the knee, nearly severing the popliteal artery. Profuse bleeding commenced immediately, yet Johnston seemingly felt nothing, and the blood filled his boot rather than flowing out where someone might have seen it. Only when Johnston suddenly swooned, went pale, and started to fall from his saddle did Harris become alarmed.

"General, are you wounded?" he cried.

Johnston was just conscious enough to say, "Yes, and I fear seriously."

They may have been his last words. Harris quickly got him to the rear, but within scant minutes the general was completely unresponsive. As others gathered around, they got a bit of brandy down his throat, but still no one had discovered the wound. If they had, a simple tourniquet above the knee might have saved his life. Johnston had such a tourniquet in his personal effects, in fact. Instead, the bleeding continued, and by about 2:30 he was dead, the first army commander in American history to die in combat, and the only one the Confederacy would so lose. Even while his friends and staff cared for the body and tried to conceal the disaster from the trooops nearby, a messenger rode to notify Beauregard that he commanded the army now. The battle must go on.[10]

It took time to find Beauregard, and when Bragg and other Rebel commanders learned the news, at first they did not know what to do, causing a costly delay in pushing the advance and giving Grant more time to dig in. But it proved to be time gained at the expense of Prentiss and Hurlbut. Even before orders came from Beauregard, Breckinridge on the right and left, and other units in the center, moved on the Hornets' Nest once more, hammering it until well after 5 p.m. Both of the Federal flanks finally gave way, and by about 5:30 the brave defenders were literally surrounded. With Sherman having been driven back much earlier, W.H.L. Wallace, on Prentiss' right, was also in danger of being surrounded. Then a bullet passed through Wallace's head, killing him before he fell from his saddle. Minutes later isolated pockets of cut-off Federals began to surrender. Prentiss and Hurlbut had about 2,000 men left, facing several times their number encircling them. Finally those who could tried to escape the noose spreading around them. Prentiss could not, and was soon seen waving a white flag, though Hurlbut got away and was soon at Pittsburg Landing itself, where Grant assigned him the task of reforming the fugitives there for what might have to be a last-ditch stand on the river bank.

Grant could not yet know it, but the succession of disasters during the day was actually working in his favor in a perverse way. The Confederates were exhausting themselves in their uncoordinated assaults, and many units were hopelessly scrambled. Moreover, in pushing the Federals back so rapidly in places, the Rebels had moved faster than their supplies of ammunition and water. Thus, when they passed through abandoned Federal camps, all too often they broke ranks to plunder and gobble the food still warming over the fires. Prentiss, though at terrible cost, had slowed them for more precious hours, and actually distracted Breckinridge later in the day from what, had the Kentuckian but known it, was a clear open road to Pittsburg Landing. And the death of Johnston, of course, would be an enormous morale blow when it became known. As a result, the Southern momentum was considerably slowed, with nightfall approaching. Unfortunately, Lew Wallace had inadvertently taken the wrong road from Crump's Landing, and his delay seriously upset Grant, but good news came from Buell, whose long overland march from the Duck River was nearly done, and he expected to reach the banks opposite the landing that evening. Furthermore, the closer the Confederates came to the river, the more Grant could bring them under the fire of heavy guns aboard a number of gunboats anchored off shore. Certainly on their face, the events of the day looked like a shambles for the surprised Yankees, but with every minute their prospects improved. If Grant could hold out until the next morning, Buell's arrival might not only save him, but allow for a counterattack against the exhausted foe.

Once the confusion of the surrender of the Hornets' Nest passed, the Confederate high commanders met to plan their next move. Bragg, Breckinridge, and Polk met to confer, agreeing that with a bit more than an hour of daylight left, they should press forward. Though Beauregard had been notified of command devolving upon him at least an hour and one-half earlier, no orders had yet been received from him. Consequently, these front-line generals started the advance once more on their own. Their exhausted men moved slowly, even though victory seemed surely in their grasp now. By 6 p.m. they came in sight of Grant's batteries and remaining infantry massed for the final defense of Pittsburg Landing on a crest actually overlooking the landing itself. The Federals could not afford to give way another inch.

The Confederates' final advance began sometime after 6 p.m. It proved to be tough going. On the right, along the river itself, the Rebels were checked by heavy fire and their advance stalled. On their left the charge progressed farther, only to be pinned down by murderous fire from Grant's massed batteries. Hurriedly reinforcements were rushed to support the advance and get it going again. "One more charge, my men, and we shall capture them all," shouted Bragg. But then Beauregard was heard from at last. Seemingly on the verge of victory, he ordered them to break off the attack and withdraw for the night.[11]

Beauregard had never had much nerve for this attack. Moreover, he suffered considerably at the moment from a respiratory infection that sapped his energy. Out of touch with the battle's events from his position far in the rear – to which Johnston had assigned him – he feared disaster in his own ranks thanks to the seemingly huge number of stragglers that he saw. He remembered from Bull Run how demoralized even the victor can be, and convinced now that they already had a victory, he decided that the men had done enough. He would rest them, let them eat and drink, and then finish off Grant in the morning. It was the biggest mistake in a career filled with bad military judgments. When Bragg got the word, he fumed. Breckinridge, on the verge of making what he believed would be a climactic assault, complained to his staff that "It is a mistake."

Indeed it was. Though badly hammered, Grant was only then starting to feel his strength. "Not beaten yet by a damn sight," he was heard mumbling to himself that evening. Ordering his gunboats to fire steadily during the night to keep the enemy awake, Grant concentrated on getting Buell's men across the river as quickly as they arrived. By the next dawn he would have at least 17,000 of them in his lines, along with Lew Wallace's 7,500-man division, which finally arrived about an hour after the fighting on April 6 ceased. While Beauregard slept in Sherman's captured tent, full of self-satisfaction and confidence that the enemy was thoroughly beaten, Grant spent a miserable night in the rain, huddled under a tree, planning his own attack to start on the coming morning.[12]

In fact, Buell launched his own attack the next morning, apparently without discussing the matter with Grant, displaying his obvious disdain for the nondescript little man who still outranked him. When his mile-wide line advanced, Buell took the Rebels almost as much by surprise as they had taken Sherman the day before. Beauregard felt little confidence in his army, so battered and exhausted from the day before. Still he tried to stop Buell's advance with a charge by Breckinridge and Hardee. In response, Buell sent forward a counterattack that sent the Rebels reeling. Charge and answering charge rushed back and forth during the morning, but almost from the first the Federals had the upper hand, their men fresh and well supplied, while the weary Confederates found that many of their rifles would not fire from having been soaked by the rain during the night. Worse, their spirits were dampened. They went to sleep thinking that they had won the battle. Now they awoke to find a newly invigorated enemy in their front, and no end of the battle in sight. All along the line Beauregard could see the lack of enthusiasm in their faces, and the lethargy in their movements. By noon he seriously questioned whether he could ask more of them.

By 1 p.m. Beauregard came to a tentative decision, and ordered captured arms and munitions taken to the rear. He needed these spoils of war. Meanwhile he tried to rally his brigades to stop the enemy drive, and take the offensive once more for the victory he still thought within reach. They did manage a fair assault on the right of Grant's line, now held by Wallace and elements of Sherman and McClernand, but the enemy beat them back handily. Over on the Confederate center, Bragg ordered an assault that also failed to push the enemy back, and then the arrival of fresh regiments forced the attackers back in confusion. Then a renewed threat arose back on the left, and only a counterattack led by Beauregard personally managed to stop it. Yet he knew that the check was temporary. Fresh Yankee troops had been coming into the fight all day. By 3:30 Beauregard could see more rushing into the enemy lines. At several places along the line, even his brave veterans were starting to break in the face of renewed Federal advances. He gave the order to withdraw. Detailing Breckinridge to act as rearguard and cover the retreat, Beauregard put his tired, battered army on the road back to Corinth. Grant realized that his own army, though it held the field and a tactical victory, was itself too traumatized to mount a pursuit. Shortly after 5 p.m. a few Union regiments fired some desultory volleys after the retreating Confederates, and that ended the Battle of Shiloh.

The cost to both sides had been terrible. Of just over 40,000 engaged on the first day, Grant lost more than 10,000 in casualties, and for the whole battle his killed, wounded and missing totaled more than 13,000. The Confederates lost 10,700 of 44,000 engaged. In the two-day fight, 3,500 Americans lost their lives in a battle that did little credit to the foresight of either of the commanders present. Grant and Sherman allowed themselves to be shamefully surprised, though they quickly lived it down in the general euphoria over what the Union perceived as a victory. Johnston and Beauregard never had a good battle plan, and the latter plainly never had much stomach for this fight, either from illness or a fear that all the credit for a victory would go to Johnston. Sidney Johnston himself squandered his life, and though his early death in battle would engender speculation over the fate of the Confederacy had he lived, there were those even then who questioned his management throughout his tenure in command. Davis, of course, would hear none of it, and spent the rest of his life defending and honoring his dead friend's memory. When Beauregard later seemed to claim credit for Johnston's achievements, and uttered veiled criticisms of the general, it fueled a feud with Davis that lasted the rest of their lives, and seriously affected the course of command decisions in the Confederacy.

Therein lies the lasting significance of Shiloh. At the end of the campaign, the armies were where they began, only bloody and tired. But the Yankee high command emerged with laurels. Grant's role as hero was firmly cemented, and Sherman was rising along with him, each to be supported unfailingly by Lincoln. Johnston was dead, and Beauregard perilously close to being discredited, never to enjoy the confidence of his president again. Therein lay the beginnings of the internal and command problems that would plague this Confederate army until the end of the war, and seriously damage the cause itself. Shiloh would be the first and last major Rebel offensive in the region, while for Grant it was only the first step on the glory road to victory.

REFERENCES

1 *O.R.*, I, 10, pt.2, p.94.
2 Charles Roland, *Albert Sidney Johnston, Soldier of Three Republics* (Austin, Texas, 1964), pp.252-60.
3 Lewis Wallace, *Lew Wallace, An Autobiography* (New York, 1906), pp.450-58; *O.R.*, I, 10, pt.2, p.93.
4 *O.R.*, I, 10, pt.1, p.386; Johnston, *Johnston*, p.582.
5 Sword, *Shiloh*, p.160.
6 *O.R.*, I, 10, pt.2, p.404.
7 Wallace, *Autobiography*, p.461.
8 *O.R.*, I, 10, pt.1, p.404.
9 *O.R.*, I, 10, pt.1, p.278.
10 Johnston, *Johnston*, pp.614-17.
11 C.C. Buel and R.M. Johnston, eds., *Battles and Leaders of the Civil War* (New York, 1884-88), I, p.605.
12 Sword, *Shiloh*, p.368.

III
THE SEVEN DAYS'

One of the war's most painful ironies struck the Confederacy in the spring of 1862. In the course of all of American history only three army commanders would fall in battle, all in the Civil War. Two wore the gray. Each went down in this same spring. Both were named Johnston. Though the irony alone is more than enough to make the coincidence worthy of note, any comparison between the events ends there. Debate may continue to the end of time over the impact of Sidney Johnston's death at Shiloh. Though his time in command was so short, and his conduct of it so indecisive, that none may truly say how matters might have run had he lived, there is almost no doubt that those who followed him to command in the troubled Western theater were lesser men and leaders, one of them destined to be that other Johnston in time. But of the fall in battle of Joseph E. Johnston himself there is, and can be, no doubt. However unfortunate for him at the time, his wounding and removal from command was the greatest blessing bestowed upon his cause's struggle for survival. Literally, the shell fragment that struck him in the chest in the gathering twilight of May 31, 1862, changed the course of the war.

Johnston may have been the hero of First Manassas, but in the months that followed he revealed an increasing number of character and personality traits that clearly unfitted him for army command. He feuded with President Davis over matters of rank and seniority, fell under the influence of his subordinate Beauregard, became so suspicious of the Richmond government that he persistently refused to share his plans with the War Department, and often as not, in fact, had no plans. Instead, he revealed an indecisiveness and hesitation, an unwillingness to take responsibility, and a genuine obtuseness when it came to understanding the president's instructions that can only have been feigned in a man of his intelligence. As the winter of 1861-2 came to a close, Davis' confidence in him lay severely shaken, and relations between the two, though still polite, took on an increasing formality as each grew to suspect the other.

Onto this troubled tableau stepped yet another monumental ego destined to leave its mark on the war. Major General George B. McClellan owed his rank and position almost entirely to matters beyond his control or influence. Fortune always smiled on him. Gifted with unquestioned academic brilliance, he graduated second in his class at West Point when only nineteen. Better yet, he took his commission in 1846 just as the war with Mexico commenced, obtained a position on Winfield Scott's staff, and won plaudits and promotion in the land of the Montezumas. Nevertheless, he left the army in the 1850s, but when the war broke out the governor of Ohio quickly commissioned him a major general of state troops, and Washington followed suit with a formal commission and assignment to command the small army raised to invade western Virginia.

A handful of minor battles and skirmishes cleared the vastly outnumbered Confederates from the region, and though the fights were really conducted by his subordinates, McClellan received – and took – the credit. Immediately thereafter, the defeat of McDowell alaong Bull Run left Washington and the nation virtually crying for McClellan to come east. The Union desperately needed a hero in the midst of its series of disasters in the summer of 1861, and McClellan was all Lincoln had. Three years later in the war, achievements such as McClellan's in western Virginia would scarcely have attracted national attention, and garnered him little more than a letter from Lincoln and perhaps the thanks of Congress. In the dark days after First Manassas, however, it got him McDowell's command and, not long thereafter, appointment as general-in-chief of all Union armies.

This was heady stuff for a man just turned thirty-four, and Lincoln knew it. He even asked McClellan straight out if it were not too much responsibility, but the man already reveling in being hailed as the "young Napoleon" only brimmed with supreme self-confidence. "I can do it all," he proclaimed.[1]

Certainly McClellan did much in the days after he took command. He took McDowell's dispirited army and trained and molded and augmented it into a virtually new entity – the Army of the Potomac. Relentlessly he worked to equip the men with the very best in uniforms and weapons, provided the best rations he could find, and struggled tirelessly to build their morale and self-confidence into a mirror of his own. In return they rewarded him with an almost reverential love and admiration. At the same time, he built a command structure with almost unquestioning loyalty to him at its foundation. In short, he worked almost a miracle that perhaps no other man in the Union could have achieved at that place and time.

Time, of course, was part of his secret. Following the debacle at Bull Run, the conflict east of the Appalachians entered a period that in later conflicts would be called a "phoney war." Through the entire balance of 1861 and the winter that followed, virtually nothing of consequence happened. The timid and hesitating Johnston nitpicked and temporized, the frustrated Beauregard asked for assignment to the West, and McClellan took advantage of the months they gave him to form and perfect both his army and his plans. Indeed, that luxurious gift of time spoiled him, for he became so accustomed to having all the time he desired that he could never afterward be compelled to act quickly or until every laborious bit of preparation had been performed to his satisfaction.

The longer McClellan took to act with his grand new army, the more certain character flaws revealed themselves. His ego and arrogance proved positively offensive. He could not and would not stand for challenge or disagreement from anyone, and even characterized Lincoln as a "well-meaning baboon" and "an idiot." Very quickly he came to regard himself as a power unto himself, above the people, the army, even Congress and the president. Worse yet, while he looked upon his own presumed friends with contempt, he bestowed an exaggerated respect upon his foes. Whereas the Confederates in northern Virginia numbered barely more than 40,000 through the balance of 1861, McClellan happily accepted erroneous reports that magnified Johnston's numbers to 200,000 or more, even though accurate intelligence was coming in from his own officers.[2]

Belief in such exaggerated enemy strength justified McClellan in his own mind in using every bit of time possible to plan his inevitable offensive, and to his credit he planned well. In the indignation following First Manassas, the North wanted a speedy advance directly against Richmond. To capture the Rebel capital, they reasoned, would end the rebellion. McClellan shared this delusion, though he quailed from meeting the enemy head-on in battle.

Instead, he finally submitted a plan that would end the conflict by strategy, with the least risk to his beloved Army of the Potomac, now approaching 120,000 strong. He would not march his army south, overland, to drive Johnston out of his defenses around Manassas. This would only force the enemy back on Richmond, with a succession of wide rivers in between, each of which offered a natural defensive barrier. McClellan proposed to board his army on a fleet of transports, steam down the Potomac into the Chesapeake, and then make for Fort Monroe, a massive casemated masonry fortification at the tip of the peninsula formed by the York and James Rivers. This fort was one little piece of Virginia that never fell to the Confederates in the days after succession. Unfortunately, thus far its value had been chiefly symbolic, for the two rivers were so wide here at their mouths that the fort's guns could not effectively interdict Rebel traffic. The James led directly upriver to Richmond, seventy-five miles northwest, while the York flowed roughly parallel and north of the James to West Point, about thirty miles east of the capital. From there the Pamunkey, a smaller but still navigable stream, flowed northwest to its origin directly north of Richmond. The several rivers together formed a peninsula not wider than fifteen miles on average, and in places such as Yorktown barely over five.

Confident that his supply line via the Chesapeake and Fort Monroe could not be threatened, McClellan proposed to drive up this peninsula over its fairly even ground, straight toward Richmond. The Confederates would be forced to pull all of their troops out of northern Virginia to meet him, thus relieving any threat to Washington, and abandoning their carefully prepared fortifications. Moving swiftly, McClellan could get the jump on them, would have only two tiny streams to cross, and could drive toward the capital before the enemy had time to erect proper defenses. Conversely, should Johnston move his army to the Peninsula in time to meet McClellan short of Richmond, then "Little Mac" would have had time to prepare his own defenses and force the Rebels to attack him on his own terms and ground of his choosing. Moreover, thanks to the narrowness of the peninsula, the two rivers would protect his flanks, and as he advanced, either could be used as a direct line of supply more quickly and less laboriously than any overland avenue of communications. Though there were definite flaws in the plan, if executed quickly it offered considerable promise.

Unfortunately, "quickly" was a word foreign to McClellan. The initial movement went well. On March 17 McClellan began embarking his army, and within two weeks had nearly 60,000 men and 100 cannon at Fort Monroe, with more arriving every day. All that lay in his front were 13,000 Confederates in the old Revolutionary War earthworks around Yorktown, twenty miles north. But immediately McClellan made excuses as to why he could not attack. Though he initially estimated enemy numbers at Yorktown accurately when he arrived on April 2, within only a few days he reported them grown to more than 100,000 – when they had not grown at all. Possessed of a four-to-one advantage, he now convinced himself that he was himself outnumbered. No attack could succeed, he said. Instead he must take Yorktown by siege. He lost a full month, a month that gave Johnston all the time he needed to get most of his army to Yorktown, and Richmond vital time to prepare to defend the peninsula and the capital. "No one but McClellan could have hesitated to attack," Johnston reported contemptuously two weeks into the siege.[3]

McClellan never did attack. When Johnston arrived, he, like McClellan, was seized by timidity. He wanted to evacuate, but Davis insisted that he hold Yorktown as long as possible. Thus Johnston held out until May 3 when he finally ordered his men to put out of their works and retire during the night, convinced that McClellan was finally about to move. Davis was mortified at the abandonment of the position without a fight, and even more chagrined that Johnston pulled back all the way to the line of the Chickahominy River, one of the streams that crossed the peninsula, and barely ten miles from Richmond. McClellan spent the entire month in leisurely pursuit, all the time telling Washington that enemy strength was growing and that he was in mortal danger of losing his army, which of course could not be his fault. When he came himself to the Chickahominy late in May, he expressed a resolution to die with his men, if need be.

It was all bombast, of course, but now, in fact, he did face real danger. Johnston's army had now grown to nearly 75,000, most of them emplaced in the vicinity of Fair Oaks Station on the Richmond & York River Railroad, and the nearby village of Seven Pines. Worse, when McClellan arrived, he split his army by putting something less than half – about 40,000 men – on the south side of the Chickahominy. Month-long rains had so swollen the little stream that now it was crossable only by a few bridges, and thus "Little Mac's" left flank, south of the river and on the same side as Johnston's entire army, stood vulnerable. Then an especially heavy downpour on the night of May 30 so flooded the river that its waters carried away almost all of the bridges. If Johnston struck quickly, he could overwhelm nearly half of McClellan's army.

Unfortunately for the Confederates, Johnston conducted a dreadful battle at Fair Oaks or Seven Pines on May 31. Confused and disordered attacks, units marching in the wrong direction, and an overall lack of coordination showed that Johnston had not profited much by his experience at First Manassas. His own ordnance chief, Colonel E. Porter Alexander, called the whole affair "phenomenally mismanaged."[4]

Yet one supreme benefit did come out of it, and that was the errant bit of a Yankee shell that knocked Johnston from his saddle and put him out of the war in Virginia for good. As his performance in the past several months had shown, and as he would demonstrate in future years after recovering from his wound, Joseph E. Johnston was not the man to command a field army, much to the detriment of his cause. But there was another, also a Virginian and near at hand, with whom the story would be different. President Davis was on the battlefield during the fighting, and soon came to the wounded Johnston's side, their feuding forgotten in the solicitude of one old soldier for another. Fortunately the dying sun was bringing the day's engagement to a close, and as Johnston was taken to Richmond, command of the army devolved upon the next senior officer, Major General Gustavus W. Smith. But later that night, as the president rode back into the capital, he informed his companion and chief military advisor that on the morrow, he was to take command of the Army of Northern Virginia, as it was to be styled. The officer to whom Davis spoke was General Robert E. Lee.

There were many in the Confederacy who did not think too highly of the fifty-two-year-old Lee. Though he had served without interruption in uniform since 1829 and won praise and promotion in Mexico as one of Scott's favorites, he spent almost his entire career in the engineers, and had never led soldiers in battle until 1859 when he commanded the contingent of marines who attacked and captured the radical abolitionist John Brown and his raiders at Harpers Ferry. Still, his seniority alone made him automatically one of the Confederacy's top ranking officers when secession came, placing him just junior to Sidney Johnston, and just ahead of Joseph E. Johnston (the source of the latter's feud with Davis over rank). In the war thus far his role had not been exemplary. He commanded unsuccessfully in western Virginia, where his soldiers derisively nicknamed him "Granny" Lee for what they took as caution on his part. Then he superintended the erection of coastal defenses in South Carolina, leading other critics to deride such work by calling him "Spades Lee" and the "Ace of Spades." South Carolina governor Francis W. Pickens actually warned friends that Lee was not "the man his reputation makes him." Rather, Pickens declared that "Lee is not with us at heart, or he is a common man, with good looks, and too cautious for practical Revolution."[5]

But Davis saw things in Lee that others did not, and in March 1862 he brought the general to Richmond to act as his military advisor and *de facto* general-in-chief, though Davis, being Davis, never allowed any truly important decisions to be made by anyone but himself. Unlike Johnston and Beauregard, Lee knew how to get along with the president, and accepted the subordinate role of the military to civil authority. Moreover, he never argued or complained, kept Davis freely and fully informed, and even at times flattered the president's ego a bit. Diplomacy behind the lines could count for almost as much as brilliance on the battlefield in this war, and Lee would prove to be effective at both.

Quite sensibly Lee did not immediately assume command. The battle was as yet undecided and Smith knew the ground better than Lee. But no sooner did the dawn come on June 1 than Smith collapsed, virtually overcome by nervous trauma over the responsibility given him. Thus Lee assumed command the next day after both sides had withdrawn from the indecisive fighting around Seven Pines. His first act was to set his army to work strengthening the fortifications around Richmond, setting off a new round of outcry that he would not be a fighting general. But to Davis, Lee confided his intent to strengthen those works so that only a small portion of his army could man them effectively, while he would take the bulk of the Army of Northern Virginia, as he now called it, and drive McClellan from the peninsula. Davis liked this kind of talk, and gave the general his head.

During the next three weeks Lee used his spades and his brains, while McClellan remained almost stationary, still convinced that his 105,000 or more troops on the Chickahominy line were heavily outnumbered. The Army of the Potomac was divided into five corps, of roughly equivalent size, and all led by Old Army professionals. Generals Erasmus D. Keyes, Samuel P. Heintzelman, and William B. Franklin were all veterans of First Manassas. The elderly Edwin V. Sumner was the oldest of the lot, while Fitz-John Porter was the youngest, just in his thirties, and a particularly loyal favorite with "Little Mac." None would demonstrate great talent in the war ahead, and some would resign in obscurity before its close, but still among them they commanded the finest army yet seen on the continent. Unfortunately, their commander was not inclined to use it. For fully two weeks after Seven Pines, McClellan sat in his works slowly planning his next set-piece battle. Typically, he proposed to fight it with his artillery, trusting to his guns alone to drive Lee back, and then he would close in upon Richmond and bombard it into submission, cleanly, bloodlessly, without risk to himself and his precious army.

Three problems would thwart him. One was his own sloth and timidity. Another was the fearfulness in Washington. Lincoln, terrified that the Rebels would take advantage of McClellan's isolation on the peninsula to send a force overland against the capital, withheld most of the corps commanded by McDowell, keeping it to protect the Potomac line. McClellan did not really need those 25,000 or so withheld from him, but their absence gave him a perfect excuse to complain that Lincoln was to blame for the delay in his campaign, and that in the event of a Union defeat "the responsibility cannot be thrown on my shoulders."[6]

The third problem was Robert E. Lee. Part of the reason that Washington was in a panic was the brilliant Shenandoah Valley Campaign conducted that spring by Major General Thomas J. "Stonewall" Jackson. Having routed three separate small Yankee armies, Jackson and his three divisions, numbering about 17,000, were now in undisputed command of the Valley. Lee thought briefly of a holding action against McClellan while sending heavy reinforcements to Jackson to mount a counter-invasion of the North. However, the mighty Stonewall and his men were too exhausted from the rigors of their recent campaigning to sustain any such movement. But they could still fight. Instead, Lee finally decided to rush Jackson east from the Shenandoah to join the Army of Northern Virginia. McClellan was offering him a tantalizing opportunity, and Jackson could play an integral part in capitalizing upon it.

After Seven Pines, McClellan made only minor shifts in his positions. By the third week of June, the Chickahominy still cut his army almost in half. Shifting some of his units south of the stream, he left only Porter's V Corps on the northern side and somewhat in advance of the rest of the army, in an exposed position that McClellan felt warranted since he expected reinforcements from McDowell to be marching overland to link with Porter. Unfortunately, Lee's dashing cavalryman "Jeb" Stuart led a lightning swift raid around McClellan's army that discovered Porter's exposed position, and brought the news back to Lee. Porter's 30,000 men were emplaced along a tributary of the Chickahominy called Beaver Dam Creek, near Mechanicsville. They were separated from the rest of their army, and that alone made them an appetizing target. Better yet, however, McClellan was now succoring his army from a supply base at White House on the Pamunkey, almost due east of Porter. If Lee could push Porter aside, he could drive straight for White House. Denying McClellan that base would force the Yankees either to withdraw down the peninsula to the next best location for a new base – thus freeing the immediate pressure on Richmond – or else to fight to hold on to White House. To do the latter, McClellan would have to send his corps across the Chickahominy over the severely limited number of bridges, and right into the waiting guns of the Confederates, whom Lee presumed would be able to defeat them one by one.

It all depended upon his division commanders, many of them men he barely knew, and none of them truly experienced in command except for Jackson. General James Longstreet hardly participated in the fighting at First Manassas. A.P. Hill had only recently been promoted to major general after service at Yorktown and Seven Pines, but he was still new to divisional command. Major General Daniel Harvey Hill of North Carolina had fought one of the war's first small battles not far from here in June 1861, and again under Johnston on the peninsula, yet he was still an unknown quantity to Lee. Nevertheless, the commanding general would use these young leaders in a complex and closely timed offensive. He would leave the two small divisions of Generals John Magruder and Benjamin Huger south of the Chickahominy, with only about 22,000 between them, to face 75,000 Yankees across the lines. The divisions of the two Hills and Longstreet would join with Jackson, almost 60,000 strong, to strike Porter on the north side of the river. It was a great gamble, for while Lee was overwhelming Porter, McClellan could overwhelm Magruder and Huger and have a clear road to Richmond.

Consultation with Jackson revealed that his Valley command could be in the vicinity and poised for action by June 25, and accordingly Lee set the next morning as the time for the attack to commence. However, other circumstances precipitated unexpected fighting on the 25th when a Yankee reconnaissance near Seven Pines escalated into a severe skirmish in the vicinity of Oak Grove. McClellan pushed two of Heintzelman's divisions forward to within four miles of Richmond in order to secure some ground that he wanted before launching his artillery attack on Lee's lines. He had learned by now of Jackson's advance, and was sending even more predictions of gloom and defeat to Washington, washing his hands of any responsibility. Yet McClellan had finally stopped delaying and had himself set June 26 as an attack date. Had he followed through and struck first, he might severely have disrupted Lee's plans, though there is little in "Little Mac's" record to suggest that he could have capitalized on the advantage and actually gone ahead to threaten Richmond. As it was, when he learned about Jackson, he called off his June 26 attack, but then did nothing more than strengthen his White House guard and warn Porter to be vigilant. Then he sat back and let Lee run the rest of the campaign.[7]

Not surprisingly, when Lee attacked on June 26 nothing seemed to go as planned at first. His orders to Jackson were to swoop down on Porter's exposed flank at first light. When A.P. Hill heard the sound of Jackson's guns, he was to cross the Chickahominy, brushing aside a small Yankee outpost guarding the crossing, then drive through the enemy posted in Mechanicsville. Pushing them back would open the way for D.H. Hill and Longstreet to cross the river uncontested, form on A.P. Hill's left and right, and then the united Confederate line would push Porter before them and away from White House.

Unfortunately, there was no sound of Jackson's guns. It remains one of the most frustrating mysteries of the Civil War. A stickler for obeying orders to the letter, Jackson had been known to keep an entire column of troops waiting in line to march while he stared at his watch, unwilling to move one second before his instructions specified. Certainly he had his orders now, and they were specific. Yet when the sun rose, he did not move, an act that defied adequate explanation. Enemy cavalry did face him in front, but for his three divisions, they could present nothing more than a nuisance. So, too, the trees and brush felled to impede his advance presented little real obstacle to seasoned warriors who could march twenty miles in a day and still be ready to fight. But perhaps, in the end, that was it. In the past three months they had simply marched and fought too much. They covered 400 miles on foot in their Shenandoah campaign. Now they were just arrived after an exhausting combined march and jolting train trip. Even then, with Stonewall to prod them, they would have moved. But he did not. As exhausted as the rest, the indomitable Jackson temporarily ceased to function. Disorientation, apathy, and sleepiness conspired to rob him of his accustomed iron discipline. He halted six miles short of where he was to have been the night before the attack, then stayed up praying through the night instead of resting himself, and finally started marching toward Porter later than ordered. Other than a late morning message to Lee that he was running late, Jackson communicated with no one, and by 5 p.m. was still almost three miles from the battleline. There he simply put his men into bivouac and himself went to sleep without his command having fired a single shot all day. Alas, it was not to be the end of his erratic performance on the peninsula.

With Jackson seemingly off in limbo, it fell to A.P. Hill to carry the fight to the enemy. Vainly he waited through the morning to hear firing from Jackson. Finally by late afternoon he gave up waiting. It did not help that Lee had been of little or no help. He waited, too, throughout the morning and into the afternoon, seemingly frozen by his battleplan and unable or unwilling to act until Jackson was in place. Lee was still learning, and this was to be his first battle. It did not help that President Davis and other dignitaries were with him, waiting. A few months from now a more seasoned Lee would improvise, think on his feet and act, rather than allow the failure of one part of a plan to endanger all of it. But now he listened, and it was Hill who put the battle in motion by acting on his own, crossing the river, and driving toward Mechanicsville.

It was 3 p.m. or shortly thereafter that the firing finally commenced, as Hill's 16,000 advanced toward Mechanicsville. The Federals occupying the village yielded it with nothing more than minor skirmishing, but as Hill's brigades swept on through the town, they could see the Yankees posted in strong positions on the far banks of Beaver Dam Creek a mile ahead of them. Quickly the battle got out of anyone's control. Two of Hill's brigades struck at Porter's right flank, and one regiment actually got across Beaver Dam Creek, though to no purpose. The stream, though barely ten feet wide, had steep brushy banks that provided excellent defensive positions from which the Federals sent forth sheets of flame and lead. Another of Hill's brigades got enmeshed in brutal volleying at Ellerson's Mill on Porter's left center, and when a brigade from D.H. Hill finally got across the Chickahominy, it rushed to its support, only to be chewed up in like fashion.

Only nightfall put an end to a fight that had gone wrong for Lee from dawn to dark. Instead of forcing Porter away from the creek by maneuver, Lee had found himself fighting for it, and losing. There was no Jackson, no Longstreet, and no D.H. Hill. A.P. Hill had borne the fight all alone, and suffered for it. He lost almost 1,400 killed and wounded, while inflicting not more than 360 casualties on the enemy. At the end of the day, Porter held his ground, and Lee had nothing to show for his first battle but his wounds.[8]

Yet Lee's losses proved to be only tactical, for later that night McClellan gave him a strategic victory by deciding to abandon the line of Beaver Dam Creek without further fight. Though Jackson had never moved against Porter's flank, the knowledge that Stonewall was near put a fright into "Little Mac." He recognized the magnitude now of the threat to his supply line north of the Chickahominy to White House, and that alone was enough to unnerve him. McClellan did not collapse as had G.W. Smith or Jackson. But inwardly he accepted defeat, or, more accurately, he defeated himself. He decided that he would have to change his base of supply from the York to the James River. That in itself was not such a desperate move. But the York was the only way by which he could practically get his heavy siege artillery up to bombard Richmond. By shifting to the James, he tacitly admitted that he would not, and could not, pursue further his only announced plan of attack on the Confederate capital. Thus McClellan's offensive evaporated. He was still a dangerous foe if only for his strength of numbers, but in the mental test of wills between the commanders, Lee now held the initiative.

Porter began to pull out of the Beaver Dam Creek positions soon after 3 a.m. on June 27, falling back toward Boatswain's Swamp, four miles to the rear, near Gaines' Mill on Powhite Creek. There Porter formed with his left on the Chickahominy where the Powhite flowed into it and fronted by the swamp, and his line extending northward along a creek to Old Cold Harbor. His front stretched in a convex arc some two miles, giving him an advantage of interior lines, and with the Grapevine Bridge over the Chickahominy just in his rear, allowing access to McClellan on the other side. It was a strong position, but Lee, his mind like his army on the offensive, was not about to recoil from renewing the fight.

Apparently overlooking Jackson's lapse of the previous day, Lee once again planned an attack that depended largely upon the sleepy Stonewall. Hill was to follow Porter's line of withdrawal directly. Longstreet, now safely across the river, would move parallel to Hill, and between him and the Chickahominy. Jackson was to come in on Porter's right flank as he should have done the day before, while D.H. Hill was to march his division way around the left to come in on Jackson's flank and form the far left of the army, striking Porter's rear in or around Old Cold Harbor, thus cutting off his line of retreat to White House.

Hill sent his bloodied division forward around 3 p.m. The Confederates rushed past Gaines' Mill then wheeled slightly southward to strike the right center of Porter's arc. By then D.H. Hill had his division in position, but Jackson was late in arriving, and again seemed disoriented. It did not help that Porter's flank was some distance to the rear of where they all expected it to be. Instead of facing an exposed and vulnerable enemy right, they were looking squarely down Porter's guns. The failure to meet the expected seemed to confuse Jackson all the more and he simply stopped, uncertain what to do even though he could hear A.P. Hill once again in the maelstrom of battle less than a mile to his right.

Hill was fighting for his life near New Cold Harbor. As the day before, Porter held a good position behind a stream bank, while Hill's men had to advance against them across open, swampy ground. The Virginian's men had been in action almost since dawn, when they began their pursuit of Porter, and by now they were exhausted, at times actually having run to catch up with the retiring foe. When they approached Porter's main line, they came upon a rain of rifle and artillery fire. Porter had the luxury of several fresh brigades unblooded in the fight at Mechanicsville, while Hill's division was already badly winded. More than 25,000 Yankees were able to concentrate their venom on Hill's 13,000 before Jackson and the rest got into the fight, as indeed they finally did.

It turned out to be a jumbled, confused series of little local fights, as the swamp and the forests prevented any overall control by Hill. Brigades attacked and withdrew, attacked again, were broken up or pinned down, depending on the inclinations of their commanders and the severity of the Yankee fire. After a time Porter actually gained the upper hand, pinning down almost the entire division, and by 4 p.m. there was danger of the Confederate attack breaking up entirely. Only then, still waiting for Jackson, did Lee take a personal hand, ordering Longstreet into the battle to support Hill's right. Then, without orders, one of Jackson's division commanders went to Hill's left on his own initiative, and though the situation continued to be desperate, at least the faltering Rebel line stiffened. Finally, around 6 p.m., Lee finally met with Jackson himself, and the balance of Stonewall's command came into line, with little thanks to him.

Having given up on his original plan of that morning, Lee now decided to resort to a general assault all along his line. It came around 7 p.m. and it gained good ground. Perceptibly Porter's resistance to the 50,000 or more arrayed against him slackened. Rebels ran to the creek in his front, waded across, then threw their rifles up the banks and clambered up after them. Lee sensed that a critical moment was at hand. He found Brigadier General John B. Hood, who had served with him in the prewar army, and now commanding a Texas brigade.

"Can you break his line?" asked the commanding general.

"I can try," replied Hood, and he led them down to the creek, across, and up into the teeth of the tired and dispirited defenders. An advance line of Yankees gave way, and Hood rushed on to the main line. It, too, broke in the ferocity of his charge, and thus he penetrated the very center of Porter's line. Within minutes the gallant

Federal's line collapsed generally, though not in rout. Deliberately, and aided by rein-forcements sent by McClellan, Porter withdrew to the bridges over the Chickahominy, and after nightfall took his command to the other side, leaving behind 6,800 men killed, wounded, or captured. Yet Lee paid for his victory with almost 9,000 casualties, the brunt of them, again, coming from A.P. Hill's valiant division.[9]

While the fighting of the past two days went on, McClellan kept 70,000 or more men virtually idle on the south side of the Chickahominy, virtually flimflammed by the activity of the enterprising Magruder into thinking that he actually faced superior numbers. Magruder marched his troops back and forth, lit extravagant campfires, made bold reconnaissances, and used every other artifice of deception to make the foe think that his 22,000 were many times their number. McClellan happily cooperated. Indeed, by the close of the Gaines' Mill fighting, between Magruder's flamboyant histrionics and Lee's ill-managed but relentless attacks, "Little Mac" was a thoroughly beaten man. Even then – or perhaps especially then – the extent of his petulant mega-lomania revealed itself. "I have lost this battle because my force was too small," he whined in a letter to Secretary of War Edwin Stanton. "I am not responsible for this." He protested that if he only had 10,000 fresh men he could still beat Lee, when the fact was that he had almost four full army corps, better than 60,000 "fresh men" who had done nothing at his disposal. "If I save this army now, I tell you plainly that I owe no thanks to you or to any other persons in Washington. You have done your best to sacrifice this army."[10]

In fact, of course, McClellan was doing a perfectly good job of that on his own. The next day saw no general engagement, as the Federals withdrew from the Chickahominy towards the James River. Through the day Lee remained uncertain of McClellan's movements, until Stuart brought him intelligence that the supply base at White House had been abandoned and everything not removable destroyed. Still, Franklin, Heintzelman, and Sumner remained in Magruder and Huger's front, and this left Lee puzzled. He thought that cutting off the enemy from the base at White House would force McClellan either to retreat entirely, or else come north of the Chickahominy to attack him. Seemingly the Yankee was doing neither, and Lee could not foresee what McClellan was in fact trying to do – withdraw to the south to the James, near Harrison's Landing, there to erect a new base. "Little Mac" had aban-doned any idea of an offensive, but as long as those three corps menaced Magruder, Huger, and Richmond, he could not be certain what course to pursue. Thus the Federals gained a day, vital time in what was now a race to escape the Rebels' crush-ing attacks.

The next morning, June 29, Lee discovered that McClellan had pulled out entirely from the works in front of Magruder and Huger. At least the mystery was gone now. McClellan was in retreat, and obviously toward the James. Lee had already formulated a plan for putting all nine of his divisions on the march, by a bewildering variety of roads – some barely more than tracks – to try to intercept McClellan before he could reach the James and the covering fire of Yankee gunboats on the river. Once again, however, it was all simply too complex a movement even in the best of circumstances, and circumstances did not favor anything like this now on the Peninsula. Many of his divisions were tired. There were few good maps, the roads were a mire after the spring rains, and some commanders like Longstreet, Huger, and D.H. Hill were strangers to the landscape of Virginia.

Lee first caught up with elements of the Army of the Potomac by about 10 a.m., three miles south of the Chickahominy at Savage's Station on the Richmond & York River line. Yet again Jackson failed to take his position on the left flank at the proper time, and Magruder, who was to launch the attack, had to delay until around 3 p.m. Huger, who was to come up on Magruder's right was equally tardy. It did not help that there were few roadsigns, and Lee seems not to have thought of giving his division commanders local guides. Longstreet fared worst of all. Ordered to move to the far right, below Savage's Station, to cut off the Yankees' retreat to the south, Lee told him to move on the Darbytown Road. It took its name from a local farm whose occupants, thanks to queer local tradition, called themselves "Darby" when their actual name, and the sign on their fence that identified the road, was spelled "Enroughty." Longstreet, a South Carolinian unfamiliar with local customs, lost precious time trying to find the right road, and A.P. Hill, ordered to follow him, did the same.

As a result, it was Magruder alone, assisted by a few other units, who opened the battle, facing three divisions from Sumner's and Franklin's corps. Magruder was himself exhausted from the tension of the three previous days of facing a virtual army all by himself, and today he did not perform well. His assault was half-hearted, and almost ignored by some of McClellan's commanders, with the result that the Yankee retreat continued unimpeded and Lee lost, or so he believed, a real chance to cut the enemy off from the James.[11]

He tried again on June 30 near Glendale, this time directing seven divisions to concentrate against four posted by McClellan to act as rearguard while his supply trains and the bulk of the army continued their flight to the James. Again it all failed to work. Only Longstreet and the ever-combative A.P. Hill managed to get themselves to the scene of action, where they launched a series of vicious attacks through the afternoon that did push the Yankees back and inflicted serious casualties, but the Confederates themselves suffered some 3,500 or more without achieving Lee's aim. Incredibly, McClellan had abandoned the land entirely, leaving his corps to fend for themselves almost without orders while he went to the comfort of a gunboat on the James and began organizing his new supply base. His absence probably accounts for much of the Federal success in thwarting Lee's designs.

But Lee would not be deterred. His frustration showed itself early on July 1 when he exploded that "I cannot have my orders carried out!" Unmindful that his orders called for what was practically unattainable, he was unwilling to abandon his hope of crushing McClellan without one last effort. The tension of the last week clearly showed. Having tried clever strategy only to meet with repeated disappointment, he now resorted in desperation to an almost utter lack of finesse. The Federal rearguard had taken a position atop Malvern Hill, an imposing elevation where they massed eight divisions and more than 200 cannon. Looking at this position, Lee somehow deluded himself that the Federals could be driven off by a resolute attack. Longstreet seconded the idea, himself locating a position from which nearly 60 Confederate artillery pieces could bombard the Yankee lines. Most of his own divisions were in the vicinity now, including even Jackson for a change, and making his decision, Lee issued the oddest attack order of his career. His batteries might be able to punch a hole in the Yankee defenses, it said. If so, Brigadier General Lewis Armistead commanding one of Huger's brigades was in a good position to see it. He would charge "with a yell," said Lee, simply ordering his other commanders to "do the same."

It was a disaster. Federal artillery fire quickly silenced the Confederate barrage, negating the conditions for Armistead's order to advance. But Lee forgot or neglected to cancel that order. Then, quite unexpectedly, Yankee sharpshooters advanced on their own directly toward Armistead, who repulsed them and pursued. Just at that moment Magruder came on the field, armed with Lee's order to follow Armistead's lead. Unaware of the utter failure of the artillery barrage, he sent word to Lee that Armistead appeared to be advancing successfully, and a desperate Lee thought he saw a chance for victory still, and ordered an attack. Magruder went forward just before 5 p.m. The Yankee artillery mowed them down like wheat. Then D.H. Hill arrived on the left. Hearing the firing and all the yelling, he obeyed Lee's terse order and launched his own brigades into the advance against Malvern Hill. Huger, too, sent his division up against those massed enemy cannon, and Lee funneled more isolated commands into the slaughter. Only nightfall mercifully ended perhaps Lee's worst tactical performance of the war. It had been a butcher's picnic. Nearly 5,500 of Lee's men were killed or wounded, as against Federal casualties of half that number. The acerbic General D.H. Hill, especially bitter over the bulk of the losses falling in his command, declared that Malvern Hill "was not war – it was murder."[12]

When night closed on that terrible field, even Lee finally gave up further attempts to stop McClellan. In seven days of almost constant fighting – soon the battles collectively would be called The Seven Days' – he had lost a fourth of his army in killed and wounded. He had not destroyed McClellan as he hoped, and on July 2 "Little Mac" completed his withdrawal to Harrison's Landing where Lee could not assail him. Still Lee had achieved much. The threat to Richmond was ended, at least for the moment. McClellan had suffered 10,000 casualties himself, and stood with his prestige in the North seriously damaged and the confidence of Lincoln deeply shaken. True, he was still on the peninsula, but he would never mount an offensive there again.

Yet despite Lee's disappointment when he reported to Davis that he had not achieved all that he had hoped, he was the one person who could not see the greatest benefit to the Confederate States from The Seven Days'. It was the making of Robert E. Lee. Though he only won one actual battle, at Gaines' Mill, still he drove McClellan back and saved the capital against seemingly overwhelming odds. That eradicated forever all recollections of "Granny" Lee. It cemented his hold on the command of the army that he would subsequently lead to imperishable glory, an army that Joseph E. Johnston had seemed disinclined to lead at all. And there, in the end, lay the great benefaction of that shell that took Johnston out of the war for the next several months, though it was a tragically mixed blessing. Out of Johnston's blood, the South got Lee, who undoubtedly prolonged the war in the East far longer than Johnston or any other might have done. Yet out of that prolongation would come untold suffering, for The Seven Days' brought an end to the "phoney war," and the revelation of a whole new scale of vicious fighting, and the longer the Confederacy lasted in this new level of warfare, the more of its sons would mingle their blood with Johnston's. After The Seven Days', there was barely a man in the South who would not readily bleed for Robert E. Lee.

REFERENCES

1 Tyler Dennett, ed., *Lincoln and the Civil War in the Diaries and Letters of John Hay* (New York, 1939), p.33.

2 George B. McClellan, *McClellan's Own Story* (New York, 1887), pp.168-77.

3 *O.R.*, I, 11, pt.3, p.456.

4 Alexander, *Memoirs*, p.102.

5 Francis W. Pickens to Milledge L. Bonham, July 7, 1861, Milledge L. Bonham Papers, South Caroliniana Library, University of South Carolina, Columbia.

6 *O.R.*, I, 11, pt.1, p.51.

7 Clifford Dowdey, *The Seven Days* (Boston, 1964), pp.161-62.

8 *Ibid.*, pp.200-202.

9 *Ibid.*, pp.236-38.

10 *O.R.*, I, 11, pt.3, p.266.

11 Dowdey, *Seven Days*, p.283.

12 Buel and Johnson, *Battles and Leaders*, II, p.394.

IV
ANTIETAM (SHARPSBURG)

George B. McClellan showed seemingly remarkable staying power. Even after his failure on the peninsula, even after his petulant and insubordinate communications with Washington, even after his snubs to President Lincoln himself, still "Little Mac" seemed able to dominate Yankee high command. He never stopped complaining over his peremptory orders to remove his army from the peninsula and return with it to northern Virginia and the capital area. The true strategic line of advance was still via the York and James, he would argue; his hidden objections lay in being told to cooperate with a new commander, Major General John Pope, and his growing army. McClellan intentionally dragged his feet and raised every objection possible to impede carrying out his orders, and by late August 1862, as Pope was about to be thoroughly beaten by Lee at Second Manassas, McClellan was still inventing excuses to withhold two full corps that might have made the difference for the unlucky Pope.

Almost everyone saw through McClellan's behavior, yet he got away with it, especially after news of Pope's defeat reached Washington. It fulfilled McClellan's own prophecy of disaster if control of any of his troops were turned over to another, a prophecy he did his best to make happen. And thus after Pope's debacle, with the renewed hysteria over the threat of a Rebel army marching on Washington once more, McClellan came once more to the fore. Despite their anger at "Little Mac's" part in the disaster – Lincoln privately accused him of relishing in Pope's defeat – the administration asked him to take overall command of all forces once more.[1] It was a humbling moment for Lincoln; McClellan exulted in his triumph, though with customary false humility he proclaimed that "I only consent to take it for my country's sake."[2]

On September 2, 1862, McClellan once more resumed command of all Union forces in northern Virginia and Washington, receiving rousing cheers from the troops who never ceased loving him, even in the face of defeat. The euphoria could not last long, however, for the very next day General-in-Chief Halleck warned McClellan that with Pope's army cleared out of the Manassas area and Lee in the ascendant, they should expect the Rebels to capitalize on their recent success by invading Maryland and even Pennsylvania. McClellan must rush to be ready.

Rushing, of course, was not in the Young Napoleon's makeup. Organizing, on the other hand, most certainly was, and if a battle could be won on paper, McClellan was the man for the job. He took the battered but not demoralized remnants of Pope's Army of Virginia and shuffled them back with his own command to make a revitalized Army of the Potomac. His I Corps, almost entirely New Yorkers and Pennsylvanians, he gave to Major General Joseph Hooker, who won the nickname "fighting Joe" in the newspapers during the Peninsula Campaign. Its three divisions were commanded by Generals Abner Doubleday, James B. Ricketts, and George G. Meade. Old "Bull" Sumner led the II Corps, three divisions under Israel Richardson, John Sedgwick, and William H. French. McClellan's favorite Fitz-John Porter stayed at the head of the V Corps, with Generals George Morell, George Sykes, and Andrew Humphreys commanding the divisions. Franklin took the VI Corps, with Henry Slocum, William F. Smith, and Darius Couch at the head of his divisions, while another McClellan favorite, Burnside, led the IX Corps and its four divisions under Orlando Willcox, Samuel D. Sturgis, Isaac P. Rodman, and Eliakim Scammon. Old but valiant Joseph Mansfield completed the infantry complement with his XII Corps, the smallest at only two divisions under Alpheus Williams and George S. Greene. Each division in the army had its own artillery except for the XII Corps, which combined all its guns into a single separate command. McClellan also put together five brigades of cavalry as a separate mounted division, led by Brigadier General Alfred Pleasonton.

It was a magnificent army, once again well equipped, well fed, trained to perfection (for volunteers), and filled with high spirit and élan. The only question was whether or not McClellan would use it. No such quandary existed in anyone's mind about that other great force in the East, the Army of Northern Virginia. Lee could be counted on to use it, and after his performance at Second Manassas, to use it with daring and imagination. He finally abandoned the cumbersome organization by divisions that he inherited from Johnston. While not yet authorized by Davis and Congress to create formal corps, he did so informally by forming two corps-like commands. The larger went to Longstreet, the steady and dependable – if slow – South Carolinian. He inherited control of the divisions of Generals Lafayette McLaws, Richard H. Anderson, David R. Jones, John G. Walker, and the hard-hitting Hood, along with the independent brigade of the very independent "Shanks" Evans of Bull Run fame. Lee's second "corps" went to Jackson who, though apparently forgiven for his deplorable performance on the peninsula, still received the lesser command, just four divisions led by Generals Richard S. Ewell (who lost a leg at Second Manassas and was replaced by Alexander R. Lawton), A.P. Hill, John R. Jones, and D.H. Hill. Each division had its own artillery, and each corps an artillery reserve. As usual, Lee's gallant cavalryman Stuart led the division of horse.

Even if Lee had not been the pugnacious fighter that he proved to be, events in 1862 would have forced him to follow up his double gains over McClellan and Pope by taking the offensive. Domestically, the victories heartened the Southern people, who were just now realizing that this would not be the brief war their politicians had promised. The close call around Richmond had taken some of the pomposity out of their attitude, replacing it with a sense that they could still win their independence, but only by beating the Yankees and beating them again until the foe no longer had the stomach for fighting. Furthermore, having regained most of northern Virginia, they must move quickly to maintain their hold. Yet the ground just gained had been ravaged by the armies after a year of war, and could not sustain Lee's need for provisions. He must draw his rations elsewhere. Then there was the international dimension to consider. The South desperately needed European help in winning its independence, yet Britain and France were slow to lend their potentially decisive aid, each waiting to be sure it would be backing a winner. The victories of the spring and summer worked to this purpose, but it would be even more effective if the Confederacy demonstrated that it could take the war to the enemy on its own homefront.

All of these influences and more combined toward the inevitable logic of invading the North. There Lee could draw fresh supplies and make the Yankee civil population feel the hard hand of war. There he could draw the foe away from any advance back into Virginia. And a victory gained there must assuredly convince world powers that the Confederacy was a safe bet for formal recognition and military assistance.

Never willing to waste a moment, Lee put his campaign in motion the very day that he notified Davis of his intention. Indeed, the precise details of the movement were still forming in his mind as his legions took the road northward to Leesburg. The next day they reached and began crossing the Potomac at White's Ford, twenty-five miles northwest of Washington, and already well in McClellan's rear. It was a heady moment for Lee's ragged veterans. At last they would give the enemy to know how it felt to play host to a hostile army.

General Halleck had predicted exactly what Lee would do, and warned McClellan on the very day that Lee told Davis of his plans. Confirmation reached Washington the next day as witnesses reported seeing the Rebels crossing the river. Almost immediately Lincoln gave McClellan orders to put the army in the field, and "Little Mac" acted with unwonted alacrity, immediately putting the lie to Lee's prediction of a several-week paralysis. The Army of the Potomac was in much better condition and morale than he realized. McClellan was still reorganizing the army, and refitting and equipping it. Now he worked feverishly, and by September 7 was actually ready to move in response to Lee.

Other than the alacrity with which it happened, this was exactly what Lee wanted. He could have moved into Maryland by the Shenandoah, masking his march and keeping the enemy in the dark longer. But he wanted to make McClellan pull out of the Washington defenses to have to chase him, and thus the wily chieftain virtually broadcast his line of march. But what he secretly intended was that once at Frederick, Maryland, with McClellan rushing to catch up, he would then turn west, cross the low range of the Catoctin, to South Mountain. It could be crossed only at a few gaps, most notably Turner's and Crampton's. By crossing over, then closing those gaps behind him, he would leave McClellan trapped on the eastern slope while Lee was free to rest his army, receive supplies sent up via the Shenandoah, and then move northward into Pennsylvania. When an exhausted and attenuated Yankee line finally caught up to him to fight, Lee could then force McClellan to fight on ground of Confederate choosing, and at a great disadvantage.

This is almost exactly how it worked. Lee entered Frederick on September 6, to stay for five days. There the men rested and replenished their haversacks from Maryland's abundant fields. Lee watched with pleasure as the Army of the Potomac moved slowly toward him, being still more than twenty miles distant by September 9. But what did not please the Confederates was what did not happen at Harpers Ferry. Having effectively cut it and its garrison off from Washington, he had expected that its defenders would abandon the post without a fight, leaving its munitions to Lee. Furthermore, in the event of having to abandon the invasion, his natural line of retreat would be via Harpers Ferry into the Shenandoah. He could not leave that garrison, small though it was and commanded by the drunkard Dixon Miles of First Manassas infamy, in his rear. He decided now to take it since it would not leave of its own accord. He gave Jackson the job of taking nearly half the army, by three separate routes, to strike Harpers Ferry from all sides simultaneously. Jackson was given such overwhelming force that they expected to accomplish the task quickly, by September 12, after which Jackson would march north to meet Lee west of South Mountain to resume the campaign.

It was a brilliant, if desperately chancy, conception, but Lee had already divided his army in the face of the enemy before and emerged the victor. He only had 50,000 with him now, though, and if McClellan's army caught up with Longstreet before Jackson returned, the Rebels would be outnumbered three-to-one.

Fortunately, McClellan, though moving, moved slowly and thus gave Lee time. McClellan continued to organize his army even while it moved. He created three "wings." Franklin commanded the first, his own VI Corps and an additional division. Sumner took the center wing with the II and XII Corps. And Burnside led the right wing, his own IX plus the I Corps. Porter and his V Corps remained behind to guard Washington for the moment, but still McClellan has almost 85,000 men on the move. Even then, he believed that Lee had at least 100,000, and probably more.[3]

By September 11 McClellan was only fifteen miles from Frederick, now convinced that Lee actually had 150,000. Though reports of Jackson's movement toward Harpers Ferry reached him almost daily, he remained uncertain about Lee's overall intentions, knowing only with certainty that Lee had left Frederick. Many around him, including McClellan himself, seemed to think that Lee was already retreating back toward the Potomac. Thus when McClellan finally marched into Frederick on September 12-13, his own plan of campaign remained unformed. There could not have been a more propitious time for one of his aides to walk into his headquarters on the morning of the 13th to hand him a dispatch from General Williams, commanding the XII Corps. An hour or so earlier, a corporal in one of his Indiana regiments stumbled upon a bundle of three cigars lying in the grass near his camp. The wrapping turned out to be no ordinary paper, but an actual copy of Lee's order detailing the plan for taking Harpers Ferry, and his own intended movements. The news was stunning. McClellan held in his hand exact details on where every Rebel division was, was headed, and its timetable. Lee had divided his army into two weak halves, and armed with this information, McClellan could move to defeat him in detail with overwhelming force. "Now I know what to do," he exclaimed. "Here is a paper with which if I cannot whip Bobbie Lee, I will be willing to go home."[4]

But then McClellan proceeded to fritter away all the fruits of his good fortune. Instead of moving immediately, as he wired Lincoln he would do, he wasted nearly a full day before putting his army on the road again. He expected to reach South Mountain on September 14 and fight Lee the next day, while sending Franklin's wing to save Harpers Ferry. He still believed that the half of the army with Lee equaled or outnumbered his other two wings, but expressed himself more than willing to risk a fight.

Just then Lee was being severely inconvenienced by more than the lost order. The Harpers Ferry expedition fell seriously behind schedule. Even the overwhelming numbers committed to the side operation, and the equally monumental incompetence of Dixon S. Miles, did not make it the easy walkover that Lee expected. The Rebels first approached on September 12, driving a garrison of Yankees from nearby Martinsburg before them. But it took time for all of the Confederates to come up, and lesser Yankee commanders, in spite of Miles, put up a better resistance than expected. The defense continued through the next two days, and only on the morning of September 15 did the beleagured garrison finally surrender. Jackson bagged 11,500 prisoners, thousands of rifles, more than 70 cannon, and tons of munitions and materiel. One of the few casualties on either side was old Miles himself, mortally wounded by one of the last artillery shots fired. Jackson promised to lead five of his divisions toward a junction with Lee later that same day, while A.P. Hill would remain behind to oversee getting prisoners and materials off to safety before leading his division north.

Lee should have been pleased, but if so he kept it to himself. He was starting to realize that he and his army faced the potential for serious trouble. He had nine divisions in his army, and had committed six of them to the Harpers Ferry operation.

That left only two under Longstreet and one of D.H. Hill's as the balance of his command, and Longstreet had mistakenly taken his two all the way to Hagerstown, ten miles north of where Lee wanted them. His command was split into three isolated portions, and McClellan – while still agonizingly slow – was moving quicker than Lee anticipated. Indeed, the day before Harpers Ferry fell, McClellan had an opportunity to hit several separated portions of the Army of Northern Virginia at once. A man of real moral courage might have taken them all.

On September 14 McClellan put his army on the road out of Frederick toward's Turner's Gap, while Franklin's corps marched in desultory fashion a few miles to the south, on a parallel route to Crampton's Gap. When the main van approached Turner's, led by Jesse Reno, now commanding Burnside's IX Corps, there was nothing in front of them but D.H. Hill and two brigades. But those Rebels were determined to fight, for the gap meant everything to Lee just then. Hill and his gallant 2,000 fought like demons, often hand-to-hand, delaying McClellan's advance for more than two hours. Then the Federals blew their advantage by calling a lull in the fight to wait for the arrival of more supports. That gave Hill's other brigades time to reach the gap, with Longstreet hurrying to join him. In the end, when the Federal attack renewed, both the I and IX Corps were involved, with still a heavy numerical advantage over the Confederates. Hill and his supports managed to set up sufficient defenses that held off the enemy advance until nightfall.

Seven miles to the south, Franklin made an equally tardy approach to Crampton's Gap, and it is well that he did. The gap had been virtually undefended until General Lafayette McLaws rushed his division from Harpers Ferry. Though Franklin still outnumbered McLaws four to one, he believed himself to be the underdog, and withheld his attack, giving the Confederates ample time to rush their reinforcements. Franklin did not attack in the end until well into the afternoon, and then only pushed it hesitatingly. Nevertheless, by nightfall he had forced the Rebels out of the gap and into the valley beyond. But there he stopped, unwilling – or too afraid – to follow up his success. He had gotten himself between two halves of Lee's army, giving McClellan a clear road to victory. Instead they all decided to wait until the morrow to plan their next move.

Lee would not wait. Knowing the danger that faced him, he decided that night to abandon Turner's Gap and pull his army together. The next morning, with Jackson soon to be on the road, he ordered all of the remaining divisions to concentrate near Sharpsburg, seven miles northwest of Turner's Gap and eight miles due north of Harpers Ferry. It was a good location for a concentration. Sharpsburg sat astride a number of roads running to all points of the compass. The village itself lay barely a quarter mile west of Antietam Creek, a stream just wide and deep enough to discourage crossing anywhere but at three places. The Upper Bridge sat more than two miles northeast of town. More than a mile downstream, and directly opposite, was the Middle Bridge. Three-fourths of a mile further down lay the Rohrbach Bridge. There was one good ford just below the Upper Bridge, and two more well below the Rohrbach. Still, with only about 15,000 men with him when he selected Sharpsburg, Lee was wise to pick a place that offered only limited crossings. That alone would put McClellan at a disadvantage, and help even the disparity of odds. Furthermore, the ground just west of the creek offered a slight rise or ridge along the Hagerstown Turnpike, running north to south through the village, and directly parallel to the creek. Lee could position his thin ranks along this high ground, thus commanding the bridges and fords. Along the way a succession of woods, fences, "sunken" roads, and more, offered good defensive terrain.

It was clear that Lee came to Sharpsburg to defend. It was not what he had wanted for his campaign's climactic battle, but in the circumstances, with his army fragmented and heavily outnumbered, and with McClellan reacting faster than he had hoped, any thought of himself taking the offensive was totally impracticable. Of course Lee was always a dangerous opponent, and never more so than when in trouble. But for now he had taken risk enough in simply deciding to stay on Yankee soil. Moreover, his position offered serious vulnerabilities as well as strengths. The Potomac ran in an arc only a mile or so west and south of Sharpsburg, swinging eastward to the point, four miles below the village, where the Antietam flowed into it. The two streams made a peninsula of sorts, but one that was open at the top. Lee could not hope to prevent McClellan from crossing the Antietam at every point upstream – he simply did not have enough men. The Yankees would get across somewhere on his left flank; that was a given. So Lee selected the best ground he could find, about a mile north of Sharpsburg, and there anchored his left, virtually abandoning the Upper Bridge to McClellan. But the gray chieftain's far greater vulnerability lay at the opposite end of his line. If the Yankees could get across the Rohrbach Bridge, or thereabouts, and force their way just 1,500 yards on the other side, they could take the road leading to Harpers Ferry, cutting off Jackson's marching divisions. Worse, if McClellan could press a bit farther to the Shepherdstown Road, he would cut Lee off from all avenues of retreat to the other side of the Potomac and safety. Take those roads, and McClellan would have Lee trapped with his back to an uncrossable river. Even a bad general could make of that an end to the Army of Northern Virginia.

Whether or not McClellan was that bad a general remained to be seen, but when he brought the advance of his own column up to the Antietam on September 15, he showed no signs of hurry. Instead, as he had all along, he proceeded to make Lee the gift of vital time. McClellan did nothing for the rest of that day, and spent all of September 16 studying and thinking, playing with the perfect alignment of his own corps, and methodically planning what was to be, in fact, his very first offensive battle.

Even McClellan could appreciate the weakness in Lee's position, while he continued to entirely misapprehend the weakness of the Rebel army. "Little Mac" planned to mass for an attack on Lee's left where he would not have to contest a crossing for the Antietam, while at the same time – more or less – moving across the bridge in front of the enemy right. Neither attack, however, was to be coordinated, and neither seemed aimed at the possible isolation of Lee from support or retreat. Instead, revealing his utter immersion in the past, he planned a Napoleonic massed cavalry attack on Lee's center should either of the flank assaults achieve success. McClellan seems utterly to have missed the lesson of the last year of warfare that the rifled shoulder arm had made cavalry charges obsolete. He also seemed unconcerned that his mounted men would still have to ride no more than four abreast across the Middle Bridge, right into the face of Rebel cannon, in such a charge. It was absolute foolishness. With the time and men at his disposal, even McClellan should have been able to produce something better.[5]

Making matters worse, he proceeded to tamper with his high command just the day before the fight. He broke up Burnside's wing, making Hooker independent, and returning Burnside to the command of the IX Corps, whose commander, Reno, had been killed at Turner's Gap. Now Hooker was to handle the attack on Lee's left, and Burnside the attempt to turn back the enemy right. Furthermore, Hooker was to be backed up by Sumner with the II and XII Corps, but they were all to be subject to Hooker's orders, effectively removing "Bull" Sumner from command. Franklin was to form the reserve, along with Porter's recently arrived V Corps and, of course, Pleasonton's cavalry. All combined, excluding non-combatant ranks, McClellan had about 75,000 fighting men at hand – five times what faced him across Antietam Creek.

Lee's dispositions by nightfall on September 16 revealed just how weak he was, and just how daring. Longstreet commanded his center and right, a long thin line with only the three divisions of Walker, Jones, and D.H. Hill right in the center along a sunken road. When Jackson and the first of his divisions arrived that afternoon, Lee placed them on his far left after McClellan's movement of Hooker across the Upper Bridge in broad daylight gave away his intent to strike Lee there first on the morrow. Jackson put Jones' division in a small forest known locally as the West Woods, just to the left of the Hagerstown road, with Lawton on the right behind a cornfield. Hood took position in Jones' rear in the wood alongside a Dunker Church. Even the addition of elements of Jackson's command from Harpers Ferry still only brought Lee up to 26,000 by nightfall. He desperately needed those absent divisions of McLaws, Anderson, and A.P. Hill.[6]

It was a restive night on both sides of Antietam Creek. Rarely in this war did two armies come this close without immediately launching into one another. Lee and McClellan stared at each other fully a day and a half, taking their time, making their dispositions. Thus their men knew when the battle was going to start, and that when it did commence, everything would be in place for each to do the maximum damage to the other. No one exactly predicted that the next dawn would inaugurate the bloodiest single day in American history, but most sensed that it would be something very definitely out of the ordinary.

They would argue over who fired the first shot, a pointless exercise, since there were probably dozens of "first" shots, all uncoordinated. The artillery started it sure enough, even while the morning fogs were still lifting. Within a few minutes, around 6 a.m. or later, Hooker began to move forward, driving straight along the line of the Hagerstown Turnpike toward the Dunker Church. Meade moved in first, heading toward the cornfield where he ran into a Virginia brigade that held him at bay despite repeated assaults. Hooker soon had Doubleday and Ricketts with their divisions ready to go into the fight, elements of the latter's division going straight into the high standing corn stalks toward unseen Confederates. They were slaughtered. The brigade in the actual field lost a third of its number in the next few minutes and soon left the field – and the battle – for good.

What caused the fearful toll in that brigade was a lesson that no one seemed yet to have learned after more than a year of war. Generals were sending their regiments and brigades in one by one, instead of attacking in mass formation to take advantage of their numbers. Rickett's lead brigade went into the cornfield with no supports at hand, and thus allowed the enemy – outnumbered overall – to concentrate their fire on the isolated unit. Then in the two brigades sent to support the advance, one brigade commander was wounded and the other turned and ran in terror, leaving them temporarily leaderless.

Soon Lawton sent a new brigade to support the by-now badly blooded defenders of the cornfield, launching a counterattack that regained some ground for a time. The nature of the fighting became brutally intense, though not yet hand-to-hand. Some regiments almost ceased to exist, the 12th Massachusetts taking 67 percent casualties in one hour. Finally the fighting for the cornfield settled as each side held to opposite fringes of the acreage and kept firing at the other. The fury of the past hour had simply exhausted them. Meanwhile, Doubleday went forward toward Jones in the West Woods. Barely had fighting begun when Jones himself was put out of action, and General W. E. Starke had to take over from him, only to fall himself soon thereafter with mortal wounds. Before that happened, however, Doubleday's people ran into a seemingly solid wall of flame and lead as they hit the western edge of the cornfield and the West Woods just across the Hagerstown road. Only persistence gained them a grasp on the edge of the woods, a perch from which to launch further drives forward. Starke fell in an attack aimed at driving them out. Even as he was carried from the field, dying, he had the fleeting satisfaction of knowing that he had succeeded. He had stopped the Yankees cold in his front.

Yet the situation was desperate. Lawton had been so badly mauled in the cornfield that he could not hold on much longer. Jones' division, now being led by a colonel, still held its grasp on the West Woods, but the Federals could clearly overlap his left, and worse, the line was so weak at the cornfield now that his right could be turned too. Fortuitously, at this moment, just after 7 a.m., Hood brought his division screaming up from the rear. Barely halting to form ranks, they hammered into the

Federals in the cornfield and the East Woods on its right and drove forward. Hooker, stunned by the ferocity of the attack, threw in the last of his corps reserves and finally called on Mansfield's XII Corps for reinforcements. The level of fighting in the next half-hour became the most brutal yet seen on the continent.

Hood's men almost reclaimed the entire cornfield, only to have Meade's last brigade destroy them. One regiment lost 80 percent in only a few volleys. Finally, by about 7:30, Hood began to fall back, still stubbornly holding on to a piece of the East Woods. Both Jackson and Hooker were exhausted, beaten to tatters in ninety minutes. The Yankee lost a third of his numbers in killed and wounded; Jackson lost nearly as great a percentage, and Hood's division was so mauled that, when asked where it was, he sadly replied, "dead on the field."[7]

McClellan's battleplan – such as it was – already lay severely compromised with the halting of Hooker. This meant that Mansfield and his XII Corps must now go into the fight, not to capitalize on Hooker's success, but to redeem him from utter exhaustion. Mansfield himself led them forward at about 7:30, coming in on Hooker's left and advancing straight into the East Woods. It was a confusing movement, passing through the wood without benefit of good roads or reconnaissance. His right elements actually swung in behind Hooker's battered left. Still, the fresh Yankees came on the field almost in time to make a difference. When Hood saw them coming he began to pull out of the cornfield, even though reinforcements were on their way to him from D.H. Hill. The fighting became particularly unmilitary, with nothing like formations and lines, but small clusters of men taking cover behind bushes, fences, trees, and rocks. It was not one battle, but thousands of small personal fights. One of those Confederates scored a big victory when a bullet from his rifle slammed into General Mansfield's chest, mortally wounding the old man. Alpheus Williams succeeded to the corps command at once, and he continued to try to funnel reinforcements into the fight. In the continuing maelstrom, the corporal who originally found Lee's lost order himself fell with a bad wound. Finally, after a North Carolina brigade fled in terror, a Yankee charge drove through the cornfield to come to hand-to-hand blows with the Rebels. Finally about 9 a.m. the weight of numbers told decisively, and the Confederates began pulling back, abandoning the West Woods, the cornfield, and the woods to its east. For three brutal hours they had done their duty and held Lee's left flank against overwhelming odds. They could hold no more.

Lee implored Hood to hold on, for off on the road to the south he could see the head of McLaws' column not more than a mile away. But before they could arrive, Hood and Hill had been pushed back clear to the Dunker Church, and slightly beyond, and only the fortunate intervention of another bullet, this one taking Hooker out of the battle with a wound, brought a temporary lull in their advance. Hooker left the field believing that the battle was almost won.[8]

At almost the same instant, old General Sumner began to bring his corps up for the fight. Unfortunately, having given only the vaguest orders the day before as evidence of his battleplan, McClellan now exercised almost no control at all over the fight once it commenced. He did not tell Sumner where to go, and left it almost entirely to the old man himself despite "Little Mac's" own loudly proclaimed belief that Sumner was little better than a fool. Certainly "Bull" Sumner did have more of bravery than brains. Around 9 a.m. when he started his divisions forward, he seemed to have little thought more than to drive straight toward the first enemy he saw. Instead of moving around to back up the remnant of the I and XII Corps, he simply moved straight west. Their route took them across the cornfield, where the advance was retarded by the efforts of the men to avoid stepping on the windrows of dead and wounded. Indeed, to some it looked as if the field – every stalk of corn had been clipped by bullets and charging feet – was somehow alive, a bubbling, crawling thing of waving arms and legs and quivering chests.

Sumner placed Sedgwick on his right, marching his men across the cornfield to run into the remnants of Hill and Hood, while Samuel French's division moved in the center, directly south of the Dunker Church. And on the left came Israel Richardson's division, heading almost southwest directly toward that sunken road that extended perpendicularly eastward from the Hagerstown Turnpike.

Sedgwick came in for a drubbing first, striking the Rebel line just as the first of McLaws' reinforcements were rushed to the scene by Lee. The fighting was terrible, and the Confederates steadily pushed Sedgwick back. Sedgwick himself fell wounded, along with one of his three brigade commanders, and half of his division was put to rout as Lee craftily – and partly by luck – got exactly the right number of men in just the right spots to hit him in front and flank. In the end, the Southerners drove Sedgwick back more than three quarters of a mile, where the battered Yankees set up a defensive line and abandoned the offensive, content merely to hold their position against the Rebels.

With Sedgwick's repulse, the focus of attention would turn now to the divisions of French and Richardson. They were about to face the balance of D.H. Hill's division placed along that so-called sunken road. In fact, it was nothing more than a wagon track, but years of traffic had so worn it down that the road surface lay three or four feet below the farm land on either side. It offered a natural earthwork fortification, from which the Rebels could fire in perfect concealment at any approaching foe. Hill had two brigades in position along its nearly half-mile length, along with the remnants of several other commands, and more on the way, maybe 2,500 in all, to meet the 5,700 in French's line.[9]

The men in the Sunken Road were told to hold their fire until the enemy was close enough for them to see the buckles and badges on their belts, and then to aim at them. The Rebels did as they were told, and when their first volley poured out, it devastated French's lead brigade. In the 4th New York, 150 men went down at a single volley. Even Colonel John B. Gordon, commanding an Alabama regiment in the road, felt sickened by what he saw. "The entire front line, with few exceptions, went down in the consuming blast," he recalled. Another Rebel colonel thought he saw the Yankees fall "as grain falls before a reaper."[10]

French's first brigade recoiled in tatters, only to be followed by the second and third brigades in turn, each to meet the same beating. In little more than half an hour, French took 33 percent casualties in his division. The Sunken Road had almost put him out of the battle for good.

Like a magnet, the sudden fury of the fighting along Hill's line attracted to it men from adjacent areas, especially with the battle on the Confederate left now quietening to a stalemate. Richardson was soon rushing toward the field at the same time that Lee was sending Anderson's division up to Hill's support. Rapidly the Sunken Road was shaping up to be the central contest of the battle, and all the while, as Lee gambled everything, McClellan kept tens of thousands inactive, unwilling to gamble at all.

There was no lull in the savagery as reinforcements arrived. Rather, the volleys from the road, the din of artillery brought up by the Yankees, and the savage assaults, continued almost unabated. Very quickly, despite their good position and their reinforcement to perhaps more than 5,500, the Southerners began to take desperate losses. General Richard H. Anderson fell almost as soon as he arrived with his division. One of Hill's brigadiers fell with a mortal wound, his successor being killed instantly immediately afterward, and the gallant Colonel Gordon soon fell with a facial wound that bled profusely into his hat. Unconscious, he might probably have drowned in his own blood had another bullet not fortuitously opened a hole in the bottom of his hat that allowed it to drain.

Still they mauled Richardson's men as they came into the fight, brigade by brigade. The Sunken Road devoured the first outfit sent in as it had everything before. But then Richardson's second brigade moved around to the far right of the road and outflanked Hill's position. Since the road formed a salient extending outward from the main Southern line, this right flank was "in the air," and dangerously exposed. Coincidentally, confusion in the main line along the road was running high. At the same time, Federals in front of the Rebel line launched yet another limited attack. The combination of such influences panicked the right of the line and it collapsed. At almost the same time, the left began to give way, too. In a few minutes the whole Southern line began abandoning the position that had visited such havoc on the foe for the past two hours.

Fortunately, over on the left Longstreet was mounting a weak yet determined charge that took Richardson's advancing Yankees in their own right flank, and though they pushed it back, still the Rebel movement slowed the Federal advance beyond the Sunken Road. Then Hill and others put together a much stronger counterattack, this time themselves charging against a foe now taking cover in that same road. Hill himself carried a rifle into the fight, as they all desperately tried to hold the Yankees at bay or drive them out while awaiting the arrival of more reinforcements. Finally enough artillery arrived to stabilize the pitifully thin Rebel line. Fortunately for Lee,

McClellan had sent almost no cannon to support his own assaults, and after a while Richardson had no choice but to pull back, away from the hard-won little road that was soon to be called Bloody Lane. Behind lay 5,600 Americans of Blue and Gray, dead, dying, or wounded. Within only a few minutes, Richardson would join them with a wound that eventually proved mortal. And still it was only about 1 p.m.[11]

A strange relative quiet settled over the field during the next several minutes. The fighting in the area of the cornfield was over for the day, and Sumner and McClellan now tacitly abandoned any idea of pushing through Lee's center at Bloody Lane. Inevitably, then, the focus of attention shifted to Burnside and his IX Corps, who had spent almost the entire morning as spectators. After all the reinforcements rushed to support the rest of his line, Lee had only the 3,000 men of David R. Jones' division left to protect the southern half of his line. Fortunately they had excellent ground on their side of the creek, and McClellan on the other. With all the ground he had to protect, Jones could spare only 400 to guard the Rohrbach bridge. But the bridge itself worked to his advantage. The ground leading down to the creek was steep on either side. This gave the Rebels a wonderful field of fire on any foe marching down the opposite slope to the bridge. Then the span itself would allow no more than four men at best to move abreast, exposing them for its entire 125-foot length to concentrated fire from rifle and well-placed artillery fire. It might have been possible to move through the creek itself, but with water four feet deep and more in places, it would slow the columns even more than the bridge. Nowhere else on the field at Antietam did Lee enjoy such an advantage of position and terrain. A handful could withstand a legion on ground such as this.

That is what they did. Burnside did not get orders from McClellan to start his movement until 10 a.m., hours after the fight at the other end of the line commenced. When Burnside sent forward the first of his brigades, with orders to rush over the bridge under fire and secure it, they got lost and then pinned down by Rebel fire without ever seeing the span. Meanwhile, a whole division under Rodman was sent far downstream to find a ford and get across, then come up and take the foe in flank, but nothing could be heard from them. In fact, McClellan's and Burnside's reconnaissance had been so shamefully inadequate that they hardly knew where the fords were, and despite all the time at their disposal on the day before, no one seems to have thought of finding out just how deep they were. In the end Rodman had to march two miles downstream before he found a crossing, and that cost valuable time.

Well after 11 a.m. Burnside sent in the next assault, and this time the Yankees found their way to the bridge, but not one of them ever set foot on it. Confederate volleys and artillery threw them back in complete confusion. But by now Jones' men were desperately low on ammunition, and exhausted from more than three hours of firing. When the next wave of men hit the bridge, it did not get across at first, but then slackening Rebel fire gave the bluecoats a further opportunity and they started to pour across in great numbers. In the face of their advance, Jones' tired little band was forced to withdraw. The bridge – forever after called Burnside Bridge – lay securely in Yankee hands.

During the next hour more Federals poured across, soon to see Rodman and his division marching toward them from the south after making their crossing. Now McClellan ordered Burnside to press the advance without delay. But Burnside lost another hour in shifting his troops about, and further time thanks to not having prepared reserve ammunition earlier. As a result, the IX Corps was not ready to move again until about 3 p.m. McClellan, meanwhile, was doing no better. Desiring that the attack on Sumner's front be pressed again, and now supported by the arrival of Franklin and the VI Corps, he finally went himself to the front from his headquarters east of the creek. But he easily allowed the now-beaten Sumner's pessimism to influence him into abandoning any further thought of an offensive on that part of the field.

Finally at 3 p.m. Burnside started out again, outnumbering Jones by three to one. In spite of gallant resistance, the Federals gained ground almost constantly, driving northwestward toward Sharpsburg itself. Some elements of Rodman's command actually reached the Harpers Ferry road itself where the fighting became hand-to-hand in places. Lee's right was about to collapse, and some Yankees even penetrated into the outskirts of Sharpsburg itself by about 4 p.m. Lee personally viewed the desperate situation, seeing only one thin brigade now standing between Burnside and the rear of the battered and exhausted Army of Northern Virginia. Should the Yankees break through, the Confederates would probably collapse completely even if the timid McClellan did not press them on the rest of their front. And given Burnside's position, all retreat across the Potomac would be cut off. Lee could only try to escape to the north with an army exhausted, out of food and nearly out of ammunition, to face a pursuing Federal horde. The other alternative would be surrender.

Then he saw troops marching off in the distance to the south. It was A.P. Hill. In a case of timing unparalleled in warfare, he was bringing his exhausted division up at exactly the right place and time to save Lee, after marching seventeen miles in the past eight hours. Without pausing to rest, Hill slammed into Burnside's exposed left flank, and within half an hour the IX Corps offensive came to an end. Lee sent reinforcements from the quiet spots elsewhere on the line, especially hurrying battery after battery to Hill's assistance. Meanwhile, seeing his advantage, Lee tried to launch his offensive with Stuart over on the far left. It never really got off the ground. Meade, though battered, was still too strong for the Rebels to make any headway. The best Lee could do in the waning hours before nightfall was to push Burnside back almost to the bridge once more, and there the armies settled into the exhausted and dazed sleep of men who have raced through hell.

It had been the bloodiest day of the Civil War – of all American history, in fact. It would be some time before all the bodies were counted, the gaps in the ranks identified and tallied. In the end, McClellan lost 2,108 killed, 9,500 wounded, and several hundred missing, more than 12,400 in sum. Lee was not far behind with 1,546 dead,

7,750 wounded, and more than a thousand missing. On both sides, many of the missing were probably also among the dead, though never identified.[12]

With an audacity that only Lee could display – backed by a streak of undoubted stubbornness – the gray chieftain refused to withdraw from the field that night, though all good sense should have dictated that he leave quickly. He had been lucky to survive September 17, having through circumstances and overconfidence gotten himself and his army into the most dangerous spot they would ever experience during the war. Only his own skill, the bravery of his men, and the indescribable folly of McClellan kept him from disaster. But Lee had to get his wounded off the field and on their way south to the Shenandoah. He still had to evacuate much of the captured materiel from Harpers Ferry. And he would not admit defeat easily. In fact, of course, the battle was tactically almost a draw, but considering the overwhelming odds against Lee all through the day, his merely holding out must be considered a victory of sorts, the more so considering the terrible damage he inflicted on his foe. But the battle certainly put an end to his northern invasion far short of his hoped-for goal of reaching the Susquehanna. Strategically, Lee had been beaten. He had no choice but to move back to the safety of Virginia. That would be fine with McClellan, whom Lee contemptuously dared to attack him again on September 18. But McClellan was himself psychologically a beaten man, defeated by his own paranoia and timidity. He would not make a move to follow up his footholds on both the Confederate flanks, nor would he do a thing to impede Lee's subsequent retreat, despite having two fresh corps at his disposal.

On September 19 Lee recrossed back into Virginia, and the campaign was over. With it died Confederate hopes of influencing fall elections in a war-weary North. Perhaps with it, too, died the always slim chance of European recognition and assistance. They would not risk backing a losing side. If the South was to achieve its independence, it must do it on its own before they would help.

REFERENCES

1 Dennett, *Lincoln and the Civil War*, p.45.
2 McClellan, *McClellan's Own Story*, pp.535, 566.
3 *Ibid.*, I, 19, pt.2, pp.264-65.
4 McClellan, *McClellan's Own Story*, p.573.
5 *Ibid.*, pp.588-90; *O.R.*, I, 19, pt.1, p.30.
6 Stephen Sears, *Landscape Turned Red* (Boston, 1983), p.174.
7 John Gibbon, *Personal Recollections of the Civil War* (New York, 1923), pp.83-84.
8 *Report of the Joint Committee on the Conduct of the War* (Washington, 1863), I, p.582.
9 Sears, *Landscape*, pp.236-38.
10 John B. Gordon, *Reminiscences of the Civil War* (New York, 1903), p.87.
11 Sears, *Landscape*, pp.253-55.
12 *Ibid.*, pp.295-96.

V

FREDERICKSBURG

It was said of Ambrose Burnside that, when he was born, at first he refused to breathe. The infant could only be coaxed into taking air – and thus life – by tickling his nose with a feather. Whether or not that really happened on May 23, 1824, is a matter of conjecture. That the story exemplified the career of this engaging yet sadly ill-starred man cannot be denied. He attended West Point with McClellan, the two becoming fast friends. Yet while McClellan won glory in Mexico, Burnside arrived just momentarily too late to participate. Thereafter he served a few years on the southwestern frontier before resigning his commission in 1853. He had invented a new breechloading cavalry carbine, and he began an ill-fated manufacturing enterprise that turned out excellent weapons, but found few takers. When the business folded, his old friend McClellan found a job for him with his own railroad firm.

Indecision seemed to dog Burnside's every move. In civilian life he was left standing literally at the altar by a fiancée who changed her mind at the last moment. Then when the war came, he took the colonelcy of the 1st Rhode Island, and very quickly afterward became a brigade commander, seeing his first action at First Manassas, where his performance, while personally brave enough, showed little of imagination or enterprise. Nevertheless he rose quickly, certainly not harmed by his close ties to the meteoric "Little Mac." And Burnside looked like the era's idea of a bold commander. There was about him somewhat of the air of the corsair. Tall, hearty, with a big smile and inevitably winning, cavalier ways, he sported on his face massive muttonchop whiskers to which a bit of word play with his name gave a lasting sobriquet, "sideburns." Following the Bull Run fight, he soon became a brigadier general, then major general, and had led a successful operation on the North Carolina coast early in 1862 that won Lincoln's notice. Indeed, after McClellan's dreadful performance on the peninsula, the president had offered command of the army to Burnside, who turned it down with expressions of unfitness for such a high responsibility. A few months later in early September, with Lee threatening the North and no one other than McClellan to turn to, Lincoln again offered the command to Burnside instead, and again he declined. "I was not competent to command such a large army as this." he would protest. Lincoln should have listened to him, for in this war, on those rare occasions when an officer said he was not equal to army leadership, he usually proved to be right.[1]

But in the weeks following Antietam, as McClellan did nothing while the country cried for action, Lincoln increasingly saw Burnside as his only alternative. McClellan had to go, of that Lincoln was sure. He knew it in his heart long before he decided to act. He visited the army early in October in the hope of impelling McClellan to take the offensive once more, yet while outwardly he remained affable and encouraging, inwardly he seethed, especially at the patrician "Little Mac's" obviously condescending manner to his rough-born president. One morning when out looking at the troops in the field with one of his friends, Lincoln bitterly asked if the other recognized what lay before them. "It is the Army of the Potomac," said the other.

"So it is called," the president replied through his teeth, "but that is a mistake; it is only McClellan's bodyguard."[2]

It could not remain so for long. During the next month all McClellan achieved was to take eight full days to get his army across the Potomac – Lee had done it in a single night after Antietam. Lincoln had hoped that McClellan might drive straight south, placing himself between Lee in the Shenandoah and his communications with Richmond, thus cutting the Rebels off from their base of supply and succor. That could force Lee to give battle on McClellan's terms or risk fatal isolation. But by November 4, almost seven weeks after Antietam, the Army of the Potomac was only twenty miles into Virginia, while Lee was speeding around in a great arc to cut off any approach to Richmond. Indeed, that same November 4, Lee had Longstreet and his corps in place at Culpeper Court House, squarely between McClellan and Richmond. The opportunity was lost, and Lincoln decided that this would be the last lost opportunity lost by McClellan. The next day Lincoln issued the order relieving McClellan from command. An emissary from the War Department went first to Burnside and practically forced him to agree to succeed to the command. Then they called on McClellan and handed him the order of removal. He took it well, though he would never see the justice of it, putting his downfall down to the spite of petty men like Lincoln and Halleck who were jealous of his genius and popularity. On November 11 he left the army, never to return to it, or the war, again.

Behind him McClellan left a Burnside almost on the verge of tears, and not just out of sadness for his friend's dismissal. Burnside *knew* that he had no business commanding an army. At Antietam he had showed not a whit of imagination, rigidly following every order given him to the letter and no more, refusing to think or act without explicit instructions. Like a great, cuddlesome, stuffed bear, he looked grand but had little depth. Thankfully he had a few days after receiving the news of his elevation before he actually took the reins from his predecessor, and this gave him time to try to take in the situation before him.

Lee had boldly split his army yet again, keeping Jackson in the Shenandoah to guard that vital back door to central Virginia, while moving Longstreet east. Thus while the latter could provide a roadblock to a Yankee move toward Richmond – which Lee did not expect, given the known sloth of the Yankee commanders – the former posed a seeming threat of yet another invasion sweeping out of the valley and into Maryland once more. Of course, the Confederates just then were entirely incapable of such a movement, but the Yankees did not know that, and Lee was happy to use the time their fears gave him to rest and rebuild his own army.

McClellan had had a plan of sorts for his snail's-pace campaign, but upon considering it in his new position as army commander, Burnside decided to abandon it for one of his own. He intended to concentrate his corps in the Warrenton area, just west of the old Manassas battleground, then make a diversionary move toward Culpeper Court House, about forty miles southwest. Immediately thereafter, he would in fact move the entire army due south to Fredericksburg on the Rappahannock River. That river was one of the few great natural barriers in his way, with Richmond just fifty miles beyond. He believed that he could move quickly enough to accomplish this before Lee could bring up Longstreet to get in his way, and certainly before Jackson could arrive in case a battle should develop.

Of course, Burnside was revealing the worn-out thinking that somehow taking the Confederate capital would put an end to the Confederacy, which was utter nonsense. When McClellan threatened to take the city back in May and June, Davis and his government made considerable preparations for abandoning Richmond if they had to, but no one even mentioned the loss of the cause as a contingency or a possible result. Lincoln knew better, and tried to persuade Burnside that Lee, and not Richmond, was the strategic objective to be desired. But the president was anxious not to demoralize a commander so freshly come to the job, and in the end gave in to Burnside's proposal, only pointing out that if it were to succeed at all, "Burn" must move and move quickly.

Like his old friend before him, Burnside first turned his attention to organization, though not with McClellan's flair. Nor did he learn any of the few lessons that "Little Mac" seemed to have gained from seeing certain men in action. Burnside returned to the "wing" concept, though he called them Grand Divisions, created three, and gave them to the unlikeliest of men. The Right Grand Division he gave to Sumner, who almost all agreed was a poor commander at best. McClellan's opinion was on record. He would have his own old II Corps, now led by General Darius Couch, Burnside's IX, under General Orlando Willcox, and most of Pleasonton's cavalry. The Center Grand Division commander posed an even more odd choice, for it was Hooker, and

Burnside hated him, believing him responsible for the breakup of his own wing prior to Antietam. But Hooker was a senior officer now, recovered from his wound, and an acknowledged fighter. Burnside had almost no choice but to give him such a command, to include the III Corps led by General George Stoneman, the V Corps now led by General Daniel Butterfield after Washington relieved Porter from command just days after McClellan's fall, and some attached cavalry. Finally, the Left Grand Division went to Franklin, who had showed positive sloth and bewilderment during the Antietam Campaign. He took Hooker's old I Corps, now under the brilliant General John F. Reynolds, the VI Corps led by William F. Smith, and a brigade of cavalry. Additionally Burnside had the XI Corps commanded by General Franz Sigel back at Centreville in reserve, and Mansfield's old XII Corps under Slocum way out at Harpers Ferry.

Significantly, not a single one of all these generals would be exercising the same command as at Antietam. Every single corps commander was new on the job, and so were two of the three Grand Division commanders, and even Sumner had never actually exercised such a level of responsibility in action. And, of course, Burnside himself had never led an army of 100,000 or more men before. In fact, all told, with a host of new recruits and units swelling the ranks, Burnside could count more than 120,000 of all arms, more than even McClellan had managed in actual field operations.[3]

Perhaps because of his consuming self-doubts, Burnside felt he needed to divorce himself from McClellan by a new organization and a different plan of campaign. Certainly he set a different tone by his willingness to move quickly. Just the day after Washington approved his plan, he had Sumner on the move. Early on November 15 old "Bull" set out and showed that without McClellan to slow them, these veterans could march. In just sixty hours they covered the forty miles to Falmouth, on the Rappahannock, just opposite Fredericksburg, with Lee nowhere in sight and clearly unprepared for such a decisive swiftness. Indeed, Sumner actually reached the Rappahannock nearly a full day before Lee knew with certainty which direction old "Bull" was headed. By then it was too late. Burnside showed just as much alacrity in getting the rest of his army on the march, and by November 20, the entire Army of the Potomac was on Stafford Heights, staring across the river at the spires of Fredericksburg.

And there he stopped. While Lincoln and the War Department began to breathe a long-needed sigh of contentment at finding a general who would move swiftly and decisively, Burnside figuratively shot himself in the foot by being inflexible, unable to think and adapt on the spot in reaction to circumstances. There were no bridges at Fredericksburg any more, though there were fords upstream some distance. But even a good ford can slow down the crossing of large bodies of troops. Burnside, of all people, knew after his hours and hundreds of men lost trying to get across a bridge just how vulnerable men were in midstream, especially a wide river like the Rappahannock. Thus, from the first he never contemplated using the fords. Rather, he ordered from the War Department a massive train of pontoon boats. Lashed together and anchored in the stream, overlaid with planks and earth, they would form floating bridges for his army. With good engineers to construct them, such bridges would take only a few hours to erect, and since Burnside expected to beat Lee to the river, he anticipated little problem for the bridge-builders from hostile fire.

The trouble is, when Sumner reached Falmouth, there were no pontoons to be seen, even though Burnside had Halleck's assurance that the pontoon train would arrive at the same time as the Right Grand Division. "Bull" Sumner may not have been an imaginative man, but he could think in a straight line, and his only line of thinking at the moment was to get across the river and take the heights above Fredericksburg before Lee could beat him there. Finding no pontoons, he sent word to Burnside that he could cross at one of the upstream fords and still take the town without a fight.

Burnside refused. Storm clouds threatened, and he feared that a heavy rainfall could isolate Sumner on the south side of the stream before the balance of the army arrived to cross. Besides, the pontoons had been promised, they had the jump on Lee, and they could afford to wait. The bridging material would arrive any minute.

In fact, another week passed after Sumner's arrival before the pontoons finally appeared, a fatal week lost that lays a heavy burden of responsibility on Burnside for what was to follow. For in that week Lee rushed Longstreet to Fredericksburg, arriving late on November 21, more than three days after Sumner first stared across the river from Falmouth, and almost 48 hours after Burnside and the rest of the Federals began to arrive. If only he had sustained his initiative a little longer, Burnside could have been a full day on the road toward Richmond ahead of Longstreet, forcing Lee to rush to battle with Jackson still a hundred miles away. Not for another twenty months would a Yankee commander manage to steal such a march on the masterful Lee.

Caught by surprise, Robert E. Lee would not waste a moment in attempting to recover the ground lost. He had not been happy about McClellan's replacement. Why should he, when he had so easily and consistently outwitted the Young Napoleon. "I fear they may continue to make these changes," he told Longstreet, "until they find someone whom I don't understand."[4] Certainly he underestimated Burnside at first, but as soon as he received definite word of Sumner's movement, he sped Longstreet on his way and called to Jackson to leave the Shenandoah. As soon as Longstreet actually reached Fredericksburg on November 21, he immediately began digging in on the long ridge behind the city, preparing to meet the Federals if and when they tried to cross.

But for Burnside, crossing meant pontoons. Then when they started to arrive on November 24, he proceeded to wait another seventeen days before putting his plan in motion, even though he had 120,000 to not more than 40,000 with Longstreet. Meanwhile, Lee wisely advised the citizens of the city to evacuate. The Federals had not shelled the town as yet, but should a battle start, the townspeople would be directly between the fires of the two armies. For the first time in the Civil War, the conflict had come to the doorsteps of a significant civil population.

Why Burnside waited is a matter of some conjecture, but as much as anything it was mental paralysis. He had only one plan, and the delay of the pontoons and Longstreet's arrival upset that. He seemed unable to think. Sensing the stalemate, Lincoln summoned Burnside to two meetings late in the month to discuss what could be done next. They produced little satisfaction, and in subsequent days, as Burnside discussed plans with his generals, their confidence in him seemed to wane – if, indeed, they had ever felt any. Early in December Burnside hit upon the idea of sending one of his Grand Divisions about twelve miles downriver to Skinker's Neck, to cross there and then move up against Lee's flank at Fredericksburg. No one felt great enthusiasm, and Burnside himself soon abandoned the plan, deciding instead that he could cross the river immediately below Fredericksburg.

On the face of it, the idea seemed utter folly. Any such crossing would be done under the eye of Lee himself, who was hardly likely to sit back and quietly allow the building of pontoon bridges. Furthermore, his position behind Fredericksburg was positively formidable. Fredericksburg sat on a descending plain that stretched less than a mile from a long, steep ridge down to the river. The ridge, in fact, was a series of steep hills – Stansbury's, Cemetery Hill, Telegraph, and Prospect. Directly behind the town proper sat Marye's Heights. Along its face ran another of those slightly sunken roads, this one fronted by a stone wall. Below the town the countryside gradually opened up away from the river, offering more room for maneuver, but still favoring any defender.

Lee at first scattered his divisions widely to cover all contingencies, expecting that Burnside would naturally try to cross either upstream or downstream in order to take him in flank, and in order not to have to cross in the face of Rebel artillery fire from those heights behind the town. He placed Jackson, when he arrived, on his right, with D.H. Hill's division far downstream, Ewell's old division now commanded by General Jubal Early at Skinker's Neck, A.P. Hill about three miles from Longstreet's flank and fully six miles south of Fredericksburg, and William Taliaferro's division several miles beyond Hill, all designed to provide maximum protection against what Lee most anticipated, a downstream Yankee crossing. Longstreet's five divisions stretched out over four miles, from Anderson immediately behind Fredericksburg, through Robert Ransom, Lafayette McLaws, George Pickett, to Hood. Even though reinforcements from other theaters and hurried recruitment had swelled Lee's numbers to almost 90,000 – the largest army Lee would ever field – still this abnormally long defensive line meant that his legions were spread thin.

Burnside would boast to Franklin that he believed he knew where all of Lee's divisions were placed, and felt confident that he could get his flanking movement across and on to high ground below Fredericksburg before Lee could act. Having gotten the jump on the Confederate master once, Burnside showed uncharacteristic self-confidence in believing that he could do it again. But then, Burnside had little choice. His sloth and inflexibility had squandered all the benefits of his lightning advance to the Rappahannock. Now, unless he was simply to turn back and abandon the campaign, to meet the wrath of Lincoln and the Union, he must give battle. A crossing upstream offered – to his mind – no opportunities, while a downstream crossing, if successful, would give him a chance to push Lee's right flank back and away from a line of communication and retreat to Richmond. If it all seemed reminiscent of his own role at Antietam, Burnside seems not to have been bothered by the comparison. He had to act.

Finally late on December 9, Burnside wired the War Department of his intention to attack two days later. The fluid state of conditions on the other side of the river had changed his plans once again. Burnside now believed that Lee was too well prepared for a crossing below the city. As a result, Burnside now proposed to cross directly in the enemy front right at Fredericksburg. There was some minimal logic to it. From his own position on Stafford Heights overlooking the Rappahannock, Burnside's artillery could completely command the city itself, making it almost impossible for Lee to mount any substantial infantry maneuver to hinder the bridge-builders. The engineers would only have to brave distant Rebel cannon fire from Marye's Heights, and the attentions of snipers and sharpshooters placed in some of the buildings of the town itself. Burnside believed that such an attempt would take Lee by surprise, and several of his generals agreed – or he said they did.

He proposed to run three sets of bridges at once. The uppermost would cross directly at the northern edge of Fredericksburg, the next a mile downstream at the city's southern edge, and the third a mile beyond at a slight bend in the river, just below the mouth of a stream called Deep Run that flowed in from the Confederate side. Sumner and his Grand Division was to lay the uppermost bridge and move directly against Fredericksburg. Burnside gave Franklin the task of crossing on the lower sets of bridges, to move across the more open ground to strike Lee where Burnside thought him most vulnerable. Hooker and his entire Grand Division were to remain on the east bank in reserve, a move that could be interpreted as Burnside's revenge for Hooker's part in the breakup of his old wing before Antietam.[5]

There was more than a little outspoken criticism of the plan. Most of Sumner's officers frankly told Burnside that to cross the river and then move straight up against Lee's entrenched infantry and artillery on Marye's and the other heights would be nothing less than suicide. Nevertheless, Burnside was not to be deterred by dissent. He spent much of December 10 drafting the final attack orders to his commanders. Sumner was to move straight across his bridges and up against the Rebels emplaced on the heights beyond. Hooker was to cross after him, but without any specific part in the battle other than to be ready to support either Sumner or Franklin. Franklin was to bridge the river, get across, and then move directly west to get to the roads connecting Lee with Richmond. Once they were in his possession, he would turn northward to strike Lee's flank. Yet these were all the orders his commanders got. Burnside gave them no specific instructions on how or where to fight, and offered no coordinating influence between them. Having told them where to go, he blithely left everything else up to his generals.

Late on December 10, the engineers moved their pontoons and other equipment up close to the river in the darkness. Some even tried a diversion by ostentatiously cutting trees and making a great deal of noise down near Skinker's Neck, hoping to deceive Lee into thinking that the bridging attempt would be made there the next day. It did not work, however. In Fredericksburg itself, McLaws could see and hear enough to conclude that the enemy would try a crossing right in his front, and at around 4:30 a.m. on December 11 he fired two signal guns that alerted the rest of the army that the fight was about to begin. With more than 200,000 men at arms in the vicinity, it was to be, in terms of the size of the armies, the biggest battle ever fought in the hemisphere.

The bridge-builders needed all the protection they could get, and an early pre-dawn fog helped them at first. Before long, however, McLaw's sharpshooters posted in lofts and upper stories through the town began to take aim as the brave engineers started their work of placing and anchoring their pontoons in full view and range of the foe. Casualties began to fall immediately, and for the next several hours almost no progress was made on the upstream bridges as Rebel fire drove the engineers back time after time. Even artillery bombardment ordered by Sumner failed to drive out the pesky sharpshooters, though 9,000 shells were thrown into the town, setting ablaze several of its buildings.

Finally one general suggested that infantrymen use the pontoons as boats and row themselves across to the other side to stop the sniping long enough for the bridges to be completed. Regiments volunteered for the work, and almost without a casualty the first wave rowed across, outflanking McLaws' advanced sharpshooters and tying down their fire. That allowed more men to row over, and finally the engineers themselves were able to complete their work. The same plan worked both for the upper bridges for Sumner, and the middle bridge at the south edge of town. Nevertheless, the attempt to cross had consumed most of the day, and what remained of daylight after the bridgeheads were secured had to be devoted to driving the Confederate snipers out of the town, house by house. Only after nightfall did the remaining Rebels pull back to their main lines on the heights, leaving Fredericksburg to Burnside. A mere 1,600 Southerners from William Barksdale's brigade had held up Burnside for an entire day.

At least Franklin's men did not encounter any difficulty getting their bridges "thrown" across the river near Deep Run. Lee had not expected a movement at that spot, and thus the engineers managed to work almost unimpeded. By 11 a.m., while Sumner's men were still pinned down by Barksdale, Franklin had completed two bridges, and later that afternoon he sent his first brigades across. Unfortunately, virtually unopposed as he was, he did not push getting more of his command over with speed, for he might have turned northward and severely worried Lee, perhaps even relieving the pressure on Sumner to allow a crossing on that front earlier. But Franklin had no specific orders from Burnside – none of them did – and so once across he simply protected his bridgehead and settled down to wait until the next day, when with Sumner finally across, they could renew the advance in concert.

Of course it was only yet another gift of time to Lee, who needed it. He had posted himself on the summit of Telegraph Hill, from which he could see almost all of his line except the far right under Jackson, and here he watched with satisfaction the check given to Sumner throughout much of the day. Still he did not act decisively to keep Franklin from getting across, and while it is possible that he wanted to have the foe between his high ground and the river, there was little point in such a maneuver since, even if he should defeat Burnside, the Federals could simply retreat back across their bridges and defy him from the heights on the other side. More likely, Lee felt secure with only Franklin coming across between Longstreet and Jackson, hoping to pinch him between the two, and also he still seems to have feared that the main Yankee flanking move would come at Skinker's Neck, where he still had the bulk of Jackson's power poised for defense.

Only after nightfall, once satisfied of Burnside's real intentions, did Lee start to shift his troops for the battle that was shaping for the morrow. He brought A.P. Hill and Taliaferro up from their extended positions to extend Longstreet's right, but still left Early and the other Hill far to the right, just in case Skinker's Neck should still pose a problem.

He need not have worried. Even with all of his sloth of recent weeks, Burnside did still have a bare advantage. After all, he heavily outnumbered Lee, and by nightfall of December 11 he had the means to get most of his army across the Rappahannock. Even Halleck, from Washington, sent an urgent wire begging that Burnside get as many people over as possible during the dark hours, in case of a counterattack in the morning. Burnside, however, would not be rushed. Nor did he give his Grand Division commanders much more in the way of detailed orders for the next morning. Afterward he would simply say that it was his intent that Sumner should hit the heights as a diversion, while Franklin rolled up the Rebel flank. Yet instead of being ready to do so at dawn, Burnside occupied much of the morning daylight hours by giving the Rebels a grand spectacle as they watched division after division march in full view down to the bridges and across to the other side. The II Corps crossed at Fredericksburg first, followed by the IX Corps, Couch's command taking position as the far right, with Willcox on his left extending almost down to Deep Run. On Franklin's front, the VI Corps crossed first, followed by the I Corps, but it took until well into the afternoon before they were all over and in line, Smith's veterans resting with their right at Deep Run, and Reynolds on his left.

Lee gave them all the time they wanted. Secure in his positions atop the high ground, he could take advantage of Burnside's tardiness to move Early and D.H. Hill the ten miles or more to the impending battle now that Franklin's might on the Deep Run line relieved anxieties that the enemy might be committing more troops farther downstream. Well before nightfall on December 12, he knew that this was where the battle would be fought.

By dawn on December 13 Lee had almost all of his Army of Northern Virginia united once more. The arrival of Hill and Early extended Jackson's line to nearly two miles in length. Stonewall took position on a wooded crest running from one to two miles back from the river. Stuart's cavalry protected his right, while his left bent backward to take advantage of better ground. Hill held the left, while D.H. Hill, soon to be joined by Early, held the right, with Taliaferro in reserve. Lee needed depth in his line here, for the ground favored the defensive less than elsewhere, and he expected Franklin to make the major push. Longstreet, meanwhile, extended his line from A.P. Hill's left, for almost five miles, through the successive divisions of Hood, Pickett, McLaws, Ranson, and Anderson.

By nightfall of December 12, Sumner had about 27,000 men, backed by 30,000 reserves under Hooker, facing Longstreet's 41,000 on the heights behind the town. Jackson had barely 39,000 in his deep lines, looking across at almost 51,000 under Franklin. And up along Stafford Heights to support the Federal advance would be 147 cannon lined up in neat rows, their bulging caissons and ammunition chests ready for a day's work, while another 190 guns actually went across the river with the attacking columns.

With this enormous mass of power at his disposal, Burnside proceeded to try to win the battle without using it, and without risk. He kept his commanders ignorant of their attack orders until just after dawn on December 13, giving them no time to prepare, and actually contradicting the plans he had discussed with them the previous day. He instructed Sumner to use but a single division, and that to march straight into the mouths of Longstreet's guns to seize Marye's Heights. Franklin, with more than 50,000 at his disposal, was also to use but a single division, this one to seize Prospect Hill, an eminence on Jackson's far right. He reasoned that taking these two high points, backed by artillery placed thereon, would force Lee to abandon all of the line in between, which meant virtually his entire position. The plan was ludicrous, conceived in a vacuum that apparently did not realize that Lee might take advantage of the limited assaults to concentrate his own numbers against them. As for the rest of the army, its sixteen divisions were essentially to act as a "reserve" for two.[6]

Despite his disappointment at the orders he received around 7 a.m. that morning, Franklin – who favored a massed attack straight at Jackson's center – gave Reynolds the task of sending out the division for the job, and Reynolds chose his friend and fellow Pennsylvanian Meade. Even here choices were bad, for Meade's was the smallest division in the corps, but he took the assignment and prepared with speed. By 8:30 he was ready to advance.

Meade moved forward with dispatch, his skirmishers encountering enemy fire almost at once. Before long he came in range of Jackson's artillery pieces on the heights beyond. Taking casualties, slowed by sunken roads and fences that had to be borne down, Meade and his division still continued in their halting progress, followed now by Gibbon, whom Reynolds had placed on Meade's right rear as a support. Seeing Stuart's cavalry off in the distance to his left, Reynolds had to position Doubleday's division to face the Rebel horse and protect the left flank of his infantry. Already, though still only Meade was principally engaged, the whole I Corps was in motion.

There followed an artillery duel of an hour or more as Rebel batteries played heavily on Meade and Gibbon. Still they got within less than half a mile of the crest of the ridge in their front before the enemy on top opened on them in earnest, stopping them in their tracks. There they stayed for the next two or more hours, unable to move until renewed Yankee artillery fire softened the foe enough for Meade and Gibbon to press on. Finally, well after 1 p.m. they reached the foot of the slope and started pushing their way up into the face of A.P. Hill's infantry.

The initial impact of Meade's advance took Jackson by surprise. He slammed into General Maxcy Gregg's brigade and dispersed it, killing Gregg in the process. Portions of brigades on both of Gregg's flanks were broken up as well before a Rebel countercharge struck a gap between Meade and Gibbon and drove them back. The Yankees pulled back as fast as they had advanced. Gibbon fell with a painful wound, and Meade lost a brigade commander killed on the spot. Fortunately a reserve division from the III Corps rushed up and stopped the Southern counterattack, buying time for Meade and Gibbon to retire nearly to the river after their severe mauling. By 2 p.m. the fighting quieted, and though Franklin's men maintained a somewhat advanced position from where they started, the fighting on his front was essentially done for the day. He had tried to execute Burnside's inane order, had failed, and would not move again without positive orders that never came. Meade lost 1,853 and Gibbon 1,267. Combined with other units involved, their casualties totaled 4,861, while A.P. Hill and Early, who did the bulk of the fighting, lost 3,400.[7]

All of that blood had been essentially wasted, but it was nothing when compared to the bloodletting taking place at the other end of the battlefield. Longstreet had dug his divisions into a fearfully strong position. He put his artillery in the best positions, clearing for them wide fields of fire. His infantry took advantage of every terrain feature to provide cover, especially that stone wall along the forward slope of Marye's Heights. McLaws and Ranson held most of this ground. Immediately behind the stone wall, the strongest position of all, sat the brigade of General Thomas R.R. Cobb of Georgia, a troublesome politician who first served in the Confederate Congress but got so fed up with President Davis that he sought a field commission instead.

Against this line, Sumner ordered Couch and the II Corps to make the advance. Couch, in turn, entrusted the mission to French's division, already emplaced in the streets of Fredericksburg itself. They were not to advance until word came of success by Franklin, but by late morning, when Burnside still heard nothing favorable from his left, he told Sumner to go ahead.

It was just past noon when the first lines of blue marched out of the outskirts of town and started up the soft incline towards Marye's Heights some 800 yards distant. Their first obstacle, not quite halfway to the stone wall, was a drainage ditch that, unfortunately, could be crossed only on bridges. The moment the Yankees left the cover of the town's buildings, they came under the fire of Longstreet's artillery, suffering substantial losses almost from the first. Soon thereafter those who got past the initial barrage came into range of the Confederate rifles. They, too, started to exact their toll. Cobb's Georgians, joined behind the wall by a North Carolina regiment, poured forth sheets of flame from behind their stone rampart.

Incredibly, French's men continued to advance, despite the great gaps opening in their lines. They actually got within 200 feet of the wall before they were propelled backward at last. As they retired, they passed through French's second brigade, which went into the advance only to meet the same treatment, and so did a third that followed. In barely an hour, French's division was put out of the battle for good. The next II Corps division, this one led by General Winfield Scott Hancock, took their place. He took even worse casualties than French, though he pushed the advance to within 150 feet of the wall. Behind that stone barrier the Rebels were standing four deep now, firing by ranks and almost without let-up. In front of them lay literally thousands of dead, dying, and wounded, along with scores of others who were not touched, but who did not dare rise to run to the rear for fear of being hit. Those who could get away left behind them some 3,200 casualties, with more yet to come.

Couch's third division, led by First Manassas veteran Oliver O. Howard, met nearly the same fate when it followed Hancock forward. When supporting units from other corps tried to move in on Couch's left to take some of the heat off him, they came under a withering Rebel artillery fire that left them, too, badly blooded. Nevertheless, Burnside, badly out of touch with a battle he never had under control from the moment of conception, continued to expect his right to press on until it took the heights. To support another push, Burnside sent word to Franklin to make an all-out assault over on the left, while telling Hooker to send two F Corps divisions against the stone wall. After seeing the front for himself – which Burnside never did – Hooker went back to his commander and begged that the order be withdrawn. Burnside refused. Meanwhile, Franklin never made his ordered assault, perhaps receiving it too late to do any good as the early December twilight began to settle. But by then two more divisions were on their way to doom against the stone wall, and in their wake after repulse the grisly total carnage before that rude wall came to more than 6,300. After six successive assaults, each one in division strength, the 6,000 men behind that wall had repulsed almost 40,000 Federals. Watching it all from his command post atop a nearby height, Lee felt torn between the elation at what his men were achieving against such odds, and the awful price in suffering being paid out on that field. "It is well that war is so terrible," he said to those around him. Otherwise "we should grow too fond of it."

Hooker echoed Lee's sentiments, though in the bitterly brutal words of a man who knew he was getting orders from an incompetent. "Finding that I had lost as many men as my orders required me to lose," he reported, "I suspended the attack." Nevertheless, only full nightfall made it safe for his men trapped by enemy fire before the wall to creep back to safety.

Sporadic firing continued along the line even after dark, but it came without direction or purpose other than to discomfit the Yankees trying to reform their disorganized regiments and brigades. Burnside sent one unblooded division of the V Corps forward under cover of darkness to bivouac close to the stone wall preparatory to an anticipated dawn assault, but they found they could hardly find a place to lie down for the carpet of bodies of dead and wounded beneath their feet. In the sharp cold of that night, wounded and dying men suffered intensely as they lay bleeding into the near-frozen ground. The living took the frozen bodies of the dead and rolled them around into human breastworks against the fight to resume in the morning. Meanwhile, elsewhere along the line, ill-clad Confederates crept out to scavenge coats and blankets from the dead.

Dawn brought terror to the Yankee division when the lifting fog revealed how close they were to the wall. The Rebels fired immediately, pinning them down, and there they stayed for the rest of the day, not returning fire, but only trying their best to disappear into the hard earth. The night before Burnside and his generals discussed the situation. At first "Burn" intended to renew the attack, reportedly even claiming that he would lead his old IX Corps into the assault in person. Sumner argued strenuously against more fighting, however, joined heartily by the disgusted Hooker. Franklin's position almost certainly echoed the other Grand Division commanders', and in the end Burnside gave in, his resolution weak as always. But having taken Fredericksburg itself, the commanding general decided not to yield it by pulling back to Stafford Heights. Should he want to launch a new offensive after reorganizing his army, he would just have to cross and take the town again. So there they sat in the relative safety of the city for two days while their general pondered his next move.

Only on December 15 did Burnside ask for a truce to retrieve the dead and care for wounded who had now spent almost 48 hours suffering out on the field. Later that night he finally decided that it served no purpose to remain in Fredericksburg any longer, and during the dark hours recrossed his battered legions and took up his bridges behind him. There would be no more contesting the enemy on this front. Lee could have the victory.

The cost to the Army of the Potomac had been truly awful: 1,284 killed, 9,600 wounded, and 1,769 missing and either dead or prisoners. Against this 12,653 total, Lee suffered just 5,377, including 603 killed and 4,116 wounded. They were the most lop-sided casualty figures of any major battle of the war, reflecting just how strong was Lee's position, and how unimaginative Burnside's handling of the fight.[8]

There was cold cheer in the Union camps a few days later when Christmas came. A month later Burnside would try to move again, this time sending his divisions upstream with the hope of effecting an unopposed crossing and then sweeping down on Lee's left flank but heavy rains left the army literally stuck in the mud, a fitting end to Burnside's soggy leadership. As 1863 dawned, the Army of the Potomac was still waiting for the man who could lead it to victory over Lee.

REFERENCES

1 *Report of the Joint Committee*, I, p.650.
2 Sears, *Landscape*, p.325.
3 Edward J. Stackpole, *Drama on the Rappahannock* (Harrisburg, Pa., 1957), pp.77-78, 276.
4 James Longstreet, *From Manassas to Appomattox* (Philadelphia, 1896), p.201.
5 Stackpole, *Drama*, pp.126-28.
6 *O.R.*, I, 21, pp.76-80.
7 Stackpole, *Drama*, p.194.
8 *Ibid.*, pp.196-7

VI

STONES RIVER (MURFREESBORO)

In the "Old Army," as Civil War officers called the service, as it was before 1861, a hilarious story was told and retold at the mess table about one of their more distinctive old comrades, Captain Braxton Bragg. Everyone knew of his irascible nature. Men often and easily came to hate him. During the Mexican War one unknown enemy actually placed a lit artillery shell under his cot in an attempt to assassinate him. The try failed, but everyone knew about it. The story they all told, however, was of a different sort. At one of his Old Army posts, it maintained, Bragg had been serving as post quartermaster when the post commandant was temporarily called away. As senior officer, Bragg became interim commandant as well. Representing the interests of his actual field command, Bragg submitted a request for certain supplies. In his capacity as quartermaster, Bragg approved the request and submitted it to . . . himself as post commander. And in that last capacity, he denied the requisition! The episode led one of his superiors to exclaim to him that having argued with everyone else in the army, "you are now arguing with yourself."[1]

It was certain that Bragg did not get along with people, especially subordinates. His execrable health, which included undoubted mental instability, affected his attitude and demeanor, making him unable to brook dissent or well-meant criticism. Instead, he was an easy mark for sycophants and flatterers. The same personality traits also made him a virtual martinet, wedded to regulations and discipline, and absolutely ruthless in the punishment of offenders. A host of apocryphal stories gained credence when he became a Confederate general, some maintaining that he had a soldier shot for an infraction as minor as killing a chicken.

Yet behind every myth may lay a seed of truth. Bragg was not inherently a cruel man, only a sick one, and sicker still in his mind after the failure of his October 1862 campaign into Kentucky. After taking command of the troubled Army of Tennessee as it was styled in the months following Shiloh, and Beauregard's relief from command in June 1862, Bragg ruthlessly set about reorganizing the brigades and divisions and instilling his form of iron discipline. That done, he led them north in the attempt to wrest Kentucky from the enemy, an abortive attempt that failed through his own errors and those of subordinates. But when Bragg retreated back into Tennessee afterward, he could not accept the responsibility for his defeat as Lee did after Antietam, or even Burnside following Fredericksburg. Rather, Bragg sought others to take his blame, and he turned to his subordinates Polk and Hardee, thus commencing a war within his own high command that never abated.

He also blamed a man who was not in the campaign, Breckinridge, who through administrative errors and inter-commander rivalry – none of it of his doing – was not able to join Bragg for the invasion. It had been thought that the presence of this most prominent of all Kentuckians would rally the men of the Bluegrass to the Southern banners. When Kentuckians, in fact, proved to be little better than indifferent to Bragg's "liberating" army and gave it neither material support nor manpower, he quickly formed a lasting resentment toward them, including even Breckinridge and the Kentucky brigade in his division. There could not have been a worse time for a man in Breckinridge's 6th Kentucky Infantry to leave ranks to go home and help his widowed mother get in a crop. He was caught, returned, and quickly tried for desertion. On December 20 Bragg approved the court's finding of guilty and ordered the man shot on the day after Christmas. No amount of pleading from Breckinridge and other officers could dissuade the general, who supposedly remarked that Kentuckians were too independent, and he would shoot them all if he must to maintain discipline. Breckinridge accused him of murder, and men in some Bluegrass regiments came near to mutiny. In the end, on December 26, the unfortunate private went to his death. He might have died only a few days later anyhow as the Kentucky brigade fought for its existence, and Bragg battled viciously to hold on to middle Tennessee. But thanks to incidents like this, when Bragg went into the fight, he was already at war with his own army.[2]

Bragg was a man who, by temperament, saw enemies everywhere, and given his personality and character, he might have been right. But as 1862 waned, and as he looked over his shoulder for foes in his own camp, he had to keep a watchful eye on a more formidable opponent in his front. While the failure of his Kentucky offensive had not produced any decisive victory for either side, even after abandoning the Bluegrass state, Bragg still occupied much of northern Alabama and a great deal of the central portion of Tennessee that, previously, had been in Yankee hands. Worse, many in the North believed that Bragg and his whole army could have been taken out of the war by a more aggressive commander than Buell. In the end, Buell became the highest ranking casualty of the campaign, as public outcry and his own army's disaffection led to his replacement by Lincoln on October 24. It did not help that Buell was also very tight with the out-of-favor McClellan. Six days later a new commander took over, with his mission very clear – follow Bragg and retake what had been lost.

William S. Rosecrans brought a varied background to high command, yet like almost all army commanders in the war, there had been little to prepare him for this. After doing commendably at the Military Academy, he served eleven years in the Old Army before poor health forced him to resign. He devoted the next several years first to the coal industry, then to making coal oil. Like so many other former officers, he came out of retirement when the war commenced, and rose quickly to become one of McClellan's principal subordinates in the western Virginia campaign that made "Little Mac's" reputation. Indeed, the minor victory by which western Virginia was taken from the Rebels in 1861 was actually more Rosecrans' work than McClellan's. Nevertheless, "Old Rosey" as his men began calling him, also saw his fortunes rise. His successful defense of Corinth, Mississippi, in October 1862 won further laurels, and thanks to this, when Lincoln needed a successor to Buell, Rosecrans got the nod.

He took command of an army in some disarray, with enlistments expiring in some units, and others whose men had not been paid in months. Its old designation as Army of the Ohio was discontinued when he was assigned, and instead it was to be known temporarily as the XVI Corps. Ever afterward, however, it would be called by another designation to come early in 1863: the Army of the Cumberland.

It was a splendid army, though barely half the size of the giant assemblage that Burnside took over in the East. Rosecrans divided it into three wings. The Right Wing went to Major General Alexander M. McCook, one of Ohio's amazing family of "fighting McCooks" that provided three brothers who became generals, and another cousin who wore the stars. Following McCook would be three divisions, each with their particular distinction. The first belonged to a hot-tempered officer with the ironic name of Jefferson C. Davis who, in an altercation earlier that year in Louisville, shot and killed a fellow general. The Second Division under General Richard W. Johnson was made up entirely of western men from Illinois, Ohio, and the like, except for one lone regiment of Pennsylvanians. The Third Division went to General Philip H. Sheridan, a short, combative, ruthless little fellow destined to make a great name for himself later in the war.

The Center Wing belonged to Major General George H. Thomas, a Virginian who placed loyalty to his Old Army uniform and flag above his state sympathies, though it cost him the undying enmity of his entire family for the rest of his life. Lovell Rousseau commanded Thomas' First Division, James Negley the Second, Speed Fry the Third, Robert B. Mitchell the Fourth, and Joseph J. Reynolds the Fifth. Thomas' wing was thus the largest in the army. The Left Wing, like the Right, had but three divisions, commanded by Thomas J. Wood, John M. Palmer, and Horatio Van Cleve, all under the command of Major General Thomas Crittenden. While each division in the army had its own artillery, and some a smattering of cavalry, the bulk of the mounted units made up a division of cavalry led by General Davis S. Stanley. Rosecrans had to struggle mightily to get stragglers in, units reorganized and armed, and the army in marching trim once more, and he had little time in which to do it. Still, by late December he had about 64,000 of all arms at hand. He would leave one of Thomas' divisions to guard his base at Nashville, but that still gave him just short of 60,000 for his coming campaign.

He must start that campaign soon, too. Rosecrans felt pressure from Washington to take an offensive against Bragg within barely two weeks of assuming command. "The government demands action," said Halleck, and when Rosecrans had not moved by early December, the general-in-chief threatened him with removal.[3]

Well aware that Lincoln wanted his armies to advance all across the map before winter set in, Rosecrans was finally forced to start forming offensive plans of his own. Clearly his objective was to be Bragg and his army. Following the retreat from Kentucky, Bragg concentrated his Army of Tennessee in and around Murfreesboro, Tennessee, some thirty miles southeast of Nashville. An important road intersection, the little town also sat astride the Nashville & Chattanooga Railroad, a chief supply line for the Confederates. From this position, Bragg offered a constant threat to Nashville, but could also easily move east or west, either to outflank the capital, or else to move against Grant to the west, or far to the east to reinforce Lee, though such a move was never in his thoughts.

Indeed, Bragg himself was busily putting his own army to rights, despite being forced to work with subordinates who despised him and for whom he felt little affection. He had but two corps in the Army of Tennessee. The I Corps was more commonly known by the name of its commander, Leonidas Polk, the wire-pulling old friend of President Davis who had yet to demonstrate any justification for wearing a uniform at all, much less commanding half an army. Happily, at least Polk had competent division commanders beneath him. Jones M. Withers led four brigades of Alabamians and Mississippians, and brought excellent Mexican War experience to his position. So did General Benjamin F. Cheatham commanding four brigades made up almost exclusively of fellow Tennesseeans. Cheatham was a proven fighter, though too fond of the bottle. The II Corps belonged to Hardee, the seasoned old professional, and the only man present who probably deserved to command the army itself. Breckinridge commanded his first division, a mixed one of five brigades composed of men from seven different states. The second division answered to General Patrick R. Cleburne, Irish by birth and Arkansan by adoption, and the most brilliant division commander in this army. A third division under John P. McCown was temporarily attached to Hardee, adding three more brigades to Breckinridge's five and Cleburne's four, and making Hardee's the larger half of the army. Finally, Brigadier General Joseph Wheeler, a favorite of Bragg's whose abilities were overstated, led the three brigades of cavalry with the command.

Bragg would continue to tamper with and adjust his organization well through the middle of December, but then he had little else to occupy him, for his only strategy at the moment was simply to stay put at Murfreesboro, and wait for Rosecrans to come to him. Besides, he had almost perfect confidence in the natural defensibility of his position, and of the ability of his more than 50,000 men to hold on to it.

Murfreesboro itself may not have been as good a place as Bragg thought. Certainly strategically it left much to be desired, for it was easily outflanked on either side, as good roads led from Nashville to points well below Bragg's position, points from which his communications could be threatened and his army approached from flank or rear. Bragg did not overlook this, and by late December had Cleburne and most of his cavalry out guarding the routes that offered Rosecrans an opportunity, while keeping Polk and the balance of Hardee with him at Murfreesboro. Thus in case of a threat he could shift his forces from one side to the other to meet an enemy advance.

Rosecrans offered Bragg just such a choice when finally he put his men on the march out of Nashville on December 26 after spending most of his Christmas planning and talking with his generals. What they settled upon was a plan designed to confuse Bragg as to their intentions. The three wings of the army would move in three different directions. Crittenden would take his wing and march straight toward Bragg on the Murfreesboro Pike. Meanwhile, McCook would move almost parallel and several miles to the west toward Triune, fifteen miles west of Bragg. Thomas was to move straight south, on McCook's right, then turn east to strike what Rosecrans believed would be the Confederate flank. "Old Rosey" felt confident. "We move tomorrow, gentlemen," he told his top generals that Christmas night. "Make them fight or run! Strike hard and fast! Give them no rest! Fight them! Fight them! Fight, I say!"[4]

McCook moved out first at 6 a.m. the next morning. It was not to be quite as pleasant a march as the men in the ranks expected, for the unusually mild December weather they had been enjoying suddenly came to an end, replaced by cold winds and rain showers. Nevertheless, the Yankees made good progress, and by nightfall McCook's advance elements were almost within sight of Triune, while Crittenden approached Lavergne, halfway to Murfreesboro. The movement left Bragg confused and uncertain as to the foe's real goal, and as a result he was hesitant to act, though he continued to believe that Rosecrans would make his main thrust at Murfreesboro. Consequently he planned his few movements accordingly. The next morning a dense fog prevented the Federals from getting an early start, and it was past noon before McCook resumed his advance, only to have it stopped minutes later by a driving storm of sleet. Nevertheless, by nightfall they had taken Triune without a fight and extended their lines somewhat beyond, with Thomas coming up on their rear, and Crittenden pressing easily through Lavergne and on to Stewart's Creek, less than ten miles from Murfreesboro.

It was all going Rosecrans' way so far, despite the weather, but by now Bragg no longer felt any doubt that Murfreesboro would be his objective, and that night the irascible Confederate set about arranging his defensive lines. Murfreesboro sat on the east side of Stones River, little more than a mile from the banks of the twisting stream that ran generally north and south. The Nashville-Murfreesboro Pike came in directly from the northwest, crossing the river a mile and half above the town, while three other roads approached from a westerly direction, and the Salem Turnpike came up from the southwest. If Bragg was to hold on to the town and the rail line that served it – and him – he determined that he had better meet Rosecrans on the other side of the stream where possible, and there he posted the bulk of his army. He put Cleburne's division of Hardee's Corps on the far left, covering the Franklin Road, with their left resting on a westward bend in the river, and a brigade of cavalry extending to the south for cover.

On Cleburne's right, posted through a series of woods, Polk's Corps extended for a mile and a half across the open side of a wide eastward bend of the river, their right resting on the stream. Revealing his fear of vulnerability on his right – the river could be forded almost anywhere – Bragg posted Breckinridge's division of Hardee's Corps on the east side, its left meeting with Polk's right across the river, and its line extending almost at right angles eastward across the northern approach to Murfreesboro. Besides providing protection on that flank, this also put most of Breckinridge's brigades in a good position to cross the river at any of the bridges to reinforce Polk in the center. It was a poor position, not least because several hundred yards in front of Breckinridge sat Wayne's Hill, a commanding eminence that even rudimentary reconnaissance should have told Bragg he must have.

There Bragg sat for the next three days without molestation. Rosecrans would not move or fight on a Sunday, and wanted to rest his army besides, so they remained comparatively idle on December 28. The next day the Federals continued their march, and by that afternoon came in sight of the Confederates drawn up in their positions. Before nightfall skirmishing began when Federals approached Breckinridge's outposts near Wayne's Hill after wading across Stones River. Quickly the sporadic firing took on intensity, and then an advance by a line of blueclad infantry threatened to take the hill itself, together with the Kentucky battery that Breckinridge had posted there after seeing Bragg's error in not occupying the eminence earlier. Only a timely countercharge by regiments from Breckinridge's old First Kentucky "Orphan" Brigade turned back the Yankee assault. Nightfall put an end to any further contact, and the Federals withdrew to the west bank of the river and their main van once more.

If Bragg had only known that at the moment he faced only a third of the Army of the Cumberland! Crittenden's wing had arrived, but Thomas and McCook had not, and the latter lay more than a mile away. A swift Confederate attack might have done incalculable harm to Rosecrans, but Bragg could not know it just then. Rosecrans worked repeatedly during the night to get McCook up, but he delayed and did not arrive until well into December 30, with the result that another day went by with nothing more than isolated skirmishing. But when night fell on that day, the two armies were virtually complete, and in place not more than a few hundred yards apart in the darkness. There was no doubt that the morrow would bring a great battle.

Rosecrans' army occupied a line almost four miles long, stretching from a position opposite McCown's division, now in advance of Cleburne on the Confederate left, thence along the edge of a dense wood, through fields and more woods, to the Nashville Turnpike and the bank of Stones River nearly a mile downstream of the spot where Breckinridge's line hinged on Polk's. McCook held the Federal right, opposite Cleburne and McCown. Thomas occupied the center, and Crittenden the left. There was much that Bragg could now tell about the enemy's line as he peered across at the moving brigades, but he believed that Rosecrans might be weak on his right flank, just where Bragg had himself shifted McCown and Cleburne from Hardee some time before. That settled his mind on taking the offensive early the next day. Hardee's two divisions would strike the enemy right, while Wheeler's cavalry rode around and got in his rear. Polk would advance as well, and simultaneously, the purpose being to keep Polk's right anchored on the river, and advance the rest of the army, wheeling around to the right and pushing Rosecrans before them until he had his own back to Stones River. Wheeler would cut off his retreat via the Nashville Turnpike, and then they could destroy him in detail. It was, of course, an utterly impossible plan, calling for perfect coordination, no breaks in his own lines, and an advance of some five miles by Bragg's own left wing.

As frequently happened in this war, Rosecrans was planning almost the same battle as his foe. He intended to launch his assault early in the morning, and to move against Bragg's right flank. He would send elements of Crittenden's wing across the river once more, smash into Breckinridge, and push him back into the town. Then Thomas would attack in his front to keep Bragg's center occupied, and in the end they would roll up his right completely while forcing him back across the river. His plans set, "Old Rosey" went to bed along with his army, and all of them, North and South, on either side of Stones River, did their best to take warmth and shelter from the winter cold. The initiative in the battle to come on the dawn, given the similar nature of the attack plans, would go to the general who moved first.

They were all up at about the same time, well before dawn, but Bragg struck first. Shortly after 6 a.m., McCown got his 4,400 Texans, Georgians, Tennesseeans, Arkansans, and a single North Carolina unit, into line and moving forward through the morning fog. Cleburne put his division, just as strong, 500 yards behind the first line as they set off for Rosecrans' right flank. It was exactly 6:22 a.m. when the Federals of Brigadier General August Willich's brigade, Johnson's Division, of McCook's wing, saw them coming. The Rebels got within 200 yards of the Yankees' line before firing broke out, and by then it was almost too late for the Federals to resist them. Within five minutes the brigade of General Edward Kirk, on Willich's left, virtually collapsed, leaving the wounded Kirk himself on the field. The Confederates swarmed over his artillery and then pressed on to hit Willich, now badly exposed by Kirk's retreat. The retreating and demoralized men of the other brigade badly disrupted Willich's men as they raced through his camps. Willich himself was away and his brigade lay in the hands of a temporary commander. With all this going against them, his Indiana, Illinois, and Ohio regiments gave way quickly one after the other. Willich himself, riding hard to rejoin his command, fell into Rebel hands, along with fully 1,000 other prisoners taken from the two brigades, as well as eight cannon. Rosecrans' right almost ceased to exist and it was not yet 7 a.m.[5]

But even now the impracticability of Bragg's wheeling plan manifested itself. When an enemy retreats precipitately, an attacker follows to press the advantage. Only Willich and Kirk's brigades did not cooperate by pulling back in the direction of the wheel. Instead, they withdrew off to their rear and right. McCown, in following them, was pulled off course, actually lengthening the Confederate line and as he moved forward while Cleburne tried to wheel behind him, it naturally brought the latter into the front line. Worse, all along the line men could not keep their pace properly, for to make the wheel men on the right were to move at a walk, while those on the left nearly had to run. The result was soon a ragged line broken by a number of gaps, with men and officers fumbling in the mist to reform their lines. For some time Cleburne did not even know that he was no longer behind McCown, but up on the front, and did not discover it until he smacked into Jefferson Davis' first brigade commanded by Colonel Sidney Post.

The disintegration of the original right flank brigades gave Post time to prepare his brigade to meet an attack. Thus he was ready when the Rebels hit, and managed to offer at least a passing resistance before half his brigade gave way, soon to be followed by the rest. The Confederates, though blooded now and starting to lose their momentum, pressed on. By 7:30 the fleeing Federals had started to reform behind a few fresh regiments and held for a few minutes before a renewed Rebel onslaught literally ran over them, putting all five of the Yankee brigades on Rosecrans' far right in precipitate retreat. Within just ninety minutes of opening the battle, McCown and Cleburne had pushed the enemy flank back more than a mile.

Now John Wharton's brigade of Wheeler's cavalry rode around the end of the shaky new Yankee position and struck the already demoralized enemy. Whole regiments simply gave up in the face of it, while others tried their best to melt still further into the woods. Wharton even came close to capturing McCook's entire ammunition train until a fortuitously timed Yankee cavalry countercharge stopped the Rebel horsemen.

By now the din of firing grew greater off to the Confederate right, as Polk's attack began to encounter the next division in the Federal line, Sheridan's. Things were not going quite as well here for the aggressors. Cheatham's division was supposed to move out at the same time as Cleburne advanced, but its commander, whom many witnesses that day believed to be drunk, did not act until prodded by Bragg, and then nearly an hour late. That gave Sheridan in his front time to prepare after seeing the debacle over on his own right. Worse for the attackers, Cheatham failed to make his advance in strength, as ordered. Instead, he sent his brigades forward one at a time, with the result that Sheridan could concentrate his fire on each in turn. The result was a severe check that sent Cheatham's first brigade reeling back, though not without cost. The immensely popular General Joshua Sill, commanding one of Sheridan's brigades, fell with a bullet through his brain.

Minutes later Cheatham sent in his next brigade, only to receive like treatment, though in a follow-up charge the Rebels gained some ground on Sheridan's right. Then Cheatham sent in his third brigade at about 8 a.m., to strike the remnant of Sill's brigade. The coming attack was presaged by a virtual stampede of rabbits flushed by the advancing Rebels, and running back and through the Federal line. This time the Yankees were ready. They stopped the Rebel brigade cold with a withering volley not fifty yards from their line. Half an hour later the Rebels struck again, but Sheridan had feverishly strengthened and repositioned his lines to meet the attack. Once more the Southerners came to a halt in the face of heavy fire, and then Sheridan sent forward a fresh brigade to counterattack. The enemy in his front rapidly withdrew.

With the Federals on his own right continuing to fall back in the face of McCown and Cleburne, Sheridan had to pull back to a new position while the Confederates regrouped for another assault. Then he had to do so yet again, and in the end selected a line along a cedar forest so thick that when the Confederates advanced once more and drove their way into the woods, no one could control the battle. Exercising command became impossible. No one could see even an entire regiment in the dense growth, and it became one of those confused, intensely private battles between men in small groups or alone. But Sheridan held on, and by 9 a.m. or thereafter, the momentum of Cheatham's ill-managed attack was spent. The cost to Sheridan had been terrible, but he finally provided an anchor for Rosecrans' ravaged right, and brought to a halt the seemingly irresistible Confederate juggernaut.

Rosecrans had been at his erratic best thus far in the battle. At first he hardly paid any attention to the sound of firing from McCook's front. His mind was set on his own attack on Bragg's right. But when he heard the intensity of the firing grow too rapidly, and spread too quickly toward the center of his line, he realized something was wrong. As the first intelligence of the collapse of Davis' division reached him, he immediately sent a supporting division from Thomas off to reinforce the threatened area. Then his excitement overtook him and he began riding everywhere, giving a flurry of orders to anyone at hand, sometimes to cross-purposes, and certainly confusing his subordinates. As his own right withdrew further and further, he finally committed almost all of his reserves in building a line a mile or so below the Nashville Turnpike, which was obviously the enemy's goal.

Inevitably the Rebels came on again, this time moving more in concert, and with the addition of a fresh brigade to the three that Cheatham had already sent into the fight. At about 10 a.m. they struck the hinge formed by Sheridan's right, and the newly arrived reinforcements sent by Rosecrans, while McCown's and Cleburne's veterans continued their swing around to press the right half of the hinge further back. The attack pressed on with renewed success, aided now by ammunition running low along the Yankee line and McCook's supply trains nowhere within reach. Before long Sheridan found himself fighting the foe on three sides, and dangerously close to being surrounded. There was no alternative but to get out, and quickly. That left the division of Lovell Rousseau, just arrived to hold the far right, alone and isolated. He was no coward, but speedily realized that he would be overwhelmed from all sides if he, too, did not pull back.

Bragg had done little in the way of managing his battle so far that morning. When initial reports indicated that McCown, Cleburne, and Cheatham were progressing successfully, he turned his own attention to the center of the Yankee line directly in his front. There the enemy had a firm foothold in a wood locally known as the Round Forest. As the right half of "Rosey's" line fell back further and further, this point became increasingly important, for if a breakthrough could be made there, virtually astride the Nashville road, then the faltering right would be cut off from the rest of the army and caught between two fires, while the other half of the Yankee line would be trapped between Bragg and Stones River. If he could take the Round Forest, Bragg could win the battle and destroy an enemy army utterly.

The first real activity in the vicinity did not come until 8 a.m., well after the battle on the Federal right was going badly. General Palmer, of Thomas' wing, realized that he was in a vulnerable position and moved his division forward a few hundred yards toward better ground. Negley was supposed to be advancing on his flank, but once Palmer was on the move he found the other officer's division moving away instead, having just seen Sheridan's line off to the right about to give way. Palmer, too, tried to move back, but in so doing created a gap in the line just at the Round Forest. Into this he sent the brigade of Colonel William B. Hazen of Ohio. Hazen moved quickly, and soon had his men erecting breastworks of fallen brush and branches to resist the oncoming Rebels.

Within a few minutes the first wave of Confederates from Polk's Corps ran into the fortified wood. The defenders had an excellent, unrestricted field of fire from their wooded shelter, and they tore apart the first wave, General James Chalmers' Mississippi brigade. For half an hour the brave Confederates stood in the open, trading volleys with Hazen, before losses forced them to retire. Chalmers himself fell wounded, and his dead and wounded so littered the ground that later that patch of field became known as the "Mississippi Half-Acre."[6]

Though some of the Mississippians held on, by 9:30 Chalmers' brigade was finished. There followed a half-hour lull during which Hazen received reinforcements and he used the time well to enhance his impromptu breastworks. Then the Tennessee brigade of General Daniel S. Donelson, of Cheatham's division, came on the field, the only one of Cheatham's brigades not already embroiled in the fight with Sheridan. Moreover, this was the last fresh brigade west of Stones River. It achieved marked success at first, driving away some of Hazen's supports, but others soon appeared in their place, and though the situation looked critical for a time, Hazen held out. Suddenly the Round Forest took on the same magnetic aspect of the Sunken Road at Antietam, or the Hornets' Nest at Shiloh. Units from all sides seemed attracted to it almost by telepathy as the Federals dug in to hold on, knowing that if they were routed here, the game was lost and they would all be, in the slang of the day, "gone up."

General Milo Hascall of New York arrived with a regiment and, being senior officer in the forest, took command. "The position must be held, even if it cost the last man we had," he wrote a few days later. They all fought on desperately, losing track of the number of times Polk's battered brigades came at them until, by about noon, the Southern assault finally exhausted itself. Once again, the failure to concentrate their numbers on large-scale attacks had wasted Rebel strength.[7]

The responsibility ultimately was Bragg's. All through the morning he exercised little or no control over the fight, leaving it to his subordinates to carry out their attack orders of the night before. Yet all the while he had Breckinridge's five brigades on the east side of Stones River doing nothing. At first this seemed justified, because portions of Rosecrans' left wing had recrossed the river just as they had the night before, and reports of their presence came to Breckinridge around 7 a.m. This seemed to threaten a possible attack. Soon after, things began to crumble on the Yankee right; however, these Federals recrossed to their own side of the river, but Breckinridge's scouts failed to report this to him. Thus a lack of good information kept him tied on that portion of the field until late morning, when intelligence finally revealed that the ground between the Kentuckian's division and the river was clear of all but skirmishers.[8]

Shortly before noon Bragg finally called on Breckinridge for one of his brigades to come assist Polk's attack on the Round Forest. Two were immediately dispatched instead, but then Bragg changed his mind. Suddenly fearful once more of an attack on Breckinridge, Bragg canceled the order, and instead started to send two brigades to support the Kentuckian. By 1 p.m. Breckinridge had definitely determined that he faced no threat. Fortunately, he had not recalled his first two brigades, and now Bragg ordered him to bring two of the three remaining brigades across to join with Polk. He obeyed instantly, but when Breckinridge brought the last two of his brigades across, he found that Polk had not waited for his entire division to arrive, but had sent the first two brigades in as soon as they appeared. Once more a piecemeal approach allowed Rosecrans' concentrated fire to take telling effect, and Beckinridge's first two brigades were reeling back in disorder even as he came on the scene.

Polk now sent Breckinridge in with his two fresh units, and they finally did little better than those before, but as the daylight was waning rapidly, they came out of the advance with substantially fewer losses. Had they but known what was happening on their own left flank, they might have pressed harder, for almost at this same time, Cleburne and McCown, and portions of other units, had made one more massive push that finally forced Rousseau back right to the Nashville Turnpike. One last rush, especially if supported by a firm push at the Round Forest, and the road was theirs for the taking, with all the fruits of victory that might attend. But those battle-weary Rebels did not have it in them. With darkness falling, they had literally fought from dawn to dusk. They simply could not go on, and instead almost spontaneously they began to fall back, leaving behind them the Federals and a much relieved Rosecrans.[9]

The battle was done for the day, and Rosecrans was lucky to have an army at all. Bragg had battered him almost to pieces along fully two-thirds of his line, and the only consolation – though he did not then know it – was that he had battered Bragg just as badly. "Old Rosey" called his generals to him and conferred on what they should do. The only choices were either to stand where they were and try again, or else retreat. Reports differed on who advocated what, but at the end of the conference the commanding general decided to remain. Well after midnight he ordered Crittenden to occupy a high ridge on the west bank of Stones River, roughly opposite the original position of his childhood playmate Breckinridge. Elsewhere he had his men dig in where they were after straightening their lines. Rosecrans seems not to have had much of a plan for renewing the battle; he only knew that he refused to leave the field unless Bragg drove him away.

Bragg, meanwhile, felt confident of victory, and at first expected January 1, 1863, to dawn with the fields and woods in front of him cleared of the foe. But when he found Rosecrans still there, he did almost nothing, allowing his army to rest after the exertions of the day before. That was fine, but all the while his men could see the enemy digging in, which meant that when the attack was renewed, the Yankees would be even harder to drive away.

By early morning on January 2, Bragg's reconnaissance indicated to him that Rosecrans might be intending yet again to advance on Breckinridge's position, the only direction from which a threat to the Confederate army could now come. Not that Rosecrans was in a position to mount an offensive, but Bragg did not know this with certainty. Further, still hoping to drive the enemy from the field, Bragg concluded not illogically that having failed to do so everywhere else, this area off to his right was the last logical place to try. Unfortunately, Rosecrans anticipated this when he ordered Crittenden to occupy those heights opposite Breckinridge. The Kentuckian's own reconnaissance this morning confirmed the strength of Crittenden's position, and especially the presence of a considerable amount of artillery on that ridge.

Nevertheless, Bragg summoned Breckinridge shortly after noon and ordered him to take his division and drive the Federals out of his front and back across the river. It was madness. Both Hardee and Polk opposed the plan, arguing that the Federals in the Kentuckian's front offered no real threat, while the Federal strength building on the west bank of the river's high ground certainly did. If Breckinridge drove the enemy back to the river, he would have to stand his ground under the fire of those

Yankee guns. "My information is different," said Bragg, and insisted on the attack. Some later believed that the assault was a punishment to Breckinridge for failing to join in the Kentucky campaign, or even for standing up to Bragg in the matter of the executed soldier. A few believed that Bragg secretly hoped to see the general killed.

When Breckinridge went back to his brigade commanders with the orders, they were close to mutiny. General Roger Hanson, commanding the Kentucky "Orphan Brigade," fumed that he would personally kill Bragg, while others urged Breckinridge to challenge Bragg to a duel. Even worse, Bragg now, at the last minute, forced the Kentuckian to accept General Gideon Pillow, a hopelessly incompetent old politician and schemer, to supersede one of his veteran brigade commanders. Breckinridge did as he was told, readied his brigades, and at 4 p.m. led them forward at Bragg's signal.

Just over 5,000 men commenced the advance; fewer than 3,500 came back. At the very outset Pillow turned coward. Breckinridge found him cowering behind a tree. Then two-thirds of the way across the ground to be covered, Hanson went down with a mortal wound, Breckinridge himself standing beside him trying to hold the severed artery in his leg to prevent him bleeding to death. Almost from the first the advancing division came under heavy fire, and it got more intense the closer they came to the river. Crittenden had massed 45 pieces of artillery on the heights across the river, and as soon as Breckinridge pushed the Yankees in his front off a hill some distance in advance of Wayne's Hill, his men came in for the full force of the shelling. Worse, by now it was 4:30 or thereabouts, and already the light was failing. Sleet started coming down, hitting the men in the face and blurring their vision. Then when the Federal brigade in their front pulled back entirely, while others retreated across Stones River, the Confederates spontaneously became caught up in the pursuit. Despite Breckinridge's efforts to keep them in hand, they raced down to the river after the fleeing foe, only to bring themselves under the murderous fire of that artillery high on the opposite bank. It cut them to pieces. Within a few minutes, the attackers started to stream back to their starting point, and by 5 p.m. it was all over, Breckinridge himself riding along his reforming lines with tears in his eyes as he saw the great gaps. He never forgave Bragg.[10]

There the battle ended. Late that night Bragg met with all of his ranking generals, and they were not yet decisive about what to do next. But on January 3, when Bragg received reports that Rosecrans' cavalry was moving around his flank, he finally decided to abandon his position and retreat. The movement took all night, and soon the Army of Tennessee was on its way several miles south to the Duck River, and a new line of defense that it would occupy for much of the winter. For his part, Rosecrans was more than happy to hold his position, having recovered some of middle Tennessee and seen the enemy leave his front.

It was a curious battle. Neither commander fought it well. Tactically Bragg held the upper hand all through December 31, and finished January 2 with the same ground he started it with. Nevertheless, he felt forced to abandon the field, which gave

Rosecrans, almost by default, the strategic upper hand. Certainly Lincoln was anxious for the news of anything resembling a victory, following the failure at Fredericksburg and a stalemate out west on the Mississippi. He gave Rosecrans his heartfelt thanks, and to the day he died remained grateful. Earning him that gratitude were the 13,000 killed, wounded, and missing, from the Army of the Cumberland, losses substantially greater than the 10,000 suffered by Bragg. But the incalculable damage done within Bragg's army by Bragg himself more than made up for the disparity. In the aftermath of the battle, Hardee, Polk, Breckinridge, and a host of other ranking generals literally went to war with Bragg over his conduct of the fight, and his subsequent attempt to lay blame for the failure to destroy Rosecrans at their feet. Those battles in headquarters tents and in the newspapers and halls of the War Department in Richmond would have repercussions far outlasting the military impact of the bloody winter days along Stones River.

REFERENCES

1 Glenn Tucker, *Chickamauga* (Indianapolis, Ind., 1961), p.75.
2 William C. Davis, *Breckinridge: Statesman, Soldier, Symbol* (Baton Rouge, La., 1974), pp.331-32.
3 *O.R.,* I, 20, pt.2, pp.60, 64, 123-24.
4 Cozzens, *No Better Place*, p.46.
5 *O.R.,* I, 20, pt.1, pp.316, 325-26.
6 Cozzens, *No Better Place*, p.153.
7 *O.R.,* I, 20, pt.1, pp.560-61.
8 Davis, *Breckinridge*, p.336.
9 *O.R.,* I, 20, pt. pp.678-81, 722, 784, 884-85, 891-94.
10 Davis, *Breckinridge*, pp.343-44.

VII

CHANCELLORSVILLE

"**M**r. President, I am not 'Captain' Hooker, but was once Lieutenant-Colonel Hooker of the regular army," said Lincoln's visitor in the summer of 1861. "I was lately a farmer in California, but since the Rebellion broke out I have been here trying to get into the service, and I find that I am not wanted. I am about to return home, but before going I was anxious to pay my respects to you, and to express my wishes for your personal welfare and success in quelling this Rebellion. And I want to say one word more. I was at Bull Run the other day, Mr. President, and it is no vanity to me to say that I am a d . . . sight better general than any you had on that field." Almost on the spot Lincoln made him a brigadier.[1]

At least, this is how "Fighting Joe" Hooker remembered the episode more than eighteen years later, but like so much of his bombast during his military career, the story is probably more weighted toward conceit than accuracy. For one thing, he had never been a lieutenant-colonel in the Old Army. Indeed, he almost did not make it into the service at all. His intemperate mouth almost got him evicted from the Military Academy before his eventual graduation in 1837, then later during the Mexican War, though his field performance was good and won him brevet promotions to higher rank, his open criticism of General Scott made even more trouble for him in the post-war army. That may have accounted for his banishment to the tranquil but almost soporific service on the Pacific coast, the same posting that nearly made an alcoholic of Grant and helped bore Sherman into leaving uniform. In 1853 he finally resigned his commission – as a *captain* – and bought a farm near Sonoma, California. Despite the lushness of the soil, Hooker was not molded for farming, and dabbled in a number of small enterprises and minor public positions. In 1859, as California was being torn along with the rest of the nation, he took the colonelcy of a militia regiment – a commission that he misrepresented to Lincoln as being in the old Regular service – and two years later, when war broke out, he borrowed money to make the trip to Washington to scramble for a place in the new army. Unfortunately, when he went to the War Department, he found that the general-in-chief at that time was his old antagonist Scott, who was quite happy to put Hooker's ambitions right at the bottom of his already long list of priorities.

If his later account of the interview with Lincoln is at all accurate, Hooker also misrepresented something else – his lack of vanity. In an era of towering egos, still his conceit loomed monumental. It was what gave him the self-confidence and – he felt – the right to go over the heads of his superiors as he chose, just as he did in going directly to Lincoln. Hooker's ends always justified his means, in his mind, and if jumping channels, disobeying orders, intriguing, wire-pulling, or outright lying would accomplish his goals, he did not shrink from the task. Then there were other rather compatible elements of his character that did not endear him to many. His was a personal as well as professional vanity. He was undeniably good looking by the standards of the time, six feet tall, robust, fair, with a rakish air that easily attracted the ladies. Indeed, his intemperance in that line soon became the talk of the army. Contrary to an old myth, the term "hooker" as applied to a prostitute does not derive from Joseph Hooker's fondness of the ladies. It predates him by many years and comes from a section of New York locally known as "the Hook," where they were once concentrated. But the fact that the myth took hold so quickly and tenaciously is ample evidence that such an association surprised no one.

His fellow officers resented his notional publicity, especially after the North fell in love with his sobriquet "Fighting Joe," which originated, in fact, in a typographical error. A compositor at the New York *Courier and Enquirer* received a report of an engagement on the peninsula with the heading "Fighting – Joe Hooker," which was meant only to indicate that the text following was to be integrated into an existing article as up-to-date information on the general's part in the battle. Instead, the compositor left out the hyphen, and set up the article as a free-standing piece with a headline reading "FIGHTING JOE HOOKER." Though the general disliked the sobriquet, the public loved it, and after a time his objection to the title was probably nothing more than an exercise of his occasional false modesty.[2]

It was his ruthless scheming that most offended Hooker's associates. Chaffing at being a part of Burnside's wing during the campaign leading up to Antietam, Hooker was widely believed to have politicked with McClellan to get himself and his corps an independent status just before the battle. Then when Burnside later assumed command of the Army of the Potomac, Hooker almost flagrantly set out to undermine him. He wrote to influential men in the War Department, complained about Burnside to important Congressmen on key committees, circulated stories – probably exaggerated – about the inefficiency within the army, and especially after Fredericksburg lost no opportunity to disparage his commander. At the same time, he sowed discontent within the Army of the Potomac itself, especially in his own command. By January 24, 1863, Burnside's outrage was so great that even in the act of resigning his own command of his army, he sought to strike out at his greatest internal foe. Calling Hooker "guilty of unjust and unnecessary criticism of the actions of his superior officers, . . . and having . . . endeavored to create distrust . . . , made reports and statements which were calculated to create incorrect impressions, and for habitually speaking in disparaging terms of other officers," Burnside issued an order dismissing Hooker from the service "as a man unfit to hold an important commission."

Nevertheless, the next day, when Lincoln accepted Burnside's resignation, he offered the army command to Hooker in his place and quashed the dismissal. After almost two years of trouble from Democratic high commanders like McClellan, the Republican Lincoln and his cabinet liked the apolitical Hooker. And after the battles of 1862, there was no doubt that he would fight. Lincoln had tried a man like Burnside who doubted his own abilities, and who went on to justify those doubts. Maybe a supremely confident fellow like Hooker could actually achieve something.

Just the same, the president felt little comfort in his choice, and some doubts of his own that he did not hesitate to share with the Army of the Potomac's new commander. Just the day after receiving the command, Hooker received a summons to meet privately with Lincoln. Very probably Lincoln told him in person what he later that day put in a confidential letter to the general. "There are some things in regard to which I am not quite satisfied with you," said the president. Hooker was ambitious which was not of itself a bad thing, "but you have taken counsel of your ambition, and thwarted [Burnside] as much as you could, in which you did a great wrong to the country." Moreover, Lincoln had heard more than once Hooker's boastful claims that the country needed a dictator to see it through its crisis. In spite of such sentiments, Lincoln gave him the command, reminding him that only "those generals who gain successes can set up dictators." He expected such success from Hooker, "and I will risk the dictatorship." Yet Lincoln made it clear that he feared Hooker far less than he feared *for* him. "The spirit which you have aided to infuse into the army, of criticizing your commander and withholding confidence from him, will now turn upon you," he warned. "Neither you nor Napoleon, if he were alive again, could get any good out of an army while such a spirit prevails in it." Lincoln would help as much as he could, but Hooker must be careful not only to his front, but also his back. "And now beware of rashness," the president concluded in an almost paternal tone. "Beware of rashness, but with energy and sleepless vigilance, go forward and give us victories."[3]

Hooker maintained the Grand Division organization inherited from Burnside, but made some changes in commanders. Couch now succeeded to command of Sumner's old Right Grand Division, with Oliver O. Howard now leading its II Corps and John Sedgwick the IX Corps. Hooker's own Center Grand Division went to Meade, with Daniel Sickles now in command of the III Corps and George Sykes taking over the V Corps from Butterfield, whom Hooker had made his chief of staff. The Left Grand Division went to William F. "Baldy" Smith, with Reynolds still leading the I Corps and Newton in charge of Smith's old VI. Sigel's XI Corps and Slocum's XII Corps became a Reserve Grand Division, led by Sigel. Cavalry and artillery Hooker parceled out to each of the Grand Divisions, for a time breaking up the former unified mounted command. Less than two weeks after taking over, however, Hooker did away with the Grand Divisions altogether. He recombined all of the cavalry into a single corps under Stoneman, while the abolition of the divisions meant that Couch, Meade, Smith, and Sigel all reverted to their old corps commands, respectively the II, V, IX and XI. All of this displaced other officers, and through seniority Sedgwick now had to be given the VI Corps, and when Sigel objected to being reduced in command, he went on extended leave and Howard took his XI Corps. At the same time, Hooker dispatched Smith and the IX Corps to Fort Monroe, Virginia, as a diversion, hoping that Confederate fears of another move up the peninsula would lead Lee to send men from his own army to protect Richmond. It worked, as Hood and Pickett and the 13,000 men in their divisions were soon on their way to the capital. Yet this and some threats to Confederate North Carolina constituted practically all of Hooker's strategic maneuver in the final weeks of the winter.

Hooker inherited a virtually static military situation when he took command. The Army of the Potomac still perched on Stafford Heights, overlooking the Rappahannock, glaring across at Lee. The hard winter made each suffer alike, and the inactivity led to a relaxation of drill and discipline on both sides of the stream. Indeed, when the river was not frozen over, the enlisted men carried on a brisk trade back and forth, Rebels trading tobacco for Yankee coffee, all of the commerce passing in little sailboats blown across on the winds. Still Hooker worked tirelessly to rebuild the equipment and morale of the men in the ranks, as well as their numerical strength, for absenteeism and desertions by the disheartened rose to alarming proportions, approaching ten percent of the army at one stage.

Lincoln came to visit the army in person as April dawned, and there Hooker paraded his magnificent legions for the president. Everyone noted in Hooker's conversation his repeated use of expressions such as "when I get to Richmond," or "after we have taken Richmond." To some the general boasted that he almost felt sorry for the enemy. "I have the finest army the sun ever shone on," he boasted. "My plans are perfect, and when I start to carry them out, may God have mercy on General Lee, for I will have none." The president found it disturbing. "That is the most depressing thing about Hooker," he told a friend. "It seems to me that he is overconfident."[4]

Again, what Hooker and Lincoln said in private is not known, but within days of Lincoln's visit the general presented in written form his final operational plan. He would send his cavalry upriver, to cross some twenty miles northwest of the armies, at or near Kelley's Ford, then to drive south, cutting off Lee from Richmond, after which Hooker would cross at Fredericksburg with the main army. Threatened front and rear, Lee would have to retire to the west, his only avenue of retreat. But no sooner did Hooker put his horsemen on the road than torrential rains fell, raising the river level, and making the whole strategy impracticable for the moment. The general called off the campaign, and for the next two weeks men both blue and gray slogged about in almost non-stop downpours. Hooker decided simply to make occasional threats along the river at its several crossing places, all the while keeping an eye out for a weak spot where he might cross quickly without loss, and for weather to allow him to move. Nevertheless, all along Lee confidantly predicted that if and when the Yankees tried to cross the Rappahannock, they would do so upstream of Fredericksburg.

While Lee anticipated at least that much of Hooker's design, he did not at all foresee the radical change in the Yankee commander's overall strategy that developed during those dreary wet weeks in April. By about the 24th or 25th at the latest, he had completely reformed his plans. No more did he think of pushing Lee aside and striking for Richmond. Now he wanted Lee's whole army itself. He would send infantry marching up to Kelley's Ford, where they would cross, then march down the opposite bank, driving the Rebels away from United States Ford and Banks' Ford, respectively just seven and four miles upstream. Then he would send more infantry pouring over those now undefended crossings and the whole group would hit Lee's left flank on the heights at Fredericksburg, while other legions crossed the river below the city and moved up on Lee's other flank as well as cutting him off from Richmond. Hooker hoped to use his superiority in numbers, along with rapid movement, to trap Lee with his back to the river.[5]

It was an excellent plan, *if* the Yankees moved swiftly and silently, and *if* Lee was slow to respond and remained content to stay at Fredericksburg facing the Federals left to occupy his attention. Certainly Hooker wasted no time in setting things in motion. On April 26 he directed that the XI, V, and XII Corps leave at dawn the next day for Kelley's Ford, expecting them to arrive by afternoon April 28. Couch was to take two of his three divisions up to the vicinity of United States and Banks' Fords, while leaving one division very ostentatiously in their camps opposite Fredericksburg to make Lee believe no one had left. Hooker hoped that Lee would sense the threat to the two lower fords and detach men to protect them, without spotting the main crossing to be made at Kelley's. This would also weaken the remainder of the Rebel army to be dealt with at Fredericksburg itself. That portion was to be the responsibility of Sedgwick, whom he temporarily placed in command over the I, III, and VI Corps. Reynolds was to cross the river at Fitzhugh's Crossing four miles downstream from the city, before dawn on April 29. The VI Corps would move at the same time over Franklin's Crossing, two miles closer to Fredericksburg, while the III Corps would follow one or the other of the first two, depending upon which crossing had been more easily and completely effected. They were all to drive inland toward the Telegraph Road, Lee's chief link with Richmond. Meanwhile, if informed that Lee had detached much of his army to meet the threats from the upper fords, then Sedgwick was to attack the remainder at once.

Just where the actual fighting would commence depended upon how quickly Lee ascertained what Hooker was about, and how quickly he responded. The men crossing at Kelley's Ford would have to move straight south, once across, and after six or seven miles would come to the Rapidan, which flowed into the Rappahannock from the west near United States Ford. They must get to the Rapidan and across it at Germanna or Ely's Fords before Lee moved to stop them. If they did, then they would march almost immediately into a dense, tangled forest known locally as the Wilderness, and crossable only on the few turnpikes and "plank" roads – literally roadbeds of wooden planks laid over log rails to evade the mud beneath. Just a few miles south of Germanna and Ely's Fords they would come to the Wilderness Tavern on the Orange Turnpike. Then they would turn due east. If Lee and his army did not confront them by that time, they could still expect to meet with him anywhere along the turnpike, perhaps a few miles further at Wilderness Church, perhaps two miles beyond, at Chancellorsville.[6]

With luck, Lee might not meet him at all, for the Rebel chieftain, for all his gifts for outthinking enemy commanders, seems not to have anticipated Hooker's strategy. On same day that Hooker was issuing marching orders to his corps commanders, Lee still held to his notion that the enemy would send his cavalry on a wide upriver sweep, while advancing the rest of the Army of the Potomac directly across against him at Fredericksburg – essentially the plan Hooker had abandoned several weeks before. There may have been something of wishful thinking in this, too, for Lee was hardly in a position to counter the more ambitious movement that Hooker had set in motion. The detachment of Hood and Pickett to meet the threat of the IX Corps on the peninsula reduced Lee's tally by 13,000, and he had sent Longstreet to command them as well. This left Lee personally directing the remaining I Corps divisions of Anderson and McLaws, with an effective strength of less than 18,000. Jackson's II Corps was intact, with the divisions of A.P. Hill, Robert Rodes commanding in D.H. Hill's absence, Early, and Raleigh Colston standing in for the absent Isaac Trimble. This corps totaled just over 38,000, and with the artillery and Stuart's cavalry division, gave Lee a grand total of just under 61,000. Even though Lee discounted reports that put Hooker's strength at 150,000 or higher, he still would not have been surprised by morning reports from mid-April that showed just under 134,000 Yankees present for duty. Thus Lee knew that Hooker could meet him two for one. As it was, he had Jackson spread out over about two miles of the works immediately below Fredericksburg, while McLaws' division held the heights behind the city itself. Anderson's men were spread out as far to McLaws' left as seemed prudent, with only elements of Stuart's cavalry thrown several miles west trying to watch the upper fords. In the face of Hooker's might, Lee was in no position to do more than await the enemy's first move. Fortunately he still enjoyed that impregnable position at

Fredericksburg itself, another reason he hoped that the enemy could come straight at him as Burnside had done.[7]

The movement to Kelley's Ford, despite heavy rain, went brilliantly. The XI and XII Corps arrived by the late evening of April 28, to find that there would be no repeat of the administrative bungling that ruined Burnside's campaign. Their pontoon bridge materials were already there waiting for them, and so was Hooker himself. By 10 p.m. the first regiments were marching across the bridges, and the few Rebels on the other side were quickly captured without getting news back to Lee. Orders for the next day went out quickly, with Meade to take the V Corps straight for Ely's Ford on the Rapidan, while Howard and Slocum marched for Germanna. Movement on April 29 was slower, hampered by the dense country and the clogging effect of tens of thousands of soldiers on the limited roads. Even though the Yankee advance was now being observed by Stuart's scouts, they still misinterpreted it as a move to make a wide sweep around Lee rather than a direct march on his army's left flank. Thus by nightfall, Meade had crossed the Rapidan unhindered while Howard and Slocum straddled Germanna Ford.

Hooker had achieved his first goal successfully. He was south of the Rapidan without opposition, with virtually all of Lee's army still in its works at Fredericksburg. One more good day like the past two, and it might be too late for the Confederates to do anything, especially with Sedgwick starting to put elements of his half of the army over the river at Franklin's and Fitzhugh's Crossings that same day. The best Lee could do was warn Richmond of the movements on both his flanks and ask for any available reinforcements. He still did not divine Hooker's true intentions, or the real strength of the column advancing toward his left. Only after dark did he learn of the crossing of the Rapidan, and only then did he realize the immediate danger. At once he knew that the enemy would be heading toward Chancellorsville, for only there could Hooker pick up the Orange Plank Road, or stay on the Orange Turnpike, the two routes that led to the rear of his position at Fredericksburg. That same evening he sent urgent orders to Anderson to take two brigades and part of another and race to Chancellorsville to hold those roads.

Anderson himself reached Chancellorsville at about midnight, and around 8 a.m. the next morning, April 30, army engineers arrived to help him start erecting a line of defenses. Since the turnpike and the plank road ran roughly parallel to one another, and actually came together again about four miles east of Chancellorsville near Tabernacle and Zoar Churches, he pulled his weak line back to this point. It still protected both roads, and also put him that much closer to assistance from Lee.

Hooker's right wing corps marched on throughout the day, Slocum in the lead, followed by Howard, while Meade moved south from Ely's Ford to take a position in their front, occupying Chancellorsville by nightfall. Meanwhile, Couch finally crossed the II Corps at United States Ford and came in on Meade's left. By the time it was dark they had a well-established line nearly four miles long along the turnpike between Chancellorsville and Wilderness Church. In fact, Meade reached the objective at around 2 p.m. that afternoon, and showed uncharacteristic elation when Slocum came up. "This is splendid," he said. "We are on Lee's flank, and he does not know it. You take the plank road toward Fredericksburg, and I'll take the pike, or vice versa, as your prefer, and we will get out of this Wilderness." Meade smelled victory. But Slocum, the senior officer, stunned him with news that, on orders from Hooker, he was now assuming command here, and they were to halt their advance with hours of daylight ahead of them.[8]

Hooker was starting to lose his nerve. The previous evening he had Butterfield send Sedgwick a message that Hooker hoped to make Lee fight him "on his, Hooker's, own ground." Such terminology naturally implied going on the defensive and waiting for Lee to come to him, and now the orders to Slocum to stop the advance sounded like more of the same. Commanders and soldiers alike were dumbfounded by the order, and not a little chagrined. That same afternoon Hooker gave even more evidence that he would not attack. He issued a congratulatory address to his army proclaiming that given the position they now occupied, Lee must either "fly" or leave his entrenchments and attack them. Furthermore, in the orders he issued for May 1, the only references to attacking related to Sedgwick's portion of the army. Hooker seemed to intend standing idle and letting Sedgwick do the work of driving Lee back to him.

He need not have bothered, for that was exactly what Lee decided to do on his own. By late on the afternoon of April 30, when no strong movement had been made against his Fredericksburg lines, Lee decided that the main threat must be from Hooker's corps advancing toward Chancellorsville. He determined to leave one brigade of McLaws' and one division of Jackson's, under Early, to face the masses under Sedgwick. To the remainder he gave orders to move at daylight to join Anderson at Tabernacle Church. By midnight, the advance elements were nearly there, with the rest marching through the night. Lee would take the battle to Hooker.[9]

The III Corps started to cross at United States Ford in the morning, and shortly before noon Meade started slowly moving forward once more, though Hooker had no intention of attacking. Rather, he was simply planning to take up a more forward defensive position.

Meanwhile, when Stonewall Jackson arrived on the scene at Anderson's line, he almost immediately began to think of taking the offensive. No sooner did he relieve Anderson at Tabernacle Church than he began to push his first units forward, along both the turnpike and the plank road. By 11:30 he had covered about the half the distance to Chancellorsville on both roads when finally he came in sight of the enemy at last. Before him on the turnpike was Sykes' division of the V Corps, with the balance of Meade's corps more than a mile north on a back road, and separated by dense growth. Facing Sykes, Jackson had the brigade of General William Mahone. A mile southwest, on the plank road, the brigade of General Carnot Posey faced practically the entire XII Corps. It was not an enviable position for the Confederates, no more than 12,000 men – including others rushing to the scene – facing 40,000 under Meade and Slocum. Nevertheless, it suited Jackson. He kept right on advancing, and around 11:40 a.m. the first firing finally broke out. By early afternoon, however, more and more of Jackson's divisions arrived, until there were 40,000 on the spot or near at hand, with still more coming up behind. All told, Lee took the bold gamble of committing 50,000 men, five-sixths of his army, to the move to meet Hooker's threat. And now, with the battle just in its first minutes, they were even on the deception score. Hooker had fooled Lee and massed more than half his army on the Rebel left flank. But today Lee had left a sixth of his to hold down Sedgwick, while Hooker still believed that the bulk of the Army of Northern Virginia remained at Fredericksburg. It was to be a battle of surprises.

"I trust that God will grant us a great victory," Jackson said to "Jeb" Stuart just after noon. It was indicative of Jackson's mood. Despite being heavily outnumbered, he thought only of winning the battle. During the next hour or so, the units on both sides rapidly came up as the battlelines began taking shape. On the plank road Jackson kept his left well advanced, while his right on the turnpike fell back to less than a mile in advance of the Zoar Church, and soon extended into the Wilderness in an arc covering the church and the road to Fredericksburg behind. But the Federals were not for giving him much fight. Instead, Hooker ordered Sykes to pull back towards Chancellorsville, and gave similar orders to Slocum on the plank road. Unfortunately, Sedgwick had not yet launched the demonstration called for at Fredericksburg, and in the absence of that, Hooker feared – quite rightly – that Lee would have too many divisions free to meet him here in the Wilderness. Thus, again, the commanding general shifted from a tentative offensive to the defensive. By 2 p.m. Hooker gave up any idea of offering battle. "Have suspended attack," he notified Butterfield. "The enemy may attack me."

Soon thereafter critics would accuse Hooker of being drunk that afternoon, and that this accounted for his erratic actions and loss of nerve. But several of his generals steadfastly denied that he had consumed anything alcoholic all day. Rather, he simply lost his nerve. He had been counting on Lee to passively fall back before his advance. Indeed, his whole campaign was predicated on the Confederates behaving exactly as he expected, and up until the previous day, they had. But Jackson coming straight for him on the two roads upset Hooker's predictions. Never seriously considering that an outnumbered foe might attack him, he now thought of nothing but getting his corps back to their fortified positions of the day before in and around Chancellorsville.

Late that afternoon Hooker gave orders to re-establish the lines of the previous night, with some small modifications. Trees were felled to provide fields of fire for the artillery, obstructions were placed in advance of the infantry lines to slow an attacker, and the men dug themselves into the hardscrabble soil. By midnight they were stretched out on a line five miles long. Commencing on the far left it was anchored by Meade extending from Scott's Ford on a bend of the Rappahannock, almost due south. The V Corps line ended just short of the turnpike, about three-quarters of a mile east of Chancellorsville. There Meade linked with portions of Couch's II Corps that completed the line to the turnpike. But at that point Couch's men formed a salient, as the line turned abruptly west along the pike itself to Chancellorsville. Slocum's XII Corps then took up the line, extending it in a wide bulge south of Chancellorsville, swinging back up to the road something less than a mile east of Wilderness Church. There Howard's XI Corps took it up, Howard's front running westward along the road, past the church and nearby Dowdall's Tavern, and halting nearly a mile west of them. The whole line was based upon the assumption that all of Lee's strength in any attack would be concentrated against Chancellorsville from the plank road and the turnpike. As a result, Howard and the far right flank, seemingly unreachable, were left literally "in the air" and unprotected. This did not seem to bother Hooker. "It is all right, Couch," he told the II Corps commander that evening. "I have got Lee just where I want him; he must fight me on my own ground." Couch was not comforted. "I retired from his presence with the belief that my commanding general was a whipped man."[10]

The fighting had been little more than skirmishing during most of the day, with casualties few, but Lee anticipated that on the morrow, May 2, he would have to make a real push now that he had most of his forces on the field. Indeed, several of his generals, including Jackson, believed that Hooker would actually pull back across the Rappahannock during the night, but Lee held no such fears. Indeed, he seems to have believed that Hooker might launch a renewed offensive on the morrow, probably coordinated with a massive push by Sedgwick. Only a Confederate stroke beforehand could pre-empt such a movement, and that evening Lee and Jackson conferred as to how and where to move.

Hooker seems to have felt a little insecurity about Howard's flank, for that same night he ordered Reynolds and the I Corps to leave their position and come join this half of the army, but that movement would require many hours. If Jackson moved quickly, he could easily beat Reynolds to Howard's right. And Jackson would strike with massive force. Lee assigned him fully three-quarters of the men at hand, all of Jackson's own II Corps plus enough elements from other commands to total almost 32,000 and 112 cannon. The boldness of the plan was breathtaking. Lee was dividing his army in the face of an enemy that outnumbered him by about three-to-two. With no more than 12,000, he would stay and demonstrate against Chancellorsville, buying time and diversion to allow Jackson to make a march of nearly nine miles from their existing right flank, all of it in full daylight. If Hooker should strike while Jackson was somewhere off on the Brock Road, the result could be disaster. But Lee knew how to smell fear and irresolution in a Yankee commander. Not only was such a movement indicative of the gray chieftain's boldness; it also announced his contempt for his opponent.

Hooker began to get a glimmer of what Lee might be about when his pickets reported numbers of Rebel troops seen marching off that morning. He even warned Howard to look out for his right flank. Unfortunately, Hooker did not know, as he should have, that there was a two-mile gap between Howard and their Rapidan River crossing at Ely's Ford. Should the enemy pass through that gap, the army would be in great danger. Unfortunately, too, Howard never had been, and never would be, much of a general.

Neither was Daniel Sickles. As the morning wore on, he, too, got reports of sightings of Rebel soldiers marching off toward the right. The trouble was, as he viewed it, this meant they were probably retreating. As a result, with Hooker's permission, he advanced his III Corps from Slocum's right on the turnpike, more than a mile south to try to intercept Jackson's columns. Unfortunately, by that time virtually all of Stonewall's divisions had passed well to the south, on their way to the Brock Road, and Sickles' movement only succeeded in stretching the Yankee line into a new, deeper salient, and leaving the joint between Slocum and Howard thin and very vulnerable.

Throughout the morning and afternoon, Lee remained content to make his presence known by sporadic artillery firing and threatening movements in Hooker's front, without actually offering battle. Later in the afternoon he did send in McLaws to harrass the Yankees on the turnpike, but again only to hold Hooker's attention to this front. Meanwhile, Jackson's tired and hungry veterans pressed on. He seemed everywhere, eyes flashing, leaning forward over his horse as if bending into the wind. "Press forward, press forward," he called out incessantly. He even placed guards with bayonets at the rear of every regiment to prod forward the stragglers.[11] Incredibly, despite his hopes for secrecy, reports of Jackson's march came into Hooker and Howard all through the morning and the afternoon, but were either misinterpreted or ignored. Howard himself, around 3 p.m., laughed derisively at reports that a substantial body of the foe was seen moving in his front. They could not possibly be there, he replied, and did nothing more. As for Hooker, by now he had convinced himself that all the information of movement by the Rebels indicated a retreat, and he sent Sedgwick a peremptory order to attack and take Fredericksburg. "We know that the enemy is fleeing," he said in triumph.

By 3 p.m. Jackson's first division neared its destination, with the other two closing up quickly. As the legions came on to the turnpike from the Brock Road, they turned right, to the east, and he put them into a formation stretching two miles in length and three lines deep. There were to be no bugle calls, no shouted orders, no cheering Jackson as he rode along the lines. By about 5 p.m. they were ready, with still a couple of hours of daylight ahead. Howard's unprotected right flank lay half a mile ahead of them, with his corps stretched out along the turnpike beyond. Jackson could hit him front, flank and rear, all at the same time. "Are you ready?" Jackson asked Rodes, commanding the front line. The simple reply "Yes" launched the attack.

Never before or after in this war was there anything like it. Within seconds they encountered Howard's scanty outposts and swept them over. And now, from every point on the charging Southern line came cheers, bugles, and the high-pitched "Rebel yell." The first thing Howard's men saw was hundreds of deer, rabbits, and other forest creatures, scampering toward them to escape the wall of men and iron sweeping through the wilderness. "It was a terrible gale," Howard later remembered. "The rush, the rattle, the quick lightning from a hundred points at once; the roar redoubled by echoes through the forest; the panic, the dead and dying in sight, and the wounded straggling along; the frantic efforts of the brave and patriotic to stay the angry storm." From all points, though there was isolated and heroic resistance, the men of Howard's corps simply melted away in the face of the Rebel onslaught.[12]

After barely fifteen minutes, batteries were being captured, regiments and whole brigades put to rout, and entire divisions disrupted. Less than an hour after Jackson launched the attack, Howard's men were streaming back toward Wilderness Church, and they did not stop when they reached it, but kept right on going. Jackson pressed on after them, now with renewed vigor because they could hear the sound of artillery several miles to the east, sign that Lee had commenced his demonstration against the other end of Hooker's line. Nothing could stand before the Rebel onslaught. Jackson pushed the foe back to the church, down to Dowdall's Tavern. Incredibly, just two miles east, at Chancellorsville, Hooker was sitting on the porch of his headquarters unaware of the calamity on his right. No one seems to have thought to send him word of it, and atmospheric conditions temporarily kept him from hearing the mounting sounds of the fighting. They only got their first hint of the disaster when a staff member stood in the road and happened to turn his field glasses to the west, toward Dowdall's. "My God," he shouted, "here they come!" Hundreds of fugitives could be seen streaming towards them in the distance.[13]

Elements of the II Corps and Reynolds' I Corps, just arrived at United States Ford, rushed to stem the rout, literally pushing their way through masses of XI Corps fugitives clogging all the roads, but still no semblance of a defensive line was finally established until close to nightfall as Sickles pulled back from his southern salient to form on Slocum's right, while elements from Meade and Couch reversed themselves to face the new threat from their rear. But shortly after 7 p.m. Jackson's advance stopped anyhow as his own units became badly disorganized by their long march, precipitate advance, and the tangled countryside. Still, Hooker was in a desperate situation. His command at Chancellorsville was literally formed into a circle, with Jackson to the west and Lee south and southeast. His only remaining line of communications was a single road leading northeast to Scott's Ford and United States Ford, and vulnerable to either of the two wings of the Rebel army. About 9 p.m. Jackson gave A.P. Hill orders to do just that, then Stonewall himself rode off to his left, north of the plank road, to reconnoiter. In the gathering gloom, edgy men of the 33rd North Carolina accidentally fired on the general and his party. Three of them actually hit Jackson – one in the right hand, another at his left wrist, and the third in his left arm between the shoulder and elbow. The first two wounds were painful, but minor; the third shattered the bone and severed an artery. Jackson's panicked horse started to run toward enemy lines, dashing Jackson's face into a low-hanging tree branch before he regained control. It seemed to take forever before others got him from his horse, brought up a litter, and took him to the rear, pale and in pain. His only words were to encourage them to keep up the fight and complete the victory.

With Stuart acceding to command of the II Corps, efforts were made to renew the push, but by this time night had fallen so completely that little remained to do. By midnight the lines lay about where they were at Jackson's wounding. There was no sleep on either side of the lines that night, as Confederates raced to bring everything up to the front, and Hooker and his generals frantically sought to consolidate their precarious position and get more reinforcements on the field. Lee urged Stuart to press on around south of the Yankees and push them out of Chancellorsville, allowing the two wings of the Army of Northern Virginia to reunite. When dawn came, however, it was apparent that Sickles still stood in the way of such a junction, and though Sickles eventually pulled out of his own accord, Stuart would not link with Lee for some time.

Instead, for the balance of the day Stuart slugged it out along the line of the night before, and some Federal units even managed to push him back with spirited counterattacks as they struggled to hold on to Chancellorsville. Shortly after 9 a.m., Stuart drove a dangerous wedge into the center of the line facing, penetrating to within a quarter mile of Chancellorsville. Hooker himself was standing on the porch of the Chancellor house in the village just then, when a Rebel artillery projectile struck a post against which he had been leaning, splitting the post and sending half of it bouncing off his head. At first his men thought him dead, but he soon revived, though only to suffer intense pain thereafter. Before long he put Couch in command of the army, and never afterward exercised any positive control over it.

By late morning, the Federals were starting to recover, and Meade actually sat poised upon what was now an exposed Confederate left flank. When he met with Couch to discuss what might have been a devastating attack on Stuart, however, Couch informed him that in turning over the command, Hooker's last order had been to leave the field. With Sedgwick making no progress in front of Fredericksburg, Hooker was not willing to remain here taking a beating any longer. To the combative Meade, the news came as a shock, but there was no choice but to comply, and from that moment onward, the Federals directed all their efforts at pulling out of Chancellorsville and back toward the Rappahannock. Behind them, Lee and Stuart once more joined forces, and around noon were preparing to continue the pursuit and press the enemy into the river when Lee got word of heavy fighting far to his right rear. At last Sedgwick was attacking Fredericksburg.

Sedgwick's had been a difficult and frustrating role through most of the past few days. His orders from Hooker were to move against the enemy in his front when the proper opportunity presented itself, which it never seemed to do. Worse, Hooker's instructions had been either too discretionary, or else not discretionary enough. All through May 1 Sedgwick awaited any action in his own front until assured that Hooker was achieving success, yet at the same time Hooker said he withheld pushing his advance any further until he learned of Sedgwick taking Fredericksburg. Thus May 1 was entirely wasted. Not until the next afternoon did Hooker issue a direct order for Sedgwick to cross the river, and then it was to follow up what Hooker then thought was a retreating foe. It was too late to do anything effective that night, but Sedgwick did push in the midnight hours, moving forward his units already across at Franklin's Crossing until they hit the Confederates placed on the high ground. Slowly they pushed the thin line of Rebels back into the defenses of the town itself, and then Sedgwick started preparing for a general assault, and at 10:30 finally sent his divisions forward.

Once more Federals charged up toward Marye's Heights and the stone wall, and after a bloody and hotly contested half an hour, the wall was gained. He drove on toward Chancellorsville, having penetrated the center of the thin Confederate line, but only got as far as Salem Church, about three miles west of Marye's Heights, before he ran into Lee with most of the I Corps. Though he had nearly 20,000 fresh troops that morning in moving against the Fredericksburg line, Sedgwick broke through with only about 5,000, and then ill-advisedly raced ahead of the rest of his command, so that when he hit Salem Church with his 5,000, he was no match for Lee, whose 10,000 would otherwise have been outnumbered had Sedgwick taken more time. But being kept out of the battle for the past two days by Hooker's wavering, Sedgwick was anxious to get into the fight now and not to wait about.

Lee stopped him cold at Salem Church, and meanwhile the rest of the Confederate line he had torn through now lay in his left rear, threatening his hold on Fredericksburg. When night fell and more and more Rebels rushed to his front, Sedgwick sensed that he might be in trouble, and began preparations to abandon Fredericksburg, bring all of his troops up to his current vicinity, and then fall back northward toward the Rappahannock, where he could hold a secure grip on Scott's Ford in case he had to recross. Lee, meanwhile, did not have everything in position to mount a major assault on Sedgwick until about 5:30 on the afternoon of May 4, but when he did, despite spirited resistance, Sedgwick felt forced to withdraw, and by nightfall stood with his back to the river and the ford. Hooker, still occasionally giving orders despite being in a delirium much of the time, could have come to his aid, for the 75,000 men in his wing sat idle all day long, content to catch their breath. But he did nothing, too stunned by the defeat of May 2-3 to move or act. Thus Sedgwick was on his own.

Late that night Hooker decided to order a withdrawal north of the Rappahannock. He had no more fight left in him. Indeed, in later days his own summation of his conduct of the campaign was that for once in his life, Hooker had lost faith in Hooker. He had let Lee beat him by beating himself, and after what started as a brilliant campaign, he had nothing at all to show for the 17,000 casualties suffered, as against 12,800 for Lee. Lincoln was almost beside himself when he got the news. "My God, my God, what will the country say!" he wailed. "What will the country say!" Yet again the Army of the Potomac had been thrown back by that insurpassable barrier, the Army of Northern Virginia. After fully two years of war, the Federals stood no closer to Richmond that they had in 1861, and all they had to show for their efforts were the thousands of dead.

But the Confederates suffered, too. On May 10, 1863, at Guiney's Station, ten miles south of Fredericksburg, Stonewall Jackson died of complications from his wound. Ironically, bullets from his own men had inflicted perhaps the greatest injury yet suffered by the Confederacy. Lee could only shake away his tears and remark with anguish that he had lost his right arm. It was a dear price to pay for a battle won.

REFERENCES

1 San Francisco, *Chronicle*, November 1, 1879.
2 John Bigelow, Jr., *The Campaign of Chancellorsville* (New Haven, Conn., 1910), pp.4-6.
3 John G. Nicolay and John Hay, *Abraham Lincoln, A History* (New York, 1890), VII, p.88.
4 Noah Brooks, *Washington in Lincoln's Time* (Washington, 1879), pp.50-51; Bigelow, *Chancellorsville*, p.108.
5 *Report of the Joint Committee*, IV, p.145.
6 Bigelow, *Chancellorsville*, pp.173-79.
7 *Ibid.*, pp.132-33, 136.
8 R.M. Bache, *Life of General G.G. Meade* (Philadelphia, 1884), p.260.
9 Bigelow, *Chancellorsville*, pp.232-33.
10 *Ibid.*, p.259.
11 *Ibid.*, p.275.
12 Oliver O. Howard, *Autobiography* (New York, 1907), I, pp.368-70.
13 A.C. Hamlin, *The Battle of Chancellorsville* (Boston, 1884), p.148.

VIII

VICKSBURG

One of the greatest ironies of the Civil War is that while most of the world's attention then and later was focused on the scant 100-mile corridor between Washington and Richmond, a region in which the status quo barely changed for the first three years of the conflict, whole states and regions were being won and lost out in the so-called West. The fall of Forts Henry and Donelson claimed Kentucky and half of Tennessee for the Union. The Yankee victory at Shiloh solidified that gain and added to it part of northern Mississippi, while the Stones River draw at the dawn of 1863 gained more of middle Tennessee for the Union. Meanwhile, the seizure of New Orleans closed the mouth of the Mississippi to the Confederates, and thereafter the Yankees moved steadily to take control of more and more of the great river. Baton Rouge fell to them in the summer of 1862, though they later abandoned it, and to keep them downriver, the Rebels erected a formidable river bastion on the bluffs at Port Hudson. Upriver, meanwhile, the Yankees did better, moving steadily south from that point. By the summer of 1862 they controlled everything as far down as Memphis.

Indeed, for one brief moment that summer, they almost took the entire river. A combined army and navy movement from both above and below came perilously close to meeting in the middle, threatening to capture Vicksburg, Mississippi, the greatest Rebel stronghold on the river. Had the city fallen, the entire western Confederacy – Texas, Arkansas, and western Louisiana – would have been cut off, and the resources of men and material that poured from the trans-Mississippi would have been denied to a hungry Southern war effort. Happily for the South, the attempt failed, and by late fall the Federals had pulled back, below Baton Rouge on the south, and to Memphis on the north. That left just 300 miles of the river in Rebel hands. In infantryman's terms, that was a long way. For any invader that could move by water, however, it was a matter of barely two days' travel.

This was hardly lost on the unassuming little man who took as his task the capture of Vicksburg. U.S. Grant was an authentic national hero following Shiloh, even despite the criticism of having been taken by surprise. When Halleck was transferred east to become general-in-chief, his departure left Grant with virtually a free hand in determining his course, though there was never a doubt that he must make Vicksburg his ultimate objective. "To dispossess them of this," he said, "became a matter of the first importance."[1]

Unfortunately, before leaving, Halleck divided his army of some 120,000 by more than half, including the sending of Buell into eastern Tennessee and, eventually, galloping after Bragg in Kentucky. Left with only 50,000 placed throughout western Tennessee and northern Mississippi, Grant actually found himself briefly on the defensive as Rebel attempts to strike the divided portions of his command led to an engagement at Corinth in early October, where Rosecrans repulsed General Earl Van Dorn and won himself promotion to the command of the Army of the Cumberland.

The Southern failure at Corinth led Richmond to replace Van Dorn with a new man, Lieutenant General John C. Pemberton. It is one of the perversities of this war that a remarkable number of the highest ranking men on each side were natives of the other. Samuel Cooper, the senior general in the entire Confederate Army, came from New Jersey. Winfield Scott, first general-in-chief for the Union, was a Virginian. Pemberton fitted the mold, being a Pennsylvanian by birth. He finished at the Military Academy in 1837, and remained in the Old Army thereafter, fighting in Mexico and out on the Plains where he probably first attracted the notice of then Secretary of War Jefferson Davis. When the war came, his political conservatism and his marriage into a Virginia family persuaded him to go against his section and join the Confederacy, after which he served both in Virginia and South Carolina.

Pemberton found things in a dismaying state when he reached his new command. Making his headquarters at Jackson, fifty miles east of Vicksburg, he soon discovered that very little had been done in the way of protecting and fortifying the river city. He had only about 24,000 men, many of them of very questionable reliability, and far too few heavy cannon to emplace in the batteries he would build on the bluffs overlooking the Mississippi. In addition, he also had to concern himself with Port Hudson. Within a few months he put the defense of the latter in the hands of Major General Franklin Gardner (a native of New York!), which freed him to concentrate on his primary responsibility, Vicksburg.

Pemberton worked almost night and day during his first month in command, and he put everyone else to work, too. No home or front yard was immune from being commandeered for his purposes, whether for an earthwork or a new battery emplacement; no idle soldier was safe from being given a spade and made to work alongside the slaves at the digging. Van Dorn, unpopular thanks to his vanity and insobriety – not to mention the philandering that would see him assassinated in a few months by a cuckolded husband – was not missed by anyone, but the incessant toil that his successor visited upon Vicksburg was not welcomed either. Still, Pemberton raised morale in the city's civilian population as well as in its small army. Even his opponent Grant, who had known him in the Old Army, expressed respect for his new adversary. "He was scrupulously particular in matters of honor and integrity," said Grant, remembering an episode in Mexico when despite great discomfort, Pemberton refused to disobey an order prohibiting junior officers from riding, even though almost all rode anyhow. "This I thought of all the time he was in Vicksburg and I outside of it; and I knew he would hold on to the last."[2]

Grant did not let knowledge of Pemberton's determination hinder his own resolve to take the river fortress. Within only weeks of the change of Confederate commanders, Grant was planning his movement south. His first move was to shift his headquarters from Jackson, Tennessee, south to Grand Junction, almost on the Mississippi border. Then he started a massive buildup of supplies across the border at Holly Springs, which he would use as a base for his invasion of Mississippi. With 30,000 he marched there, and soon ordered his trusted subordinate Sherman to join him with two more divisions. Pemberton was facing them some fifty or sixty miles to the south, having advanced from Vicksburg to meet the threat, but Grant had to postpone his own further advance until his base at Holly Springs was sufficiently built up that he could depend entirely upon it rather than a long supply line that currently ran clear back to Kentucky.

Furthermore, as he looked long and hard at the situation before him, Grant decided that a lone overland advance offered too many dangers. Sherman had been proposing using the Mississippi instead, making a direct campaign against Vicksburg. Grant did not favor it at first, but by early December he modified his own plans to include Sherman's. He would make a combined campaign of it. He sent Sherman back to Memphis to organize a separate wing that would soon total some 32,000. With this small army, Sherman would move downriver on transports and, with the assistance of gunboats commanded by Captain David D. Porter, make a landing at or near Chickasaw Bluffs just north of Vicksburg. Grant, meanwhile, would move overland, engaging Pemberton's army and thus weakening any resistance to Sherman. It was an able plan, each wing advancing in support of the efforts of the other.

And it probably would have worked but for the disliked Earl Van Dorn. He had made his own headquarters at Holly Springs back in October, and knew the ground well. Now, though he no longer commanded the department, but led only Pemberton's 3,500-man cavalry division, he could still influence the campaign. On December 20, 1862, with virtually no warning, he swept down on Holly Springs out of the winter dawn. In a lightning raid, he swiftly overwhelmed the 15,000-strong garrison Grant had guarding his supply base, and then put the torch to all of the

Federals' carefully assembled provisions and munitions. Perhaps more than $1,500,000 worth of materiel went up in smoke. At almost the same time, more Rebel cavalry, led by the peerless Nathan Bedford Forrest, raided deep into northwestern Tennessee and tore up some sixty miles of track on the single railroad line that connected Holly Springs with Columbus, Kentucky, the embarkation point for all of Grant's supply and communications.

Unfortunately, by this time Sherman was already on his way down the Mississippi to carry out his half of the program, and Grant could not get word of the disaster to him. Thus, expecting that Grant would have Pemberton fully occupied in northern Mississippi, Sherman was not prepared for what he met on December 26 when he marched his men ashore after steaming into the Yazoo River a few miles north of Vicksburg. Rain hampered his march toward the city, and after two days he came up against Chickasaw Bluffs. The next day, after a morning-long shelling, he sent his men forward in a pointless assault that saw 1,700 of them fall as casualties, against a mere 187 Confederates. All of those defenders were supposed to be occupied elsewhere by Grant, but now they stopped Sherman cold, and the next day, as he heard the sounds of trains bringing more and more Rebels into Vicksburg, he decided to abandon the campaign.[3]

There was more misfortune immediately to follow. Lincoln had unwisely yielded to political pressure by making an important Democratic politician, John McClernand, a major general senior to Sherman, and assigned him to command on the Mississippi, though subordinate to Grant. McClernand arrived just as Sherman was steaming back upriver from his unsuccessful expedition. Intensely ambitious and scheming, McClernand immediately took command and planned and put into action his own operation against Fort Hindman in Arkansas, without consulting Grant or informing him until it was too late. Sherman and Porter fought the entire affair in January, took the fort, and thus gained a good foothold on the west side of the river near the mouth of the Arkansas River, but McClernand immediately took credit for the entire affair. An indignant Sherman and Porter begged Grant to come and take command personally. Otherwise they would find it unbearable to work with McClernand, and there was no telling what the inept fellow would do next in what was obviously a personal campaign not to win the war, but to win sufficient glory to win the White House one day in the future.

Finding that so many were "distrustful of McClernand's fitness to command," Grant saw the wisdom of their wishes, and on January 30, 1863, he came to Young's Point, just a few miles north of Vicksburg, and on the opposite bank of the river from the city. Here he superseded an irate McClernand, and now, he later recalled, "the real work of the campaign and siege of Vicksburg commenced."

Once he had his forces from Tennessee downriver with him, Grant's overall command totaled just over 60,000. Leaving his XVI Corps back in Tennessee for the time being, he reorganized the forces at Young's Point into three new corps – the XV commanded by Sherman, the XIII by McClernand, and the XVII to be led by James B. McPherson. That done, he proceeded to take a fresh look at how he might take the prize. Any idea of a simple assault across the river was out of the question. A crossing would have to be made under the fire of those massive batteries now staring over at him from the bluffs on the east side. The only practical approach was to strike at the city from the Mississippi interior, and preferably from its rear, so that the garrison would have its back to the river with no line of retreat. Unfortunately, the ground north of the city was so favorable to the defenders – as Sherman had discovered – that a campaign from that direction stood little chance of success, or at best would lead to a long siege, which Grant did not want. The country south of the city was more open and level. He could move and maneuver there. The trouble was that Porter's fleet of gunboats and transports had to be there to ferry his army across, and Porter could not get his flotilla past the several miles of batteries on the bluffs.

With the onset of winter and the rainy season, Grant had time to work out the problem before the ground would be dry enough for active operations, and this allowed him to try a succession of plans for getting Porter downriver. Just below Young's Point, the Mississippi made a deep bend eastward, then abruptly doubled back on itself, forming a peninsula of Louisiana land that jutted some seven miles into Mississippi. Vicksburg sat on the east bank, just opposite and slightly below the tip of that peninsula. Grant could easily march his army across the base of the peninsula, bypassing Vicksburg entirely. But his fleet could not go overland. An earlier commander (one General Thomas Williams) back in the summer of 1862 had faced the same dilemma, and he tried to solve it by cutting a canal across the base of the point of land that would allow ships to get below Vicksburg without steaming around that wide bend. The canal was never finished, but now Grant set men to work once more on the digging. He never actually expected much from the enterprise, but it kept the men busy. Even with the Mississippi running high due to rains, it refused to send sufficient water through to float Porter's boats. Ironically, years later the Mississippi shifted its course on its own, carving out a new path directly through Grant's unsuccessful canal, and leaving Vicksburg practically high and dry. But that was much too late to help the Federals.

Even while his "ditch" continued to defy completion, Grant looked to other possibilities, always with a view to getting his army and Porter's fleet below the city. A series of streams and bayous, often little more than sluggish swamps, meandered through the Louisiana interior west of the Mississippi. Some thirty miles upriver from Young's Point, Lake Providence sat a scant half-mile west of the great stream. Bayous flowed into it from the south, connecting in turn with the Tensas River, and then eventually led to the Red River, which merged into the Mississippi near Port Hudson, more than eighty miles below Vicksburg. The bayous were shallow and filled with trees growing out of the bottom, while thousands of others, dead or dying, further blocked any passage. Nevertheless, Grant set McPherson to work clearing a path through all of this, and when a passage was finally cut to connect the lake with the Mississippi, the river flowed in with such force that it flooded wide areas and helped to clear its own path. Nevertheless, Grant would never use the route. It still required Porter's vessels to chart a tortuous route more than 400 miles long as it wound back and forth, and should the river fall, so would the level of the bayous, leaving the gunboats stranded in the mud. It could not be risked.

But another risk, formerly unthinkable, suddenly looked much better, and it came about almost without anyone noticing. Late in January, a Confederate supply steamer arrived in Vicksburg, having come upriver from the Red and run past a few Yankee guns on the west bank below the city. Though hit once or twice, she was hardly injured. The move taught Grant and Porter two lessons: they must somehow stop supply traffic from reaching Vicksburg; and it was possible for a vessel, moving swiftly, to run past batteries with minimal damage. Porter decided to send one of his gunboats, the *Queen of the West*, on a daring run past Vicksburg's batteries to get below and interdict enemy supply. On February 2 she ran down just after dawn, suffered a mere three hits from all the batteries above the city, set fire to a Rebel steamer, and then passed the batteries below the city with only twelve more hits, none of them serious. Though the ship was lost a few days later when run aground, still she had shown what could be done. Porter sent another past the batteries, this time at night, without difficulty. This one, too, was lost soon thereafter, but neither casualty negated the salient fact that Porter could expect to get his ships past Vicksburg after all, probably under cover of dark, and with an acceptable risk of damage. A few days later he even sent a barge disguised as a gunboat floating down the river past those same batteries, and though they did their best, they could not inflict more than minor damage. Now Grant knew he could get his army across the river once he marched it south.

The question was when. Meanwhile, other opportunities presented themselves. Grant found more than 150 miles upriver from Vicksburg a place called Yazoo Pass, once a route inland on the east side to the Coldwater River. If flowed south into the Tallahatchie, and that in turn kept on south until it flowed into the Yazoo, which ran right down to Vicksburg. If the route could be cleared, transports could carry Grant right to Vicksburg's back door, and all that had to be done was break through a 100-foot natural levee that separated the Mississippi from the pass. The whole journey for his men would be almost 700 miles, when they started from Young's Point and went upriver, only to turn around again and come down the new, winding route. On February 3 a charge of explosives blew a hole in the levee, and the Mississippi spent the next several days pouring a flood of millions of tons of water through, widening the opening and inundating the Coldwater and Tallahatchie. Grant then sent 4,500 men aboard transports on their way south. Unfortunately, almost from the first they encountered natural obstacles and mile after mile of trees felled into the streams by Confederates who anticipated the move. In nearly a month of cutting their way south, the Federals got no further than the mouth of the Tallahatchie, where a hastily erected

Confederate Fort Pemberton stopped them cold. By late March, Grant ordered them to return.

Now it was Porter's turn for a bayou expedition. He found that, in the flooded countryside north of Vicksburg, he could get up the Yazoo a few miles to Steele's Bayou, steam northward through to Black Bayou, then north on Deer Creek, to the Sunflower River, which then flowed back south into the Yazoo. This roundabout route bypassed the portion of the Yazoo above Vicksburg that the Rebels had fortified. It also cut into the Yazoo below Fort Pemberton, allowing a way to get troops ashore north of the city but without passing any batteries. It would take Porter 200 miles on two long sides of a triangle, to finish at a point just thirty-five miles east of where he started, but it appeared to be a good gamble. In the end, it turned out to be a fiasco, as Porter got well stuck in the thick undergrowth of Deer Creek.

The one that finally worked was a variant of ideas already tried. Those bayous running through the interior of Louisiana, even if not deep enough to accommodate his gunboats, could still handle the much more shallow draft transports and barges. Part of the army could move aboard them while others carried ammunition and supplies and the balance of the infantry marched across the marshy land. Once below Vicksburg, they could be ferried across by the steamers, and all with the assistance and cover of Porter's gunboat fleet. Porter, Grant decided, could safely risk running his vessels past Vicksburg during the night. Grant would cross his army to the Mississippi side somewhere near Grand Gulf, sixty miles below Vicksburg, march inland, then turn north and attack Vicksburg from the rear.

Grant set the plan in motion on March 31, when the first of McClernand's corps began their march into the bayous. But then another disaster struck. The level of the Mississippi, so high from the winter rains, suddenly fell. The bayous now would not even handle the most shallow draft vessels. As always, Grant refused to be deterred. Instead, Porter would simply have to take everything with him past the batteries. Well after dark on April 16, the flotilla started downstream. They were not yet abreast of the river when the Confederates spotted them and opened fire. What followed Porter could only liken to a trip through hell. One by one, during almost two hours, the ships ran the gauntlet of fire. But when Porter counted bows afterwards, only one transport had been lost. Six nights later the six remaining transports made the run, and five made it. So far so good.

Grant had intended using the gunboats to force Rebel fortifications at Grand Gulf to yield so he could cross his army. Porter wisely persuaded him not to risk the transports in a river crossing under fire, and Grant decided instead to cross at Bruinsburg, ten miles further south. It was a good idea, and by April 30 Grant was ready to start sending McClernand and McPherson and their corps on the most difficult one mile of Rebel territory a Yankee army ever had to cross – the Mississippi. And after all the time and effort taken to embark those troops, the crossing was almost an anti-climax, for Grant made it virtually unopposed. By evening on May 1, both corps were on the east bank, while Sherman remained above the city, making a demonstration against the bluffs along Chickasaw Bayou to keep Pemberton from sending any men south to resist the landing. It had all worked brilliantly. At the same time, Grant had launched another diversion, sending Colonel Benjamin Grierson and 1,700 Federal cavalry on a raid from La Grange, Tennessee, all the way down to Baton Rouge. The troopers were to travel 600 miles in sixteen days, tear up nearly sixty miles of railroad, disrupt telegraph lines, and destroy tons of enemy supplies and weapons. Moreover, the lightning raid kept all of the Confederate cavalry in Mississippi busy looking for Grierson, and away from Grant as he made his crossing.[4]

The entire operation had been one of the most brilliant in the history of warfare, but Grant did not pause to congratulate himself. He moved, and quickly. He marched immediately to Port Gibson, pushed aside the small force of defenders, and that, in turn, forced the Grand Gulf garrison to evacuate to avoid being cut off from any line of retreat. Then he moved on inland and northeasterly, heading for the state capital at Jackson. If he was successful and took it, he would break Vicksburg's only remaining rail line of communications. Then he could turn west, knowing that Pemberton would be cut off from not only supply, but also any reinforcements, and march straight west against Vicksburg.

Pemberton knew that he stood increasingly in a bad way now. He wired to Joseph E. Johnston, now in charge of his area, for reinforcements, or at least to move with whatever forces were at hand to threaten Grant's rear and keep Vicksburg from being cut off. Johnston, true to form, did next to nothing, though Bragg's army was then sitting around Tullahoma spending its most idle summer of the war. All Pemberton could hope to do was keep his army in the field, avoid being bottled up in Vicksburg, and pray that Johnston would develop some courage, or that President Davis would intervene. Both proved to be idle dreams.

Grant waited for Sherman to make the long trip south through the bayous and across the river. When he arrived on May 8, the reunited army totaled more than 40,000, and with it the Yankees continued their drive. "The road to Vicksburg is open," he told Sherman, a glory road on which he believed nothing could stop them. Indeed, it could not. By May 12 they were at Raymond, just fifteen miles southwest of Jackson. There they met and repulsed a ragtag force trying to stand in their way. The next day Grant sent McPherson straight north to cut the Southern Railroad line at Clinton, Vicksburg's link with Jackson. Then McPherson would turn east as Sherman himself marched on Jackson. Again it all worked beautifully, and two days later the state capital flew United States flags. Leaving the city's factories and warehouses in smoldering ruins, Grant launched McPherson and McClernand on the road to Vicksburg the next day.

All Pemberton could hope to accomplish now was to stop Grant somewhere along the road before he could reach Vicksburg. On May 16 he met the foe on and around Champion's Hill, twenty miles west of Jackson. Finally he had heard from Johnston that help was on the way, and he must delay Grant to give time for them to arrive. To do so he took a grave risk, and brought 23,000 of his troops – virtually the whole army – out to meet the foe. Combined forces of McClernand and McPherson were there to meet him, and in a battle lasting from mid-morning until well into the afternoon, Pemberton actually achieved some early gains, but could not hold on to them. A Federal counterattack put one whole division to rout, and it could not make its way back toward Vicksburg. Instead, it moved below and east of Grant in hopes of meeting the relief column.

Pemberton suffered heavily. He took 3,800 casualties in the fight, and lost that whole division. With the balance, he could do nothing but retire. The next day he mounted a brief rearguard action at Big Black River Bridge, but had to retire once more after little more than an hour. That afternoon Pemberton and his dispirited soldiers filed back into their earthworks surrounding Vicksburg and dug in even deeper, realizing that now there was nothing left to them but to withstand a siege until Johnston should arrive.

Grant was to get there first. On the evening of May 18, McClernand and McPherson began to see the spires of the city, topped by the cupola on the Warren County courthouse. By the next morning, the Federal line had spread itself along the entire eastern face of the defensive lines held by Pemberton's 31,000 remaining soldiers, a line more than five miles long.

The works Grant faced at Vicksburg were among the most formidable to be seen anywhere in the war up to this time. They had been planned eight months before, on three quarters of an eliptical arc stretching from Fort Hill, overlooking the Mississippi directly north of the city, northeast to the Stockade Redan, then south through a series of other redoubts and lunettes, to South Fort, two miles below the city. Every road into Vicksburg had a fort guarding it, and in between all of these works ran a deep line of trenches with firing ramparts, and often obstructions like sharpened stakes or felled trees, even wire, to slow or halt an enemy charge. Pemberton had placed batteries in commanding positions, and thanks to the hills surrounding the city, there were many places in which the works sat on such an elevation that any attempt to attack would be suicidal.

It was another reason why Grant wanted to take it now before the Rebels could dig in even further. At 2 p.m., May 19, his signal guns launched the attack. The fighting became at once furious, and rare for Civil War engagements, hand-to-hand in places. All along the line isolated Federal units actually reached the outer edge of the enemy parapets, only to be unable to go further or hold on. Sherman saw men falling "as chaff thrown from the hand on a windy day." The repulse did not deter Grant, who ordered another, better coordinated attack for May 22. He let his artillery bombard the defenses continually beforehand, both to soften them up, and to keep the Confederates from sleeping. Porter's gunboats were out on the river adding their long-range shells to the din of the cannon.

At 10 a.m. the signal sounded once more, and in went all three corps: Sherman from the northeast, McPherson on *his* left, and McClernand on *his* left. Some men actually carried ladders, so steep were the outer walls of the enemy parapets, while others brought planks to throw across ditches and trenches. Sherman's men met the worst of it, since they moved against the most difficult terrain. Enemy fire soon halted them, though they struggled valiantly time after time to get into Stockade Redan. When they were forced to halt at the bottom of the slope leading to the works, Confederates lit artillery shells and threw or rolled them over the parapets as grenades.

McPherson met a galling fire, too, and got no farther. Only McClernand enjoyed a measure of success when he took a redoubt guarding the railroad. Yet resistance was so great that he had to ask that Grant order Sherman and McPherson to renew their stalled assaults to take the pressure from him. Grant did as asked, but it availed nothing. McClernand held on to the Railroad Redoubt through most of the day, but by evening a Confederate counterattack drove him out. Once more night fell with no advantage gained, but Grant had more than 3,200 casualties in the bad bargain "without giving us any benefit whatever," he later lamented.[5]

It would be the last wasted attack. That night Grant concluded that "the nature of the ground about Vicksburg is such that it can only be taken by a siege." He hoped it would take no more than a week.[6]

In fact, it took another six weeks. From May 23 onward, Grant maintained an almost constant bombardment of the works and the city itself. The soldiers burrowed even deeper into their trenches, while the townspeople soon sought shelter in impromptu caves dug into hillsides. The streets became a virtual no man's land, dangerous for everyone alike, including animals and even pets, for as the supplies of food dwindled, soldiers and civilians were forced to turn to anything they could find. When the cattle were gone, they turned to horses, then mules, and finally even dogs and cats. By the beginning of July, even the city's mice and rats found their way into pots. As Grant steadily extended and strengthened his line around the city, the plight of those inside his steel coil became ever greater. Pemberton was not strong enough to attempt to break out, and besides he had orders from Davis to hold Vicksburg at all costs. All he could do was hope that Johnston would arrive in time, and by late June that tardy general was believed to be approaching Jackson. Perhaps he would arrive in time. But then Grant sent Sherman with more than 30,000 back east to meet and stop the relief column, and in fact Johnston would never get any closer than Jackson. "The fall of Vicksburg and the capture of most of the garrison can only be a question of time," Grant told Washington late in June.

The siege wore hard on Blue and Gray alike. Grant's army grew through reinforcement to 77,000, greater than at any time during the campaign. Pemberton, by contrast, saw his own numbers dwindle through exhaustion, death, and desertion, to a mere 28,000 or more. Even the mules and rats ran in short supply, and the Vicksburg *Citizen* had to start printing on wallpaper.

By the end of June, Grant's engineers were digging tunnels under the Rebel works and exploding massive powder charges that sent men and earth flying into the sky. It became increasingly obvious to Pemberton that time was running out. On July 1 he asked his generals what they advised, and the next day they replied with near unanimity that there was no alternative. That night Pemberton asked Grant for an armistice to discuss terms of surrender.

The two met the next day in a tense interview that almost saw a proud and hurting Pemberton call it all off. Only tact by his subordinates, and the generous and humane terms offered by Grant, saved the proceedings. Rather than make prisoners of the Vicksburg garrison, Grant would release them on their paroles not to take up arms again until exchanged officially for released Federal prisoners of war. As a final gesture of respect, Grant also agreed to allow the garrison to march out of the defenses before the Federals marched in, thus honoring a vow of Pemberton's that no Yankee soldier would set foot in Vicksburg while his army was there. What Pemberton could not get was an agreement to postpone the ceremony for a day. Grant wanted it to happen on July 4, a symbolic day for the Union now to be made the more so.

It all happened the next day. Vicksburg changed hands. A Confederate army simply ceased to exist, and all that remained in the way of the Yankee takeover of the Mississippi was Port Hudson, which fell within the week. In Washington a jubilant Lincoln exulted that "the Father of Waters again goes unvexed to the sea." The Confederacy was cut in half, and in Richmond a War Department official lamented that "the Confederacy totters to its destruction."[7]

REFERENCES

1 Grant, *Memoirs*, I, pp.392-94.
2 John C. Pemberton, *Pemberton: Defender of Vicksburg* (Chapel Hill, N.C., 1942), p.14.
3 William T. Sherman, *Memoirs* (New York, 1875), I, p.292.
4 *O.R.*, I, 24, pt.1, pp.33-34
5 Grant, *Memoirs*, I, p.531.
6 Carter, *Vicksburg*, p.233
7 Frank Vandiver, ed., *The Civil War Diary of General Josiah Gorgas* (Tuscaloosa, Ala., 1947), p.146.

IX

GETTYSBURG

The accidents of history give nobility to the commonest of men and turn rude country crossroads into names that echo through the ages. Men like Alexander of Macedon and places such as Rome may have been ordained from inception for greatness, but for most people and locations such recognition comes as nothing more than the fickle choice of chance. But for the events that made them, Napoleon would be forgotten, U.S. Grant would never have risen above being a face in the crowd, and even Lincoln would have remained an obscure prairie lawyer. But for chance, little-known places like Bull Run and Shiloh would still be nothing more than wide spots on forgotten country roads. Even when men tried to plan in advance those locations that the events they controlled were about to immortalize, chance robbed them of the choice.

If one of the army commanders involved had had his way, the greatest engagement of the Civil War – and perhaps of all American history – would have come down to us as the Battle of Pipe Creek. But men could not plan for greatness, and "Pipe Creek" would never be emblazoned on the battleflags of Blue or Gray or stir the memories of old veterans and serve as a rallying cry for the patriots of later generations. Armies sometimes move on a momentum all their own in their lurching, swaying paths to meet, and the tens of thousands who might have let their blood to make Pipe Creek immortal missed each other there and collided some twenty miles north instead, giving their nomination for fame to a dull Pennsylvania crossroads at Gettysburg.

Despite the fact that no one could predict where the armies were to meet next after Chancellorsville, a certain logic virtually dictated that they should clash again on Northern soil, and that the victorious Lee should be the aggressor. In part, the reason was personal and emotional. Lee, after a year in command of the Army of Northern Virginia, had become accustomed to victory. McClellan, Pope, Burnside, Hooker – he had beaten them all. Only once did he taste defeat, and that was on Yankee ground at Antietam. Lee was a very human man for all his growing stature as a Confederate demigod. To himself and the South he had proven almost everything, except that he could meet and beat the foe on their own ground. Lee, the man, needed a successful invasion of the North.

Lee the general needed it, too. He had beaten Hooker, but he had not removed in any way the continuing threat to Virginia. And if Lee could bring Hooker to battle and decisively defeat him on Union soil, the humiliation and dismay might discourage the Northern population from continuing what was already an increasingly controversial war.

In fact, Lee had an old plan worked out a year before with Jackson, and perhaps even originally inspired by the lamented "Stonewall." A variation of it led to Antietam, but now Lee worked on the original notion of moving the entire army into the Shenandoah Valley, then closing off all gaps to keep the enemy in the dark as to his movements. While Hooker still sat in northern Virginia, Lee could slip quietly and quickly northward through the Valley, cross the Potomac, and suddenly appear in Maryland. Before Hooker could react, Lee would have his divisions marching into Pennsylvania, heading for Harrisburg and the Susquehanna River. It meant leaving Richmond exposed, of course, but Hooker would not dare march on the Confederate capital with a Rebel army threatening his own. He would have to abandon Virginia to go after Lee.

It was a tremendous gamble, the kind of chance that Lee could make with conviction, but it took him much of May to convince President Davis to go along. Only after a long meeting on May 26 did Lee finally have approval, and still Davis wavered in the days that followed. Lee did not, however, and arduously made his preparations, mindful that time could be blood.

Feverishly Lee gleaned reinforcements from throughout Virginia and the Eastern seaboard. He reunited the old I Corps with the return of Longstreet, who now once more commanded three divisions: McLaws' Georgians, South Carolinians, and Mississippians; Pickett's all Virginia division; and Hood's Alabamians, Georgians, Texans, and the one and only regiment from the trans-Mississippi in Lee's army, the 3rd Arkansas. The death of the irreplaceable Jackson eventually led Lee to replace him at the head of the II Corps with the solid though unimaginative Richard S. Ewell, just barely recovered from the loss of a leg the previous summer. He, too, had three divisions. The cantankerous yet combative Jubal Early led a mixed command of Louisianians, Virginians, Georgians, and North Carolinians. Edward Johnson commanded the division that had been Ewell's, and Jackson's before him, almost all Virginians, with one Louisiana brigade and some North Carolinians and one Maryland unit. And Robert Rodes, who brilliantly led Jackson's great flank attack at

Chancellorsville, led a division of three North Carolina brigades, plus one from Georgia, and one from Alabama. Furthermore, Lee created a new III Corps made up of units from the other two corps, along with new additions, to be commanded by the superlative A.P. Hill. Richard H. Anderson led five brigades hailing from as many different states – Alabama, Georgia, Virginia, Florida, and Mississippi. Major General Henry Heth – said to be the only general that Lee addressed by his given name, though no one knew why – led North Carolinians, Virginians, Mississippians, Alabamians, and the only Tennessee regiments with the army. And William Dorsey Pender, at a mere twenty-nine one of the most loved and respected generals in the army, commanded two North Carolina brigades, and one each from South Carolina and Georgia. Every division in the army had its own artillery, and each corps an artillery reserve. Meanwhile, "Jeb" Stuart continued to command the army's cavalry, seven patchwork brigades of varying size, all but two from Virginia, and six batteries of light and mobile horse artillery.

All told, and including small units that he would pick up during the early stages of the coming campaign, Lee could count 80,000 or more of all arms, though he still knew himself to be outnumbered by those Yankees glaring at him from the other side of the Rappahannock.

Despite his humiliating defeat at Chancellorsville, Hooker still commanded those Yankees. The Army of the Potomac, though discouraged by its defeat, remained strong. Except for the XI Corps, the men had fought better than ever before, and most acknowledged that what Lee defeated in the recent battle was their commander, and not themselves. The chagrin was greatest at the several corps headquarters, where Hooker lost the confidence of almost all of his commanders. Speculation that he would be relieved ran wild almost as soon as the retreat from Chancellorsville was finished, and Couch, Slocum, and Sedgwick started what amounted to an incipient cabal when they approached Meade with assurances that they would gladly serve under him instead. Hancock, Sickles, Sedgwick, Couch, Reynolds, and others, were all spoken of as possible successors. yet Lincoln stood by Hooker through the balance of May, not so much out of conviction that he could bring a victory, as from an unwillingness to have yet another change of commanders so soon. By waiting to relieve him, he hoped psychologically to diminish the emotional impact of the recent defeat in the North. Still, on June 2 Lincoln asked Reynolds confidentially if he would take the command. The Pennsylvanian declined, chiefly because he feared too much political interference in his handling of the army. Receiving this refusal, Lincoln apparently decided to back away briefly. Hooker was handling the army well again. Perhaps he could retrieve his own and his army's fortunes if given another chance.[1]

Indeed, in June, just as Lee was starting to put his plans in motion, Hooker launched a small offensive with his cavalry, sending Pleasonton with 11,000 cavalry and 3,000 infantry on a raid across the Rappahannock. Hooker had word that elements of the Army of Northern Virginia had been pulling out of their camps on June

2 and the days following. Fearing a raid – not a major invasion – Hooker sent Pleasonton toward Culpeper Courthouse, where he believed Lee was concentrating supplies for the raid. The result was an engagement on June 9 between Pleasonton and Stuart's 10,000 cavalry near Brandy Station. The inconclusive fight failed to reveal to Hooker the true extent of the mounting threat, and it proved to be his only attempt to take control of affairs. For Lee, it only served to make him more determined to move and move quickly, lest Hooker or some successor might strike again with more determination. The very next day he rushed Ewell and his corps toward the Shenandoah, with the rest soon to follow.

The move came with lightning swiftness. In three days Ewell's advance approached Winchester; in a week Lee's entire army was in the Shenandoah. Hooker, reacting to the enemy movement, shifted his army west toward the Blue Ridge, but lack of information prevented him from taking any more decisive steps, while his own tardiness and hesitation made the situation even worse. The Confederates captured almost the entire Federal garrison at Winchester, dispersed the Yankee defenders at Martinsburg, and clearly were on the move northward in strength. Yet Hooker faced with this overwhelming body of evidence, could not decide what to do. "His role now is that of Micawber," wrote Hooker's provost marshal, " 'waiting for something to turn up.'" Even after 4,500 men were lost at Winchester, Lincoln continued to stand by Hooker, not out of confidence so much as unwillingness to replace a commander now that the enemy was on the move. Changing horses in midstream would be dangerous, said the old adage; changing generals could be disastrous.[2]

Instead, Washington tried its best to reinforce Hooker from other commands in Virginia and Maryland, until by late June, Hooker had at his disposal over 100,000 men. But by that time, Lee had crossed the Potomac and was marching through Maryland once again. He sent Stuart and most of the cavalry on a sweeping ride around the eastern side of Hooker's army, between him and Washington, to sever communications, capture and destroy supplies, and put even more panic into an increasingly nervous Union government.

By now, because of Hooker's reluctance to move decisively, Lee stood considerably north of him, with his army spread out on the roads between Frederick, Maryland, and Chambersburg and York, Pennsylvania, while the Army of the Potomac still remained in northern Virginia. Lee was at least two days ahead of him, maybe more. On June 25 Hooker finally put his own army in motion northward, and sent Reynolds rushing ahead in command of the I, III, and XI Corps. The next day the balance of the Yankee army started crossing the Potomac on the race to catch up with Lee. In two days they covered up to forty-five miles, reaching the vicinity of Frederick by evening on June 27.

But that same evening, other events came to a head. From a variety of motives – fear of fighting Lee again, feuding with Halleck, bluffing that went wrong – Hooker sent in his resignation. Lincoln had no choice but to accept it, and probably felt little or no reluctance, except for the act coming in the middle of a crucial campaign with the armies on the move. Wisely, he did not consult his cabinet or political advisors about a replacement. There was not time, and even asking such a question would be to invite political turmoil. Instead, Lincoln took counsel only of himself, and that night issued an order placing Meade in command. With little enthusiasm, but with an unquestioning soldier's obedience to orders, Meade accepted the post – one he would hold for the next two years, making him the Army of the Potomac's sixth and last commander.

Certainly Meade presented nothing at all imposing or inspiring to those who saw him. Tall, slender, with thin graying hair and a generally schoolmasterly look, he utterly lacked the sense of style that made men like McClellan and Hooker the favorites of the men at times. Moreover he possessed a wickedly acid tongue, with a temper that gained him a reputation as a "snapping turtle" with many of his associates. Neither timid nor impetuous, he was a cool, methodical old professional who enjoyed almost universal respect among his peers.

At once Meade met with Hooker to take the command and learn the latest of the situation. Though he took over at a most difficult time, at least Meade had the advantage of assuming command of a magnificent army. It was little changed from the days at Chancellorsville just a few weeks before. Reynolds led the I Corps, with three divisions. Hancock had the II Corps with three more. The inept Sickles still held the III Corps and its two divisions. George Sykes now assumed command of the three divisions making up Meade's old V Corps, while Sedgwick remained at the head of the VI Corps' three. Howard, who never on merit deserved command of the XI Corps, still led it, though after Chancellorsville its three divisions were the smallest in the army. Slocum still had the XII Corps' two divisions, and Pleasonton commanded three divisions of cavalry. Every corps had a brigade of artillery attached, while there was also an army artillery reserve with an additional five brigades of batteries. In all, what with detachments left along the march to date, its numbers now ran to about 95,000.

The very date of his appointment, Meade told Washington that he would march directly for the Susquehanna, keeping always between Lee and Washington. He did not intend to move directly for Lee, but rather wished to be in a position to force Lee to turn and fight him on ground of his own choosing. By dawn on June 29 Meade had the whole movement planned and under way, intending to cross into Pennsylvania the next day if necessary. Then he learned that Longstreet and Hill were at Chambersburg, moving toward Gettysburg, while Ewell's corps occupied both Carlisle and York. Thus Lee was spread out on a triangular line more than fifty miles long at its base between Chambersburg and York, and extending twenty-five miles northward to its apex at Carlisle. Elements of Ewell's corps were within striking distance of Harrisburg, the state capital, barely twenty miles above Carlisle. If they took it and destroyed the Baltimore & Ohio bridge they would disrupt the union's major east-west transportation route. Should Lee get his whole army north of the Susquehanna, he could prevent Meade from crossing in his rear and wreak havoc on the North. Thus Meade's rapid march toward Lee's rear, to make of his own army such a threat that Lee must turn from his invasion to deal with Meade. And now, seeing the Army of Northern Virginia spread out at those three points of the triangle, Meade could also see that if Lee should try to concentrate his army for a battle, the shortest route for all three arms would be for them to move to their center – almost exactly at the Gettysburg crossroads.

Rapidly the momentum of events began to take over. Just as Meade put himself in a position to threaten Lee's rear, Lee himself had decided to abandon attempts to get across the Susquehanna, though he came close enough for elements of Ewell's command actually to cool their feet in its waters. Lee now decided that he must concentrate his scattered corps. Meade, meanwhile, deciding that his foe was gathering his forces to strike a blow at the Army of the Potomac, chose several possibilities of battlefield, preferring a line along Pipe Creek in northern Maryland that offered excellent defensive terrain. Nevertheless, in the hope of striking elements of Lee's army and defeating them in detail before they were reunited, he issued orders directing a concentration of his own corps at Gettysburg. The result is that by dawn of July 1, both armies were rapidly converging on the same little town, Lee swooping down from the north by four major routes, and Meade moving up from the south on five separate roads. All told, there were eighty-eight brigades of infantry and over 600 cannon on their way to Gettysburg – 93,500 Federal soldiers and about 75,000 Confederates. Because of their advanced positions, Reynolds and A.P. Hill would likely be the first to reach the little town that had never expected the war to come to its doorsteps.

Gettysburg sat some thirty miles southwest of Harrisburg. It was not an old town by Pennsylvania standards, nor a large one, and enjoyed few advantages to its benefit other than its being the chance converging place of a number of important roads leading more or less directly to most of the major cities in the region. Indeed, it was nearly impossible to move east to west or north and south through Pennsylvania without passing through the sleepy town, and all traffic south from Harrisburg had to tread its dirty streets. Ridges and hills dominated its landscape. Less than a mile to the west ran Seminary Ridge, running north to south for more than two miles. Parallel to it, and commencing immediately below the town, ran Cemetery Ridge, its northern end punctuated by Cemetery Hill, and its southern end, two miles distant, by a rocky, wooded eminence called locally Little Round Top, and just below it by the even bigger Big Round Top. The roads over which Lee's corps were converging would bring them in from the north, northeast, and northwest, directly toward the town and the upper reaches of Seminary Ridge. Meade's columns, marching from the south, southeast, and southwest, would almost all be arriving on either side of the Round Tops, with the high ground of Cemetery Ridge before them immediately for the taking. Only Reynolds with his I Corps was marching in from almost due west, on a route bound to make him collide with Heth as he returned on the Chambersburg Pike from the northwest.

The first guns sounded shortly after dawn, as Heth moved toward the outskirts of town only to encounter pickets from General John Buford's brigade of cavalry posted on the Chambersburg Pike. Obviously heavily outnumbered, Buford sought only to fight a delaying action, to slow Heth's advance while Reynolds came up. Reynolds himself arrived several hours later, around 10 a.m., and begged Buford to hold on until his first division should arrive. Reynolds at once apprehended how important Gettysburg would be for Meade, and started issuing orders designed to erect a defensive line to hold out until the rest of the army could come up. Reynolds was practically fighting on home ground here, being a native of Lancaster, a town just forty miles to the east.

When the first regiments began arriving, the general himself led them into place one after another. All along it was evident that he could do no more than fight a holding action, and then a chance bullet from a Rebel gun struck the valiant Pennsylvanian in the head, killing him in the saddle. His subordinate Abner Doubleday immediately assumed command. Each side gained some success, turning back the right wing of the other, and Heth found himself in a quandary. There were more Yankees here than he expected, and quickly the fighting escalated as such engagements tended to do. Hill sent forward reinforcements, and before long, what had been intended as merely a foraging raid on a scantily defended town had turned into a substantial firefight, magnetically attracting more and more men to the front. By noon, as Reynolds spent the last minutes of his life expanding his defensive line, Hill and Heth, wisely or unwisely, were already deciding for Lee where the great battle of the campaign would be fought.

Not long after Doubleday assumed command, and while the Federals enjoyed better than expected success in holding back the growing gray lines, Howard arrived on the field. Being senior, he immediately assumed command, with hardly any idea of what to do. He had seen Cemetery Hill on his way to the front, however, and well recognized the strategic importance of its commanding height. Making it his headquarters, he hurried his divisions on their march to the fight, no doubt mindful that after their disgrace at Chancellorsville, the veterans of the XI Corps had a score to settle with Lee, and something to prove to themselves and the army. By early afternoon the entire I Corps was on the field, and two of the three XI Corps divisions, with the third soon to arrive. But by now Heth's full division was on the line, with Rodes' rushing into the fight as well, and Early's division of Ewell's corps coming in from the northeast. The result was that, by 3 p.m., the Federals were faced with enemies on a wide front in a semicircle extending from due west, all across to the northeast, and in numbers that for the moment outnumbered their own.

Rapidly the fighting became intense as the Rebels pressed to envelop both Yankee flanks. Rodes led the attack, sending all five of his brigades – 8,000 strong – forward, with Heth on his right and Early on the left. In the first action, Howard's line stopped the attack and severely mauled Rodes' center. But the Confederates pressed again, and in time Early got around the right rear of the XI Corps, striking them at their most vulnerable spot, just as Jackson had done less than nine weeks before. The attack crushed the right of the Federal line, leaving the defenders no choice but to pull back from their position north of Gettysburg. Otherwise the Rebels could get between them and the town and cut them off from the rest of Meade's army advancing from the south. But then the simultaneous advance of the rest of the Confederate line turned any attempt at an orderly withdrawal into a shambles. It was not the panicked rout of Chancellorsville, especially for the I Corps, but neither was it a calculated affair. Instead, the men simply broke up in regiments and companies and raced back to the streets of Gettysburg, sometimes stopping to deliver fire on the way. Howard sent instructions to reform on the slopes of Cemetery Hill, but he did not need to. It was the only obvious choice in the direction in which the Rebels were driving them.

The rush through the town proved to be even more disorganizing, as the men scrambled to reach the high ground below. The narrow streets broke up their units. Some left ranks to plunder, others to hide. Wagons and animals jammed crossroads. Men simply found themselves lost and unable to find their way out. And all the while the pursuing Rebels were right behind them. Hundreds were captured, and others had to take refuge to escape being made prisoners. Brigadier General Alexander Schimmelfennig, commanding Howard's XI Corps third division, was cut off from his command during the retreat and forced to hide in a small pig barn off Baltimore Street, where he remained for the rest of the battle, being brought food by its owners when they came to feed the swine.

Happily, when the ragged remnants clambered up Cemetery Hill, they found a fresh brigade on the summit, with the cool, composed Winfield Scott Hancock there in person setting up a new line of defense. Meade had sent him ahead with orders to take command on the scene, since Meade wisely had little use of Howard's skills. To his credit, Howard uncomplainingly yielded and cooperated admirably with Hancock thereafter. The II Corps commander's presence put spine back into the disheartened men of the I and XI Corps as he dug in determined to hold his ground. He sent a division off to the east of Cemetery Hill, to Culp's Hill, upon which he decided to anchor the right of the Federal line, and then, assisted by Brigadier General Gouverneur K. Warren, Meade's chief engineer, Hancock prepared to fight to the end if need be.

By now it was perhaps 5:30 in the afternoon, and more reinforcements were approaching, the XII Corps coming in towards Culp's Hill, and Sickles and his III Corps at last marching up the Emmitsburg Road from the south towards Hancock's much more vulnerable left, now trying to stretch down to Cemetery Ridge. Nightfall would be upon them in a couple of hours or more, and Hancock felt some assurance that he could hold his position until dark, by which time Meade would arrive to take command and decide whether to fight or retire. It had been a near thing for the

Yankees that afternoon. Only the valiant yet costly fighting of the I Corps had held the line long enough to have Cemetery Hill ready to occupy. It cost them dearly, with nearly 65 percent casualties out of the 8,500 Yankees who started the battle. Yet they managed to inflict almost 40 percent losses on the 16,000 men of Hill's corps who opposed them. The I Corps almost ceased to exist, but won imperishable glory by its heroic stand.[3]

Lee himself reached the battlefield around 2 p.m., but did not exercise much direct command of the following assaults because he had not yet seen the ground, whereas Heth and Rodes knew it better. By late afternoon, with Hill now present, too, Lee started to exert more control, deciding that he would have to fight Meade here. Yet he did not yet have a battleplan – there had been no time to formulate one – and not all of his army was yet on the scene. He needed time to make a plan and for Longstreet and Ewell to arrive. Nevertheless, in looking at the Yankees as they withdrew up Cemetery Hill, he realized immediately that he must drive them off that important elevation before Meade got sufficient reinforcements on the scene to make the hill impregnable. But when he sent the just-arrived Ewell a request to attack the hill, it was just that – a request and not an order – and Ewell decided that he could not achieve the goal and did not try.

Thus the first day of the gathering fight came to an end, and rapidly balances started to shift. Though barely 12,000 Federals remained of the 18,000 who started the day, more rapidly arrived. The XII Corps came on to the east side of the field. Sickles started coming into view on the Emmitsburg Road, and shortly after twilight settled in, there were perhaps 27,000 in the blue line, now commanded by Slocum. Meade himself rode through much of the night, only arriving on Cemetery Hill before the next dawn. The contrast between him and some of his predecessors in army command became immediately apparent. While McClellan or Hooker would have struck a heroic pose and uttered some bombastic boast to show his courage and inspire the army, Meade simply asked his senior generals on the field about their positions. Hearing that they felt themselves strongly placed, he said simply that this was good, for they were all too committed to pull out now. He would fight Lee here and that was all there was to it.[4]

The previous day Meade had directed his efforts to getting all of his corps on the several roads towards Gettysburg, leaving it to his capable subordinate Hancock to manage the fight. Once on the scene, the commanding general immediately made a personal reconnaissance of his position and the available ground for the coming battle. He rode almost to Little Round Top, then turned north along Cemetery Ridge, to Cemetery Hill, and then east to Culp's Hill. He did not fail to see that along this route he could occupy an almost unbroken ridge of high ground, roughly in the shape of a fishhook: his left near the Round Tops at the "eye" and his line running north up the shank until it curved to the right to the barb at Culp's Hill. It meant a line three miles long, but it would have the advantage of "interior lines" – Meade could shift troops from one end of his line to the other by cutting across the axis of the arc, while Lee, whose line would naturally have to be longer, and with fewer men, would have to march men the long way around the arc to reposition his forces.

When the sun began to peer over the back slopes of Cemetery Ridge, Meade had his I and XI Corps remnants on Cemetery Hill, and two divisions of Slocum's XII Corps on their right at Culp's Hill. On Howard's left Hancock put his three II Corps divisions in line along Cemetery Ridge, and on his left sat Sickles and the III Corps. Only Sickles was not sitting where Meade wanted him. Through a combination of imprecise orders from Meade, and Sickles' own palpable lack of competence, the III Corps was not placed on the ridge south of Hancock where it would enjoy the best defensive position. Instead, for reasons that made sense to few but himself, Sickles advanced his two divisions nearly three-quarters of a mile beyond Hancock's line, extending from Hancock's left out into the lowland to a peach orchard barely half a mile from the Confederate positions on Seminary Ridge, and then arcing back in front of a wheatfield on a tangled rock outcropping known locally as Devil's Den near the foot of Little Round Top. Meade did not learn of it precisely until nearly 4 p.m., when he rode to inspect his left and saw for himself what Sickles had done. He was furious, for Sickles had put himself in a position where he was terribly vulnerable to the enemy, and in which he could only be reinforced with difficulty. He jeopardized the entire left of Meade's line, virtually making pointless the plans the commanding general had been making for an offensive. Sickles expressed regret and offered to move his corps back to the ridge. "I wish to God you could," said Meade, just as Confederate cannon announced the coming of an attack from Lee that belatedly started the day's fighting, "but the enemy won't let you."[5]

The Confederates had waited far too long to commence the battle. Lee still enjoyed a numerical advantage, as well as one in morale, when the sun set the night before, and even though Meade's reinforcements in the dark strengthened his position, every hour that Lee delayed only gave the foe more time to choose the best ground. The trouble was, unlike Antietam or Fredericksburg or Chancellorsville, where Lee had enjoyed plenty of time to study the terrain, Gettysburg was entirely new to him. He needed time to study it. Longstreet did not want to fight there at all, not liking the look of Meade's position. But Lee felt that they had to give battle now, while Meade's army was incomplete. It might be the best opportunity they would ever have to defeat him in detail. All through the night he talked with his generals and considered plans, finally deciding that the place to hit Meade was on the Yankee left, exactly where Sickles would foolishly expose his corps. This task would fall to Longstreet, whose corps was slowly coming up and was to extend itself south all along the length of Seminary Ridge. Hill's corps, battered from the previous day, would hold the center on the ridge, reaching almost to the town, where Ewell took up the line, swinging around in an arc matching Meade's. Ewell would make a demonstration against Cemetery Hill and Culp's Hill when he heard Longstreet's attack, both to occupy and keep Yankees in his front from going to Sickles' aid, as well as to press on in a concerted attack should an advantage be gained.

But so much depended upon time, and Longstreet's corps proved agonizingly slow in arriving. Still, both Hood and McLaws and their divisions were on hand by 9 a.m. Lee gave Longstreet his instructions for the manner of the attack to come, but then "Old Pete" balked. Opposed to the attack since the night before, he argued. Some later claimed that he intentionally delayed in hopes of getting Lee to call off the attack, though with McLaws and Hood still four miles from Seminary Ridge, even such a short movement required four or five hours, including final alignment, placement of artillery, and the other details involved in an assault. Confusion of troops on the road made the whole process take even longer, and in the end Longstreet was not in position and ready to attack until 4 p.m.

When the screaming Confederates rushed forward, their attack was devastating. Hood, on the far right, swept up from the southwest, crossed Plum Run, and smashed into Sickles' left between Devil's Den and the wheatfield, while McLaws hit the jutting angle of Sickles' line in the peach field from two sides at once. Longstreet battered the Federals with a barrage from fifty-four of his cannon. Immediately Sickles' men put up a stiff resistance that in the ensuing three hours would take on a grim determination. Almost from the first, their position turned critical, as one of Hood's regiments spotted the importance of Little Round Top. Big Round Top was too wooded to allow artillery to reach its summit. The smaller hill was different, however, and it appeared to be unoccupied. Guns placed there could fire down on the entire Yankee line as far north as Cemetery Hill. But as the Rebels raced up its slopes to secure it, the timely arrival of a brigade from the V Corps, just now rushing to the field after a long march, allowed Meade to hold the position until more reinforcements could reach the scene. In a furious little fight from behind boulders and fallen trees, Blue and Gray battled bitterly for the hill before the Rebels were forced eventually to retire from the scene.

Even while fighting for their lives, the Yankees on Little Round Top could see the III Corps being cut to pieces out on the lower ground to the northwest. Six full brigades and portions of a seventh hammered at Sickles. Almost immediately the casualties became dreadful. An artillery shell carried away one of Sickles' legs. Hood took a desperate wound that left one of his arms useless for the rest of his life. The men fought on almost until dark, the Federals slowly giving way, then collapsing entirely when men from McLaws' division broke through and into the rear of the right center of the shaky Yankee line. In a near panic, the survivors rushed back to the safety of Little Round Top and more freshly arrived Union reinforcements. The III Corps had almost ceased to exist. Shortly after the battle it would be disbanded.

Despite his success in destroying Sickles, Longstreet saw that it was too late for him to follow up the advantage and mount a new attack on Little Round Top itself. His men were exhausted after four hours of solid fighting, and Union reinforcements appeared to be too numerous. Besides, the fighting had spread up along Cemetery Ridge for some distance, and he had no fresh troops to lend strength to his own battered divisions. Anderson's division of Hill's corps went forward on McLaws' left, and spent most of the afternoon in bitter fighting with elements of the I, II, and III Union corps, but especially with the intrepid Hancock, who managed the defense of the ridge brilliantly and even managed a spirited counterattack late in the day that reversed some of the gains made against Sickles. When darkness fell, the Union line, though battered, was intact from Cemetery Hill south to Little Round Top. A simultaneous threat had come on the right of the line when Ewell moved against the east slope of Cemetery Hill and Culp's Hill. He sent his whole corps forward around 6:30 p.m., not in a demonstration as ordered, but in a general attack, haphazardly supported by Rodes' division of Hill's corps. The whole affair was ill-managed and uncoordinated, and at the end of the day's fighting, Culp's was still securely in Yankee hands, though threatened, while only a small piece of the down slope of Cemetery Hill fell to Early and his Virginians. The firing of skirmishers and artillery continued long after nightfall, not dying away until around midnight when finally the thousands of battered and exhausted survivors could fitfully try to sleep.

There was to be little sleep for the two commanding generals, however. Well after dark Meade gathered his senior commanders at his headquarters behind Cemetery Hill. For almost three hours he listened to their thoughts and experiences of the day. Finally they responded to three basic question: should they hold their position or retire; if they remained, should they attack on July 3 or remain on the defensive; and if they chose the defensive, how long should they stay in place awaiting Lee's offensive? The generals were almost unanimous in recommending that they stand their ground, stay on the defensive, and give Lee no more than another day to attack them before they either took the offensive or else moved away from Gettysburg. The decision taken – and Meade made it himself – they spent the rest of the night readying themselves to meet what came on the morrow. Since Lee had tried to turn both his right and left flank without success, Meade suspected that the enemy would strike his center next.

He guessed well. Lee was frustrated – frustrated by Longstreet's and Ewell's reluctance on the first two days' fighting, frustrated by struggling for the first time on ground he did not know well, frustrated by his own poor health, and most of all frustrated by the steadfast resistance of a Yankee army that he had so many times before put to rout. As a result, he was fighting arguably his worst battle of the war. He issued orders late on July 2 for a virtual repeat of that day's efforts, coordinated attacks on Meade's right and left, to launch just after dawn the next morning. But it all went wrong before it was fairly started. Longstreet, still intimidated by the Yankee position, used latitude in his orders to try a wide sweeping flank march instead, and Lee only discovered and countermanded the move at about 6 a.m., July 3. By then it was too late, for Ewell had already started his renewed assaults on Culp's Hill. Instead, Lee decided to have Longstreet make a hammering frontal assault on Meade's center on Cemetery Ridge. His men would have to march more than a mile, largely out in the open, across broad fields of milo, then up the slopes of the ridge and into the face of Yankee guns. Fixing a clump or "copse" of trees on the otherwise bare crest as the aiming point, he told Longstreet to take 15,000 men and drive themselves as a wedge into the Union center. If successful, they would have Meade's right half trapped between themselves and Ewell and Hill. Again Longstreet objected, this time vehemently, but Lee was adamant that the plan go ahead.

Given no choice, Longstreet assembled his freshly arrived division of General George E. Pickett, along with several units on loan from Hill's III Corps, especially Heth's division now led by General James J. Pettigrew following Heth's suffering a disabling wound. Brigades from Pender's and Anderson's divisions would also join in, but Longstreet would command the whole. In the end, it came to 13,500 men. Lee wanted them to advance only after a massive barrage from 159 cannon spread all along Seminary Ridge had silenced or driven away defending artillery on Cemetery Ridge. At 1 p.m. the barrage began.

Almost two hours later the Confederate guns fell silent. Surmising correctly that the shelling presaged a massive attack, Hancock had Federal artillery conserve their fire to meet the assault. But Southern commanders interpreted this to mean that they had silenced the Yankee batteries. Against his better judgment, Longstreet, when pressed by Pickett, finally nodded his head to send the assault forward. All who witnessed it, North and South alike, admitted that it was one of the grandest sights of the war. Across a front more than a mile wide, a sea of red banners fluttered above the glistening bayonets of the flower of Lee's army. It was the greatest and grandest infantry assault of the Civil War.

It was also a terrible mistake. For all his brilliance, Lee suffered one deadly flaw. When desperate, when he had tried everything else, he would resort to the frontal assault, despite his own and others' repeated experience of bloody failure of such a tactic. The deadly accuracy and firepower of the infantryman's weapon in 1863 made such an attack virtually obsolete when directed against well-placed defenders on good ground. But Lee was out of ideas.

Thanks to the momentum of such a mass of men, and to the valor of them all, Pickett's and Pettigrew's men swept in brilliant ranks over the ground before them. When they came in range of Yankee guns, fire hit them from all sides. First came the shelling, then the musketry. Throats shouting the Rebel yell, the Virginians and North Carolinians and others hurled themselves toward the wall of blue flame atop the ridge. The closer they got, the fewer their number. General Lewis Armistead was almost at the forefront of the first few hundred who actually made it to a stone wall in front of the clump of trees. He put his hat atop his sword, held high over his head, and called for his men to follow him onward. Perhaps 150 got over the wall; few returned from it. Behind them Armistead lay with a mortal wound. It was as close as they got. Gradually, then with increased momentum, the defenders pushed back the Rebels, who then had to run a deadly gauntlet of fire for another three-quarters of a mile to get back to Seminary Ridge. Lee watched them stream into his lines, tears in his eyes as his told them that it was all his fault. Behind them lay one general killed, one mortally wounded, and another wounded and captured, and nearly half of the attacking force either killed, wounded, or taken prisoner.

And that was an end to it. The bloodiest battle in American history, and the one to spawn the most enduring controversies, had cost Lee a staggering 20,451 in casualties, with losses among his officers so high that his command system would never entirely recover. For Meade, too, the damage was great – Reynolds dead, Hancock seriously wounded, and 23,049 casualties of his own. Between the two armies, the dead alone numbered more than 6,000.

As a result, the armies simply sat and glared at each other on July 4, Lee too proud to leave the field, and Meade too battered to follow up a clear advantage. Heavy rain set in that afternoon, making further fighting impracticable anyhow, and during the night Lee silently withdrew and marched for the Potomac, his invasion and all its hopes at an end. He would not set foot on Northern soil again. Meade, though criticized for failing to pursue Lee vigorously, had still achieved what no one else had done so far in this war, not even McClellan at Antietam. He had given the entire Army of Northern Virginia a crushing open field defeat. It was to be Lee's last offensive operation of the Civil War.

REFERENCES

1 Edward J. Nichols, *Toward Gettysburg: A Biography of General John F. Reynolds* (University Park, Pa., 1958), pp.220-23.
2 Marsena R. Patrick Journal, June 17, 19, 1863, Library of Congress, Washington, D.C.
3 Edwin B. Coddington, *The Gettysburg Campaign* (New York, 1968), pp.306-307.
4 *O.R.*, I, 27, pt.1, p.705.
5 Coddington, *Gettysburg*, p.346.

X

CHICKAMAUGA & CHATTANOOGA

etting aside the often overblown claims of their partisans and supporters, it is more than a little interesting to consider just how few battles most Confederate army commanders' reputations are actually based upon. Lee is the exception to this, for during the conflict he led his army in no fewer than a dozen major engagements, and far more if the Seven Days' fights and those of 1864 are considered individually. No other commander of the war except Grant came even close to this. Of his fellow Confederates, Albert Sidney Johnston had just one battle, Beauregard only portions of two, and Joseph E. Johnston no more than half a dozen, most of less than major stature. Ironically, next to Lee the one Confederate commander to lead a full army in major battle more than any other was the despised Braxton Bragg. Four times he would commit his Army of Tennessee to full-scale engagement; the first two at Perryville and Stones River. With even greater irony, in his last two battles, fought within less than ten weeks of one another, he would inflict the most complete defeat ever suffered by a Union army, and then follow it by taking the most humiliating beating in the brief but glorious history of Confederate arms. First to last, the man presented the most intriguing puzzle of any general of the war.

It all revolved around a place known only by an old Cherokee name that meant something like "crow's nest." In fact, the name Chattanooga was actually aimed at the nearby towering eminence of Lookout Mountain, but when a small city of 5,000 grew up on a bend in the Tennessee River near its base, the name quickly shifted to the town. Of little consequence before the outbreak of war, its vital rail link between the Confederacy east and west of the Alleghenies gave it a strategic importance second only to Atlanta or Richmond. Control of Chattanooga offered the key to a back door into Virginia and the front door to Atlanta. It was of great strategic value. The

Confederacy had to hold it at all costs. The price of losing Chattanooga would have been too high to contemplate.

Typically, Braxton Bragg lost it in early September 1863 without firing a shot. Following his marginal defeat at Stones River the previous January, Bragg withdrew toward the Duck River. Before long, however, he relocated to Tullahoma, on the Nashville & Chattanooga Railroad, about forty-five miles west of Chattanooga, thus protecting his supply line. Here he sat out the balance of the spring and the summer, the longest period of inactivity during the prime campaigning months of any major army in the war, a period almost matched by Rosecrans and his Army of the Cumberland. Both armies remained content to refresh and refit themselves. But then toward the end of summer, Rosecrans marched tentatively south once more, intent on taking the city more by craft than force. First he conducted a brilliant campaign of maneuver that threatened to cut Bragg off from his base, forcing him to abandon Tullahoma and pull back to the defenses on the mountains around Chattanooga. Then, sending a diversionary movement to make Bragg fearful for his right, Rosecrans moved the bulk of his army to the Tennessee River west of Chattanooga. There he crossed in late August and started to move east along its bank toward Chattanooga. Bragg, his left turned, and fearing that the enemy might now strike for his rear, abandoned the city. On September 9 Rosecrans marched in without a fight.

But then Rosecrans misjudged Bragg. Thinking that the Rebel army was demoralized and in full retreat, he was not careful to keep his own three corps under Thomas, McCook, and Crittenden, together, or at least within easy supporting distance. Instead, he left Crittenden at Chattanooga and sent the other two on widely diverging routes in pursuit of the enemy. The long high ridges of Raccoon Mountain, immediately below the Tennessee, and the even longer Lookout Mountain further south, shielded Bragg's movements from the Yankees. Moving without sure information of the foe's whereabouts, Rosecrans became reckless. He sent Thomas through Stevens Gap in Lookout Mountain, twenty miles southwest of Crittenden at Chattanooga, and McCook nearly twenty miles farther along at Winston Gap. As a result, his right and left were separated by almost forty miles of tough country. And Bragg, in fact, had all of his forces tightly in control and almost directly in Thomas' path. All that separated them was a gap in Missionary Ridge, a valley known as McLemore's Cove, and the waters of Chickamauga Creek.

It was another Indian word, this one meaning, they said, "River of Death." If so, Bragg was ready to give meaning to the name. This general, though he only ever commanded the Army of Tennessee, never fought with the same army twice. Earlier in the year he had detached the disliked Breckinridge and his division to go on Johnston's abortive Vicksburg relief expedition, and other units had been loaned out elsewhere during the summer of inactivity. But now many, including Breckinridge, were being sent back to him. Furthermore, given the static situation in Virginia with almost no activity between Lee and Meade at all, Richmond had prevailed upon Lee to send

Longstreet and most of his I Corps out to reinforce Bragg temporarily. And of course, even among those units that had never left his immediate command, Bragg's continuing war with his own commanders had led to substantial changes. Hardee, who by now loathed Bragg, had been sent to Alabama by Richmond, and partially at his own request. His corps had been broken up, Breckinridge sent west and Cleburne put under the irascible Daniel H. Hill. Hill had so fallen out with Lee and everyone else in Virginia that Davis sent him out to replace Hardee, thus placing two of the worst tempers in the army together. When Breckinridge returned, he would be assigned to Hill as well. Meanwhile, another old Bragg enemy, Leonidas Polk, remained in command of his corps, with one division under the capable but erratic Cheatham, and another led by General Thomas C. Hindman of Arkansas, now in command of what had been Jones Withers' division. Bragg also created a Reserve Corps commanded by W.H.T. Walker, with two divisions led by General States Rights Gist and St. John R. Liddell.

Once Longstreet arrived, Bragg would assign him command of a separate wing composed of two hastily organized corps. The first would go to Major General Simon Buckner, now returned from a Northern prison camp. Bragg would give him Hindman's division from Polk's corps – a clear blow at Polk – and small divisions led by Generals William Preston and Alexander P. Stewart. Longstreet's other corps would be commanded by Hood, recovered as much as he would ever be from his arm wound at Gettysburg, and now to lead McLaws, his own old division in the hands of Evander M. Law, and another under the Ohioian Bushrod Johnson. Even the cavalry fell into two separate corps, one of two divisions under the erratic Wheeler, and two others led by the incontestably brilliant Nathan B. Forrest.

Many of these units were not yet with Bragg, and there was some fear that a few might not arrive in time if Rosecrans pressed with vigor. But should they all come together, they would total about 60,000, giving them a wonderful advantage over Rosecrans, then believed to have no more than 50,000 in his three corps. For once, as at Stones River, the Confederates might go into battle with numbers on their side.

The question was where the battle should be fought. Rosecrans believed that Bragg was retreating toward Atlanta, though his basis was little more than wishful thinking, for his cavalry was bringing him almost no intelligence of Confederate whereabouts. Thus he kept his corps going ahead, Crittenden now moving out of Chattanooga and turning due south toward what was, in fact, Bragg's position several miles to his front. On September 9 Thomas and McCook were moving through their gaps, and then the next day General James Negley, commanding the second division of Thomas' XIV Corps, stumbled into the frightening sight of most of Bragg's army awaiting him as he was the first to march into McLemore's Cove. Within a few minutes Negley found himself almost surrounded. Only nightfall and more of Thomas' troops arriving saved him, as well as command confusion between Hill, Cleburne, and Bragg, that resulted in the wonderful opportunity to destroy a full division being squandered. Worse, the next day the Southerners allowed Negley and his supports to withdraw from the cove, letting yet another chance slip away. Bragg would later arrest Hindman for disobedience of orders in the affair.

Even now Rosecrans was not fully alerted to the danger facing him. He thought Negley had only encountered a rearguard. He was unaware of another similar danger narrowly averted when Bragg ordered Polk to attack the isolated Crittenden, only to have the utterly incompetent corps commander fail to carry out the order or even attempt to do so. And certainly Rosecrans had no idea at all that on September 9, the same day Crittenden occupied Chattanooga, trains in Virginia were loading the first of Longstreet's corps for the long ride to eastern Tennessee. At the same time, Breckinridge's and Bushrod Johnson's divisions were rushing to join Bragg. Walker's Reserve Corps was coming from Johnston out in Mississippi, and Buckner had brought his command from Knoxville. Meanwhile, "Old Rosey" marched blissfully onward, unaware of the combinations forming against him.

Only on the evening of September 12 did the commander finally realize his jeopardy and order his army to concentrate, calling Crittenden and McCook to rush to Thomas in the center. Unfortunately, Bragg gave him four days of unhindered time in which to do so, simply keeping his own army in check and awaiting Longstreet's arrival. But then he decided to go ahead. Walker had arrived and Breckinridge and Johnson were coming up. Rosecrans was in a beautifully exposed position. All Bragg had to do was move north along the near bank of the Chickamauga, cross Johnson, Walker, Buckner, and Forrest at any of the available fords, and he could get between the Yankees and Chattanooga. Then he could retake the virtually unoccupied city and Rosecrans would either have to attack him in his defenses, or else withdraw back towards Nashville in order not to risk having Bragg cut his own lines of supply.

Bragg intended to strike on September 18, but delays held it off for a full day, during which Rosecrans moved quickly in response to his own danger. Chickamauga Creek ran roughly north to southwest, with numerous bends and cutbacks. Rosecrans had Crittenden on the west side just behind Lee and Gordon's Mill about two miles above Crawfish Springs, Rosecrans' headquarters, on September 18. In order to speed the concentration toward his threatened left, he had halted Crittenden here while ordering Thomas to move to his support, and that night the XIV Corps marched behind and past Crittenden almost two miles in order to meet the anticipated threat from Bragg. As it turned out, no battle erupted on the appointed day either, as spirited actions with Yankee cavalrymen prevented Bragg from crossing where and when he wanted. Instead, Rosecrans used September 18 to continue extending his line northward to protect the road to Chattanooga. On into the morning of the 19th he continued rushing his scattered divisions in their concentration.

It was tangled, sometimes obscure countryside between the two armies. Admitting that he could not keep Bragg from crossing the creek in his front, Rosecrans was arraying his forces to protect his lines of retreat and to take advantage of a few natural advantages, most notably some dense woods and thickets, and a moderately commanding eminence called Snodgrass Hill. On such ground it would be difficult to control the armies for there was no point from which a commander could see all or even a significant part of his command. They would have to fight by "feel." Rosecrans, being outnumbered and caught in a bad position, knew that he would have to stay on the defensive. Bragg, with a slight numerical advantage of perhaps 7,000 and 30 pieces of artillery, would unquestionably be the aggressor.[1]

The fighting really began the next day, almost accidentally, and again heavily influenced by the Federals' lack of knowledge. Word came to Thomas that a single brigade from Bushrod Johnson's division was isolated on the west side of the Chickamauga, midway between Alexander's and Reed's Bridges. Sensing an opportunity to take out an entire enemy brigade at a quick stroke, Thomas immediately sent two brigades off to make the easy kill. He did not know that the rest of Johnson's division was lurking nearby, and when the would-be Federal attackers actually encountered that brigade, they ran into the entire Reserve Corps under Walker, supported by Forrest's cavalry. The Yankees advanced and quickly discovered their mistake. Johnson's men handily repulsed the first blue advance, but commanders on either side of the line were somewhat surprised at the ferocity of the fighting. As rapidly as possible, more reinforcements were summoned, and soon successive divisions of each army began coming on the scene at about the same time. Neither Rosecrans nor Bragg was in control just now. Rather, the battle was taking on a life of its own as the momentum of the fighting automatically drew more and more units toward the action.

Before long Walker committed both of his divisions to repulsing the first attack, and did so almost decisively, nearly capturing an entire brigade themselves. But then a fresh division from McCook came up on the Federal right and struck Walker's flank with vigor, putting renewed energy into the other battered Federals, and together they drove Walker back more than a mile, only to be themselves stopped cold when Cheatham's division of five brigades suddenly appeared, passed through Walker, and slammed into them.

It was past 11 a.m. by now, and the fighting had been going on for about two hours. Cheatham's new division almost immediately went into action with Federal General Richard Johnson's division, just south of Walker's earlier position. Soon more of Thomas' divisions appeared, being matched almost one-for-one by the arrival of more Confederate units. Late in the day, the Federal line stretched for nearly five miles through the woods and fields west of the Chickamauga. Thomas held the left, from just beyond Reed's Bridge, with two of his divisions. But then came Johnson's division of McCook's Corps, then John Palmer's division of Crittenden's XXI Corps. Then came Reynolds' division from Thomas, followed by Horatio Van Cleve's division from Crittenden, then James Negley's division from Thomas again. Off to the right came Jeff C. Davis' division from McCook, then Thomas Wood's division from

Crittenden, then Sheridan's division from McCook's once more. Obviously, the entire line was an organizational jumble, with all semblance of neat corps unity set aside in the rush to get units on the field. As a result, an informal command system went in place instead, with Thomas commanding the divisions on the left, Crittenden those in the center, and McCook the right.

Bragg's units, too, came into the line without much regard for organization. Walker's corps remained on the right, though battered, then Cheatham from Polk's corps came in on his left, followed in turn by Stewart from Buckner's, then Johnson and Law from Hood's corps, and Preston from Buckner. Breckinridge and Cleburne, Hill's whole corps, were still on their way, having been posted downriver the day before in anticipation of action at Lee and Gordon's Mill. And Hindman from Polk's corps was just on his way to Bragg's left. Thus the Rebel line ran just over three miles, from Reed's Bridge down to a bend in the Chickamauga just opposite Davis' division in Rosecrans' right center. Bragg had intentionally kept shoveling his divisions northward that morning in the hope of still getting between Rosecrans and Chattanooga, but by noon, with the strength of Thomas' attacks on Walker, it became evident that the foe knew what he intended, and that this approach was not going to succeed. Yet so fixed was Bragg on his original intent that he seems not to have credited, or even looked for, information about a wide gap in the center of Rosecrans' line. If he had sent one or two of his divisions forward at the right place and time, he could have split the Yankee army in two. Such an opportunity rarely came to a general even once in a battle, and Bragg passed this one by. Miraculously, he would get another in time.

The fighting shifted toward the center where, in spite of the failure to capitalize on the gap in the Yankee line, Bragg's divisions struck good blows, and Stewart in particular drove a deep bulge into Van Cleve's line in a brutal afternoon attack that nearly saw the Federal line break before Thomas sent Palmer and Negley to stem the break. It was a near thing, for Stewart's hammering brigades, especially the one led by Tennesseean William B. Bate, broke through to one of the two roads connecting Rosecrans with Chattanooga, and got within sight of the other before being pushed back. Only the arrival of Joseph J. Reynolds and his division finally pushed them back to their own lines.

By about 4 p.m. the fighting started to die down on Stewart and Cheatham's fronts, only to be taken up by some new arrivals on the field. Longstreet's corps, moving laboriously over the overburdened and badly worn Confederate railroad system from Virginia, actually started to arrive at Ringgold, several miles southeast of Chattanooga, on September 16. From there it was a march straight west about fifteen miles to reach Bragg on the banks of the Chickamauga. Law's division arrived first, while Hood himself with more men only came on the field about 3 p.m., while the battle was underway, and immediately assumed command of Law and Johnson. Hood was not a brilliant man, but he did have a perfect instinct for combat, and no sooner did he arrive than he pitched into Rosecrans' right with his two divisions. The fighting became brutally vicious, with whole regiments almost disappearing in the melee. Some soldiers saw an owl flying overhead with crows diving and pecking at it, and believed the spirit must be contagious. "Moses, what a country," said one Yankee. "The very birds are fighting."[2]

Hood's fight sputtered out as darkness fell, and the buildup of Federal forces on his front prevented any gains. But there was still one more attack to be made, this one in the gathering gloom of night as Cleburne brought his division on the field after a day-long march from the south. Bragg, still clinging to the idea of turning Rosecrans' right, had marched Cleburne and Breckinridge all the way from Lee and Gordon's, clear past the rear of his entire battleline, to get them on his own right. The result, of course, was two exhausted divisions by day's end.

Bragg ordered Cleburne to report to Polk, commanding the right wing of the army, and when Cleburne went forward into the fight, well after 5 p.m., he exploded out of the trees and thickets to slam into Thomas with ferocity. For half an hour the firing was as thick as any of the veterans could ever remember, and only the settling of absolute darkness brought it to a halt.

At the end of the first day's fighting, neither Bragg nor Rosecrans had achieved a thing, and the men and officers in both armies suffered low spirits that night. Rosecrans and his officers discussed the situation, hopeful that Bragg would retreat, and decided to stand their ground. There was more activity across the lines. That evening Longstreet himself arrived, with McLaws' division, commanded for the moment by Joseph B. Kershaw, marching behind and due to arrive in time for the next day's fight. Bragg decided to divide his command into two wings. Polk would command the right, consisting of Walker's Corps, Hill's Corps, and Cheatham. Longstreet was to command the left wing with Hood's corps of three divisions, Buckner's corps of two divisions, and Hindman on loan from Polk. As for a plan of battle, Bragg hardly had anything more sophisticated in mind than a general attack all along the line, starting with Polk on the far right, and then spreading to the left. Polk would begin his attack at daylight.

Of course, Polk did no such thing. Supposed to attack before 6 a.m. on September 20, he did not get things moving until almost four hours later. Confusion, bad communications, and Polk's customary obtuseness, delayed the attack inexcusably, and Bragg would not forget. Finally he had Breckinridge placed on his far right, and it fell to the Kentuckian to launch the attack.

The ferocity of the Kentuckian's attack would become legendary. His three brigades almost shattered the Federal left flank, and two of them quickly got around the end of Thomas' line, only to encounter very stiff return fire from behind breastworks. It cost him General Ben Hardin Helm, commanding his old Kentucky "Orphan Brigade," who took a mortal wound whose pain would be felt all the way to Washington, the White House, and the home of Helm's brother-in-law, President Lincoln.

Still Breckinridge hammered away, sending the normally cool and reserved Thomas into something as close to overexcitement as he ever got. He began to call on Rosecrans for reinforcements to stem the attack. Then he called again. When Cleburne took up the attack on Breckinridge's left, the pressure only got worse, and Thomas called for yet more. Then Cheatham moved in on Cleburne's left, and Thomas renewed his request for more troops. These three Rebel divisions were battering him badly, and Rosecrans tried to comply. The trouble was, as "Old Rosey" sent more and more units from his center to his threatened left, he did not pay careful attention to the rest of his line or to the precision of his orders – a fault common to Rosecrans. Finally he ordered the division of Thomas J. Wood to shift to its left. Unfortunately, Rosecrans had exploded in temper at Wood earlier for not explicitly following an order, so now Wood did exactly as he was told, even though in so doing he would leave a hole in the Federal line close to half a mile wide.

Here was Bragg's second chance of a lifetime, yet ironically, he would not capitalize upon it intentionally. With the resistance on the Yankee left being greater than he had anticipated, Bragg abandoned his earlier intent of a rolling attack, and now left it up to his line commanders to strike as opportunity offered. That was all the combative Longstreet needed to hear. There was no Cemetery Ridge in front of him this time. He had nearly 11,000 men at his disposal in the divisions of Johnson, Kershaw, and Law, all commanded by Hood, with Hindman on his left, Stewart on his right, and Preston behind him bringing the total to more than 20,000. He intended to make a massive attack.

Through sheer chance, when Johnson went forward as spearhead of the attack, he aimed almost exactly at the spot where ten minutes before Wood's Federal division had pulled out. Incredibly, after battling through some tough resistance on his right front, Johnson saw nothing to his center and left front but open country and a few scattered enemy commands on the march toward Thomas. Followed by the rest of the attacking column, Johnson swept through, pushing more than a mile to the Dry Valley road, one of Rosecrans' links with Chattanooga. Hindman came through behind him and turned left, taking Sheridan in flank and dispersing him. Behind them, more and more Rebels poured through the gap, now widened to more than half a mile. By noon, after an hour of fighting, the Army of the Cumberland was in two pieces, separated by ground it no longer held, and thousands of screaming Confederates.

The breakthrough was coming at a high cost. Breckinridge and Cleburne, who set it up with their relentless pressure on Thomas, suffered heavily. Now Hood fell with a bullet in his right leg, requiring amputation later that day. But in payment, they had the joy of seeing whole brigades of Yankees put to flight. And now as Hindman began to roll up the flank of the right half of Rosecrans' army, even more of a panic set in on the now demoralized Federals. As the remaining Confederates on the left of Bragg's line pressed forward, the divisions of Sheridan and Jeff C. Davis became disorganized and terrified at seeing the enemy coming at them from two sides and their line of retreat to Chattanooga almost cut off. In groups, then by whole regiments, they broke and ran for the rear. In no more than an hour the entire right half of the Yankee army became infused with the panic, which spread even to McCook, Crittenden, and Rosecrans himself. In a scene not repeated since the rout at First Manassas, thousands of demoralized Federals started streaming back toward Chattanooga. Rosecrans, seeing what happened, simply attached himself to the fleeing horde. So did Sheridan and Davis, though the latter managed to rally himself and some of his men and return to the battlefield by nightfall. The rest simply kept on until they reached Chattanooga. Many including Rosecrans, would never hold field command again.

Still the left half of the Army of the Cumberland held out, and now Thomas shone as he stood his ground. Now it was not merely a matter of repulsing the enemy attacks. He had to stand in order to cover the precipitate retreat of the rest of the army. Thomas' almost frantic appeals of that morning for more reinforcements helped lead directly to what was now happening, but his earlier apprehensiveness now disappeared as, in the height of the crisis, he acted with cool courage and a granite immovability. Time after time Breckinridge and Cleburne, joined now by elements of Longstreet's victorious command, hammered away at him. Thomas held his front, where Polk obligingly relaxed his pressure, and turned his main attention to his right, now turned back obliquely to meet Longstreet. On the slopes of Snodgrass Hill, and a little further to the right rear on Horseshoe Ridge, the Federals put up one of the most heroic stands of the war, well earning Thomas his later sobriquet as the "Rock of Chickamauga." He refused to move. Only darkness closed the fighting, by which time General Gordon Granger and his Reserve Corps arrived, acting on no specific orders but largely on Granger's own initiative. Having heard the sounds of the battle from his position many miles north, Granger deduced that it was not going well for his army, and rushed to the sound of the guns. He arrived in time to bolster Thomas sufficiently to hold out until nightfall. Only then did Thomas finally yield the field, now that most of the rest of the army was well on the road to Chattanooga – an army that he may well have saved.

Even Bragg must have been a bit stunned at the result. The losses to both sides were dreadful, 21,000 for the Confederates and more than 16,000 for the Federals, totals not much less than the numbers suffered at Gettysburg by much larger armies in a three-day battle. Bragg's casualties told of the ferocity of Rebel attacks and the stubbornness of Thomas' stand. Still, the field belonged to Braxton Bragg, and with it the glory of having inflicted the most complete defeat ever suffered by an army in blue.[3]

But that was not an end to it. Chickamauga was to have an echo just two months afterward, when these two armies were to meet again in circumstances completely different, yet leading once more to the near-total demoralization and rout of one of the contestants, and this time in a contest of inestimably more far-reaching impact than

Bragg's victory along the Chickamauga, the fruits of which he largely discarded by failing to go after Rosecrans.

"Rosey," of course, was delighted to be allowed to withdraw into the defenses of Chattanooga, and once there his men took heart once more, even those from Crittenden's and McCook's corps who had fled so precipitately. Surprisingly, Rosecrans did not immediately lose his command after the debacle. Lincoln always felt rather kindly towards him, chiefly because of the muted victory at Stones River, coming when it did at a desperate time after Fredericksburg. Indeed, Lincoln did not have to do anything directly about Rosecrans. Instead, he and the War Department created a new command, the Military Division of the Mississippi, encompassing Grant's Army of the Tennessee, Rosecrans' Army of the Cumberland, and the small Army of the Ohio now at Knoxville under the command of Burnside. It all went to Grant, and to him fell the decision of what to do about Rosecrans. The decision was a simple one. Though Grant never felt great regard for Thomas, he nevertheless relieved Rosecrans on October 19 and turned the army over to the Rock of Chickamauga.

It was an army that was not in a happy position. Bragg's army appeared on Lookout Mountain and Missionary Ridge in their front soon after the battle, and began a shelling that, while it did little harm, certainly did not encourage calm in the camps. Worse, Bragg soon had them virtually under siege. Chattanooga sat with its back to the east side of the Tennessee River, its only connection to the supply base at Nashville being a single rail line that moved along the same side of the river until it crossed to Bridgeport, twenty-five miles west. The rails went directly beneath the slopes of the northern end of Lookout Mountain, and when the Rebels occupied that height, the railroad was effectively cut. The only other way for supplies to get from the Federal railhead at Bridgeport to Chattanooga was by a rugged wagon road on the northwest side of the river, through rugged mountains, and always subject to raids by enemy cavalry. It was more than sixty miles long, and so difficult that only the merest fraction of an army's needs could be brought over it. Bragg was very quickly in a position to starve Rosecrans out even before Thomas took command.

Fortunately for the federals, Bragg, as usual, went back to war with his own generals as soon as Chickamauga was over. He arrested Hindman and relieved Polk. In his typical cowardly fashion, Polk blamed his own failings on D.H. Hill, but Bragg was already setting an attack on that general as well. Then Longstreet got involved, hoping to get Bragg's army for himself, and before long Richmond had a petition signed by twelve generals asking for Bragg's replacement. Davis himself came to see the troubled army in October, but only to sustain Bragg. In a series of attempts to quell the unrest, Davis replaced Polk with Hardee, and then allowed Hill to be relieved and replaced by Breckinridge. Then Buckner's corps command was abolished, and he reduced to leading a division. Longstreet was too powerful to attack in such manner, however, so in the end Bragg got rid of him by giving in to "Old Pete's" own repeated suggestions that he take his corps and leave the idle lines about Chattanooga to go take Knoxville from Burnside. This was the worst of all the feuds, for by his manner of solving it Bragg sent away nearly a third of his army. Now he was down to just two corps. Hardee commanded the I Corps with four good-sized divisions, and Breckinridge the II Corps, smaller though it, too, had four divisions. All told, Bragg had about 32,000 men in the two corps still with him after he sent Longstreet away on November 4. They had a lot of ground to cover. Missionary Ridge ran almost parallel to the Tennessee, from Tunnel Hill on the north down to its terminus at Rossville Gap three miles below. Hardee had to cover almost all of it with the three divisions of Cheatham, J. Patton Anderson, and Walker, along with Cleburne, transferred to this corps from Breckinridge's after Buckner was sent off to Knoxville to aid Longstreet. On Hardee's left Breckinridge occupied the so-called Lookout Valley between the end of Missionary Ridge and the tip of Lookout Mountain. He had just his own old division, now led by Bate, along with Stewart and a small division led by Carter Stevenson. They were spread out over a three-mile front, covering the valley, then holding the slopes and crest of Lookout. Almost all believed that they had a virtually impregnable position on those heights, and that Thomas was in serious trouble.

They reckoned without U.S. Grant. He reached Chattanooga in person on October 23 to see for himself the condition of Thomas and his army, and to do what he did best – turn adversity into opportunity. Of most immediate concern was lifting the blockade of supplies. That same evening he and his generals solved the supply problem. They laid out a line that cut the overland distance from Bridgeport from sixty to thirty miles, successfully planned the elimination of the small Rebel command holding one vital gap on the way, and by the end of the month had the route open for mountains of supplies to start coming in once more. Thanks to all the hardtack that formed a staple of their diet, the soldiers dubbed the new route the "cracker line." Over that line there also came substantial reinforcements. Sherman brought portions of his Army of the Tennessee, including most of the XV and XVII Corps. From Virginia came old familiar names in the persons of Hooker and Howard. Hooker brought the XI and XII Corps, with himself in overall command. John M. Palmer took over the XIV Corps, now reconstituted from Thomas and McCook's old commands, while other divisions from McCook and Crittenden joined with Granger to make a new IV Corps. Thomas and Sherman maintained their separate army commands, and combined they totaled more than 60,000 by mid-November.

Grant was anxious to attack and force his way out of the siege as soon as possible, and the necessary delays vexed him considerably. By November 21, however, he was determined to wait no more. He had Sherman placed on his own left, Thomas in the center holding the works of Chattanooga itself, and Hooker on the right. Originally Grant wanted to make a diversion against Lookout Mountain, while Sherman launched the main attack on Bragg's right, at Tunnel Hill. Turning the north end of

Missionary Ridge, Sherman could then sweep down its length, or pass beyond and get in the enemy rear, perhaps cutting him off from a line of retreat toward Dalton, Georgia, on the railroad to Atlanta, his own base of supply.

It did not work out exactly as Grant planned. Rain on the appointed day kept Sherman from moving out. Then information came in suggesting that the Rebels might, in fact, be pulling out. Before putting more of his plan into operation, Grant ordered Thomas to make a strong reconnaissance on November 23. Thomas was simply to move forward from his positions in Chattanooga's works and advance to the forward enemy outpost line some mile and a quarter west of Missionary Ridge, anchored on an eminence called Orchard Knob. Thomas mustered 25,000 from the Army of the Cumberland and swept them forward that morning in full view of the main Rebel lines atop Missionary Ridge. The sight was magnificently impressive, as even the Confederates later testified. It proved to be almost a walkover. The thin enemy line could hardly resist this avalanche of moving blue, and within a few minutes the Yankees swarmed over them. Grant moved his headquarters to Orchard Knob almost at once. Bragg, meanwhile, seeing the danger in his front, strengthened Missionary Ridge by drawing Walker's division from Lookout Mountain. It could not have come at a more unfortunate time, for that summit would be the next object of Grant's desiring.[4]

On the morning of November 24, Grant struck at Bragg's right and left more or less simultaneously. Sherman sent three divisions across the Tennessee north of Chattanooga and swept along Chickamauga Creek toward Tunnel Hill, now held by Cleburne and Walker. He ran into less than he bargained for. Expecting substantial resistance, he found very little, in part because he stopped short of hitting Tunnel Hill. Instead, he occupied two nearby eminences that would put him in a good position for renewing the advance the next day. At the other end of the line, however, Hooker made spectacular gains at Lookout Mountain. Thanks to fogs and mists clinging to the slopes of the steep mountain, the fight would ever after be called – erroneously – the "Battle Above the Clouds."

Hooker led 10,000 forward along the far side of the Tennessee, having previously crossed over downriver. This brought him directly against Stevenson's division posted on the summit and forward slopes. They heavily outnumbered the defenders, and even though Stevenson enjoyed high ground, it was so steep and rugged in places that it offered few advantages, and none for artillery on its slopes. Striking around 8 a.m., Hooker pushed them easily back. Finally the brigade posted at the northern base of the mountain, where it met the Tennessee, was forced to retire. With the Yankees now spilling around the base of the mountain, those on the summit and slopes were in danger of being cut off from the rest of their army. Breckinridge rode over to personally direct the defense, but outnumbered more than four to one, there was nothing to be done. The best he could do was hold out until nightfall, and under darkness' cover he withdrew everyone to the south summit of Missionary Ridge.

This left Bragg with but a single position, the three-mile front slope of Missionary Ridge. Breckinridge held somewhat more than half of it from the Rossville Gap northward, with only the divisions of Bate and Stewart. Bragg had sent Stevenson off to the right, where Hardee had Cleburne and Walker near Tunnel Hill and Cheatham and Anderson on the ridge itself. The night before, in council, most of the generals renewed their belief that their position was so strong they could not be driven off it.

Shortly after dawn on November 25, Sherman advanced once more, and this time he ran squarely into one of the stubbornest fighters in all the Confederacy. Cleburne, called by some the "Stonewall of the West," refused to yield an inch of ground. All day Sherman hammered at him, and all day Cleburne hammered right back. On into the afternoon the Federals kept trying to take that Tunnel Hill, and they never got it. Never, that is, until events elsewhere forced Cleburne to give it up.

Those other events were the absolute collapse of the divisions in the center and southern positions of Missionary Ridge. Grant did not intend Thomas to attack Missionary Ridge with his army. The heights looked too well defended. Besides, since he envisaged turning both Bragg's flanks, he would lose many of the fruits of victory if Sherman and/or Hooker got around a flank, only to find that there was no Confederate rear to strike because Thomas had pushed Bragg off the mountain. Instead, Grant only told Thomas to advance to the base of the mountain and drive in the enemy skirmishers placed there in rifle pits. This should occupy enough of Bragg's attention to facilitate the two flank attacks.

But then something happened. When Thomas paraded his 25,000 out in full view once more, and then sent them forward, the sight of all those Yankees had a demoralizing effect on the men in the lines atop the ridge. They knew their own weakness – outnumbered nearly two to one. They knew that Cleburne was taking – and giving – a beating over on their right, and they knew that they had lost the seemingly impregnable Lookout Mountain. Now this wave of blue was coming towards them. When Thomas' men reached the base of the ridge, men in the rifle pits raced back up the slopes behind them with only token resistance, and many did not stop when they got to the summit. Instead, they began disrupting the main lines as they passed through. Then the Army of the Cumberland decided not to stop. Grant did not order it, and neither did Thomas. When the veterans reached the base of the ridge, they found themselves coming under a heavy fire, and with nowhere to take refuge. They could not stay where they were. They could only retire, or go on up the ridge. The soldiers themselves and their officers on the scene took the decision out of the hands of the generals. On up they raced, impelled by fear, patriotism, anger, revenge for Chickamauga, and a simple absence of knowing anything else to do.

The result was a virtual stampede. Despite heroic efforts by Breckinridge and Bragg, both of whom narrowly escaped being captured, most of Bate's and Stewart's divisions dissolved, and those on their right began to waver as well. Whole batteries of artillery were captured, then turned against the remaining defenders. Hardee, com-

155

manding the right, suddenly found himself facing Sherman on his front and right, and Thomas on the ridge to his left. The best he could do was to hold on for a little longer until the early winter twilight brought operations to a close. Then he pulled out to follow the rest of the shattered army, with the ever-defiant Cleburne covering the retreat.

How ironic that just over two months to the day after giving the Yankees their most humiliating defeat ever, Bragg now suffered a similar fate himself. There was no explaining what had happened, he would later say, and many agreed with him. The men were defeated before the fight began, defeated by the sight of that massive army in full view, and coming toward them, bayonets glistening. Now they could do nothing but retire toward Dalton, Georgia, where they would winter while Grant relished yet another victory in a Chattanooga freed from siege. But at least the discouraged soldiers of the Army of Tennessee could take heart from one particular casualty of their bitter defeat. Three days after the collapse on Missionary Ridge, Braxton Bragg asked to be relieved from command. He would never lead troops in the field again.

REFERENCES

1 Glenn Tucker, *Chickamauga: Bloody Battle in the West* (Indianapolis, Ind., 1961), p.125.

2 Frank Moore, *The Civil War in Song and Story* (New York, 1889), p.169.

3 Tucker, *Chickamauga*, pp.388-89.

4 James L. McDonough, *Chattanooga – A Death Grip on the Confederacy* (Knoxville, Tenn., 1984), pp.113-14.

XI

THE WILDERNESS

It is a measure of just how much Gettysburg devastated both armies involved that Lee never again fought an offensive battle, and neither side could bring itself to a major engagement for almost a year afterward. Certainly Meade was willing, but the failures of subordinates spoiled one opportunity after another. As for Lee, ever-pugnacious, he simply could not offer battle on anything like an equal footing, but should the foe attack him, he could still prove to be very dangerous.

By the beginning of 1864 it became obvious that that foe would be under the overall leadership of a new man, one whom Lee had never faced. Meade had performed well, and would stay in command of the Army of the Potomac for the balance of the war. But when Washington made U.S. Grant general-in-chief following the victory at Chattanooga, all thoughts united in expecting him to come to Virginia to direct the campaign there in person. Here it was that for almost three years the Union had strategically gained nothing. Here President Lincoln needed his most victorious of commanders.

When Grant came east, his first proposal for countering Lee was both daring and novel. He wanted to send 60,000 men from the Washington area on a waterborne expedition to the coast of North Carolina and then drive west toward Raleigh through the sparsely defended North Carolina interior. By doing so he would cut most of Lee and Richmond's rail links with states to the south, while the fall of Chattanooga and Sherman's advance toward Atlanta would cut the rest. Lee would be cut off and isolated from all supply and succor, facing a powerful army under Meade, and having little choice but to fight at a dreadful disadvantage, or else withdraw toward eastern Tennessee, abandoning Virginia to the Federals. The plan also had the beauty of creating a potential new front far to the south and west of Richmond, whereas any advance by Meade over the old routes toward Richmond would mean meeting Lee on familiar ground of his choosing, and which he had well prepared with defenses.

Unfortunately, Lincoln vetoed Grant's plan for a number of reasons, not least being a fear that the daring Lee might take the opportunity to move against a weakened Washington defense. As a result, Grant had no choice but to look once more at that ground between the two warring capitals to search for a road to victory.

He approached the task with seemingly overwhelming power. The Army of the Potomac, augmented by the IX Corps commanded by Burnside (kept independent, chiefly as a consideration to Burnside himself to prevent the onetime army commander from having to serve under Meade, his one-time subordinate), numbered nearly 120,000. There were familiar old names here, along with some new ones. Gone was Reynolds' old I Corps. Hancock, recovered from his Gettysburg wound, was here at the head of his II Corps and its four divisions under Francis Barlow, John Gibbon, David Birney, and Gershom Mott. The III Corps, virtually destroyed at Gettysburg thanks to Sickles, was also gone. Gouverneur Warren, one of the heroes of Little Round Top, now commanded Meade's old V Corps, with four divisions led by Charles Griffin, John C. Robinson, Samuel W. Crawford, and James S. Wadsworth. Sedgwick and his VI Corps were here, Horatio Wright, George Getty, and James Ricketts leading its divisions. And Burnside, reporting directly to Grant and not Meade, had his old veterans in hand under division commanders Thomas G. Stevenson, Robert Potter, Orlando Willcox, and Edward Ferrero. Each corps carried its own artillery brigade. Grant's old associate from the West, Phillip H. Sheridan, assumed command of the three-division Cavalry Corps, his able subordinates being Generals Alfred T.A. Torbert, David M. Gregg, and James H. Wilson. After three years of war and despite having suffered heavy losses, the Army of the Potomac was at its height of experience and efficiency. It was never in better condition.

Denied his plan for a grand strategic movement to remove Lee from Virginia, and literally starve him towards submission without, it was hoped, inflicting or taking heavy casualties, Grant had no alternative but to drive straight for the enemy in his positions below the Rapidan River. Those positions were good ones, though Lee was vulnerable on a number of fronts, and no one knew that better than the gray chieftain himself. Detachments to other more pressed fronts had considerably weakened his army during the winter. Longstreet and two of his divisions had gone to join Bragg in Georgia and Tennessee. Now Lee asked for their return. Pickett's division had gone to North Carolina, and it, too, was returned to Lee. Eventually, by late April, he had built his forces back up to about 63,000, though in many ways it was still rather a shadow of what the Army of Northern Virginia once had been.

"Old Pete" Longstreet still headed the noble old I Corps, though until Pickett returned he had only the divisions of Joseph B. Kershaw and Charles W. Field. Richard S. "Baldy" Ewell still led the II Corps, carrying as it did the spiritual memory of its mighty Stonewall Jackson, now dead nearly a year. Ewell's health was not good since he lost a leg in action in 1862, and some feared that the "fight" that used to animate him had dwindled when he took corps command. But he had fighters under him with division leaders like Jubal Early, Edward Johnson, and Robert E. Rodes. And then there was the magnificent A.P. Hill at the head of his III Corps. He, too, suffered increasingly severe and disabling bouts of illness. Some thought them psychosomatic, induced by tension before battle, when the fact was that complications from venereal disease were slowly killing him. But when he fought, he could be a tiger in front of the divisions of Richard H. Anderson, Henry Heth, and Cadmus Wilcox. Then there was Lee's cavalry, still led by the boldest cavalier of them all, the brilliant – if erratic – Jeb Stuart. Wade Hampton, Fitzhugh Lee, and William H.F. Lee commanded his mounted divisions, every one of them a dangerously capable cavalryman.

Despite being outnumbered nearly two-to-one, Lee possessed a few advantages, chiefly his position on the south side of the Rapidan. Grant would have to cross to get to him, and that always gave the defender some edge. Lee knew the ground intimately; Grant and Meade did not. Indeed, he even entertained hopes of being able to strike an offensive blow at the Yankees, as he had the year before on almost this same ground at Chancellorsville. Should he have to stand on the defensive, his greatest asset would be the tangled growth of woodland and bush known locally as the Wilderness, an almost impenetrable wall of vegetation crossable only on a few roads, some of them barely more than paths. Lee could use this to hold off twice his numbers, he believed. Furthermore, if the armies became mired in this jungle, then Grant's heavy superiority in cavalry and artillery would be neutralized.

Grant decided inevitably to risk the march through the Wilderness, even though old hands with the Army of the Potomac tried to warn him that "you don't know Bobby Lee!"[1] He was not certain about either Lee's numbers or his positions, but as April waned and plans for his other armies' advances into Georgia and the Shenandoah approached execution, he could delay no longer. By about May 1 he made the final decision. On May 4 he would send the Army of the Potomac across the Rapidan and into the Wilderness.

The plan depended upon much, including an expectation that the Yankees could get through the Wilderness before the Confederates could stop them. If Grant's leading elements could make the seven miles to Germanna Ford and nearby Ely's Ford, get the pontoon bridges up, and get across before Lee reacted, the Wilderness lay barely more than six miles beyond. One stolen march, half a day's head start, would be all he would need.

The Wilderness itself lay immediately below the Rapidan, and stretched for miles along its south bank, extending several miles southward from the river. Only a few roads offered passage. The Orange Turnpike and the Orange Plank Road crossed it from west to east, converging near the Wilderness Church and then passing on to Chancellorsville. From the Germanna Ford the Germanna Plank Road extended down to Wilderness Tavern, beyond which it merged with the Brock Road. This, the Ely's Ford Road about two miles to the east, and a lesser track about a mile to the west, offered the only useful routes north to south. Almost everything else was thickets of second-growth oak and pine.

Just after midnight, in the first minutes of May 14, 1864, the Federals started their move.

By about 6 p.m. that day, the Army of the Potomac was well on its way. Warren held the important intersection near the Wilderness Tavern. Sedgwick was over the river and in position on his right, while Hancock had his corps in and around Chancellorsville. Burnside was on his way to Germanna Ford, and Lee had apparently been caught napping.

So it seemed. In fact, Lee anticipated that the foe would attempt such a crossing, and was already moving to counter it when Grant's legions left their camps. Still the Yankees had a good start on him, but their interpretations of his own movements were faulty, and the reconnaissance conducted that evening, especially by Wilson, was so flawed that they failed to discover that Ewell had moved his II Corps to within four miles of the V Corps on the Orange Turnpike by nightfall. As for Longstreet and Hill, Grant and Meade had no certain information of their whereabouts, though Grant took it for granted that by now Lee knew of his movements and would be speeding to meet him.

It had been a rushed day for the Confederate leader, to be sure. First certain intelligence of the Federal crossings came to him sometime before 9 a.m. He had Ewell in motion by noon. Hill started out even earlier, with much farther to go, and Longstreet moved shortly afterward. Though neither the I nor III Corps could be expected to reach the Wilderness on May 4, at least Ewell could come close enough to be available once Lee decided upon closer inspection just how he should react. Indeed, even as he rode with Hill toward the scene, Lee was formulating his plans based upon the limited information coming in to him from his cavalry outposts. Grant might be either attempting to reach Fredericksburg and move from there toward Richmond, or he might march through the Wilderness, then turn south and west and attempt to strike Lee's left, turning it and getting between the Confederates and Richmond. Either eventuality would be dire. It was not until well into the early hours of May 5 that Lee finally decided that Grant intended to march into and through the Wilderness, heading perhaps towards Spotsylvania Courthouse, and the decision buoyed his spirits. Grant would bog himself down just as Hooker had the year before, and when Lee ate breakfast that morning with an old friend, General A.L. Long, Long found him "in the best of spirits" and expecting to be able to repeat the victory at Chancellorsville, perhaps even inflicting greater damage on Grant than he had on Hooker.[2]

At the moment, however, Lee had to face some daunting statistics. The Federals had fully ten divisions in his front; he had just five at hand, and those understrength.

Worse, Longstreet could not be expected to be on the scene before nightfall, nor would Anderson from the III Corps. Hill's other two divisions could not get up before noon, and that left just Ewell and the II Corps for him to work with that day. Lee was too outmanned, with his army divided, even in the protective thickets of the Wilderness, to make a serious move against Meade on May 5, yet if he waited until the rest of his forces arrived, the Yankees might keep on marching and emerge in the open country below, ready to turn and strike his own flank that afternoon.

The best he could do was to send Ewell and Hill forward that afternoon in what amounted to a reconnaissance in force. He would give them orders not to bring on a general engagement, though any opportunity to delay the Federal march should not be passed by. Meanwhile he would wait for Longstreet and Anderson to come up on his own right flank, and on the morrow would use them to swing around the Yankee left, he hoped, and smash them if they did not get out of the Wilderness first. Daring as always, Lee sensed that the advantage of the ground might allow him to do what he felt he did best – take the offensive.

While Lee was making his decision, Grant and Meade arose on May 5 intent upon continuing their basic plan. Indeed, having set this in motion, Grant seems to have left most of the actual planning and detail to Meade, and he in turn left much of it to his staff, quite properly in both cases. Both of the infantry columns were to keep moving on their roads, Warren and Sedgwick moving south from Wilderness Tavern toward Parker's Store on the plank road, a distance of about three miles, and Hancock continuing on from Chancellorsville until he could turn southwest on the Catherine Furnace Road. This would bring him out of the Wilderness on a route headed toward Lee's left. If he got out of the woods, that is.

By 5 a.m. the troops were on the march, but within an hour Griffin reported to headquarters that he could see the forward elements of Ewell's corps moving toward him on the turnpike. Soon Griffin saw the Rebels go into infantry line and heard them start skirmishing. Meade himself arrived on the scene shortly after 7 a.m. and peremptorily ordered Warren to attack at once. Thus the march was halted almost without a shot being fired, something Lee might only have prayed for. Now, instead, the Federals themselves went into line of battle. At the same time, Meade ordered Hancock to halt his own march, in order that he did not inadvertently move out of supporting range. Ironically, even though Meade suspected that the Confederates might only want to delay his march, he stopped it himself now. Nevertheless, Grant accepted Meade's judgment, as he almost always accepted the judgment of a commander on the scene if he trusted him. "If any opportunity presents itself for pitching into a part of Lee's army," he wrote in a message to Meade, "do so." Grant did not know exactly where all of the Confederate army was just then, but he did believe that Lee could not have it all with him on the Orange Turnpike. This meant that, even with the terrain working against him, he would still have a great numerical advantage and might destroy a part of the enemy before the rest arrived.[3]

Unfortunately it took Warren some time to get his corps in line and ready for the attack, due in part to the general's own apprehension of acting before he was fully prepared, and also because of the terrain. In front of him was a maze of small streams, marshy bogs, thickets, and dense woods. Nowhere would his men be able to see more than a hundred yards or so to their front, except along the turnpike. Worse, during the agonizing minutes that it took Warren to get ready, word began to come in from Wilson's cavalry, farther south near Parker's Store, of action in the vicinity of the Chewning farm, action that soon resulted in Wilson being forced back. Before long it became apparent that the advance of Hill's columns was approaching on the plank road. Should the III Corps veterans get past the store, they would actually be barely a mile distant from Warren's exposed left flank as he was deployed to advance against Ewell.

This changed the situation at once. While the horsemen fought furiously to hold back Hill's advance, Grant personally arrived on the scene in Warren's rear, not at all pleased with the fact that more than two hours had passed and still Meade had not gotten the V Corps to attack. Now their flank was threatened. Grant knew that this was the time to make a major tactical change. He abandoned the original intent to march through the Wilderness, and instead ordered an immediate attack from each of Warren's divisions, supported by other units from Sedgwick's VI Corps. Some of Sedgwick's other units were directed to head for the plank road to hit Hill, and he sent orders to Hancock to hurry units of his II Corps along the Furnace Road to its intersection with the Brock Road, there to join the assault on Hill. In a few short minutes Grant's reaction to the threat transformed the campaign.

It still took some time for the Federals to mount their first assault, but when it came the Rebels found it "furious." In front of Ewell's column was Johnson's division. "Old Club Foot," as some of his men called General Edward Johnson, formed his four brigades at right angles to the turnpike not long before the Yankee wave hit them. When the antagonists joined, his line held except for John M. Jones' brigade of Virginians, who broke and ran for the rear, Jones himself taking a mortal wound as he tried gallantly to rally them. Happily, Early's division came up just as Johnson's line started to waver, around 1 p.m. At once both sides began to understand what fighting in this dense vegetation would be like. One Yankee described getting only "occasional glimpses of gray phantom-like forms."

As Early arrived on the scene, Joseph Bartlett's brigade of bluecoats were starting to swarm through the center of Johnson's line. Ewell sent the brigades of John B. Gordon and Junius Daniel to the right of the line, and in a swift counterattack they struck the flanks of the advancing Federal penetrating wave and turned it back. Indeed, Gordon pressed the Yankees so hotly that he pushed them back to their own starting point until he found himself on a line with the Federal front. Behind him, the field over which he had advanced caught fire from gun flashes, and soon the flames began to consume wounded and dead Federals just as Ewell's counterattack consumed Warren's advance. Soon the flames hit the cartridge boxes on the belts of the dead and dying, exploding them like volleys, tearing the bodies in half and leaving in their wake a scene from the *Inferno*. Men rushing to help the wounded could not find them in the choking smoke. Meanwhile, the flames, fanned by a stiff breeze, swept across the field like a wave, so that in a few minutes it had burned itself out, consuming all the dry grass and sputtering out in leaves and twigs at the forest edge. When the flames subsided, Blue and Gray returned to their work.

Finally Gordon and the others halted their counterattack, seeing Warren's line before them thoroughly demoralized and beaten back. In the breathing time given them, the battered Union veterans of V Corps regrouped, while Ewell turned his attention to readying himself for what he perceived as a threat to his left by Sedgwick's arriving VI Corps. "Baldy" was still heavily outnumbered, with but 13,500 men in line to face Warren's and Sedgwick's combined 39,000 or more.

By about 3 p.m. Grant was trying to get the army in control to send forward a general attack, and was largely directing affairs, having lost some confidence in Meade. Unfortunately, the terrible terrain, the unexpected check to Warren, and the miscarriage of orders doomed his efforts to achieve concert of motion. Instead, the offensive that Grant wanted rapidly slowed. He did not know for certain where Hancock was, and kept sending him orders to attack when, in fact, the II Corps was not yet on the field. In fact, it was 4 p.m. or afterward before Hancock had his corps in position across the plank road, facing Heth's Confederates before him. Even now, Hancock could only get two of his divisions – Birney's and Mott's – on the line, joined by Getty's division from the VI Corps. Heth had only four brigades facing him, but once again the terrain favored the defender, though he was outnumbered some 17,000 to 6,700.

Hancock's attack went in shortly after four o'clock, Getty taking the first fire from Heth's concentrated Confederates, and suffering for it. Despite their numerical superiority, the Yankees were handled badly by volley after volley from the well-placed Southerners. Getty soon had to call on Birney for more reinforcements, and the whole attack soon degenerated. Mott's units became almost bewildered as they tried to get into line through the tangled maze of growth. General Alexander Hays fell at the head of his brigade as volley met volley along the plank road. Hancock himself had to try to rally some of Mott's disorganized men as they raced to the rear, but by 5 p.m. or shortly afterward the attack had failed.

Undaunted, the combative Hancock struggled to renew the attack as his other divisions under Barlow and Gibbon reached the front. Warren, to his right, was extending his line to link with the II Corps, and Grant decided now that the major effort of the day should be Hancock's renewed advance, as he sent an additional division to assist. By about 6:30 Hancock was ready, though fighting had never entirely stopped during the interval since the last advance. By now the sun was setting over the smoke-blackened treetops, but the fury of the firing only grew as the Federals went in again. Hancock arranged his brigades so as to envelope Heth's line on both flanks. Sheer weight of numbers now threatened to overpower Heth and his veterans, badly battered already after their earlier fighting. It was a struggle for them just to hold on until nightfall could close the battle. Lee sent them two more brigades to help hold the line, but they were not enough, and two more were dispatched. It became almost a foot race to see who would arrive first – the relieving brigades, or the Yankees rushing through the brush to get around Heth's flanks. Almost miraculously, the Rebels got there in time. Around 7:30 Barlow's rush to get around Heth's right was met and stopped, and a similar move against Heth's left was stymied soon afterward. The Rebels might not be able to hold their position through the night, but at least they could hold on long enough for darkness to prevent any further exploitation by Hancock. And even as they struggled, the Confederates knew that Anderson and Longstreet were on the way and would be with the army on the morrow.

Over on the Federal right, Sedgwick's attempt to hit Ewell's left flank met with similar fate, though the Confederates halted him at considerable cost, including the mortal wounding of General Leroy Stafford commanding one of Johnson's brigades. They turned back Sedgwick's first assault by Horatio Wright's division, then counterattacked. In the end, the preponderance of Federal might pushed them back again, and there the fighting died down to a steady skirmishing while Grant shifted his attention to Hancock's grand assaults.

By 9 p.m. the fighting had settled to skirmishing all along the line. If either side held the upper hand, it was Grant, who still had massive uncommitted numbers, with Burnside on the way, and a good lodgment on the enemy right.

That night Grant, unwilling as ever to abandon a line of attack once commenced, decided that the massive assault that failed to materialize on May 5 should be attempted the next morning, now that almost all of the Army of the Potomac would be in position. He had intelligence that Longstreet still had not joined Lee, and knew that May 6 would be his best chance to strike a telling blow before "Old Pete" brought his I Corps to Lee's aid. He directed that at 5 a.m. Sedgwick would demonstrate to hold Ewell in position, while Hancock hammered once more around Hill's flank and Burnside and other elements drove through the gap now thinly filled between the two Rebel corps.

Nevertheless, as the first hints of dawn came on May 6, Ewell took the initiative by sending forward a modest-sized attack at 4:30 that took the Yankees quite by surprise. He did not have the manpower to make it a decisive strike, but it was enough to stun the enemy. Sedgwick and Warren sent forward a counterattack that saw most of the lost ground regained, but when they came up against "Old Club Foot" Johnson's breastworks, three successive charges came to an end at the muzzles of his guns. By this time, Hancock's attack had jumped off at 5 a.m., and Grant's plan for a massive offensive was well underway.

Sedgwick and Warren were supposed to play an essentially passive role for the rest of the day, though heavily engaged. Yet it did not work out as Grant had planned. Ewell held out sufficiently that he was able to lend a brigade to the fighting elsewhere on the line, which is exactly what Grant hoped to prevent. Worse, Longstreet was approaching the field as the sun rose, and was well within the sound of the guns when the grand attack jumped off. It would be now a race to see if the Yankees could press their advantage before they had to face the fresh I Corps.

Indeed, everything seemed to miscarry. Besides the V and VI Corps roles' coming to naught, the ever inept Burnside failed utterly in his part of the plan. With a wide gap still existing between Ewell and Hill, the IX Corps could have plunged through and cut Lee in half. Instead Burnside ran over ninety minutes late in getting his men into position, and even then brought only one division. Hancock's men were heavily engaged by that time and achieving dramatic gains against Hill's right flank. If Burnside could have attacked in force and in time, the Army of Northern Virginia might very probably have ceased to exist.

Hancock moved precisely at the appointed time and though encountering heavy resistance, soon saw that they would be able to push over Hill's weakened and outnumbered positions. The Federals struck like a storm on both the Confederate front and left flanks. "Our left flank rolled up as a sheet of paper would be rolled without power of resistance," a North Carolina colonel confessed. Between them Birney and Wadsworth swept over seven of eight defending brigades in their fronts as Hill's line simply collapsed. As Birney pursued, he gradually extended his own left until it overlapped what remained of Hill's right. Hit front, left, and right, at the same time, the III Corps turned in rout by 6 a.m. Lee and Hill were there to see it happen, and Lee at least was reported to have resorted to "rough" language in attempting to rally the men that few ever heard him use. Hancock drove the Confederates for nearly a mile along the plank road, and was so elated with his success that he exclaimed to one of Meade's officers that "we are driving them most beautifully . . . be-au-ti-fully."[4]

Unfortunately, the failure of Burnside soon took the euphoria from Hancock's spirits. There was worse to come. As elements of Hill's command streamed back on the plank road, they encountered the head of Kershaw's division. Longstreet had arrived. The news put resolution back into Hill's veterans, and before long, though routed, they formed ranks once more. Kershaw at once spread his command out on the south side of the plank road while Field came up on his left. Without stopping, Longstreet's tired veterans slammed into Hancock in a vicious assault that stopped the Federal attack in its tracks. Lee himself apparently attempted to lead Hood's old Texas Brigade into the fight, but was deterred by shouts of "Lee to the rear," and the apparent refusal of the men to go forward until their beloved commander took himself out of harm's way.

By 8 a.m. Hancock's advance had been brought to a halt, and Longstreet was pushing back his own right flank, while Wadsworth's Federals were being shoved back on the left, Wadsworth himself falling with a mortal wound. But Grant and Hancock were not discouraged yet. Grant sent one of Burnside's idle divisions to bolster the II Corps, and Hancock himself speedily worked to reform his battered corps and renew the attack. It was a valiant effort, but hampered by exhaustion, limited visibility, the timidity of Burnside and Gibbon, and a growing "fog of battle" that hereafter impeded almost every effort at decisive action. The Army of the Potomac simply was not reacting quickly and efficiently to orders, and the morale boost given the Confederates by Longstreet's arrival, with Anderson right behind him, swung the pendulum of initiative on the south end of the line to Lee. Indeed, sometime after 9 a.m. Longstreet started purposefully extending his own right around Hancock's left, and the II Corps had to look out for its own safety.

By 10 a.m. Grant had seen his whole plan thwarted. Consequently he ordered Sedgwick and Warren to halt their holding action against Ewell and start erecting defenses instead. He would send reinforcements to try to get Hancock moving again. But Lee, sensing a momentary advantage, was moving ahead of him now. He quickly sent what he could to strengthen Longstreet, who had held three brigades out of the heaviest fighting in order to use them as an offensive reserve. Now "Old Pete" shifted them to his right under cover of the heavy woods on a route previously reconnoitered. It was almost a repeat of Jackson's Chancellorsville maneuver, though in miniature. Federals detected fragments of the movement, but too late to do anything about it. The Rebels surged forward, yelling at the top of their lungs to magnify the impression of their numbers. They hit with terrible effect, for the Federals had not erected breast-works to protect their flank, and by 11:45 Longstreet was rolling up Birney's flank. Before long Hancock ordered him to withdraw. Providence almost gave the Yankees another chance when, in another repeat of Chancellorsville, an errant Confederate volley struck Longstreet and a party with him. General Micah Jenkins went down mortally wounded.

But now Lee intervened. Longstreet had been preparing another, more massive flank attack that he believed could achieve Hancock's rear and turn the whole tide of the battle. Lee now cancelled that movement, no doubt lacking confidence that it would succeed without Longstreet to manage it. Instead, in a desperate move reminiscent of the order for Pickett's charge at Gettysburg, Lee decided upon a major assault on Hancock's center. But at 4:15 the gray chieftain sent his men forward only to see the attack broken up without great difficulty by the II Corps veterans, and with appalling losses to the Rebels. It would be Lee's last open field infantry assault.

By the time Lee's attack failed, Grant had given up pursuing the battle further. The Wilderness and Robert E. Lee were too formidable as opponents. But unlike his predecessors, he was not going to turn around and give up the campaign. This indecisive fight was just a check, not a defeat. Even an early evening attack on Sedgwick's right flank by the brigade of the enterprising John B. Gordon – an attack that actually put Grant's right wing in near panic – came to nought. Grant simply sent more troops from elsewhere, and the reserves and darkness put an end to it.

They put an end to the Battle of the Wilderness as well. The armies entrenched and stared at each other the next day, but then Grant started the series of side-stepping flank marches that were to take him through Spotsylvania, to the North Anna, Cold Harbor, and eventually to Petersburg. Though he could not decisively defeat Lee in the field he forced the wily Confederate to dance to his tune until almost a year later the two great generals finally met in peace at Appomattox. Neither they nor their battered veterans ever forgot the horrors of fighting in the Wilderness. Nor did they forget the more than 17,000 casualties left behind by the Army of the Potomac, and the 8,700 or more of Lee's men who would not fight again. Their sacrifice had decided little. Lee could not stop Grant, and Grant could not yet destroy Lee. The final decision would have to wait for other fields. The Wilderness, in the end, like the ground that hosted the battle, was just a tangled, confused, and painful, stopping place along the way.

REFERENCES

1 Horace Porter, *Campaigning with Grant* (New York, 1897), p. 39.
2 A.L. Long, *Memoirs of Robert E. Lee* (New York, 1886), p. 327.
3 O.R., I, 34, pt. 2, p. 403.
4 Edward Steere, *The Wilderness Campaign* (Harrisburg, Pa, 1960), p. 330; Theodore Lyman, *Meade's Headquarters, 1863-1865* (Boston, 1922), p. 94.

XII
MOBILE BAY

The civil war was very much a family affair. More than a dozen sets of brothers became generals on one side or the other, and some families had a son on each side who reached high command. The Lees of Virginia produced four generals, as did the McCooks of Ohio. But no single family on either side so dominated the land war the way the sons of David Porter virtually defined the battle for control of the waters. Porter had been one of the young nation's first naval heroes, and he spawned a generation of seamen whose careers came to fruition just as North and South went to war. William Porter, though not well-liked and nicknamed "Dirty Bill" by associates, was an early influence in the gunboat engagements that won the upper Mississippi and the opening of the Tennessee and Cumberland rivers for Grant. His more brilliant brother David Dixon Porter became Grant's most dependable captain in the move down the Mississippi to take Vicksburg, and went on to distinction through the balance of the war, though like "Dirty Bill" he had a scheming, dark side that could turn against anyone who threatened his ambitions, including even yet another brother, the best "Porter" of them all – David Glasgow Farragut.

He was an orphan boy from Tennessee only a few years old when the first David Porter adopted him and took him to sea. There he quickly became a favorite, alternately admired and resented by the Porter stepbrothers who later followed their father into the navy. When the war came, some doubted his loyalty, especially since when on land he had made Virginia his home. But there was never a doubt about allegiance in his own mind, and less than a year after the start of the war he was the Union's premier naval hero after capturing New Orleans, exciting the admiration of all the North, and the jealousy of his step-brother David, who spent much of the rest of the war writing back-stabbing letters about Farragut to the Navy Department in Washington.

By 1863, Farragut was a rear admiral commanding the West Gulf Blockading Squadron, and charged with controlling the entire Gulf coastline of Texas and Louisiana. His task, on paper, was a simple one – to stop all blockade-running traffic into and out of Rebel ports. New Orleans was already safely in Yankee hands, thanks to Farragut, but there were a few other places where blockade-running traffic continued at a brisk clip as the sleek, fast steamers slipped through the cordon of Union warships. By January 22, 1864, when Farragut returned after a five-month absence , the most significant remaining rebel-held ports were Brownsville and Galveston in Texas, and Mobile, Alabama.[1]

Of them all, Mobile was the prize, and for a host of reasons. It provided a vital link in the Confederacy's fragile transportation network. At least twice, once before Stones River, and again prior to the Battle of Chickamauga, significant numbers of Rebel troops had been shifted from Mississippi to Tennessee, and the only way for them to go was by rail from Jackson to Mobile, and then up the Alabama River to Selma, to pick up the rails again to go on to Atlanta. Take Mobile, and that link was broken. Mobile was also a key to holding nearby Pensacola, Florida, and its navy yard just fifty miles east, which had only recently been retaken from the Rebels. Then, too, with Sherman expected to launch a drive for Atlanta in the spring, Mobile would be a vital point of origin for supply for Joseph E. Johnston's defending Confederates. Deny him that, and his only other seacoast link for receiving succor by rail would be Charleston, South Carolina, itself under threat. More than that, of course, by those same links, vital war materials coming through the blockade into Mobile could reach other parts of the South. Closing that port would help to starve the vital center of the Confederacy.

Mobile had been one of Farragut's objectives even before he was ordered north back in August 1863. Indeed, before leaving the Gulf he had left instructions on how an attack on the harbor should be carried out should the time and circumstances prove auspicious, but in his absence, nothing more could be done than to maintain fewer than a dozen warships patrolling off the harbor mouth. But by late December, disturbing intelligence came to Washington of a massive new ironclad, the *Tennessee*, being built by the Confederates to defend the bay. Worse, there were mounting reports that this ship and other lesser gunboats being built by the enemy intended to sally out of the bay to attack the blockading fleet, composed almost entirely of wooden vessels. After the experience of the C.S.S. *Virginia* virtually destroying two wooden warships at Hampton Roads on March 8, 1862, and only being prevented from wrecking more the next day by the arrival of the U.S.S. *Monitor*, Union naval authorities were understandably worried.[2]

Farragut was the man to send. He reached New Orleans and his flagship *Hartford* on January 22, and found a report there that largely confirmed what he had seen himself two days before when he steamed past Mobile and made a personal reconnaissance. In order to control Mobile Bay, he would first have to run a deadly gauntlet of firc. The entrance to the bay was a little more than half a mile wide, and guarded on the left, or west, by Fort Gaines on massive Dauphin Island. The main ship channel lay on the opposite side of the opening, and wooden pilings had been driven into the bottom extending out from Fort Gaines to force any traffic to run very close to the opposite side, right under the guns of massive Fort Morgan on Mobile Point. The fort mounted at least 48 cannon, 28 of them great monsters ranging from 10-inch seacoast mortars and columbiads to terrible imported British guns that threw shells weighing 160 pounds. Farragut had run past forts before, of course, and knew it could be done as he had done it on the Mississippi. However, he had never run a fleet past this kind of armament, nor right under the guns, at 1,000 feet or less – virtually point-blank range.

Should he get past the forts, he then would have to contend with the enemy vessels. Of the *Tennessee*, reports came in constantly, and though they varied, still they presented a picture of a dreadful adversary, with an iron ram, protected by at least six inches of ironcladding, and mounting four 10-inch smoothbores and two massive 7.5-inch rifles. Then there were its consorts, the steamers *Morgan* and *Gaines* and *Selma*, the ram *Baltic*, the ironclad *Tuscaloosa*, and a sister ship, the *Huntsville*. All told they mounted 47 cannon of varying description, and though they were all of the ersatz kind of armoring that was all the Confederacy could produce, still they were better protected than any of Farragut's vessels. In a battle, his fleet could throw more weight of iron, but against some of these ships it might not be effective.[3]

Farragut went to work preparing for an attack as soon as he arrived. Unlike others, he had no fears of the enemy attacking his blockading fleet, but he believed from the start that he needed ironclads of his own to neutralize the *Tennessee* and the other ships that his own vessels could not meet on equal terms. Unfortunately, he found it difficult to get Washington's attention as the opening of the spring overland campaigns approached. "I fear that I shall lead a life of idleness for a month or two," he lamented in February 1864, "as the Government appears to plan the campaigns, and Mobile does not appear to be included just yet." Meanwhile, "I shall have to content myself going along the coast and pestering all the people I can get at." By March he had some fourteen vessels off Mobile, but none of them other than the *Richmond* were truly powerful ships. "I am expecting ironclads from the North," he said sadly, "but God knows when they will arrive.' 'I only ask for two, and will go in with one." Alas, he would have a long wait.

Part of the problem was the absence of land forces, for any attack on Mobile to be effective it would have to be undertaken as a combined operation. Farragut could steam into the harbor past the forts any time he chose, but there would be little point. Even if he took out the enemy fleet, he could not batter down those forts. They must be attacked from their landward sides, with Farragut bombarding them from the water. Then the garrisons would be forced to capitulate. Unfortunately, he could not get Washington to assign even a few thousand to the task as every available man was sent to Grant or Sherman, or Nathaniel Banks' soon-to-be-launched expedition up the Red River of Louisiana. And so the long, weary months wore on. By May, with Banks' campaign a shambles, Sherman locked with Johnston in north Georgia and Grant and Lee battling through Spotsylvania and on to the North Anna River, the frustration really told on Farragut. "I have written to the Department time and again about the ironclads," he complained, "but it is of no use; they will listen to nothing until the fight is over at Richmond."[4]

It should have come as some little compensation to him to know that his opposite number in Mobile got little more out of his government, and for the same reasons. While all eyes focused on the epic battles in Virginia and Georgia, Major General Dabney Maury commanding land forces in and around Mobile, and Admiral Franklin Buchanan commanding its fleet, were almost entirely on their own. In February, Maury had about 10,000 of all arms scattered among his fort garrisons, but feared that they were barely more than half of what he needed. His counterpart Buchanan, however, faced a much more difficult situation. The enemy may have been afraid of him, but he knew the truth of the situation, one that ran throughout the Confederate Navy – not enough of everything, and poor quality to what there was.

A veteran of years of service in the US Navy and a friend of Farragut before the war, Buchanan was one of the South's few naval heroes, exclusively because of his command of the C.S.S. *Virginia* during her near-destruction of a Federal fleet in March '62. Badly wounded during the fight, and not a young man to start with, the Marylander remained a rugged, determined fighter, whose enemies through most of his Mobile Bay command were shortages. He worked constantly with the overburdened Naval Gun Foundry and Ordnance Works at Selma, Alabama, to produce the armor and guns for the *Tennessee* and the other vessels at his command. They could turn out no more than one cannon per week, the first one for the ironclad coming in mid-January 1864. The armament for each of his vessels had to be made specifically for its ship, for matters of weight, length and caliber could make a cannon suitable for one vessel quite unsuitable for another, all of which further slowed the manufacturing. Still, the *Tennessee*'s armament was almost complete by the end of January, and one of her lieutenants could boast that "she is a splendid vessel," though he feared an old hand "will almost swear about some of her arrangements." Buchanan would almost swear at his inability to get good officers. He had only two young lieutenants, no midshipmen, and only two "green" mates, a doctor, and a young inexperienced paymaster. "So we go," he lamented.[5]

Buchanan even had to procure his own propellers from Selma, and shells for the guns, though the demand for cannon was so great that Selma had no time to manufacture projectiles. Besides shortage of officers, Buchanan also had not nearly enough seamen for his fleet, and begged Maury to release to him any infantrymen who might have had riverboat experience. Army–navy rivalries arose, and only an order from the secretary of war at Richmond finally got Maury to turn loose the men Buchanan needed. Then came the cladding of the vessels with plates of iron, two inches thick and about 10 inches square, another time-consuming and laborious process. Also, it tended to make all of them very heavy and low in the water, especially the massive *Tennessee*. When that ship came down the Alabama River and tried to enter the harbor for the first time, it was found that she rode too low in the water to get over the sand bar at the river's mouth. Not until late May did Buchanan get her across. Meanwhile he kept his men busy, some of them being occupied with taking small copper barrels and filling them with gunpowder to make "torpedoes" – actually mines detonated either on contact, or else by an electrical spark sent from batteries on shore. During the spring and early summer, Confederate engineers placed these in several locations in the main ship channel to await any Yankee vessels that dared to enter.

Once equipped, not everyone shared Buchanan's optimism for his fleet. An officer on one of his vessels, the *Baltic*, complained to a friend that "between you and me, the *Baltic* is as rotten as punk, and is about as fit to go into action as a mud scow." The old admiral almost worked himself to death performing all the functions of midshipmen, lieutenants, on up to flag captain, in the absence of good officers. Every day he worked from dawn until 3 p.m. in his office, then made the rounds of the navy yard to see to the armoring of the *Nashville*, the building of "camels" to help float the *Tennessee* over the bar, the mounting of guns, stockpiling of ships' stores, and more. He even had hopes that a mysterious new "torpedo boat," designed by John P. Halligan and built at the Selma works, would be able to join him. Just thirty feet long, it held a crew of only five, and was powered by a very small and compact steam engine. But when it chose, the boat could submerge. Powered underwater by the crew turning a crank propeller, it could steal up to a vessel, attach a torpedo to the hull, set a timed fuze, then move away before the explosion. Perhaps thinking of the old myth of the monk who drove the reptiles from Ireland, its builders called it the *Saint Patrick*. It would never see action.[6]

By late June, one of the local army commanders believed that Buchanan looked "humbled and thoughtful" by the frustrations he had faced and the state of some of his ships. The *Baltic* was considered a waste, and others thought the *Nashville* a failure. By late July, the latter still did not have its armor cladding, and on the last day of the month Buchanan was still struggling to have a defective steering apparatus repaired, while relations with Maury remained icy. But time for preparations had run out.[7]

Through a spring and early summer as frustrating as Buchanan's, Farragut finally began to see his plans for an attack approach fruition. "I have long since given up all hopes in the Department of the Gulf," he wrote on June 13, in some excitement at the army's continued lack of interest in cooperating against Mobile and its forts. But at least his own strength grew gradually. And then, following the failure of Banks' campaign in Louisiana, he looked to others for army cooperation, and got it. Major General Edward R.S. Canby, commanding Federal forces at New Orleans, began gathering troops to send for the operation. He hoped to send almost 5,000, commanded by the gallant Gordon Granger of Chickamauga fame, and rapidly the general and the admiral evolved their plans. Finally, too, the long-awaited ironclads began to arrive. By June 1 the *Galena* appeared, an ungainly experimental model that still carried heavy armor. By the end of the month the monitors *Chickasaw* and the *Winnebago* came off Mobile, while the monitors *Manhattan* and *Tecumseh* were on their way.[8]

By the end of July Farragut had his attacking fleet almost intact. He was also getting up-to-date intelligence on enemy obstructions and torpedoes planted in the harbor. "Things appear to be looking better," Farragut confessed on July 15. As soon as the monitors all arrived, he would "take a look at Buchanan." Indeed, he believed that with the seas calm, the days long, and the weather excellent, Buchanan was even then passing up his golden opportunity to bring the *Tennessee* and the others out to attack the wooden fleet before the arrival of the ironclads. "If he won't visit me," said Farragut with typical mock humor, "I will have to visit him."

No later than July 18, Farragut formulated his attack plan, a variant of the tactic he used in running his fleet past Port Hudson the year before. He would take fourteen of his gunboats moving in a column two abreast, into the main channel and past the forts. The four monitors would steam alongside in a single file, between the rest of the fleet and Fort Morgan, acting partially as a screen, but chiefly with a view to turning due east past the fort, to attack the *Tennessee*, moored behind Mobile Point. Once past the forts, the rest of the gunboats would divide their attention between taking on the rest of Buchanan's fleet, and assisting the infantry landed on Dauphin Island to attack Ford Gaines.

During the last week of July, a flurry of orders issued from Farragut's headquarters aboard the flagship *Hartford*, as he awaited only the last of his two monitors and the troops steaming from New Orleans for the land attack. The soldiers, only 2,400 in the end, with Granger in command, left New Orleans on July 29 and arrived three days later. This left only the last monitors to arrive, and Farragut awaited anxiously for the *Tecumseh*, the last one due to come. He had expected her on August 1, and had planned to make his attack on August 3. Bitterly disappointed when he lost that opportunity due to her failure to show, he resolved to give her two more days to come, or else he would go without her. "When you do not take fortune at her offer," he said, "you must take her as you can find her." With or without that last ironclad, August 5 would be the day.[9]

Happily the *Tecumseh* arrived the next day, and Farragut could make the attack at full expected force. He landed Granger's troops on August 3, to give them two days to move up Dauphin Island and occupy the defenders of Fort Gaines. That would remove most of the pressure from one fort, leaving only Fort Morgan to worry about. Orders went out through the fleet. "Strip your vessels and prepare for the conflict," he said. All unnecessary spars and rigging must be brought down and stowed. Splinter nets must go up on the starboard side, showing that he expected the worst fire to be that from Fort Morgan, which would pass on their right. The nets were to catch bits of flying debris that shell explosions could turn into deadly missiles. The positions of the men at the wheels were to be barricaded to protect them from being hit while steering the vessels, and the ships' engines were to be given some cover by laying sandbags and chains on the decks above them, to inhibit plunging fire from the fort. Other chains were to be draped over the sides amidships to stop shots from enemy vessels from penetrating to the boilers and machinery. They would get as close as they could to the fort before opening fire, but when it opened on them, they would return fire immediately. And they must watch for the torpedoes, which were believed to be marked by a line of black bouys on the west side of the channel. There were no definite reports of torpedoes on the east side.

The *Brooklyn* would go in first, with the *Octarora* lashed to her port side. Behind them, left to right in pairs, would come: *Metacomet* and *Hartford; Port Royal* and *Richmond; Seminole* and *Lakawanna; Kennebec* and *Monongahela; Itasca* and *Ossipee;* and *Galena* and *Oneida.* On their right the monitors would go in with *Tecumseh* leading, followed by *Manhattan, Winnebago,* and *Chickasaw.*[10]

Farragut wanted to go in just as dawn was breaking and the flood tide's force would add to their speed. The night before everyone in the fleet knew what was coming. "God grant that we may have good luck," wrote a marine corps private aboard the *Hartford.*[11]

The boatswains called everyone out of their hammocks at 3 a.m. on August 5. By 5:30 the vessels were lashed together and with steam up, they began their run toward the mouth of the harbor under a dark and cloudy sky, a light breeze behind them. They moved slowly, the progress of the faster gunboats retarded by the heavy ironclads beside them. The Rebels in Fort Morgan first saw them about 6 a.m., and fifteen minutes later opened fire. The *Tecumseh,* last of the fleet to arrive, was the first to return fire. Well before the first of the Yankee vessels came close to the fort, Morgan's guns were delivering a rapid shelling, concentrating chiefly on the gunboats and ignoring the ironclads. Inside the harbor, orders immediately called all hands to quarters, and the *Tennessee* began to get up steam as its gun crews prepared their pieces.

Brooklyn drew the first fire, as Captain Alden, her commander, and his men expected they would. Indeed, this is why they virtually demanded of Farragut that their ship, and not his, should lead the line. They would not risk their commander, and he could not refuse them, especially viewing the fact that *Brooklyn* was the only ship that had a torpedo boom or "catcher" affixed in advance of her bow, expected to explode the devices harmlessly before they came in contact with the ship's sides. If the other vessels followed behind in line as ordered, *Brooklyn* would sweep a clean path for all of them. As soon as his guns came to bear on target, Alden returned fire with his starboard battery, firing grapeshot that appeared to nearly silence Fort Morgan's batteries for a time, by driving their gun crews below to safety.[12]

Then it happened. *Tecumseh*, leading the line of ironclads, got about 300 yards ahead of *Brooklyn*. In such a position, and moving to starboard of her, the monitor gained no advantage at all from the other ship's torpedo boom. She was only about 150 yards from the beach, having just passed the tip of Mobile Point, when she struck a torpedo directly amidships. The water rushed in in a torrent, and Captain T.A. Craven immediately ordered the crew to abandon ship. But there was no time. Only twenty-two men and officers managed to get out of the hatchway at the top of the turret. Craven himself stood at the foot of the ladder to safety about to climb, when he stepped aside to let one of the crewmen go first. That was the last man out. In helpless horror, the men on the rest of the leading vessels saw the *Tecumseh* simply roll over and go down, as one described it, "like a shot." With her went Captain Craven and the rest of the crew.[13]

Even as he watched in horror, Captain Alden saw that his own ship had somehow gotten alongside what appeared to be a line of other torpedo buoys, and at once he stopped advancing and started to back out of the presumed danger. This stalled the whole line of ships, and an impatient Farragut did not want to wait. Besides, while they stalled, the *Brooklyn* and *Hartford* were coming under a renewed and heavy fire from Fort Morgan. The admiral himself, to have a better view of the action, actually stood high in the rigging near the top of the flagship's main mast, reportedly lashed in place so that he would not fall to his death if wounded. It was a foolish way to expose himself, but it gave him a sight that few others could enjoy. "I witnessed the terrible effects of the enemy's shot and the good conduct of the men at their guns," he said with pride a week later, "and although no doubt their hearts sickened, as mine did, when their shipmates were struck down beside them, yet there was not a moment's hesitation to lay their comrades aside and spring again to their deadly work."

In an instant Farragut ordered *Hartford* to take the lead. He sent his ship steaming right between the buoys that had worried Alden. There is more of legend surrounding this event than any other episode in the entire story of the Civil War at sea. Farragut believed that the buoys did, indeed, mark torpedoes. Certainly the destruction of the *Tecumseh* showed them to be in the vicinity. But he also had intelligence suggesting that the devices may have been in place for longer than the assumed six months it took before water seepage or other causes inactivated them. It was worth the risk to get his attack going again. Exactly what he said in ordering the movement forward will never be known precisely, but from all accounts the meaning was clear. "Damn the torpedoes" was what he meant, and exactly what he proceeded to do.

It was about 7:50 when Farragut and the first ships got past the fort. Now they could see the Rebel fleet bearing down on them, the *Tennessee* coming from its moorings on the east, and the *Morgan, Selma* and *Gaines* directly ahead. Farragut ordered *Metacomet* to cast loose her lashing and go after *Selma. Morgan* and *Gaines* immediately made for the protection of Fort Morgan's guns, however, and the ships coming in behind Farragut were not quick enough at separating to go after them. As a result, *Morgan* escaped later that day, but the fire from Yankee ships succeeded in disabling the other vessel, forcing her crew to run her aground, where they would later destroy her to prevent capture.[14]

The *Metacomet* chased the *Selma* back up the bay, taking fire from the Confederate's stern gun, and giving it back for more than an hour, until at about 9:10 the Rebel vessel's wounded captain struck his colors and surrendered his vessel. Meanwhile, Farragut ordered the rest of his fleet, once safely past the guns of the fort, to come to anchor north of Dauphin Island and about a mile distant from Fort Gaines. And then, about 8:45, they saw the *Tennessee* steaming toward them, Buchanan in command.[15]

There had been no real close action thus far in the morning for the Rebel ironclad. Buchanan traded shots with the Yankee boats as they passed the fort, and hovered nearby apparently with the intention of ramming one or more if the opportunity presented itself, but the ponderous weight and inadequate engine of the ship made her too slow to maneuver competitively with the faster Federal ships. Buchanan tried first for the *Hartford*, seeing Farragut's flag flying over her. She evaded him, and so did the *Brooklyn*, and before long the Confederate admiral simply saw the enemy line of ships steam away from him, content to leave him behind while going after the easier marks of his other gunboats.

But old Franklin Buchanan was every bit as much a fighter as David Farragut. Shortly before 9 a.m., he turned his prow toward the anchoring fleet and asked for full steam from his engines. As they lumbered on their way toward battle, some of his seamen stood atop the iron-plated casemate of the vessel. "It looked to me that we were going into the jaws of Death," one young engineer, John C. O'Connell, wrote that night.

Farragut realized at once that Buchanan's intent was to ram the *Hartford* if he got the chance. Immediately he signaled to the remaining monitors and *Ossipee, Kennebec, Monongahela,* and *Lackawanna* to join the flagship in attacking not only with their guns, but also with their bows, hoping that by ramming they could bring Buchanan to a halt. *Monongahela* struck first, to no effect, and when *Lackawanna* rammed the ironclad she almost crushed in her own prow, without doing significant damage to the enemy. *Hartford* took the next turn, glancing alongside the *Tennessee* without inflicting injury, but then pouring a withering broadside into her iron sides as they passed. "It was the warmest place that I ever got into," a Rebel seaman recalled, and as the minutes wore on, it got worse.

Steaming around to the ironclad's port side, *Monongahela* rammed her once more, and then a 15-inch shot from *Manhattan* broke through the enemy's iron plating and almost penetrated to the interior of the ship. It was enough to send young O'Connell below with an iron splinter in his shoulder and more in his leg. Then another shot followed hard upon the first. Buchanan had ordered his executive officer, Commander

J.D. Johnston, to steer for Fort Morgan once more since the ship was taking on water, but Johnston found that the exposed steering chains that operated the rudder had been damaged and the *Tennessee* could not answer her helm. He went to report this to Buchanan, only to find that another shot, probably from *Manhattan*, had struck the aft gun port while a seaman tried to get the port stopper unjammed. The seaman was literally blown to pieces, another man took mortal wounds, and a fragment of shell or iron hit Buchanan in the leg. The admiral immediately ordered Johnston to take charge.

There was not much left to command. *Tennessee* could no longer steer. Then her smokestack was shot away, so reducing the necessary draft for the furnaces that Johnston could barely keep up steam to make headway. Though his men loaded the guns valiantly amid the din of Yankee iron exploding on the outside of their casemate, defective primers prevented most of the guns from firing, while the aft pivot gun could not fire at all thanks to all three of its port-stoppers being jammed shut by Yankee fire. The temperature inside the ship rose to 140[deg] or more, and then Johnston saw the enemy vessels crowd around and literally surround his ship. For the next half hour the Yankees poured a constant fire into the casemate shield, while Johnston rarely if ever returned fire at all. Then the *Ossipee* backed off to get up a full head of steam for a devastating ramming. Looking out at this, Johnston ran to Buchanan to ask if he should yield.

"Do the best you can, sir," answered the admiral, "and when all is done, surrender." Johnston returned to the gun deck, looked out to port, and saw the *Ossipee* bearing down on him. That was all he needed. He sent a white flag up the staff of the brave and battered *Tennessee*, though not quite in time for the charging *Ossipee* to slow down, and she struck a final, glancing blow that fortunately caused no further injury. By 10 a.m., the Battle of Mobile Bay was over.[16]

Almost immediately Farragut put the badly wounded Buchanan aboard a ship and sent him off to Pensacola with many of the other wounded from Union and Confederate ships alike. Buchanan's leg would be saved. All told, thanks to her heavy iron sheathing, *Tennessee* lost only two killed, and nine wounded. Aboard *Selma* another eight were killed or mortally wounded, and seven others injured. Thus total casualties in the Confederate fleet amounted to ten dead and sixteen wounded. By contrast, Farragut took much heavier losses, fifty-two killed and 170 wounded. Hardest hit was the *Hartford* with nearly a quarter of the losses, and the *Brooklyn* the same, being largely the losses suffered by fire from the fort. *Oneida* never got fairly into the fight, taking a shot from Fort Morgan that penetrated her boilers and left her helpless, dependent upon her consort *Galena* to tow her to safety. But none of these figures included the dreadful loss of life aboard the *Tecumseh*. For weeks afterward Farragut would be uncertain just how many men died in her, since no accurate monthly strength report had been filed recently. Yet almost certainly she took down with her at least ninety, including sixteen officers and seventy-four men.

The defeat of the Confederate fleet did not, of itself, take Mobile for the Union, but it made the rest possible. Granger took Fort Gaines three days later, and Fort Morgan fell on August 23 after a combined land and naval bombardment by Farragut and Granger. Though the city of Mobile itself remained in Confederate hands for several months to come, the loss of the bay put an end to the blockade trade into that port and the taking of the *Tennessee* virtually closed the book on Southern attempts to resist Yankee control of its coastal waters. Never again in this war would mighty ships do battle with mighty fortresses. Never again would ironclad and wooden warships challenge each other for supremacy in this war. Indeed, it would be one of the last fleet fights in all naval history conducted chiefly by wooden vessels. As such, it spelled more than just the end of one of the Confederacy's last sources of supply. While cinching the starvation even tighter around the South, Farragut's victory at Mobile Bay brought down the curtain on the age of wood and sail.

REFERENCES

1 US Navy Department, *Official Records of the Union and Confederate Navies in the War of the Rebellion* (Washington, 1906), Series I, Volume 21, p.53. Cited hereafter as *O.R.N.*

2 *Ibid.*, pp. 4, 12, 30-31.

3 *Ibid.*, pp. 35-36.

4 *Ibid.*, pp. 95, 121, 122, 141, 300.

5 *Ibid.*, pp. 859, 863, 871, 872, 878.

6 *Ibid.*, pp. 35, 748, 877-78, 886, 896-97, 902-903, 931.

7 *Ibid.*, pp. 903-904, 906, 909.

8 *Ibid.*, pp. 318, 332, 344.

9 *Ibid.*, pp. 378, 388, 400, 403.

10 *Ibid.*, pp. 397-98.

11 C. Carter Smith, ed., *Two Naval Journals: 1864* (Birmingham, Ala., 1964), p. 43.

12 *Ibid.*, pp. 417, 445; Smith, *Journals*, p. 5.

13 Smith, *Journals*, p. 43; *O.R.N.*, pp. 490-91.

14 *O.R.N.*, pp. 417, 419, 444.

15 *Ibid.*, pp. 442, 443.

16 *Ibid.*, pp. 418, 576-77, 580; Smith, Journals, p. 5.

XIII
NASHVILLE

Pity the poor Confederate Army of Tennessee. No army of the Civil War, not even the hard-luck Army of the Potomac, suffered under such a succession of sad and inadequate commanders. The statistics of its series of commanders is eloquent. Jefferson Davis created only seven full rank generals for field service during the war. The Army of Northern Virginia used only two of them during the entire course of the war, Lee alone commanding for three of the four war years. But this great army of the West went through no fewer than five. Its brightest hope was probably Albert Sidney Johnston, whose tenure was so brief and ill-starred that none then or later could say with certainty whether or not he might ever have realized his promise. Beauregard gave up any hope of victory at Shiloh, then abandoned his army weeks later, leaving it to its turbulent year and a half in the hands of the hated Braxton Bragg. Many thought that promise returned when Joseph E. Johnston at last replaced Bragg in December 1863, but the following campaign for Atlanta only revealed him to be the Johnston of old – timid, lacking in moral courage, and contentious. Where Bragg spent most of his time fighting his own generals, Johnston spent his falling back and fighting with Richmond. On July 17, 1864, after months of this behavior Davis quite rightly relieved him of his command. Quite wrongly, alas, he replaced him with the newest and youngest of the Confederacy's full generals, John Bell Hood.

That Davis could turn to Hood reveals just how desperate he was for a commander. He could not take Lee from Virginia. Bragg was out of the question. Davis himself so loathed Beauregard that he could not be considered, and the only other available full general, E. Kirby Smith, was already in command of a virtual empire west of the Mississippi and could not be spared. Davis might have looked toward someone like Hardee, but he had declined the army command once before, and now

Davis considered that refusal permanent. He needed someone who had the will for a fight, unlike Johnston who seemed only to avoid combat and give up ground. Of all the corps commanders with that army in the summer of 1864, only Hood seemed to have the spirit. The sad-eyed young Kentuckian, just turned thirty-three, also had the stomach for flattery and sycophancy. Recovering in Richmond from the loss of his leg at Chickamauga, he lost no opportunity to ingratiate himself with the president, and once back with his corps, he wrote frequently to Davis to complain of Johnston's hesitation. Finally fed up with the latter, Davis gave his army to Hood, along with promotion to the temporary grade of full general.

At least Hood did fight. He had the courage to use his army, but alas, not the brains. He was not a stupid man. Rather, he lacked the temperament or maturity for headquarters leadership. Removed from his proper position at the head of a division, Hood as a commander could not gain the respect of his corps commanders, and alienated many of the rank and file by intimating that they lacked the courage or fortitude to attack the foe. Certainly he gave them enough opportunity to practice, for he launched a series of offensives as soon as he took command of the army. Yet he also gave them ample cause to fear to attack, for his tactical plans were so fuzzy and undeveloped that time after time his men suffered terribly for it. Indeed, after assuming command, Hood lost every battle he fought, and in September had to give up Atlanta to Sherman to prevent losing his army with it.

Even then, however, the bold commander continued his aggressive tactics. Having lost Atlanta, Hood moved his army quickly north of the city to threaten Sherman's railroad communications back to Chattanooga. As a result, Sherman went after him with most of his army, and gradually they maneuvered their way back almost to Dalton, where the campaign for Atlanta began. Very nearly from the first, Sherman suspected that Hood might try to force him out of Georgia entirely by striking even beyond Chattanooga, to Nashville, and early on he assigned General George H. Thomas to take a division of the XIV Corps back to organize a defense for the Tennessee capital and its vital supply warehouses.

Hood, in fact, did not have very definite plans, one of the consistent drawbacks of his generalship. At first he hoped only to force Sherman to withdraw back to the Tennessee border, and there engage him in battle, perhaps with a view to driving the enemy out of Chattanooga. It seemed to work well at first, encouraging the Confederate commander to think in much bolder terms. Richmond had approved his initial plans. But now, by mid-October 1864, he realized that Sherman simply outnumbered him too overwhelmingly to allow for any hope of success in an attack. Besides, Sherman now began to indicate a disinclination to keep following him once they were in north Georgia. In fact, Sherman had decided not to pursue Hood any farther. The Federals still held Atlanta, and were still between Hood and Chattanooga. In fact, the confident Sherman chose now simply to pretend that Hood and his army did not exist. Sherman would turn his attention elsewhere and leave

Hood at his back. Thomas could take care of him if he posed any kind of threat. Meanwhile, Sherman would march toward Savannah and the sea.

Hood, too, realized that he had achieved nothing by his maneuver. Now he needed to do something far more significant if he was to achieve anything with his army before the winter came to close down operations. How long the idea gestated in his mind no one knows, but by the end of the second week of October his mind was set. He would take his army quickly across the northeastern corner of Alabama, up to the Tennessee River, cross it, and strike deep into middle Tennessee, driving toward Nashville. If he could meet and defeat Thomas and any others in his way, he could take Nashville with all its supplies, then continue his triumphant march into Kentucky, driving all the way to the Ohio River. Victorious there, he could then turn east, cross the Appalachians, and either join with Lee, or else strike the Yankee army besieging Petersburg from the rear. It was the sort of grandiose plan that only an immature commander could devise.

Unfortunately, Hood did not move quickly, even though he had himself made speed with one of the essentials of his plan. He moved out of Gadsden, Alabama, on October 22, reaching Tuscumbia nine days later. There he would cross the Tennessee River, but he lost a precious twenty days waiting for supplies that a better prepared commander would have had arranged in advance. Only on November 21 did the Army of Tennessee once more march northward and cross over the line into its name-sake state. What lay ahead of him was a hastily assembling variety of commands and commanders. Sherman had sent the IV Corps, under General David Stanley, and the XXIII Corps, led by General John Schofield, to Pulaski, Tennessee, sixty miles south of Nashville. Thomas, meanwhile, had three divisions of the XVI Corps on their way to him, and a host of small garrisons and posts throughout middle Tennessee to draw from. All told, including the force at Pulaski under the overall command of Schofield, he could look for about 60,000 men to meet Hood's 40,000 or more.[1]

Hood's line of march northward would take him several miles to the west of Pulaski, and Schofield at once saw the possibility that the enemy could get between him and Nashville. At once he pulled back toward Columbia, on the Duck River, where his own line of withdrawal and Hood's line of advance converged. It was a near thing, with Schofield just getting to the river crossing first on November 24. Hood's advance elements were there the same day, but it was three days before the entire Army of Tennessee arrived, and by then Schofield was too well entrenched for Hood to risk an attack.

Undaunted, however, and showing a return of the aggressiveness that he had lost for so long at Tuscumbia, Hood concluded to march east a few miles, cross the Duck, and then strike for Spring Hill, fifteen miles north of Columbia. If he got there first, he would once more have a chance to cut Schofield off from his line of retreat, and outnumbering the Federals by 40,000 to about 26,000, he could hope for a conclusive victory.

Once more it turned into a race as Schofield realized Hood's intentions and himself made for Spring Hill. Once again it came down to a whisker of a difference between survival and disaster for Schofield. On November 29 Hood himself led most of his army across the river and on the road for Spring Hill, coming in sight of it by mid-afternoon, with some 25,000 men at hand or nearby. In Spring Hill there were but 5,000 Yankees. But then came an afternoon and evening of mistakes, confusions, and poor coordinating command at many levels, most notably Hood himself. The result was that the attack was stopped when only fairly begun, and Schofield escaped. Hood would ever-after blame General Cheatham for the failure to catch the enemy. Uncharitably, he would also blame the army itself for being "unwilling to accept battle unless under the protection of breastworks." If the army felt that way, it was due more to Hood than anyone else, for his fruitless waste of men in his attacks around Atlanta.[2]

In the end, Schofield marched almost all of his army up the road to Spring Hill and beyond, within sight and sound of the waiting Rebels, and one of the most spectacular opportunities of the war went wasted. The next morning there was nothing for the Confederate to do but follow. About 3 p.m. that day, November 30, Hood's advance ran into Schofield, now positioned in and around the town of Franklin, and this time the two armies neither missed nor evaded each other. A ferocious battle ensued, lasting for five hours or more, and well after nightfall. If he needed any further proof of his error of thinking about the valor of his army, Hood here saw it disproved. With a fury that can only come from courage, his divisions hurled themselves at Schofield's lines time after time. To inspire the men, their generals risked themselves with absolute recklessness, and it took a heavy toll. Five fell killed or mortally wounded, among them the irreplaceable "Stonewall of the West," Patrick Cleburne. In no other battle of the war did either side suffer such a fearful loss of general officers. It gained nothing. Schofield held out, withdrawing toward Nashville during the night while Hood tried to reorganize his battered legions, intent on pressing on.

By now, Thomas was frantically assembling forces from all quarters to defend Nashville. The XVI Corps reinforcements arrived on December 1, joining the 10,000 infantry and 6,000 cavalry already there. Thomas armed clerks and carpenters and every customarily non-combatant soldier at his command in the quest to defend the city. Men returning from furlough, many of whom had gone North to vote in the recent election, arrived just in time to be commandeered, along with ambulatory hospital patients, and anyone else capable of holding a rifle. By the time all of Schofield's men reached Nashville, Thomas' whole force totaled close to 60,000.

Thomas gave them an improvised organization. Thomas J. Wood, the same general whose strict obedience to an order led to the rout at Chickamauga, now commanded the IV Corps and its three divisions. Schofield reverted to command of the two divisions of the XXIII Corps now with the army, while General A.J. Smith led the three divisions of the XVI Corps. Several brigades, including some black units, made up a Provisional Detachment under General James Steedman, and the old Nashville garrison, including a brigade from the old XX Corps and a scattering of other units, followed General John F. Miller. One of Grant's favorites, the young Major General James H. Wilson, commanded four small divisions of cavalry. Quite clearly, they would all have to fight well in defense, but in case of an offensive, Thomas would naturally turn to the old veterans in the three infantry corps.

Nashville sat on the south side of the Cumberland River, much of it within a bend in the stream. In the years since Federal occupation in early 1862, much work had been done in constructing fortifications and earthworks extending across the open side of the bend, while the river protected the city's back. Several roads led on to the city from the southward, most notably the Hillsborough Pike, the Granny White Pike a little more than a mile east of it, and the Franklin Pike about two miles further east. Thomas' actual communications with Sherman in Georgia were via yet more roads southeast of the city. It was a lot to cover defensively, even with 60,000, especially when many of them were untrained and inexperienced, convalescent, or even civilian.

Thomas went about it with characteristic deliberation. Never rash or impulsive, nor inspired, "Old Pap" as the men called him was, rather, rock solid, methodical, and unhurried. When he saw that Hood, now reduced to probably no more than 25,000 effectives, followed Schofield and then commenced setting up defensive lines around Nashville, Thomas had to know that all the advantages lay with the Federals. The trouble was, Thomas had only a few thousand troopers, and very few good mounts. Consequently, he decided to risk waiting until more cavalrymen and horses could reach him before mounting his attack.

This did not sit well with Washington, or with Grant, who never enjoyed a great fondness for Thomas in the first place. He especially feared that Hood would withdraw and get away if Thomas did not attack quickly. The day after Hood reached Nashville, Grant urged Thomas to attack, and on December 6 he sent a direct order to do so. Still Thomas delayed. "There is no better man to repel an attack," Grant said of "Old Pap," "but I fear he is too cautious ever to take the initiative." Others in Washington began to suggest to Grant that Schofield should replace Thomas. Still Grant continued his urging until December 9, when he finally ordered Thomas to turn over his command. But by then a terrible freezing rain storm had blanketed the Nashville area under a virtual sheet of slippery ice, making any movement impossible. Grant relented, recalling his order, but two days later told Thomas to attack, ice or no ice. Soon thereafter he dispatched Major General John A. Logan to Nashville with orders to take command from Thomas if the army had not attacked by the time he arrived.[3]

As he prepared for his offensive, Thomas arrayed his forces all across his front. On his left, at the eastern line of defenses, he placed Steedman. Schofield and his corps came next, stretching toward the center, where Schofield's right met Wood's left. At Wood's position the line turned back to the right, taken up by Smith's corps and then, on the extreme right, by Wilson's cavalry positioned alongside the Cumberland. Having taken his time to prepare for an attack, Thomas devoted considerable thought to his precise plan for the offensive, and when he met with his commanders on December 14, everything had been as well thought out as any battleplan of the war. It was quite simple. Along Hood's entire front, the Federals were to make demonstrations in force to pin down the enemy infantry. Then Smith and Wood would deliver a major hammer blow against Hood's left in their front. At the same time, Wilson would attack with his cavalry. Meanwhile, Steedman was to make a secondary attack on Hood's right, which Thomas felt might have been weakened in the last few days. Schofield would remain in reserve, ready to exploit any advantages, and also perhaps as punishment for being Grant's presumed pet. They would advance on the next day, December 15.

Thomas had little idea of the true plight of Hood and his army. Running out of supplies, short of men and material, Hood had led the Army of Tennessee to Nashville because he simply did not know of anything else to do. Thoughts of Kentucky were out of the question now, yet to retreat back into Georgia would mean moving toward Sherman, with Thomas in his rear. Hood never had many practical strategic ideas, and now he was fresh out of any of them. He could only think to wait here at Nashville and hope for reinforcements from faraway Texas, and hope that he could repel a Yankee attack. With this in mind, he put his men to work building a line of defenses and redoubts. Despite the bitter cold, in spite of poor clothing, lack of shoes and tools, the poor Confederates struggled with the cold earth to erect their works.

Hood's army reflected a lot of changes since its last winter battle in Tennessee a year before, even since Atlanta. All of the corps commanders were new since Chattanooga. The erratic Cheatham now led one corps, composed of three divisions, two of which had lost their commanders at Franklin – Cleburne and John C. Brown. Only Breckinridge's old division had the same general it had a year before – William B. Bate. Hood placed Cheatham on the right of his line, between the Franklin Pike and the Murfreesboro Pike. Thinly manned, Cheatham's works could not quite reach to the banks of the Cumberland.

On Cheatham's left sat the three divisions of Lieutenant General Stephen D. Lee's corps, under Generals Edward Johnson, Carter Stevenson, and Henry Clayton. Lee's line extended to the left to the Granny White Pike, and both he and Cheatham took position just below Brown's Creek, which flowed left to right across their front and emptied into the Cumberland. The creek in front of them, and the line of low hills on which they erected their works, gave the outnumbered Confederates at least some advantage of ground. Meanwhile, to Lee's left sat the corps of Lieutenant General Alexander P. Stewart, three divisions led by William W. Loring, Samuel G. French, and Edward C. Walthall. Stewart extended Lee's line from the Granny White Pike to the Hillsboro Pike, then angled southward along the latter, his position protected by a series of earthwork redoubts constructed along the pike. None of them were finished as yet but at least they afforded some protection. But a three-mile gap existed between Stewart's left and the Cumberland River to the west of Nashville, and all Hood had to fill it was one division and one brigade of cavalry – a woefully inadequate force for such a task.

Indeed, both Hood's army organization as well as his dispositions revealed the pitiful weakness of the Army of Tennessee. Through intrigue and politics, transfer, or death, gone now were the old experienced corps commanders like Hardee, D.H. Hill, Breckinridge, and others. Cheatham had been at the head of his corps for only two months. Lee took over Hood's old corps in July when Hood took command of the army. Stewart was the senior in corps command, having replaced Polk after his death in June. As for the divisions under them, it was all a mish-mash. On Cheatham's three divisions, only one, Cleburne's old command, had the same organization as a year before. Brown's and Bate's divisions were a patchwork of brigades formed out of Breckinridge's and Hardee's old corps. Lee's corps retained far more integrity of organization, Stevenson's and Clayton's divisions being intact since Chattanooga, and Johnson's almost so. Polk's old corps, now under Stewart, had only rejoined the army during the previous campaign, and was itself reconstituted from several other commands. Worse, none of the corps commanders and only two of the nine division leaders had exercised that level of command for a full year. The war and its own internal strife had battered the high command of the army to pieces. Regiments were placed in brigades with others they did not know, men and officers no longer had the old bonds of long service together, and they were all tired, cold, and hungry. Worse, they were in front of Nashville with nothing to gain, spread too thin to hold their line, and led by a general in whom they had only shaky confidence. That Hood himself realized his weakness is evident in the works he had them build. That line of redoubts running south along the Hillsboro Pike was his tacit admission that he could not hold the left of his line with the great gap covered only by his cavalry. He expected the enemy to seek his weakness and strike him there.

Thomas had seen the same things, and would oblige Hood if he could. "Old Pap" arose early on December 15. Happily a modest thaw in the weather had come. The ice was gone and the ground, though mired and boggy, was at least passable. Moreover, with the change in temperature, a fog blanketed most of the field covering the Federal's early movements. Still, the Rebels certainly heard the shrill bugles that called their foes into line well before dawn, and there was no concealing the clank and bustle of tens of thousands of men, animals, vehicles and guns, moving into position.

Thomas intended to move Steedman's command forward against Hood's right flank first. In the predawn fog, Steedman formed his men and moved them into position. Off to his right, others moved as well, most of Thomas' army leaving their works and marching out to the positions from which they would launch their demonstrations and attacks. It took time in the mist, but by about 8 a.m., they were all ready.

Across the way, the Confederates were up, too, and back at work on their redoubts. Lee was even then sending a note to Stewart warning that "I think you may look out for a demonstration on your left today." Whether it was precognition or simple military instinct, Lee could not have been more correct. Within minutes he heard the sound of Steedman's guns as the battle commenced.[4]

It went well for Steedman at first. His skirmishers pushed forward and rather handily drove in the Confederate outposts. But then the Federals came up against the first of the earthworks, and their initial assault, though 4,300 strong, was driven back in considerable disorder, and successive charges against Cheatham's line fared no better. Shortly before noon Steedman relaxed his pressure, having he hoped, achieved his goal of diverting Hood's attention away from the main Federal attack shortly scheduled to strike Stewart.

It did not work. Indeed, Hood anticipated what was coming at least two days before, and had already reinforced his cavalry covering the ground from the Hillsboro Pike to the Cumberland. The actual Yankee attempt to get around his flank launched shortly after Steedman's demonstration began. Wilson had about 12,000 cavalrymen, a quarter of them dismounted, and his orders were to move out of the works and strike almost straight south, keeping just in the right of General Smith's XVI Corps infantry, which would move directly against Stewart's lines along the Hillsboro Pike. Unfortunately, the fog and some confusion among Smith's troops delayed the movement until about 10 a.m., but once it started, it operated perfectly. Smith pivoted his left on Wood's right, and swung his corps like a door on a hinge, sweeping across the muddy ground to strike Stewart. Meanwhile, Wilson moved straight against the pitiful Rebel commands trying to hold that three-mile gap between Stewart and the river. With only a tiny division of cavalry – in fact a mere seven regiments – and a single infantry brigade with only the strength of an undersized regiment, to contend with, Wilson met virtually no opposition worthy of the name.

The Yankee troopers drove the foe straight back from them, and incidentally, further away from the rest of Hood's army. Then they moved for Stewart. No one hurried. Thomas' plans had been deliberate and meticulous, and he instilled this same sense in his subordinates. It was as if they had a wounded bull tethered. There was no need to rush. Rather, they would move slowly and decisively, in order that all their blows might tell, and the destruction of the trapped foe would be complete.

The first of Stewart's works came under fire shortly after the advance began. Smith brought up artillery and started to pound the redoubt prior to a successful infantry charge. By about 12:30, Wood started to bring his right-most brigades into the action as well, and they easily swept over the advanced Rebel defenses. Then the same technique was applied to each of the other redoubts in turn, artillery barrage first, then infantry assault to follow. Redoubt Number 5 fell, at the very left end of Stewart's line on the Hillsboro Pike. Then they turned northward, up the pike to Redoubt Number 4, and though it gave them more resistance, still it, too, fell. Now, as previously ordered, Schofield and his corps in reserve marched across Smith's rear to take position on the extreme right of the Federal army. This put them in position to press Hood's collapsing left even harder, while also freeing Wilson's cavalry to strike out farther south then sweep up and take Hood in the rear. It was all going according to plan.

Now with the two redoubts taken, Smith came up against the infantry of Walthall's division placed behind a stone wall that ran nearly 1,000 yards along the Hillsboro Pike. The Federals shelled them mercilessly, then launched a massive infantry assault that drove its way across the pike, moving northward toward the rear of the balance of Stewart's corps and Lee's. Though Stewart tried valiantly to establish a line to meet the oncoming enemy, the attempt proved fruitless, and Stewart and Lee only barely got their remaining divisions out in time before the Federals swept everything before them. By late in the afternoon, the withdrawing Confederate left had pulled back to the Granny White Pike, almost a mile from where it began the day. Only nightfall prevented Schofield and Smith from pressing it even farther.

Hood faced a terrible predicament. His left had all but collapsed, and his right had been battered somewhat early in the day. Wood did advance against his center in the afternoon, but it was a half-hearted attempt that Hood ought to have read as a demonstration and nothing more. Now with darkness descending over the field, he faced his army's greatest crisis since Missionary Ridge. His line was too long, even after the day's contractions. He pulled part of Cheatham's corps out of line on the right and moved it to the far left, and later in the evening issued orders for the balance to follow. This corps, still fresh and relatively unblooded, would hold his left now. Hood set it up along the Granny White Pike, with Bate's division placed on an eminence called Shy's Hill, somewhat in advance of the pike. The remnant of Stewart's corps was pulled back almost a mile from its position in the center, to form a new center extending from Granny White almost to the Franklin Pike, and there Lee was ordered to put his corps in position to hold the right flank, anchored on Peach Orchard Hill. When the cavalry finally succeeded in rejoining the main army that night, Hood put it on Cheatham's left to help hold the Granny White Pike, Cheatham's only available line of retreat. Lee and Stewart, in case of disaster, were to withdraw on the Franklin Pike.

Of course, the disaster was already upon them, and it was Hood. Having come this far with nothing to accomplish, he now compounded his folly by refusing to see that his army was in mortal danger of being not just beaten, but destroyed. The only reasonable course open to him was to get out during the night. By swift marching and hard rearguard fighting, he might have gotten the army back to safety south of the Tennessee, though his utter lack of cavalry, and Wilson's 9,000 mounted troopers operating at will on his flank and rear, might have made even that impossible. Instead, Hood doomed his army by deciding to remain for another day.

Thomas, too, had much on his mind that night. He wired Washington of the day's events, receiving in return thanks from the War Department and from Grant, who realized that now Logan would not have to supersede "Old Pap." "Push the enemy now," said Grant, "and give him no rest until he is entirely destroyed."[5]

It almost could not have gone better for the Yankees. The advance began at about 6 a.m. as Wood and Steedman moved into the works abandoned by the enemy the night before. Over on the Federal right, Schofield skirmished briskly with Cheatham throughout the morning while the other Federal forces moved forward, but by noon no actual engagement had yet erupted. Once again, Thomas took his time. As the afternoon began, Thomas personally called at all points along his line, making certain that everything was in place as he wished. Meanwhile, throughout the morning he kept up an almost constant artillery bombardment of the whole Rebel line, but concentrating especially on Shy's Hill, where Bate's position formed not only a corner of the Rebel line, but a salient at that.

Once more Thomas ordered demonstrations against Hood's right. Wood sent several strong feints against Lee's position on Peach Orchard Hill, and finally launched a four-brigade attack that the defenders barely beat back. But not before Lee sent Hood a plea for reinforcements. The army commander faced a terrible choice. There was no serious activity in front of Cheatham other than skirmishing. He could pull troops from there to support Lee, but what if Thomas then attacked Cheatham? Of course, it was exactly what "Old Pap" had in mind. At 2 p.m. Hood sent one of Cheatham's divisions to Lee, only to find that by the time it arrived, Wood's attack had been beaten back. Consequently, about 3:30 Hood sent it on its way back across the two miles to its original position. Before they could return, however, Schofield and Wilson finally struck.

The Yankee cavalryman, with his dismounted troopers, ran right around the left flank of Cheatham's line and started to deliver an enfilading fire into the rear of the Confederate line. At the same time, Schofield attacked across a broad front, while Smith struck due south with part of his corps, hitting Shy's Hill. The Rebels under the valiant General Bate were caught in a hopeless predicament. Smith in their front right, Schofield on the front and left, and Wilson in their rear. Wilson's cutting of the Granny White Pike eliminated their only direct line of retreat. If the enemy pushed on to the Franklin Pike, they would have no way out at all.

Seeing this, Bate's old veterans did not have the will to put up the kind of resistance normally expected of these seasoned fighters. Instead, they began to break by pairs and groups, racing for the safety of the Franklin Pike. Others tried valiantly to hold out, but to no avail. Smith broke through to the right of Shy's Hill, and Wilson swept up from the south. Bate's division simply all but vanished. Then the smell of victory swept over to the rest of Smith's corps facing Stewart. Seeing the triumph to their right, they rushed forward without orders. Seeing the debacle on their left, Stewart's corps did not try to stand, but almost as one man got up and ran for safety "in the wildest disorder and confusion." Then the panic spread to Lee's corps on the

Confederate right. Some tried to hold out, but the Yankee attackers penetrated the lines so quickly that Johnson's division was cut off and virtually swallowed. Those who could turned to join the fleeing horde on the Franklin Pike.[6]

Only a heroic rearguard action by one staunch brigade managed to hold a position just east of the Granny White Pike long enough for Cheatham to get most of the remainder of his corps past and over to the Franklin Pike. Others managed to cover Lee and Stewart's withdrawal, and before long some modest order re-emerged out of the chaos of the day's fight. But it was clear that this army was terribly beaten, and still in mortal danger. All that saved it was a determined stand by Hood's pitiful little cavalry command. It managed to stall Wilson's advance long enough to prevent him from cutting off all routes of escape. Had this dramatic effort failed, Hood would have been surrounded.

Now on the frantic flight back toward Franklin, Lee covered the retreat, and did so skilfully, while Hood sat that night in his tent alternately crying and pulling his hair with his one good hand. Already the irrepressible soldier wit of Johnny Reb was re-emerging from the bitterness of defeat, and during the terrible days that followed, as the army continued its retreat, boys sang a version of the "Yellow Rose of Texas" that ended with the lines:

You may talk about your Beauregard
   and sing of General Lee,
But the gallant Hood of Texas played hell
   in Tennessee.[7]

"Played hell" he had, indeed. Even though he managed to get his army back to the Tennessee, the march was one long rearguard action, made the worse by the intense cold, the lack of food, and for many Rebels an absence even of shoes. For years afterwards men would tell of bloody footprints on the frozen ground. They reached the river on Christmas and crossed the next day, then marched for their ultimate destination at Tupelo, Mississippi. The next day Thomas abandoned the pursuit. Of the nearly 70,000 men at his command, Thomas had actually used about 50,000, and suffered losses that were almost negligible – a mere 387 killed, 2,562 wounded, and 112 missing. Against this total of just 3,061 Yankee casualties, Hood's losses were staggering in proportion. He had no more than 24,000 of all arms at hand. In the aftermath of the battle, he and his commanders were so disorganized that they never compiled or filed reports of their losses. But Thomas recorded at least 4,462 Rebel prisoners taken, including three generals, and fifty pieces of artillery. Killed and wounded can only be guessed at, but Hood's overall loss must have been high, for three weeks later the army mustered only 15,000 men. Thus Hood's killed and wounded must have come to nearly 5,500, and his loss overall amounted to nearly forty percent of his army.[8]

In later years extravagant claims would be made about the Battle of Nashville: that it was perfectly planned and executed – which it was not; that it destroyed the Army of Tennessee forever – which it did not; and even that it was *the* decisive battle of the Civil War, which is patently absurd.[9] The real war between the Appalachians and the Mississippi had been over since the fall of Atlanta, awaiting only Confederate realization of the fact.

Nashville, however, did decide the fate of John B. Hood. Humiliated, he asked to be relieved in January, and thereafter saw no active service. The army command then went for a time to Richard Taylor, but very soon Lee's and Cheatham's corps were sent to Georgia to be joined with a command under Hardee. Together they reconstituted the Army of Tennessee once more, and left with no other alternative, President Davis once again put Joseph E. Johnston at its head. Less than four months later, with Johnston commanding, and with Beauregard and Bragg in attendance, it would at last surrender, surrounded by the ghosts, living and dead, of the commanders who had been so much a part of its infrequent triumph and its almost continual turmoil. Of its four commanders still living, only Hood was not there.

REFERENCES

1 Thomas R. Hay, *Hood's Tennessee Campaign* (New York, 1929), pp. 77-78.
2 John B. Hood, *Advance and Retreat* (New Orleans, 1880), p. 290.
3 *O.R.*, I, 45, part 2, p. 96.
4 *Ibid.*, p. 691.
5 *Ibid.*, p. 195.
6 *Ibid.*, pp. 439, 698.
7 Sam R. Watkins, *Co. Aytch* (Nashville, 1882), p. 229.
8 Hay, *Nashville*, pp. 179-80.
9 Stanley F. Horn, *The Decisive Battle of Nashville* (Knoxville, Tenn., 1956), pp. vi-vii.

EPILOGUE

One of the great errors made by even the greatest of commanders in this war was the notion that there could be such a thing as one, great, decisive battle. It was an obsolete notion, applicable perhaps in the time of Napoleon, but not to a massive conflict on the scale of this one. Individual battles and campaigns may have had decisive influences on the course of the war, but no one engagement could end it, short of actual extermination of one or the other of the participants involved.

And thus it was that the conflict wore on even after such seemingly climactic contests as Gettysburg and Nashville. Indeed, for Grant and Lee, their first meeting in Virginia in May 1864 was only to be the beginning of a year-long confrontation, one that could hardly have disappointed any of those who always wondered what would happen when the Gray chieftain met the Yankee juggernaut. Both men were accustomed to taking chances, both were conditioned to expect victory.

Following the inconclusive meeting in the Wilderness, Grant forced Lee to fall back to Spotsylvania, presaging the approach he would take for fully a month, seeking always to turn Lee's flank and get between him and Richmond. If he succeeded, all was good. If he did not, it could only be because Lee fell back before him to protect his lines of communication. Thus, either way, Grant emerged the victor strategically, if not tactically. Thus their dance of death undulated steadily southward: Spotsylvania, The North Anna River, The South Anna. May passed away, with the armies around Cold Harbor, near where Lee and McClellan had met two years before during the Peninsula Campaign. Here Lee finally stopped Grant cold for the first time. After several days of indecisive skirmishing, Grant launched a massive assault on June 3 that he later acknowledged as the greatest blunder of his career. He sent whole divisions forward in a frontal assault against Lee's entrenched positions, despite Grant's own career-long penchant for avoiding such unsophisticated sledge-hammer tactics. The result was completely disastrous, with thousands killed and wounded in a single hour of combat for no gain at all.

Yet nothing ever deterred Grant from his greater purpose. Stymied at Cold Harbor, with Lee securely between him and Richmond, Grant conceived one of the most daring and skillfully executed movements of the war. Completely fooling Lee, he pulled the Army of the Potomac out of its lines, marched it east and south of Lee, and crossed it over the James River. Lee only discovered what had happened more than a day later, when Grant was moving against Petersburg, south of Richmond. If he took that fortified city, he would have virtually all of the enemy capital's rail links with the rest of the Confederacy at his mercy, a back door to Richmond, barely twenty miles away, and Lee in a position where he had nowhere to retreat to. But subordinates bungled the attack. Stout resistance by a scratch force led by Beauregard, and Lee's hurried reinforcements, saved Petersburg through tense days of assault. By then, surprise was gone, and Lee moved most of his army into the fortifications surrounding the city. A distressed Grant realized that he might have another siege on his hands, and when a massive assault launched on July 30 failed to achieve its purpose, he admitted that he had no alternative but to besiege the Confederates. The battered Army of the Potomac, after three months of almost daily fighting, was too weary to do more.

But if Grant was tied down, Sherman certainly was not. Following the capture of Atlanta in September, he decided in the end not to bother about Hood, but to strike out across country through Georgia. His goal was to cut the heart out of this breadbasket of the Confederacy, sever rail lines, destroy industry, and drive to Savannah and the Atlantic. Taking Savannah would deny the South yet another of its ports, and virtually cut off Florida and Georgia from the upper South. There was little to resist him, though the gallant Hardee used what local defense forces he could muster to slow the Yankee advance. Nevertheless, by Christmas 1864, Sherman could wire Lincoln that Savannah was in Union hands.

That done, "Uncle Billy" Sherman turned north, his goal now to drive through South Carolina, ravage its resources for continuing the war, and disperse or destroy the remnants of the enemy left before him. In January Hardee was joined by the corps of Stewart and Cheatham, all once more under the command of Joseph E. Johnston. In the ensuing Campaign of the Carolinas, Johnston futilely attempted to stop Sherman. By the time they met in the one and only real battle of the campaign, at Bentonville, North Carolina, in March 1865, it was obvious that Sherman could go where he pleased and do what he wished. The only hope for the Confederacy in the East now was for Johnston to evade Sherman and march north, while Lee broke out of Petersburg and moved south. If they could link their forces, they would still have a considerable army of 60,000 or more, and might hope to defeat first Sherman, then turn and drive back Grant and Meade's Army of the Potomac.

The impending fall of Petersburg on April 1, 1865, forced Lee to prepare for such a move. While the government evacuated Richmond, he put his proud old Army of Northern Virginia on the road to join Johnston. Grant though was too numerous, and his cavalry, now led by Sheridan, kept getting ahead of the Rebels, forcing them always to go farther west before they could turn south. Finally on April 8, when Lee camped in and around Appomattox Courthouse, he saw the glow from Yankee campfires on all sides of him. He could go no further. The next day, in the parlor of the home of Wilmer McLean, who had left his house at Manassas in 1861 in order to get away from the war, the two generals met. The peace that came of their meeting started the slow process of bringing the war to an end.

Sherman and Johnston met next, on April 26. After several days of negotiations, this time involving both Davis' fleeing government, and the Union War Department in Washington, Johnston, too, surrendered. His capitulation would have been easier had it not been for one of the last casualties of the war. Twelve days earlier, President Abraham Lincoln went to the theater, never to return.

There were still other armies, of course. In May Richard Taylor surrendered the last of the Rebel armies east of the Mississippi. The next month the trans-Mississippi army of Kirby Smith was surrendered in New Orleans. Perhaps the last surrender or organized troops came on June 23, when Confederate Indian cavalry gave up out west of the great river. Yet it was not until many months later, in November, that the last of the surrenders came, when the commerce raider C.S.S. *Shenandoah*, cut off from news and unaware of the collapse of the cause, finally surrendered itself to British authorities in Liverpool.

It took a long time for Jefferson Davis and some of his advisors to admit to themselves that it was all over. Throughout their long flight south from Richmond, they continued to envision marshaling their remaining forces to continue the fight elsewhere, at first, in the Carolinas, then after Johnston surrendered, off in southern Alabama. Taylor's surrender made that obsolete, and even as he was captured in Georgia on May 10, Davis was hoping to reach the trans-Mississippi and Kirby Smith, to continue the fight, as long as there was one Southerner with a weapon in his hands, reasoned Davis, the fight could go on.

In the end, he even considered sending the disbanded men from the armies into the hills to continue the conflict on guerrilla terms. Happily, such a form of war, which inevitably must have degenerated into something ignoble compared to the heroic stand made by the Confederate armies, never came to pass. Generals and soldiers alike admitted that it was all over, and Davis finally had no choice.

It had all been more than trauma enough for the Union, which hereafter ceased to be called that in preference for United States. Secession had been tested and failed, and where the former implied unity by consent, the latter clearly proclaimed ineradicable nationhood. It was fitting, considering what bound North and South together as a result of the war. There was all the suffering they had endured, the hardship and privation. There was all the heroism and sacrifice they displayed, not just as partisans, but as Americans.

Even more than this, however, there was the bloodstained land to bind them together. Johnny Reb and Billy Yank had made streams run red as they poured virtual rivers of their blood on the ground for their causes. "Bloody Run," "Bloody Pond," the "Bloody Angle," "Bloody Lane," and a host of other sanguinary new names on the land testified to where they had been and what they had done. The geography of North America would never be entirely the same. Rivers had been diverted, hills leveled, whole forests denuded, and the fields of a million farmers sown with lead and iron. Mountain tops once reserved for the wolves, were now to be the haunt of old veterans and men too young to fight, who came as tourists to see where it all had happened. Fields made battlefields, were soon to become parks, there to host the future millions who, like their ancestors, could never entirely turn loose of this war. For too much passion, too many horrors and so many sacrificed lives would ensure that these places would live on in the thoughts of those who came after.

In the wake of the surrenders North and South began the final tally of the cost for their quadrennium of madness. More than 600,000 dead. Over one million wounds inflicted. A whole generation of maimed and crippled men left to live out their days however they could. A section of the country ravaged of all its resources: material, agricultural, and human. An angry scar across the landscape and the soul of its people, a scar that could never be erased. Four million Americans, once enslaved, were now free, with little but their freedom and the clothes on their backs. An old question about the nature of the Union and the relation of the states to the Federal government had been settled at last. The old Union was gone forever, washed away in a flood of blood and tears, but faith still remained in many to create a new America.

And most of all, there remained the nagging question. Had it all been worth the price? Within weeks of Lee's surrender, Union soldiers met on the old Manassas battlefield, where the first full-scale, but still rather haphazard fight had taken place those years before, to dedicate one of the very first monuments to commemorate the dead and what they died for. It was only the first of thousands of such ceremonies, to be repeated on every great battlefield of the Civil War, a continuum that still endures to this day. And always when they come to the bloodied land, now peaceful beneath the sod that covers the dead and their sacrifice, always they wonder. Had it all been worth the cost?

PART 2
COMMANDERS

I
THE "OLD ARMY"

In the late spring of 1861, in the infant western city of Los Angeles, a sad group of old friends gathered for the last time. They met at the home of Captain Winfield Scott Hancock and his wife Ada to bid farewell to half a dozen of their number who were about to embark upon the overland journey to the new Confederacy. All had resigned their commissions in the United States Army and were preparing to don a different uniform, one that meant they might have to fight against their old friends in blue who were seeing them off at midnight on that day, June 16.

Leader of the traveling party was Albert Sidney Johnston, colonel and brevet brigadier general, until recently commander of the Department of the Pacific. He had resigned back in May, hoping to stay out of the coming war entirely and become instead a farmer in southern California. When that failed, he thought to go to Texas to try again and, ostensibly, this was why he was leaving in company with the others. There was no question, however, about his companions' intent. Lewis Armistead, George Pickett, Richard B. Garnett, and the others were going to take commissions in the Confederate Army. Despite his peaceful hopes, Johnston would too, and in only a few weeks.

At the end of the evening, as tears began to well in the eyes of all present. Johnston asked his wife to "sing me one or two of the old songs you used to sing." She obliged, treating the company to "Mary of Argyle" and "Kathleen Mavourneen." She sang sadly, saying that in her heart she feared all cause for singing was gone. All around her the old friends put on brave smiles that covered, all-too-imperfectly, what Ada Hancock felt were "hearts that were filled with sadness over the sundering of life-long ties, and doubts as to the result of their sacrifice."

Finally Armistead, a North Carolinian, could contain himself no longer. He wept openly. The tears spread throughout the gathering. It was time to go. Armistead gave Ada a small satchel with some personal effects, asking her to open it only in the event of his death, and then to send the contents to his family. To Hancock he gave his new, unworn major's uniform, commenting that "he might sometime need it." Then, in farewell, he stood before Hancock, put his hands on his shoulders, looked him squarely in the eyes, and spoke through his tears. "Hancock, good-bye," he said. "You can never know what this has cost me." Praying that he might be struck dead rather than have to fight his old friends, he and the others rode off into the warm California night.[1]

It was a scene oft-repeated from ocean to ocean in the small 16,000-man United States Army – in what, after the outbreak of civil war would ever-after be called, fondly, the "Old Army." It was an odd fondness, for it grew out of years of service in an under-funded, often ill-equipped corps that demanded loneliness, hardship, Job-like patience, and almost unrelenting self-sacrifice from its officers. No wonder the years of isolated duty at frontier outposts, the incredibly slow advancement for junior officers and the oppression of superannuated old commanders, and all the other frustrations of a seemingly unappreciated service, tended to forge a bond among those who endured it all. Theirs was a very small world. When the war broke out, there were only 1,098 serving officers in the entire Old Army. Inevitably their social and family ties became exaggerated, especially in outposts where there might not be more than half a dozen officers with whom to associate. While not everyone might have felt as desolated as Armistead, still when the war came, the destruction of the small world that had been all they knew cost them all.[2]

"I always found them the same," a British visitor wrote of the American officers he met in 1852; "gentlemen-like and agreeable."[3] It is remarkable, considering what they endured. They were soldiers in a nation that had never liked armies and always maintained a suspicion of a professional military. The overwhelming majority of them had been educated at public expense at the United States Military Academy, leading to a dual resentment, from taxpayers who objected to the cost, and from would-be volunteer officers who found their aspirations stunted or eclipsed by a super-abundance of West Point graduates.

The Old Army had always been small, rarely more than 10,000 of all ranks, and frequently less since the War of 1812. That alone severely limited the chances for advancement of any young officer hoping to find promotion. Worse, the Military Academy yearly turned out more graduates than there were vacancies to fill, especially in peacetime. Since the country had enjoyed decades of peace, interrupted only by war with Mexico and an occasional Indian conflict, vacancies through casualties were few. Instead, graduates accepted brevet – essentially honorary – rank, and a place on a waiting list. The final, and worst contributor to making that list a long one was the complete absence of a mandated retirement policy. An officer could remain in service as long as he chose and so long as he seemed relatively healthy. When Colonel John

Walbach, commanding the 4th Artillery, died in his command in 1857, he was ninety-three years old and had been continuously in the service since 1799. The 4th Infantry was led by Colonel William Whistler in 1861. He had been in the army since 1801, and had taken command of the regiment some sixteen years before, when his aged predecessor died of exertion on the field after giving the regiment its first field drill in a number of years.[4]

In fact, the "fogyism" in the army's upper levels was so bad that half of the colonels commanding regiments in 1823 were still in command two decades later. When the war broke out in 1861, the army's commissary general, George Gibson, had been in the same post since 1818, and stayed there until his death on September 29, 1861. Indeed, half of the chiefs of the War Department's bureaus when Fort Sumter was fired upon had been in office since before the Mexican War.[5] More telling than this was the fact that at the time of secession there were only four line officers of general rank in the army, and only one of them, William S. Harney, was under the age of seventy! On average they had spent forty-seven years in the service, and Winfield Scott, aged seventy-four, had been in uniform since 1808. The oldest, Brigadier General John E. Wool, was seventy-seven when war broke out.

No wonder then that one official estimate provided to the secretary of war speculated that a new West Point graduate would wait eight years to make first lieutenant, another ten years to receive a captain's bars, and two decades more after that to become a major. Twenty more years would see him promoted lieutenant colonel and then, finally, colonel . . . after almost sixty years in uniform. An 1842 graduate of the Military Academy, fresh from his education and training, proud of his new uniform and anxious to serve and get ahead, could expect to wait into the next century before he got to command a regiment, if he lasted. No wonder that an outfit like the 4th Artillery was called "the immortal Regiment" – not for its heroic deeds, but from the fact that most of its lieutenants – junior officers – were already gray-haired![6]

Even for those officers who could handle the stultifying effects of years without a promotion, the concomitant problem of inadequate income often proved too much to bear. Just four years before the outbreak of the war, a second lieutenant's pay of $300 per year was exactly what it had been in 1812, forty-five years earlier. In the earlier years of the century the only way to get more pay was to obtain promotion – hardly a glowing prospect. Later on, special allowances for clothing and victuals and other amenities had the effect of increasing income even without promotion, but still almost every officer began to look after a few years at the attractions of more remunerative civilian employment. The rate of resignations among lieutenants and captains, as a result, was continually high, providing the only steady source of vacancies for new West Point graduates, and leading to an actual shortage of junior officers in some regiments. In fact some infantry companies were left with no officers to command them. In the year 1836, just over 18 percent of the officers in the Old Army resigned. Of the 117 who left, 97 were West Point men, and all but seven were junior officers. Low pay and no advancement had been simply too much for them, and only the war with Mexico in the late 1840s would bring some of them back into uniform.[7]

This effect of the hardship of military service put the lie to an old canard that West Point only educated the sons of the wealthy and influential. To be sure, many officers did come from well-established old families with good political ties to the Senators and Congressmen who gave the appointments. But for every Robert E. Lee whose family name and connections assured him an appointment, there were a dozen others who went because they could not afford any other education, because they really wanted to be soldiers, or because they had no choice. Hiram Ulysses Grant went because his father made him go, and while at the academy saw his name changed forever to Ulysses S. Grant. Another who would be known by a different name, Thomas J. Jackson of Virginia, went there because the education was free. By the 1840s, most claimed that their families were in "reduced circumstances," though just prior to the Civil War the number of cadets who admitted to independent wealth went up sharply, indicating perhaps that the growing sectional crisis was attracting the sons of the planters in the South who would soon have to fight to keep their wealth.[8]

Whatever their family background, by the time of the Civil War the West Point men dominated the officer corps of the Old Army. In 1861, out of the 1,098 commissioned officers in uniform, 744 were Military Academy graduates.[9] Naturally enough, most were from the classes that finished their schooling after the Mexican War, but again, the absence of any retirement policy allowed for a number of septuagenarians as well. All of the general officers in service had been born before the Military Academy was founded in 1802, and none of them had attended. Of the roughly 350 non-West Point graduates who were officers in 1861, almost all had received special appointments from civilian life, or else had originally been elected or appointed leaders of state volunteer regiments raised during the Mexican and earlier conflicts. Such men, if they performed well, were often commissioned into the Regular Army after their volunteer units had mustered out. Thus it was that the commanding general of the army, Major General Winfield Scott, had been appointed by President Jefferson in 1808. The other generals, William Harney, David E. Twiggs, and John E. Wool, had all been similarly commissioned, and all but Harney were veterans of the War of 1812.[10] Ironically, not one of the men in command of the Old Army had ever had so much as a single day of professional military training. Whatever they knew they had learned on the field of battle.

But there were a host of other, younger officers in 1861 who had learned their trade more systematically, though unlike Scott and the other generals, these younger men for the most part had more military education than military experience, thanks to years of relative peace. The overwhelming majority, in fact, had never led in the field or in combat anything more than a company of less than 100 men, and there were less than two dozen in uniform who had ever commanded a regiment. In the four years that followed 1861, however, many of these inexperienced officers would be leading brigades, corps, and even armies. Men whose biggest pre-war command in action might have been a squad, would find themselves leading tens of thousands.

Their names were little known outside the Old Army at the time, but they would be heard from in the war between the states. Gouverneur K. Warren finished second in the class of 1850 and eleven years later was only a first lieutenant teaching mathematics at the Military Academy. First Lieutenant Alexander McD. McCook, 3rd Infantry, class of 1852, was teaching infantry tactics at the academy. From the same class came George Crook, now a first lieutenant in the 4th Infantry serving in a Californian outpost. James B. McPherson graduated first in the class of 1853 and went into the elite corps of Engineers, but he was still only a lieutenant when war broke out. Philip H. Sheridan ranked thirty-fourth in McPherson's class and the two were good friends, but he had never gotten a single promotion and was still a junior lieutenant in Crook's regiment. Sheridan's classmate John Bell Hood of Kentucky was a lieutenant in the 2nd Cavalry. Oliver O. Howard finished fourth in the 1854 class, but 1861 found him still a lieutenant teaching mathematics at West Point with Warren. Wesley Merritt, class of 1860, was in the 2nd Dragoons, while James E. B. Stuart, known to friends as "Jeb," served as a lieutenant in the 1st Cavalry out in Colorado. Four of these obscure officers would command armies in the war just starting, and the rest would lead army corps. A few of them would become immortal by their deeds.[11]

Considering the frustrations they endured and the life they led in the Old Army, it is little short of amazing that these men were still in uniform when the war came. As one officer observed, civilian life could look very alluring to men who, naturally enough, would prefer that they "not be dragged into the wilderness to be either stationed there separate from their families, or fighting the Indians in unhealthy climates, where nothing can be gained but everything lost – health, reputation, money."[12]

There were inevitable consequences of such a life. With little to do in their off-duty time, officers turned to drinking and gambling, quarreling with each other, fighting bureaucratic battles with higher authorities, and sometimes even dueling. In 1852 an officer of the 4th Infantry observed that every day all of the officers in his regiment except two were drunk, and the commander liked to pile furniture in the center of a room and set fire to it when inebriated.[13]

Typically, an officer's quarters might be a bare room with no furniture, he having to provide it all for himself. At best he would have a cot, a table and one or two chairs, and perhaps a shelf for possessions provided for him. Anything else he had to buy out of his own pocket. If he were fortunate enough to be stationed at one of the eastern forts or garrisons, the officer could at least look forward to the opportunity to visit New York or Baltimore or Charleston, and other civilized centers of activity and entertainment. If less fortunate, as most fresh officers were, a man would find himself posted to Arkansas or Colorado, or the Pacific northwest, where the overriding experience was monotony. An officer in Arkansas felt himself "buried in oblivion," and another concluded after eleven years of frontier duty that, "no amount of money could induce me to remain in such a state of isolation from society."[14]

Many found solace and company in religion, though the majority ignored any kind of formal church attendance. Churches did not exist near many outposts, and few garrisons were large enough to merit their own army chaplain. Most often the officers simply had informal prayer meetings in their own quarters. Meanwhile, many found other ways to use their abundant free time. Intemperance was epidemic in some regiments, to the point that some officers literally drank themselves to death, while others got drunk at their funerals. Even though much exaggerated in later years, the problems of young Captain U.S. Grant were typical of many who found the isolation from friends and family so depressing that it could turn otherwise sober men to the bottle. Grant resigned his commission in 1854 after his drinking to while away lonely months on the Pacific coast got him in trouble.

Officers quarreled over rank and seniority, over leaves and furloughs, over the few white women of marriageable age in their vicinity, over politics and religion and gambling. They often argued with neighboring civilians. Courts-martial were common occurrences as officers pressed charges against one another, providing one of the frontier service's chief forms of entertainment. Many an officer like Jefferson Davis and Thomas J. Jackson became so disillusioned and disgusted over the quarreling that they resigned. Those who stayed in the army not infrequently turned to violence. Dueling was officially outlawed in the military, but that did not stop a host of challenges being issued and accepted, and duels being fought. In 1845 Lieutenant P. G. T. Beauregard challenged a fellow officer over a minor matter of supply. John C. Frémont did the same during the Mexican War, and as late as 1856 a bloodless meeting between brother officers took place in the Wyoming territory.[15]

No one summed up the hard side of Old Army service better than Captain John W. Phelps of the 4th Artillery. After two promotions in twenty-three years of service, and after one miserable posting after another, he declared in 1859 that "I am suffocating, physically, morally and intellectually – in every way." "Fairly, gasping for fresh outside air", he said he felt like a brother officer who a few days before begged, only half in jest, "to be taken out and hung for the sake of variety." Phelps resigned his commission just weeks before John Brown's raid on Harpers Ferry, Virginia, electrified the nation and helped set the states on the road to disunion. Eighteen months after his resignation, with the country going to war, Phelps was given a commission of brigadier general and more than enough to do that monotony was never a problem for him again.[16]

Phelps represented a type, a resource for both sides of trained officers that in 1861 was to be of great importance in supplementing the corps of currently serving commanders. Indeed, officers who had resigned their commissions and returned to private life probably had a greater impact on the war than any other class, chiefly because many of the commanders of the major armies, especially for the Union, were men who were out of uniform when Fort Sumter was fired upon. U.S. Grant was failing almost as badly in private business in 1861 as he had as an officer. The war was literally his salvation, and he was delighted to accept the colonelcy of an obscure Illinois regiment in 1861, hardly suspecting that he would end the war as general-in-chief of all Union armies. His chief lieutenant in the war, William T. Sherman, had also resigned from the army, leaving in 1853 after thirteen years' service. He, too, failed in business and the law, and in 1861 was running a streetcar company in St. Louis when war came and the government offered him the command of the 13th United States Infantry. George B. McClellan spent eleven years in uniform before resigning his captaincy to become a railroad manager. Then overnight he became a major general of Ohio volunteers after Fort Sumter. Thomas J. Jackson, after resigning in a huff in 1852, taught young cadets at the Virginia Military Institute and was regarded as an eccentric fanatic nicknamed "Tom Fool." When war came, he found himself a Confederate brigadier by June 1861, and a month later the holder of a rather less derogatory nickname, "Stonewall." These are only the most outstanding. Literally scores of others of lesser note were out in the land working as planters and farmers, lawyers, businessmen and politicians; a tremendous potential reserve of experience and ability, good and bad. The armies that were to be formed in the aftermath of secession would depend heavily upon them.

Some of these men shared a common role with yet a third potential source of leaders for the coming war, many of them men without West Point or other formal military training. Every state North and South boasted numerous publicly and privately supported militia organizations, founded for a variety of reasons ranging from fraternalism to an enthusiasm for drill competitions, to a rising militarism in the face of the sectional friction. While a number of West Pointers did take prominent positions in such organizations, most notably Simon Buckner, who resigned in 1855 from the army and in 1861 was adjutant general of the Kentucky State Guard, most of the militia officers were drawn from local men in private life. As a result, their training and ability varied dramatically.

Best known of them all was probably E. Elmer Ellsworth, leader of the Chicago Zouaves, a spectacularly skilled volunteer company that he raised before the war and led in exhibitions and competitions throughout the North. Coming to Washington with his friend and newly elected president Abraham Lincoln, he soon organized another company, the New York Fire Zouaves, so-called because many of its members were firemen. Ellsworth had no formal military training at all, and was a prime example of the dilettante officer whose enthusiasm for things military sprang from a love of the show and finery. His record inspired many others. That is not to say that he was not a brave and patriotic young man, for he became, in fact, the first Union officer to die in the war, being shot dead by a secessionist in Alexandria, Virginia, on May 24, 1861, as he tried to take down a Confederate flag. Ellsworth's lasting contribution to the war came from his unit continuing in service as the 11th New York.

North and South there were a number of other such young men, and older ones as well. Frequently, men with good political connections achieved high positions in their pre-war state militias, and these, too, provided a limited source of potential officers. While few might have any practical field experience with an army, they did at least know much of the inner workings of a military organization and how to administer one, almost as important to a leader as ability to lead in battle. Alpheus S. Williams was president of Michigan's state militia board with the rank of brigadier, and readily in place for transfer into the Union's volunteer army. In Tennessee, Benjamin Franklin Cheatham served as major general of state militia before the war, making it only natural that he would be commissioned a brigadier in the Confederate service as soon as Tennessee seceded. And elsewhere down the line, as private military organizations offered their services to one side or the other, company officers were accepted and commissioned wholesale. The South was blessed to get the services of New Orleans' famed Washington Artillery and the Washington Light Infantry of Charleston. Lincoln, by the same token, readily extended commissions to the leaders of the civilian military companies in the North.

The same was occasionally the case with the officers at the private military academies. Many Northern states had such institutions, and almost all of the Southern states possessed them, such as the Virginia Military Institute, the Citadel at Charleston and the State Seminary of Learning and Military Academy in Louisiana. When war came, of course, many of the instructors and academy officers immediately volunteered. Thus Thomas J. Jackson left V.M.I. to take a commission as colonel for the Confederacy.

Finally there remained the largest single source of leaders, and the most difficult to tap predictably. Out in the great multitude of private citizens, among the bankers, cotton brokers, lawyers and doctors, farmers, store clerks, and even simple day laborers, there lay an undoubted reservoir of raw, native talent. There were brave men who could rise to leadership, win the trust and respect of their men, the approval of their superiors, and use it all to help win battles. But finding these officers-to-be would be the most costly and time-consuming search of all, for they could only be found through trial and error, by testing and retesting, the way a dairyman let his cow's milk sit and waited for the cream to rise to the top. There was cream out there in the millions of untried young men of America. By 1861 the time had come for it to rise.

"No act of my life cost me more bitter pangs than mailing my resignation as a captain in the United States Army," lamented Henry Heth of Virginia, "separating myself from those I loved, bidding adieu to my splendid company, my pride, and the finest regiment in the army."[17] It was a commonly held and expressed emotion. Not infrequently, other friends in the Old Army attempted to persuade Southern men not to go South. When Lieutenant Edward Porter Alexander reported for duty in San Francisco to his close friend Lieutenant James B. McPherson, there was no question that the Georgian Alexander intended to leave the army. He talked with McPherson telling him of his intention and asking him to accept his resignation.

"Aleck if you must go," said his friend, "I will do all I can to facilitate your going. But don't go." He promised that Alexander would be able to remain on the Pacific coast, far from the war, honorably continuing his service without having to fight against his own people.

"Now this is not going to be any 90 days or six months affair," McPherson continued. If Alexander went South, with his training he would certainly wind up in the front lines. "God only knows what may happen to you individually," he said, "but for your *cause* there can be but one possible result. It must be lost." McPherson tried to explain how Alexander's promotion would be rapid as other officers were drawn away to the war. He even suggested that the Georgian could make good investments in the expanding land business in San Francisco.

"In short, remaining here you have every opportunity for professional reputation, for promotion, and for wealth," McPherson concluded: "Going home you have every personal risk to run and in a cause foredoomed to failure."

Alexander was deeply impressed by McPherson's words. "A crisis in my life was at hand," he recalled later. He was utterly helpless to avert it, however. "Mac," he cried, "my people are going to war, and war for their *liberty*. If I don't come and bear my part they will believe me a coward – and I will feel that I am occupying the position of one. I must go and stand my chances."

"So I wrote my resignation of my beautiful position in the Engineer Corps," Alexander remembered. McPherson gave him a leave of absence to return to the East to await its acceptance, and then as his last gesture of friendship, helped arrange Alexander's passage home at a reduced steamship rate. The two never met again. Alexander would serve with the Confederates in Virginia, from First Manassas all the way to Appomattox; McPherson, during the Atlanta campaign in the summer of 1864, would be the only Union army commander to be killed in the field.[18]

The only Confederate army commander to be killed, Kentuckian Albert Sidney Johnston, had faced the same dilemma as Alexander, and only came to the same conclusion after painful deliberation. He had been a nationalist all his life. A West Point graduate in 1826, ranking eighth in his class, he gave distinguished service in the Black Hawk War of 1832, then resigned and joined the Texan revolutionaries in 1836, becoming their senior brigadier. He led a Texas regiment in the war with Mexico, and then re-entered the Old Army in 1849 and had risen to the brevet rank of brigadier general by 1861. The blood in his veins was as red, white, and blue as that of any other officer in the army. As a result, unlike Alexander, he hoped that he could simply stay out of the coming Civil War by remaining in California and resigning from the army. But the old ties to Texas began to pull at him. While he resisted all attempts by Southern sympathizers to get him to turn over public property to them while he was still in command at San Francisco, refusing to dishonor the uniform he still wore, once he resigned and went to Los Angeles to take up farming he could no longer turn a cold ear to the entreaties from Texas. He had resigned rather than have to bear arms against the Lone Star State. At the same time, men in Washington were trying to hold up acceptance of his resignation as they tried to persuade him to withdraw it, and promised that he would receive an important command in the volunteer army being formed.

Thus pulled and torn from both sides at once, Johnston in the end decided that he had to follow his heart into the Confederacy. "It seems like fate," he told a friend, "that Texas has made me a Rebel twice."[19]

Yet in the minds of many, most tragic of all was the decision faced by Robert Edward Lee. His had been a distinguished, yet typically frustrating, Old Army career. Graduating second in the West Point class of 1829, Lee came of an honored old Virginia family, served his trying time on frontier posts before the Mexican War, but emerging from that conflict with a considerable reputation. Yet by 1861, after thirty-two years in the army, he was a colonel in the 1st Cavalry, with nowhere to go until some of the older generals died or retired. Then came the outbreak of the war. With all of the line generals too old for active service, senior men like Lee and Johnston were the ones Lincoln would have to turn to for the command of his armies. On April 18, 1861, Lee was called to a meeting in Washington, where an emissary of Lincoln's told him that the President wanted to know if Lee would take the command of the major army to be raised in the East.

Few men have ever had to face such an agonizing test of ambition against loyalty. Lincoln was offering what Lee had sought all his professional life, the capstone to any military man's career, and one offered to precious few. But just the day before, Lee's beloved Virginia had voted to secede. Inevitably the Commonwealth would join with the new Confederacy, and just as inevitably, any Union army seeking to put down the rebellion in the East would make Virginia a battleground.

"I declined the offer," Lee wrote later, "stating, as candidly and courteously as I could, that though opposed to secession and deprecating war, I could take no part in an invasion of the Southern States." As soon as the interview concluded, Lee went to the office of his mentor, friend, and commanding general, Winfield Scott, and expressed his intention to resign. Two days later he sent in his resignation. He apologised to Scott for not bringing it in person and for taking two days to make himself write it. It had been, he confessed, a "struggle to separate myself from a service to which I have devoted all the best years of my life." "Save in defense of my native state," he concluded, "I never desire again to draw my sword." The next day a message came from Virginia's governor asking Lee to come to Richmond to discuss the state's defense. Inevitably, Lee would be drawn into the war.[20]

Not all of the anguish of torn loyalties fell to the lot of Southern-born men in the Old Army. Many a Yankee found himself caught between conflicting emotions. John C. Pemberton of Pennsylvania was a West Pointer who served twenty-four years in the military. But he had married a Virginia girl in 1848, and the ties to an adopted family were great enough to persuade him to cast his lot with the Confederacy. Franklin Gardner was a New Yorker who finished at the Military Academy in Grant's class, and was a lieutenant colonel in 1861 when he resigned to go South, following political principles rather than geographical loyalties. Two years later Pemberton and Gardner would command, and lose in siege, the two main Confederate bastions on the Mississippi: Vicksburg and Port Hudson. Both would be accused of treason to the South due to their Northern birth. Both were innocent.

And there were loyal Union men of Southern birth who faced equal heartache. Stephen Hurlbut was born in Charleston and lived for thirty years in South Carolina, but when war came he became a Yankee brigadier. Even more dramatic is the story of William Terrill of Virginia. A West Pointer, he stayed with the Union and rose from captain in the 5th Artillery to be a brigadier general in 1862. His brother James was a brigadier general in the Confederate Army. Both brothers would be killed in the war. Equally heart-rending was the choice faced by another Virginian, George H. Thomas, who served as a major in the 2nd Cavalry before the war, his commanders including Albert Sidney Johnston and Robert E. Lee. In January 1861 he had applied for the position of commandant of cadets at the Virginia Military Institute, perhaps hoping to stay out of the coming war, and feeling as did a few at that time that Virginia might not secede, and her sons not be called on to fight the Union. However, he went through some kind of political or emotional epiphany that spring, and in the end turned down the offer of a high command from Virginia's governor in the days before Fort Sumter. Within a few months he was a Federal brigadier, and would finish the war as commander of one of the two major armies that defeated the Rebellion. His family in Virginia never spoke to him again. His portrait still hung in the family home, but his sisters turned it to face the wall.[21]

So there was more than enough anguish over choices to go around in the continent in 1861. If any place was to symbolize it best, however, one needed to look no further than the small garrison of Old Army men out in the middle of Charleston Harbor in Fort Sumter. Almost to a man they were career military men, mostly West Pointers, put in the most awkward spot of all. Their commander, Major Robert Anderson, was a Kentuckian, married to a Georgia woman, and a personal proponent of slavery and states' rights. Yet he had been given the trust of this command by the army that had been his life. All he had to do was turn it over bloodlessly to the Confederates who were ringing him with batteries, and he would be a Southern hero. Lieutenant R. K. Meade of Anderson's garrison was a Virginian, a young officer with a bright future before him. Even more than Anderson, he sided with the South. How would he behave if the Confederates opened fire on Sumter? Many in both nations expected them to do as another Southern-born officer in a position of trust had done. Old David E. Twiggs of Georgia was seventy, and one of only four general officers of the line in the Old Army. He commanded the Department of Texas in 1860, and early in 1861 he listened to his Southern loyalties. He turned over his command to the state forces of Texas, along with all of his stores and armaments and men. It was an act of clear treason, for he had not bothered to resign his commission first, and for it he was vilified in the North and even in some quarters of the South, and almost universally throughout the Old Army. It was an act without honor.[22]

But Anderson and Meade were different sorts of men. When the guns opened up on Fort Sumter on April 12, 1861, both did what almost every Old Army officer could be counted upon to do . . . his duty. Indeed, while some suspected Meade in particular, he actively joined in helping man the few cannon that returned the fire of the Confederates commanded (by now General) P. G. T. Beauregard. As for Anderson, he manfully held out until the wooden portion of his fort was in flames, and his supplies were running out. Only then did he capitulate. All of Sumter's defenders were later given a hero's welcome when they returned to the North. Anderson became a brigadier and served the Union cause faithfully until his broken health forced him to leave active duty in 1863. And Lieutenant Meade soon resigned his commission, but took one in the Confederate Army instead. Having more than honorably fulfilled his duty to his first country, he would soon give his life for his second.

Those old friendships that were broken, some forever, by the coming of the war would remain among the most heart-rending of its casualties. They all had to choose their own way. "How strange it is," wrote new Confederate Brigadier General Braxton Bragg to his old friend Captain Henry J. Hunt, who would one day be a Yankee brigadier responsible for all of the artillery of the Army of the Potomac.

"We have been united in our views of almost all subjects, public and private," continued Bragg. "We still have, I trust, a personal regard for each other, which will continue whatever course our sense of duty may dictate, yet in one short year after exchanging at your house assurances of friendship, here we are, face to face, with arms in our hands, with every prospect of a bloody collision. How strange."[23]

How strange, indeed, lending all the more poignancy to that little dinner party in far off Los Angeles on June 16, 1861. Though they never spoke together in peace again, Hancock and some of his friends would meet once more in a strange way. On July 3, 1863, at Gettysburg, Pennsylvania, when General Robert E. Lee launched the biggest infantry assault of his army's career, he hurled it at the center of a fortified Union line commanded by Major General Winfield Scott Hancock and his II Corps. Leaders in the assault were Major General George Pickett and Brigadier Generals Lewis A. Armistead and Richard B. Garnett. Garnett fell amid a storm of bullets and smoke and was never seen again. Armistead, his hat atop his sword so his men could see him, actually penetrated the Union line and had laid his hand on one of Hancock's cannon before he took a mortal wound from the Federal line. His last request before death was to see Hancock, one it was not possible to grant for Hancock himself had just received a near-mortal wound from Armistead's attacking Confederates.[24]

REFERENCES

1 Ada Hancock, *Reminiscences of Winfield Scott Hancock* (New York, 1887), pp.69-70; Charles P. Roland, *Albert Sidney Johnston, Soldier of Three Republics* (Austin, Tex., 1964), p.252.

2 E. B. Long, *The Civil Day by Day* (New York, 1971), p.709.

3 Edward M. Coffman, *The Old Army* (New York, 1986), p.102.

4 *Ibid.*, pp.49, 99.

5 Frank J. Welcher, *The Union Army 1861-1865: Organization and Operations: Volume I, The Eastern Theater* (Bloomington, Ind., 1989), pp.2-4.

6 Coffman, *Old Army*, p.49.

7 *Ibid.*, pp.50, 52.

8 *Ibid.*, pp.47-8.

9 *Register of Graduates and Former Cadets, United States Military Academy* (New York, 1948), pp.386-8.

10 Ezra J. Warner, *Generals in Blue* (Baton Rouge, 1964), pp.209, 430, 573-4; Ezra J. Warner, *Generals in Gray* (Baton Rouge, 1959), p.312.

11 George W. Cullom, *Biographical Register of the Officers and Graduates of the U.S. Military Academy* (Boston, 1891), III, pp.254, 323, 329, 333, 356, 362, 369, 375, 509.

12 Coffman, *Old Army*, p.54.

13 *Ibid.*, p.63.

14 *Ibid.*, p.81.

15 *Ibid.*, pp.70-1.

16 Coffman, *Old Army*, p.67; William H. Powell, comp., *List of Officers of the Army of the United States from 1779 to 1900* (New York, 1900), p.529.

17 James L. Morrison, ed., *The Memoirs of Henry Heth* (Westport, Conn., 1974), p.149.

18 Gary W. Gallagher, ed., *Fighting for the Confederacy, The Personal Recollections of General Edward Porter Alexander* (Chapel Hill, N.C., 1989), pp.23-5.

19 Roland, *Johnston*, pp.250-2.

20 Douglas Southall Freeman, *R. E. Lee* (New York, 1934), I, pp.436-7, 441, 447.

21 Warner, *Generals in Blue*, pp.496, 500-1.

22 Warner, *Generals in Gray*, p.312.

23 Coffman, *Old Army*, p.96.

24 Hancock, *Hancock*, p.70.

II

OFFICERS & GENTLEMEN

While no precisely accurate tally exists, it is clear that at least 5,085 separate regiments, battalions, companies, legions, and batteries saw service in the American Civil War. While no accurate tally exists of the total number of officers who served in those units, on staff duty, and in the departments and bureaus that provided support services, obviously the number had to be enormous. A workable estimate would be about 140,000 individuals who at varying times served as commissioned officers during the course of the war. Many more held unofficial rank in informal guerrilla commands and in some of the local home guard units that were never absorbed into the formal Union or Confederate services. Due to the high rate of battlefield attrition among officers, the actual figure might be higher by several thousand. Far more important, however, is the fact that a nation with little military tradition found itself, in a comparatively short span of time, facing the task of finding this many men who were or could be made into leaders. It was a tall order indeed.

To their credit, and quite logically, both governments turned first to the professionals, to current and former officers of the Old Army, and especially those with West Point training. Both sides knew that such men would not be enough, but they could form the nucleus of experienced leaders around whom a much larger officer corps could form, as volunteer commanders were added to the army. And from the outset, the high level vacancies created in the new regiments and brigades were chiefly to be filled by these professionals. Thus it was no surprise that many of the more esteemed Old Army officers found themselves wooed by both sides in what at times almost amounted to a bidding war in which the prize was not money, but rank. Simon Buckner of Kentucky was offered brigadier generalcies by both Lincoln and Davis in the summer of 1861. He sided with the latter. Another Kentuckian, Ben Hardin

Helm, was offered first a major's commission in the Union Army, then took the colonelcy of a new Confederate infantry regiment. Robert E. Lee, of course, had reportedly been offered command of the Union Army by Winfield Scott but took the command of Confederate Virginia's state troops instead. Even as he was resigning his commission to go to the South, Albert Sidney Johnston was wooed by Washington to remain in the Federal service, to no avail.[1]

Once the men of the Old Army had made their choice of whether or not to serve, and for which side, there remained for most the sometimes daunting task of simply getting to their respective armies. The 1,000-odd officers were scattered all across the continent, with more than a third of them in the far West, some of them more than a thousand miles from their destinations. Further, for many there was a gnawing uncertainty for families that were back in the East, as well as a personal anxiety, especially on the part of Southern-born officers. With news traveling very slowly, many officers who determined to cast their fortunes with their native states did not know for weeks whether or not their states had seceded. The only "rapid" communication came by way of the famed Pony Express, which sent its riders from the westernmost telegraph line at Fort Kearny, on the Platte River in the Nebraska Territory, on to the Pacific coast.

On "pony day," as they called it, the officers and men in the frontier garrisons assembled at the post trader's store or perhaps company headquarters at the appointed hour for the rider to arrive. Captain John Gibbon, 4th Artillery, joined others at Camp Floyd in the Utah Territory, looking anxiously across the level sagebrush plain to see the tell-tale streamer of dust in the distance raised by the rider's pounding hooves. If the express was late, officers climbed atop the store for a better view, all ears cocked for the magical cry "here he comes." As the news from the East became more and more dire prior to the firing on Fort Sumter, the faces on pony day were the more anxious. When the first news of the outbreak of hostilities did arrive, Gibbon noted how all within hearing of the officer reading the dispatch were "serious and thoughtful."[2]

For men of the South, when news of their native states' secession came through, or for those who had decided to take Confederate service in any case, the sometime pain of the decision was at least compensated for by the immediate control they could take of their own destiny. A simple letter of resignation, once posted, freed them of any sense of further obligation or necessity to wait around. They were free to make their way to the Confederacy, saying farewell to their remaining brothers of the Old Army who had to wait where they were for orders to come.

Thus it was that Albert Sidney Johnston made his journey all the way from Los Angeles to Richmond, Virginia, the Confederate capital after May 1861. While he may have equivocated about simply staying out of the war altogether, once his adopted state of Texas seceded he knew he had to go. After the tearful party at the Hancock home on June 16, he joined with the others in a daunting trek across the southwest by horseback that took them to Fort Yuma, then along the Gila River, south on the Rio Santa Cruz to Tucson, then due east to Picacho on the Rio Grande. It was more than 800 miles, on foot and horseback, and in the worst of the summer, when daytime temperatures could rise above 120[deg]F in the deserts. It took more than a month for the trip, and once in Texas it took Johnston another month to reach New Orleans, and another week, perhaps, to get to Richmond. In the end, he had covered more than 2,000 miles in two and a half months to reach the capital. He went straight to the executive mansion, only to learn that President Jefferson Davis, his old friend, was upstairs ill. But Davis was awake, and he heard the traveler's boots in the hall below. "That is Sidney Johnston's step," the President exclaimed. "Bring him up." In less than a week, Johnston was a full general and the second ranking officer in the entire Confederate army.[3]

Literally dozens of other officers preceded or followed Johnston in the exodus of Old Army men to the Confederacy. While few others traveled so far or through such danger and hardship, still each had his story. James Longstreet of South Carolina was a major and paymaster of the post at Albuquerque, New Mexico Territory, when the war came. Here, too, the men stood atop the quartermaster's office roof to look for the dust raised by a coming mail wagon. When the tragic news arrived, and Longstreet and others made their choice to "go South," many of their old friends who remained loyal to the Union rode out on the trail with them a few miles, "which only made the last farewell more trying" for Longstreet. They rode across the territory to the Texas line, stopping in El Paso to find everyone singing "Dixie" and "The Bonnie Blue Flag." Even then he had another 500 miles to travel before he could take trains on to Richmond. Ironically, his chief traveling companions were two Yankees heading home, and for whom he provided protection. Once in Richmond, Longstreet applied at the Confederate war department on June 29 for an assignment in the pay department, having as he said "given up all aspirations of military honor." Two days later he found himself commissioned a brigadier general with orders to go to Manassas. In time the would-be paymaster became what Robert E. Lee called "my old War Horse," the longest serving and most dependable of the corps commanders of the Army of Northern Virginia.[4]

An officer whose Civil War career would be intricately linked with Longstreet's had a considerably different experience in reaching the Confederacy, and clearly a different strategy about his resignation. Lieutenant Edward Porter Alexander of Georgia knew that his resignation was inevitable the moment Georgia seceded. He was stationed in far away Washington Territory, however, and shortly expected orders for his company to return to the East. However, he decided to wait until the army had ordered and moved him back before he turned in his resignation. The expected orders came, and he and his family embarked aboard a steamer bound for San Francisco, whence he would take passage on another ship to Panama, cross the isthmus by rail, then board another steamer to Washington.

But once in San Francisco, Alexander's plans were totally upset by that same harbinger of bad news that had set so many on their way east, the Pony Express. Orders arrived canceling his trip to the East, and instead assigning him to Alcatraz Island in the bay. "I was very sorry for this," he recalled, "because it precipitated my resignation & compelled me to pay my own expenses for the journey." In short, Alexander had hoped to stay in the United States service long enough for it to pay to get him home so that he might then resign and join the Confederacy.[5]

Like many others, Alexander made the trip home by ship. So did Hancock, though his was a different destination and destiny. For all of them who chose that route, there was nearly as much excitement and danger as for those who went overland. For some the peril was more imagined than real. Rumors abounded of events in the East, but there was little hard information. When Hancock procured an American newspaper in Panama, he had to read it aloud to everyone in the cabin, so starved were they for war news. More unsettling were the stories of Confederate warships prowling the sea lanes hoping to intercept ships from California that might be carrying gold. When his ship was almost home, steaming off the North Carolina coast, an unidentified vessel did approach, and Hancock hastily organized some of the passengers for defense, while other Old Army friends bound for the Confederacy looked on in amusement. Alexander, too, encountered the rumors of Rebel warships, but on his vessel there were so few Unionists that no defense could be organized. In the event, no threat appeared, but they were almost lost in a severe storm, and after that two crewmen were killed in accidents.[6]

Even these dangers might have seemed as nothing compared to the frustration of the loyal officers who did not resign, and as a result had to sit at their posts awaiting news and hoping for orders to report to the East. It would have been unnatural for these men, most of whom had only known peacetime service with its boredom and glacial rate of advancement, not to be anxious to participate in the excitement in Virginia and elsewhere. There careers could be made, promotion won, and real experience gained. After the news of Fort Sumter, said Gibbon, "days and weeks now dragged their slow length along and all eyes were turned eagerly eastward for more news, while orders for our recall to the States were anxiously awaited." Every succeeding pony day brought more news, none of it good for the Union, and produced more and more excitement and frustration among the men. They were torn between anger at what was happening to their country, and fear that the war would end too soon for them to participate. When finally Gibbon's orders arrived, he was directed to march 1,200 miles to Fort Leavenworth in Kansas. Stores and supplies that could not be carried with his marching column were sold locally, and all excess arms and ammunition were destroyed. On July 27 they started on their two months' dusty march, and four days later were startled to see a Pony Express rider hastily hand a slip of paper to an officer as he raced past. All gathered to hear the man read an account of the battle of July 21 along Bull Run, near Manassas, Virginia, the war's first major engagement. He read of the initial success of Irvin McDowell's Union army as it pushed back the Rebels commanded by Beauregard and Joseph E. Johnston. When the reader paused for breath, one disgusted listener muttered, "Great God, the thing will be over before we get there." But then the reader went on, told of the Confederate counterattacks, the timely arrival of reinforcements, and the ultimate rout of McDowell's army. "Good God," muttered the same incredulous listener, "there will be no government when we get there."[7]

Once Gibbon's column reached Fort Leavenworth, more personally tragic news began to reach the Old Army men. Few were touched by it as Gibbon, when he opened two months' worth of mail. He learned that his three brothers were all entering the Confederate service, following their allegiance to North Carolina, which had seceded. He never saw or spoke to them again until after the war. When he finally reached Washington, he met the same sight that confronted so many of his brother officers. The army and the country were in disarray. "Everywhere were troops, camps, baggage-wagons, the sound of martial music, and saddest of all, the constant boom of distant guns which told the story of our distracted country."[8]

George Crook felt the same way as that muttering officer on the plains when, ordered to come east, he reached Panama and heard the news of what later became known as First Bull Run. "We all felt that the war would be over," he recalled, "and a bluer set of people could not well have been found."[9] It was almost as frustrating for some officers who did not have to make a long journey to reach the armies. Lieutenant Cyrus Comstock, on the faculty at West Point, had to sit idly by and watch other officers ordered to the gathering army at Washington, while he sat and continued teaching his classes. Officer after officer left before him. A new class was graduated in May 1861, and almost every new lieutenant would be going to war. "We who are still here expect to be sent any day," he wrote hopefully, but by late June he was still seeing others from his faculty and members of his own graduating class getting promotions and assignments. In July he went to Washington on his own to seek a field assignment, but returned dejectedly to West Point "as a fixture." At last on July 26 his orders came, and a man who would become one of U.S. Grant's most trusted and effective staff members two years later finally got to go to war.[10]

For a number of officers, even those already in the Regular Army, personal politicking had to be resorted to in order to get a field assignment. Never in any other conflict in American history was personal influence – local, financial, family, and other connections – to play so large a role in determining who was to receive a commission. Never before or afterward did the ingenuity or persistence of the prospective officer himself have so much to do with his success in getting a place – often more to do with it, in fact, than any training or experience he might have had.

When George Crook finally reached Washington, he had been given a captaincy in the 14th Infantry, a new Regular Army regiment. But all around him he was seeing others being made colonels and even generals in the volunteer armies being raised.

Since the War Department apparently intended to fight the war chiefly with volunteers enlisted for ninety days' service – and later for three years or the duration of the war – rather than by expanding the Regular Army, it was obvious that advancement in the few Regular units would be little faster than before the war. Thus the overwhelming majority of officers like Crook sought appointments from the governors of their home states. Crook first went to Washington hoping to see President Abraham Lincoln. He went in company with Brigadier General Robert C. Schenck, a fellow Ohioian, who had never had a day of military service in his life. But he had been an influential campaigner for Lincoln's election, and his brigadier's star was his reward. Now he sought to use his political influence on behalf of Crook. Lincoln told them that in a cabinet meeting the day before, it had been agreed to allow 100 Regular officers to take volunteer commissions, but when Schenck suggested one for Crook, Lincoln gave an excuse that he probably had to use hundreds of times in the months ahead. He never interfered with the running of any branch of the government, he said, any more than he would try to mend a watch. Should he "put his foot into it," as he said, it might never run again. So he referred them to the adjutant general's office. There Crook was told that to get a volunteer commission he would have to have a state governor make application for him. At once he telegraphed the governor of Ohio, and a few weeks later he found himself in Columbus, the state capital, taking command of the 36th Ohio Infantry as Colonel Crook.[11] It was a routine to be repeated again and again both North and South.

Yet with barely 1,100 actual serving officers in uniform when the war broke out, and with 300 of those resigning to go South, demand for leaders clearly outstripped supply. Even counting West Pointers who had left the service and might be brought back, such as Grant and Sherman, that only offered another potential 200 or so for the Union, and even fewer for the Confederacy. Lincoln's initial call for 75,000 volunteers after the fall of Fort Sumter would alone require at least 2,500 officers, easily double the number of trained men currently in uniform or in retirement. Obviously he and Jefferson Davis would both have to lean heavily on state militia officers, private military school faculty and graduates, and even politicians who, if nothing more, knew how to run election campaigns and might just be trainable for military campaigns as well. In the end, both governments utilized a host of means in choosing officers. The rule of the day was that there were *no* strict rules of procedure. What was policy was simply whatever means succeeded in getting a man a commission.[12]

G. Moxley Sorrel was a Georgian with no military experience other than his being a private in the Georgia Hussars, a Savannah militia company. His company offered itself to the Confederate service after Fort Sumter, but Davis was so besieged with similar offers that he could not arm and equip all the volunteers, and many companies were put off. Sorrel determined to get into the war any way he could, and so went on his own to Richmond to "seek employment." Even with the influence of a brother in the surgeon general's department, Sorrel could get nothing in the way of an appointment, and consequently went to visit his father's farm in Fauquier County, just ten miles from the army being built by Beauregard near Manassas. Sorrel's father had just days before met Beauregard's adjutant, Colonel Thomas Jordan, an acquaintance from years earlier. "This was my opportunity," said the young man. He went to Jordan to plead his case. Nothing happened, and Jordan kept him waiting as the days led up to July 21 and the First Battle of Bull Run. That morning, awakened by the sound of the guns, Sorrel was delighted to be handed a note from the adjutant ordering him to report to a new brigadier, James Longstreet, as an aide with the rank of captain. Incredibly, young Sorrel got his commission and his first taste of battle on the very same day, though Longstreet's brigade was left out of almost all the fighting, and Sorrel's first impressions of his commander were drawn from seeing him throw his hat on the ground, stamp his feet, and curse the luck of being left out of the fight. Sorrel would be at Longstreet's right hand for nearly three years, then would himself become a brigadier.[13]

Alpheus S. Williams of Michigan was a major in a large company of state militia when the war commenced, and was almost immediately made brigadier general of state volunteers. Such a militia rank, however, carried no weight in the rapidly growing United States volunteer service, for generals could only be commissioned by Washington. He went to the Capital and met Lincoln, Secretary of War Simon Cameron, and a host of other influential men. "I have the promise of an appointment," he wrote home in July. In a few weeks he had his generalship, and was already politicking to get command of just the right brigade.[14]

The whole subject of such politically motivated appointments would be a sore one for both Lincoln and Davis. In the Union Army especially, literally hundreds of commissions would go to men with no military experience or ability at all. Lincoln's was a coalition government, his majority made up not only of fellow Republicans, but also of so-called "War Democrats," men who put commitment to saving the Union above party loyalties. The latter were specially important, for their influence could deliver votes to sustain the administration. Consequently, from among their number several men immediately achieved high command.

The very first major general of volunteers appointed by Lincoln was Benjamin F. Butler of Massachusetts. He had opposed Lincoln's election in 1860, but immediately supported the war effort after Fort Sumter, and was so influential that Lincoln had to give him a high command. As a result, Butler outranked for a time every other general in the army except Winfield Scott and George B. McClellan. Failing ever to demonstrate any real command ability, he was an obstacle to every subsequent general-in-chief until Grant finally removed him in 1865. Equally troublesome to Grant was John A. McClernand, a Democrat from Illinois made brigadier and later major general. In the same way, twelve members of Ohio's influential McCook family, all of them brothers or cousins of a former law partner of Lincoln's second secretary of war, Edwin M. Stanton, became Union officers. Six of them became generals.[15]

Nathaniel Banks of Massachusetts, a thoroughgoing incompetent militarily, was made a major general the same way as Butler, and then for four years lost almost every engagement he fought, often in command of actual armies. So useful were his services in raising troops and money for the war effort, however, that Lincoln felt justified in retaining him.

Jefferson Davis, too, had his problems with political generals and other officers. To his credit, and perhaps reflecting his own experience in the Old Army, and later as President Franklin Pierce's secretary of war in the 1850s, his judgments were somewhat better than Lincoln's and he issued commissions to politicians and influence holders more sparingly. Bombarded incessantly in the early years of the war for appointments, Davis, despite his protestations of making decisions solely upon individual merit, handed out quite a number of places to old friends, the sons of friends, and prominent state and local politicians. Indeed, the power to appoint generals he reserved exclusively to himself throughout the war, and only two career politicians ever achieved high rank from him, Howell Cobb of Georgia, and John C. Breckinridge of Kentucky. Cobb had been a Congressman, Speaker of the House, Secretary of the Treasury, and in 1861 a close contender for President of the Confederacy. Though he had no military experience, happily he turned out to be a good field officer. Breckinridge, former Vice President of the United States and Lincoln's chief opponent in the election of 1860, proved even better, becoming one of the premier volunteer generals of the Confederacy.

But for every good political appointee, at whatever level, there were two or three who proved worthless. The war tended to weed out most of them, either by dismissal as with Butler, or resignation, as with McClernand. A marginally more reliable source of commanders North and South would be the men who led pre-existing militia companies. As it happened, they often tended to be prominent in local public affairs as well, thus affording to Lincoln and Davis a double advantage. Many of the units, such as the North Santee Mounted Rifles of South Carolina, formed themselves when the sectional controversy heated up in the final months of 1860. Arthur Manigault was elected captain of the unit, and when Confederates started building batteries ringing Fort Sumter, Manigault became an aide on Beauregard's staff and oversaw much of the construction. From there it was only a short step to the colonelcy of the 10th South Carolina Infantry, and thereafter a distinguished combat career that led to a general's stars. Though not a true professional with formal training, Manigault's exposure to militia training and command gave him at least enough background when opportunity afforded to best display his leadership abilities.[16] Far more remarkable would be John B. Gordon of Georgia. With no military experience at all, he was elected captain of the "Raccoon Roughs," which later became a part of the 6th Alabama Infantry. Four years later Gordon would be a major general and commander of a corps in Lee's army.[17]

The genesis of Gordon's career illustrates the manner by which the overwhelming majority of officers were chosen, North and South, especially early in the war. In a nation that was fiercely democratic, that did not entirely trust the professional military, and that always vocally lauded the ability and judgment of the "common man," volunteer regiments both North and South had the long-held tradition of electing their officers. Practice varied from unit to unit, but typically the men in each company of infantry or cavalry would choose among themselves their captain and two lieutenants. If one man had been especially important in raising the company, or if as was often the case he had paid to arm and equip the company out of his own pocket, then almost certainly he was elected the captain. The captains, in turn, voted from among their number to choose a major, a lieutenant colonel, and a colonel to command the regiment. Again, a man signally responsible for recruiting several of the companies might expect the colonelcy, or else the governor of the state might have indicated a preference, for the governor in the end had to issue the actual commissions. In many cases, men of new regiments purposely left their colonelcies vacant to give the governor a chance to exercise his best judgment.

Inevitably in many regiments the electioneering took on a carnival atmosphere when more than one candidate sought a commission or if there was no clear favorite from the start. Liquor and other inducements could flow freely, along with promises of rapid promotion for the lower ranks. Sometimes even money changed hands. "Our election has not yet come off," wrote a new Johnny Reb, "and to one who like myself is not a candidate it is a time replete with feelings of disgust and contempt." Everywhere he turned, he found his favor courted, and himself hugged and coddled by would-be officers. "I never dreamed before that I was half as popular, fine-looking, and talented as I found out I am during the past few days."[18]

Highhanded methods were commonplace. One Yankee colonel simply called a regiment together, informed them that he had had their *acting* officers mustered in as permanent, "not knowing of any objection" on their part, and then asked the men to ratify his act. "No one *daring* to object," complained one soldier, the colonel was sustained. "This is called an election!" he decried. "What a farce!"[19] Another disgruntled man in the 3rd North Carolina told how his company's first lieutenant pushed through the election of a second lieutenant. "Men, there are two candidates for office, and there is but one of them worth a damn," he bellowed, "and I nominate him." Directing that all in favor of electing his nominee should come to the position of shoulder arms, the lieutenant then ordered the entire host to "company, shoulder arms!" Declaring the election unanimous, he turned the company over to its new lieutenant to dismiss.[20]

If the men of a company or regiment found they did not care for their officers once elected, there was nothing they could do about it until the regiment's term of service expired. Early in the war most units enlisted for twelve months' service, expecting the conflict to be short. When the war continued, and their enlistments expired, most regiments re-enlisted for three years or the duration of the war, and now they elected officers again. Thanks to having had a year's experience in observing themselves and their officers in action, the men made decidedly better selections the second time around.

When men found that they could not abide the original choices made, little but mutiny could help them, and that was dangerous. When the 4th New Jersey formed, one company fought against the captain somehow imposed upon it and tried to elect its own candidate, but the result was a poisoned atmosphere in the company that spread to much of the rest of the regiment.[21] One Mississippi company called the Madison Guards rebelled and disbanded in displeasure at the regimental officers elected, and not infrequently the disappointed aspirants for commissions themselves left the service immediately.[22]

Ironically, some who did not seek office and yet found themselves elected company officers, considered leaving the service too, only out of terror. Notified of his selection as lieutenant of his North Carolina company, Walter Lenoir quailed. "Oh! that I could but once have gone to school for two or three months as a diligent student of the company and battalion drills," he lamented in his diary.[23] It did not help that most of the company officers elected had long been known to the other members of the company either as friends, business associates, childhood playmates, or even brothers and cousins. "It was a trying ordeal for the officers," wrote one Texan, when they had suddenly to exercise authority and arbitrary control over young men they had known on an equal footing since youth.[24] The brother or friend long accustomed to cuffing the ears or tousling the hair of a fellow, could find it very difficult to salute and obey him without a smirk or question just because he had been made an officer.

But an overwhelmingly greater obstacle for thousands of the newly elected regimental officers was their utter ignorance of what an officer was supposed to do. The strutting about in bright buttons, sash and sword and gleaming boots, came easily enough, but the business of command was as good as a foreign language to them, and some of it, in fact, was foreign, many of the drill evolutions being called by French rather than English names. Unfortunately, in all the rush to go to war, neither side made any provision to give officer training to the newly elected or appointed leaders. Whatever hasty education the new officers received was strictly of an ersatz and informal variety. Some regiments – usually those with an experienced Regular Army colonel appointed to command – set up their own schools to train men in the manual of arms, drill evolutions, and the duties and deportment expected of an officer. With no system or uniformity, however, the students often learned nothing more than the weaknesses and prejudices of their teachers.

Some states like Michigan did establish camps of instruction, and sent their officers to them first before the enlisted men followed. More often than not, however, fresh officers and men were both simply dumped into the maelstrom of camp life and training and left to learn and fend for themselves. The results were usually comical and not infrequently tragic.

For starters, the officers, especially at the company level, were often hardly more educated than their own illiterate men. Drill maneuvers of the simplest kind could not be performed because the men did not know the meaning of the words, and because frequently enough there were enlisted men who literally did not know right from left. One ingenious officer devised the system of tying hay to the left feet of his men, and straw to the right. Then, instead of commanding them to march "left, right, left" and so on, which many could not understand, he simply called orders for "hay-foot, strawfoot." The technique was a success and achieved a wide usage in both armies.[25]

Worse still, many men given sudden power were not able to grasp fully the difference between the use and abuse of it. Early in 1862, the lieutenant of Company E, 4th Kentucky, abused and mistreated one of his privates. Only the intercession of now General Breckinridge brought a remedy. On another occasion that spring, a different officer ordered a private to sweep out the officer's tent. When the private refused, he was put in the guardhouse until Breckinridge learned of it and ordered the officer to apologize to him and sweep out his own tent. Occasionally the men themselves turned the tables on abusive commanders. When a North Carolina captain put one of his men in the guard house, other soldiers got even by catching the captain when he was drunk. "We put him in the Sh-t House," wrote the offended private, "so we are even." And in 1863, the men of the 55th Georgia deposed their colonel and rode him about camp on a rail until he promised better behavior and was allowed to resume command.[26]

There was a great deal of routine involved in being an officer – making out reports, inspections, roll calls, promulgating general orders from headquarters, specifying guard details, and more. Throughout many of the volunteer regiments, there would always be complaints of these and other functions not being performed in a routine and timely fashion. Throughout the war there would be repeated complaints of laxity made by army inspectors. The Confederates attempted to do something about it by instituting competency examinations in 1862, but they were ever haphazard, and the simple needs for more officers in a hurry due to the attrition of disease and the battlefield always placed untried and untrained men in hundreds of vacancies every month.

The inevitable result of such inexperience was embarrassingly evident in the early months of the war. At drill especially, most regiments were like unto the mute leading the deaf. Infantrymen at bayonet drill stuck each other in the back when orders were garbled. Cavalrymen inflicted more saber wounds upon themselves and their horses than they ever later visited upon their enemies. There were a number of accepted drill manuals available, especially *Rifle and Infantry Tactics* by William J. Hardee, now a general in the Confederate Army. But others with conflicting ideas were also used, and it wasn't until 1862 that the War Department in Washington issued a new standard manual by Silas Casey.

Some of these new officers, it seemed, could not even count. The adjutant of the

First Kentucky Brigade, Breckinridge's first command, had to be reprimanded when he detailed more men from the 5th Kentucky for camp and police duties than the regiment actually mustered. A Pennsylvanian complained of "a total lack of system about our regiment." Everything was late, there was little or no anticipation of the needs of the future, and good managers in the form of officers seemed to be in dire want. "We can only be justly called a mob & one not fit to face the enemy."[27]

The results of all this inexperience were nowhere more evident than on the drill field. Trying to keep the men in proper step while putting them through ill-understood maneuvers with orders often mispronounced, all amid choking dust and under the eye of superiors, could be an inordinately difficult task. A man in the 14th New Hampshire told of the preening officers "who had been cramming Casey for a fortnight," vainly trying to make it all work on the parade ground. "That the men got into a snarl, a tangle, a double and twisted, inextricable tactical knot, is tame delineation," he wrote. "The drill caused a great deal of serious reflection."[28]

Men in the ranks coughed so much that officers' commands could not be heard. If a rabbit jumped out of its nest in front of the tramping men, all discipline could dissolve as the boys took off after the potential meal. Orders passed down the ranks became garbled. When a Rebel major sent back word for the men at the rear of his column to close up at the double-quick, it finally reached the stragglers as "double quick back there." Suiting action to word, the rear of the column promptly turned around and marched off at high speed in the opposite direction, leaving the major in command lying on his back, kicking his feet into the air, and swearing "benedictions of an unusual kind for a Presbyterian elder."[29]

It did not help that many amateur officers felt free to choose their own particular set of drill instructions. When time came for battalion drill of more than one company at a time, and one captain had trained with Hardee and another with Casey or Winfield Scott's old manual, the result could be chaos. More than one officer simply skirted the whole issue by abandoning military jargon and telling the men plainly what he wanted them to do. Seeing his command approaching a mud hole, and not knowing the proper commands to have the men march around it, one finally shouted, "Boys! Break up, scoot the hole, and git together on t'other side." In the end, one Tennessee colonel used three commands: "Form line", "Forward march", and "Fix bayonets." Colonel Robert Preston of the 28th Virginia apparently saw nothing incongruous about ordering his men: "Fall in Twenty-eighth, fall in! If you don't fall in, I will march the regiment off and leave every one of you behind!"[30]

Not infrequently the men in the ranks were openly disrespectful or laughed at the expense of an inexperienced and confused officer. "Drill is aching funny," wrote a New Hampshire boy. "Mistakes are corrected by making still worse mistakes. The men in the ranks grin, giggle and snicker, and now and then break out into a coarse, country hee-haw." When an inordinately youthful lieutenant rode in front of his men for the first time, wags shouted from the rear, "And a little child shall lead them," to peals of laughter. The laughs turned to groans the next day when the lieutenant published an order for a twenty-mile practice march. "And a little child shall lead them!" it read, "on a damned big horse!"[31]

Indeed, as insubordinate and disrespectful as many of the enlisted men could be toward a novice officer, the position of company and even regimental commander could be anything but pleasant. "My post is no sinecure," lamented a Mississippi captain. "My hands are full – perfectly full. I have no hope of being a popular Capt. I am only trying to make a good one." The good ones were appreciated in time by their men, and respected. For the rest, the common soldier North or South had little use. "I wish to God one half of our officers were knocked in the head by slinging them Against A part of those still Left," declared one Yank. Another proclaimed late in the conflict that "had it not been for officers this war would have Ended long ago." Confederates could be just as critical. While one declared his colonel "an ignoramus fit for nothing higher than the cultivation of corn," another Reb from Florida achieved even greater heights of invective, pronouncing his officers "not fit to tote guts to a Bear."[32]

No wonder that many officers could not take the pressure of their new job, nor the disapproval of their men, and chose to resign. The rapid formation of the armies, and their launching into active campaigning with barely a few weeks for training, quickly separated those who could stand the frustrations from those who could not. While the Regular Army officers, whichever side they chose, knew what they were getting into when it came to training and leading men, the unskilled volunteer officers who were to form the overwhelming majority of this war's leaders had no alternative but to learn by doing, and it was a hard school of experience that awaited them in America's bloodiest war. There were many who might have agreed with one officer from Texas who found he could not take the strain, and resigned. "If he had to associate with devils," he had said, "he would wait till he went to hell, where he could select his own company."[33]

REFERENCES

1 Warner, *Generals in Gray*, pp.38, 132; Roland, *Johnston*, pp.249-50.
2 John Gibbon, *Personal Recollections of the Civil War* (New York, 1928), p.3.
3 Roland, *Johnston*, pp.252-60.
4 James Longstreet, *From Manassas to Appomattox* (Philadelphia, 1896), pp.29-33.
5 Gallagher, *Alexander*, pp.22-3.
6 Hancock, *Hancock*, pp.73-5; Gallagher, *Alexander*, pp.30-1.
7 Gibbon, *Recollections*, pp.5-7.
8 *Ibid.*, pp.9-10.
9 Martin F. Schmitt, ed., *General George Crook, His Autobiography* (Norman, Okla., 1960), p.83.
10 Merlin E. Sumner, ed., *The Diary of Cyrus B. Comstock* (Dayton, Ohio, 1987), pp.230-5.
11 Schmitt, *Crook*, pp.83-5.
12 Coffman, *Old Army*, p.92.

13 G. Moxley Sorrel, *Recollections of a Confederate Staff Officer* (New York, 1905), pp.21-6.

14 Milo M. Quaife, ed., *From the Cannon's Mouth; The Civil War Letters of General Alpheus S. Williams* (Detroit, 1959), pp.16-8.

15 Mark M. Boatner, *The Civil War Dictionary* (New York, 1959), p.526.

16 R. Lockwood Tower, ed., *A Carolinian Goes to War: The Civil War Narrative of Arthur Middleton Manigault* (Columbia, S.C., 1983), pp.9-10.

17 John B. Gordon, *Reminiscences of the Civil War* (New York, 1904), pp.4, 26.

18 Bell I. Wiley, *The Life of Johnny Reb* (Indianapolis, 1943), p.20.

19 Bell I. Wiley, *The Life of Billy Yank* (Indianapolis, 1952), p.24

201 James I. Robertson, Jr., *Soldiers Blue and Gray* (Columbia, S.C., 1988), p.13.

21 James I. Robertson, Jr., ed., *The Civil War Letters of General Robert A. McAllister* (New Brunswick, N.J., 1965), p.30.

22 Wiley, *Johnny Reb*, p.20.

23 Robertson, *Soldiers*, p.51.

24 *Ibid.*, p.51.

25 Robertson, *Soldiers*, p.49.

26 Davis, *Orphan Brigade*, pp.54-5; Wiley, *Johnny Reb*, p.242.

27 *Ibid.*, p.54; Wiley, *Billy Yank*, p.26.

28 Francis H. Buffum, *A History of the Fourteenth Regiment, New Hampshire Volunteers* (Boston, 1882), p.45.

29 Robertson, *Soldiers*, p.52.

30 Robertson, *Soldiers*, pp.50-1.

31 *Ibid.*, p.49.

32 *Ibid.*, p.51; Bell I. Wiley, *The Common Soldier of the Civil War* (New York, 1973), pp.87-8.

33 Robertson, *Soldiers*, p.53.

III

UNDER THE MARQUEE

"**A** captain does not only his own, but all the thinking of the company," lamented an officer of the 125th New York. "A captain has as much to do as – in fact, he is practically – the father of ninety children. Men in camp, sensible men, lose all their good judgment and almost their good sense; they become puerile, and come to the captain on a multitude of silly, childish matters."[1]

In other words, this new business of being an officer and a gentleman in an army of volunteers was no picnic. Even the Old Army men were ill-prepared for it – indeed, they may have been even less prepared for it than the men who were commissioned out of civil life, for the Regulars were accustomed to Regular enlisted men who did not question orders, who recognized and respected the chain of command. This new army of volunteers, imbued with the old Jacksonian spirit of individuality, was a different thing altogether. An officer did not command the regard of his men by divine right. He had to earn it.

This situation was always difficult because from the very outset the officer had a number of marks against him in the men's eyes. He was paid more. He received a much better allowance of rations, or pay allowances that enabled him to buy better food than his men. Whereas most of them – infantry anyhow – had to walk, the average officer was mounted. The officer did not have to obey the same restrictions to camp that applied to the men. He lived in a larger and better furnished tent or winter quarters, and the frequent rules against drinking and gambling did not necessarily apply to him. However much the enlisted men may have liked a man when they first elected him to company or regimental office, sooner or later at least some came to resent the markedly different status of a man who was, in their eyes after all, no better than they were. Only years of service in the field, tempered by performance in battle and a demonstrated concern for the welfare of the men in the ranks, would eventually win for an officer the approbation of the men he commanded.

Certainly the men in command did live a different life. "It seems queer, though, and almost magical," wrote the new brigadier Alpheus S. Williams when he joined his brigade in October 1861. The officers' encampment was on a lovely hillside, eight or ten tents being for Williams and his staff and escort. Nearby were the tents for the officers' servants, and even the horses were sheltered in woods under the shade of a tent fly. "Altogether it is a delightful spot," he concluded, "especially towards sundown when the bands of the regiments strike up for the evening parades and the hillsides in front are covered with moving bodies of troops and the bugle calls from the neighboring brigades float up the valleys and are echoed along the hillside."[2]

Even then, Williams could complain of hardship . . . of a sort. When he and his three wagons of impedimenta reached the camp, no one offered assistance. Of himself, a captain, two lieutenants, and three servants, only Williams and the captain had ever pitched a tent. Still they got their tents erected, then settled down and opened their mess chest to a dinner of broiled ham and soda biscuits, lamenting that they could not find fresh meat or bread. At the same time, most of the men in the ranks were sleeping crammed into crowded circular tents that held a dozen packed in like spoons, and eating salt pork or pickled beef and hardtack. No wonder many of the men commenced the war with an immediate resentment of their leaders.[3]

It was much the same all across the country in the early days of the war. Even in the Confederacy, where in time supplies would be so tight that the officers lived little better than the men, at first there was an abundance of everything. The men of Charleston's Washington Light Infantry went to the front taking their black servants and valets with them, lived in crisp white canvas tents with spacious accommodation, and dined from hampers sent by family and friends and filled with cakes and cheeses, fresh coffee and tobacco, champagne and beer and wine, and the finest of smoked meats. Often they had their own musicians to serenade them. The Washington Artillery of New Orleans went to war in bright awning striped marquees, set up on raised wooden floorboards to get them out of the mud and dust.

The daily routine in these officers' quarters varied considerably from regiment to regiment, army to army. For Williams and his staff it began with reveille at sunrise, after which his servant William served all of the officers good strong coffee. An hour later he served breakfast. By 8 a.m., the morning reports of men present for duty, absent without leave, on sick call, and so forth, began to arrive from the several regiments in his brigade, all of them prepared by officers who had to arise earlier than Williams and awaken their men for roll call. The morning reports out of the way, the lieutenants and their sergeants began making out copies of the day's orders for the regiments, filling out leaves and furlough papers, requisitions for quartermaster or commissary stores. Then orders would come down from division for Williams' officers to copy and distribute through his regiments.

Once he had seen and approved a consolidated report of those present for duty for his entire brigade, Williams mounted his horse to start his daily rounds of his command, usually not returning until noon or later for a meal before remounting and continuing his inspections. "In this way the days seem short," he wrote home, "and by eight or nine o'clock we are all in bed."[4] To his wife he would complain that "according to the custom of the army I am obliged to live and travel in considerable state." A guard was detailed for him every day by each of his regiments in turn, every time he came or went turning out to present arms. A mounted orderly followed him everywhere, and whenever he approached the camps of one of his regiments, shouts of "The Brigadier General" would result in a guard of a hundred or more rolling out. He had to ride past and review them, repeating the same performance with each regiment. "I go through this process at least once a day," he complained.

More onerous were all the petty details to which he had to attend, or which he oversaw his subordinate officers in attending. He even had a special clerk detailed to help with the paperwork. All issues from the quartermaster's or the commissary's stores required his approval. His signature appeared on every leave and furlough, every order for a court-martial, and all reports. "In short, everything for 5,000 men has to pass under my supervision." And at that, he believed that he had streamlined the process from what many other brigade and regimental commanders went through, so much so that he still found time to visit each of his regiments daily, look in on the condition of the camps and hospitals and kitchens, and attend personally to the special reports turned in each day by field officers designated to review all the complaints and suggestions that needed acting upon within the command. To get everything done satisfactorily, he frequently stayed up late on the nights when the moon allowed a few extra hours.[5]

Even the poor volunteer officer who tried his best to master his sudden new "craft" faced considerable obstacles, not the least of which were the frequently contemptuous Regulars who often commanded the regiments or otherwise oversaw the training of new company commanders. There was nothing worse, wrote Yankee Thomas W. Higginson, than the experience of having "some young regular army lieutenant ride up to your tent at an hour's notice, and leisurely devote a day to probing every weak spot in your command – to stand by while he smells at every camp-kettle, detects every delinquent gun-sling, ferrets out old shoes from behind mess-bunks, spies out every tent pole not labelled with the sergeant's name, asks to see the cash balance of each company fund, and perplexes your best captain on forming from two ranks into one by the left flank." Yet Higginson and others had to admit that, unpleasant as they were, these inspections "are the salvation of an army."

A few senior commanders recognized that this teaching was especially important for volunteer officers, and that special schools of instruction were needed. These were sporadically operated, however, depending chiefly upon the whim of the individual camp commander. Some form of system was introduced on July 22, 1861, when the

Congress in Washington enacted a bill in response to the chaos at Bull Run, making provision for the establishment of a military commission in every department, charged with examining all volunteer officers to adjudge their competency. The act showed some immediate salutary effects, for many officers who knew themselves unequal to their commissions resigned rather than go before the examining boards and suffer the possible humiliation of dismissal. A man who did not appear for his scheduled examination automatically failed. By November 1861, for every officer discharged by the boards, nearly three others resigned voluntarily.

Of course the new system had its faults, not the least being that since it was created by politicians, it suffered from political influences that hampered its full and impartial operation. The overwhelming majority of officers being dismissed or forced into resignation were from the lower grades; very few colonels and no generals were affected. Though they could be no better schooled or able than the lieutenants and captains, the men with high rank had connections that the examining boards did not want to offend.[7]

Occasionally more drastic measures were necessary to deal with inept or insubordinate volunteer officers, as when General George B. McClellan had perhaps a score of them from one regiment sent to the prison at Fort Jefferson in the Dry Tortugas to labor until they changed their ways.[8] But by and large the examining boards accomplished much of what they were intended to do. A side effect was that governors and others raising regiments showed more discretion in their appointments, rather than risk having their appointees later discharged by the boards. Thus, generally with plodding pace, the organization and discipline of the volunteer officers and their men gradually improved. And as officers were removed by discharge or battle, the soldiers slowly acquired much better judgment in voting for their replacements. Making things easier, the War Department began to print instructions on the forms and blanks that some services required officers to fill out. In the ordnance service, for instance, these instructions were "so simple and so minute that it seems as if, henceforward, the most negligent volunteer officer could never make another error." Of course they did, just the same.[9]

And no examining board or set of instructions could protect either Union or Confederacy from the relentless operation of the seniority system. The higher an officer's rank from the beginning, the less his chances of being dismissed for incompetency or removed from command thanks to wounds or death. And when such a man, a colonel or a general, did leave the service, the system dictated that someone of high seniority replace him. In short, many of the inept early commissioned leading officers could not be displaced by any means. "Beneath the shadow of their notorious incompetency all minor evils may lurk undetected," complained a lower officer. "To crown all, they are, in many cases, sincere and well meaning men, utterly obtuse as to their own deficiencies, and manifesting all the Christian virtues except that of resignation."[10]

It did not help that among many of the volunteer regiments, men and officers chose not to recognize that a difference existed between them. When Major General Richard Taylor inspected a new Texas cavalry regiment joining the Confederacy, he at first thought them well disciplined since their camp was so quiet. Then when he got to the center of the group of men, he discovered that their silence was due to their intent concentration on their colonel whom he found seated beneath some trees on a blanket, "dealing the fascinating game of monte." Only grudgingly did the colonel stop playing cards and start playing commander. "Officers and men addressed each other as Tom, Dick, or Harry," lamented Taylor, "and had no more conception of military gradations than of the celestial hierarchy of the poets."[11]

When they did learn to recognize those gradations of rank, men and officers in each army knew them by different insignia. By regulation, and almost without fail, all Union officers wore their insignia of rank on rectangular shoulder straps rimmed with gold bullion, worn one on each shoulder of their dark blue uniform blouse or tunic. A second lieutenant, the lowest form of officer, wore plain shoulder straps that were blank inside the bullion border. A first lieutenant was recognized by a single gold bar at each end of the strap. A captain wore a pair of bars at each end. A major showed a gold oak leaf front and back on his strap, and a lieutenant colonel the same, except that his leaf was silver. A full colonel had a single silver eagle in the center. Among the grades of general, a brigadier wore a single gold star in the center of his epaulette, a major general wore two, a lieutenant general three. Only U.S. Grant wore three stars during the war, and shortly afterward he was given a fourth.

Officer insignia in the Confederate Army was entirely different, and probably made so solely for the sake of the difference, and perhaps to avoid confusion early in the war since several regiments in the South wore blue uniforms.

All badges of rank in the Confederacy were ordered by regulation to be worn on the front sides of the stand-up collar on the officer's blouse. A second lieutenant wore a single horizontal gold stripe on either side; a first lieutenant two stripes, one above the other; and a captain three. For a major, a single five-pointed star replaced the bars. A lieutenant colonel wore two stars on either side of his collar, and a colonel three stars. Thereafter, however, it got a bit confusing, for even though the Confederate Congress eventually authorized four grades of general – brigadier, major, lieutenant, and full general – it never amended its original specifications for insignia when only the brigadier grade existed. Thus, all generals of all grades were to wear three stars, one larger one flanked by two smaller, encased in a gold wreath. Further, the Confederate law specified distinctive – yet imprecise – cap and sleeve markings. Lieutenants of both grades were to wear gold braid or "frogging" one wale (ridge of cloth) in width. For a captain it was two wales wide, and the same for a major. A lieutenant colonel and a colonel both wore three wales of braid, and all ranks of general four. Each officer's uniform kepi, a short cap with a brim in front, was to carry vertical side stripes in number corresponding to the sleeve braid. It was a more complex insignia system than the Federals, and less precise. Worse, a combination of scarcity of materials and/or seamstresses, and the idiosyncratic nature of the officers themselves, meant that regulations were honored almost as much in the breach as in the observance of the law. Many former U.S. officers simply continued to wear their Old Army uniforms, as did Thomas J. Jackson for a time. Many more, uniformed by their states before Confederate regulations were established, wore shoulder straps, or epaulettes and collar insignia. The sleeve braid never saw light of day on a majority of Southern leaders, and neither did the kepis, full brimmed slouch hats being more practical for field service. And even among the highest ranking officers observance was lax. Robert E. Lee and Joseph E. Johnston, both full generals, never got around to encircling the three stars on their collars with wreaths, and only Johnston wore the sleeve braid. Had not their men recognized them by sight, these army commanders might have been mistaken for colonels.[12]

North and South, there were also arrangements of buttons to denote rank, but these were often misleading, for men who won promotion frequently did not bother to rearrange their buttons. Also, in the Union Army the practice of awarding brevets might entitle a man who was only a major to wear the insignia of his brevet rank, which could be colonel or even brigadier. It was not all quite as complex as Taylor's reference to the "celestial hierarchy of the poets," but to men entirely new to military etiquette, it could certainly be confusing.

Perhaps the frequent disinclination to recognize the differences in rank sprang in part from many of the volunteers' initial refusal to admit an obligation to pay attention to officers. Here was the new officer's chief hurdle. Most of his men believed, as one soldier put it, that enlisted men were the equals of their leaders, "and not a few . . . the superiors." One Yankee volunteer general found his men completely ignorant of "the proper deference due superior officers," and it was worse in the more individualistic Confederacy, where one observer noted that it took years to teach the privates "to give unquestioning obedience to officers because they were such."[13]

As a result, initially many inexperienced officers tried to deal with their men by staying their friends, by assiduously denying their own different status. "Gentlemen of the Banks County Guards," one Georgia captain suggested, "will you please halt." A firmer hand than that would be needed for real effective command, but it took the green officers many months in camp and field to acquire the self-confidence to take such a hand with the men.[14] Less wise were those who sought from the outset to control their men by the imposition of bullying or flagrant exercise of rank. "Tell a soldier that he must not do a certain thing or go to a certain place," wrote a Rebel Texan, "and he will immediately want to know the reason why and begin to investigate." Consequently, in the training of these volunteers, the officers had to exercise considerable judgment of how far they could be pushed before they would push back. Lieutenant Colonel John Beatty went past that line with his 3rd Ohio. When he approved court-martial sentences for men who broke camp rules, he was vilified in the unit. Insubordination broke out, and a mutiny ensued after he punished a soldier for drunkenness. Only by dint of staring them down did he prevent open rebellion, but later he lost them again when the ineffectual colonel of the regiment went back on a promise to resign rather than have Beatty press charges against him. The men liked the loose – indeed, non-existent – rule of the colonel, and when he decided not to resign 225 of the men in the ranks signed a petition that called for resignation from Beatty instead. Only by unyielding steadfastness did Beatty manage to hold on to his command.[15]

Even when they did not actually mutiny or rebel, the men knew of ways to show their lack of approval of their officers, and especially of men with inflated egos. Not a few swell-headed blue-bloods from Massachusetts or South Carolina openly showed a disdain for the common men in the ranks. Colonel Charles S. Wainwright of New York was not at all embarrassed to denounce the indiscriminate mixing of the social classes in the army, and the inclination of privates to "hobnob" with their betters. Seeing so much in the army that took place on "a purely democratic footing" was disgusting to him. Some Massachusetts units even dismissed officers for fraternizing too much with the private soldiers, and in the Confederate army soldiers often complained of the officers setting themselves above and apart. "The officers above the rank of captain knew but little of the hardships of war from personal experience," complained a Virginian. "They had their black cooks[un]. . . . The regimental wagons carried the officers' clothes, and they were never half-naked, lousy, or dirty. They never had to sleep upon the bare ground[un]. . .; the officers were never unshod or felt the torture of stone-bruise."[16]

Consequently, the men struck back however they could. In Virginia, one regiment put on black-face minstrel shows in which the most ludicrous characters were clearly recognizable as parodies of unpopular officers. A major in the 20th New York was taken by a group of his men and tossed into the air repeatedly from a tent fly. A stuffy New York captain of the 9th Infantry found his men openly derisive. They shouted insults and taunts at him when he tried to form them for parade, hanged and burned him in effigy, and drew rude caricatures of him on the walls of his own tent. Finally he was virtually a prisoner in his own quarters, fearful to venture out lest the baiting continue. In the end he resigned. "Nothing," said one soldier, "was more keenly relished than a joke on an officer."[17]

Even a less aristocratic and otherwise well-liked officer had to be wary not to allow momentary harshness or a loss of temper or demeanor to poison his relations with his men. When a Massachusetts officer thoughtlessly whistled for his young drummer to come to him, the boy belligerently replied that he was not a pet and would not come when whistled at. If the men in a company or a regiment decided that they did not respect an officer, they could affront him either by refusing to salute when he passed or, just as often, by offering in mockery exaggerated responses to his orders. Even more galling to an officer was the occasional barracks "lawyer" who found in the army regulations a weapon to use against him. When a Virginia lieutenant ordered his company to dig a trench, he himself returned to the comfort of camp. After a time, so did many of his men, arguing that they had worked as hard as the men on either side of them. The lieutenant found that John Casler was the ringleader, and immediately started cursing him to his face. "You must not curse me," Casler retorted, "or I will report you to headquarters." In the end the officer apologized for his intemperance. "An officer can punish a private," Casler well knew, "but he dare not curse him. That was one advantage a private had over an officer."[18]

Even in obeying orders without rebellion, an unpopular officer the men could torment. One man gave a sentry orders so exhaustively complete and minute that the sentry felt his intelligence had been insulted. Instead of protesting, he simply carried out his orders as given – exhaustively and minutely, to the point that the offending officer was forced, by literal interpretation of the instructions, to dismount himself in the center of a stream.[19]

Not many of the soldiers appreciated the fact that a lot of the volunteer officers themselves were painfully aware of their ignorance and lack of experience. The more conscientious ones did their best to study or otherwise learn quickly what they needed to know. Colonel Roger Hanson sat up for several nights in late 1861, studying in his tent with his brigade drillmaster, as the teacher instructed him in the latest regimental and brigade drill by moving kernels of corn around on a table. Many a young man like Lieutenant Samuel Craig would go off alone into a field or deep wood, and there read from Casey or Hardee the necessary commands to drill the men, shouting the orders at the mute trees. A few even wrote their required orders on small pieces of paper, then read from them – perhaps concealing them by their saddle, when drilling on parade. Unfortunately for the colonel of the 5th Wisconsin, when he did this his horse spooked at noise from the band, and all his notes fluttered to the ground. Parade had to halt while he picked them up and got them resorted into proper order.[20]

Besides learning what to say to the men when on parade, every officer had to wrestle with the question of his own personal deportment and the example he set. Forbidden by regulations from excessive drinking or gambling, or other vices, and liable to punishment if guilty, the private soldiers would not long tolerate similar behavior in officers. Certainly the same temptations that lure a private or non-commissioned officer could work upon the spirit of one of his commanders. "Temptation was around me in a thousand forms," wrote a Mississippi lieutenant. "In none of these things did I indulge."[21]

Drunkenness, especially, outraged the men, not because of insobriety itself, but because an officer could get away with it without punishment often as not, while that same officer might very well impose harsh sentences on the men in the ranks caught drinking. A man of the 10th Confederate Cavalry wrote of seeing his colonel "always drunk when he can get whiskey," and in the 61st Illinois one lieutenant was damned by a soldier as a "mean, pucelanamous, low bread, nigerdly, unprincipled drinking sot." When a captain with too much liquor in him became insulting and berated and harrassed a guard who had challenged him at the picket line, a number of other soldiers came to the rescue and collectively yanked the inebriate from his horse, beat him thoroughly, and sent him afoot back to his camp.[22]

An officer also had to be careful not to fall into other habits of his men, or to become even a passive participant in their vices, for fear it would give them a weapon to use against him. In every army there were orders prohibiting foraging in neighboring farmyards, and officers were duty bound to enforce both the regulations and punishments. However, when part of the booty from such stealthy expeditions was mysteriously left beside or inside a company officer's tent, all too often he was not too diligent about finding the offenders. Instead, officers and men evolved a little bit of play acting in which the officer regularly made stirring and ferocious speeches before the men denouncing such infractions and promising the direst of penalties if any were caught transgressing. But the men well knew he was saying it only as a matter of form, and kept right on with their mischief. An Ohio colonel who found his men robbing haystacks fumed at the men, then rode away and told others met along the way that they would have to hurry if they wanted to get any hay. The colonel of the 14th Wisconsin near Vicksburg, Mississippi, spoke his warnings so hyperbolically that none of his men could mistake his real intent. "Boys, you have heard the orders," he shouted. "Now I don't want to see a d—d man touch any of them sheep we just passed, and these hogs, I don't want to see any one touch them. Break ranks!" Quickly the men went to work, and later that day the colonel himself discovered a fine ham in his tent.[23]

Many officers simply turned a blind eye, rationalizing their men's behavior by considering the poor rations the government furnished them, and the undoubted fact that the war was all the enemy's fault anyhow, and enemy civilians should pay the price with their livestock and fence rails. And worse, a few commissioned men actually participated in the transgressions. An Ohio lieutenant helped some of his men steal hogs, and was later caught eating a rib by his major. His incredible explanation was that "it rained pieces of fresh pork this morning." Yet the major, smilingly it must be assumed, accepted the excuse, and later accepted a nice chunk of pork from the lieutenant.[24]

The point was, however, that sooner or later an officer who joined with the men or condoned their depredations tended to lose their respect. Certainly he lost whatever healthy quotient of fear or awe there might have been that gave him an edge in exacting obedience when it really mattered. And such a man also lost the respect of his fellow commanders, for though it was a very large army, North or South, it was still a rather small, closed society in which nothing stayed secret for long. "The men talked about the officers, and the officers talked about each other," wrote a New Yorker, "in a manner that led strangers to believe that like Ishmael of old, 'Every man's hand turned against his neighbor, and his neighbor's hand against him.'"[26]

After the first few months in camp, army life took on a routine a bit more relaxed than the days of initial training. In the Confederate Army of Tennessee in north Georgia in the early months of 1864, the officers saw that their men had breakfast first before drilling them for ninety minutes at regimental or company evolutions. Then after lunch and time taken for details and camp policing, another ninety minutes of drill by battalion and brigade, with occasionally a drill of an entire division or even corps. On Sundays brigade commanders inspected their men, and looked over all equipment and impedimenta, including wagons and ambulances, animal harnesses, even blacksmiths' forges. "Having little else to do," wrote one Rebel officer, "all our time was devoted to such duties as tended to improve the men as soldiers, and added to the efficiency of the army." It was good for all concerned, for Brigadier General Arthur M. Manigault observed, even at this late date, that "soldiers are proverbially careless, and officers of our army, those of the line particularly, were scarcely any more careful than their men." Unlike many officers, North and South, Manigault made his command engage in daily target practice, something that, unimaginably, was never taught to recruits with any system or science.[26]

Most armies devoted more time than usual to drill and other such matters when in winter quarters. Since the armies could only campaign seriously in the spring, summer, and fall, the cold months of the year they stayed stationary, usually building semi-permanent quarters of logs and tents combined. Officers, too, lived in such dwellings, and many found a cosy sort of comfort in them. "You probably think living in tents in the winter is a killing thing," Alpheus Williams wrote home in February 1863. "But it is vastly more pleasant and comfortable than you in a warm house imagine." Of course, he did have to stoke his little stove constantly to keep off the cold, but still he was not uncomfortable. Certainly he did not complain. Instead, he lamented, "think of my poor 600 men on picket out in front, and the thousands around so poorly sheltered." Williams was a beloved officer, thanks to his concern for his men.[27]

Across the lines, the routine of officer life took on much the same aspect, though one feature of Confederate officers was the number of them – especially colonels and generals – who had their wives and even children with them when not on active campaign. The wife of Colonel and later General John B. Gordon was a frequent sight in the camps of the II Corps, and a frequent annoyance to his commander General Jubal A. Early. Yet Early had to admit, as he did publicly to Mrs. Gordon, that "General Gordon is a better soldier when you are close by him than when you are away, and so hereafter, when I issue orders that officers' wives must go to the rear, you may know that you are excepted."[28] The wives of men like Breckinridge, Joseph E. Johnston, and many others were frequently with the armies, providing not only comfort to their husbands, but also serving as nurses and comforters for the wounded, writing letters for illiterate soldiers, and simply bringing to men away from home a little genteel feminine company. The other thing that a Southern officer could expect that few Yankee counterparts endured was a good snowballing in winter. For some reason Johnny Rebs felt this a peculiar right of theirs. "All distinctions were leveled," wrote a Georgia colonel, "and the higher the officer the more snow balling he received." Occasionally it got a little out of hand, and captains came out with black eyes and missing teeth, often the injuries reflecting the low standing of the officer concerned.[29]

On the other hand, there was one unique experience that only Northern officers would have in this war – leading black troops. It is one of the great ironies of the Civil War that the Negro, and especially the slave, was the *sine qua non* of the conflict. Without slavery, there would have been no war. Yet once the conflict had commenced, blacks – slave or free – had almost nothing to do with it for at least the first two years. Very few Yankees went to war to end slavery, and very few Southern men went to war to protect the institution. To the former the idea of emancipation and freedom for the Negro was an abstraction, while to the latter the continuation of slavery hardly mattered because only one in a thousand Confederates ever owned a slave or had any personal stake in perpetuating slavery. The fact is that a host of motivations sent these men out to be officers and gentlemen – adventure and glory-seeking, misplaced nineteenth-century romanticism, boredom, even embarrassment at staying behind while so many others went to war. But only a very small portion of Union officers were fighting for abolition or emancipation or for anything connected with the Negro. They went to war chiefly out of patriotism, to defend the Union and remove the stain on the national banners left there by what they saw as the treasonable rebellion of the South. By the same token, Southern men became Confederate officers not to defend slavery or the shadow-issue of states' rights, nor even for the most part because of any sense of Southern nationalism. They donned their uniforms and led men into battle simply to protect their homeland, which, in their eyes, was being invaded by a hostile foe bent on conquest. On both sides, interest in or concern for the slaves did not enter into more than a tiny fraction of the decisions to become an officer.

Even Lincoln's Emancipation Proclamation of January 1, 1863, was more a move to make the Union cause a holy war for freedom for all than a real involvement of the nation's blacks in the contest. But that involvement was bound to come, for no sooner had the war begun than prominent abolitionists in the North began to clamor for free blacks to be allowed to go to war to fight for their brethren's freedom. At first the raising of Negro regiments was such a politically dangerous issue that the Lincoln government would not entertain the idea. Knowing that if black soldiers were enlisted they would, of course, not be integrated into white regiments, Negro leaders even proposed that "efficient and accomplished" white officers be selected to command them. Still Lincoln would not dare act. But by late 1862, with losses in his armies mounting, and with tens of thousands of runaway Southern slaves coming into Yankee lines for refuge, something had to be done. That fall, while he was issuing his preliminary Emancipation Proclamation, he quietly authorized the raising of a single black regiment in Union occupied territory in South Carolina. From that modest start, eventually more than 186,000 Negroes would take service for the Union.[30]

An adverse reaction from many was immediate. "A decided majority of our Officers of all grades have no sympathy with your policy," a Wisconsin commander told Lincoln. "They hate the Negro more than they love the Union." Nevertheless, enlistments went at a brisk pace in the new Bureau of Colored Troops, and that emphasized the immediate need for officers to train and lead them.

Eventually some 7,000 whites would become officers of the regiments officially designated United States Colored Troops – generally shortened to U.S.C.T. They came from a variety of motivations. At first, the government and the Bureau assiduously sought out men who felt committed to black freedom and who actually wanted to help blacks work and fight for abolition. They wanted men who would be proud to lead Negro soldiers, men who were helping to make a grand social and moral statement. A number of able and experienced non-commissioned officers from white volunteer regiments were so selected, and for a time it appeared to some that the caliber of leaders in the U.S.C.T. would be better than in the white regiments, because influence and ambition could not get a commission out of the examining boards, only intelligence and ability. Unfortunately, such men were not a sufficient source for all that were needed. Eventually, far more men came to the U.S.C.T. regiments for the opportunity to obtain high promotion and better pay, or simply because they saw it as a quicker way of winning the war. In many white regiments, a sergeant might never rise to a commission, but by taking a commission in a black unit he had a much brighter future. "I would drill a company of alligators for a hundred and twenty a month," one man admitted, while others sought the commissions because an officer – unlike an enlisted man – could resign at will. Becoming an officer in a U.S.C.T. unit, thus, was a faster way out of the army altogether.[31]

However he obtained that commission, the white officer in a black unit faced some very special challenges. Almost all had to overcome their own prejudice toward Negroes, their attitude that blacks were essentially children, and that former slaves would not fight. A few officers actually viewed their men as victims, defrauding them of pay, and others berated them, and even sexually assaulted the wives or sweethearts who were near camp. Indeed, there were many tests of character faced by such officers that would not have presented themselves in white outfits. Then, too, the officers also had to cope with the derision and prejudice of fellow officers in the regular volunteers. This especially, helped lead to the resignation of many U.S.C.T. leaders. Fortunately, more remained however.

In many regiments, a genuine bond grew between men and officers. Perhaps it arose from the special nature of their service, under the eyes of the world, in which each had to prove himself worthy of his place. Colored regiments were often more difficult to manage than others, and training and discipline required special patience. More patience was required when in proximity to white regiments, for many would not conceal animosity and prejudice. Fights were a constant problem, and insults hurled at the Negroes a daily occurrence. But now and then a U.S.C.T. regiment did so well that it won the approval, if not the respect, of fellow white soldiers. When his black regiment peformed ably at drill, a colonel wrote proudly that "even the N.Y. Cavalry in the street forgot to say 'Nigger.'" It was a small victory.[32]

When it came to battle, the black regiments did well enough to win commendation, and by war's end a few dozen blacks themselves became officers, the highest being Major Martin Delaney of the 104th U.S.C.T. Perhaps it was seeing this that led the South to the greatest irony of the war.

On March 23, 1865, the Confederacy authorized raising black units with white officers to lead them. The promise was that freedom would be granted to any slaves who enlisted, and surprisingly there was some small measure of enthusiasm for the plan. At one military hospital, sixty out of seventy-two slaves said they would volunteer should their masters agree. The press in Virginia, North Carolina, Georgia, and elsewhere, endorsed the desperate last-minute measure, and in Richmond itself the work of raising a Negro unit actually got under way.

By March 27 there were thirty-five recruits drilling daily, fully uniformed and equipped, under their new white officers Major Thomas P. Turner and Lieutenant Virginius Bossieux. Moreover, a dozen of the recruits were not slaves at all, but free blacks apparently fighting for their native state. General Lee, especially, endorsed the idea, hoping that the full quota of 75,000 slaves could be enlisted, creating virtually a new army.

But unfortuantely for Lee, the experiment was too late for the Confederacy and too soon for Southern society. Richmond fell ten days after the enabling legislation passed, and the Confederate Negro units being raised never saw action. Indeed, the only violence they did experience came when they drilled on Cary and Twenty-first Streets in Richmond. Crowds of citizens gathered on the sidewalks and jeered and spat at both the black soldiers and the white officers who led them.

REFERENCES

1 Robertson, *Soldiers*, p.122.
2 Quaife, *Williams*, p.18.
3 *Ibid.*, p.18.
4 Quaife, *Williams*, p.20.
5 *Ibid.*, pp. 22-3.
6 Thomas W. Higginson, "Regular and Volunteer Officers," *Atlantic Monthly*, XIV (September 1864), p.353.
7 Fred A. Shannon, *The Organization and Administration of the Union Army 1861-1865* (Gloucester, Mass., 1965) I, pp.186-7.
8 George B. McClellan, *McClellan's Own Story* (New York, 1886), p.99.
9 Higginson, "Officers," pp.354-5.
10 *Ibid.*, p.354.
11 Richard Taylor, *Destruction and Reconstruction* (New York, 1879), p.126.

12 George B. Davis, et al., comps., *Atlas to Accompany the Official Records of the Union and Confederate Armies* (Washington, 1891-1895), Plate CLXXII.

13 Gerald F. Linderman, *Embattled Courage; The Experience of Combat in the American Civil War* (New York, 1987), pp.37-9.

14 *Ibid.,* p.40.

15 Robertson, *Soldiers,* p.124; Linderman, *Courage,* p.41.

16 Linderman, *Courage,* pp.229-230.

17 *Ibid.,* pp.48-50.

18 *Ibid.,* p.51; John O. Casler, *Four Years in the Stonewall Brigade* (Dayton, Ohio, 1971), p.193.

19 Linderman, *Courage,* p.54.

20 Davis, *Orphan Brigade,* p.50; Robertson, *Soldiers,* p.127.

21 Linderman, *Courage,* p.122.

22 Robertson, *Soldiers,* pp.126, 129.

23 Linderman, *Courage,* pp. 188-9.

24 *Ibid.,* p.190.

25 Robertson, *Soldiers,* p.128.

26 Tower, *Manigault,* pp.163-4.

27 Quaife, *Williams,* pp.165-6.

28 Gordon, *Reminiscences,* p.319.

29 Wiley, *Johnny Reb,* pp.63-5.

30 Joseph T. Glatthaar, *The March to the Sea and Beyond* (New York, 1985), pp.3, 10.

31 *Ibid.,* pp.10, 39-41.

32 *Ibid.,* pp.279-80; Robert F. Durden, *The Gray and the Black* (Baton Rouge, La., 1972), pp.268, 270, 274-5.

IV
THE TEST OF LEADERSHIP

"OH, EVERYONE is brave enough," wrote one Federal speaking of the officers in his army; "it is the head that is needed." How right he was. In all the preparation, sometimes amounting to months of training and campaigning before a unit saw its first action, it was the intelligence of their leaders that accomplished or failed to accomplish their preparation for battle. And when finally an officer led his men into the fight, for all that personal courage was a necessity, still more requisite was a cool head and the ability to think under the severest kind of pressure man can experience. Many a brave soldier got himself and his men killed through bold foolishness. The commander who knew when to temper his courage with discretion, who knew how to control his men by means other than mere personal example, who knew how to control himself, was the one who achieved the greatest goals with the means available to him.[1]

Much had to do with simply knowing how to control the men, whether on the march or before going into battle. Mere use of the authority of rank was rarely effective, for the simple fact was that most of the volunteers never equated rank with the right to command, and they always felt at liberty to question the directives of an officer if they did not agree. Thus the martinet had a difficult and often insurmountable task before him. Simply stated, the men would never yield. If they could not stymie him one way, they would find another. In the worst extremity, if their claims be believed, they threatened to, and perhaps did, exact their revenge in battle.

"Many a wearer of shoulder-straps was to be shot by his own men in the first engagement," wrote a Massachusetts boy speaking of the expressed intentions of comrades in the ranks. However, once under fire, most men found themselves occupied pretty much full-time by the enemy, so the threats may have been hollow. Still, many enlisted men believed that such things had happened, and the stories were told and retold, and no doubt magnified, in hushed tones around the campfires. "Such officers," said one man referring to a martinet he had seen, "received a stray ball occasionally on the field of battle." Indeed, some claimed to know officers who were afraid to go into battle at all, and not from fear of the enemy. If it actually happened, no one can say with certainty. It is known, however, that General Charles Winder, a regulation-bound Confederate stickler who repeatedly meted out humiliating punishments to his men for minor infractions, was so hated and despised by his private soldiers that they "spotted" him. In other words, he was marked for death in their next battle. "The next fight," wrote one Virginia private, "would be the last for Winder." Indeed it was, though he fell to a Yankee cannon ball before his own men could shoot him, if in fact they really intended to do so.[2]

Undoubtedly some officers were killed by their own men. But for the most part such extreme means were not necessary. They could get an offending commander's attention much more effectively by less violent means. Many were the companies that staged mock funerals in camp, with the officers they disliked hanged in effigy before being placed in a gaudy coffin covered with dire records of his offenses. Seeing how his men felt about him, many a tyrannical commander either changed his ways or else resigned before the mock coffin had to be exchanged for a real one.[3] When such means did not achieve success, the men could go farther, as when they fired a volley through the tent of Rebel General Allison Nelson out in Arkansas in 1862. Firing just above his head, their volley had the desired effect, and he quickly loosened his oppressive rule.

At the same time, an officer dared not be too easy or lenient with his men, else he could not command their respect, and only hope that they would obey important commands without question. Consequently, the leader had to walk a fine line between being sufficiently detached and authoritarian to remind the men that he was different, while at the same time not assuming to be so self-important that the men still did not think of him as one of them. He had to understand and to some degree empathize with their problems – even if he could do little to remedy complaints, he had to appear to sympathize with them. He had to be very reluctant to criticize their faults openly, and show a lot of discretion in doling out reprimands or punishment when required. He had to be able to read his men to anticipate how they would accept his actions, and most of all, he had to fall back upon cold and final military law only as a last resort. That was a lot to expect even from Regulars who were accustomed to command. When it had to come from civilians-turned-officers, more often than not it sprang from basic instinct for leadership rather than training.[4]

The trick was to instill a little bit of fear along with respect, and it came more often in isolated gestures than from the daily regimen or drill. On the march men were generally under orders not to fire their weapons, nor even to have them loaded. When one man shot down a buzzard, his lieutenant immediately and profanely reprimanded him in front of his company. Later during a halt, the officer returned and apologized to the offender for losing his control. Thus he had achieved two ends. His initial outburst showed that there was fire in the man, and that similar infractions in the future might elicit the same response. His apology showed him to be a man of good heart and fair play, and won him the admiration of his men. Another time, when he found his sentries asleep, instead of upbraiding them, he simply concealed their rifles, then woke them with shouts that the enemy was coming. Their consternation, confusion, and finally embarrassment at not being able to find their rifles at a seemingly critical moment, were enough to teach them a lesson. A Confederate captain from Alabama, en route to Virginia, found one of his men drunk in a barroom and refusing to go any farther with his company. A regular barracks lawyer, the private pointed out that the company had not yet been officially mustered into service, and therefore the captain could not compel him to do anything. Wisely the captain agreed, then pointed out that the soldier was wearing an Alabama state uniform, the property of the state. Even if the soldier was not under the captain's orders, the uniform was. "That uniform is going to Virginia with me and the Company," he declared. "I will have that uniform stripped from you at once and turn you loose in the streets without it." Given the prospect of being abandoned in the nude in a strange city, the drunk speedily gave in and went on to Virginia.[5]

The purpose of mastering this kind of human psychology was all, in the end, directed to making the enlisted man a part of a team, his company, regiment, and ultimately his army, and all to prepare him to be his most effective when he went into battle. This was one of the things that many enlisted men never understood; that all of the boring routine was designed, not just to keep him occupied, but to condition him to immediate response to an order when his own and the lives of his companions might depend upon it.

However much success at it the officers might think they were having when the armies were in winter quarters or field camp, they could quickly discover that the men would behave differently when on the march or heading toward the enemy. Whether 100 men or 100,000, they were easier to control in the confines of an encampment where sentries and provosts could keep an eye on them. But string them out over miles and miles of dusty country roads, marching past wells when they were thirsty or well-stocked farmhouses and barns when hungry, and the men proved almost impossible to control. Every farmer's fence rails looked like excellent firewood, and henhouses and cornfields appeared to be there for the taking. Many Confederates, specifically ordered not to take farmers' hogs, simply decided to call the hogs bears instead, and then gleefully boasted of the abundance of wild "bears" they shot and ate on the march.

Straggling – lagging behind the rest of the company by not maintaining the rate of march – was epidemic in both armies. Officers of every rank had constantly to ride along their lines urging the men to keep up. The two most frequently heard words out of the mouth of Confederate General Thomas J. "Stonewall" Jackson were "close up, close up," as he pushed his infantry forward. Sometimes a frustrated commander even drew his saber and smacked the laggard on the head or shoulders to force them forward, though not without risk. One officer made ready to strike a slow soldier with the flat of his blade, and was told "put up your sword or I'll shoot you."[6]

As busy as he was when his command lay in camp, an officer's duties seemed to multiply ten-fold when the army was on the march. Often no more than two or three days' notice were given from army high command. The officers had to see that the prescribed number of rations were issued for the march, cooked if necessary before leaving, the ordered rounds of ammunition passed out, any defective or missing weapons and equipment replaced, and the men carefully inspected one last time to weed out those who could not stand the march. The officer supervised the breaking down of the encampment, the storing of impedimenta not being taken on the march, saw that the company wagons – if there were any – were in shape to haul tents and heavy baggage, and looked to the condition of the horses and mules. A week's worth of inspections, it seemed, had to be accomplished in a single day. Moreover, there were constant demands from higher authorities for daily – even hourly – status reports, mostly to soothe the nerves of anxious regimental and brigade commanders who fidgeted before the final jump-off of the campaign. The last evening before the march began, the company and regimental officers had to circulate through all their encampments, calming the anxieties of the enlisted men, perhaps exchanging stories and jests with them, maintaining quiet so that sleep – for those who could – might come early.

The day of the march the whole column might be up at 3 a.m., not because commanders really expected to march at that hour, but because the larger an army, the longer it took to get it moving. If the column were only a few regiments, it might get going with relative dispatch. If it were an army of 50,000 or more, then it would move in several columns from four or five different general encampments, using parallel roads when possible rather than stringing itself out endlessly on a single road. Even then, a single column of a division or a corps might stretch out for miles, with any event along the way that caused a delay – a narrow bridge, a halt for water, men breaking ranks to pick berries by the roadside – being transmitted back down the line and exaggerated. Thus the march was often a series of fits and starts, with the officers all the while riding or walking along the line trying to keep the men from bunching up, leaving the column, or simply stopping when tired. Whereas a single man could easily walk twenty miles a day, a marching column of any size could rarely achieve half that. This was why officers really needed horses. In battle, almost everyone moved afoot. But on the march a commander had to ride back and forth almost constantly to maintain some sort of control. Enlisted men resentful of walking while their company commanders rode might have thought differently at the end of a ten- or twelve-hour day spent constantly in the saddle.

Matters became more tense for everyone as the column approached the intended scene of action, especially if the battle was already underway and the men had heard the boom of the cannon for hours, and the rattle of rifle fire as they neared the conflict. Then, too, the wounded coming to the rear, the demoralized or cowardly who skulked away from the field, the riderless crazed animals, and the other scenes of carnage, all could conspire to dishearten the soldier, especially men going into their first fight. Thus with every step towards the battlefield, the challenge to maintaining discipline and order became greater.

Those final hours before the fight, when officers and men alike knew that they were about to launch themselves into the inferno, could be either the most difficult of all or – oddly – the easiest, for many men achieved a kind of peace and calm before battle, especially the veterans. It was now that the individual strengths and personalities of the company and regimental officers revealed themselves most fully. The martinets stayed in their tents or busied themselves with issuing orders and even punishments, right up to the last minute. The officers who understood leadership more perceptively walked among their men, encouraging them, comforting those with the inevitable premonitions of death, and attempting to assure all that each would do his duty, not show the white feather, help achieve a victory, and emerge unscathed from the fight. The officer knew, of course, that for many his words were hollow or meaningless, but still it often helped the men to hear his reassurances just the same.

Sometimes they made speeches or issued more formal pre-battle orders that sought to arouse the patriotic fervor of their commands. The exhortations could vary as widely as the literacy and background of the officers themselves. Some were quite brief. "You love your country, you are brave men, and you came out here to fight for her," a New Hampshire major told his men. "Now go in! Forward!" Others indulged in overly lengthy and florid addresses that traced the history of the political differences leading to the present war, reviled the foe for his exclusive role in bringing on the contest, and promised the men an easy and speedy victory if they would only do their duty. "Your general will lead you confidently to the combat," Albert Sidney Johnston declared on April 5, 1862, before the Battle of Shiloh, "assured of success." In fact, they lost the battle, and he lost his life.[7]

And, for reasons known only to themselves, a very few officers took the opposite approach, perhaps thinking that the worse the picture they painted of what lay ahead, the more the men would be relieved if it turned out to be not so bad. "They are strongly fortified," said a colonel to his men. "They have more men and more cannon than we have. They will cut us to pieces. Marching to attack such an enemy, so entrenched and so armed, is marching to a butcher shop rather than to a battle. There is bloody work ahead. Many of you boys will go out who will never come back again." With talk like that no wonder his men were so dissatisfied with him that he was forced to resign.[8]

In the last minutes before the fight, the officers felt exactly the same emotions as their enlisted men. Tension. Dry mouth and throat. Sweaty palms. A hollow or empty feeling in the pit of the stomach. Enhanced senses of hearing and smell. A faintly electric quavering that ran from shoulder to shoulder through the center of the chest, sometimes causing a brief quiver or shake. The feelings that men of all times have felt in all wars. If the officer was more fortunate than his men in these moments, it was only because they had little to do but wait, while he could be busy with last-minute duties and arrangements right up to the firing of the first gun.

The actual place of an officer in battle in the Civil War varied widely, chiefly according to rank by regulations, but more by temperament of the individual officer. While army rules did not so specify, most professional and volunteer generals in time came to understand that their presence was most important behind the lines, not to save them from danger, but to have them where they could stay in touch with all of their units and maintain some control over their part of the battle. It was difficult to do, of course, for men of that era, regardless of rank, felt it unmanly to stay in safety when the fighting was going on. But it was foolhardy for generals to risk going into battle. Johnston did it at Shiloh, personally leading a balky regiment into the fight, and taking a mortal wound in the offing. He felt that the personal example of the cool and collected commander leading his men to the foe would have a calming effect on his unblooded volunteers in this, their first action. Indeed it did, but it may have cost the Confederacy the battle. Men like U.S. Grant and R.E. Lee, who were every bit as brave, knew where they belonged and stayed there. Grant never tried to take personal part in the actual fighting, and Lee apparently only attempted to do so once or twice in the desperate days of 1864, and then his men wisely refused to risk him. "Lee to the rear," they shouted, and he obeyed. For every fighting battleline general like Nathan Bedford Forrest who survived the maelstrom, at least two others fell in the fight, causing a continual drain of experienced officers at the highest levels of command. In Lee's Army of Northern Virginia, the losses of generals in battle practically crippled his command system after Gettysburg.

Corps and brigade commanders, too, belonged at the rear, and sometimes stayed there. Only the regimental colonels really had any business going into the fight with their men, and even they were better used by staying close to the battleline, but out of fire. It was the company captains and lieutenants, however, who truly belonged with their men. Whether charging on the attack, or standing to meet an enemy assault, the company officers had to be right there to inspire the men, hold them in line – with their swords and pistols if necessary – and rush in reserves to fill gaps in the line or transmit instructions from higher command. Years after the war, however much they may have revered their colonels and field officers, the men in the ranks most remembered the bravery – or the failings – of their immediate company officers. These were the leaders the men lived with, saw every day, came to know and respect – or despise – and trust. When his lieutenant or captain stood toe-to-toe with the enemy, the private knew he was in good hands. Let that officer quail or fail to share the risks of his men, and he had lost them. Thus it was that the losses among company officers in this war would be the greatest of any of the commissioned ranks. These captains and lieutenants had to pay a great price indeed for their little bits of gold braid, their shoulder straps or collar bars, and their $300 per year plus allowances.

Every officer, of course, carried side arms. He was entitled by regulations to a saber and a pistol, though the variety of both was wide. In the Union Army a standard field officer's saber was the model 1840 cavalry or 1840 light artillery saber, or variations of one or the other, though many officers preferred to furnish their own blades from such makers as Ames of Chicopee, Massachusetts. More ceremonial than practical, the officers found – like the cavalrymen who were issued sabers – that it was most useful for spitting meat or hacking brush. Very few saber wounds were inflicted on an enemy in this war. In the main, the officer carried it overhead to signal the advance, or to show where he was, or else used it to persuade skulkers and cowards to return to the line. He may have treasured his sword as a symbol of his office, but he rarely trusted his life to it.

Far more useful was his pistol. It was no mere symbolic weapon, but one that allowed him to add his firepower to that of his men. Again, a host of varieties went into action in the hands of officers, but on both sides they most often came down to one of two types, either a .36 caliber or a .44. The larger bore was favored more by infantrymen, and the chief providers were Colt and Remington. Naval officers and many cavalrymen were issued the lighter .36 model, again usually a so-called Colt "Navy." Yet for often sentimental reasons, or because nothing else was available, many men carried side arms that were clearly out of date. General Breckinridge went to war with a brace of single-shot H. Aston pistols that he had carried in the Mexican War. Confederate General Joseph E. Johnston actually went into battle wearing the saber his father had carried as a hero of the Revolution. In the Southern armies, especially, where scarcity was the order of the day in all articles of equipment, an officer might wind up carrying anything from a rusty old flintlock to a shotgun. Pistols ranged from antiquated smoothbores to the exotic French-made Le Mat, with a revolving cylinder carrying eight .40 loads, and a separate barrel underneath that fired a single .18 gauge shotgun blast. A few officers even had to provide their own side arms because Richmond could not furnish them, and the confusion of dozens of different calibers and ammunition requirements made supplying these officers a headache that was never fully eased.

Ironically, the bayonet was another weapon that inflicted almost negligible wounds in this war. The fact was, by the time one line closed with another, either the attacker or the defender was on the verge of breaking and withdrawing. Hand-to-hand combat as pictured in the paintings of the day was a rare occurrence, thus making the bayonet obsolete so far as causing casualties. But symbolically, the long, brightly polished, sharp blade had an intimidating effect on men who saw a whole line of them advancing toward them. As a result, the fear of the bayonet often accomplished far more than its actual use. How well Civil War commanders understood this psychological advantage to the weapon is arguable. Certainly they never stopped expecting their men to be well trained in the arcane exercise of bayonet thrust and parry, though not one soldier in a hundred ever had to do it for real.

By the time the first bullets started to whistle over their heads – all Civil War soldiers tended to fire high and waste inordinate amounts of ammunition – the tension was so great for both officers and men that the actual start of combat came almost as a relief. At least now their waiting was over. Indeed, some were so anxious to get into action and end the waiting that they ran to get to the battlefield. "We were repulsed the first charge," wrote an officer of the 59th Georgia, "because the men were so completely exhausted when they made it." They had run nearly a quarter mile to get into the fight.[8] Just before the Battle of Ball's Bluff, in October 1861, the men of Alpheus Williams' brigade were "cheering all the way" as they approached what they thought would be their first fight, and Williams confided privately that they were in "excellent spirits, better, I confess, than I was."[9]

The battlefield quickly became a confusion. The thick, white smoke from the black powder weapons tended to hang low, like a fog over the ground. The more guns that fired, the sooner much of the field was obscured to vision unless the wind was brisk enough to blow it away. The electric booming of the cannon and the flat, low crackling of thousands of rifles made orders nearly impossible to hear. In time, men and officers often could neither hear nor see one another, and maintaining control of even a company – much less a regiment or a brigade – could be more a matter of chance than design. In the First Battle of Bull Run, one captain went into battle leading his company, and when the smoke cleared discovered that only two of them were still with him, but that along the way he had somehow picked up a surgeon, a staff clerk, three cavalrymen without their horses, a confused artilleryman, and one very bemused chaplain.[10]

With the first moment under fire, every officer had to face a basic question within himself. What sort of leader was he to be? Would he lead, or follow; be an example to the men by taking a leading part in the actual fighting, or play the less romantic but perhaps more effective role of a good behind-the-lines manager? The fact was that both officers and men in this war expected that the leaders would lead by example, that they had to show their own bravery not only to win the respect of their soldiers, but also to inspire them to emulate such conduct. And for most, this meant that the officer had to risk his life intentionally by exposing himself to enemy fire, often even in ways not risked by his men. To some it came instinctively as the battle-lust seized them; for others, it was a calculated pose.

In Kentucky, in 1862, Colonel John Beatty ordered his 3rd Ohio Infantry to take cover from a storm of Confederate artillery fire while he remained standing. He did it intentionally. The regiment had caused him a lot of trouble, been insubordinate and disrespectful. "Now," he found after his display of bravery, "they are, without exception, my fast friends."[11]

The gallant young Major John Pelham kept his Confederate artillerymen under cover from an enemy fire, while he not only exposed himself, but sat atop his horse for a better view of the battle unfolding, and all the while maintaining a perfect calm and composure. It won the hearts of his men, who would afterwards follow him anywhere.

The stories of such conspicuous bravery abound from both sides. Particularly affecting is that of Colonel John B. Gordon, commanding that same 6th Alabama that he had entered as a private. But now it was the spring of 1862, and he was leading it into its first real battle, at Seven Pines, Virginia. Early on the morning of May 31, the brigade of which they were a part hurled itself against Yankee breastworks. Gordon, to be seen by his men, rode his horse in the attack, his adjutant mounted beside him. The instant that Gordon spurred his animal over the enemy works, his adjutant fell dead at his side. Gordon reformed his men under fire and sent them forward in another charge to pursue the retiring Federals. Then his lieutenant colonel fell dead. The regiment's major, also riding, went forward with the line and took a fatal ball. Gordon was the only field officer left, and his soldiers later declared that they could hear Yankee gunners shouting, "Shoot that man on horseback." By this time six of his twelve companies had lost their officers as well, and their brigade commander had also fallen. "Still I had marvellously escaped", Gordon remarked. Then he passed his younger brother, lying shot through the lungs, it appeared fatally. But there was no time to stop, "no time for anything," said Gordon, "except to move on and fire on." Then his horse was killed under him, and Gordon had to slog on foot through a near swamp, to find that his regiment had become separated from the rest of the brigade.

"My field officers and adjutant were all dead," he later recalled. "Every horse ridden into the fight, my own among them, was dead. Fully one half of my line officers and half my men were dead or wounded." Men were fighting from water, knee- and hip-deep, moving against a solid line of blazing Yankee rifles, with reinforcements swelling the Federal number. Gordon sent a flanking force under one of his remaining captains to stall the reinforcements, only to lose that captain and most of his men. Finally, orders came for Gordon to withdraw. Gordon alone of the field officers was alive. Of the forty-four line officers, only thirteen were left, though one of them, Gordon's brother, did survive his wound. And of the few Alabamians in the enlisted ranks who came through the fight alive, few indeed were those who did not thereafter think of John B. Gordon as a charmed god of war whom they would follow anywhere.[12]

Men like Gordon were often special cases for another reason. Men with wide military experience before the war often did not have to prove themselves overmuch.

Volunteer officers like Gordon found themselves put more on their mettle to show themselves worthy of their rank. But those whose commissions came due to political influence or connections very frequently had to overcome considerable animosity on the part of their men and subordinate officers, and ostentatious bravery was frequently the quickest and surest means of achieving this. Breckinridge, who had never experienced a day of battle in his life prior to Shiloh, exposed himself repeatedly wherever he went on that field. Struck by spent balls – bullets that had lost the force to penetrate or do more than inflict a bruise – and feeling more than one bullet pass through his clothing, the newly created general from Kentucky seemed to dare death that day. Part of his behavior was simply bravery or imperviousness to danger, for he showed the same calm and unstudied indifference on every battlefield on which he fought. But also a measure of such behavior certainly came from the need to show his men, also in their first battle, that he deserved their respect and complete obedience.[13]

On the Union side Carl Schurz received a brigadier's commission solely because he was a vocal and influential German-American who could help rally thousands of his fellow countrymen to enlist. By "displaying courage in battle," he wrote, he was able to dispel the objections of his men. A Confederate officer from France, the Prince de Polignac, took a generalship, and was so resented by men who thought he got high rank thanks only to aristocratic birth, that the men dubbed him "Pole-cat" and openly ridiculed him. But when the time came and they saw him cool and brave under fire for the first time, they thereafter "got on famously."[14]

Moreover, once such a man did prove himself, it was still occasionally necessary to reinforce his image as courageous and cool. Major General Richard Taylor received his Confederate commission for no discernible reason other than the fact that he had been Jefferson Davis' brother-in-law. As a result, he found himself much resented, even though he became a creditable battlefield commander. In 1863, in Louisiana, engaged in a sharp engagement, he saw his troops wavering and clearly in danger of giving way should the enemy attack. "It was absolutely necessary to give the men some *morale*," he concluded. Consequently, he mounted a breastwork in clear sight of the enemy, took out paper and tobacco, and coolly rolled a cigarette, lit it, and then walked back and forth atop the parapet casually enjoying his smoke. "These examples," he concluded, "gave confidence to the men, who began to expose themselves."[15]

Sometimes an officer even stood out to embarrass his men into doing likewise. General Daniel H. Hill once reprimanded a skirmisher for taking cover, then made the man stand beside him, under fire, and load his own rifle for Hill to fire back at the enemy. In time, such actions could have the effect of making the enlisted men ashamed to be cautious or take cover when their officers so brazenly showed themselves. It was a risky, and ultimately costly example to set, but it was what was expected by the private soldier who, seeing himself as intrinsically the equal of any officer, felt it undue to be asked to take any risks that an officer would not gladly share.[16]

Indeed, when their officers did not spontaneously exhibit such courage, the men in the ranks had their ways of testing, of drawing out whether a man was a hero or a coward, and woe to him if he proved the latter. Cowardice among themselves the men would tolerate occasionally, especially if a man had performed well in battle before. Everyone, they reasoned, could lose his nerve now and then. But for an officer to turn "yellow" was the most public form of humiliation. He was not a face in the crowd like a private. Thus when an officer was truly conspicuous, the men never forgot.

For the rest of their lives, the survivors of the 54th Massachusetts, a black regiment commanded by Colonel Robert G. Shaw, told of how they watched Shaw lead them in the attack on Fort Wagner, South Carolina, in the summer of 1863. In a nighttime assault, he led his men forward under orders not to fire a shot until they closed with the Confederates, emplaced behind a massively formidable sand and earthen fortress. Shaw led the regiment, walking at first. To begin with, long-range artillery opened up on them, without effect. Shaw kept walking. Within 200 yards of Fort Wagner, the defenders opened fire, and men started to fall. Shaw drew his sword, raised it over his head, and rushed forward calling for a charge. All across the remaining sand he was in front of his regiment, and when they reached the fort's sandy rampart, he was perhaps the first to race up its steep slope into the enemy's rifles and cannon. The last the men ever saw of him was his silhouette against the starry sky, sword in hand, atop the parapet, before he fell dead inside. A leader did not have to give his life to inspire his men and win their confidence but, like Shaw, he had to risk that chance sooner or later.[17]

And should the officer show fear or cowardice, the men would not let him forget it. Indeed, few commanders who lost their nerves managed to stay in power for long. At Stones River, in January 1863, in Tennessee, Breckinridge caught Brigadier General Gideon J. Pillow hiding behind a tree when the brigade he had begged to command was going into battle. Pillow was one of Jefferson Davis' political appointees, and Breckinridge rather publicly ordered him from his cover and out on to the field with his men. Pillow, who had also showed cowardice the previous February when he abandoned his command at Fort Donelson and escaped to safety while they were forced to surrender, would never hold a field command again.[18]

For all the cowards – and there were many – the number of the brave was one hundred fold, but somehow the stories of the timid or weak achieved inordinately wide currency just the same. Sometimes the men thought they could spot a coward even before their first battle, and looked especially askance at young officers who appeared foppish or overly concerned about rank and military etiquette. Virginians in 1862 noted such a young man, and sure enough, just as the next battle was commencing, he ran away, only returning several days later. The colonel of the regiment sarcastically asked the man how the battle had gone for him when he was eighty miles to the rear of it, then dismissed him.[19]

Along with this gradually acquired sophistication in judging their officers, the men in the ranks also began to discern between those whose qualities included bravery but not good judgment. This was when the "everyone is brave enough; it is the head that is needed" lament was heard. When Lieutenant General John Bell Hood, one of the most ferocious division commanders in the Confederate Army rose to the command of the Army of Tennessee, there were many who felt ill on the outlook. Hood had the heart of a lion, said one of his subordinates, but with it went "a Wooden Head." He was "simply a brave, hard fighter," but that he possessed personal daring no longer seemed to guarantee to the men in the ranks that he was also smart enough to lead them well. As events were to prove; for at Franklin, Tennessee, late in the war, he almost destroyed his army through a number of senseless attacks. No wonder that afterward, to the tune of "The Yellow Rose of Texas," men of his army changed the final lines to "the Gallant Hood of Texas played Hell in Tennessee."[20]

In time, too, many officers learned that so far as their careers were concerned, often there was little to gain by conspicuous bravery, for battlefield promotions were effectively non-existent. Grant is known to have made only two during the war, and in the Confederate service there were probably none, since Davis steadfastly held on to the exclusive authority to commission and endorse promotions. There were no medals to win in the Southern cause, though the Union did create the Medal of Honor in 1862. Unfortunately, the criteria for its award were always ambiguous. Extraordinary heroism could win one, but so could simply capturing or even picking up a Rebel battleflag. In the 27th Maine, 864 were issued as an inducement to re-enlist, though only 300 actually did so. The only man in history to be awarded the medal twice was Lieutenant Thomas Custer, brother of General George A. Custer. In the last week of the war he twice captured Confederate flags from overpowered regiments, and received a medal for each banner.

But of bravery, in the end, there was more than enough to go around, and chivalry, too, though many of the nonsensical old notions about glorious war dissolved in the blood-sodden fields of Virginia and Tennessee. It was just as brutal for an officer as for an enlisted man. The sight and stench of a battlefield after the fight did not distinguish between the eyes and nose of a private or a general. The disillusionment, depression, shame, guilt, and exhaustion that battle's aftermath imposed on almost everyone also struck the officers. They were not immune to the effects of what they saw; unlike their men, however, they were expected not to show it.

Like their men, however, they never lost their humanity. Out in Virginia's Shenandoah Valley in 1862, a Pennsylvania private had just drawn a bead on the dashing Confederate cavalryman, General Turner Ashby, Stonewall Jackson's right-hand man. Before the Yankee could pull the trigger on a certain shot, the colonel of his regiment knocked aside the private's rifle, thus saving the unsuspecting general. "Ashby is too brave to die in that way," said the colonel.[21]

Ashby would die in battle that same year anyhow, but an act of nobility by a foe preserved him for the South a little longer, and at the same time revealed a great deal about the kind of men who led soldiers North and South into the war. Those soldiers were well served by those they served.

REFERENCES

1 Theodore H. Lyman, *Meade's Headquarters, 1863-1865* (Boston, 1922), p.139.

2 John D. Billings, *Hardtack and Coffee* (Boston, 1888), p.152; David H. Donald, ed., *Gone for a Soldier: The Civil War Memoirs of Private Alfred Bellard* (Boston, 1975), pp.187-8; Casler, *Four Years*, p.102.

3 Linderman, *Courage*, p.53.

4 *Ibid.,* p.56.

5 *Ibid.,* p.55.

6 *Ibid.,* p.51.

7 Robertson, *Soldiers*, pp.215-6.

8 *Ibid.,* p.219.

9 Quaife, *Williams*, p.24.

10 Robertson, *Soldiers*, p.219.

11 John Beatty, *Memoirs of a Volunteer, 1861-1863* (New York, 1946), pp.139-40.

12 Gordon, *Reminiscences*, pp.56-8.

13 William C. Davis, *Breckinridge: Statesman, Soldier, Symbol* (Baton Rouge, 1974), p.313.

14 Linderman, *Courage*, p.45.

15 Taylor, *Destruction and Reconstruction*, pp.130-1.

16 Linderman, *Courage*, p.46.

17 Peter Burchard, *One Gallant Rush* (New York, 1965), pp.137-8.

18 Davis, *Breckinridge*, pp.343-4.

19 Linderman, *Courage*, p.47.

20 *Ibid.,* p.162.

21 *Ibid.,* p.70.

V

THE ARMIES THEY LED

It is certainly no surprise to discover that neither North nor South was prepared to wage a massive continental war in 1861. Besides the pitiful number of men actually under arms at the dawn of 1861, the military organization in Washington was barely more than adequate to handle the few thousand Regulars of the Old Army, while the new Confederate government, of course, did not even exist, and therefore, neither did any kind of military management. That both sides evolved, under the worst sort of circumstances, a complex military organization, and the equally complicated civil hierarchy to run it, is a testament to the ingenuity and resourcefulness – and occasional folly – of both Union and Confederacy.

The North, of course, started with a distinct advantage. Even though its War Department was not much compared to what it would be by 1865, still it was a lot more than Jefferson Davis had to start with when he took office. By contrast, on inauguration day in 1861 Abraham Lincoln did at least find a functioning though antiquated military establishment. At its head sat a cabinet officer, the secretary of war, and here as so often political and military policy intertwined. One of Lincoln's first acts was to appoint a new secretary, and he chose Simon Cameron of Pennsylvania. The choice was an entirely political one, for Cameron had no military or administrative experience at all. But he was a powerful Republican who traded his influence in the election of 1860 for the promise of a cabinet post. He would last less than a year, when a combination of military reverses to Union arms, and the scandals over corruption in the War Department, led to his replacement on January 15, 1862, by Edwin McM. Stanton. Stanton, too, lacked military experience, but he had served as attorney general in the previous administration and, though a Democrat, was an able and effective administrator. Indeed, he proved to be the most effective of all Lincoln's cabinet ministers, and held his post for the balance of the war and beyond.

The secretary of war was not expected to be a master strategist. While different incumbents would see the office in varying ways, for the most part the secretary was the one responsible for implementing the policy of the civil leaders through military channels. He was much involved with raising new regiments, using the military to quell civil unrest when necessary, facilitating the transfer of large numbers of troops from one region to another via civilian railroad or other transportation, and, indeed, consulting with the president and top generals on broad military policy and objectives. Most of all he needed to be an able executive, and Stanton was superb.

Chief responsibility for grand strategy for the war effort rested at first with the commanding general, so long as Lincoln had confidence in him. Until November 1, 1861, that meant Lieutenant General Winfield Scott who, despite his age and more than twenty years in his position, was still a brilliant man. Too corpulent and infirm to mount a horse or take the field, he was a desk general, planning strategy and leaving it to the younger men to carry out. He it was who first conceived the plan that, effectively, was followed by the Union for four years to victory: controlling Southern shipping with a tight blockade, while seizing the Mississippi and its southern tributaries to split the Confederacy into pieces and squeezing them between river and ocean, the so-called "Anaconda Plan." By the end of 1861, however, Scott was maneuvered out of his office by the younger and immensely popular Major General George B. McClellan. In many ways the opposite of Scott, McClellan was a brilliant army administrator and a timid battlefield commander, yet his success in organizing and training the Army of the Potomac in 1861 was so great that Lincoln made him general-in-chief.

McClellan proved to be a great disappointment, though part of the problem was that no one had a clearly defined idea of what a commanding general was supposed to do. Fearing that his new responsibilities were interfering with getting the Army of the Potomac into the country to fight, Lincoln relieved McClellan in March 1862 and returned him to the field. For four months Lincoln and Stanton ran the army themselves before calling on Major General Henry W. Halleck in July 1862. A noted military intellectual known as "Old Brains" in the Old Army, he had been a disappointment on the battlefield yet was known as a brilliant administrator. Unfortunately, he became, instead, a pettifogging bumbler whom Lincoln once called "little more than a first rate clerk." Now dubbed "Old Wooden Head" by subordinates, he shone only in imposing order and discipline in the military staff departments, but while he held his office, Lincoln and Stanton were forced to continue to act essentially as their own general-in-chief.[1]

When U.S. Grant was promoted to the reactivated military rank of lieutenant general on March 9, 1864, he became at once general-in-chief, and Halleck thereafter served as chief of staff, his responsibilities reduced to adapting Grant's and Stanton's decisions into the detailed orders necessary for an army with nearly a million men under arms. In a later time, an army of such size would not think of existing without a sophisticated top staff system in place, but in the Civil War, the organization to manage the huge armies always advanced several steps behind the growth of those armies.[2] Once Grant took command, Lincoln happily bowed out of military affairs almost entirely, having at last found the man he needed.

Primitive as army organization was in 1861, still there were a number of subordinate hierarchies within the War Department necessary to maintain the armies in the field. Each of them was stretched beyond its means in the early days, and often beyond the abilities of the officers who commanded them. For most of the war there were ten general staff departments or bureaus, each with specific – though often conflicting – functions, headed by independent officers rather than members of what would later become known as a general staff.

Probably more influential than any other department head was the adjutant general of the army. It was he who dealt most often and most intimately with the secretary of war, transmitting reports from field commanders, managing recruiting, assigning new officers to positions, and promulgating the directives of the president and secretary. He did not make any policy on his own, other than department policy, but the effectiveness with which Lincoln and Stanton's policy was carried out had much to do with the ability of the adjutant general. For the entire war period, fifty-seven-year-old Brigadier General Lorenzo Thomas held the post. He had been Scott's chief-of-staff for several years before the war, and perhaps for that reason he seemed a good choice for adjutant, but Stanton was never happy with him, and after 1863 sent him away from Washington on errands while Colonel E.D. Townsend did his job as acting adjutant general.[3]

Continuing the seeming policy of elevating the older officers to staff and department heads, perhaps to get them out of the field, Scott and Lincoln made Colonel Randolph B. Marcy inspector general, responsible for all kinds of inspections required throughout the army, from morale to desertion to military contractors. Happily, Marcy served well, won promotion to brigadier, and remained inspector general until 1881. Often closely involved with Marcy would be the judge-advocate general who oversaw courts-martial and courts of inquiry. There were two incumbents, though elderly Joseph Holt of Kentucky held the post the longest, and was a civilian given a military commission solely to enable him to become judge-advocate general.

While the men in the ranks, and even officers so long as they stayed out of trouble, had little contact with or appreciation for these departments, the other bureaus of the War Department were vitally important indeed. The chief of the Ordnance Department had the responsibility for procuring and distributing all of the weapons issued to the men, from small arms to the heaviest cannon, along with appropriate ammunition and impedimenta. He bought some, and oversaw the manufacture of the rest. The first incumbent, Henry K. Craig, had been in the Old Army nearly fifty years when war erupted, and he resigned less than two weeks after Fort Sumter fell. His successors, James W. Ripley, George D. Ramsay, and Alexander B. Dyer, each had relatively short tenures. Ripley was sixty-eight when he took office, and Ramsay sixty-one. Only the younger, forty-six-year-old Dyer was up to the strains of the office, which he took over in September 1864 and where he continued until 1874.

If the men in the armies were to eat properly, they depended upon the competence of the commissary general of Subsistence, who purchased and distributed all rations of any kind. The department was in the hands of George Gibson when the war began, he having held the post since 1818. Colonel and later Brigadier General Joseph O. Taylor, brother of President Zachary Taylor and uncle of Confederate General Richard Taylor, succeeded Gibson at the age of sixty-five, and died in office, to be succeeded by Brigadier General Amos Eaton, the most effective of the lot, and the only one not born in the 1700s!

Hand in hand with the commissary general went the work of the quartermaster general and his department. Uniforms, camp equipment, horses and fodder, and everything else not already supplied by Subsistence or Ordnance, came through the quartermaster general, and here, thankfully, a good, capable, young and healthy man was found almost from the start. When Sumter was fired upon, Brigadier General Joseph E. Johnston held the post, but he resigned and went south when Virginia seceded. An acting quartermaster filled in for a few weeks, and then the post was given to (later Brigadier General) Montgomery C. Meigs, arguably the most effective department head in the War Department. A career officer, amateur photographer, and brilliant engineer who oversaw the building of the new House and Senate wings in the 1850s, as well as the dome, on the Capitol, he handled the expenditure of over half a billion dollars on his own authority during the war, accounting for every cent spent. He was the only department head to be made a major general in honor of his services.

Less dramatic, though certainly indispensable to the welfare of the men, were the officers in charge of the Medical and Pay Departments. While four men held the post of surgeon general during the war, it was William Hammond who held it the longest, and made the greatest impact. He revitalized a somnambulant department, organized the first ambulance corps, brought young and skilled surgeons into the army, and also stepped on so many toes that he was ousted in 1864. The Pay Department also had four incumbents, none of them particularly distinguished, and none of whom rose above colonel. At least they were all honest in handling hundreds of millions of dollars in military payrolls.

Several departments concerned themselves with specific branches or functions of the armies in the field. The Corps of Engineers, under a chief engineer, was responsible for providing the officers and expertise for the construction of fortifications, bridges, roads and railroads, and the like. Elderly Brigadier General Joseph G. Totten, who had held the post of chief of engineers since 1838, continued to hold it until 1864, when sixty-six-year-old Brigadier General Richard Delafield succeeded him.

Closely related was the Corps of Topographical Engineers, indeed so closely related that in 1863 it was abolished and merged into the Corps of Engineers, where its survey and map work was most useful anyhow. The newest staff department was the Provost Marshal's, established in 1862, and created to handle the apprehension of deserters, traitors, the institution and maintenance of punishment within the camps for infractions, and eventually the administration of conscription, or the draft. Two officers, neither very popular, held the office of provost marshal general.

Finally, in 1863, an informally designated signal officer was commissioned chief signal officer of the newly created Signal Corps. The first incumbent of this important post was Colonel Albert J. Myer, who along with Edward Porter Alexander invented the "wig-wag" system of signaling by flags before the war. He used observation balloons, the telegraph, and signal towers, to gather and transmit intelligence. He was transferred in 1863 and his department essentially phased out under his successors.[4]

All of this, in some instances moving haltingly and at a snail's pace, and in others with alacrity and skill, had to support the efforts of some two million men who wore the blue. Conservatism and a reluctance to accept change, always typical of entrenched military high command, was rife throughout the bureau chiefs. At Ordnance the adoption of repeating weapons, those using self-contained cartridges as opposed to more time-consuming cap and ball systems, improved rifled small arms and cannon, and almost everything else that later generations would look upon as an advance in the evolution of weaponry – were all resisted. In the quartermaster's department, despite Meigs' extraordinary efforts, defective supplies and unsound horses for the cavalry were a constant problem. Indeed, to solve the latter, in 1863 a special Cavalry Bureau was established. Pay was often late, especially at more distant outposts. Maps, when there were any at all, proved insufficient thanks to the Federals' unfamiliarity with Southern terrain. Yet for all their shortcomings, their conservatism and obstructionism at times, the War Department bureaus more often than not accomplished what they were supposed to achieve. For the officers in charge it was about the least glamorous service a man could endure, sitting at a desk in Washington while the reputations and promotions were being won out in the field. But most of the incumbents were old Regular Army men, used to dull service with slow advancement and little emotional reward. The fact that many of them were too old to serve elsewhere in the service does not lessen the thanks they were due for enduring the tedium of department staff work.

The War Department itself was only the beginning of the total organization of the Union war effort, for somehow from that central point all the operations on the whole continent had to be overseen, managed and directed. When the war began, it appeared that, if only a short conflict, the existing geographical division of the army's command might suffice, but as the conflict escalated and more and more men went into the field to campaign for ever smaller sections of territory, it soon became abundantly evident that a more sophisticated territorial organization was going to be needed.

At the very beginning of the war, there were only seven territorial divisions comprising the entire United States and its territories. The Department of the East included everything east of the Mississippi, from Canada to the Gulf of Mexico. Most of the old Louisiana Purchase, much of it still not organized into states, constituted the Department of the West, while the balance of the country was divided into departments that coincided with their namesake states or territories: Texas, New Mexico, California, Utah, and Oregon. It was a peacetime organization designed to cope with managing Indians and furthering admission of western territories to statehood.

Secession quickly changed all that. Meeting the requirements of increased attention to affairs east of the Mississippi, the western departments began to expand and combine, while the old Department of the East became increasingly fragmented, into four departments by June 1861, six a year later, nine by June 1863, and eleven in June 1864, until the war's end. The more important military operations became in a region, the more attention they required, and territory was accordingly reduced to prevent distractions upon the commander of the military forces in that region. By war's end, the number of formal divisions was further subdivided into more than 60 departments, generally named for a river or geographical feature. These, too, evolved considerably as territory was won or lost, and as field operations shifted to other scenes. Some were as large as the huge Department of the Missouri, while others were nothing more than administrative jurisdictions as small as the Department of Key West. Within each department, its military forces, if they were large enough in size to merit being called an army, were given the same name as the department. Thus from the Department of the Potomac came the fabled Army of the Potomac, and from the Department of Tennessee the mighty Army of the Tennessee.[5]

The formation of those armies themselves also evolved. When the war commenced, there was no intent in Union military planning for any subdivision of an army larger than a brigade, usually constituted of four or five regiments and an artillery complement. But as the armies grew prior to First Manassas, such an increasing number of brigades could become difficult for an army commander to handle, and so they were formed into divisions, each division to contain from two to four brigades. Still the armies grew bigger, so that by July 1862 it was necessary to formalize what a number of army commanders had already done informally on their own. Divisions were joined together to make army corps, usually consisting of between two to four divisions. They were numbered with Roman numerals from I through XXV, plus a Cavalry Corps. Other informal organizations appeared from time to time, as at the Battle of Fredericksburg in December 1862, when army commander Major General Ambrose Burnside consolidated his several corps into three "grand divisions." However, by war's end the standard descending order of organization throughout the Union Army was army, corps, division, brigade, regiment, and company. No specific regulations prescribed the exact rank of the commander of the larger groupings. Major generals always led the main armies, but in a smaller department a brigadier could command. Corps almost always had a major general at their head, but again brigadiers were seen occasionally. Many major generals also led divisions, mostly men with junior commissions, though a number of brigadiers also held such command. Brigades were exclusively the province of brigadiers and quite a few senior colonels, and, of course, regiments were led exclusively by colonels except in the case of a temporary absence from duty.

The chain of command was almost always clear to any officer. Especially important – particularly when viewed in comparison to the working of the Confederate command system – was the fact that a department commander reported directly to his military division commander, and the latter to the general-in-chief. Both Lincoln and Stanton were in the main very good about not circumventing the chain of command by sending orders directly to a lower level commander, and by-passing his superiors. It was the only sure way to prevent confusion and cross-purposes.

Throughout this whole increasingly sophisticated system, there really existed two kinds of army, not as separate field forces, but mixed together. There were the Regulars and there were the volunteers. While the Lincoln government looked primarily to volunteers from the states to swell its armies and fight the brunt of the war, the old career Regular service also saw some expansion. By war's end the Regular Army had grown to six regiments of cavalry, sixty batteries of artillery, one engineer battalion, and nineteen regiments of infantry.[6] Still, taken altogether, their numbers did not amount to much more than a good full-sized army corps. Rather than keep them all combined, however, the War Department parceled them out among all of the field armies, occasionally in complete brigades, but more often mixed into brigades, the theory being that they would provide a professional, steadying influence on the volunteers. Many of the Regular units never even got into the war, being left out in garrisons on the western frontier to maintain order.

It must have been a frustrating service for many of the officers, as they saw former brother officers who had resigned to take volunteer commissions rise in rank. For the fact is that men who stayed in the Regulars during the war tended to experience the same glacial advancement as before the war. Of the 1,098 Regular officers serving at the start of the war, 767 remained loyal to the Union. Of their number, only 142 eventually became generals, and almost all of them did so by leading volunteers. Some 161 who were captains at the commencement of the war were still captains or majors at the end. By contrast, of the 102 Military Academy graduates who had left the service before the war, then enlisted in 1861, 51 – exactly half – became general officers. Perhaps the only consolation many of the unpromoted Regular officers would have – and they had to wait until after the war for it – was the fact that when the volunteer armies were disbanded in 1865 and 1866, almost all of the Regulars who had achieved high rank in the volunteers reverted to their pre-war rank, or perhaps a step or two above. Thus George Custer finished the war a major general of volunteers, but a year later he was only a lieutenant colonel second in command of a cavalry regiment.[7]

Across the lines in the new Confederacy, a very similar and at the same time very different military command system appeared. It owed its peculiar organization to two overwhelming influences: the model of the old United States War Department prior to the conflict, and President Jefferson Davis. Indeed, no assessment of the Confederate army in any of its facets, particularly its officer corps, can fail to take into account the pervasive influence of the man who led the country.

Jefferson Davis, despite having been a distinguished Senator and spokesman for Southern rights, always saw himself at his core as a military man. He attended West Point, served in the Old Army for several years, and then after resignation came back into the field in command of a Mississippi volunteer regiment during the Mexican War. At the Battle of Buena Vista he distinguished himself and his regiment, and contributed materially to the victory by an otherwise ill-advised formation in which he placed his men in an inverted "V." Fortunately, the Mexican cavalry that charged him was repulsed, and Davis became a hero. Then in 1853, when President Franklin Pierce took office, Davis became his secretary of war.

That moment of glory at Buena Vista never left Davis. Ever after he assumed that he knew and understood the management of an army in the field as well as or better than anyone else. When he took office as president of the Confederacy, consequently, he interfered far more than Lincoln did in the actual operations of his armies, leading one wag to quip that the Confederacy perished "because of a 'V.'"

The irony is that, however much he denied it, Davis was at heart an administrator. Throughout the Civil War, all the while complaining that he dreaded paperwork, he immersed himself in it and actually made much more of it for himself than was necessary. Having served as secretary of war, he naturally felt that he knew how to set up his own War Department, and indeed he did pretty well. But then he proceeded to run it largely himself, instead of leaving the details to his cabinet secretaries. Davis had the sort of mind that could not delegate even the smallest detail, for fear that if left to someone else, it would not be well handled. As a result, he almost worked himself to death, suffering dreadful health and exhaustion during most of the war. Yet even at war's close, when most of his letters opened with an apology for lateness in replying because of the burden of all his correspondence, he would still repeatedly spend up to an entire afternoon personally penning remonstrances of fifteen pages or more lecturing some subordinate on fine points of military law, aimed always at pressing the conclusion that Davis was invariably correct. It is certain that no man in the Confederacy devoted himself more heart and soul to the cause, or made that cause and his own name more synonymous. Davis' loyalty and dedication to duty are beyond question. Unfortunately for the fate of the South, his temperament, personality and general character simply did not suit him to be a chief executive, and the reasons why this was so are amply demonstrated in the overall makeup and management of his War Department.

It was an incredible challenge. Everything in the new Confederacy had to be created out of nothing. Not surprisingly, one of the very first acts of the new Provisional Confederate Congress was to create a War Department. Indeed, it was done just three days after Davis' inauguration as President on February 18, 1861. In the initial legislation, just four bureaus or staff departments came into being, reflecting the most immediate and obvious needs of the army to come: Adjutant and Inspector General's Department, Quartermaster General's, Commissary General's, and a Medical Department. The secretary of war presided over all – theoretically. In actual practice, Davis ran it himself.[8]

As a result, whether by design or unconsciously, Davis repeatedly chose as cabinet ministers for the department men who had few skills, little reputation or experience, and poor health. Thus all were totally dominated, offering little or no resistance to his daily involvement in their responsibilities. Not surprisingly, he went through six war secretaries and four assistant secretaries, creating more turnover than in any other cabinet position. Leroy P. Walker served until September 1861, resigning largely due to poor health. Judah P. Benjamin, formerly attorney general and later to be secretary of state, filled in for seven months until George W. Randolph took over. He, too, left from poor health that would kill him five years hence, and also out of frustration at the president's high-handed meddling. Gustavus W. Smith filled in for a very few days, having previously suffered a nervous breakdown when he briefly commanded the Army of Northern Virginia. Then he was succeeded by James A. Seddon, who served for more than two years and suffered from a frail constitution. Only the final incumbent, Major General John C. Breckinridge, enjoyed both good health and a stature that made it impossible for Davis to treat him as a clerk as he had the others. But by the time Breckinridge took office in February 1865, the cause was lost.

In the staffing and initial operations of those first four departments, Davis showed a weakness for old cronies and ineffectual appointees that would plague the War Department throughout the war, As adjutant and inspector general, he appointed Samuel Cooper, who had held the same position in the Old Army until secession. That, alone, made him seem a logical choice. But he was sixty-three years old, had never held a field command, and was tired and weak-willed. A department employee, Robert Kean, head of the later established Bureau of War, characterized Cooper as ignorant and incompetent and kept in office solely thanks to Davis' preference for "accommodating, civil-spoken persons of small capacity." Though he was, in fact, the senior ranking general in the entire army, Cooper was regarded and treated by most subordinates as a mere cipher.[9]

Two men held the post of quartermaster general. Colonel Abraham C. Myers was effective but fell out of favor with Davis, apparently over a remark attributed to his wife. In 1863 Davis replaced him with Brigadier General Alexander R. Lawton, who found the post so uncomfortable that he soon wanted to resign, but stayed on until the end of the war.[10]

Where Davis' weakness for old friends really hurt was in his appointment of Brigadier General Lucius B. Northrop to be commissary general. All aspects of feeding the armies came under his control, and Northrop early showed himself to be an incompetent. Worse, he had been on permanent sick leave from the Old Army since 1839! But he and Davis had been friends at West Point, and despite almost four years of clamor against Northrop, Davis refused to replace him until February 1865, when Breckinridge made Northrop's dismissal a condition of his accepting the cabinet post. Breckinridge – not Davis – then replaced Northrop with Brigadier General Isaac M. St. John, and in a matter of weeks the remaining men in the field were being better supplied than they had in months, all too late of course.[11]

Only in the Medical Department did Davis make an initially happy choice. Surgeon General Samuel P. Moore served from July 1861 until the end of the war, supervising hospitals, medical officers, and acquisition of precious medical supplies. His performance, under terrible conditions, proved to be excellent.

Considering that Davis was essentially a regulation-bound kind of administrator, it is much to his credit that he demonstrated a willingness to evolve his War Department to suit changing needs. Thus when it was evident that functions required more than the existing departments, he expanded the War Department. In 1861 he created the Engineer Bureau, a Bureau of Ordnance and Ordnance Department, and a Bureau of Indian Affairs (the Confederacy had no Interior Department, where Indian matters would normally be handled). The next year there was even more growth, with the creation of the Signal Bureau, the Army Intelligence Office, the Bureau of Exchange, and the Bureau of Conscription. In 1863 there appeared the Niter and Mining Bureau and the Bureau of Foreign Supplies, and in 1864 the Office of the Commissary General of Prisoners was created.[12]

Each office, headed in all cases by an officer with the rank of colonel or brigadier, had its own very specific area of influence, and many were tailored to the peculiar needs of the Confederacy's strained and ill-equipped war effort. Indian Affairs, unlike the Federal bureau of the same name, was concerned not with keeping the Indians west of the Mississippi peaceful, but instead with attempting to persuade them to join the Confederate forces in the conflict; with some success it has to be said.

Contrary to the name it held, the Army Intelligence Office did not deal in confidential information, but rather acted as a kind of Red Cross, keeping track of sick and wounded and getting information to families of soldiers. It was the Signal Bureau that dealt with the clandestine; one of its branches being the shadowy "Secret Service," its operations still only imperfectly known.[13]

The bureaus of Exchange and Conscription both attacked the problem of manpower, though from different directions. Early in the war, and again toward the end, cartels went into effect providing for the exchange of prisoners of war. Such exchanges took place on a one-for-one basis based upon rank, a private being worth one private, a general worth one general, and so forth. A lieutenant might be worth several privates, and a general worth several lieutenants. The Bureau of Exchange was to handle all this, but when prisoner exchange was brought to a halt by the Federals in 1863, the bureau had little to do. Conscription, on the other hand, oversaw the drafting of men of military age under the several conscription acts passed in Richmond. Even more specialized was the function of Niter and Mining. Reliant upon what it could make internally for much of its munitions, the War Department took over supervision of the mining of raw materials like lead for bullets, and niter for gunpowder. What could not be made domestically had to be brought in by the Bureau of Foreign Supplies through the blockade. And as the prisoner exchange system broke down and the number of imprisoned Federal prisoners continued to mount, a cabinet level bureau to feed and care for them came into being, though shortages prevented it being very effective.[14]

Borrowing from the organization he had known so well as Pierce's secretary of war, Davis organized the Confederacy into a number of territorial commands, as did Lincoln. Like the Washington government, the Confederates also saw the number of departments grow in reaction to the course of military affairs. In the summer of 1861 they had only the Department of Texas, the Indian Territory (now Oklahoma), Department No. 1 encompassing chiefly Alabama, Department No. 2 containing both banks of the Mississippi from Tennessee nearly to Baton Rouge, and then a massive unnamed territory that embraced literally all of the rest of the Confederacy clear to the Atlantic. It was an ungainly organization to say the least, but with no enemy armies threatening anywhere except in northern Virginia, and the only western threat the control of the Mississippi, the lopsided organization briefly suited its purpose. Six months later there were eight departments, the borders between them badly blurred. By the summer of 1862 everything west of the great river had been redesignated the Trans-Mississippi Department, virtually a third of the Confederacy. Eighteen months later the Confederacy east of the river contained ten departments, those beyond the Appalachians grouped into a still larger Western Department. At the end of the war the departmental organization was bizarrely laid out, with the Department of Tennessee and Georgia commencing at Tallahassee, Florida, on the Gulf of Mexico, then extending several hundred miles north before turning west at the Tennessee line and continuing on to the Mississippi River. Though more than 600 miles long, with a dog-leg to the left at Tennessee, it was in places only 50 miles wide.[15]

As with the Union forces, the individual military command within each department constituted its "army." However, an unfortunate flaw in Davis' adherence to his department system was that each commander was an independent entity, responsible only to the War Department. Therefore, if a Yankee threat or invasion appeared in one department, the threatened commander could not require a neighboring commander to come to his assistance. Only Richmond could do that. Since there was no general-in-chief until 1865, when Robert E. Lee assumed that position, and since there was no chief-of-staff even, only Davis – acting through the secretary of war – could compel one department leader to aid another. This was the way Davis wanted it, and only heavy pressure from his Congress finally forced him to accept a general-in-chief, too late for the move to have any effect.

Because of a greater variation in rank in the Confederate service, there was more variety among army commanders. Grades of general officer ran from full general to lieutenant general, major general, and brigadier. A department and its army, depending upon size, could be commanded by a man of any such grade. In the case of officers who fell out of favor with Davis, such as P.G.T. Beauregard, a man with a very big rank might sometimes find himself in command of a very small department. In Beauregard's case the Georgia and South Carolina coastal defenses in 1863. The armies themselves, as with the Federals, generally took their name from their department, as with the Army of Northern Virginia, Army of the Trans-Mississippi, and so forth. Within those armies, the same organizations such as corps, divisions, and brigades, existed as in the Union forces, and were generally commanded by officers of comparable rank. However, with the high rate of attrition among Rebel officers, it was far more common for men of lesser rank to hold higher commands.

And like the Union, the Confederacy had basically two military organizations, one very large and all-important, and the other negligibly small. On February 28, 1861, the Confederate Congress, then still in Montgomery, Alabama, created the Provisional Army of the Confederate States, abbreviated to P.A.C.S. It was the direct equivalent of the volunteer forces of the North. The legislation allowed the Confederacy to accept regiments of volunteers provided from each of the states, and acknowledged its obligation to feed and pay for them for their term of service. That term, at first, might be only twelve months, but by 1862 only regiments enlisted for three years or the duration were being accepted. Later legislation also provided for the recruiting of more such units, but all were officially a part of the P.A.C.S., and the commissions of almost all officers, even most generals, were provisional. If and when the war should end – successfully, of course – all P.A.C.S. officers and men would return immediately to civilian life.[16] Of the 750,000 or more men who served the Confederacy during the war, virtually all were provisional.

But there was another force: the Confederate Regular Army. At least, such a standing professional army was dreamed of. Considering Davis' West Point and Old Army background, it is hardly surprising that – expecting his new nation to survive for a long time – he would want to establish a Regular force of his own. Consequently, on March 6, 1861, the Congress authorized the "Army of the Confederate States of America," calling for one corps of engineers, one corps of artillery, one regiment of cavalry, and six infantry regiments. The War Department staff departments previously authorized were a part of the Regular Army system. Initially only brigadier generals were authorized, but soon that was changed to recognize the full general rank and five were appointed in 1861 – Cooper, A.S. Johnston, Lee, J.E. Johnston, and Beauregard.[17]

Almost from the first, a Confederate Regular Army appeared to be a futile effort. As in the Union, men did not want to enlist for specific mandated periods of time in the Regulars when they could go into the volunteers and leave service as soon as the war was over. Regulars fulfilled an enlistment commitment no matter what happened in the war. Further, because of the very small size of the service, promotion for officers would be just as slow as in the Old Army. While the legislation called for 15,003 men and officers of the Regulars, in the end only about 1,000 enlisted men and 750 officers and cadets were actually raised, and as the very high proportion of officers would suggest, most were not needed for the few soldiers enlisted, and were instead allowed to serve in the P.A.C.S., where Regular officers with low commissions could often become colonels and generals of volunteers.[18]

In the end, not one single complete regiment was raised. About five companies did serve intact throughout the war, but more often the Regulars enlisted were scattered among other state regiments and only a few dozen Regular officers stayed in the service through the course of the war. A number of other ostensibly "Regular" units did come to life, in all twelve separate regiments and battalions of cavalry, nine regiments and battalions of infantry, and five regiments and battalions of engineers. However, most were simply formed by consolidating the depleted remnants of several volunteer regiments later in the war. Mixing companies from more than one state in such a regiment, the War Department could not decide what state designation to give them, and so called them "Confederate" instead.[19]

Part of the Regulars' problem was confusion in the War Department. With a Provisional Army, a Regular Army, and a shadowy and ill-defined "volunteer" army of state militia that served only within the confines of their native states, cross-purposes abounded in determining where appropriations should go, with the P.A.C.S. consuming so much that there was little left over. Indeed, due to monetary restraints, Regular recruiting stations were closed in July 1861 and never reopened. At one point in 1864, kindly but vague old General Samuel Cooper apologized for being unable to appoint a man into the service, explaining that "there have been no appointments in the regular army for several years, there being no regular army." The adjutant and inspector general had forgotten the Regulars.[20]

Yet the officers who made up over forty percent of the Confederate Regular Army became, like their Old Army counterparts in the new Union volunteer forces, a major vertebra in the backbone of the P.A.C.S. The Confederacy did not live long enough to build a lasting military tradition, but in its brief, blazing four years of life, its officers, like the men they led, and like the men they fought, built a legend.

REFERENCES

1 Warner, *Generals in Blue*, pp.196-7.

2 Welcher, *Union Army*, p.4.

3 Warner, *Generals in Blue*, p.503.

4 Welcher, *Union Army*, pp.2-4.

5 Davis, *Atlas*, Plates CLXII-CXLXIX.

6 Frederick Dyer, *A Compendium of the War of the Rebellion* (Des Moines, Iowa, 1908), III, pp.1,689-1,716.

7 Boatner, *Dictionary*, pp.495, 673-4.

8 Henry P. Beers, *Guide to the Archives of the Government of the Confederate States of America* (Washington, 1968), p.134.

9 Edward Younger, ed., *Inside the Confederate Government; the Diary of Robert Garlick Hill Kean* (New York, 1957), pp.xxx-xxxi.

10 *Ibid.*, pp.89-90.

11 Warner, *Generals in Gray*, p.225.

12 Beers, *Guide*, p.134.

13 *Ibid.*, pp.152, 210, 233.

14 *Ibid.*, pp.233, 237, 243, 246-7.

15 Davis, *Atlas*, Plates CLXII-CLXXI.

16 Beers, *Guide*, p.301.

17 Richard P. Weinert, "The Confederate Regular Army," *Military Affairs*, XXV (Fall 1962), pp.97-8.

18 *Ibid.*, pp.106-7.

19 *Ibid.*, p.107; Joseph H. Crute, Jr., *Units of the Confederate Army* (Midlothian, Va., 1987), pp.65-72.

20 Weinert, "Regular Army," p.107.

VI

CLASSROOMS OF CONFLICT

However much North and South may have failed to recognize and act upon the need for systematic training of their volunteer officers, both sides never let up in their steady production of professionally trained men to send forth for leadership in their armies. The United States Military Academy at West Point continued its operations without interruption, and so did the United States Naval Academy, though its proximity to danger in secession-sympathizing Maryland necessitated its temporary removal to Newport, Rhode Island. Across the lines, of course, there had never been a Confederate military academy before the war, but the host of Southern military schools, especially Virginia Military Institute and the Citadel, kept right on graduating young cadets who went almost immediately into Southern armies. More than that, Jefferson Davis and his government even created a new floating Confederate Naval Academy, and made some provisions for the appointment and training of cadet infantry officers. Amid the turmoil of a nation torn apart and bleeding, the schools were still teaching young men to be officers.

West Point, of course, led all the rest for the sheer number of graduates that it turned out and for the number that it contributed to the armies, especially the Union. Young men graduating in the early 1860s had been fortunate enough to attend in what many later called West Point's golden years. General Winfield Scott was inordinately fond of the school, meaning that it had his ardent and influential support. The faculty had almost all been trained by Sylvanus Thayer, the man whose vision of the school stamped it and every graduate, practically since its founding. Coming out of a long peace-time era in which many in Washington questioned the need for the Academy, it was now the darling of politicos. "The graduates of that institution contributed in an eminent degree to our unexampled career of success," declared

Secretary of War William Marcy, making West Point an appropriate repository for all the trophies of war taken from the Mexicans. From wanting to see the school torn down, many old opponents now looked to it as a center of Army history and tradition. Even new barracks and class buildings were constructed, and the intellectual cream of the Old Army's officers were sent there to be instructors and administrators.[1]

In the 1850s West Point had enjoyed a series of good superintendents, most notably Robert E. Lee, who took over in 1852. Following him in 1855 came Captain John G. Barnard. Barnard would later achieve distinction as an engineer, and by war's end was chief engineer on Grant's staff. Following him came Major Richard Delafield, who had previously held the superintendency, and who in the war to come would be chief of engineers. By 1861, another new superintendent, Pierre G.T. Beauregard, had taken command, but within only a few days he was relieved because of his decided Southern sympathies, and replaced by Delafield once more. Delafield, his scholarly face rimmed by pure white hair, sideburns, and beard, looked more like a school teacher than an officer anyhow, but he would not remain long in command.

The course of instruction at West Point during the Civil War did not differ substantially from the kinds of classes that cadets had studied for decades. Sciences – natural and physical – mathematics, history and the like made up the liberal arts aspect of the regimen. In military sciences, every cadet was exposed to engineering, infantry, cavalry, and artillery studies and tactics, and for most some studies of French, in order to master the latest European military manuals. Classes continued through fall and spring terms, with a summer encampment a traditional event before the war, and one especially essential once hostilities commenced.

But as the excitement mounted in the later winter of 1860 and spring of 1861, it became more and more difficult to keep the cadets' attention fixed upon their course of study. War fever seized almost all of them. "I can think of nothing else," one young man wrote to his girlfriend. It was the same with his classmates. "Everything is cast aside. The professors complain bitterly about the deficiency of cadets in their recitations and the superintendent says that something will have to be done about it. I imagine the only way to prevent it is to stop the war."[2]

When the South Carolina batteries fired on Fort Sumter, all West Point cadets came to a final examination not previously a part of the school's studies. Secretary of War Simon Cameron immediately ordered that all cadets, officers, and faculty at the Military Academy should swear an oath of allegiance. It was essential to weed out at once the disloyal and the wavering. The new plebe class, the first year cadets, were the first required to so swear, and it was an affecting scene. Under the assumption that there would be some who would refuse the oath, causing some drama, most of the Academy's upper classmen were present as well, to witness what happened. The plebes gathered in the chapel before the assembled military and academic staff, all in full uniform. Their names were read aloud, and each of the plebes stepped forward to swear his oath. The first time a Southern boy refused, fellow Southerners stamped their feet in applause, while the rest of the assembly of spectators began a loud hissing. Ten young men could not take that oath, and were soon dismissed. The Civil War had begun to split "the corps."[3]

Of course, the decision of whether to go or stay had been faced by men at the Academy as far back as January 1861, a few days after South Carolina seceded in December. One young man actually asked Beauregard during his brief tenure if he should resign. Still hoping to stay himself, the superintendent counseled the boy, "Watch me, and when I jump, you jump. What's the use of jumping too soon?"[4]

Some had already "jumped." On November 19, 1860, Henry S. Farley of South Carolina became the first cadet to resign. Another South Carolinian followed him four days later, then a Mississippian, and an Alabama boy who had risen to first sergeant and who wept when he said goodbye. As the resignations continued into 1861, the lame-duck president James Buchanan ordered that all cadets suspend studies on February 22, George Washington's birthday, to go to the chapel and hear read to them Washington's farewell address, and to think upon his admonitions of "the immense value of your national union." Later that evening, cadets of opposing viewpoints began to shout cheers for the Union or for Southern rights from their windows. A few weeks later, when the war began, the first shot – a signal shell – was fired by a West Point graduate, Lieutenant Wade Hampton Gibbes, class of 1860. And the second shot came from a new Confederate lieutenant who never quite graduated, Henry S. Farley.[5]

The Academy was in a turmoil for a few days after the outbreak of war, cadets ignoring regulations, missing classes. Then came the oath, and the forcing of resignations from those who would not support the Union. As a result, March and April were bitter months of heart-wrenching partings of close friends, many of whom would never meet again except in battle.

In the end, out of 278 cadets at the Academy at the beginning of November, 65 left either by resignation or from being discharged for refusing to take the oath. More annoying to Federal authorities were the six cadets who graduated in the accelerated classs of May 1861, and then resigned a few days later, obviously having waited to get their diploma at United States expense. This brought on yet another oath, this one specifically stating that the cadet held the law and authority of the Union above that of any state. This precipitated two more dismissals. As evidence of how agonizing such a fateful decision could be for a man of 21 who had only recently been a boy, one of the last two cadets to refuse later changed his mind and went into the Union army.[6]

Both the departure of so many ungraduated cadets, and the growing needs of the burgeoning army in the field, impelled the War Department to accelerate the rate of graduation of cadets. There was resistance at first, for Secretary of War Cameron thought he saw in the large number of West Pointers – 306 in all – who either resigned from the Academy or from service in the army, "an extraordinary treachery displayed," and asked if it "may not be traced to a radical defect in the system of education itself." The criticism did not last for long, especially when supporters of the Academy reminded critics that at least 66 Southern-born graduates had not resigned but remained firm to the Union.[7]

Indeed, soon the War Department was singing the tune that accelerated graduation was a necessity, for there were not enough officers for all the places to be filled – exactly the opposite of the pre-war Old Army experience. In his annual report for December, Cameron recommended "that immediate provision should be made for increasing the corps of cadets to the greatest capacity of the Military Academy." Whereas there were only 142 students at that time, Cameron urged that the number be raised to 400, and that funds be spent to increase that to 500. "It is not necessary at this late day to speak of the value of educated soldiers," he said, forgetting his earlier calumnies on the Academy.[8]

By the end of 1861, two classes had been graduated ahead of time: the class of May 6, with 45 cadets, and the class of June 24, with another 34. Those first two wartime classes would leave their mark. Standing first in the May class was Henry A. DuPont, later a distinguished artilleryman. Ranking third was Orville E. Babcock, who served as Grant's aide by the end of the war and won a brigadier's brevet. Adelbert Ames, fifth ranking, became a leading division commander, and Emory Upton, eighth, achieved a single star and proved to be one of the most distinguished soldiers of the post-war army. Number seventeen was Judson Kilpatrick, much disliked and troublesome, but eventually a major general of cavalry with Sherman in Georgia. Seven of the forty-five would be killed in battle, one of them having later become a Confederate officer.[9]

The June class achieved no less distinction. Alonzo Cushing won immortality by his defense of Cemetery Hill on July 3, 1863, at Gettysburg, where he gave his life. Six others of his class met their deaths in the war, and the man who ranked at the very bottom, thirty-fourth, courted death time and time again, but would only find it at the hands of the Sioux eleven years after the war ceased. George A. Custer would become the youngest major general in his nation's history.[10]

Thereafter the classes continued to turn men out for the hungry regiments. The class of 1862 gave twenty-eight, including Ranald S. MacKenzie who would become a brigadier when only twenty-four and later one of the greatest Indian fighters of the West. The next class brought forth twenty-five graduates, and the class of 1864 another twenty-seven. They were the last to see Civil War service, for the 1865 class graduated on June 23, 1865, after all of the hostilities had ended.[11]

Thus the U.S. Military Academy graduated just 159 officers during the war, though the total body at any time was over 200; never close to Cameron's hoped-for 500. Far from reducing its appropriations, as might have been inferred from remarks made in 1861, Congress augmented funds earmarked for the institution, so during the last year of the war its expenditures exceeded $200,000, a twenty-five percent increase over its annual average expenditures for the previous twenty years.

Thus it was that the United States Military Academy emerged from the Civil War with enhanced prestige, and a considerable momentum for growth in the last half of the century. Though the total number of its graduates that made up the Union Army's officer corps might have been small as a percentage, their influence went far beyond their numbers. Every one of the major army commanders would be a West Point man, and most of the corps and department leaders as well. Grant, Sherman, Sheridan, Thomas, and more, the men who won the war, all learned much of their craft at the Academy, and so did that small legion of lesser officers like Cushing, who served them so well. And Lee, both Johnstons, Beauregard, Bragg, and the rest of the Confederate high command owed their schooling to the same institution. Indeed, the story of West Pointers in the war could be taken for the story of the war itself, for they were never out of the big action.

Perhaps because so many leading Rebels were graduates, and certainly because of the long-standing military tradition in the South, the new Confederacy was not yet even established before leading secessionists began to call for a Southern military academy. On January 26, 1861, the Mississippi secession convention passed a resolution calling on its representatives in any new confederation "to use their influence to have a military academy similar to that of the United States at West Point." Once the Confederacy was formed, its Congress waited only until May 16, 1861, to approve an act providing that cadets could be appointed by the president on an interim basis, "until a military school shall be established for the elementary instruction of officers for the Army." Not long thereafter, on October 7, 1861, in a treaty concluded with the Cherokee Indians, one of the inducements used to woo the tribe into an alliance with the Confederacy was the promise that one Cherokee youth would be selected every year "to be educated at any military school that may be established by the Confederate States."[12]

For all the good intentions, certainly heartily approved by old West Pointer and now President Jefferson Davis, the South simply never had the time or the wherewithal to set up its own military academy. The act allowing Davis to appoint cadets was as far as Congress got, and he did, indeed, appoint quite a large number. They were attached as supernumeraries to existing volunteer or Regular companies, where the cadets, presumably, learned just as much of the art of war as would allow them to be commissioned into active service. Several of them went on to become second lieutenants in the Regular Army, and probably even more took commissions in the P.A.C.S.[13]

Fortunately for Davis and his cause, he had other sources of excellently trained young officers. The South literally teemed with private and state military schools. Furthermore, a number of colleges and universities offered intensive courses of military instruction, meaning that there were actually thousands of non-West Point-trained men in the Confederate reservoir of potential officers. Indeed, looking just at the field officers – regimental men of colonel's, lieutenant colonel's, or major's rank – in Lee's

Army of Northern Virginia, it appears that out of a total of 1,965, some 208 or ten percent were graduates of such schools. Adding to that the 73 West Point field officers gave Lee a very respectable nucleus of trained leaders.

They came from everywhere. In Lee's command there was one from the La Grange Military Academy, 14 from the Georgia Military Institute, 37 from the Citadel (formally known as the South Carolina Military Academy), and 156 from another institution that caused the Union an especial degree of discontent. Indeed, when asked why the war was taking so long, one unsubstantiated account says that Lincoln replied that he could win the conflict a lot faster, "were it not for a certain military school they have which supplies them with trained officers." Lincoln may not have said it at all, but even if he did not, certainly he and everyone else knew what school he would have been talking about: the Virginia Military Institute.[14]

Founded in 1839 at the picturesque Shenandoah Valley town of Lexington, it was referred to by locals and graduates as "the V.M.I.", and it rather quickly acquired a sense of tradition and esprit rivaling that of West Point. In its 22 years of operation before the outbreak of war, almost 1,000 young men entered its ranks, and 455 actually graduated. At the same time, the 523 who dropped out before graduating had almost all stayed in school from six months up to two years or more, thus acquiring much of the basic training and knowledge of the graduates. Furthermore, all but 35 of the 978 cadets who entered prior to the war came from Virginia, thus ensuring that their loyalties would take them into the Confederacy almost to a man.

Most of them did not stay in the military after graduation. Indeed, perhaps as few as two dozen were all that made careers in uniform, while the rest returned to civilian life. Many stayed active in local militia organizations, however, and all remained a part of an "old school" network just as powerful as West Point's. It was certain that if a war came, and any V.M.I. men achieved high position, they would call upon a host of fellow graduates.

In 1861, after Virginia seceded, there was a host of them ready to be called. Out of 882 alumni of the V.M.I. living in July of that year, at least 740 took arms for the South, a staggering eighty-four percent. The impact of their service can be determined just by looking at the commands they held. Of sixty-four units of all arms that Virginia gave to the war in its first year, twenty-two – more than a third – were commanded by V.M.I. graduates. Those not commanded by V.M.I. men often had a number of former cadets in their ranks. Beyond doubt, such alumni proved to be the dominant force in the officer corps of the Army of Northern Virginia, where all but a few of them served. When Major General George Pickett's Virginia division of fifteen regiments charged across the Pennsylvania fields to their high water mark at Gettysburg on July 3, 1863, thirteen of those regiments were taking orders from graduates of the V.M.I. No wonder then that V.M.I. came to be called "the West Point of the Confederacy."

All told, some eighteen men of the Institute became generals in the war. At least

95 commanded regiments as colonels, another 65 served as lieutenant colonels, 110 became majors, 310 held captaincies, and among both grades of lieutenant there were 221 alumni. Many more served in the ranks without commissions, leading to one informed estimate that as many as 1,796 former cadets or alumni of the Virginia school fought for the Confederacy.

Since there were only 978 former cadets and alumni at the beginning of the war, this staggering figure of 1,796 reveals something else about the school. Unlike West Point, which thanks to Congressional legislation limiting appointees had a restricted class size, the V.M.I. turned out a huge increase in cadets and graduates. Between 1861 and 1865, as many cadets entered the school as had gone there in all the previous twenty-two years.

When the war came, there was quite a lot of practical experience in store for the cadets and alumni. For the latter, immediate commissions awaited most. Confident that a V.M.I. training had equipped the graduate with the necessary essentials to exercise firm command, to train raw volunteers into effective soldiers, and to lead them in camp, field and battle, Jefferson Davis and Virginia's Governor John Letcher commissioned hundreds. Even alumni returning to far-flung places like Tennessee and Alabama, found themselves receiving ready commissions from other states' governors, for the V.M.I.'s education was recognized throughout the South.[15]

As for the cadets currently enrolled when war broke out, that first summer proved an active one. Classes traditionally graduated on July 4 every year, though that quickly changed since Confederates were uneasy about observance of what had been a national holiday before the conflict. Even before their graduation, however, the class of 1861 got a taste of the war when, on April 21, 1861, the whole corps left for Richmond to undertake duty drilling Confederate volunteers. The leader who rode at their head was their professor of philosophy and artillery tactics, Major Thomas J. Jackson. Once in Richmond, the corps effectively disbanded, as the young men expecting to graduate in a few weeks took service with the Confederacy. As a result, on July 4, though they were no longer at the Institute, the V.M.I. declared the class of 1861 officially graduated as of that date. On December 6, 1861, the Institute did the same thing for the men who would normally have gotten their degrees as the class of 1862.

In fact, the Institute was not able to reopen until January 1, 1862. Those cadets not already enlisted or graduated returned, and a number of new "rats," as first-year cadets were called, entered. Almost immediately their continuing association with Jackson re-asserted itself. When he was a professor he had not been well-liked. One cadet challenged him to a duel. Another reportedly attempted to assassinate him, and most of the boys ridiculed his queer ways by calling him "Tom Fool," or mocked his eyes with the nickname "Old Blue Light." But by May 1862 he was no longer either of those things, but had a new sobriquet. As "Stonewall" Jackson, bearing the name he had won at the first Battle of Bull Run or Manassas, he was ordered off into the

Shenandoah to drive out three separate Federal armies. He did it, in part with the assistance of the corps of cadets. They accompanied him on the march to the Battle of McDowell, though they saw no actual combat, much to their chagrin.

That campaign was also the last time they saw Jackson. A year later, on May 15, 1863, the corps turned out once more as the formal escort to take Jackson's body to his resting place in Lexington's cemetery, after his mortal wounding at Chancellorsville. Six weeks later, on July 3, the Institute graduated its class of 1863.

Three more times the boys and young men were called out for emergencies, once in August when Federal raiders threatened and again in November and December for two more Yankee raids. Yet neither time did they see action. But then came May 1864, and what would ever-after be for the V.M.I. its most treasured tradition and legend.[16]

A Federal expedition commanded by Major General Franz Sigel set out to wrest the Shenandoah from the Confederates, destroy its crops, and use the Valley as a back door into the heartland of Virginia, at the same time as U.S. Grant and the Army of the Potomac were launching a major overland thrust at Lee and Richmond. The Shenandoah, known to Virginians simply as "the Valley," lay almost entirely undefended. As a result, except for harassing by Rebel cavalrymen, his march south was almost unimpeded. Still thanks to Sigel's timidity and questionable competence, it was a leisurely advance. That gave the Confederate department commander in faraway southwest Virginia, Major General John C. Breckinridge, time to assemble a small scratch force to meet Sigel. It was vitally important to stop the Yankees before they got to Staunton, a major supply and rail connection, and also an avenue to Lee's rear while he faced Grant's forces.

Rapidly Breckinridge forced his small command of a few thousand Confederates toward Staunton. Knowing himself badly outnumbered, he sent orders to the superintendent of the Virginia Military Institute, General Francis H. Smith, to turn out the entire corps of cadets. He hoped that he would not have to use them, but if necessary, use them he would. On May 11, 1864, jubilant at the prospect of seeing action, the 258 cadets and their instructor-officers left for Staunton, where they met Breckinridge the next day. Two more days of marching brought them to the vicinity of New Market, a sleepy Valley farming community just then occupied by the advance elements of Sigel's army of 6,200. Breckinridge, with less than 5,000, including the cadets and some elderly reserves, decided to attack.

The next morning the Confederates seized the initiative and never let it go. Breckinridge formed his men in line and pushed north, driving back Sigel's outposts, and then elements of his main army. That morning the general had posted the cadets in reserve, stating his intention to keep them out of the battle if at all possible. All through the morning and early afternoon he lived up to his intent.

But then late in the afternoon, as he pushed toward the main Yankee line atop Bushong's Hill, a hole opened in the left center of his line just as the enemy was about to mount a countercharge. Frantically Breckinridge looked for some other unit to fill the gap. There was none available but the corps of cadets. His adjutant Charles Semple saw tears in Breckinridge's eyes. "Put the boys in," said the Kentuckian, "and may God forgive me for the order."

The "boys" went in, and some were no more than boys. The oldest cadet in the battle was 25; the youngest was a bare 28 days past his fifteenth birthday. Bravely they moved into the gap in time to help repulse the Yankee assault. Then, in company with the rest of Breckinridge's line, they swept up the slope in front of them, through mud so sticky it sucked the shoes from their feet, and moved straight toward an enemy battery. In the face of the charge, the whole Federal line retreated so quickly that one gun from that battery was abandoned just as the cadets reached it. The jubilant cadets swarmed all over the field piece, exulting in their trophy as Breckinridge rode up to them crying, "Well done, Virginians! Well done, men!" Then he immediately took them out of the line again to act as reserve, while his army continued the pursuit of the beaten Sigel.

It was one of the most significant small battles of the war, and the corps of cadets had played a prominent part in it. Breckinridge may indeed have called them "boys" when he ordered them into the line, but after their charge he called them "men."

They suffered like men, too. Five fell dead outright, and five more would soon die of their wounds, while forty-seven others felt the enemy's lead and steel. In all, the corps suffered almost twenty-two percent losses, comparable to many a veteran regiment in a major battle. A week later, when the corps arrived in Richmond to aid in its defense, President Davis himself addressed the cadets and paid tribute to their valor.

Still, the war was not done with the men from V.M.I. In late May the governor assigned them to duty with local defense troops in and around Richmond. Then came word that another raid had struck the Shenandoah, and this time there had been no Breckinridge to turn it back. On June 7 the cadets were ordered back to the Valley to defend Lynchburg, and by the ninth they reached Lexington where, two days later, they took part in the feeble defense of the city against the advancing Federals under Major General David Hunter. Overpowered, the Confederates abandoned Lexington, and Hunter wreaked vengeance for New Market. He burned the barracks at the V.M.I. almost to the ground, so that only its masonry walls still stood.

Their school destroyed, the corps went back to Lynchburg to take post in its defenses, and then late in June returned to the burned-out ruin of their school. Undaunted by war's visitations, there on June 27, 1864, fourteen members of the class of 1864 – all New Market veterans – were graduated while the rest of the cadets were furloughed. Reassembled in October, the corps spent the rest of the war in and around Richmond, where they took temporary quarters for the Institute at the city almshouse. Studies continued until March 1865, when again authorities ordered them out into the field, though they saw no action. On the night of April 2, as

Richmond was being evacuated, the Institute's faculty disbanded the corps at the almshouse and sent the boys home.

Yet with incredible resilience, the Virginia Military Institute could not be held down for long. In October of 1865 classes resumed in Lexington, and the work of rebuilding the Institute began. On July 4, 1866, having returned to its traditional graduation day, ten cadets of the class of 1866, all New Market veterans, took their diplomas. As late as 1870, the last of the New Market boys to finish their education at the V.M.I. got their degrees. And on January 16, 1875, by an act of the governing board of the Institute, diplomas were awarded to all remaining New Market cadets who, for whatever reason, had not been able to complete their studies. Many of them had left the corps to take commissions in the Confederate Army.[17]

Just the afternoon of the day of his fatal wounding, Stonewall Jackson had been talking of the Institute, and his expectation that in the Battle of Chancellorsville, then under way, the influence of his old school would be substantial. "The Virginia Military Institute will be heard from today," he told a friend, and indeed it was. The V.M.I. was heard from on every battlefield of the Army of Northern Virginia, and with many of the other field armies of the Confederacy as well. But for all the generals and colonels and other field officers who would take their training at Lexington with them on those immortal fields, the Institute's place in the Civil War would always be remembered most for what its 258 cadets did at New Market. No class at West Point during the war came even close to the kind of real training by experience as that acquired by the cadets at the V.M.I.[18]

No one was more aware of that than the faculty and students of the Institute itself. In May 1866 the five cadets killed and buried at New Market were brought to the parade ground in front of the burned out barracks for re-burial. Thereafter every year on that site and on the anniversary of the battle, May 15, an affecting ceremony was to take place. Before the assembled corps of cadets, standing at attention, the roll of the corps was called. On that date ten additional names were called with the roll, but those ten, the killed and mortally wounded from New Market, were represented by a living cadet. As the names were called out, the corps and a large audience of civilian onlookers remained hushed.

Every year for generations, the corps retraced the march to New Market in May, and on the field of that memorable battle called out the names of the dead, as a living reminder of an era when schoolboys both North and South studied in the shadow of war, a reminder of boys who quickly became men, and who rose through their bravery and devotion to duty to cast a shadow of their own in that great conflict.

REFERENCES

1 Thomas J. Fleming, *West Point, The Men and Times of the United States Military Academy* (New York, 1969), p.126.

2 *Ibid.*, p.154.

3 *Ibid.*, p.155.

4 *Ibid.*, p.148.

5 Cullum, *Officers*, II, p.513.

6 Fleming, *West Point*, pp.156-7.

7 U.S. War Department, *War of the Rebellion: Official Records of the Union and Confederate Armies* (Washington, 1880-1901), Series III, Volume 1, p.309.

8 *Ibid.*, p.703.

9 Cullum, *Officers*, pp.520-48.

10 *Ibid.*, pp.548-69.

11 *Ibid.*, pp.570-609.

12 War Department, *Official Records*, Series IV, Volume 1, pp.81, 327, 685.

13 Weinert, "Regular Army," p.98.

14 Richard M. McMurry, *Two Great Rebel Armies* (Chapel Hill, N.C., 1989), p.99.

15 *Ibid.*, pp.100-3.

16 William Couper, *The V.M.I. New Market Cadets* (Charlottesville, Va., 1933), p.ix.

17 William C. Davis, *The Battle of New Market* (New York, 1975), pp.122, 147, 195, 197; Couper, *Cadets*, pp.x-xi, 6-7, 254.

18 Douglas S. Freeman, *Lee's Lieutenants* (New York, 1943), II, p.554.

VII
LEADERS AT SEA

There has always been a forgotten Civil War, a realm of endeavor in which the services of officers and men are little known and more often ignored. Perhaps it should not be much of a surprise, considering that the role of the navies, North and South alike, was very much a passive one through the bulk of the conflict. Only one or two so-called "fleet" engagements occurred in the entire war, almost all on the Mississippi River, and there were only a handful of individual ship-to-ship combats. Most of the hostile actions of Union and Confederate warships were against unarmed merchantmen or blockade runners. Certainly the blockade of the Southern coastline made a significant contribution to eventual Rebel defeat, just as the activities of Confederate commerce raiders on the high seas distracted enemy vessels from the blockade while Rebel gunboats on the rivers and harbors of the South helped impede the advance of Lincoln's armies. Nevertheless, this was a war fought and won and lost primarily on the land. As a result, even in their own time, the men who led the navies of North and South found themselves often ignored or forgotten. To posterity and history they are, for the most part, all but lost.

Certainly when the war clouds formed in December 1860, those men were as much in the minds of the political leaders as the officers of the Old Army. There was as yet no Confederate Navy, and that of the United States looked even more pitifully small and scattered than its military. When South Carolina seceded in December, President-elect Abraham Lincoln could look to a mere forty-two vessels actually in commission, only twelve of which made up the Home Squadron in American waters. Worse still, of these twelve, only a scant four were berthed in secure Northern ports. Only 7,600 men of all ranks made up the rolls, and of their number, 1,554 were commissioned officers.[1]

Even as a few warships began to return to home ports with the rising of the crisis, the navy felt the same strains of loyalty that tore apart the Old Army. There were naval bases all around the South, from Norfolk, Virginia, with its vital navy yard, down the Atlantic coast to Key West, and along the Gulf of Mexico at Mobile, Alabama; Pensacola, Florida; and elsewhere. The security of all, when and if war came, would depend upon the loyalty of the officers in command, and of those loyalties the government in Washington could not be entirely sanguine.

While not as popular a vocation as the military, still the naval service enjoyed considerable prestige in the old South, and a sizeable proportion of those 1,554 serving officers when secession commenced were natives of the seceding states. Which way they would "jump," as Beauregard had put it, became a primary concern of the Navy Department in Washington. It needed these trained and experienced men to command its ships; at the same time it recognized that, as with the army, the U.S. Navy would be regarded as a prime resource of officers for any new Confederate Navy that might emerge.

Just as the strains on loyalties and oaths taken severely demoralized the Old Army, so it very quickly began to break down the naval officer corps. In January 1861, Captain Samuel F.I. DuPont wrote of being "sick at heart" as he witnessed the scene in Washington. He was "astounded to see the extent of the demoralization, not only in every department of the government, but among the officers of the Navy."[2] Already the resignations were coming in at an alarming pace. In the month of December 1860 eleven resignations arrived, almost all lieutenants and midshipmen, and all but four from the just seceded state of South Carolina. Nine of that eleven would later take commissions in the future Confederate Navy. As more states voted to leave the Union, that initial trickle became a seeming flood. In January 1861 another forty resigned. Twenty left in February, and another thirty-seven in March. With April, the firing on Fort Sumter, the secession of Virginia, and the certain outbreak of war, 114 officers left the service, followed by another 120 in the next three months. All told, by the end of 1861 at least 373 naval officers had given up their commissions.[3]

The decision whether to go or to stay in the old service proved to be every bit as hard for the old Navy men as for their brothers in the Army. Promotion had been even slower in the old Navy, and many an ambitious young officer of Southern blood or sympathy might look for speedy advancement to the new Confederacy. That very December 1860, as the news of the secession of South Carolina reached Washington, forty-seven-year-old Lieutenant David D. Porter of Pennsylvania first heard it from the wife of a prominent Southern politician. "We will have a glorious monarchy," she declared of the expected Southern nation, "and you must join us!" Teasingly, Porter mused that such treason might earn him a title like "Duke of Benedict Arnold." But the lady was serious. "Nonsense," she answered, "but we will make you an admiral."[4]

Porter, having no sympathy with the South or its cause, was not tempted, but certainly others were. Even his own stepbrother, Captain David G. Farragut, felt to some degree the conflicting tugs of nativity versus loyalty. Farragut had been born in Tennessee, yet lived much of his life in Virginia and married a woman from the Old Dominion. Politically conservative, he had near relatives living in the Deep South and almost all of his in-laws were Southern sympathizers by birth and inclination. But he had also spent nearly fifty years in the old Navy. He honored its traditions and had participated in some of the stirring events that had become those traditions. In the end, though suspected of being pro-Confederate both North and South, and even in his own Navy Department in Washington, he emphatically took his stand with his uniform.[5] In time he would become the Union's premier seaman, and its first admiral.

But there were others who could not stay. Indeed, Lieutenant J. R. Hamilton of South Carolina was the very first to submit his resignation, doing so on December 1, 1860, even before his own state seceded. His very next act was to publish in several newspapers a call to other officers of Southern birth to resign. Going even further, he suggested that officers commanding vessels should bring their ships to Southern ports and surrender them to local secessionist authorities. A few weeks later, Captain V.M. Randolph of Alabama, a man with nearly fifty years of service, showed up at the Pensacola Navy Yard in command of a band of secessionists and forced its surrender. He had only submitted his resignation two days before, and since it had not yet been accepted by the Navy Department, he was still a commissioned United States officer when he took arms against his service.[6]

In the end, the old Navy would find itself particularly hard hit exactly where it hurt the most, among the younger mid-level officers who would be expected to take the bulk of the warship commands in the coming war. While there were 93 serving captains – then the Navy's highest rank – only 15 eventually left, and of them twelve joined the Confederate Navy. Certainly they were missed, but most were elderly, and several too feeble ever to take shipboard commands. From the next level, however, 34 out of 127 commanders resigned, 29 of them taking Rebel commissions. Even worse, out of the 351 lieutenants then serving, 89 departed. Of the 123 commanders and lieutenants who turned in their commissions, only 15 did not don the Confederate gray, and it was those who did that formed the overwhelming majority of those who would one day command their own ships in service of the South. For the Union, which would commission hundreds of ships before war's end, the loss of this pool of potential captains was the biggest blow of all.[7]

Among those who left were some of the finest talents of the old Navy. Matthew F. Maury had achieved international reputation as an oceanographer. Franklin Buchanan, after years of distinguished service, was commanding the Washington Navy Yard. Commander Raphael Semmes, though 52, was one of the brighter lights in the Navy's constellation. All went south with their states. With them went a host of others who would win fame in the years ahead: Catesby R. Jones, John N. Maffitt, John Taylor Wood, John McI. Kell, and more. Had they remained in the old Navy, their services to the Union would have proved invaluable.

Unfortunately for Lincoln, much of the damage had already been done before he even entered office, and before his new Secretary of the Navy, Gideon Welles, could do anything about the flow of officers out of the service. When Welles did take office, he was shocked. "I found great demoralization and defection among the officers," he wrote. "It was difficult to ascertain who could and who were not to be trusted." Worse than that, he saw many good officers still undecided who were being assiduously courted by secessionist friends. As a result, Welles remained suspicious even of staunchly loyal men like Porter and Farragut for some time after all doubt of their position had disappeared.

Warnings constantly came to Welles – many anonymously – questioning the loyalty of this officer or that. Then, when the firing on Fort Sumter accelerated the rate of resignations, he finally took positive action. Prior to that time, the Navy Department had routinely accepted resignations without comment or castigation. After Sumter, however, almost every officer ranked lieutenant or above who submitted his resignation did not have it accepted. Instead, the Navy Department formally dismissed him, a treatment that carried with it an ages-old stigma to any career navy man. In short, while the department could not prevent a resignation, it could make it as painful as possible to do so. Further, Welles virtually forced the resignations and dismissals of many, by requiring that all naval officers take an oath of allegiance, just as the army had done. Those who could not in conscience take that oath had little choice but to leave the service.[8]

For those who stayed loyal to the Union, a huge task remained ahead of them. From its pitiful beginnings in 1861, the Union Navy would grow by the end of the war to include 51,500 men and officers and nearly 700 ships of all classes. Just the civilian employees maintained by the Navy Department in 1865 equaled more than double the entire 1861 manpower of the whole Navy. Lincoln's ships would ply every navigable river on the continent, and every ocean of the world. All of this required a degree of organization previously unthought of, as well as a host of officers to make it all work.[9]

Welles stood at the top of the organization. A Connecticut newspaperman with no prior naval experience, Welles proved to be an able administrator. With fourteen clerks and messengers, he oversaw the work of his office and of four sub-offices, those of the Assistant Secretary of the Navy, a Solicitor and Naval Judge Advocate General, a Commissioner of the Naval Code – essentially a codifier of naval law – and an Office of Naval Records and Library.

Of far more importance to the men out on ships and shore stations, however, were the thirteen bureaus in the department that directly influenced the lives and careers of naval officers. The Bureau of Construction, Equipment, and Repairs did exactly what its title implied until July 1862 when it was broken up into several smaller bureaus for greater efficiency. One of those was the Bureau of Construction and Repair, another the Bureau of Steam Engineering, and a third the Bureau of Equipment and

Recruiting. A Bureau of Medicine and Surgery did as its name would suggest, and was the only bureau not commanded by an officer of commander's rank or higher, being led instead by surgeons.

The Bureau of Navigation oversaw five sub-offices, partly scientific and partly catch-all, including the Naval Observatory, the Naval Almanac Office, the Chaplain Corps, and the Naval Academy. Its most conspicuous operation was the Office of Detail, which oversaw the assignment of officers to their posts. All naval cannon were handled by the Bureau of Ordnance, and another bureau dealt with Provisions and Clothing. The technology of the age mandated the creation of the Bureau of Steam Engineering, and the developments of the Civil War itself led directly to the establishment of the Office of the General Superintendent of Ironclads, which oversaw construction of all of the behemoth warships built, except for a few serving on the Mississippi that were laid down by the separate Office of the Superintendent of Ironclad Gunboats.

Finally there were other bureaus to administer, such as those of Yards and Docks, Naval Boards and Commissions, and the Marine Corps, which was then, as later, a part of the Navy. The men in charge of all these several bureaus varied widely in rank and service. Yards and Docks was commanded by Rear Admiral Joseph Smith, a veteran of decades of service. Commanders of the Bureau of Ordnance included two captains, a commodore, and a rear admiral. Thus it went throughout these branches of the Navy Department, though in general its department heads were not quite as superannuated as those in the War Department at the beginning of the war.[10]

Of course, the Navy's real front line was comprised of those officers and men on squadron and station duty. As with the Army, the naval forces of the Union were organized geographically, though instead of departments and divisions, Lincoln's seamen served in squadrons and flotillas. As a general rule, the squadrons patrolled the coastlines and high seas, enforcing the blockade, while the flotillas operated on the rivers, chiefly in cooperation with the army in joint operations. The first of the squadrons was the Atlantic Blockading Squadron, covering the Atlantic coast from Virginia to Florida. In September 1861, however, in response to the increased activity on this line, it was divided into North Atlantic and South Atlantic Blockading Squadrons. Similarly, the whole line of the Gulf of Mexico was originally the assignment of the Gulf Blockading Squadron, but soon that too was divided, into East Gulf and West Gulf squadrons. Out on the broader oceans, the West India Squadron patrolled the West Indies protecting Yankee commerce from raiders. The Pacific Squadron, the African Squadron, ships in the Mediterranean and off South America and elsewhere, all did similar duty. Of the flotillas, these were more informal, including the Potomac and James River Flotillas. Unlike the actual geographical squadrons, which remained permanent throughout the war, the flotillas sometimes came and disappeared according to need and circumstance. What started as a Mississippi flotilla came in time to be designated the Mississippi River Squadron.[11]

The highest rank at the time of the outbreak of the war was rear admiral, most of them elderly men with forty years or more of service. Just below them came captains, then commanders, then lieutenant commanders, and then lieutenants. Surgeons, were above assistant surgeons, and assistant surgeons came next, followed by paymasters, masters in line of promotion, chaplains, engineers, and professors of mathematics, all of whom were either masters or ensigns. Then came midshipmen and acting midshipmen. The Marine Corps ran the same ratings as the Army, from second lieutenant up to the commandant, a colonel. The degree of specialization is evident.

Just as bewildering to an army man would be figuring out a naval officer's rank by looking at his insignia. They wore both shoulder strap and sleeve markings on their dark blue uniform coats. A rear admiral showed eight gold stripes circling each cuff, with a star above the topmost stripe, and two stars on his shoulder strap, showing him the equivalent in rank to a major general. When the Civil War began, there was no official rank of commodore, it having been simply used as an honorary title for any officer of whatever rank commanding a flotilla of ships. But in 1862 it was recognized as a fixed rank immediately below that of rear admiral, to be recognized by seven cuff stripes and a single star on the shoulder. The captain wore six stripes and a silver spread eagle on his shoulder strap. Each of the succeeding ranks wore successively one sleeve stripe fewer, and the correspondingly lower shoulder insignia the same as that of equivalent army officers, right down to the level of the ensign, whose one stripe and shoulder strap showed him to be the equal in status to the Army's own lowly second lieutenant.

The remainder of the men such as gunners, boatswains and the like, were so-called petty officers, the equivalent to non-commissioned officers such as sergeants in the military. As such, they were not technically officers, and it is just as well, for the confusion was bad enough already. Furthermore, all of the officers in line positions wore a silver foul-anchor either in the center or at each end of their shoulder straps. Staff officers – the paymasters, engineers, etc – wore special insignia indicating their function instead of foul-anchors. Paymasters wore an oak sprig, engineers wore a cross made of oak leaves, chaplains a silver cross, professors an oak leaf and an acorn, and surgeons nothing at all. Midshipmen wore shoulder-knots in lieu of straps.[12]

All such insignia were honored for the most part, though officers showed just about as much individuality in their adherence as did their brethren in the Army. Especially confusing would be the sleeve stripes, for their width varied greatly according to the whim of the wearer, and often sleeve ornamentation lagged behind the rank displayed on the shoulder.

The men wearing those uniforms and insignia were in a very large measure amateurs so far as naval service went. Of the 1,554 commissioned officers in uniform in December 1860, 353 had left the service either by resignation or dismissal. That left just 1,181. Eliminating the petty officers and midshipmen, that left only 876, including chaplains and paymasters, and other staff officers not really trained or in line to take line commands.[13] And of those remaining, many were under suspicion for, while 373 men, mostly Southerners, had resigned or been dismissed, another 350 of Southern birth had chosen to remain in the Navy. In the higher ranks, from lieutenant upward, from which vessel commanders could be expected to come, Southerners in the old Navy split almost man for man, 126 leaving while 127 stayed.[14]

What this meant was that every commissioned line officer who was loyal would be needed, and promoted midshipmen and Naval Academy graduates would have to fill the places of those lost in the war. The Navy could ill afford to waste a trained or experienced commander on staff duty. As a result, a host of civilians would be commissioned into the Navy as ensigns and masters to fill those posts as paymasters, chaplains, and surgeons of all grades. Such men, like their counterparts in the military, were volunteers as opposed to regular Navy. Their commissions were to be for the term of the war only.

Just as the Navy was strange to these volunteer officers, so were they an oddity to the old regular men. "We don't get a great many sailors from the prairies," an old commodore told Keeler. For his part, Keeler was pleased with what he found in his fellow officers. "There appeared to be more real earnestness of purpose & less of that swagger & bluster & rowdyism about them than among many of the land officers I have met with," he wrote. As for the new Navy suit he was required to wear, "I felt awkward enough at first in mine, . . . but I am getting used to it now," he wrote. "Bright handsome uniforms are so common here that scarcely any notice is taken of them."[15]

The same was not necessarily the case across the lines in the Confederacy. There the sight of men in naval uniform would always be an oddity, only because there were so few officers in the first place, and because uniforms were even more scarce in the second. Of course, when the secession crisis began, there was no Confederacy and no Southern navy. Instead, for a brief time, each of the seceding states that had coastlines and ports had its own state navy. Three days after the inauguration of Jefferson Davis, on February 21, 1861, the new Congress in Montgomery, Alabama, passed an "act to establish the Navy Department," and authorized Davis to appoint a Secretary of the Navy. His choice was Stephen R. Mallory of Florida, a lawyer and former United States Senator who, like his Federal counterpart Welles, had little experience of naval matters other than his chairmanship of the Naval Affairs Committee in the old Senate. Yet he proved to be one of Davis' most fortuitous choices as a cabinet minister, and at once he set about organizing his department along lines very similar to that of the United States Navy.[16]

Instead of bureaus, Mallory's department subdivisions were called "offices," and in the end he set up four basic departments: Orders and Detail, Ordnance and Hydrography, Provisions and Clothing, and Medicine and Surgery. Each was headed by a resigned U.S. Navy officer, the first two by captains. Their functions are self-evident. Orders and Detail performed exactly the same duties as the Office of Detail in

Welles' navy. Ordnance and Hydrography handled cannon, the construction and placement of "torpedoes," or underwater mines, the collection of navigational information, and for the want of anywhere else to place it, the supervision of the Confederate Naval Academy. Provisions and Clothing dealt with uniforms, provisions and stores, and pay, while Medicine and Surgery oversaw the appointment and assignment of ships' doctors and the acquisition of supplies. Additionally, and in response to the need for the Confederacy to build its own ships, Mallory later created an office for a chief constructor and of an engineer in chief to acquire machinery. Finally, the fledgling Marine Corps was also placed under Mallory's control. Further, in response to the crying need for warships, Mallory was also authorized to maintain naval representation in Europe, where his agents could purchase ships.[17]

Like Welles, Mallory divided his new navy into geographical commands, calling them squadrons. There would eventually be squadrons assigned to the James River in Virginia, a North Carolina Squadron, a Charleston Squadron, a Savannah River Squadron, Mobile, Mississippi River, Galveston, and Red River Squadrons, and several informal lesser commands of no permanence. Since commerce raiders on the high seas operated almost entirely independently, they had no specific designation as commands, roaming where they chose in search of Yankee shipping. The squadrons, meanwhile, had the task of protecting rivers and harbors, and of breaking the blockade when possible. In almost every case, a captain commanded a squadron.[18]

The subject of officers arrived on Mallory's desk as soon as he took office. On March 16, 1861, Congress authorized him to appoint four captains, four commodores, thirty lieutenants, ten surgeons and assistant surgeons, six paymasters, and two chief engineers. Very quickly, however, it became evident that there would be a greater need for officers, and a greater supply thanks to resignations from the Union Navy. Many, of course, were too old to be useful on the line. "A number of old officers, past service, disdaining to eat the bread of ignoble pensioners upon the bounty of the United States," wrote Captain Raphael Semmes, "came South, bringing with them nothing but their patriotism and their gray hairs." However much they might have been useful in a fully staffed and equipped modern navy, these old gentlemen were for the most part unsuited to the sort of hardship and improvisation that Confederate service would require.[19]

Mallory dealt with the problem by creating two navies, as did the Union. The Regular Confederate Navy accepted all resigned U.S. officers at equivalent rank and gave them assignments, most of the older officers becoming office heads. Then in May 1863 Congress established the Provisional Navy, and Mallory then selected from the Regular Navy list those younger and more vigorous officers for active commands, at the same time being able to give them increased rank in the Provisional list. In effect, the Regular Confederate Navy became, as Semmes called it, "a kind of retired list."[20]

In the end, well over a thousand men served the Confederate Navy as officers, though there were never more on duty at a single time than in April 1864, when the rolls listed 727 active officers and twenty-six others shown absent from duty. All told, perhaps 500 vessels of all description flew the Rebel flag during the war, but only a few dozen were really major ships requiring a full complement of ship's officers. Most were converted ferry boats and river steamers, of small size, with small crews, and as a result, there were always more senior grade officers than there were commands.[21]

The order of rankings in the Confederate Navy for officers very closely paralleled that of the old U.S. Navy, and officers moved up, if at all, very slowly, and only through the death, resignation or dismissal of superior officers. The number of positions at each grade was set by act of Congress, and the maximum of 798 of all grades above petty officers was set in April 1862. Not all of those posts would be filled, however. Congress authorized four admirals, for instance, yet only one, Franklin Buchanan, was ever so appointed. Of ten captains authorized, nine were appointed, and only one of them had resigned as a captain from the U.S. Navy. Confederate regulations did not allow for commodores, but an honorary rank of flag officer filled the same purpose for men commanding fleets or squadrons. Below the captains came the commanders, then the lieutenants, and unlike the Federal service they were broken down into first and second lieutenants. There was no lieutenant commander nor were there to be ensigns, but there were the same masters, engineers, surgeons, paymasters as in the Yankee service.[22]

Regulations called for all these officers to wear steel gray uniforms with rank indicated by shoulder straps and sleeve stripes, cap insignia, and buttons on the front of the frock coat. Since the rank of admiral was created after the clothing regulations were set, and since they were not later amended, there was no specification for an admiral, but presumably it would have been the same as that of a flag officer, with four gold stars on the shoulder and on the front of the cap, and four gold stripes on the cuff, the topmost having a loop. Two rows of nine buttons ran down the front of the coat. A captain wore the same coat, except that there were three stripes on the cuff, the top one looped, and three stars on cap and shoulder strap. A commander wore two stripes of gold lace and two stars on cap and shoulder, and a lieutenant one stripe together with one star. A master wore a stripe of lace with no loop and no stars, while a passed midshipman had no stripe at all but three buttons on his cuff and his shoulder strap consisted of a strip of gold lace, while a foul-anchor adorned his cap.

Among the staff ranks the officers wore the same uniform as a master, excepting only that a single stripe of varying widths or else cuff buttons denoted rank of surgeons, paymasters and the like. Surgeons wore black straps with olive sprigs, and so did paymasters except that their straps were green. Engineers wore dark blue straps with oak sprigs denoting rank. Surgeons' caps showed wreaths of olive leaves or stars, depending upon length of service and rank, while paymasters wore exactly the same cap insignia. Engineers, however, had the letter "E" embroidered on their caps.[23]

Since the Confederacy always had more officers than ships and postings, there was never a shortage of manpower. Of the 798 officers authorized, 281 could be drawn from the resigned U.S. officers who enlisted with the Confederacy. While several of the latter would be on the Regular rolls, and therefore essentially inactive, still it is evident that Mallory had fewer than 500 appointments to make, and the majority of these would be of midshipmen attending the Naval Academy, and therefore not on line duty. For the rest, there was never really a need for an active recruiting effort, as able civilians were brought into the service as and when they were required.

The Confederate Marine Corps, like its Yankee counterpart, never really amounted to much, since there was little need for them. The role of marines in most instances was to help with boarding enemy vessels in battle, but no such action ever took place in the Civil War. Otherwise, they did guard duty, or were detailed to help work guns in battle, or else went ashore on raids and cutting out expeditions.

The only source for replenishing trained officers lost due to battle or resignation were the naval academies. The United States Naval Academy had been established in 1845 at Annapolis, Maryland, and there it continued until May 1861, when the tenuous state of Maryland politics made a move judicious. That month the Navy Department moved the Academy to Fort Adams near Newport, Rhode Island. Five months later it moved again to quarters in the Atlantic House, a hotel, and there it remained until after the close of the war. All of their books, instruments, and other articles of learning went with them. Upper classmen lived in the Atlantic House, but the first and second year boys had to live aboard the schoolships *Santee* and *Constitution*, anchored off Goat Island. Meanwhile, the Academy's Annapolis grounds were taken over by the Army for the defense of Maryland.[24]

When the outbreak of war came and there was an initial need for more officers to replace those who had resigned, the class scheduled for graduation in 1862 was detached from the Academy for special duty. They never returned and were never graduated, though always thereafter treated as graduates just the same. Those who stayed behind at the Academy studied seamanship, naval construction, tactics, practice exercises, signals, swimming, gymnastics, ordnance and gunnery of both field and naval variety, fencing, algebra, geometry, trigonometry and calculus, steam engineering, astronomy, navigation, surveying, physics and chemistry, mechanics and applied mathematics, English literature, history and law, French and Spanish language, drawing, and chart-making. It was, to say the least, a rigorous program of study. Commodore George S. Blake served as superintendent throughout the war, assisted by a naval and civilian staff and faculty of about 90. The student body itself, like that of West Point, was governed by the Congressionally mandated limit of one cadet per year to be appointed by each senator and congressman, plus ten appointments at large and one from the District of Columbia, all at the discretion of the president.[25] Because of the rigid system of promotion through vacancy only, none of the graduates of the wartime classes had an opportunity to achieve much in the way of distinction, and few even rose above their graduated rank of passed midshipmen by 1865.

The case was a little different to the south. On March 16, 1861, President Davis was authorized to appoint midshipmen, and a month later the limit was set at 106. By 1865 that limit had risen to 150, though through the course of the war a total of nearly 200 young men were so appointed. Many failed to pass the courses, or else left to join the army, accounting for the attrition. However, it was not until later in December 1861 that Congress mandated "some form of education" for midshipmen. The following spring, Congress provided for the appointment of midshipmen cadets by representatives and senators, as well as the president, and in May 1862, with no funds or location for a permanent Academy campus, the ship C.S.S. *Patrick Henry* was officially designated as the Confederate Naval Academy. To superintend the new school, Mallory selected Lieutenant William H. Parker, and ordered that the school-ship be moored off Drewry's Bluff on the James River. There the boys could study, while at the same time manning the ship – which was a fully operational sidewheel steamer – in the defense of the James.[26]

At once it became evident that the schoolship was not sufficient to house all the appointees. Extra cabins were constructed ashore at Drewry's Bluff, and alterations were made to the *Patrick Henry* – called simply *Patrick* by the boys – to accommodate more midshipmen. Still only about half of the 106 appointed cadets could live aboard the ship. As a result, Mallory began to rotate the young men, those on the *Patrick* alternating from time to time with others stationed ashore or out at sea. The boys had to be at least 14 years of age but not more than 18, and were made to pass examinations in reading, writing, spelling, and math. Once admitted as midshipmen cadets, they had to study under the tutelage of the officers commanding their ships or shore stations until the *Patrick* was ready to receive them. In fact, with alterations and other kinds of delays, actual classes aboard the ship did not commence until October 12, 1863.[27]

The studies of each of the four classes were clearly prescribed, and were essentially the same as the program at the United States Naval Academy, only with the addition of political science. The boys met in two recitation rooms for their classes, working at blackboards with their math problems, or stepping outside for gunnery or small boat drill on the rifled and smooth-bore cannon on deck. They could also engage in sail drill and engine work, or go ashore and practice infantry tactics. "Hard study is the order of the day," Midshipman Hubbard T. Minor confided to his diary. The boys were awakened at 7 a.m., with breakfast an hour later, and then studies until 2 p.m. After a lunch, the boys spent the rest of the day drilling or studying practical applications of their studies. There was little time for recreation, and getting a pass to go ashore was not easy. Poor Minor, after only two weeks at the Academy, lamented that he walked the deck for hours longing "to be once more at home among those who love me so well & who now mourn over my wearisome stay." Homesickness could strike anywhere.[28]

It did not help that the accommodation and fare were pretty miserable. Their uniforms were of coarse and uncomfortable gray cloth. "The food they had to eat," remembered a new midshipman, "was, at first, revolting to me." There was no variety to speak of. "If it was not a tiny lump of fat pork," declared cadet James M. Morgan, "it was a shaving of fresh meat as tough as the hide which had once covered it,with a piece of hardtack and a tin cup of hot water colored by chicory or grains of burned corn, ground up, and brevetted *coffee*." Worse, almost half of the midshipmen at any time seemed to suffer from chills and fever thanks to the cold and damp on the river, but few were excused duty. Instead, they were allowed to lie on deck while the shivers persisted, then stood up and returned to duty. No wonder tempers ran extremely short at times, with at least one challenge for a duel issued but never consummated.[29]

Yet all the frustrations aboard the *Patrick* could be forgotten in an instant when a professor was lecturing in the recitation room and the boom of distant cannon was heard. For as Midshipman James M. Morgan would declare, that ship was "the most realistic war college that ever existed." The boys were literally in the line of fire. With the Union fleet just miles down the James River, threats and alarms were frequent. It was nothing for a professor to interrupt a math lecture by asking a student to "kindly step outside and find out for me which battery it is that has opened up." Indeed, even more than the boys at the Virginia Military Institute, the young cadets at the Naval Academy were called upon for active service, and almost everyone volunteered when asked. As a result, the active assignments became rewards, given to the best scholars. Sometimes the boys manned shore batteries near Drewry's Bluff. They laid mines, assisted in boarding parties to capture enemy vessels, and even took a hand in defending against Federal land movements. In consequence several midshipmen lost their lives in action.[30]

In the end, their most noted service came in April 1865, when Richmond fell to Grant. Taking part in the evacuation, they burned the old *Patrick Henry* to prevent it falling into enemy hands, then Lieutenant Parker led them off with the fleeing government as a guard for the Treasury and the Confederate archives, which duty they manfully performed until May 2. On that day, at Abbeville, South Carolina, with the Treasury disbursed to the remaining soldiers accompanying the fleeing government, Parker disbanded them and the Confederate Naval Academy came to an end. Parker's last sight of them was as they melted into the shadows, carrying with them bacon and beef, and army bread, to help them get home.[31]

In the end, only two classes graduated, totaling in all a mere forty-eight midshipmen. Many more simply did not have time enough to complete their studies and examinations before the war closed. Much of the cream of Southern youth was here, including the sons of General Breckinridge and Captain Semmes, along with Lee's and Pinckney's and others from the leading families. Theirs had been a noble attempt, under the most adverse conditions possible, and the conduct and training of a number of midshipmen assigned to the various ships and squadrons, as well as the behavior of the boys who escorted the government on its last journey, bears testimony to the caliber of the students and the school they served.[32]

For all of the officers, whether midshipmen or masters, commodores or captains, the life of a serving commissioned leader was governed by his branch of service and posting, and each had its distinctive features. Officers on blockade duty saw a different sort of war from those in the river flotillas and squadrons, officers on ironclads had a more varied existence and routine than those aboard conventional ships, while the men on the cruisers or the men on shore stations lived in yet other environments.

What they all had in common was boredom, for there was little to do when not on duty. Fortunately, therefore, shipboard routine was very well organized and generally followed, so that, at least, the officer knew what to expect from each day and could plan for his free time accordingly. For the most part, that leisure time was occupied with spinning tales, writing letters home, and exactly the same sort of activities that men at war in all times have used to fill their idle hours. Aboard the Confederate warship *Chattahoochee* in Georgia, for instance, things were so quiet that there was but one mail call a week. This ship was a dull assignment, with no action and no prospect of action, so the men were anxious for any diversion. Lieutenant William Whittle undertook to have local cobblers make bargain rate shoes for his friends in Richmond to save them money. Others complained that they had no prospect of promotion, while some idly dreamed of glories that would never materialize. The *Chattahoochee* was still under construction and consequently her officers lived ashore in temporary quarters, like many Rebel officers in a number of ports when not at sea. At least these men ate well and as one wrote, "have as elegant table as one would wish." Better yet, many officers could visit the nearby plantations and mix into the local social life. And when finally the *Chattahoochee's* officers moved on board their ship, the local belles repaid their visits, finding that the seamen had decorated their quarters with flowers, and even damask cushions upon which the ladies were seated while they all enjoyed strawberries and pound cake and a cream tea.[33]

Across the lines, aboard the U.S.S. *Monitor*, Paymaster Keeler found things a bit different. That was because, being on a Yankee ship in enemy territory, he had to live aboard his vessel. For all who did so on ironclads, North or South, life could be unpleasant. Asked how he liked life on a warship, he replied that, "I have made the discovery that there are some things about it not very romantic." For one thing, aboard an unheated ironclad, on winter mornings he had to arise and eat breakfast in the wardroom with the temperature at 35[deg]F, "shivering so that one can hardly find the way to his mouth." At night, between cold linen sheets, he shook "till I thought the frame work of my berth would be shaken apart." Relief only came in the morning with hot water in his washbowl, after which he and other officers frequently went to the engine room "to thaw out," it always being warm there. At least eating was not a problem, as "we have the best of food provided." On a ship like an ironclad with a small complement of officers, they all ate together in a single mess in the wardroom, contributing proportionately to the purchase of their victuals out of their own pockets. Eventually steam heaters were installed in the wardroom.[34]

A boatswain's whistle roused the ship at 5 a.m., though off-duty officers could sleep until 8 a.m. or thereabouts when awakened by their servants for breakfast, for many did manage to engage young Negro boys as valets and the like very cheaply. Then after a day of regular duties, Keeler and others would spend their evenings in reading or conversation or writing, much the same as the men of the *Chattahoochee* and virtually every other warship not cruising.[35]

Of privacy there was little on any ship. "As far as sounds are concerned," complained Keeler, "we might as well be in one room." Even as he wrote in his cabin, he could hear every word being spoken in the adjacent wardroom and other cabins. Only the captain had claim to more spacious and private quarters, though on a few vessels other officers enjoyed some elbow room as well. Aboard the Confederate commerce raider *Alabama*, her boarding officer George T. Fullam found the "ward room furnished with a handsome suite of state rooms." What a far cry that was from the verdict of Lieutenant James Baker of the C.S.S. *Huntsville*. "She is," he said of his ironclad, "terribly disagreeable for men to live on." An officer on another Rebel ironclad, the *Baltic*, despaired of finding comfort. "I begin to think that in our Navy it does not exist," he lamented. Aboard the ironclads especially, in the summers it was oppressively hot and humid, with condensed water dripping from overhead and everything in any way organic mildewing. Ventilation was non-existent, and whenever possible the men and officers slept out on deck, or ashore.[36]

About all the officers could say as a class, North or South, was that their standard of living was better than that of the lower ranks. The great leveler, when and if it came, was battle, for then all shared the same risks, though here, at least, the ironclad officers had a measure of reward for their otherwise miserable existence. Behind their iron shields, they were far less likely to suffer injury from enemy shot or shell than their comrades aboard wooden gunboats or ocean-going cruisers.

With numerous variations due to size of ship and kind of service and action, North and South saw generally the same routine. With battle imminent, the captain stationed himself on his quarterdeck, or wherever the wheel and compass were to be located. Ironclads did not have quarterdecks, and when Franklin Buchanan took his C.S.S. *Virginia* into battle at Hampton Roads, Virginia, on March 8, 1862, for a time he actually sat atop the casemate on an armchair, fully exposed. On Federal ironclads, the captain stood in the armored pilot house, communicating by messengers or through a speaking tube. The executive officer, a clerk, midshipmen, and a master, were with the captain as well, all to carry out his orders.

Out on the gun decks, or inside the casemate or turrets on ironclads, lieutenants commanded the gun divisions. Depending upon the size of the ship and the number of cannon and lieutenants, a division could be one gun or six or more. The lieutenant saw that the cannon were cast loose from deck moorings and prepared for action. Sometimes marine officers assisted, though usually they commanded smaller deck howitzers or else placed their men in rigging or at gun ports to act as sharpshooters.

Another lieutenant commanded the powder magazine and saw to its disbursement to the gun divisions. Meanwhile down in the engine room, the chief engineer and his assistant engineers operated the steam engines if the ship had them. Sail-driven vessels had men detailed from the gun divisions to handle changes of sail during combat. The wardroom now became a hospital. The remaining officers posted themselves wherever the captain detailed them.

As was often the case otherwise, the ironclad service had some special features. More officers were free to command gun divisions, since there were no sail parties to lead. The *Virginia* had an officer for every gun in her battle with the *Monitor*. Also these additional officers were thought necessary to command boarding parties, for every ironclad commander expected to batter his opponent with gunfire, then possibly ram him, and in the end board to capture. It never happened in practice.[37]

As for the experience of battle itself, there is little to say. An officer aboard a cruiser or open-deck gunboat felt very exposed, and saw not enemy soldiers firing at him with rifles, but mighty cannon billowing forth fire and smoke in his direction. It was a mitigating fact that most ship-to-ship or shore-to-ship actions took place at some distance, even more than a mile away. It was mostly the ironclads that got to close work, and aboard them the experience was not unlike a 19th century man's concept of hell itself. Deafening roars of his own cannon rang in his ears. His gun deck filled with unventilated smoke that made his eyes tear and his throat parch. The drumming of the engines made the firmament vibrate beneath his feet, while now and then the deafening crash of enemy shells against his iron armor could send him reeling from the concussion. And all the while, only the captain and his pilot could see where they were going or what was happening. The lieutenants at their divisions just kept firing blindly through the gun ports when so ordered.

Happily those scenes were rare in the life of a naval officer. Most Confederate vessels of all classes never fought in more than three engagements in the war, while most Yankee ships chased unarmed blockade runners or bombarded shore positions that often did not return fire. For all its hellish nightmare quality in action, the navy, North and South, was not an inherently dangerous place – just boring.

REFERENCES

1 William S. Dudley, *Going South: U.S. Navy Officer Resignations & Dismissals On the Eve of the Civil War* (Washington, 1981), pp.7, 19; E.B. Long, *The Civil War Day by Day* (New York, 1971), p.719.

2 Dudley, *Going South*, p.4.

3 *Ibid.*, pp.16-7, 37, 42, 44, 45.

4 David D. Porter, *Incidents and Anecdotes of the Civil War* (New York, 1885), pp.8-9.

5 Charles Lee Lewis, *David Glasgow Farragut* (Annapolis, Md., 1943), I, pp.288-9.

6 Dudley, *Going South*, pp.5-6.

7 *Ibid.*, pp.34-40.

8 *Ibid.*, pp.8-13.

9 Long, *Day by Day*, p.719.

10 Kenneth W. Munden and Henry Putney Beers, *Guide to Federal Archives Relating to the Civil War* (Washington, 1962), pp.453, 458, 461, 484-5.

11 *Ibid.*, pp.486-92.

12 *A Naval Encyclopaedia* (Philadelphia; 1881), pp.155, 826; Francis A. Lord. *Civil War Collector's Encyclopedia* (Harrisburg, Pa., 1963), pp.142-3.

13 Dudley, *Going South*, pp.34-55 *passim.*

14 J. Thomas Scharf, *History of the Confederate States Navy* (New York, 1887), pp.32-3.

15 Robert W. Daly, ed., *Aboard the USS Monitor: 1862* (Annapolis, Md., 1964), pp.xiv-xv, 4-5, 9.

16 Scharf, *Navy*, p.28.

17 Tom H. Wells, *The Confederate Navy: A Study in Organization* (University, Ala., 1971), pp.13, 46, 74, 91, 95, 107, 118.

18 Beers, *Guide*, pp.345-64.

19 Scharf, *Navy*, p.29; Raphael Semmes, *The Confederate Raider Alabama* (Greenwich, Conn., 1962), p.29.

20 Semmes, *Raider*, pp.29-30, 30-1.

21 Wells, *Confederate Navy*, p.19.

22 *Ibid.*, p.20; Scharf, *Navy*, pp.33-4, 819-20.

23 Wells, *Confederate Navy*, pp.153-8.

24 Munden and Beers, *Federal Archives*, pp.465-6; Mame Warren and Marion E. Warren, *Everybody Works But John Paul Jones* (Annapolis, Md., 1981), p.8.

25 Warren and Warren, *Everybody Works*, p.56; *Naval Encyclopaedia*, pp.14-5.

26 Wells, *Confederate Navy*, pp.67-9; G. Melvin Herndon, "The Confederate States Naval Academy", *Virginia Magazine of History and Biography*, LXIX (July 1961), p.304; William H. Parker, *Recollections of a Naval Officer, 1841-1865* (New York, 1883), p.324.

27 Herndon, "Academy", p.306; Hubbard T. Minor Diary, October 12, 1863, U.S. Army Military History Institute, Carlisle, Pa.

28 Herndon, "Academy", p.309; Minor Diary, October 30, November 10, 1863.

29 James M. Morgan, *Recollections of a Rebel Reefer* (London, 1918), p.205.

30 *Ibid.*, pp.202, 206; Herndon, "Academy", pp.309-10.

31 Parker, *Recollections*, p.365.

32 Herndon, "Academy", p.316.

33 Maxine Turner, *Navy Gray* (University, Ala.,1988), pp.66-7.

34 Daly, *Monitor*, pp.19-20.

35 *Ibid.*, pp.22-3.

36 *Ibid.*, p.26; Charles G. Summersell, ed., *The Journal of George Townley Fullam* (University, Ala., 1973), p.5; William N. Still, *Iron Afloat* (Nashville, 1971), p.100.

37 Wells, *Confederate Navy*, pp.144-8.

VIII
A THOUSAND GENERALS

One of the reasons that the naval officers, even in their own time, seemed so overlooked, was the fascination felt then and later with the seemingly more dashing army officers bravely leading their soldiers into battle. No image of the Civil War proved to be more powerful in the American mind, North or South. And for all of their self-proclaimed egalitarian spirit of the "common man," the fact is that most Americans of the era – like Americans of all times – were captivated chiefly by the doings of the high and mighty. There were none who were higher or mightier than the men who carried stars on their shoulders and collars. The generals of Blue and Gray were the true focus of almost universal attention throughout the war, eclipsing all officers of other ranks. The word on everyone's lips after a battle was not what privates or lieutenants did. It was what this or that general did. Indeed, the generals' names became in time synonymous with their commands. To millions of ears, the name "Lee" meant the Army of Northern Virginia, and at every command level down the line, to say that a certain general went into action or was defeated, meant that his brigade or division or corps had done so. To the population at large, and even to many of the private soldiers who served them, the generals *were* the armies.

There would always be a problem, then and later, in simply determining how many generals actually served in the war. The trouble is one of definitions, especially with the Confederates. According to Jefferson Davis' Congress, only officers appointed by the president could be generals, and in most cases those appointments had to be ratified by the Senate. In actual practice, Davis nominated an officer and sent his name to the Senate for affirmation or denial. Sometimes, through oversight, a desire for more information, or simply adjourning before acting, the Senate failed to vote on a nomination. And when the Senate was in adjournment, Davis could appoint generals and hold sending in their nominations until the Senate reconvened.

All of this is simple enough, and the officers so nominated or appointed pending nomination and approval have incontestable claim to having been generals. Yet a host of other claimants appeared during and after the war to considerably confuse the matter. In the far-off Trans-Mississippi Department, where communications with Richmond could be cut off for months, commanding General E. Kirby Smith, through necessity, began to appoint generals on his own in his army, asking Davis and the Senate to approve them later. It was the only way to avoid waiting sometimes months to put a man in a vacancy. Some Davis and the Senate approved, but others were never acted upon, and these latter cannot be deemed genuine general officers.

Finally, there were a number of old Confederates who simply took to calling themselves "general." Often in wartime correspondence a man would be called by that title though he had never been promoted. They may have been so called though confusion, or because they commanded brigades – the usual post of a brigadier general – or perhaps because, as with the old honorary naval rank of commodore, some regarded a man in command of a force as a general regardless of his rank. After the war this confusion became compounded by the tendency of elderly officers to "promote" themselves. In their last years, Major Generals Joseph Wheeler and John B. Gordon both claimed to have been made lieutenant generals. Manifestly, neither was, and Gordon signed his own parole at Appomattox as a major general. Further, a number of colonels, like Charles Crews of Tennessee, wore the wreath and stars collar insignia of a general even though never so promoted. Men seeing them during the war, and their uniformed photographs afterward, naturally assumed that such men had been appointed. Worse yet, the United Confederate Veterans, the influential and universal Rebel veterans organization in the years after the war, had a policy of giving its officers the title of "general," even though few of these veterans had ever been more than lower level officers, and many had been private soldiers. Finally, a number of state militia officers held the rank of general, as with Francis H. Smith of the V.M.I. or M. Jefferson Thompson of Missouri.

Out of this mass of confusion, debate can go on interminably. However, after assessing all of the claimants, the best criteria appear to be the fact of appointment, nomination, and confirmation, and officers appointed and nominated but, for whatever reason, not confirmed. Looking at the case in this fashion, there are 425 men who can be said certainly to have held one of the four grades of generalship in the Confederate service.[1]

They were truly a mixed bag of characters. There was a French nobleman, a former vice president of the United States, the son of a president and the grandson of another, alongside farmers and clerks. Many were Northern born, some with brothers in the Union Army. Quite a few had some prior military experience of whatever kind, and at least 146 held diplomas from the United States Military Academy.

Remarkably, three of them had formerly been officers in the U.S. Navy! This was the blend of the rank.

In age they ranged widely. The oldest of all was David E. Twiggs, who was seventy-one when commissioned into the Confederate service. Born in 1790 in Georgia, he was the fourth oldest general officer on either side in the war, and just about the least distinguished of the lot. Suspected even by Confederates after his treasonable surrender of Texas to the Rebels, without bothering to resign his commission, he achieved nothing as a Confederate major general. Indeed, he died of old age less than two months after accepting his commission.[2]

At the other end of the age spectrum was young Brigadier General William P. Roberts of North Carolina. Enlisting at age nineteen, he rose through the ranks to be colonel of his regiment in 1864, and on February 23, 1865, Davis appointed him brigadier. If legend may be believed, so impressed was Robert E. Lee with young Roberts' performance on the battlefield, that he gave the twenty-three-year-old new general his own gauntlets.[3]

They were big men and small. Brigadier General William R. Peck, appointed just five days before Roberts, stood six feet six inches tall and weighed well over 300 pounds. Probably the smallest was young John C.C. Sanders of Alabama. Just past twenty-four when appointed, he apparently stood no more than a few inches above five feet. Ironically, Peck, the biggest target of any Confederate general, came through the war unscathed while Sanders, the smallest, was wounded once in 1862, and again mortally just three months after his promotion.[4]

For some the war was a family affair. Jerome Bonaparte Robertson of Kentucky was forty-seven when he became a brigadier late in 1862. Two years later his twenty-five-year-old son Felix H. Robertson was also appointed a brigadier. Young Felix had another minor claim to fame, in that when he died on April 20, 1928, he was the last surviving Confederate general officer. He might not have enjoyed that honor if an investigation into his chief claim to infamy had been prosecuted more rigorously, for he was also the only Southern general to be investigated by the War Department for the murder of wounded and captured enemy soldiers, chiefly blacks. Only the end of the war impeded then Secretary of War Breckinridge from concluding the investigation. Obviously no saint, Robertson had also delivered perjured reports on command in 1863 in an effort to discredit then-General Breckinridge, which no doubt added some zest to the war secretary's investigation.[5]

Matt and Robert Ransom were brothers from North Carolina. Robert Garnett of Virginia, the first general killed in the war, was a cousin to Richard Garnett who died leading a charge at Gettysburg. Hugh and Ben McCulloch of Tennessee both became Confederate brigadiers, and so did the Starke brothers, Peter and William of Virginia. Ben McCulloch and William Starke were both killed in battle. Surely the best known close relations to achieve generalships were Robert E. Lee and his two sons William H. F. Lee and George Washington Custis Lee. The latter, Lee's elder son, went to

West Point, and served most of the war on President Davis' staff, where he rose to major general, largely to flatter his father no doubt. The younger son, called "Rooney" by the family, had field experience becoming the youngest major general in the Confederate service, due to his abilities leading a division of Stuart's cavalry.[6]

For others, family connections were less fortunate. John Rogers Cooke of Missouri took at least seven wounds before being promoted to brigadier in November 1862, and was widely acknowledged to be one of the best junior generals in the South. Yet his greatest wound was that his father, Philip St. George Cooke, was even then a major general in the Union Army. Major General James E.B. Stuart felt that same wound, for Philip Cooke was his father-in-law. Also in the Army of Northern Virginia was James B. Terrill of Virginia. On May 30, 1864, he fell killed in battle, the day before his appointment as a brigadier was confirmed by the Senate. Eighteen months earlier his brother, Brigadier General William R. Terrill, was killed at the Battle of Perryville fighting for the Union. Probably best known of all the brothers divided by the war, however, were George and Thomas Crittenden. George, an experienced West Point graduate, became a major general in the army commanded by Albert Sidney Johnston, but resigned under a cloud in late 1862. His brother Thomas became a Yankee major general, and was commanding the XXI Corps at the Battle of Chickamauga when it was routed, effectively ending his career. Ironically, their father, Senator John J. Crittenden of Kentucky, had authored and pushed the last attempt at sectional compromise before war broke out. Its failure helped to set the nation on the road to armed conflict, and his sons to opposite sides of the battlelines.[7]

In their antecedents, the generals were just as varied as in their families and vital statistics. Breckinridge, of course, had been vice president under James Buchanan from 1857 to 1861, and was the highest ranking United States official to take arms with the South. As a result, he was under indictment for treason in the Union. Richard Taylor, the son of President Zachary Taylor, became a lieutenant general, while a grandson of Thomas Jefferson, George Wythe Randolph, became a brigadier after leaving his post as Secretary of War in 1862. There was foreign royalty of a sort in the general called "Pole-cat" by his troops, Camille Armand Jules Marie, Prince de Polignac, of France. And there was native American "royalty" in the person of Stand Watie, a chief of the Cherokee nation, who led many of his followers as Confederate cavalry and won a brigadier's star for his effective efforts.[8]

A Rebel general's nativity could have occurred literally anywhere on the map. While naturally most of the generals came from the Southern states, a score and more hailed from New York, New Jersey, Ohio, Pennsylvania, and even in the case of Zebulon York, from Avon, Maine. Polignac, of course, came from France, and Ireland contributed in Patrick R. Cleburne and Patrick T. Moore two very distinguished leaders. Devonshire, in England, gave Collett Leventhorpe, who got his appointment as brigadier in February 1865, though for some reason of his own he declined it.[9]

They came from all walks of life. Besides statesmen like Breckinridge, there were former governors such as Henry Wise and William Smith of Virginia, and a host of other lawyers and jurists who, indeed, made up the largest single professional group among the Confederate general officers, some 129. Surprisingly, professional soldiers or men with extensive experience or military training trailed just behind at 125, though in fact, some 272 of the 425 had some sort of military experience, if only of the brief militia sort. But of the remaining 153 men to become generals, they came from a host of professions. A third had been bankers or merchants and manufacturers. Nearly another third had been farmers and planters. Only 24 could be called professional politicians, while the remainder came from such diverse occupations as education, civil engineering, medicine, and clergy, peace officers and Indian agents, the Navy, and the press. There was even one man, Robert C. Tyler, the most mysterious of all the generals, whose only pre-war occupation appeared to be as a soldier of fortune. Certainly the most unique pre-Confederate occupation of any Southern general, however, was that of Frank C. Armstrong, appointed brigadier general on January 20, 1863. Two years earlier he had been an officer in the Old Army, and chose to remain with it through August 1861. As a result, he fought *against* the Confederates at First Bull Run before resigning to become one of them, a living example of the old adage that said "if you can't beat them, join them."[10]

Wherever these men came from, they eventually took appointments into one or more of the four grades of generalship authorized by the Confederate Congress. The most numerous, naturally, was the lowest grade, brigadier general. In all some 328 rose to that grade, ranging from young Roberts all the way to the sixty-year-old John H. Winder, who was made responsible for Union prisoners. Overall they averaged just over thirty-six, though seventy-one were under thirty at the time of their appointments. Many were distinguished, among them John Hunt Morgan, the dashing and colorful – if troublesome – cavalry raider from Kentucky who led numerous raids into Union territory before he was killed in a surprise attack by Federals in 1864. Almost equally as noted was his subordinate and friend, Brigadier General Basil W. Duke, who succeeded to Morgan's command. At the twilight of the war, he commanded the military escort of the fleeing President Davis and cabinet, and after the war became one of the premier writers on the Confederate experience.[11]

At the next level of command, there were seventy-two major generals, of whom Twiggs was the oldest and "Rooney" Lee the youngest. Interestingly they were still a relatively youthful group, average age running thirty-seven, barely a few months older than the brigadiers. Here is where the greatest battlefield reputations of the war may be found. "Jeb" Stuart, John B. Gordon, Joseph Wheeler, Patrick Cleburne, Frank Cheatham, George E. Pickett, Sterling Price, and more and more. These men commanded the divisions, and sometimes the corps, of the mighty armies of the Confederacy. Few who lacked real ability rose to this station.[12]

More rarified still was the fraternity of lieutenant generals, for only seventeen held such rank. Here the widest sort of variety showed itself. The oldest was fifty-four-year-old Leonidas Polk, formerly Episcopal bishop of the Southwest, and a man of almost no military ability at all. Yet he was a West Pointer and, more importantly, an old friend of Jefferson Davis. The youngest was Stephen D. Lee, who was just twenty-seven when appointed. In between there was the cranky and irascible Jubal A. Early, a profane bachelor who apparently detested women yet may have fathered several mulatto children out of wedlock. There was Richard Taylor, who had no military experience other than having been General and President Zachary Taylor's son – and who was also a brother-in-law to President Davis. Nevertheless he showed real talent in a difficult command in Louisiana. Better known were some of Lee's warhorses, men like James Longstreet and Richard S. Ewell and A.P. Hill. Hill was killed in action just as the war was closing, at the same time that he was dying of complications from venereal disease. Out in the western theater there was the capable William J. Hardee and, above all, the incomparable Nathan Bedford Forrest. With no schooling or experience of war at all, Forrest rose from private in the 7th Tennessee Cavalry to become probably the most instinctively talented cavalryman of the war.[13]

At the very top, in the rank of full general, they were all West Point men, all eight of them. Senior in grade, and also the oldest, was sixty-two-year-old Samuel Cooper, who spent his war in Richmond and never saw active service. Of the others, they were a distinguished if flawed lot. Robert E. Lee stood without peer. Albert Sidney Johnston was killed at Shiloh before he could demonstrate if Davis' trust in him was well-placed. Joseph E. Johnston and P.G.T. Beauregard started the war brilliantly, then frittered away much of their time petulantly feuding with an equally argumentative Davis. The great genius of Johnston, widely proclaimed then and later, never appeared on the battlefield, for he rarely risked battle. There was almost no debate on the command merits of Braxton Bragg, however, an absolute disaster as commander of the Army of Tennessee, a man who fought his own subordinates more than he fought the enemy, and who owed his continuation in command to his friendship with Davis.

Far to the west sat Edmund Kirby Smith, another crusty commander who became a virtual king in the trans-Mississippi domain that was called by some "Kirby Smith-dom." Smith was never an able or experienced battlefield commander, but he ran the administrative nightmare of a province one-third the size of the Confederacy with remarkable success, and was one of the very last to surrender. As for the last and most junior of the full generals, he was John Bell Hood, a daring and bold fighter who simply was not smart enough to command an army, as he demonstrated by nearly destroying the Army of Tennessee when he took its command for a time from Joseph Johnston. Hood owed his position, as much as anything, to his shameless flattery of President Davis, as well as to Davis' own loathing of Johnston.[14]

Certainly within this group as a whole there were all the vices and virtues to be found. Even generals were not immune to temptations and vanities, or worse. They could be a contentious lot, and challenges to duels were occasionally issued. Brigadier General John A. Wharton of Tennessee was killed when a cavalry colonel shot him under strange circumstances, and in a formal duel General John S. Marmaduke shot and killed General L.M. Walker. They could be venal, too, as charges of theft and willful dishonesty occasionally attested. Certainly Earl Van Dorn was no saint, invading the sanctity of at least one married woman's bedroom, and losing his life for it.

Van Dorn also suffered another far more common vice, drinking. Alcohol was common enough before the war in the South, and many an officer had developed a taste for it. The pressures and sometimes fears of high command led a few to excess. Breckinridge was accused of drunkenness on two occasions, though his enemy Bragg was the accuser; the charge therefore may be false. But Breckinridge's fellow division commander Major General Frank Cheatham was frequently seen drunk by a number of witnesses. George B. Crittenden resigned his commission in some disgrace after losing first a battle with the enemy at Mill Springs, Kentucky, in January 1862, and then a fight with the bottle that led to his relief from corps command shortly before Shiloh. Perhaps the most noted of all inebriates, however, was Brigadier General Nathan G. Evans of South Carolina. Known as "the most accomplished braggart" in the Confederate Army, he was also a prodigious drinker, having a specially detailed orderly who followed him everywhere carrying a "barrelita" of whiskey for his personal use. Twice he went before courts-martial, once for drinking and again for disobedience, and in 1863 he was finally removed from command, though he was certainly one of the premier fighters in the service.[15]

Worse was cowardice, and certainly there were a few who showed it. Probably best known and most notorious was John Floyd of Virginia, senior commander of Fort Donelson, Tennessee, in February 1862. When surrounded by the enemy, he turned the command over to a subordinate and effected his own escape, abandoning his command. Worse yet, Floyd's immediate subordinate, General Gideon J. Pillow, proved to be just as cowardly. He, too, turned over the command to the next subordinate, Simon Buckner, and then made good his escape with Floyd. Floyd would be so censured in the Confederacy that he never again held a position, and on March 11, 1862, President Davis summarily relieved him of command. Pillow, an experienced old political wire-puller, managed to hang on to his commission, though suspect, and at the last minute even got command of a brigade in Breckinridge's division during the Battle of Stones River, Tennessee. But his cowardice there ensured that his field command days would be over for good.[16]

But for every act of cowardice on the part of a Rebel leader, there were scores of individual demonstrations of great bravery and heroism. Armistead's, leading his men right up to the summit of Cemetery Hill at Gettysburg, can never be forgotten, nor can Albert Sidney Johnston's coolness under fire at Shiloh be anything other than bravery, however ill-advised. In an age when leaders were expected to inspire by example, most of these men did just that, though at terrible risk to themselves. Thus fell Johnston and Armistead. Thus was Jeb Stuart lost in 1864, A.P. Hill a year later, Leonidas Polk to a cannon shot in Georgia, and McCulloch and Terrill. Thus fell Stonewall Jackson to shots by his own men in the dark at Chancellorsville.

Indeed, the attrition among the general officers was appalling, and a major source of the weakness in the command structure of Lee's army after Gettysburg. For so many of his experienced brigadiers had been killed or otherwise put out of action due to wounds, that men who had months before been captains were now leading brigades. In all, 77 of the 425 generals were killed or mortally wounded in battle, almost twenty percent. Another nineteen died in service from other causes, yet the true extent of the loss is even greater than it at first appears, for of the total 425 generals, many never held field command and therefore never risked enemy fire. Factoring such officers out of the equation would raise the percentage of field officers killed to fully one quarter or more. Unfortunately, the bravest were the most likely to be hit, and thus many of the best leaders were destined to fall, while several of those not killed suffered disabling wounds. Richard S. Ewell lost a leg as a result of a wound, and was never as effective in corps command again. Hood, bold to rashness, lost a leg at Chickamauga and the use of an arm at Gettysburg. Francis T. Nichols of Louisiana lost his left arm in 1862 and his left foot at Chancellorsville.

Thus their bravery was costly. Forrest, arguably the boldest of all, was wounded several times in the war, yet so fierce a fighter was he that he is believed to have personally killed more enemy soldiers than any general of the war. He even killed one of his own officers in a quarrel, though only after the officer had shot him in the hip.

Not so fortunate were many other wearers of the stars. Without doubt, the worst day of the war for the corps of Confederate generals came at Franklin, Tennessee, on November 30, 1864. In a massive frontal attack on the Yankees, Hood at his rashest almost shattered his army, and when the casualties were counted, five of his generals were found slain: Hiram Granbury, States Rights Gist, John Adams, Otto F. Strahl, and worst of all for the Confederacy, Patrick R. Cleburne. That night they were laid out in a row on the porch of a nearby house, while a sixth, Brigadier General John C. Carter lay mortally wounded. Bravery in this war came at a terrible price for leaders.[17]

It was a price paid by both sides, for almost everything suffered by the generals in Gray was felt by their foes in Blue. Indeed, they even shared the initial confusion as to just who really was a general, though from a much different cause. Long before the Civil War, with promotions governed by vacancies at higher levels, and with deserving officers staying in grade seemingly indefinitely, the War Department adopted a system of brevets. Essentially, it meant that conspicuous service, almost always in action, could be recognized with an honorary promotion by brevetting an officer. A captain could be brevetted to major, or even higher, though he only exercised the regular rank of captain unless there were other captains in his command. Then, thanks to his brevet, he would take charge as senior officer.

Unfortunately, when the Civil War got going in earnest, the brevet system got out of control as political and personal influences came to bear while there were thousands of officers hoping to make a record for themselves. No tally of the total number of brevets awarded to officers exists, but it would certainly run to 10,000 or more!

Just as confusing was the fact that an officer could possibly hold four different ranks simultaneously. A Regular Army captain might have taken a commission as a colonel in the volunteers, though his Regular commission still remained active. Good performance on the battlefield could lead to a brevet promotion to brigadier general of volunteers and, at the same time, brevet promotion to major in the Regulars. Worse, officers were entitled to wear the insignia of their brevet ranks, which confused everyone. On top of that, two pre-war Regular officers, one subordinate to the other, could find their positions reversed in the volunteer service, and compounded by brevets if they held the same volunteer rank. Thus a brevet brigadier of volunteers would outrank a colonel of volunteers who might, in the Regular Army, be his own superior.[18]

In the end, some 1,367 men received brevet promotions to brigadier or major general of volunteers or Regulars during the war, men who never received actual appointment to those ranks. Thus they do not figure in any tally of true generals. Of those genuinely promoted to wear the stars, however, there were 583.

They represented the same mixed bag as their foes across the lines. Oldest of the lot was John E. Wool, born just a year after the close of the Revolution, and fully seventy-nine when he finally retired in 1863, having done two years' excellent service in the Civil War. Old General Winfield Scott, of course, and Edwin V. Sumner were both born a few years after Wool, Scott in 1786 and Sumner in 1797. Scott never took the field, being too old and corpulent, but Sumner became the oldest active general officer of the war, rising to major general and command of the II Corps of the Army of the Potomac, which he ably commanded in the 1862 Peninsular Campaign. At Fredericksburg that December he commanded Burnside's Left Grand Division, and was on his way to a new command in the West when he died in March 1863, aged sixty-six.

At the other end of the scale was a young man who set a record never yet equaled or exceeded in the United States Army, Galusha Pennypacker – entitled to remembrance if only for his odd name – was elected captain of his company of the 97th Pennsylvania Infantry in August 1861, aged seventeen. Three years later, thanks to able service, and though only twenty, he was colonel of the regiment. He served so well during the Petersburg Campaign that he rose to command of his brigade, took four wounds in battle, and finally felt enemy shot a fifth time in the January 1865 assault on Fort Fisher, North Carolina. "The real hero of Fort Fisher," a superior called him, and his reward came on April 28, 1865, when he received an appointment as brigadier general, thirty-four days before his twenty-first birthday. It made him the youngest general in American history, and, staying in the Regular Army after the war, he became the youngest regimental colonel in its history.[19]

Overall, as with the Rebels, the Federal generals were young men, as it required the vigor of youth to stand the rigors of field and campaign. The men who became the premier leaders all shared relative youth. U.S. Grant was thirty-nine when he donned his first star. William T. Sherman was forty-one, George H. Thomas forty-four, and Philip H. Sheridan just thirty. On average the brigadiers had passed their thirty-seventh birthday when commissioned, making them just a year older than their Rebel counterparts. Yankee major generals averaged thirty-nine, two years older than Confederates of the same rank, though it must be kept in mind that the advanced years of a very few old men like Scott, Sumner, Wool, and others considerably raised the average.

Largest of all of them was very probably old Winfield Scott himself, who stood six feet five inches and probably weighed in excess of 300 pounds. As for the smallest, figures are uncertain, but "Little Phil" as Sheridan was often called, barely passed five feet in height, and was usually photographed standing alone, or else seated if in a group, no doubt to avoid accentuating his diminutive stature, which would have been the way he wanted it.[20]

Not nearly so many sets of brothers or fathers and sons became Yankee generals as in the Rebel service. John and Napoleon Buford of Kentucky were half-brothers. The former, commanding a cavalry division in 1863, was the first to resist the Confederates at Gettysburg, and may have saved the battle by buying time for infantry to come to the battlefield. His brother served creditably in the western theater of the war. Two other brothers, David and William Birney, had been born in Alabama, but their father, abolitionist James G. Birney, moved them north at an early age. Both became lawyers, yet thanks to their influential father, and their early stand by the Union, each obtained a volunteer commission. By February 1862 David was a brigadier, destined to become a major general with a rather distinguished record until felled by malaria in 1864. Brother William went into the United States Colored Troops, received a brigadier's commission in 1863, and later commanded a division in Grant's army at Appomattox.

However, all families, North or South, were outdone by the McCooks of Ohio. Alexander McCook became a major general and commanded the XX Corps, suffering irreparable damage to his career at Chickamauga, along with Crittenden. His younger brother Daniel McCook led his brigade up the slopes of Kennesaw Mountain, Georgia, on June 27, 1864, and took a mortal wound, dying on July 17, just a day after his appointment as a brigadier. Their oldest brother was Robert L. McCook, made brigadier in March 1862 after a distinguished performance at the Battle of Mill Springs, only to be ambushed and mortally shot under mysterious circumstances by Confederate partisans a few months later. And a cousin of the three brothers, Edward M. McCook, also became a brigadier, serving with Sherman in Georgia in 1864. The stars on the shoulders of this particular family truly made a constellation.[21]

Before the war these men destined for leadership had seen a wide range of experience and circumstances. Quite a number came from Europe, especially from Hungary and the Prussian states, refugees from the political upheavals of 1848 and later. Franz Sigel, Carl Schurz, Julius Stahel, Albin Schoepf, Alexander Schimmelfennig and Wladimir Krzyzanowski were only some of the immigrants who became Yankee generals. Several had genuine military experience. Others were simply appointed out of political expedience, to encourage immigrants to enlist in Union regiments. Few achieved distinction, though that had nothing to do with their nativity. Ireland, too, contributed a dozen generals, just as did Germany. Others came from Canada, France, Great Britain, Russia, Spain, Sweden, and even one from Switzerland.

Few of them had quite the distinguished antecedents of Breckinridge or Taylor or the other more aristocratic Rebel generals. None were sons of Presidents, though a few would later become Presidents – U.S. Grant, Andrew Johnson, Rutherford B. Hayes, Benjamin Harrison and James A. Garfield. Certainly there was a fair share of Senators and Congressmen. Among the most interesting of backgrounds was that of Ivan Vasilovitch Turchinoff, later simplified to John Basil Turchin. Born in Russia in 1822, he attended the Imperial Military School and became a colonel of the Imperial Guard, serving on Crown Prince Alexander II's staff during the Crimean War. Made a colonel and later a brigadier, he brought Russian attitudes toward war to the South, riding roughshod over soldiers and civilians alike, including women. Eventually he was court-martialed and dismissed, but then reinstated by Lincoln, and ended the war with the nickname "Russian Thunderbolt" thanks to his hard-hitting skill in battle.[22]

By and large, the rest of the generals showed much the same profile as their foes. Professional soldiers made up a substantial plurality of 194 out of the 583, while all-told 217 men who attended West Point donned stars. Just behind them ranked the lawyers and jurists, with former merchants and businessmen accounting for almost the same. Far fewer planters and farmers became generals than in the Confederacy, attesting to the generally less rural nature of leading men in the Union. As for the rest, however, almost the same proportions of general occupations occurred North as South of Mason and Dixon's line.

Except for the politicians, just over five percent of Confederate generals were professional politicos. In the Union Army that rose to over eight percent, and considering the subsequent military quality of the men as demonstrated in the field, it is apparent that Lincoln's choices were not nearly so good as Davis'. While at least half of the political generals in the South performed creditably, and some like Breckinridge were outstanding, very few in the North rose above mediocrity. Some were absolute disasters. Sigel became a major general, yet lost almost every battle he ever fought, and ran away from at least one. Nathaniel Banks repeatedly showed an almost complete lack of command ability, yet led one army after another until the 1864 failure of his Red River Campaign. Probably most notorious of all was Benjamin F. Butler in the East and the scheming John McClernand in the West. In April 1864, chief of staff

Henry Halleck actually wrote to his friend Sherman that "it seems but little better than murder to give important commands to such men as Banks, Butler, McClernand, Sigel, and Lew Wallace, and yet it seems impossible to prevent it." Indeed, it was impossible, and only later in the war, with the Union clearly on the road to victory, were the political generals weeded out.

There were only two grades of generalship, excepting the unique case of Grant's promotion to lieutenant general. Most numerous, as in the Confederacy, were the ranks of the brigadiers, some 450 in all. Youngest, of course, was Pennypacker, while the oldest was probably Daniel Tyler, already a sixty-two-year-old brigadier in the Connecticut state militia when the war began. Many distinguished themselves, especially younger men like the brilliant cavalry raider Benjamin Grierson, who led his 1,700 cavalry on a daring expedition through the heart of Rebel Mississippi in April-May 1863 as a diversion during Grant's Vicksburg Campaign. Others did a different kind of service like John A. Rawlins, who spent the whole war on Grant's staff, constantly watching him for signs of a return to the bottle, advising as friend and fellow officer, becoming in Grant's words "the most nearly indispensible" man on his staff.[23]

Of the major generals there were 132, with Wool the oldest and twenty-five-year-old George A. Custer the youngest – indeed, the youngest in American history. Here were the most storied commanders of the war – men such as Sherman, Sheridan, Thomas, McClellan, Hooker, and more. They were the ones who commanded not only the corps but also the armies, that eventually fought their way to victory.

Of course, not every Yankee general was a hero. Cowardice, intemperance, avarice, perhaps even treason, showed up in their number. Three of them would be court-martialed and dismissed for various offenses. Brigadier General James H. Ledlie commanded a brigade in the IX Corps and then a division, and was in charge of it at Petersburg when an assault was ordered on July 30, 1864. When his men went forward, with no assistance in preparation for the assault by their general, he sat huddled back in a bomb-proof dugout. He resigned in disgrace a few months later. With him at the time was another division commander of the IX Corps, Edward Ferrero. He, too, cowered in the bomb-proof, sharing a bottle of "Dutch courage" with Ledlie. Irish-born Brigadier General Thomas F. Meagher was a notorious inebriate, who died two years after the war when he got drunk and fell off a steamboat into the Missouri River.

Most ignoble of all, however, was the performance of Brigadier General Justus McKinstry of New York. A career officer, he made brigadier early in the war, and then took charge of the quartermaster's department in Missouri. Quickly he extorted huge sums from contractors dealing with the Army by helping them to sell their goods at highly inflated prices. When his chicanery was finally discovered, he was cashiered in 1863 after a year in jail.[24]

Yet bravery and self-sacrifice they also had aplenty, and the cowards and poltroons were only a fraction of their number. For generations men would tell and read of the exploits of Joshua L. Chamberlain of the 20th Maine. At Gettysburg his performance would win him the Medal of Honor. Six times he felt Rebel lead, and was believed to be mortally wounded at Petersburg when Grant gave him a field promotion to brigadier. Jokingly in later years he would quip that he was "not of Virginia's blood; she is of mine," after having been hit so many times on the state's battlefields. It was no wonder that Grant accorded to him the high honor of formally receiving the surrender of Lee's Army at Appomattox. Ranald Mackenzie, only twenty-four in 1864, led a brigade and then a division of cavalry so magnificently that Grant was moved to remark that he thought the young man, "the most promising young officer in the service."

So many of them were gallant, so many compassionate, so many showed the virtues that all men aspired to, that it is difficult to choose from among them. Even when hostile generals themselves met, they acted like men born to lead, and few episodes illustrate this more than the wartime meetings of two pairs of opposing generals.

At Gettysburg, on the first day of the fight, July 1, 1863, Brigadier General Francis C. Barlow led a brigade of the XI Corps that was driven off Cemetery Ridge by the Confederates. It was his misfortune in the retreat to be struck by a bullet that left him virtually paralyzed for several hours, and he was believed dead or dying and left where he fell. When the advancing Rebels swept over his position, Brigadier General John B. Gordon came upon Barlow. Asking Barlow's name, and thinking him bound to die, Gordon had him put on a litter and carried to the shade, where he promised to send Barlow's letters to his wife and tell her how he died. Showing every tenderness, Gordon fulfilled Barlow's wish. But unknown to Gordon, Barlow eventually recovered. Fifteen years later they met by chance, and formed a friendship that lasted almost twenty years.[25]

More touching still were the last hours of Major General Stephen D. Ramseur. A West Point cadet in the class of 1860, he took arms with the Confederacy, and at the October 19, 1864, Battle of Cedar Creek in the Shenandoah, was commanding a division in Jubal Early's army. Near the close of the battle, while rallying his troops to hold fast, he felt a Yankee bullet enter his right side and puncture both lungs. His men put him in an ambulance and sent him to the rear, but when the rest of the army began to retreat, Ramseur was stalled, and at nightfall the Yankee cavalry pursuers had caught up with him.

They took him to Union General Sheridan's headquarters, where Sheridan's own physician looked at him and judged the wound mortal. Soon the word that Ramseur was there spread in the Union high command, and his old friends and classmates from West Point came to gather around him. Off and on through the night they kept vigil at his bedside. Henry A. DuPont came. So did George Custer and Wesley Merritt, while Sheridan himself frequently looked in on his dying foe. Finally the next morning, when Ramseur breathed his last, he did so made comfortable by the ministrations of an enemy doctor, and surrounded by his old friends. Later that day, while this one dead general was sent off to his family, the other generals who had attended him returned to the business of the war.[26]

REFERENCES

1 Warner, *Generals in Gray*, pp.xiv-xix.

2 *Ibid.*, p.312

3 *Ibid.*, p.258

4 *Ibid.*, pp.231, 268.

5 *Ibid.*, pp.260-1; Davis, *Breckinridge*, p.460.

6 Warner, *Generals in Gray*, pp.99, 100, 179, 184, 253.

7 *Ibid.*, pp.61, 65, 302; Warner, *Generals in Blue*, p.100.

8 Warner, *Generals in Gray*, p.241

9 *Ibid.*, p.185

10 *Ibid.*, pp.xxi-xxii, 13, 313.

11 *Ibid.*, p.xxv.

12 *Ibid.*, p.xxv.

13 *Ibid.*, pp.xxv, 92.

14 *Ibid.*, p.xxv.

15 *Ibid.*, p.332; William C. Davis, *Battle at Bull Run* (New York, 1977), p.163.

16 Warner, *Generals in Gray*, p.90; Davis, *Breckinridge*, pp.343-4.

17 Warner, *Generals in Gray*, pp.xviii-xix.

18 Warner, *Generals in Blue*, pp.xvi-xvii.

19 *Ibid.*, pp.xviii, 365-6.

20 *Ibid.*, p.xviii.

21 *Ibid.*, pp.34-5, 53-4, 294-7.

22 *Ibid.*, pp.511-12, 603-4.

23 *Ibid.*, p.342.

24 *Ibid.*, pp.150, 277, 303-4, 318.

25 John B. Gordon, *Reminiscences of the Civil War* (New York, 1903), pp.151-2.

26 Gary Gallagher, *Stephen Dodson Ramseur* (Chapel Hill, N.C., 1985), pp.164-5.

IX
THEY ALSO SERVED

All too often forgotten, then and later, was the fact that few of these generals of the Civil War, or the colonels commanding regiments for that matter, could have functioned as effectively as they did, were it not for the services of the members of their staffs. These men consulted and advised, carried messages and carried out orders, handled almost all of a commander's communications and correspondence, became his friend and confidant, sometimes his alter ego, and in times of dire necessity even replaced the field commander in battle. They saw to his needs and comforts, such as they could, defended him against calumnies and enemies in his own camp if they felt loyal to him, or helped to fan rumor and innuendo if they did not. It would be too much to say that a staff could make or break a commander, but without good men at his side, and without their trust and confidence, even the best of leader's abilities would be seriously impaired.

The whole concept of a staff was dangerously underdeveloped when the Civil War erupted. Because colonels and generals in previous wars had led comparatively few men in camp or battle, often a commander needed no more than a quartermaster and a military secretary to handle his everyday working needs, taking care of much of the work himself, instead of delegating it to others. That was fine in the Mexican War, when a whole field army might number fewer men than in a good-sized Civil War infantry division. When the conflict did erupt in 1861, however, the necessary internal military organization developed just as slowly, and just as much behind the times, as did much of the military technology. Retrospect clearly suggests that in 1861 all soldiers should have been armed with rifled weapons, but they were not, thanks to the conservatism and inertia of entrenched old ranking officers. Similarly, with the prospect of armies that could number 100,000 or more, leaders entrusted with brigade, division, and especially corps and army command, should have had staffs two and three times the size of those they used. In part they were limited by army regulations specifying the staff officers allowed, and in part by their own inability to delegate or to foresee the needs of their very modern kind of war.

In actual practice, the size of a staff depended upon the level of the commander involved. A colonel commanding a regiment, whether infantry or cavalry, generally had the smallest of all. While there were variations, especially in the Confederate service, the colonel might have an adjutant, a clerk – not a commissioned officer – a surgeon, a quartermaster, and occasionally a chaplain. Sometimes the surgeon had one or two assistants, also commissioned, but that essentially would be all.[1]

At the next level of command – brigade – both war departments recognized the need for more officers, in part because of the nature of most brigades early in the war. A brigadier could expect the same adjutant. With as many as 5,000 rather than 1,000 men on his hands, like a colonel, the brigadier usually also divided the supply functions in two, appointing both a quartermaster to oversee all of the materiel needs of the command, and a commissary officer to see to the feeding of the men and animals. There would also be a surgeon, sometimes a chaplain, and one or two aides-de-camp, often volunteer civilians but frequently commissioned lieutenants, to do whatever tasks came to the general's mind.

When that general rose to division command, he would need all of the above, and also the addition of an ordnance officer, since most divisions contained their own artillery batteries. At this level, too, the general might also find an engineering officer to oversee construction of defenses and battery emplacements, and perhaps even a topographical engineer to help survey landscape and prepare military maps. And should the general rise to corps or army command, then he would have the largest staff to be found in this war: two or three aides, a chief engineer, a chief quartermaster, a chief of ordnance, a medical director or chief of surgeons, a judge advocate general for dealing with military policy and law, a provost marshal for maintaining that law in the army, a chief of artillery who oversaw actual field command of the batteries, whereas the ordnance chief looked after the acquisition and disbursement of the weapons, a chief commissary of subsistence, an adjutant general, an inspector general, and perhaps even others. Often a commander divided his assistants formally or informally into a personal and a general staff, the personal staff consisting of aides, military secretary, and adjutant. Rarely, however, did any officer designate yet another staff member later considered essential – a chief of staff.

Throughout much of the war a well-developed prejudice against staff officers flourished in both armies. In part it was well-founded, for a considerable number of staff appointments went to men who, like the political generals, had high connections or family ties to thank for their commissions rather than training or ability. Furthermore, there could be an annoying degree of self-importance displayed by some of these men. Attached to headquarters, where food and accommodations and pay were better, without having to suffer the worst rigors of the march and often not called upon to set foot on the battlefield, they sometimes almost flaunted their clean smart uniforms before men whose dress showed the rough wear of the field. They rode while thousands walked. Often they were youngsters still in their teens or early twenties – especially the aides – who showed the immaturity of their years by lording their status over the poor common soldier. Worse, those who had the good fortune to serve a distinguished commander like Lee or Sherman sometimes displayed the puffed-up conceit or pride that more than anything else alienated the common soldier, and even fellow officers. At the same time, commanders often passed along to their staffs their own demeanor and temperament. Bragg's staff could be just as gruff and quarrelsome as he was. The unjustifiably egotistical and pompous Federal Major General John C. Frémont, stationed in St. Louis, surrounded himself with a staff that many thought more akin to a palace guard in their high-handedness and finery.

Not because of such men, but in spite of them, did the rest of the staff officers North and South achieve whatever degree of respect and admiration they received, and for many that proved to be considerable. Indeed, a number of them rose to become generals in their own right, and some of note. E. Porter Alexander began the war as a signals officer, and later became chief of artillery for corps commander James Longstreet. His exemplary services were rewarded with a brigadier's commission. John Rawlins, Grant's trusted staff officer, became a brigadier, and so did others of Grant's military family. Several of Lee's officers achieved generalships, including William Pendleton, R.H. Chilton, Armistead L. Long, and Walter H. Stevens. Often, when a staff officer rose to high rank like this, he left staff work to take an active field command, as did Long, but more frequently he remained where he was. Indeed, in some cases the promotion to generalship was a reward for good staff service, and not an indication that higher authorities felt the recipient capable of independent command.

For the overwhelming majority of staff officers, however, theirs was unsung and obscure service. The generals and colonels got the headlines, while the field officers on active service received all of the glory and opportunity for speedy advancement. Staff work was tedious for the most part, often involving longer hours than those of the enlisted men and their leaders, and carrying with it the added frustration of having to please many masters at the same time. And perhaps to an even greater degree than field officers, the men of the staff had to suppress their own hurt feelings when their superior overruled their decisions.

In response to their forgotten contributions, some staff men became practically belligerent in their assertions of their worth. None more typified this than the quartermasters, nor with more justification. If there was any staff officer who meant something to the soldier in the ranks, it was the one or ones who fed and clothed him. Asserting that his department was "the most important by far of all the staff," Yankee quartermaster J.F. Rusling neatly summed up what he did for the soldiers. "The

Quartermaster's Department," he said, "houses and nurses the army; makes its fire and furnishes its bed; shoes and clothes it; follows it up, with its outstretched and sheltering arms, dropping only mercies, wherever it goes; carries, even to its most distant and difficult camps, the food it eats, the clothing it wears, the cartridges it fires, the medicine it consumes; and finally, when 'life's fitful fever' is over, constructs its coffin, digs its grave, conducts its burial, may even erect a head-board to mark the spot where 'sleeps well' the departed hero, and keeps besides, by special Act of Congress, a record of the time and place of his interment, for future references of his friends."

In the Confederate Army, he had to deal with more than sixty different forms, sometimes filed singly, and other times in confused combinations, just in order to carry on the routine business of his department. There was a form for forage, another for fuel, one for wagons and harness, and a host of others required every time any sum of money was disbursed. All incidental expenses of an army passed through the quartermaster, even postage.

In the Union, where everything, including manpower, was available in greater abundance, the quartermaster and his counterpart the commissary could carry on their duties in relative security. Their foes to the south, however, faced a distinct challenge in the face of constant shortage, poor transportation, and lack of funds. One typical Rebel quartermaster could speak for all. Captain N.A. Birge, quartermaster at Monroe, Louisiana, from 1862 onward, first of all had to supervise a railhead at Monroe that connected it with Vicksburg to the east, thus making him a transportation officer. Further, he oversaw several steamers on the Ouachita River in order to get his materiel where the railroad did not go, chartering the boats from their civilian owners and paying with government funds. Then he managed 54 wagons in trains that covered the rest of his far-flung territory. All of these arteries of transportation were in constant operation simultaneously, and Birge directed and paid for all of it, using a mountain of those sixty-plus forms. Every month he had to file a grand consolidated report of all his department's activities, and frequently he found himself so overtaxed just with management that he did not have time to prepare the lengthy report. His superiors' solution to his problem was to assign him three additional reports to make each month. Truly, an army did move on paperwork, even in those days when already the red ribbon used to wrap folded and docketed official documents in the military had come to be called "red tape."[2]

Honesty and character were also an essential element in a good quartermaster or commissary; for as seen in the case of General Justus McKinstry, ample opportunity presented itself for mishandling government funds. Confederate Commissary General Lucius B. Northrop, hardly competent himself, frequently thought he saw signs of dishonesty in others. One supply officer, a Major Lanier, complained to a friend that Northrop had too little confidence in him. "I told him," the friend wrote to Northrop, "that you were probably under the impression that he drove fast horses – gambled occasionally – kept a woman – and drank a quart of whiskey per day – all of which he says is *true*, but nevertheless thinks himself capable of making a good officer and promises to do his duty."[3]

The Confederate quartermaster, especially, also had to suffer the righteous wrath of the citizenry. As rations inevitably became scarce, impressment of civilian food-stuffs became necessary. Though sanctioned by Congress, still it was destined to be a controversial and hated policy, and the staff officer responsible in a department or an army could become a very unpopular fellow. "The Government has employed an army of barnacles to go out in swarms like the locusts of Egypt," one editor said of the impressment officers. "Many of these agents knew no more of business than a Comanche Indian knew of mathematics."[4] For an officer who might think himself the most important of all in a general's military family, being called a "barnacle" and a "locust" for his efforts seemed a pitiful reward.

Far less disliked – indeed, generally well-regarded – was an entirely different staff officer common to both armies, the chief of engineers or topographical engineer. Rarely did an officer below the level of corps or army commander have one, but he could be indispensable, especially for an aggressive commander like Stonewall Jackson, who used geography as a weapon of war just as potent as the rifles of his men. Jackson, in fact, had two such men on his staff, the first being Captain James K. Boswell, and then when Boswell became chief engineer, Jackson found another, Jedediah Hotchkiss. It was on March 26, 1862, as Jackson was planning his legendary Shenandoah Valley Campaign, that he summoned Hotchkiss to him. "I want you to make me a map of the Valley, from Harper's Ferry to Lexington, showing all the points of offence and defense in those places," Jackson said, thus commencing the career of the most noted military map-maker of the Civil War. He would hold the post as topographical engineer successively on the staffs of Jackson, A.P. Hill, Richard S. Ewell, and Jubal A. Early, almost until the very end of the war, producing maps that were the very model of what a field officer wanted to know of terrain.[5]

Very quickly Hotchkiss and Boswell became best friends, working closely together in their dual role of mapping positions and advising Jackson on the best places for lines of defense. Jackson listened to them time after time, and was rewarded by signal successes, for he had little ability of his own to "read" a landscape for its military mer-its, but great ability at planning a battle once he understood the terrain. As a result, Hotchkiss developed the habit of taking his maps to Jackson and verbally explaining them. Sometimes his services could extend considerably afield from topography, as when Hotchkiss asked permission to go into a nearby town to buy himself a hat, and Jackson asked that he buy him one too.[6]

Meanwhile, Boswell, as chief engineer, served yet other staff functions, at the same time as being an indispensable friend to Hotchkiss. The chief engineer constantly rode around his commander's lines, studying positions of troops and batteries, look-ing for weaknesses or missed opportunities, and suffering with the interference of superior officers who thought they knew better. Once Jackson took command of the

II Corps, one of his division commanders was Major General D.H. Hill, always an able general though quarrelsome. Hill insisted on laying out his own defensive lines near Virginia's Rappahannock River in the winter of 1862-3, instead of following Boswell's advice, and only the agreement of Jackson led to an order for a change. As a result, Boswell seemed to spend a great deal of time working with – and being patient with – Hill, "who interferes as usual," the engineer wrote in his diary, "and insists on acting as engineer." Finally on January 5, 1863, Boswell had taken all he could. "I am disgusted," he declared, "and will let him take his own way." Relenting – and because it was his duty – Boswell tried again to be useful to Hill. One morning he rode around Hill's lines with the general, but later wrote in dismay that "as usual he thinks every point which he visits last the most important to be finished without delay." Other generals could be equally frustrating. A few weeks later Boswell helped General Robert Rodes construct an emplacement for an artillery battery above the Rappahannock. Rodes wanted breastworks eight feet high erected along the river bank. "I think it perfectly useless," complained Boswell, and Jackson agreed with him, but would not interfere. Surely few of those who scoffed at the easy life of the staff officers ever appreciated the emotional frustrations of men who sought to do the best job possible, only to be thwarted by superior officers who lacked experience, knowledge, or other things but rank.[7]

And staff officers were not entirely immune from danger, either, though Boswell seemed to think so. "Strange as it may seem," he wrote to an aunt on April 21, 1863, "not one of Genl. J's staff has ever been killed, though I doubt not they have been as much exposed as the staff officers of any Major Genl. in the army. I suppose his prayers have shielded us." Perhaps they did, but not for long. Just eleven days later, on the first day of the Battle of Chancellorsville, Boswell and other staff officers accompanied Jackson on an evening reconnaissance. Confusion in the darkness led to some of their own men firing on the mounted party. Jackson went down with two wounds, one in his hand and the other in his arm, which proved to be fatal. At the same time, three bullets struck young James Boswell. One hit his leg, and might have been of no great danger. But the other two went straight to his heart and killed him instantly. His dear friend Hotchkiss did not know at first of his loss, but when he returned the next morning he found Boswell lying peacefully as if in repose. Hotchkiss took his dead friend to a nearby cemetery and there saw him interred. "The charmed circle in which General Jackson and his staff moved," lamented a heart-broken map-maker, "is broken & the break is a heavy one." In the service of a bold battlefield general, staff work was no safe refuge from an enemy ball.[8]

Indeed, staff officers not infrequently found themselves ordered into battle by their general, to take command of a regiment – even a division or more – suddenly deprived of its leader. At the Battle of Baton Rouge, on August 5, 1862, Breckinridge sent a mere captain of his staff to take command of a brigade after all of his brigadiers and several colonels had been put out of action in the fighting. Certainly there were higher ranking field officers available, but in a command crisis like that, a general needed to have someone whom he understood, and who implicitly understood him, in charge, for he could not take time to get intimately acquainted with some junior field officer he might only have met in passing. More than anyone, Grant would use members of his staff at times to fill temporarily vacant places in high field commands, and some of his staff later went on to command virtual armies of their own.[9]

Surely one of the most frustrating staff assignments in either army was that of a command's policeman, the provost. Usually hated when they did a good job, and generally accused of corruption or favoritism when they wielded a loose rein, the provosts North and South had probably the most thankless staff assignment of all. Most provosts only appeared on the staffs of generals commanding corps and armies, and occasionally at divisional level. Also, wherever there was a stationary command, be it a fort or garrison, or a territorial department, a provost organization emerged. Command confusion sometimes ensued, for the provost might report to his commanding general, or to the general's adjutant, as well as to the provost marshal of the army. When brigades had provosts, they reported to the divisional provost, who reported to the corps provost, and so on. The question of who was in charge arose more often for these beleagured policemen than for any other staff officer.[10]

His duties, depending upon the command he was attached to, might range from combating spying and espionage, maintaining command discipline, looking after transportation, enforcing the draft, providing guards for hospitals, prisoners of war, and headquarters, to placing guards over public and private property, overseeing the comings and goings of citizens within the command, running courts-martials, and even sometimes overseeing troop movements. That was not all. He could also be ordered to manage shipping, oversee the impressment of local supplies and, in the case of the Confederates, local labor in the form of slaves. He had to receive and provide escorts for prisoners of a special nature, put down drinking within the command and prostitution near it, act as jailor for soldiers caught breaking camp rules, gather intelligence and manage friendly spies, practice espionage and misinformation campaigns against the enemy, look after men away on furlough to make sure they returned, hunt down deserters, and in the greatest extremity, conduct executions and the resulting burials.[11]

To be sure, a provost's position offered some compensations, especially early in the war. Even Davidson admitted that in 1861 he had "quite an easy time" at his post. It was behind the lines, safe from battle, was provided with generally comfortable quarters and good food, and an almost perfect freedom to come and go as the provost officer pleased. Others found it just as pleasant at first, especially the freedom to move about, one provost commenting how he "would have more privileges on the road." Indeed, these extra "privileges" were often a source of the resentment that others felt for the provost officers. In times of scarcity, one Texas provost even boasted of the great supply of fresh pork that he could obtain.

But in time all this changed. The resentment of the citizenry soon manifested itself as they encountered provost interference in their lives and mobility. It was a situation made worse by the inevitable fact that the power that provosts had over others sometimes went to their heads. "It seems that instead of these disgraceful, lawless, unfeeling and impolite *men*, not Confederate soldiers in the strict sense, being at the front," complained one citizen to President Davis, "they . . . are running around over town and country insulting even weak unprotected women." Another lamented that the provost officers were an "unnecessary annoyance," and "of no possible benefit to the country."

Soldiers in the ranks were no less cynical. They regarded provost duty as just another way to avoid combat. "Lords ascendant," one man complained, "they loll and roll in their glory." Many a commander lamented having to deal with them. A staff officer with Beauregard in Mississippi in 1862 declared that such officers' ineffectiveness was not willful, "they being in most cases men of inferior intelligence."

The general lack of respect that soldiers usually feel for any policeman assigned to curb their behavior showed amply in their attitude toward this maligned officer. "As may be supposed," wrote Brigadier General Arthur Manigault, "they were not regarded with any very kindly feeling by the men, who never lost an opportunity of sneering at them, or letting off some witticism at their expense." Throughout the army, a provost officer and his men would be jeered at and resented, sometimes running a gauntlet of insults. Manigault recalled, "the scorn and contempt with which the Guard passed by, in the most profound silence." By the end of the war, Confederates especially, were displaying sentiments felt throughout the armies of both sides. "A great and growing evil," they said of their provost officers, "a source of almost boundless oppression." Only now and then did a provost, like Lieutenant Colonel John P. Bull of Major General Sterling Price's staff, hear such words of compliment as "able, energetic and efficient discharge of his duties."[12]

No chief ordnance officer or chief of artillery had to suffer the kind of obloquy heaped upon the provost. Indeed, the ordnance man was far more likely himself to be the one complaining for, like the engineer, he was a specialist assigned to perform his duties to the best of his knowledge and ability, and yet always subject to being overruled by a general officer who might know little of artillery tactics and usage, or worse some political general who know nothing about it at all. Major Thomas Ward Osborn served as chief of artillery in the Army of the Tennessee, on the staff of Major General Oliver O. Howard. He took his assignment in August 1864, and a month later wrote that, "since I came to this army I have made a complete revaluation in the artillery organization of this Army and Department." He was appalled. "I found its organization bad, or more exactly I found it without organization." That was sad enough, but when he instituted reforms, he met constant opposition. "What I have done has been against the wishes of the division and corps commanders." He found batteries scattered about, two or three to each division, and subject to the division commander.

Osborn reorganized all of the batteries into a separate brigade within each corps, simplifying command considerably. Yet he only accomplished it because he had Howard's backing. His predecessors had tried the same thing, but been thwarted by Howard's predecessors.[13]

Far worse, though, was what Osborn saw of the way his superiors used the batteries in the field. "The ignorance of some of our general officers in regard to the proper uses of artillery is simply stupendous," he declared that September, echoing the frustration of engineer Boswell with Hill and Rodes. When Osborn complained to an infantry brigadier who had placed his battery several hundred yards in *advance* of his infantry line, with the enemy apparently about to attack, the general replied "What is artillery for if not to protect the infantry?" He had completely missed the essential function of artillery, but poor Osborn could only shake his head.

The position of chief of artillery was no place for the retiring. The officer was almost constantly in the saddle when on campaign, seeing to the placement and supply of both the field pieces of the army, and the men who served them. He was part quartermaster, part engineer, and at times part field commander. Indeed, in recognition of the responsibility of his position, the ordnance chief or chief of artillery was the staff officer who more often than any other rose to the rank of brigadier general, North and South. "I have this work now on my hands to perform," wrote Major Osborn when he assumed his new assignment in August 1864, "and I will do it regardless of how much there is of it."[14]

Of the rest of the staff members in a general's military family, the surgeon and the judge advocate, and the aides, where there were such, suffered far less in the way of internal frustration or external criticism. The performance of their duties was governed by the resources available to them and the degree of trust and support they received from their commander. Yet of all of the staff officers, there was one who stood above the rest in stature if not in rank; the one most trusted, most intimately associated with the general in command. That, of course, was his adjutant.

If ever there was a catch-all post, this was it. Definitions were almost impossible. For one thing, his official title was "assistant adjutant general," since there was only one true Adjutant General, and he was on the War Department staff. One former incumbent "A.A.G.", as such staff officers were usually called, did attempt a half-serious, half-jest description of the requirements for the post. He "should be a man well posted in all arms of the service, know the right flank from the left, and from the front to the rear. He should be able to tell, without hesitation a jackass battery from one of one-hundred pounder Parrotts; should be able to ride a horse without falling off, and to handle his saber and revolver without wounding himself or killing his horse. He should know how to write both the name of the commanding general and his own; the larger the letters the better. He should be an adept in military correspondence, and be able with Chesterfieldian courtesy to apply the cold steel of official rebuke to subordinate commanders."[15]

Like others, the adjutant was denied the luxury of remonstration or gainsaying his commander's instructions or whims. Stonewall Jackson was notorious among his staff for odd and demanding behavior, as his new adjutant Captain Henry Kyd Douglas found out in 1862 soon after taking his assignment. One evening at midnight, Douglas saw Jackson send for Boswell without specifying the nature of his need. Expecting to have to ride off to some threatened point, Boswell dressed for the field at that late hour, only to find on reaching Jackson that the general wanted to know the distance from one point to another, information Boswell could easily have sent by message. Then after Boswell had returned to his quarters and prepared for sleep again, another summons came from Jackson fifteen minutes later, asking for the same information, this time in writing. "I learned afterwards that occasionally his staff officers were subjected to petty ills of that kind."[16]

It could be an exhilarating service at first. When Douglas joined Jackson's staff "and got my first taste of its delightful excitement," Jackson immediately began using him for transmitting important communications. Never thinking of the difficulties he was imposing on Douglas, Jackson one evening handed him a message and instructed him to take it to a detachment "on the other side of the Blue Ridge Mountains, somewhere near Culpepper." "My heart stood still with amazement," Douglas remembered. "For a moment I was stampeded, paralyzed. I had never been over a foot of the country and had only a vague idea that Culpepper was somewhere beyond the mountains; but how to get there I could not imagine." He had already been twenty-five miles in the saddle that day. It was dark, raining heartily. "But a young man soon rallies," the captain declared. "I was being weighed in the balance right there and I determined to throw all my weight on the scales." That was what made a good adjutant. As for Jackson, when Douglas rode off, the general bid him "a successful and pleasant ride!" not devoting an instant's concern to what he was sending the young man into. That, oftentimes, was what made a good general. Douglas successfully completed his mission, riding over 200 miles in four days. Yet when he reported his mission completed to Jackson, expecting some word of praise, all the general said was, "Very good. You did get there in time. Good night." Douglas was outraged. "Refusing to be comforted by the staff, who knew the General better, I threw off my heavy, soggy clothes and retired in grievous disappointment to an uncomfortable bed." The next day, when Jackson appointed him to the position of inspector general, all was forgiven.[17]

In a larger organization, such as a corps or army, the A.A.G. very often served the function of a chief of staff, even if not officially so designated. G. Moxley Sorrel served as such for Longstreet in the I Corps of the Army of Northern Virginia, and the degree of trust that had to arise between general and adjutant is well illustrated in their working relationship. "The General left much to me, both in camp and on the field," wrote Sorrel. "As chief of his staff it was my part to respond to calls for instruction and to anticipate them. The General was kept fully advised after the event, if he was not near by at the time; but action had to be swift and sure, without waiting to hunt him up on a different part of the field." Changing the position of a brigade or a division in battle was a grave responsibility, he knew, "but it often has to be faced by the chief of staff officer if the general happened to be out of reach."[18]

Thus was the adjutant to be seen everywhere his commander went. Often he was an almost comical sight, like Grant's adjutant and military secretary Parker, a Seneca Indian sachem, who stayed glued to Grant's side, carrying a portfolio with the necessary military papers over his shoulder, and a little boxwood inkwell tied to a buttonhole in his jacket. Yet Grant happily paid tribute to the assistance he got from Parker. "The only place I ever found in my life to put a paper so as to find it again was either a side coat-pocket," he said, "or the hands of a clerk or secretary more careful than myself." That was what adjutants – indeed all staff, in the end – were for.[19]

At the topmost levels North and South, the staffs of Grant and Lee present an interesting contrast, not only of the capabilities and functions of the officers assigned, but even more so of the way in which the generals used them.

Back in 1863, during the Vicksburg Campaign, Assistant Secretary of War Charles A. Dana came to Mississippi to inspect Grant's army and, so most believed, to spy on Grant for the War Department. Certainly the snobbish civilian revealed an instant disdain for many of the rough-hewn western characters that served on the general's military family. "A curious mixture of good, bad, and indifferent," he reported of the staff, "a mosaic of accidental elements & family friends." He approved of Rawlins and of Inspector General James H. Wilson, who by war's end would command a small army of his own as a lightning cavalry raider. Yet among the others, Dana disparaged one "worthless, whiskey drinking, useless fellow," and another who "violates English grammar at every phrase. Indeed, illiterateness is a general characteristic of Grant's staff," Dana would assert incorrectly.

What Dana did not immediately see was the way Grant used his staff to relax, all the while testing them and improving them. In the evenings the whole group would sit around a camp fire singing and spinning yarns, while Grant sat quiet, smoking a pipe or cigar, listening but not participating. If Rawlins, notoriously profane, began to swear, the rather straightlaced Grant would "good-naturedly remonstrate with his chief of staff for using too vigorous and sulphurous language," observed Parker. Rawlins would stop, but soon forget himself, and Grant would simply pretend not to hear him. In short, it was an almost typical civilian family scene, with Grant the father, and from that he drew stability when away from home. But he also watched these officers, observed their strengths and failings, and gradually through the war kept the good ones and replaced the others. By war's end, many of his staff officers were in fact brigadier and even major generals, trained specialists at their individual functions, and full participants in his strategic planning. Grant may have made all of the final decisions, but the informed views of his staff were the raw materials from which he fashioned the strategies that took him and the Union forces to victory.[20]

By contrast, Lee was a very different sort of general, and his staff reflected the fact. With only a couple of exceptions, his staff officers were lieutenant colonels or lower ranks, and the size of his staff considerably smaller than Grant's. In many cases, moreover, the men on his staff were not exactly outstanding. His chief of artillery, for instance, William N. Pendleton, had been found unfit for field command of artillery, and consequently promoted to staff command instead, "a well-meaning man," thought Sorrel, "without qualities for the high post he claimed." The situation was much the same on Lee's general staff throughout the war, perhaps because Lee was loath to pull good men out of active field command where their services were more immediately needed. The trouble with this was that it left Lee himself often having to perform the tasks that abler staff officers should have been doing for him.

On his personal staff, however, Lee had better men, yet the three most close to him – Charles Venable, Charles Marshall, and Walter H. Taylor – were all civilians with no military training. The first two spent the most time with Lee in the field, Marshall being especially useful for handling the paperwork with which Lee never had much patience. Taylor, youngest of all, eventually became Lee's principal aide. Selected more for their personalities and temperaments than their military skills, Lee's staff were congenial and productive, but they were never planners in the way Grant's officers were. Their duties were the performance of details, not the proposal of ideas. Lee relied upon himself for that. Rarely did he have a council of war or a general staff planning session. He carried on his own shoulders the burden of strategic and even tactical thinking, as well as overseeing the myriad other great issues of supply and ordnance and engineering that trained and effective officers should have handled for him. The only real function that Lee's staff had in common with Grant's officers was the use Lee put them to for relaxation. Lee needed them for that far more than Grant, for by doing so much himself, Lee was almost always tired, even exhausted, and very frequently ill, as his overtaxing workload put strains on an already weak heart. Grant, by contrast, was usually rested, relaxed, and able to push himself physically to great limits without impairing his health, because he left the details to his staff.

Worse still, on several battlefields, most notably the Seven Days' Battle and at Gettysburg, Lee suffered reverses largely through terrible staff work, with no one coordinating the execution of orders. Lee tried to manage it all himself, and it was simply too great a task for one man, even one whose staff often referred to him as "the tycoon." Lee looked at running an army the way his predecessors in previous wars had seen it, as the responsibility of the man at the top. Grant looked at the same challenge, and saw it as generations of the future would see it, presaging in his military family the general staffs of the next century.[21]

Years after the Civil War, a British writer summed up what these men faced, when he wrote that a staff officer was like unto a trouser button. "There are few to praise it while it goes on with its work," he said, "and very few to abstain from cursing it when it comes off."[2]

REFERENCES

1 Rufus Dawes, *Service with the Sixth Wisconsin Volunteers* (Marietta, Ohio, 1890), p.13n.

2 *Ibid.*, pp.10-2.

3 Richard D. Goff, *Confederate Supply* (Durham, N.C., 1969), p.127.

4 *Ibid.*, p.54.

5 Archie P. McDonald, ed., *Make Me a Map of the Valley* (Dallas, Tex., 1973), p.11.

6 *Ibid.*, p.xxi.

7 James K. Boswell, "The Diary of a Confederate Staff Officer," *Civil War Times Illustrated*, XV (April 1976), p.31.

8 *Ibid.*, p.38; McDonald, *Make Me a Map*, p.xxiv.

9 Davis, *Breckinridge*, p.321.

10 Kenneth Radley, *Rebel Watchdog, The Confederate States Army Provost Guard* (Baton Rouge, La., 1989), p.11.

11 *Ibid.*, p.336.

12 Tower, *Manigault*, p.166.

14 *Ibid.*, pp.4, 27, 29.

15 William H. Armstrong, *Warrior in Two Camps: Ely S. Parker* (Syracuse, 1978), p.88.

16 Henry Kyd Douglas, *I Rode with Stonewall* (Chapel Hill, N.C., 1940), p.48.

17 *Ibid.*, pp.49-50, 54.

18 Sorrel, *Recollections*, p.129.

19 Armstrong, *Ely Parker*, p.103.

20 T. Harry Williams, *Lincoln and his Generals* (New York, 1963), p.312.

21 Jeffry Wert, "[un][un]'The Tycoon': Lee and His Staff", *Civil War Times Illustrated*, XI (July 1972), pp.11-8; Williams, *Lincoln and His Generals*, p.313.

22 Radley, *Watchdog*, p.233.

X

OFFICERS BEHIND BARS

One danger that all officers faced, whether field or staff, was the ever-present possibility of being taken prisoner. Only those posted far, far behind the zones of military activity could be considered safe, and on a few occasions even these men were not immune to capture by daring raiders. The number of officers of both sides actually taken prisoner is undetermined, but at least 13,000 or more Confederates were captured during the war, and the number of Yankees must have been the same or greater. Thus, perhaps 25-30,000 or more men wearing gold on their collars and shoulders soon found themselves thrown into the rude and uncomfortable position of no longer being in command of anything, including their own destinies.

It could be a frightening and unnerving experience, being taken prisoner, though most officers, being used to composure under trying circumstances, seemed to handle it well enough. Major Abner Small and his regiment were a part of Grant's forces besieging Petersburg, and in August 1864 were ordered out on a raid on the Weldon Railroad. Early in the expedition they came face to face with strong Rebel resistance, and when a gap opened in the Yankee line, the enemy poured through it and surrounded Small and his men. "I found myself looking into the muzzle of a gun with a determined face behind it," he recalled.

With a curse on his lips for the Union blunder that got him into such a fix, Small went with his captors to the rear, where first he tried to persuade them to let him go. Then he was taken to talk with Confederate Major General William Mahone, who grilled him for information on Grant's position and numbers. "General," said Small, "you are too good an officer to expect me to give you correct answers," and Mahone only smiled and ordered him taken away. While enlisted men could, and often did give information to the enemy after capture out of guileless innocence, few officers could ever be expected to answer questions.

As he was taken toward Petersburg, Small first hid his watch, knowing that he would likely be stripped of any valuables, as indeed he was later. Once in Petersburg, he was marched down streets lined with old men and women and children "who vied with one another in flinging insults and venom." The women were the worst, he thought; "they spat upon us, laughed at us, and called us vile and filthy names." It was a far cry from the respect and deference an officer had come to expect.

Finally they reached Petersburg's neighbor to the north, Richmond, and marched at once to an old ship chandlery now known as Libby Prison, the most notorious of the Confederacy's prisons for Yankee officers. "We were received at Libby Prison as if at a palatial hotel," Small wrote. Courteously they were asked for their names for the register, then asked if they had any valuables that they wished the commandant to put in his safe for security's sake. Then each man went to a room at the rear, where "a little puppy named Ross went through the clothes of every prisoner," taking whatever money or valuables he could find. They went to that room one by one, and none returned to tell the rest of what to expect, allowing Ross to pillage them freely. Only when they were shown to their quarters in the large second floor rooms did the men compare experiences and learn what had been done to all of them. "We cursed our keepers from that hour."[1]

Robbery of prisoner officers was not official policy North or South, but since in both armies the best men in character were usually at the front, those left behind to act as prison guards were less likely to scruple over the belongings of an enemy. Yet there were exceptions. Confederate Captain William C. Thompson fell into Yankee hands late in 1864 in Tennessee, and early in 1865 found himself transferred to a prison in Nashville. With him he was carrying $4,000 in Confederate currency, a pocket knife, and a fine gold pen with silver appointments. Being ill, he was taken to the prison hospital and hid his valuables under his pillow. A hospital official came up to him, commented upon the Masonic pin that Thompson wore, and asked if, indeed, he were a Mason, and then inquired if the Rebel had any valuables. "I told him they were under my pillow," said Thompson. "He took these and left, much to my satisfaction, for I knew he would care for them." Indeed he did. True to his fraternal oath to care for a fellow Mason in distress, Phillip Grove of the 92nd Indiana later returned, discussed Masonry awhile, then warned Thompson which guards to beware of, and commenced smuggling little extra bits of food to him. Learning that Thompson's brother was in another prison hospital in Nashville, Grove managed to get Arthur Thompson transferred to be with his brother, and then smuggled in whiskey to help ease the pain of Arthur's recent amputation. Thereafter, "Grove always saw to it that we shared in the food and refreshment that the kind ladies of Nashville brought to the hospital from time to time." Such kindness was not common, but happened enough to ease the natural hatred of prisoners for their keepers.[2]

Another Confederate, Captain Samuel Foster of Texas, felt absolutely incredulous when captured. A member of the garrison of Fort Hindman, Arkansas, besieged by a Federal gunboat fleet and land troops in January 1863, he wrote in his diary that "there was excitement sure enough." Then, as the bombardment was beginning to cut the defenders to pieces, someone raised a white flag. "It was the only intelligible thing we could do," lamented Foster. The Confederate flag came down, and white sheets, towels, even handkerchiefs were upraised to stop the firing. Soon an enemy officer came among them and ordered them to stack their arms. "No one had ever given us a command in that manner before," said Foster. "The order struck us with awe. We were affronted with the reality that we were prisoners."

Then came a dangerously tense few minutes. The Yankees corraled the prisoners into a group and surrounded them with guards. "The entire Yankee army seemed to be standing around us," thought Foster. Captors and captured began to glare at one another. "Their guards had to fight hard to keep a space between them and us," Foster observed. "The men of both sides began hollering across to each other." Only night-fall relieved the tense moment, but even then it was still very difficult for officers who had until a few hours before been men in command to realize and come to terms with their changed status. "Had the sentinels not been so close, with their glistening bay-onets," Foster recalled, "we would have been unable to fully realize the situation. One look at them satisfied anybody. Their presence told us that what had happened had not been a joke."[3]

Eventually they reached Columbus, Ohio, which would be their prison home. Late at night, one by one, they were led into a small building where everything of value, money and pocketknives particularly, was taken from them. Then they were released into the prison compound. There was no organization. In the dark men began calling the names of their old friends and messmates, seeking to re-establish their pre-captivity society in some way. "Three hundred men created quite an affair," thought Foster. "We got together, separated, mixed ourselves up, then got together again. The entire situation was humorous." Only when the whole mess was con-cluded did they finally settle down to start living as prisoners of war. They washed. They ate the rations provided: bread, beef, vegetables, and coffee. "Things suddenly did not seem so bad after all." Then a Federal officer assembled them and returned their knives – unless they were large enough to pose a real threat – and their money. Men with over $100 had their money held for credit for their purchases at the prison's sutler's store. Then he read them the prison rules. Lights out at 8 p.m., and no noise thereafter. No coming within ten feet of the stockade. Assemblies every morning and evening. "We finally began to understand how things were going to be like in this prison," wrote Foster of that moment. "At least, we were getting to know what they expected us to do. I guessed everybody would do it."[4]

At the beginning of the war, when no one had any concept of its ultimate scope or length, no special provisions were made on either side for handling officer prisoners. They usually just occupied separate quarters in the same prisons with enlisted men, and sometimes with civilian political prisoners as well. Thus it was at Fort Warren in Boston Harbor. It began with some 750 men, most of them Confederates, being transferred from other sites. Many of these were an elite sort of captive, some of the Rebel officers being very wealthy and influential. Officials allowed them to form informal "messes" of half a dozen or so, assigning them to comfortable group quarters, while the private soldiers were crowded into a large single room. Not long thereafter, officers were allowed to roam free on the island the prison sat upon, giving their parole not to attempt to escape, thus allowing them exercise and fresh air. Some 100 of the less affluent officers from North Carolina contributed some sixteen cents apiece per day to a general fund that purchased luxuries to augment their beef and pork diet.

In general they all had two meals a day, and one wrote that "our closet is never without crackers, cheese, bologna, sausages – fruit cake, plain cake – coffee, tea." None of the private soldiers in Fort Warren ate so grandly, and it proved to be a source of no little resentment. Large contributions of clothing and foodstuffs came from friendly Southern sympathizers in the North, and the officers were allowed to share them. Some officers even had curtains and floor coverings in their quarters. Few Confederate commissioned officers elsewhere in the war would enjoy a standard of prison living to equal that of the Fort Warren occupants. The prisoners even got along merrily with their guards, frequently joining in song and story. One Yankee lieutenant was presented with a gold-headed cane by his prisoners when they finally left the fort. When General Simon Buckner and others arrived at Fort Warren after their capture at Fort Donelson, the commandant actually had tears in his eyes when he explained to Buckner that he had orders to restrict his movements within the fort. In the end, almost all of the officers were exchanged and sent back to their own lines in 1862 and 1863, and no officers were incarcerated there again until after Gettysburg. When new officer prisoners arrived thereafter, they found a strict new commandant and a new set of rules, much at odds with the way the prison had run earlier. Still conditions were better at Fort Warren than at any other prison North or South, as attested by the fact that only twelve prisoners died while being held there.[5]

But Warren was the exception to the much harsher rule that prison, even for officers, was not a pleasant place. Once the Federal War Department appreciated the numbers of prisoners it would have to deal with, it began establishing a host of camps around the country, and decided that all – or virtually all – Rebel officers should be consolidated at one place. For this they selected an island in Lake Erie, opposite Sandusky, Ohio. Johnson's Island was essentially barren when authorities began construction of their new prison on its 300 acres, and by June 1862 its occupants were almost exclusively Confederate officers. In all at least 12,000 prisoners would pass through its gates during the war, from lowly lieutenants all the way to prominent generals like Isaac Trimble and James J. Archer, captured at Gettysburg. Henry Kyd Douglas would wind up there for a time, as would several other generals, and a host of lesser mortals. Their captors confined them in wooden barracks, each room having a wood stove that proved effective except in the bitterly cold winter storms on the lake. They had bunks with straw mattresses, and about three blankets per man. The commissary issued clothing to those who could not buy any from their sutler, or who did not receive gifts from friends at home, and food was both plentiful and of generally good quality. "Our men," wrote one inmate, "live as well in the way of eating as we ever did." Only late in 1864, when Federals began to hear exaggerated stories of the ill treatment of Federal prisoners in the South, did a harsher regime reduce rations in retaliation.[6]

Incarcerated for long periods of time, especially after prisoner exchange was discontinued, the officers found much to occupy their time. They made articles of every description – rings and charms from shells, furniture from available scrap wood, even a violin. One industrious man, having smuggled a glass lens into camp with him, somehow got chemicals and used a tin can lid as a plate, sensitized it with the chemicals, and exposed it in a crude camera that he built, making an ambrotype portrait of a fellow officer. In their evenings, when weather permitted, they played games, chiefly a variant of the still new baseball. "I don't understand the game," one officer complained, "but those who play it get very much excited over it."

In the winter they had snowball battles, including one memorable contest when General Trimble led one side against another commanded by Missouri militia General M. Jefferson Thompson. Ironically, Thompson was taken prisoner in the fight, giving him the dubious honor of being a prisoner within a prisoner. They read and played cards and chess, received newspapers, and wrote home. Indeed, thanks to the fact that the prison was almost entirely populated with officers, and therefore far more literate than the enlisted men of their army, more prisoner-of-war letters were written from Johnson's Island than from all the other Confederate prisons in the North. As for reading, in the end they built a lending library of up to 800 books and magazines. They formed a minstrel band and a theatrical group of players. Thanks largely to the quality of their conditions, the officers at Johnson's Island enjoyed a prisoner death rate less than half that of the other camps where enlisted men were kept.[7]

As the war progressed, like most prisons, Johnson's Island's population far outgrew its original intended limits. Expected to house about 1,000, the compound at its peak held over 3,200. Inevitably such overcrowding led to hardships, but on the whole, other than their restricted activity, the officers led lives not materially worse than they would have had had they not been captured. For many, the worst feature of prison life at Johnson's Island was being ordered about by young Yankee enlisted men. "Fall in, boys, I'm in a hurry," an impudent eighteen-year-old sergeant might yell at captains, colonels, and even generals, "his seniors in age, rank, position, and everything that constitutes a man, soldier, and gentleman," complained one indignant officer. It was, however, a small cross to bear.[8]

322

"As prisoners our days seemed endless," lamented a Rebel at one of Nashville's many prisons. "We were watched, spied upon, and continually checked by the guards and watchers," he wrote. "We couldn't get any news of the war. All reports were gloomy." That was very much the usual routine for officer prisoners, North or South. When Captain James Bosang arrived as an inmate of Washington's Old Capitol Prison, he also encountered another of the ever-present enemies of prisoners – lice or bedbugs, sometimes called "chinches" by the prisoners. His first night started comfortably enough, but then "I seemed to have hardly gotten to sleep when I awoke itching and burning with something crawling all over me with thousands of hot feet." When he arose, brushing the vermin off himself, he looked about and, by the dim light of a gas jet burning in the room, "could see them by the hundreds, chinches, all over me, all over my bed." The rest of the night he hardly slept, and in the morning gave his clothes and bed a thorough picking over, only to have the same experience the next night. Finally, studying the problem dispassionately, he saw that the only way for the insects to reach him was by crawling up the legs of his bed. Consequently, he obtained four cups, placed one leg of the bed into each of them, then filled them with water. "Oh, the good, undisturbed sleeping I had," he crowed later. "I found but very few that even attempted to swim and they were drowned."[10]

The Confederacy, too, eventually established prisons intended strictly for officers, the largest and best known being Libby. Unlike Johnson's Island or Fort Warren, Libby afforded absolutely nothing in the way either of comfort or privacy. Most captured Federals had to run the same gauntlet of insults and leering civilians that met Major Small, before they got to Libby. Upon arrival, many found themselves placed in a first floor room with 200 or more crowded into a space 30 feet by 70. "The floor is an inch deep in thick black greasy slime which we cannot remove," Captain William Wilkins wrote in his diary. "A horrible odor pervades the apartment." An open privy stood at one end of the room, while the walls were covered seemingly "with the slops & excretions of the hundreds of men confined overhead." There was almost no ventilation, lice and vermin all over the men, no place to sleep except upon the slimy floor, and no blankets, soap, towels. Meals came twice a day, and drinking water was brought from the nearby James canal, "hot and of a very foul taste."[11]

Daily life very quickly took a dreary and monotonous tone. Wilkins started keeping a diary "to divert my mind from constantly dwelling on my sad fate and on the hardships which surround me." Almost immediately the men grew weak from want of exercise in their jammed quarters. "We are so crowded as scarcely to have standing room." Their rations he found reduced to "very greasy soup in the morning & a tainted boiled beef at 4 p.m.; bread at both meals & no more."

Frequently some prisoners were kept incommunicado from the rest, but quickly a system of slipping notes through cracks in the board walls and floors, or bribing guards to carry information, evolved. Different men bore their boredom and trials in very different ways. One sat with his face buried in his hands all day, day after day.

Another walked the floor constantly "like a caged wild beast." General Henry Prince stayed buried in his blankets most of the time, while others played cards. Wilkins, for variety, tried to change his "employments" frequently. He would walk, smoke, play cards or checkers, and sleep, to get through the day. In his diary he would write "Thank god another day is done."[12]

Especially demoralizing was the constant presence of death. Sickness and disease and malnutrition killed hundreds, and the room in which they were laid out was directly beneath the first floor that housed Wilkins and many others. Through the crevices in the floor they could look every day on the faces of the deceased. Worse, as Wilkins found, "the sentries stationed around our windows are so anxious to shoot a 'Yankee' that yesterday they kept cocking & aiming their muskets at any of us who even looked out of the window." One captain, washing in the morning, came too near a window and was shot in the wrist and stomach by a guard outside. At times the guards chose to deny delivering to the prisoners the packages that were sent to them by family and friends at home. Further, officers from the army of the very much detested Federal General John Pope, such as Wilkins, were placed in what he called the "black-hole" on that first floor, while other officers from other generals' commands were assigned to the cleaner and healthier upper floor rooms. "How long, O Lord," Wilkins would supplicate, "how long!"[13]

In fact, Wilkins was one of the lucky ones. With the prisoner exchange system still in operation in late 1862, he was finally "traded" for an officer of equal rank in a Federal prison, and released and sent home on September 24. Wilkins, ironically, would be recaptured eight months later, only to find himself yet again in the "black-hole."[14]

A year later, in December 1863, Brigadier General Neal Dow became an inmate at Libby, and for generals the treatment could be very different. Late in 1863 he noted that he and other ranking officers "continue to receive great numbers of boxes containing supplies." Dow found himself the recipient of two whole trunks filled with goodies from home – clothes, coffee, tea, sugar, ham, preserved meats, preserves, jellies, nuts, stationery, molasses, and even condensed milk, chocolate, and beef extract for soup. He also received blankets, and was allowed to purchase other commodities from a local market. First he sold United States "greenbacks" to guards and others at a ratio of one dollar for fifteen dollars in Confederate scrip. With some $19,000 of the Rebel "shin-plasters," Dow and others purchased potatoes at $30 a bushel, flour at $200 a barrel, and sugar at $6 a pound.[15]

Then on December 14, 1863, prison officials announced that no more packages from home would be allowed, and the next day purchases from the local markets were prohibited. On a cold Christmas Day soon thereafter, the prison authorities could provide no wood for heat or cooking, so Dow and others broke up their tables and benches for fuel. New Year's Day, 1864, marked six months of captivity for Dow, yet he was not despondent. While others like Wilkins became disheartened by the failure to exchange them speedily, Dow wrote that he was "entirely patient, because exchanges are not at present, for the interest of our country or cause." Meanwhile he spent all of his time reading and writing. Somehow he got books like *Tom Brown at Oxford* and Azel Roe's *Like and Unlike*, while other lesser officers were unable to obtain reading matter. One of his difficulties – there were few for Dow compared to the men confined on the lower floor of Libby – was that he was a general, and therefore had to be exchanged for a Rebel officer of like rank. As it happened, in the summer of 1863 Robert E. Lee's son Brigadier General W.H.F. "Rooney" Lee was taken prisoner, and in January 1864 negotiations commenced for a trade of the two brigadiers. It would not take place until March 14, and then only as part of a special exchange. Federal authorities had executed two captured Rebel officers for some reason, and Libby officials were going to kill two Yankee captains in retaliation. Hearing that, the Federals threatened to execute General Lee and another officer. Finally bloodshed was averted by trading Dow and two captains for Lee and two equivalent officers.[16]

One of the few differences in the life of Union and Confederate officers was that when captured, unlike enlisted men who experienced the same horrible conditions North or South, Yankee officers enjoyed very significantly worse treatment than Confederates. It was not in the main intentional, but rather simply a condition of the general shortages of everything in the South, for officers and enlisted men alike. Nowhere was this more evident than in the most hellishly notorious of all Civil War prisons, Camp Sumter, better known by the name of the small town nearby, Andersonville.

Both officers and enlisted men were kept at Andersonville, with no formal differentiation between the quarters or treatment accorded to them. It was simply one rather small stockaded compound, with a sluggish little rivulet flowing through it, no shelters, no sanitary facilities, miserable food, no clothing, and little or no attempt by guards and officials to improve matters. Indeed, they could not, for they lived not much better than their prisoners. As a result, in order to provide some kind of meager enhancement to their execrable rations, the prisoners soon developed an internal system of trade, barter, and commerce. Newly arrived officers could sell their blankets, tobacco – almost anything – in return for food hoarded by others. Some men specialized in buying and selling food. The guards helped a bit, by bringing in tobacco, eggs, and things, concealed on their persons, and "sold" at exorbitant rates when they entered the compound. And the prisoner officers detailed to carry the dead outside every day often had opportunities to effect trade with Southerners they met, bringing their goods back when they returned.

Indeed, such articles were so prized and brought such good "prices" that a subordinate trade appeared inside the prison, selling "chances" to go outside with the dead. "In this way," wrote one colonel, "the dead soon became articles of merchandise and were bought and sold." Since the daily death rate was up to 100 or more, there were plenty of chances to escort a corpse. The best spot to buy was with one of the first corpses each day, for those escorts got to the traders outside first and acquired the best articles for resale inside the stockade. "It soon became the custom for the price of a corpse to be written on a piece of paper and pinned to the rags of the corpse." The first bodies could bring three dollars each; the last bodies on a busy dead-detail day might go for only fifty cents. Worse, those who bought the latter corpses had to sit by them well into the afternoon awaiting their turn to go out for the burial, "and when it did come to your turn to go the stench of your corpse would make you sick and chances for trade would be slim." Prison custom was for a messmate or one who had attended the dead in his last hours to accompany the body, and he was allowed to choose two others to accompany him for the burial detail. These were the men to whom others paid their money for the chance to go out.

To their credit, even the prison guards, many of them officers, found Andersonville appalling. Major James Dunwoody Jones of the 8th Georgia Infantry, assigned to Camp Sumter in 1864, put it very simply. "Thirty thousand men in a stockade are apt to suffer more or less," he wrote years later. Only a few of them were officers, but they suffered right along with the rest. Most of the officers sent to the Deep South went to a camp near Columbia, South Carolina, that contained some 1,250 of them. Jones was eventually detailed from Andersonville to take the command of the interior of this stockade, and he could not conceal his delight at getting away from Camp Sumter. "To me this was one of the most pleasant episodes of the war," he wrote of his South Carolina service. "I soon made fast friends, I believe, of every officer in the prison."[17]

Undoubtedly Jones' friendships were formed thanks to his humane and friendly treatment of his fellow officers in adversity. He helped one of his prisoners carry on a pre-war love affair with a Columbia lady, even smuggling her photograph into the camp for him. As a result, when the end of the war was approaching, some of his prisoner officers from Illinois urged him to come north with them, offering even to provide him with some land and livestock to get him going. Gratefully Jones declined. Certainly theirs was one of the more unusual relationships between captors and captives, but it was not by any means unique. Officers on both sides returned courtesy for courtesy, and the better of them took neither pleasure nor advantage from seeing fellow officers in adversity.

But still, captivity was captivity, and especially onerous at Libby or Andersonville. Understanding this, Major Jones had told his prisoners at Columbia that "it is your privilege to try to get away, just as it is my business to keep you." "I never punished a man for trying to escape," Jones recalled proudly.[18]

And escape they did. From every prison North or South where the officers were kept, some managed to get away. At Fort Warren Lieutenant Charles W. "Savez" Read, a Rebel blockade runner and adventurer, chipped his way up an abandoned chimney in his cell to get free, then stole a small sailboat to get away. Unfortunately, as soon as he was on the harbor he was recaptured. Another attempt that failed came when Captain Thomas H. Hines sent a special Bible to the mother of his friend Captain John Castleman, then incarcerated in a prison in Indianapolis. The Confederate Hines, an agent operating behind Union lines, took the book to a binder in Chicago, had it unbound, put four small saw blades made of watch spring steel inside the new binding on one side, and $3,000 in Yankee currency inside the other. He marked certain passages in the Book of John, chapter XIV, as hints to Castleman, the most telling being, "Let not your heart be troubled; believe in God, believe also in Me." "Me" in this case meant the Bible but, though he found the money and the saws, Castleman decided not to attempt to break out.[19]

His friend Hines, however, was an old hand at escaping from prison, having taken a leading part in one of the most famous break-outs of the Civil War. In the summer of 1863, Rebel raider John Hunt Morgan led his cavalry across the River Ohio and into Indiana and Ohio. Quickly the Federals were on his trail, and on July 26 they brought Morgan and a few hundred of his men to a halt, forcing them to surrender. On August 1 Morgan, Brigadier General Basil W. Duke, Hines, and sixty-seven other officers were sent to the Ohio State Penitentiary at Columbus. Each found himself searched first, and all pocket knives and other useful articles were taken from them.

At first their captors placed each officer in a separate cell and prevented communication between the Rebels as much as possible. But then, between 7 a.m. and 5 p.m. the jailors released all of Morgan's officers into a single large hall where they could talk. "Many plans for escape, ingenious and desperate, were suggested, discussed, and rejected," wrote Hines. They thought of bribing the civilian guards, but gave up on that and all other schemes until late in October. One day the warden somehow insulted Hines, and the captain retired to his cell, determined not to leave it again until he had devised a plan for escape that would equally humiliate the warden. In a day he had it, aided by having recently read Victor Hugo's *Les Misérables*. Tunnels and subterranean passages were on his mind, thanks to the book, and while sitting in his cell he noticed that despite its location at ground level, and with no sunlight reaching the floor of his chamber, still the floor was quite dry and free of mold or dampness that might normally be expected if it sat directly above the earth. That meant there had to be an air chamber or basement of some kind underneath. If he could get through the floor into that chamber, then he and the others could tunnel out through the foundation to the open yard beyond, exit at night, and climb over the penitentiary walls to freedom.

Morgan agreed to the plan the next day, but there was a problem. Only prisoners on the lower floor of cells would have access to that air chamber, and then not even all of them. Thus Morgan and Hines decided to limit the tunnelers and escapers to themselves and five others. To prevent the daily inspection of his cell that was prison routine, Hines so thoroughly cleaned his room himself every day that the prison inspector no longer bothered to look in. Then associates in the prison hospital managed to smuggle to them some flat table knives. Planning to start excavating on November 4 under the rear end of Hines' cot, the Confederates looked forward to freedom, and Hines to humiliating Warden N. Merion.

When they began, they cut their way through six inches of cement, and then beneath that six layers of brick, before they reached the chamber. It turned out to be four feet high and six feet wide and to run the entire length of the cell block. Then it was time to tunnel. Running at right angles to Hines' cell, they cut through a five-foot thick foundation wall, followed by another twelve feet of grouting, then through another six-foot wall, before the tunnel was done. They halted about four feet beneath the surface of the prison yard at a point they calculated to be under a little used section of the compound.

All the while the digging continued, Hines sat on his cot above the hole in his floor, studying French and reading Edward Gibbon's *Decline and Fall of the Roman Empire*. Thus he stood guard. The men digging had reliefs every hour, and all communications were by way of signals, rapping on the floor of the cell. Meanwhile General Morgan's brother, Colonel R.C. Morgan, shredded his bed, ticking and braiding it into a thirty-foot length of rope, and attaching at its end a hook made from their stove poker.

All that remained was to cut holes in the floors of the cells of the other prisoners who were to break out, giving them access to the chamber below. This was necessary since the break had to be made under cover of darkness, when all of the men were locked in their individual cells. To do so, an accurate measurement of the length of the cell block was necessary, else in cutting the escape holes from the chamber *up*, they could end up working in the wrong place. To further his revenge against the warden, Hines tricked him into measuring the block for them. The holes being properly spaced, they were cut almost to each cell surface, with only an inch or two of cement left in place and easily kicked out when the time came.

That time was to be November 27. Having first planned to go to Canada, the Confederates changed their minds. Instead, armed with a newspaper, they saw that they could take a late evening train that would get them to Cincinnati before the cells were opened in the morning, and their absence discovered. When they were locked up that evening, General Morgan, who was kept on the upper level of cells, quietly switched places with his brother on the lower level.

The train to Cincinnati left at 1.15 a.m. The guards checked the cell block every two hours. Consequently the daring Rebels determined to break out immediately after the midnight check. After the guard had left the block, they each arranged their bedclothes to simulate the appearance of the beds being occupied, then broke through the little crust of cement, and hurried out the tunnel and broke through the earth above. Quickly they ran in the rainy darkness to the wall, threw their hook over the top of a gate, and climbed up to the top of the wall. Each wore two sets of clothes, and now they walked atop the wall to an empty sentry box, and inside took off their dirty outer coats and pants. That done, they used their rope to lower themselves to the outside, then separated into groups of two and three and walked the quarter-mile to the railroad depot, bought their tickets, and rode through the night to Cincinnati. A ferry took them across the Ohio to their native Kentucky, and from there they began to thread their various ways south to Tennessee and friendly lines. Hines was recaptured while crossing the Tennessee River, but Morgan and some of the others reached safety, Morgan writing to Hines' father of the captain's capture, and closing with the promise that "he will certainly escape." Indeed he did, and Hines, too, reached safety. Meanwhile, far behind them all at the Ohio Penitentiary, Warden Merion found on the morning of November 28 a note left behind for him, telling of the digging of the tunnel, the number of hours per day it occupied, the tools used, and a little taunt in French to show that Hines had paid attention to his studies while standing guard.[20]

While most break-outs were performed by single men or small groups like Morgan's, attempts at much larger escapes were made occasionally. One of the most ambitious was a Confederate plan to capture a Lake Erie warship and use it to free the officers on Johnson's Island. The operation actually got started, but fell apart almost at once, with not one prisoner released and the would-be rescuers fleeing back to Canada.[21]

But one massive prison-break did succeed, and it came where one might have expected it – Libby. The miserable conditions made escape an ever-present thought on the inmates' minds. The number of officers crowded together was bound to lead to numerous plans for breaking out, while the flimsy nature of the building itself invited attempts. The one that succeeded was the brain-child of an engineer, Major Thomas E. Rose, who started looking for a way out as soon as he arrived. At once he surveyed the prison. It contained four floors, each 45 feet by 105 feet. The top three were divided into three rooms each, while the ground floor was kept off limits to the men except its middle chamber, used during the day as a kitchen. Rose, looking out a window at the end of the building, saw about seventy feet away two small outbuildings. He believed that if the prisoners could somehow get access to the unused basement floor, which was partially below ground level, they could do as Hines and Morgan had done, break through the foundation, and tunnel under the open lot to the two outbuildings. Once there, they could emerge at night and take their chances on Richmond's streets.

It was easier said than done. The only access to the cellar would have to be by the floor above, yet only the central portion was open to the men for their cooking, and it would be impossible to reach the part of the cellar they needed from that position. Directly above the basement room they wanted was the prison hospital, and they couldn't break through that. Finally they devised a scheme to tunnel through the brick wall of the kitchen fireplace, angling downward so as to miss the hospital on the other side, but reaching the cellar beneath the hospital. They had to work at night, when no one was in the kitchen, using only a jack-knife and a chisel found by Rose.

329

Brick by brick, the tunnel was opened up in silence and darkness. At 4 a.m., with dawn approaching, all of the bricks taken out were carefully replaced and then the back of the fireplace covered with soot to prevent detection. It was incredibly tedious, yet finally they succeeded in reaching the cellar, only to discover that it was a haven for hundreds of vermin. "Rat Hell" they called it.

Once in Rat Hell, Rose and his companions, their number growing rapidly as the scope of the work before them became evident, stumbled for a while deciding what to do next. After several false starts and missed opportunities, they chiseled through the foundation and started tunneling. The men worked in relays in the dark and foul air. One would chisel the earth, fill a spittoon with it, while another at the tunnel mouth would haul it out by a cord, the tunneler using a cord of his own to pull the empty vessel back in for refilling. Another man used a blanket to fan air into the tunnel. To keep the men working all day long, even though there were twice daily roll calls, other off-duty prisoners were instructed to answer to the names of the absent when called. With 1,200 prisoners in all, no guard would note a voice heard a second time answering to a different name. Soon this became too dangerous, and finally they had to work only at night, which slowed progress in the rat-infested darkness.

Finally one of the diggers thought the tunnel had gone far enough, and broke through to the surface, only to find that he was still twenty feet short of the objective. Hastily they filled the opening with a coat and some earth, and pushed on forward. At last, terrified of discovery, Rose himself got back in the tunnel and refused to come out, single-handedly digging much of the rest of the needed distance in a little more than a day. Taking heart, Rose did the same thing again two days later, and after eighteen or more hours of constant digging, fainting from exhaustion, hunger, and lack of air, he rolled over on his back ready to quit. Suffocating, he dropped the chisel and beat his fists against the roof of the tomb-like tunnel. As if in response to his entreaties, the roof suddenly gave way and he broke into the cool night air above.

Rose clambered out and found that he was in a small shed, with good cover for reaching the city streets. He covered the opening with a plank and crawled back through the tunnel to tell his excited compatriots. They agreed to wait until the next night for the escape, as it was by this time almost dawn. The original fifteen tunnelers also decided to take another fifteen into their confidence for the break itself, though the rest of the prison's 1,200 inmates had been kept ignorant of the weeks-long excavations for security.

They started the next evening, February 9, 1864, shortly after sundown. Rose and the first fifteen went through and out of the tunnel without difficulty. But behind them, the word had leaked from someone in the second party, and soon hundreds of prisoners clamored for a chance to go. All order broke down, and in the end scores of men poured through the tunnel, though, incredibly, they retained enough composure to stay quiet when they exited. The prison guards never knew what was happening until the next morning when roll call showed 109 officers missing. After a series of individual adventures too lengthy to tell, sixty-one of the escapees reached friendly lines and freedom. An unlucky forty-eight, sadly including Major Rose, were recaptured and returned to Libby. For Rose, however, liberty had to wait only another few weeks, for he was exchanged on April 30, and soon rejoined his regiment, never to be captured again, and proud of his part in the "great escape" of the Civil War.[22]

For those, the great majority, who could not escape – and most never tried – there was only the long unremitting boredom of endless days and nights that seemed to lead nowhere. Their enemies were tedium, malnutrition, exposure, and disease, as well as the occasional inhumane guard. For a very few, more violent dangers lurked near, in the way of reprisals. When a Federal command murdered – for whatever reason fair or foul – a Confederate officer, the Southerners felt fully justified in executing a prisoner of equal rank as a discouragement of further outrages, and vice versa. It happened very seldom, but it did happen.

More outrageous, however, was the much-touted plan of Confederate authorities in Charleston to place several dozen Federal prisoners directly in the line of fire from their own cannon shelling the city, as a means of coercing the Union to commence exchanging prisoners without restrictions. In fact, there may have been no such intention, but still about fifty Yankee officers suddenly found themselves under their own shells. "We are exposed to the fire of our heavy guns," wrote Lieutenant Edmund Ryan of the 17th Illinois, "but as a general thing the Federal prisoners take great delight in seeing and hearing our shells drop into the heart of this rebellious city." Apparently one officer was wounded.

Soon stories of this reached the Federals, and quickly they took fifty prisoners from various compounds in the North, and sent them to Morris Island, near Charleston, where they were to be kept directly in line of fire of the Confederate cannon. Four of them were generals, including Franklin Gardner, Edward Johnson, and Basil Duke, along with M. Jefferson Thompson. The officers were shipped south but, in the end, they were not placed in harm's way and, instead, were shortly exchanged for the Federal prisoners in Charleston.[23]

But then a few weeks later, on August 15, 1864, Major General John G. Foster commanding Federal forces besieging Charleston, learned that another 600 Federal officer prisoners were being kept in Charleston under fire. Indeed they were, though not intentionally to expose them to hazard, but simply until some other place for their confinement could be found. However, having once experienced the usage of prisoners as a tool to coerce him, Foster was not prepared to believe what was, almost certainly, a genuine explanation of the presence of the 600. Accordingly, 600 Confederate officer prisoners were soon shipped to him, and placed under fire of their own guns, on Morris Island. They came to be known in the South as the "Immortal Six Hundred." For forty-five days they lived under shelling from Charleston's guns. Miraculously none were killed or seriously injured, though they suffered considerable hardship from exposure and tension.[24]

For all of these men, the happiest day of their lives would be the one on which they were finally exchanged or released. Yet even then their trials might not be over. Confederates especially had a long road home from prison, though the Federals provided most of them some form of transportation to their home states. For Federal prisoners, they were taken care of by their own kind, but that did not always promise safety. On April 25, 1865, almost 2,000 released Federal prisoners from Andersonville and elsewhere boarded the steamer *Sultana* at Vicksburg, bound for the North and home. One of them was Lieutenant William F. Dixon, of the 10th Indiana Cavalry. He was aboard as the boat steamed north, passing Memphis the next day. That night most of the men were asleep. "I was lying on the crowded cabin floor," he wrote later, "I was sound asleep and knew nothing until I was awakened by a sudden jar that threw me across the boat." The *Sultana's* boiler had exploded. Quickly fire spread as the ship started sinking into the cold, dark Mississippi. "The thought rushed through my mind," wrote Dixon, "of the long months that I had struggled for existence in prison . . . , and now that I must die an awful death."

The choice before him and the other survivors of the explosion was simple, "to either burn or drown." All around him he heard screaming, saw others jumping into the inky darkness, and clumps of scrambling men in the water dragging each other under. Only by grabbing a plank and diving in, avoiding all others, did Dixon manage to get away from the inferno. He paddled his way to the bank in the darkness, now illuminated by the fire of the ship and made terrible by the cries and screams behind him. Some even got to shore, clinging to overhanging trees, but were so weakened by the cold water that they could not pull themselves out of the river and drowned. Dixon floated on his plank some eleven miles to Memphis, where he was pulled out of the river the next morning. Behind him lay the greatest maritime disaster in American history. At least 1,238 – and perhaps as many as 1,647 – former prisoners, many of them officers like Dixon, their war and its trials over, going home, had perished. For weeks the bodies continued washing up on the banks down river.[25] There could not have been a more tragic ending to the whole tragic business of being a prisoner in the Civil War.

REFERENCES

1 B.A. Botkin, ed., *A Civil War Treasury of Tales, Legends and Folklore* (New York, 1960), pp.447-50.

2 William C. Thompson, "From the Defenses of Atlanta to a Federal Prison Camp," *Civil War Times Illustrated*, III (February 1965), p.42.

3 Samuel C. Foster, "We are Prisoners of War," *Civil War Times Illustrated*, XVI (May 1977), pp.29-30.

4 *Ibid.*, p.33.

5 Minor H. McLain, "The Military Prison at Fort Warren," *Civil War History*, VIII (June 1962), pp.34-47 *passim*.

6 Edward T. Downer, "Johnson's Island," *Civil War History*, VIII (June 1962), pp.100-3.

7 *Ibid.*, pp.104-5.

8 *Ibid.*, pp.100-12 *passim.*

9 Thompson, "From the Defenses of Atlanta," p.43.

10 Botkin, *Treasury*, pp.445-7.

11 William D. Wilkins, "Forgotten in the 'Black Hole'," *Civil War Times Illustrated*, XV (June 1976), p.37.

12 *Ibid.*, pp.36, 38-9.

13 *Ibid.*, p.40

14 *Ibid.*, p.44.

15 Frank L. Byrne, ed., "A General Behind Bars: Neal Dow in Libby Prison," *Civil War History*, VIII (June 1962), pp.62-3.

16 *Ibid.*, pp.61, 76.

17 James Dunwoody Jones, "A Guard at Andersonville – Eyewitness to History," *Civil War Times Illustrated*, II (February 1964), pp.24, 28.

18 *Ibid.*, pp.28-9.

19 Richard M. Basoco, "A Sequel: 'Savez' Read's Adventures After His Capture at Portland Harbor," *Civil War Times Illustrated*, II (February 1964), p.32; John B. Castleman, *Active Service* (Louisville, Ky., 1917), pp.176-8.

20 Castleman, *Active Service*, pp.113-22; Philip Van Doren Stern, *Secret Missions of the Civil War* (New York, 1959), pp.164-5.

21 Downer, "Johnson's Island," pp.108-9.

22 Frank E. Moran, "Escape from Libby Prison, Part I," *Civil War Times Illustrated*, IX (October 1970), pp.28-39 *passim*; Frank E. Moran, "Escape from Libby Prison, Part II," *Civil War Times Illustrated*, IX (November 1970), pp.39-43.

23 William M. Armstrong, ed., "Cahaba to Charleston: The Prison Odyssey of Lt. Edmund E. Ryan," *Civil War History*, VIII (June 1962), p.120; Basil W. Duke, *Reminiscences of General Basil W. Duke* (New York, 1911), p.378; Donald J. Stanton, Goodwin F. Berquist, and Paul C. Bowers, eds., *The Civil War Reminiscences of General M. Jefferson Thompson* (Dayton, Ohio, 1988), p.227.

24 War Department, *Official Records*, Series II, Volume 7, pp.7, 598, 625, 683; Rod Gragg, *The Illustrated Confederate Reader* (New York, 1989), pp.165-6.

25 William F. Dixon, "Aboard the *Sultana*," *Civil War Times Illustrated*, XII (February 1974), pp.38-9.

XI
THAT SPECIAL DISH

With all those tens of thousands of officers in service, most of them frequently engaged in battle, it was inevitable that some would come to stand out from the rest, men of special gifts, a genius for war, or extraordinary personal bravery. Part of it was the requisite of leadership, of setting an example for the men. Yet a special few truly rose above their brothers in arms to show what genuine heroism and bold leadership could achieve.

Of course, it was different for officers than for enlisted men. Most of the outstanding acts by the men in this war were solitary deeds, by one man alone. Officers, on the other hand, were most often leading men and thus their great deeds depended upon the collaboration of their followers. It made them none the less bold – indeed, it took a special kind of man to get others to follow him into some of the places these intrepid commanders ventured.

Yet there were a few individual officers who took their risks alone. Indeed, as examples of such heroism began to mount, both Union and Confederacy took steps to recognize their heroes. Each authorized the awarding of a medal of honor to such men, though only the North actually went beyond the authorization to present medals, the predecessor to the Congressional Medal of Honor. Authorized on July 12, 1862, the first medals went to enlisted men involved in a daring raid on Rebel railroad facilities in Georgia, but soon officers, too, began to earn them. During the course of the war some 1,520 medals would be awarded: 1,196 in the army, 307 in the navy, and 17 in the marine corps. While many were awarded indiscriminately for lesser deeds – often to be revoked after the war – the majority were earned for real valor. Most were earned by enlisted men in the army, yet of that number 301 were awarded to officers, just over a quarter. Of those given in the navy, all went to petty officers and lower ranks, while in the marine corps only non-commissioned officers and enlisted men received the medal.

Of those officers in the army to receive the award, every branch and variety of service was represented. There were chaplains and surgeons, staff officers of every description, and men of every rank from second lieutenant up. At least twelve general officers won the award, including Absalom Baird, Daniel Butterfield, Manning Force, John P. Hatch, Oliver O. Howard, and Major General Daniel Sickles, who received the award for great personal bravery amid what most critics regard as a very stupid act – the advance of his III Corps to an exposed position at Gettysburg, where the corps was destroyed and Sickles lost a leg. Some of the awards were certainly politically motivated, but the overwhelming majority, especially among the lower commissioned and staff ranks, were earned the hard way.[1]

Assistant Surgeon Richard Curran of the 33rd New York went into the Battle of Antietam, on September 17, 1862, with no orders as to where to place his field hospital. Left with no choice, when the battle began he started treating his men almost where they fell, right in the line of enemy fire. Though repeatedly ordered to the rear by other ranking officers, Curran stayed where he was needed. Sometime later, when the wounded were removed some distance to the rear, though still in range of Rebel artillery shells, Curran stayed with them, having one poor patient's leg blown away by a cannon ball even while the surgeon treated his other wound. His heroism won him the Medal of Honor.[2]

At Gettysburg there were more officers who distinguished themselves, and not just for stupidity like Sickles. Indeed, others would win the medal because of Sickles' ill-advised exposure of his corps. Second Lieutenant Edward Knox of the 15th New York Light Artillery received orders to take two field pieces to support the threatened left of Sickles' badly placed line. In his enthusiasm Knox took the guns too far, some 100 yards beyond any support, and just as the Rebels were launching a charge. He fired both pieces into them, then ordered his men to lie down and pretend to be killed or wounded. As a result, the Confederates charged right over them without stopping, and when their assault was repulsed and they passed back over Knox once more, the rash but daring artilleryman got his men and guns back to relative safety. That same day Captain John Lonergan led his severely reduced company to surround a house filled with Confederate sharpshooters, and boldly bluffed them into surrendering. He captured eighty-three, more men than in his company. Another captain, J. Parke Postles of the 1st Delaware, was already feeling ill that day, but volunteered to ride through a storm of Rebel fire to deliver an order to some Federal sharpshooters in a different building on the battlefield. Boldly riding across the field, Postles figured out that the only reason that he was not hit was that he was a moving target. That was fine so long as he rode, but he would have to stop when he reached the building to deliver his order. Consequently, when he arrived, instead of stopping, he jerked back on his rein, put the spurs to his poor horse, and thus jumped and bucked around the yard while he shouted his message to those inside. He evaded all of the enemy fire, and received a Medal of Honor for his pluck.[3]

There was just as much heroism in the western theater of the war. Few could compare with the exploits of Captain Patrick M. White of the famed Chicago Mercantile Battery. At Vicksburg, an order came directing him to take one field piece into a shallow ravine and break down a Rebel earthwork. Incredibly, all the while under fire from the foe, White and a few of his men manhandled their gun right up to within a few yards of the fort, and then calmly began battering it with cannon balls, White himself cutting the fuses so that they exploded just moments after leaving his gun. Before long he silenced an enemy cannon in the fort, set the works ablaze, and drove the defenders out, continuing to hold his ground for some time until ordered to withdraw. For their gallantry and devotion to duty, White and five of his brave men would win the medal that day.[4]

Such heroism and resourcefulness was not limited to Yankee officers. On October 13, 1862, Jefferson Davis signed into law an act passed by the Confederate Congress authorizing him "to bestow medals, with proper devices, upon such officers of the armies of the Confederate States as shall be conspicuous for courage and good conduct on the field of battle." But a year later, indicative of the scarcity of raw materials and services of all kinds in the South, the War Department still had not fixed a design for the medal nor manufactured any. Instead, so as not to postpone any longer recognition of bravery, it created a "roll of honor" to be read before the armies listing the names of the daring. That was as far as the government got.[5]

Yet there was one case of an officer receiving something more tangible, and for one of the most incredible acts of daring of the war. On September 8, 1863, Lieutenant Richard W. Dowling commanded a small garrison of forty-three men, mostly Irishmen, holding a fort guarding Sabine Pass at the mouth of the Sabine River, which flows southward into the Gulf of Mexico, forming the boundary between Texas and Louisiana. Dowling's fort stood on the Texas side overlooking the entrance to a river that would be invaluable to the Federals as a means of invading the interior of Texas. Dowling and his little command were all that stood in the way of such an invasion.

On that September day, 4,000 men of the XIX Corps appeared on transports off the mouth of the Sabine, expecting to steam up the river. To silence little Fort Grigsby, as Dowling's earthwork was called, they were accompanied by four gunboats, the *Clifton*, *Sachem*, *Arizona* and *Granite City*, mounting between them more than twenty guns, versus the four smoothbores and two howitzers in the fort. Well before dawn Dowling's lookouts saw signaling among the Federal ships, and he ordered the fort's cannon loaded and ready for action. When the sun rose, he could see the *Clifton* anchored some distance from the fort, and at 6.30 a.m. she opened fire. For an hour she kept it up, doing no damage. Then the *Sachem* entered the fight by opening fire on the little support steamer *Uncle Ben* moored near the fort. This fire, too, was ineffective, and the gunboats did not renew the firing until 3.40 that afternoon, when several of the ships approached again. It was then that Dowling opened fire for the first time, concentrating on the *Sachem*. At once one of his shots penetrated her steam boilers and she raised a white flag, out of action. Then another shot ruined the *Clifton's* steering apparatus, and she ran aground right under Dowling's guns. For twenty minutes he pummeled her until she, too, surrendered. The whole fight lasted about forty-five minutes before Dowling boarded his prizes. The other Yankee gunboats withdrew, for a time abandoning the transports, and the whole operation was cancelled by the Federals.

"This seems to me to be the most extraordinary feat of the war," district commander Major General John B. Magruder wrote two days later. Perhaps it was. With six cannon and forty-two men, Dowling had disabled and captured two gunboats with their thirteen cannon, 340 prisoners, and put the rest of the expedition to flight. A few months later the Confederate Congress would give Dowling and his men an official vote of thanks. Better yet, in the brief but desperate little battle, not a single one of his command, called the "Davis Guard," was injured in any way. Probably nowhere else in the Civil War was there such a lopsided disparity of odds going into an action, and conversely such a lopsided list of casualties.[7]

Even in faraway Richmond, President Davis was impressed. "The success of the single company which garrisoned the earthwork is without parallel in ancient or modern war," he would declare, "It was marvellous."[7] But perhaps even more memorable than the words of their president, were the tokens that Dowling and his forty-two defenders received a few days after the fight. They were simple silver medals, made from coins, with the initials "D.G." for Davis Guards inscribed on one side, and "Sabine Pass, September 8, 1863" inscribed on the obverse. Modest though they were, they were the only medals ever issued for valor to Confederate officers and men.

Such desperate stands were not entirely uncommon in this war, though rarely were they as dramatic as at Sabine Pass. For the Confederates particularly, so often outnumbered, the prospect of disparate odds frequently had to be faced. In April 1865, when Richmond and Petersburg were being abandoned and Lee and his Army of Northern Virginia valiantly tried to escape toward Appomattox, one incredibly brave band of men stalled the advance of the pursuing Federal army for hours at two tiny outposts, Forts Gregg and Whitworth. There on April 2, officers of the South discovered the cost of true leadership.

Fort Gregg was nothing more than an earthwork with a six-foot deep trench in front of it, and several piles of cannon ammunition. Semicircular in shape, it could be outflanked on either side. Nearby Fort Whitworth offered some protection, but neither was manned until the desperate hours of April 2 as Lee was starting to pull out of his lines. Brigadier General Nathaniel Harris had only 400 men, yet he divided them between these two forts, while men of the Washington Artillery of New Orleans dragged three field pieces into Fort Gregg. Other bits and pieces of commands, including Brigadier General James Lane, filtered into the forts. But then Lane had to return to his North Carolina brigade, forming a thin line some distance to the rear of the forts, and that left Gregg and Whitworth all by themselves in front of the advancing enemy. Soon the defenders of Fort Whitworth abandoned it, and only Gregg, now commanded by Lieutenant Colonel James H. Duncan and Captain A.K. Jones, under the general direction of Major General Cadmus Wilcox, remained. They had fewer than 300 troops to effect a defense. "Men, the salvation of this army is in your keep," shouted Wilcox, "Don't surrender this fort."

Soon afterward the enemy opened fire, and for half an hour an artillery barrage plowed the earthworks before the first infantry assault was seen forming. Some in the fort thought the bluecoat line three-quarters of a mile wide, numbering 9,000 or more. Then the Yankees advanced. Twice the Federals charged and were repulsed. Duncan coolly watched them reform a third time. Nearby a surgeon urged a gun captain to surrender. "Let it go as it will," replied Captain W.S. Chew, "We'll not give up." Then the third wave came forward. Duncan ordered his men to hold their fire until they could hear the enemy's boots on the hard soil between them. Then the Rebels delivered their last volleys, but the Union line kept coming, over the bodies of the dead and wounded from the earlier assaults, over the ditch, up the parapet, and into the fort. Bayonets and musket butts were the only weapons left to the defenders now. They threw bricks, even lit fuses to the artillery shells in the fort and threw them like grenades at the enemy.

Captain Jones was one of the few survivors. "The battle flags of the enemy made almost a solid line of bunting around the fort," he recalled. "The noise was fearful, frightful and indescribable. The curses and groaning of frenzied men could be heard over the din of our musketry. Savage men, ravenous beasts! We felt that there was no hope for us unless we could keep them at bay. We were prepared for the worst, and expected no quarter." For ten minutes or more the death struggle continued inside Fort Gregg, officers fighting without distinction of rank alongside their men. Then at last it was over. Duncan lay unconscious, badly wounded. Miraculously Wilcox, Jones and twenty-eight others were unhurt, out of the few who entered Fort Gregg that morning. Out on the field before them, and in the compound and ditch around Fort Gregg, lay at least 714 Yankee casualties traded for the 57 dead, 129 wounded, and thirty uninjured prisoners taken.[8] Better yet, the bravery of those officers and men had bought enough time for Lee to stabilize Longstreet's corps, time to set up a defensive line that allowed Lee to escape.

There were many definitions of heroism, and some of them might appear otherwise to be little more than pointless exposure and risk. But then, sometimes, these things had to do with a code of honor and gentlemanly conduct even older than the hatreds that brought on the Civil War, and they could only be observed with wonder.

At Gettysburg on July 2, 1863, most of the Confederate cavalry present was massed on the extreme left of the Rebel line, considerably out of the day's action. Brigadier General Wade Hampton of South Carolina commanded them, and there they sat on their horses awaiting orders. Hampton had enlisted as a private soldier, but soon raised his own command, the Hampton Legion, and rose to generalship through bravery and ability, though he had no prior training or experience. Six feet tall and incredibly muscular, Hampton was, thought one Rebel, "unquestionably the strongest man in the Confederate service." Certainly he had strength of nerve and character, as he was about to demonstrate.

Hampton was out in front of his troopers, out of supporting distance from them, when he heard a bullet whistle over his head. In a moment, looking at a belt of woods 300 yards away, he saw the muzzle flash of a rifle, and quickly heard another bullet. Instead of retiring, Hampton spurred his horse to a trot and made for the place where he had seen the flash. After going more than half the distance to the woods, he came to a high fence and, looking over it, saw at the edge of the wood a young Federal cavalryman, Frank Pearson of the 6th Michigan Cavalry. Incredibly, rather than standing behind cover, the boy had taken position atop a tree stump, no doubt to give himself a better line of fire on the Confederates. It also made him an outstanding target.

Hampton pulled his revolver, and he and Pearson fired simultaneously. Hampton sent the bark flying from Pearson's stump, while the Federal bullet lodged in a fence rail near the general. Then Hampton did something inexplicable. Clearly having the edge with his revolver, while the Yankee carried a single-shot carbine, Hampton turned his pistol upward and calmly waited for Pearson to reload. Then they fired again. It had become a duel.

This time Hampton missed, but Pearson pierced his coat and grazed the South Carolinian's chest. The Federal's gun then jammed as he tried to load another round. Looking at Hampton, he raised his right hand in a way that seemed to say "Wait a bit, I'll soon be with you." Quickly he cleaned his bore, while Hampton looked on. "The delay sorely taxed the patience of Hampton," wrote a friend, "as it would that of any gentleman who was kept waiting to be shot at." But the general would not fire until the boy was ready. It echoed a day just weeks before at Brandy Station, when Hampton charged a Yankee lieutenant intending to cut him down with his saber, only to find the Federal's sword arm was disabled and he could not defend himself. Hampton saluted him and rode away.

Now the Yankee cavalryman had his carbine ready, and the two duelists finished their private battle with a final exchange of shots. Hampton felt nothing, but Pearson dropped his weapon, his wrist hit by Hampton's bullet. Picking up his carbine, the young Yankee disappeared into the woods. Just then, Hampton felt a terrible blow on the back of his head. So caught up was he in his duel with Pearson that he did not hear the approach of a lieutenant of Pearson's regiment behind him. It was not a cowardly act. The Yankee approached with the fence between him and Hampton and knew only that here was a Rebel officer firing in the direction of his own men. He would not run the general through from the rear, for it would have been dastardly.

Yet he could not risk demanding surrender, for Hampton was a huge man who looked as plucky as he was, and the lieutenant figured the general would most likely just turn around and use the pistol in his hand. So he hit Hampton with his sword blade instead.

The lieutenant reckoned without Hampton's thick hat, thicker hair, and tough skull. Barely dazed, Hampton wheeled around anxious to use his pistol. The lieutenant turned his mount and raced away, Hampton in hot pursuit, repeatedly pulling the trigger on his revolver. Fortunately for the Yankee, every chamber refused to fire. Then the foe wheeled off toward safety through a gap in the fence and Hampton could only hurl his pistol at him, "accompanying it with some words which did not entirely become his character as a vestryman of the Protestant Episcopal Church."

There, seemingly, it ended. But there was to be a postscript. Ten years later, in 1873, Hampton's younger brother Frank met that same Yankee lieutenant in Mobile, Alabama. In fact, the officer sought him out. "Colonel," he said, "I sought your acquaintance in order that through you I might make the *amende honorable* to your brother." He had been troubled by the manner in which he struck Hampton from behind, and sought now to explain and to apologize. In time Hampton wrote to the Yankee expressing his gratification that his pistol had malfunctioned that day, and heartily accepting the Federal's apology. Further, through the Federal, Hampton commenced a correspondence with Frank Pearson, then a successful farmer back in Michigan. Pearson assured Hampton that he was happy now that he had missed him with all those carbine shots, and the general, for his part, replied how sorry he was to have wounded the young private at Gettysburg.[9]

This was individual dash on a grand scale. But most of the generals who achieved a reputation for daring did so as leaders rather than for their own personal deeds. Major General Jeb Stuart, though certainly brave and dashing, won his lasting renown through the bold raids that he led into enemy territory. Twice he rode entirely around Federal General George B. McClellan's Army of the Potomac, once on June 12-15, 1862, and again on October 9-12. Ever the daring raider, Stuart led other similarly bold enterprises against Yankee communications and supply, each one accompanied with the trademarks of his dash – swift movement, lightning strikes, the gathering of considerable plunder, and few if any casualties taken himself. Best of all, he gathered the information that his commander Lee needed in order to thwart repeated Federal campaigns. To be sure, Stuart was a flawed cavalryman at times. More than once he let the glee of taking and returning with captured goods distract him from his primary mission. At Gettysburg, when he should have been acting as Lee's eyes and ears, he was off on a pointless raid that gained nothing and may have helped cost Lee the battle. But that was an aberration in Stuart. The real man was unfailingly courageous and selfless, and whatever hardships his men suffered, he shared as well. Thus it was that he was in the thick of the fighting with them at Yellow Tavern, Virginia, on May 11, 1864, when a Federal trooper fired a .44 pistol ball into his right side. Twenty-seven hours later he died, having braved every danger to which he had exposed his men. Certainly there was a special kind of bond between such charismatic leaders and the men they led.

Equally dashing and far more productive, though less flamboyant, was another cavalryman, this time a Yankee. Though he led only one cavalry raid, it was, perhaps, the most effective of the war. He was, of course, Colonel Benjamin Grierson, whose drive through the heart of Mississippi during April 17-May 3, 1863, proved to be the greatest – and most dangerous – diversionary action of the war.

The plan grew in the mind of U.S. Grant, who wanted something to distract the attention of the defenders of Vicksburg away from his attempt to move his army below the city on the west bank of the Mississippi, then cross the river below Vicksburg and move against it from the rear. He needed to cut the rail line connecting the city with the rest of Mississippi and the Confederacy, and sufficiently confuse the foe as to what was going on to buy time to move his army. Already Grant had seen promise in Grierson, and on February 13, 1863, Grant suggested that the colonel and 500 picked men might make a raid against the railroad east of Vicksburg. "The undertaking would be a hazardous one," said Grant. "I do not direct that this shall be done, but leave it for a volunteer enterprise." Grant's friend Sherman had already recommended Grierson as "the best cavalry officer I have yet had," and Grant would come to agree.[10]

The plan evolved considerably before it actually went into action. For one thing, Grant suggested that instead of returning from the railroad raid, Grierson should push on to the south and east, into Alabama, but in the end left it to Grierson's discretion. That showed the greatest trust of all, for only the raiding commander on the scene could decide what was best; no one could predict all the variables that might combine against him, and he had to have the latitude to adjust his plans to the circumstances.

Poor Grierson, away on furlough, only reached his command three hours before they departed on April 17. There was no time to rest. Before dawn Grierson led his command, now 1,700 strong, out of their camp at La Grange, Tennessee, and soon crossed the border into Rebel-held Mississippi. For the next sixteen days, they would see no friendly faces, have no support to look to, and nothing but the enemy behind and ahead of them. Daring in the face of a daunting situation, Grierson reduced his command the third day out by sending some 175 men who were unfit for the rest of the expedition back to La Grange, instructing their leader to be as ostentatious as possible, hoping that this party might distract Rebel attention from the main column.

A day later the Confederates had gotten Grierson's trail and were after him. Thereafter it was a chase through Mississippi, with the Federal sending out decoy parties to fool the enemy as to his destination, while the Confederates slowly brought more and more troops to bear on bringing Grierson to bay. On the eighth day out, the raiders took Newton Station, on the railroad to Vicksburg, and effectively cut the line. They burned bridges, tore up rails, and destroyed two locomotives and large stores of ammunition. Then they were off that same afternoon to the southwest towards Natchez. Ahead of them the Rebels were telegraphing to all points to gather troops to cut off any avenue of escape. Traps were laid at most of the major roads. By April 30, Grierson and his men had been in the saddle day and night for two weeks without more than a few hours' rest at a time. Bone weary, they kept on until May 1, their fifteenth day out, when they came up against a roadblock in their path. At Wall's Bridge, on the Tickfaw River, an ambush had been laid. They had to cross that river or else lose valuable time, time that would allow the converging Confederates in their rear to trap them. With nothing else to be done, Grierson and his exhausted troopers attacked across the bridge and drove its defenders away in the biggest fight of the raid. But then they had to cross Williams' Bridge on the Amite River a few miles further southwest. Confederates knew it too, and began ordering troops there for another trap. But in a frustrating misadventure, the Rebels stopped for a party on the way, and Grierson's column crossed the bridge two hours before their would-be ambushers arrived. From that point onward, the raiders rode as if possessed. For twelve straight hours through the night of May 1-2, they rode without stopping, racing toward Federal lines at Baton Rouge, Louisiana. With thirty miles still to go, they pressed on again, finally reaching safety late on May 2.

What Grierson had done was phenomenal. He had ridden his command over 600 miles in sixteen days. They killed or wounded more than 100 Confederates, captured and paroled 500 more, tore up fifty or more miles of railroad, destroyed 3,000 stands of arms and considerable other stores, and captured 1,000 horses and mules. In return, Grierson's losses were three killed and seven wounded, and nine missing. On their final day of the raid they had ridden 76 miles, fought four small engagements, forded a river so deep the horses had to swim, and all without food or rest. "Grierson has knocked the heart out of the State," a friend told Grant. Grant did not have to be told. "Grierson's raid from La Grange through Mississippi has been the most successful thing of the kind since the breaking out of the rebellion," he declared. Years later Grant would be even more effusive. "It was Grierson who first set the example of what might be done in the interior of an enemy's country without any base from which to draw supplies," he wrote. His friend Sherman was more succinct. He called it "The most brilliant expedition of the war."[11]

None of Stuart's celebrated raids came close in their results to Grierson's achievements, perhaps the ultimate combination of dash and daring with positive military objectives and accomplishments. Yet it would be Grierson's only great moment. There was another leader, however, who took personal courage and military accomplishments to practically the same heights again and again throughout the war, perhaps the greatest cavalry leader ever produced in America: General Nathan Bedford Forrest. The feelings of his men said much. "As long as we followed Forrest," said one, "we were heroes."

Given his poor and ignorant background, few would have expected much of this man. Yet he possessed an authentic military genius, along with the drive that also made him a fortune before the war. Having read none of the military manuals, he felt little but disdain for them. He fought by commonsense and keen intuition. "Whenever I ran into one of those fellers who fit by note," he said of the book-learned generals, "I generally whipped hell out of him before he could get his tune pitched." He was only crudely literate, and wrote few letters. One that survives says much of his elemental view of waging war. "I had a small brush with the Enamy on yesterday I Suceded in gaining thir rear," he wrote. "They wair not looking for me I taken them by Suprise they run like Suns of Biches." While he never said that his theory of war was "to git thar fustest with the mostest," as Civil War mythology would suggest, still that elemental philosophy characterized his generalship. Along with it went incredible personal daring. Thirty Federals at least fell by his own hand. Twenty-nine horses were killed under him as he stayed in the thick of the fight time after time. Three times the enemy's bullets tore into his flesh. Nothing could stop him.[12]

Forrest's brilliance and daring shone on his very first raid, when he was just a new brigadier. In July 1862 he led 1,000 men from Chattanooga into middle Tennessee, and almost at once captured a whole brigade of Yankee infantry, some 1,200 men including General Thomas Crittenden, $1 million worth of property, and considerable cavalry stores and four cannon for his command. This done, he moved on toward Nashville, burning railroad bridges along the way, and sending such a fright into Tennessee's Union governor that two infantry divisions of Federals were detailed away from the Army of the Ohio to guard railroads. The result was to cause a serious delay in an offensive campaign that army had planned. All in all, a very successful conclusion for a new general's first independent command.[14]

Everywhere he went, Forrest led the way, absolutely fearless, absolutely confident in himself and his men. Even his enemy Sherman sent him a note congratulating "his dash" in taking Memphis, but then so discomfited was Sherman by the raider's exploits that he later turned the full force of his own cavalry to bear on this genius in the saddle. It was Sherman himself who gave the Confederate his enduring sobriquet, "that devil Forrest."[15]

Besides the cavalrymen, who had the most opportunity for daring escapades, civilians North and South thrilled to the adventures of the spies and secret agents, very often officers, who operated behind enemy lines. Unfortunately, because they dealt in a business of lies and deception, their own later stories of their adventures are highly embellished and unreliable, as if their habit of deception did not wear off when the war ended. Some even completely invented wartime careers for themselves, and invented their commissions as well. One of the best known was a woman, Loretta Velasquez, who claimed to have operated disguised as a man in Confederate uniform, and even obtained a commission as "Captain Buford." Her whole story was a fabrication.

Quite genuine, however, were many of the daring escapades of officers who rode gallant ships instead of horses. Again, perhaps because of their perpetual underdog status, the Southerners seem somehow to have provided the majority of stirring examples. One officer, Captain Raphael Semmes, made an absolute habit of bold deeds, starting on June 30, 1861, when he steamed his little raider C.S.S. *Sumter* out of Pass aá L'Outre at the mouth of the Mississippi and made for the open seas. Outrunning a Yankee warship that pursued him, Semmes embarked on a six-month cruise that saw eighteen Yankee merchantmen captured, seven of which he destroyed. Finally cornered by Federal warships in the neutral port of Gibraltar, the *Sumter* sat idle for a few months, and was later auctioned to a British firm. She was no longer needed, for early in 1863 word reached Semmes from Confederate naval authorities in Britain that a new ship would soon be ready for him, a bigger, more powerful, more formidable vessel altogether. To conceal her intentions, they called her for the moment the "*290*." To the world and posterity, she would soon become known as the C.S.S. *Alabama*.[15]

Here was a commerce raider to challenge the seas; 900 tons burden, 230 feet long and 32 feet wide. "Her model was of the most perfect symmetry," wrote Semmes, "and she sat upon the water with the lightness and grace of a swan." Her engine developed 300 horsepower, and on her decks sat six 32-pounders in broadside, while at her bow a massive 100-pounder Blakely rifle was mounted as a pivot gun, with an 8-inch smoothbore pivot aft. With 144 men and officers, she was ready to take on Uncle Sam's shipping.[16]

She did so with a vengeance, in the north and south Atlantic, the Caribbean, the Gulf of Mexico, and around the Cape of Good Hope to the Indian Ocean. She made sixty-six captures, one of them the Yankee warship *Hatteras*, which she met in open battle and sank in action off Galveston. For two years Semmes plied the seas, becoming such a terror that he and the handful of other Rebel commerce raiders eventually tied up some seventy-nine Federal warships assigned to hunt for them; Federal vessels totaling almost eighty thousand tons and mounting 774 guns, all of them vessels that Lincoln would have preferred to keep on blockade duty. Their diversion to the chase for Semmes and the others undoubtedly contributed substantially to the frequent perforations of the blockade that allowed a trickle of much-needed supplies to keep coming into the Confederacy from abroad right up to the end of the war.[17]

Finally, however, for reasons that still baffle students, Semmes took on even more than his daring could handle. Having put into Cherbourg harbor on June 11, 1864, for repairs, he found himself blockaded by the arrival of the Federal warship U.S.S. *Kearsarge*. The Yankee vessel outclassed the *Alabama* in every category; she displaced over 1,000 tons, had better engines, and mounted eight guns, all of them of substantially heavier caliber than Semmes'. He later said that "the disparity was not so great but that I might hope to beat my enemy in a fair fight." Years later Semmes also would claim that it had not been fair that the commander of the *Kearsarge*, Captain John Winslow, hung chains over the sides of his ship, making of her a sort of "ironclad," in order to protect his engines. Displaying a quaint and very impractical notion of war ethics, Semmes complained that Winslow should have warned him of this, as if a combatant was obliged to reveal his plans to a foe he was about to meet. With the chain protection on the *Kearsarge*, Semmes pouted that the ships were no longer evenly matched and that he would not have given battle. (Semmes never seemed to think it unfair that the *Alabama* completely outclassed the *Hatteras*, the only warship he defeated, or that none of the merchantmen he captured had been armed at all. For all their daring, men who lost battles in this war could find some pretty silly excuses to explain away their defeats.)[18]

On June 19, Semmes steamed out of Cherbourg to give battle. Almost immediately it became apparent that the *Alabama* was outclassed. Seven times the ships circled around each other, firing away as best they could. Semmes did next to no damage to the *Kearsarge*, but Winslow's superior gunnery gradually made a wreck of the *Alabama*. Finally, after an hour and ten minutes, Semmes saw that his ship was sinking. Sadly he ordered her abandoned, and a short while later she sank to the bottom where she still rests today.[19] Whatever may be said for Semmes' apparent poor judgment in going out to meet the *Kearsarge*, once he steamed out for battle he did so with a daring that would have done credit to Stuart or Grierson.

In the end, however, it probably belonged to an obscure gunboat captain on the Mississippi to show daring at its zenith. Isaac Brown commanded a hastily built and still incomplete Rebel ironclad, the C.S.S. *Arkansas*. She had been "completed" up the Yazoo River, a tributary of the Mississippi above Vicksburg, and in July 1862 was desperately needed to help defend the city against an assault by two combined Yankee fleets. His vessel was almost comical, an iron sheathed shed atop a hull, three guns protruding on either broadside, and one gun each fore and aft. Her armor was forged from railroad iron, and there lay her strength. On July 14 she began her journey, ready as she would ever be, down the Yazoo toward Vicksburg. Ahead of Brown there were at least thirty-seven Yankee vessels that he knew of.

The next morning Brown saw three Federal ships: one ironclad and two heavy gunboats. As he opened fire, the Yankee ships returned a few shots then turned and fled, fearing the much-rumored ironclad. As Brown pursued, he disabled the ironclad *Carondelet*, then raced on down toward the mouth of the Yazoo. When he got there he saw "a forest of masts and smokestacks." "It seemed at a glance as if a whole navy had come to keep me away from the heroic city," he wrote. Ahead of him were seven rams, five ironclads, and a fleet of heavy wooden gunboats and cruisers. He was all by himself. What he decided to do was to steam into the very center of the enemy squadrons, hugging them close so they would have to watch their fire for fear of hitting one another.

He later said he felt as if in the middle of a volcano, guns blazing all around him, smoke everywhere. He could only keep firing and steam straight towards the safety of the Confederate lines at Vicksburg. Along the way, the *Arkansas* inflicted serious injuries on at least four of the enemy ships. Steaming through a solid wall of flame and iron, Brown left the Yankee fleet behind, dazed and reeling, and brought his battered ship into the safety of Vicksburg. Later that day he would say simply that "it was a little hot this morning all around."[20] That is surely the epitomy of officers' dash and daring.

REFERENCES

1 Editors of Boston Publishing Company, *Above and Beyond* (Boston, 1985), pp.316-24.

2 *Ibid.*, p.25.

3 *Ibid.*, pp.28-31.

4 *Ibid.*, pp.34-5.

5 *Ibid.*, p.53.

6 U.S. Navy Department, *Official Records of the Union and Confederate Navies in the War of the Rebellion* (Washington, 1894-1927), Series I, Volume 20, pp.559, 561, 562-3.

7 Jefferson Davis, *Rise and Fall of the Confederate Government* (New York, 1881), II, p.238.

8 Burke Davis, *To Appomattox* (New York, 1959), pp.74-9; Douglas S. Freeman, *Lee's Lieutenants* (New York, 1942-1944), III, pp.681-2.

9 T.J. Mackey, "Hampton's Duel", *Southern Historical Society Papers*, XXII (1894), pp.122-6.

10 Dee Brown, *Grierson's Raid* (Urbana, Ill., 1954), p.8n.

11 *Ibid.*, pp.219-23.

12 Robert S. Henry, *"First With The Most" Forrest* (Indianapolis, 1944), pp.7-8.

13 *Ibid.*, p.90.

14 *Ibid.*, pp.342, 381.

15 Harpur A. Gosnell, ed., *Rebel Raider* (Chapel Hill, N.C., 1948), p.209; Charles G. Summersell, *The Cruise of the CSS Sumter* (Tuscaloosa, Ala., 1965), p.161.

16 Semmes, *Raider*, pp.33-4.

17 *Ibid.*, p.xix; Summersell, *Cruise*, p.177.

18 Semmes, *Raider*, pp.369-70.

19 *Ibid.*, p.373.

20 Samuel C. Carter, *The Final Fortress: The Campaign for Vicksburg, 1862-1863* (New York, 1980), pp.69-71.

XII

PEACE MAKERS FOR POSTERITY

It was always hard to say with certainty just who was responsible for the unfolding of events in the Civil War. Clearly the common folk, those who would provide the enlisted men of both sides, could be held little responsible for bringing about the conflict. That guilt lay with the leaders of North and South, largely the same men and class that would provide so much of the military leadership of the armies. Yet, once they went to war, the fate of battles most often rested in the end with the common soldiers. Generals and lesser officers could plan as they would, but if the men did not fight, then the contest was lost. Sometimes, as at Missionary Ridge on November 25, 1863, the foot soldiers could go beyond their officers' commands and take control of the battle on their own.

But there had to come a time when, once again, it was all out of the hands of the common soldiers, a time when they had fought the best they could and one side or the other could fight no more. When that day came, the war would be all but over. Then, again, it would be time for the officers to take over in earnest, for only they could put an end to the marching and fighting, only they could officially admit victory or defeat. To them would fall the first step in making peace.

In Virginia that day came on April 9, 1865, at Appomattox Court House. The soldiers he still had were full of fight, but Robert E. Lee simply no longer had enough of them. His once mighty Army of Northern Virginia was reduced to barely a good-sized army corps of previous days. A week before he had had about 50,000 men in the trenches around Richmond and Petersburg, facing Grant's combined armies totaling 112,000. But then after being forced out of his lines on April 2, Lee made a forlorn attempt to escape to the southwest to join forces with the remnant of Joseph E. Johnston's Army of Tennessee in North Carolina. All along that trail of tears to

Appomattox, Lee lost more men until, by the morning of that Palm Sunday, April 9, he had only 26,600. And Grant had him surrounded.[1]

In fact, even before the evacuation of the Confederate capital, some officers had made fleeting attempts at bringing hostilities to a close. Back in February Lieutenant General James Longstreet engaged in a correspondence by flag of truce with Federal Major General E.O.C. Ord. The two foes met on February 21, and agreed that if a cease fire were called, and if Grant and Lee could meet, then perhaps the two generals might work out a way of ending it all. Longstreet even suggested making it sort of a social occasion, with the wives of generals on opposing sides paying calls to their counterparts, to ease tensions while negotiations went on. It was the sort of thing that Old Army men would think of, reminiscent of the part played by officers' wives on the frontier posts in putting an end to petty disputes. When Longstreet suggested this to President Davis, the idea was approved but nothing came of it.[2]

Still, in the end, it fell to Grant and Lee. Indeed, two days before that Palm Sunday, on the afternoon of April 7, Grant sent a note to Lee through the lines. "The results of the last week must convince you of the hopelessness of further resistance," Grant said. "I feel that it is so, and regard it as my duty to shift from myself the responsibility of any further effusion of blood, by asking of you the surrender of that portion of the C.S. army known as the Army of Northern Virginia." Lee received the note when Longstreet was with him and the two were almost ready to sleep for the night. "Not yet," was Longstreet's laconic reply when Lee showed him the note. Their situation was desperate, but on April 7 there was still slim hope.[3]

Still hoping to find some accommodation short of surrender, and wishing to keep communication open with Grant, Lee replied asking what terms Grant would offer. The next morning (April 8) came Grant's response. "Peace being my great desire," he said, he would ask only that Lee's men put down their arms and give their parole not to take them up again until and unless properly exchanged. Struggling to avoid facing actual surrender, Lee replied that same day that his situation was not yet that desperate. Still, he wished that the two generals might meet to discuss the "restoration of peace." What Lee could have meant by that is a mystery, though it may be that he wanted to talk of something broader. Now that he was general-in-chief of all Confederate armies, he might have hoped to call a war-wide armistice. But all that could have done would have been to buy a little time. With the South so clearly on its knees on all fronts, the Union would hardly accept any conclusion to the war other than total victory.

Whatever Lee meant, Grant declined the interview, but his reply did not reach Lee until the morning of April 9. By then, Grant's hard-riding cavalry under Sheridan had gotten ahead of Lee's retreating columns, cutting off their escape from the van of the Union army. Now Lee was trapped, the situation changed irretrievably, and he had no choice but to send Grant a final note asking for a meeting specifically to discuss surrender. "I would rather die a thousand deaths," said the proud Lee.[4]

Their meeting itself came in the home of Wilmer McLean in the village of Appomattox Court House. Lee arrived first and was shown into a plain front parlor, where Grant joined him shortly afterward. The staff officers of the two – Lee had only Marshall with him, Grant had Parker and several other officers, including Sheridan – noticed the marked contrast between the two commanders. Lee arrived in his best and most fully appointed uniform; Grant, who had come in haste, was dusty from the ride and wearing only his customary private's blouse with insignia of his rank sewn on.

They shook hands, then each sat at a separate table. An uncomfortable Grant tried to make small talk and asked if Lee remembered their meeting once during the Mexican War. It was Lee who turned the conversation to the point. Grant repeated his simple terms, and Lee agreed. "This will have a very happy effect on my army," Lee said as he read Grant's generous terms after they were put down on paper. As a further gesture, Grant allowed that any man claiming to own a horse or mule in Lee's army would be permitted to take it home with him. There would be spring planting to do. Lee would always be grateful for Grant's magnanimity, so much so that in later years, when president of Washington College in Lexington, Virginia, Lee threatened with dismissal any faculty member who should speak disrespectfully of Grant in his presence.[5]

There was something remarkable in the way that these men who had made war like no others so instinctively embraced peace. Grant even fed Lee's starving army from his own commissary. The victor felt depressed at the humiliation of his noble foe, and ordered that the firing of any salutes in celebration be stopped immediately. "The war is over," he said. "The Rebels are our countrymen again."[6]

It was left to their subordinates to work out the details of the surrender itself. Longstreet, Gordon, and Pendleton represented Lee, meeting with Grant's men Charles Griffin, Wesley Merritt, and John Gibbon. While they deliberated, the officers of the two armies crossed the lines to look for old friends from before the war. Almost at once, the Old Army fraternity reappeared. Sheridan found Longstreet, Wilcox, and Heth, and brought them to see Grant. Major General George G. Meade, commanding the Army of the Potomac, went over to see his old friend Lee. "What are you doing with all that gray in your beard?" teased Lee. Looking back on two years of commanding his army in the frustrating attempt to bring Lee to this pass, Meade responded, "You have to answer for most of it!"[7]

Grant, tender toward Lee's feelings to the last, left for Washington before the formal surrender ceremony took place on April 12. He gave to Brigadier General Joshua L. Chamberlain the honor of formally receiving the stacked arms and furled flags of the proud Army of Northern Virginia. It is good that he did, not only for the acknowledgement of Chamberlain's outstanding record, but even more because it put Chamberlain in a place to see and record, as no other pen could have, the moving last moments of Lee's army.

Chamberlain formed his command on either side of the road leading into

Appomattox Court House, and toward the village Lee's men slowly marched. Gordon, commanding the II Corps led the way, followed by the remnants of Richard H. Anderson's and Henry Heth's commands, and then Longstreet's I Corps. In total silence they slowly marched forward along the road, heads hanging in sadness, feet dragging the dust. And then something almost magical happened. Seeing Gordon approach, Chamberlain ordered a bugler to call his men to attention, then to shift their position from "order arms" to "carry arms." To a civilian it meant nothing; to a soldier it meant the marching salute. Chamberlain was honoring Gordon's men as they approached.

And now Gordon was seized by some similar inspiration of the moment, some instinct of nobility greater than the sadness burdening him. "Gordon at the head of the column," wrote Chamberlain, "riding with heavy spirit and downcast face, catches the sound of shifting arms, looks up, and, taking the meaning, wheels superbly, making with himself and his horse one uplifted figure, with profound salutation as he drops the point of his sword to the boot toe; then facing to his own command, gives word for his successive brigades to pass us with the same position of the manual – honor answering honor."

Only men made of stone escaped with dry eyes. "Memories that bound us together as no other bond," said Chamberlain, "thronged as we looked into each other's eyes." No victor cheered. There was, in fact, "not a sound of trumpet more, nor roll of drum; not a cheer, nor word nor whisper of vain-glorying, nor motion of man standing again at the order, but an awed stillness rather, and breath-holding, as if it were the passing of the dead!"[7]

Events seemed to pile on top of one another after that, as the whole Confederacy crumbled. Charleston was finally taken by Federal authorities, and on April 14, four years to the day from the sad moment when he had hauled down Fort Sumter's flag in surrender, Brigadier General Robert Anderson returned to Sumter and raised that same flag once again. That night Union jubilation suffered a severe blow when President Lincoln made a trip to the theater from which he never returned, yet despite this the Union victory train kept on moving.

The next great meeting of the officers would come in North Carolina, and here again it was old antagonists coming together to begin peace and a life-long friendship. Joseph E. Johnston had been brought almost to a standstill by Sherman's advancing host in North Carolina. He was not trapped as Lee had been, but desperately outnumbered, and with nowhere really to go, he asked President Davis – himself in flight through North Carolina with his cabinet – to allow him to ask Sherman for an armistice to discuss surrender. Reluctantly Davis assented.

The two generals met on April 17 at the Bennett farmhouse near Durham Station. Neither had met the other previously, despite their mutual Old Army service, but, said Sherman, "we knew enough of each other to be well acquainted at once." Alone in Bennett's place, they talked. Sherman – after telling Johnston the news of Lincoln's assassination – said frankly that further resistance was pointless, and his old foe agreed. But Johnston suggested that they should go farther than the surrender of just his own army. Thinking he could get authority from Davis to surrender all Rebel forces still in the field, Johnston proposed that this form the line of their discussion. Sherman agreed, and after several minutes of open and pleasant conversation, they agreed to meet again the next day, when Johnston hoped to return with Davis' authorization.

In fact, Johnston did not get Davis' explicit agreement, but he did get Secretary of War Breckinridge to come and meet Sherman with him on April 18. First he counted on Breckinridge's well-known eloquence as a weapon in persuading Sherman to grant the best possible terms. Beyond that, Breckinridge was the only remaining cabinet member with any real influence on Davis, and might be able to persuade the president to abandon hope and accept terms embracing all Confederate forces. At first Sherman declined to meet with the Kentuckian, since he was a civil officer of a government that the Union did not recognize. However, he was also a major general, and as a military officer Sherman agreed to allow him into the conference.

The three generals talked for some time, Breckinridge speaking eloquently in favor of recognition of political and property rights for former Confederate men and officers. In the end, they agreed upon a settlement that would disband all Rebel military forces. Federal authority was to be recognized, Southern state governments were to be reorganized as soon as their members took an oath of allegiance, Federal courts would be re-established, and former Confederates would have restored to them full constitutional rights so long as they obeyed the law.

The agreement went far beyond what Grant had proposed to Lee, and reflected the war-weariness of the generals who framed it. Indeed, it was probably the most far-reaching agreement ever concluded by generals commanding armies, going way beyond the limits of their military authority. The presence of Breckinridge – in whatever capacity – gave it some measure of civil Confederate approval, but Sherman had no such power, and a few days later Washington would reject the terms entirely, starting a feud between Sherman and Secretary of War Stanton that made headlines. Given no choice, Johnston then surrendered his own army alone to Sherman on April 26, with the same terms given to Lee. Some 30,000 Confederates turned in their arms and were soldiers no more. Sherman graciously provided transportation to help most of them to get home again. Still though their attempt at being universal peacemakers had failed, Sherman and Johnston forged a personal friendship that lasted until the great Federal general's death in 1891. Present at his funeral was his old foe Johnston, who stood bare-headed in the rain as Sherman's bier passed by. Five weeks later Johnston, too, died, reportedly from a cold he took by refusing to wear his hat at Sherman's funeral.[8]

Just as they were so often forgotten during the war, so were the far western armies forgotten in their surrenders, In fact, the combined forces of Lieutenant General

Richard Taylor's 12,000 men in Alabama and the 43,000 that General Kirby Smith had in the trans-Mississippi were almost exactly equal to the numbers surrendered by Lee and Johnston. Both, as it happened, made terms with an almost unknown major general, E.R.S. Canby, a forty-seven-year-old Kentuckian whose highly creditable service had been spent almost entirely in these regions. Taylor met with him on May 2 at Citronelle, Alabama, receiving terms similar to those given Lee and Johnston. Kirby Smith never did meet Canby himself, sending instead a poor man destined to repeat an earlier experience in surrendering for timorous superiors, Lieutenant General Simon B. Buckner. Buckner met with Canby's representative in New Orleans on May 26. By this time all vestiges of the Confederate government had disappeared, Jefferson Davis and most of his cabinet were prisoners, and fighting on was nothing more than pointless. Nearly a month later, at Doaksville in the Indian Territory, General Stand Watie surrendered what remained of his Confederate Indian regiments, and in so doing made the last capitulation of a formal Rebel command. It was all over.

At least, it was all over for the overwhelming majority of the officers who had followed the Blue and the Gray. For a very few, however, the danger was not entirely past. Some military officers of the Confederacy had been indicted for treason in Federal courts during the war, but their surrender and parole virtually quashed any possibility of further prosecution. But for Breckinridge, who as vice president had been a very important civil official of the old Union, those indictments were still active, as they were for several of Davis' cabinet. Consequently, he felt it in his best interest not to be captured. First, after consulting with Sherman and Johnston, Breckinridge finished his primary mission, which was to see Confederate armies surrendered and to oversee the escape of Davis and the government. He did so as best he could, finally parting with Davis in South Carolina on May 2 and riding off with a small party of followers, hoping to decoy pursuing Federals from Davis' trail. It did not work, and Davis was taken in Georgia on May 10. When he learned of that, Breckinridge was free to make his own escape, and set off for the coast of Florida. Along the way he picked up others, including the daring Confederate commerce raider John Taylor Wood. Together they rode as far as Fort Butler, on the St. Johns River. Then loading their small party of three officers and three Confederate enlisted men and Breckinridge's servant Tom Ferguson into a small boat, they sailed the St.Johns to the Indian River, then all along the Indian – a part of the inland waterway – to its mouth. Along the way they engaged in a running gun battle with renegades living near present-day Miami, and turned pirate by commandeering at gunpoint a larger sailing boat from the hands of Federal deserters. Having tried unsuccessfully to reach the Bahamas, they now decided instead to sail out across the Gulf Stream to Cuba. They chose to do so amid one of the worst storms of the decade, and then only after eluding one Federal patrol boat, and boldly trading for supplies from another Yankee steamer. For four days they braved near-hurricane winds and seas, almost going under at least twice, before in the end they saw the coast of Cuba ahead. On June 12, 1865, they landed at Cardenas, and Breckinridge began what would be a three-and-one-half-year exile until the Universal Amnesty of Christmas 1868 allowed him to return to Kentucky without fear of molestation.[9]

While Breckinridge was the only high-ranking officer who might genuinely have feared for his life, there were many others who simply could not accept defeat, nor the prospect of life under Yankee rule. In the months after the surrenders, somewhere between 5,000 and 10,000 Confederates and their families left the South in the largest expatriation movement in American history. Almost 5,000 went to Mexico to start new lives in the settlement of Carlotta. Among them were several generals, including Sterling Price, John B. Magruder, Thomas C. Hindman, Joseph O. Shelby, and others. Several took service in the army of the Emperor Maximilian in his war against the Juarista insurgents. One of them, Brigadier General Mosby M. Parsons, along with his former adjutant, were killed by the Mexican rebels. Unfortunately for them, their attempt to start a new colony in Mexico failed, and most eventually returned to the South to try to pick up their old lives.

Elsewhere, old Confederates, again largely ex-officers, moved to settlements in Central America, and even South America, especially in Brazil, where their descendants still live. Some stayed in Cuba, while even more went to Canada. There, especially in Toronto and at Niagara, a virtual little Confederate community arose. For a time Breckinridge was their leading citizen, soon joined by Jubal Early and a host of lesser officers. Breckinridge stayed only as long as he had to, purposely living just across the Niagara River from United States soil so he could see the Stars and Stripes flying over Fort Niagara, a flag and a country he had never wanted to fight against. Early and others were there out of pure bitterness, though almost all of them, in time, would return to the South.

More of these men, almost entirely officers, crossed the Atlantic to Europe and the Near East, In the late 1860s, when the Khedive of Egypt needed trained soldiers, several men including Brigadier Generals Charles W. Field and William W. Loring took commissions in his army. There, ironically, they found themselves serving side by side with other soldiers of fortune, former officers of the Union Army.

More still went to Europe, and especially to England and France. These men were truly exiles, not there to stay but simply wandering until they could go home. Breckinridge also turned up here, and again was the leading figure for a time. His society often included men like Longstreet's old staff officer Osmun Latrobe and General Louis T. Wigfall. The Confederates, for the most part, were well accepted into European society. Prominent politicians and socialites paid them attentions and sought their friendship. Breckinridge became acquainted with Thomas Carlyle and the Archbishop of Canterbury, while others married into European society. There had been considerable sympathy in Europe for the Confederate cause, and many of the former officers were just as flattered and indulged as any exiled royalty, of which there was always a surfeit. Yet almost all of these officers, too, wanted only to go home. By 1869, most of them had.[10]

What so many of them feared when they left the South, especially those under indictments, was trial and perhaps even execution. Since there had never been an insurrection in the United States before, no one could predict what the victorious Union would do with its former enemies. The terms of Grant and Sherman, and the well-known attitude of Lincoln toward leniency, would have seemed to bode well. But then a madman killed Lincoln just in the moment of triumph, and a bitter vengeful mood swept much of the North. In such a climate, many might logically fear for their lives.

Yet they needed have no fear. Even Davis and his leading officers of government suffered no more than imprisonment for a time. None were ever brought to trial, all were released, and some even sought and obtained their full rights of citizenship again. Several officers, most of them generals, were also imprisoned for a time, most because of suspected war crimes or else because they had been involved in espionage. All of them, too, were eventually released.

In fact, after all this terrible, bloody war, with the deaths of 620,000 and untold devastation of property and civilian lives behind them, the Union, even in its vindictive mood after Lincoln's death, took as reprisal the life of only one man. He was an officer; Major Henry Wirz, the commandant of Camp Sumter, the infamous Andersonville. In what was unquestionably a miscarriage of justice, he was brought before a military tribunal some months after the surrenders and charged with intentionally starving and mistreating thousands of Union prisoners to death. Perjured testimony appeared to prosecute him, attempts were made to link his crimes with Jefferson Davis, and he was denied many of the safeguards that would have been available to him in a civil court. Worse, he spoke with a thick Swiss accent that only further aroused the xenophobic prejudices of the officers on his court. Not a particularly likeable man, still he was no war criminal, but in this court he never had a chance. The court convicted him and sentenced him to death. On November 10, 1865, while the soldiers stationed around him chanted "Andersonville" over and over again, he was hanged, the sole Confederate executed as a result of the Civil War. For Wirz it was a personal tragedy. For the reunited Union, it was evidence of the most incredible restraint ever shown in history by a victor dealing with a defeated separatist movement.

Such restraint would be needed through the dark days of Reconstruction ahead. Though its horrors have been greatly magnified by Southern writers since, still the years from 1865 to 1877 were hard ones for the South. Only with the passage of time would passions die and the men who had led the armies of the Confederacy rebuild their lives. Yet most of them did. Indeed, within two decades after Appomattox, almost all of the once-Confederate states were again firmly under the control of the men who had been captains and colonels and generals in the armies of the gray.

Gordon would become a United States Senator and later governor of Georgia. Francis Nichols became governor of Louisiana, and John S. Marmaduke won the governorship of Missouri. No one has counted the total number of former Rebel officers who became governors, Senators and Congressmen, or elected and appointed state officials, but surely it runs into the thousands. Several even became Republicans, like Longstreet and William Mahone, earning no little criticism from their old comrades in arms. And one, the oft-imposed-upon Simon Buckner, finally had a measure of repayment for the surrenders forced upon him during the war by being nominated for the vice presidency in 1896. His running-mate was one-time Union major general John M. Palmer, and though they lost, still their candidacy truly represented the unity of the re-united states. Buckner's own son and namesake would become a lieutenant general in the United States Army, dying on Okinawa in 1945.[11]

As evidence of the degree to which the officers of the Confederacy assimilated themselves into the Union once again, several of them later re-entered the U.S. Army during the Indian campaigns of the 1870s and 1880s, and most notably during the Spanish-American War. Both Joseph Wheeler and Fitzhugh Lee, major generals in the Confederacy became major generals of volunteers in 1898, and were retired, respectively, in 1900 and 1901, as brigadiers in the Regular Army. Ironically, this made them and all the other ex-Confederate officers who returned to the military eligible to receive a pension from the government they once had fought to overthrow. Only in America.

The Confederates also became active in their own veterans' organization, the United Confederate Veterans, and for decades the old officers once again held sway as the leaders of the local "camps" of the U.C.V. A succession of them acted as grand commanders, their purpose being the care and comfort of aged and infirm former soldiers, and the preservation of the story of the Confederate epic. Indeed, that preservation was on the minds of veterans of both sides. Immediately after Lincoln's assassination, a group of Union officers formed the Military Order of the Loyal Legion of the United States, generally known by its much less cumbersome acronym "MOLLUS." Originally intended as a sort of guard to protect against chaos in the wake of Lincoln's murder, it quickly turned to more peaceful pursuits. State commanderies were established in every Union state, and not many years passed before they began a systematic program of publishing papers by officers recounting their Civil War experiences. While many officers also belonged to the much larger Grand Army of the Republic, or G.A.R, only officers were allowed MOLLUS membership, and the contribution of their collection and publication of memoirs and reminiscences of the war would prove to be a major boon to historians, just as the museums they established in their commanderies kept alive for visitors the exciting years they had shared.

In other spheres, their influence was equally profound. Even more so than their former foes, the officers of the old Union virtually took hold of American politics for two generations. Indeed, in the years following the war, service in that war became almost a prerequisite for winning political office. Only two of the presidents elected during the remainder of the century were not veterans. Andrew Johnson, U.S. Grant, Rutherford B. Hayes, James A. Garfield and Benjamin Harrison had all been generals, and William McKinley, who took office in 1897 and served until his death in 1901, had been a lieutenant in Hayes' regiment. Untold governors and Senators and Congressmen, ambassadors, state legislators, and others sprang from the ranks of the veteran officers of the Union. The United States as a whole was in the firm grip of the men who had led its companies and regiments and armies in the great war for the Union.

Yet the years after the war were not glorious for all of them. When the Union armies demobilized and the nation returned to its old Regular Army establishment, men who had been major generals of volunteers reverted to their old Regular ranks. George Custer, youngest major general in American history in 1865, was a lieutenant colonel of the 7th Cavalry a year later, and in 1876 would die with it at the Little Big Horn. Mackenzie was also destined to become a famed Indian fighter, but the rigors of a lifetime of campaigning finally exacted a toll, and he died in an asylum for the insane. Poor Canby, destined to receive obscure surrenders, suffered an obscure death when three Modoc Indians attacked and murdered him during an 1873 peace negotiation. Rawlins would die in 1871 of tuberculosis, while alcoholism, hard times, or just boredom would kill others. For many of those who had suffered wounds, especially amputations, there were ahead lifetimes of addiction to morphia that started with its use as a pain killer. For every officer who parlayed his service into post-war personal and career success, there were the tragedies of men who, having tasted excitement and responsibility, could never find it again and suffered the inexorable and debilitating gradual descent back into obscurity.

Just as the veteran Yankee officers who did well, rose to greater heights than their old foes after the war, so did the Confederate officers who fared badly, do so more than the Federals. Raphael Semmes and Richard Taylor would die penniless. Forrest never rebuilt the considerable fortune he had when the war started. Bragg was living a hardscrabble existence when he fell dead on a Galveston street in 1876. Buckner did only a little better though he lived a long time and was much honored. Hindman was assassinated in his Helena, Arkansas, home in 1868, and poor Brigadier General Thomas Benton Smith suffered perhaps the worst fate of all. Captured at the Battle of Nashville in December 1864, he was being taken to the rear when, for reasons unknown, Colonel William L. McMillen of the 95th Ohio drew his sword and repeatedly hacked at Smith's head before he could be restrained. The assault left Smith's brain partially exposed, yet miraculously he lived – if it could be called living. Troubled constantly by the wound, he eventually lost his reason and spent forty-seven years in an insane asylum before dying in 1923.[12]

Whereas poor Smith died in obscurity, the already tragic John Bell Hood was under the eyes of the whole South when on August 30, 1879, already bankrupt, he died of yellow fever, along with his wife and one child.

For the officers of lower ranks, the share of success and tragedy proved much the same. Yet one thing they had completely in common with their old foes of the North, and here perhaps the former Confederate officers managed to emerge pre-eminent. Having lost the war, they almost immediately took possession of its presentation to posterity. A flood of memoirs and histories began to emerge from Northern and Southern officers alike almost as soon as the war ended. Captain Ed Porter Thompson of the old 1st Kentucky Brigade actually started writing his history of his unit in 1864, before the war was over, and hundreds more would follow. Having lost the contest by the sword, the old Confederates quickly won it with the pen. In 1876 former officers who had formed the Southern Historical Society began publishing an annual series of "Papers" that would eventually run to more than fifty volumes, providing one of the most reliable and authoritative sources of first-person accounts of the Confederate side of the conflict. Much later, in 1892, former captain Samuel Cunningham started the publication of the *Confederate Veteran* which for forty years would publish articles about the war and veterans' affairs. Jubal Early and a few other officers of the Army of Northern Virginia virtually controlled the Southern Historical Society, presenting an almost officially revealed version of Lee and his campaigns that remained influential for more than a century in Civil War historiography. Indeed, other Confederate officers who dared to write or say anything contradictory – as Longstreet did in his own memoirs – found the Society's *Papers* used as a powerful weapon against them.

The flood of individual recollections was staggering. Hood, Johnston, Beauregard, Longstreet, Early, and dozens of other generals – and hundreds of lower grade officers – wrote their memoirs. The generals were often, like those above, still fighting their old internal battles in their books. One, however, Richard Taylor's *Destruction and Reconstruction,* was of a different stripe, quickly coming to be recognized as perhaps the finest of all Confederate memoirs. For all that their old foes might publish, the portrait of the war presented in these old officers' books still remains the most persuasive version.

The Federal officers were not idle, of course. McClellan, Custer, Sheridan, and dozens of others left behind important books telling their sides of the war. Sherman wrote an unfailingly interesting autobiography, and U.S. Grant, even while dying of cancer, wrote what some regard as the finest American memoir of all time, and certainly one of the greatest books ever written by a soldier. The Federals, too, formed their societies, and more than just the MOLLUS published extensively on the Union side of the war. In the end, nearly 50,000 books and articles would be published on the conflict, perhaps a fifth of them coming from the pens of former officers of Blue or Gray. It was as if the event of their youth had been so great that they could not rid themselves of it, but had to tell and retell again the stories of those days when they all faced death.

A few years after the war's conclusion, ex-Confederate Carlton McCarthy would lament that "the historian who essays to write the grand movements will hardly stop to tell how the hungry private fried his bacon, baked his biscuit, and smoked his pipe." Indeed, for many years the story of the common soldier's war was almost completely ignored. Yet ironically, for all the voluminous memoirs they left behind, the officers of North and South, however well remembered *individually*, have been equally forgotten *collectively*. Perhaps in the flood of books about the generals, people lost sight of the contribution made by the *whole* officer corps of both sides. How the raw young lieutenant learned his drill, led his men, and bore his heavy responsibility, was just as important in determining the course of the war. By all that they left behind, the officers of Blue and Gray showed how much they believed that what they had suffered and done deserved to be kept alive in memory's shrine.[13]

REFERENCES

1 William C. Davis, "The Campaign to Appomattox," *Civil War Times Illustrated*, XIV (April 1975), pp.5, 48.

2 Longstreet, *Manassas to Appomattox*, p.584.

3 Davis, "Appomattox," p.27

4 *Ibid.*, pp.32-3.

5 *Ibid.*, pp.36-8.

6 *Ibid.*, p.41.

7 *Ibid.*, pp.42-8.

8 William T. Sherman, *Memoirs* (New York, 1875), II, pp.349-54; Davis, *Breckinridge*, pp.512-3.

9 Davis, *Breckinridge*, pp.521-40 *passim*.

10 William C. Davis, "Confederate Exiles," *American History Illustrated*, V (June 1970), pp.30-43.

11 Warner, *Generals in Gray*, p.368.

12 "Confederate Generals," *Southern Historical Society Papers*, XXII (1894), pp.65-6; Warner, *Generals in Gray*, p.284.

13 Philip Van Doren Stern, ed., *Soldier Life in the Union and Confederate Armies* (Bloomington, Ind., 1961), p.293.

PART 3
FIGHTING MEN

I
OFF TO WAR

"By gard, if I had known then as much as I do now I would [have] had a hart."[1] The lament of Private Jim Slattery of the 13th Massachusetts spoke volumes about all the trials endured and lessons learned by the three million men who would soon be living out under the open heavens, marching in unison step, and slavishly following the orders of more privileged officers they often regarded as fools. Army food was as yet an unrevealed mystery to them, as were the horrors of military medicine awaiting the sick and wounded, or the prison hells ready to swallow up the captured. The routine of army life for the common soldier would be an awakening for them all, relieved only by those inerasable traits ingrained in the nature of all America's lowly; their folk-humor, rowdiness, the love of sport and frolic, and fear of their god.

And out of their four years of war, these Johnny Rebs and Billy Yanks would forge a legacy uniquely their own. They fought and died as Americans do; the examples of sacrifice and daring they set in campaign and battle would never be surpassed. But they rarely became soldiers. They remained always simple civilians, temporarily "reassigned." Reb and Yank alike carped incessantly at the army and everything in it, and became masters at looking out for themselves.

Most of all, they knew who they were. These simple soldiers were not the planters and politicians who made the war. Yet while they grumbled about its being "a rich man's war and a poor man's fight," they did not shirk that fight. Though at the same time, they had a sense that what they did and suffered might never be recognized. Barely had the war come to an end before one proud Confederate lamented that amid all the outpouring of boastful memoirs and florid accounts of battles and leaders, few "would hardly stop to tell how the hungry private fried his bacon, baked his biscuit, smoked his pipe."[2] They accepted it as part of the lot of the common soldier, a price they paid toward a greater end. Yank and Reb alike could agree with Sergeant Ed English of New Jersey when he wrote in 1862 that, "A man who would not fight for his Country is a scoundral! I cannot get tired of soldiering while the war lasts." He had to be there, for all his unsung trials. "Though humble my position is," he wrote, "gold could not buy me out of the Army."[3]

As the war dragged onward year after year, a time would come when gold was about all that would buy a man *into* the army. The first volunteer enlistments were for terms usually of 90 days – a year at most – when everyone expected the war to end before the summer of 1861 was out. When it did not, many regiments simply ceased to exist, while many more re-enlisted, first for a year, and later on for three years or the term of the war, both North and South. But in the first great rush of enthusiasm and patriotism that followed secession and the firing on Fort Sumter, the fever to volunteer for the fight fed virtually upon itself. Thousands of young men on both sides of Mason and Dixon's line sensed intuitively what the editor in Richmond, Virginia, John M. Daniel expressed in his newspaper: "The great event in all our lives has at last come to pass. A war of gigantic proportions, infinite consequences, and indefinite duration is on us, and will affect the interests and happiness of every man, woman, or child, lofty or humble, in this country. We cannot shun it, we cannot alleviate it, we cannot stop it. We have nothing left now but to fight".[4]

When the English journalist William Howard Russell passed through North Carolina after Fort Sumter, he saw "flushed faces, wild eyes, screaming mouths," and heard men and women shouting so boisterously that nearby bands playing "Dixie" could not be heard.[5] North Carolina was ready to fight, though it was still in the Union. So was Indiana, where Governor Oliver Morton responded to President Lincoln's call for six regiments with the boast that he could furnish fifty times their number. And when a New Yorker asked a recently arrived volunteer from Massachusetts how many other Bay Staters would follow in his wake, he boasted, "How *many?* We're *all* a-coming!"[6]

Spurring them on from every press and pulpit were the fiery exhortations of the zealots who helped bring the conflict in the first place. "I hear Old John Brown knocking on the lid of his coffin and shouting, 'Let me out! Let me out!' cried the abolitionist Henry B. Stanton. "The doom of slavery is at hand. It is to be wiped out in blood. Amen!"[7] And far to the south in New Orleans, a plantation overseer offered up a prayer that, "every Black Republican in the Hole combined whorl Either man woman or chile that is opposed to negro slavery . . . shal be trubled with pestilents & calamitys of all Kinds & Dragout the Balance of there existence in misray & Degradation."[8]

Aroused by such invective, the young manhood of the nation could hardly fail to respond, North or South. The words of the Boston *Herald* thundered just as loud: "In order to preserve this glorious heritage, vouchsafed to us by the fathers of the

Republic, it is essential that every man should perform his whole duty in a crisis like the present."[9] To encourage and profit by the spirited wave sweeping over the continent, every public square and courthouse lawn sprouted mass meetings with stirring martial music, posturing politicians, swaggering young recruiting officers, and an excess of swooning damsels. Aging veterans of bygone days tottered to the stand to remind one and all of their proud traditions. At least one woman in the audience would arise and shout that she would "go in a minute if she were a man," while at a rally in Skowhegan, Maine, a company of ladies manned the village cannon and fired thirty-four rounds.[10]

Then it was time to enlist. "Who will come up and sign the roll?" shouted the recruiting officers, and forward they came, a rushing wall of young men with all the zeal of repenting sinners at a backwoods revival. The whole event played out to the tune of the most shamelessly unselfconscious display of patriotism yet seen. Even some of those in the press who did their best to encourage the feeling had to admit that at times it seemed a bit overdone. "The Star-Spangled Banner rages most furiously," wrote a Detroit editor. "The old inspiring national anthem is played by the bands, whistled by the juveniles, sung in the theatres." Indeed, he heard the anthem, "hammered on tin pans by small boys, and we had almost said barked by the dogs."[11]

They stepped forward for all manner of reasons. For some, in their enthusiasm, enlisting just seemed the right thing to do. Standing back would let down friends and community, even family, risk missing all the fun and glory and, worse, hazard the chance of being branded a coward. The pressures on a young man's pride and sense of honor were profound. Enlisting friends urged their comrades to follow them. Fathers gazed toward the rifle on the wall and lamented that they were too old to go. Worst of all were the sweethearts. "If a fellow wants to go with a girl now he had better enlist," wrote an Indiana boy.[12] The song on the young belles' lips was: "I am Bound to be a Soldier's Wife or Die an Old Maid." When an Alabama youth showed reluctance to rally to the colors, his sweetheart, angry at his behavior, broke off their engagement and sent him a skirt and petticoat with the note: "Wear these or enlist."[13]

More than this appeal to pride and shame, thousands of young men enlisted simply to see a change. The army was something different from struggling behind a plow or scrivening at a desk. War was adventure, the great adventure of their generation. There would be glory, excitement, new places to see. Many of these boys had never been outside their own home counties. The wild life of the army promised enticements that few of them had ever known. And even to men who had seen battle before, the allurement of adventure was the same. Texan Walter P. Lane was forty-five years old and already a veteran of the Texas Revolution and the Mexican War when he enlisted in 1861 as a private in a company of cavalry, "wishing," as he said, "to have a finger in that pie."[14]

Even economics played a part in luring men into the ranks. To be sure, the pay of a Union private was not particularly generous, just $13 a month, while for a

Confederate it would be $2 less. Yet North and South alike were suffering from widespread unemployment and recession, and army pay was enough to live on – and it was supposedly steady. Better yet, many states were paying enlistment bounties or bonuses to those who joined – and later those who re-enlisted – often amounting to several hundred dollars. "It is no use for you to fret or cry about me," explained Enoch Baker of Pennsylvania to his wife, "for you know if I could have got work I wood not have left you and the children."[15] It remained for the years ahead to teach Baker and others that pay would not always be as regular as they supposed. In the South some men would go a year at a time without being paid, only to find their currency so inflated that it bought next to nothing anyway.

Certainly there were loftier motives on both sides. "I tell the boys right to their face I am in the war for the freedom of the slave," declared Chauncey Cooke of Wisconsin.[16] For Cooke and many Northerners like him, the war became in time a crusade to end slavery. "Slavery must die," wrote a Green Mountain corporal, "and if the South insists on being buried in the same grave I shall see in it nothing but the retributive hand of God."[17] Some would even look upon the early years of Yankee failure on the battlefield as a punishment for acquiescing on the issue for so long. Yet their sentiments were much in the minority. Among the two million men who would wear the blue of the Union, less than one in ten felt any real interest in emancipation. And for every Federal who voiced his sympathy for the plight of the slaves, there were a legion of others who disagreed. "If some of the niger lovers want to know what most of the Solgers think of them," wrote Private Charles Babbott of Ohio, "they think about as much as they do a reble. they think they are Shit asses."[18]

Far more pervasive was the sense of duty to cause and country. In the South that meant the defense of its lands and institutions. In Virginia immediately after secession, Benjamin W. Jones found that, "the determination to resist invasion – the first and most sacred duty of a free people – became general, if not universal."[19] That determination sent him into the army, and thousands more with them.

Bred for generations to view Northerners as hypocritical fanatics bent on destroying the Constitution, most Southerners were thoroughly convinced of the righteousness of their cause. Further, theirs was a militant society, and they looked upon themselves as by nature better soldiers and fighters than Yankee shopkeepers. Defense of the South, to them, was as holy a task as the American Revolution, and the enlistees vowed to bear hardships as great as Washington's before they would fail. "I & every Southern Soldier should be like the rebbil blume which plumed more & shinned briter the more it was trampled on & I believe we will have to fight like Washington did," wrote Sergeant John Hagan of Georgia, "but I hope our people will never be reduced to destress & poverty as the people of that day was, but if nothing elce will give us our liberties I am willing for the time to come."[20]

While military inclinations did not dwell in the North in the same degree as they did below the Potomac, still they abided much in the western frontier, where

Lincoln's call for volunteers met with a more enthusiastic reception. Yet, as in the new Confederacy, militarism stood well behind a sense of duty and purpose in impelling those young men to rush forward and sign the muster rolls. "I did not come for money and good living," Private Samuel Croft of Pennsylvania wrote in 1861, looking at the glistening bayonets of his regiment. "Knowing that the bayonets are in loyal hands that will plunge them deep in the hearts of those who have disgraced that flag which has protected them and us, their freedom and ours, I say again I am proud and sanguine of success."[21] Sergeant English of New Jersey, himself the son of Irish immigrants, spoke for all, native or foreign-born: "The blind acts of unqualified generals and Statesmen have had no lasting impression on the motives which first prompted me to take up arms or chilled my patriotism in the least," he wrote in 1863. "As long as God spares my health and strength to wield a weapon in Freedom's defense, I will do it."[22]

For all the differences that brought about the war, and those that impelled the men on either side to enlist, the Northerners and Southerners who rushed to take up arms were more alike than not. They came overwhelmingly from the farms of rural America; and not just in ones or twos. Whole companies and regiments were raised in the same locality, bringing with them their own local values and customs.

Fully one half of the men who donned the blue had been farmers, and almost two-thirds of the new Confederates were trading the plow for the gun. Carpenters, clerks, laborers, and students made up much of the remainder, but in fact over 300 different occupations were represented in the Union Army, and over 100 in the Confederate. In the North, it would be rare for any trade not to have at least one member in a brigade, which afforded the new regiments a remarkable self-sufficiency in the field. When a weapon or piece of equipment fell in need of repair, there was usually someone near at hand with the experience and knowledge to set it aright. The South would suffer somewhat thanks to a lesser degree of diversity, and no one ever knew quite what to do with those soldiers who listed as their pre-war occupation that of "gentlemen."

Just as the majority on both sides were white, native-born, Protestant, and unmarried, so were they all primarily young men. Four out of five in both armies were between eighteen and twenty-nine. Many sixteen and seventeen year olds wrote the numeral "18" on slips of paper and put them in their shoes. When asked by a recruiting officer how old they were, they could say that they were "over eighteen." The youngest Confederate soldier was probably Charles C. Hay of Alabama. He was just eleven when he enlisted in 1861. He was not alone in his youth, for many other children served in the Southern armies. Indeed, after the brief fight at Farmington, Mississippi on May 9, 1862, General P.G.T. Beauregard called the "especial attention of the Army to the behavior of Private John Mather Sloan of the 9th Texas, a lad of only 13 years of age." The boy lost a leg in the fighting, but could only exclaim that "I have but one regret I shall not soon be able to get at the enemy."[23] The youngest soldier of the war, however, Private Edward Black, joined the 21st Indiana as a musician, aged nine.

While the youth of the soldiers enlivened camp life and infused an enthusiasm in battle that enhanced morale, the armies took some stability from the maturity of soldiers at the other end of the allotted three score and ten. Not all of the drummers in uniform were the children of folklore. David Scantlon of the 4th Virginia was fully fifty-two years old. A member of Virginia's Richmond Howitzers recalled knowing personally, "six men over sixty years who volunteered, and served in the ranks, throughout the war."[24] In North Carolina, in July 1862, E. Pollard joined the 5th Infantry and gave his age as sixty-two, though he was probably above seventy and had to be discharged soon after for being "incapable of performing the duties of a soldier on account of rheumatism and old age."[25] Yet once more it was left to the Yankees to reach the greatest extreme. Curtis King was the oldest soldier of the war when he enlisted in the 37th Iowa in November 1862, aged eighty.

Whatever their age, they were healthy men, inured by the hard life of the fields or the factories. The ruggedness of military life posed few challenges to their hardened constitutions. "I am well, and I think this kind of life agrees with me," a Virginia cavalryman wrote to his family in the autumn of 1861. "I weigh the same as I did when I left home – one hundred and twenty-five pounds – but all there is of me is bone and muscle, very tough and very active."[26] The men tended to be lean when they enlisted, and to stay that way. No one grew fat on army grub and marching.

Neither were they overly tall. The average ran between five feet five inches and five feet nine. The shortest Federal had to hustle some to keep up with his comrades in the 192nd Ohio. He was just three feet four inches from sole to kepi, and it would have taken two of him, end to end, to approach the tallest Yankee. Captain David Van Buskirk of the 27th Indiana stood just an inch short of seven feet, the loftiest pinnacle in a 100-man company that boasted eighty men above six feet. The 380-pound Van Buskirk was described as "a 'whale', but some of the others are whales, too, but a trifle smaller." When he was captured in 1862 and sent to a Richmond prison, Van Buskirk became such a curiosity that a Rebel entrepreneur put him on exhibit as a freak, labeled "the biggest Yankee in the world." Even President Jefferson Davis came to see him, to be astounded when the impish Van Buskirk claimed that, "Back home in Bloomington, Indiana I have six sisters." They told him goodbye when his company marched off to war, he said. "As I was standing with my company, they all walked up, leaned down and kissed me on top of my head."[27]

But undoubtedly the loftiest man of the entire war was Private Henry C. Thruston of Texas. He enlisted in a Morgan County company with his four brothers, the shortest of whom stood six feet six inches! Incredibly, this ample target served through the war taking only two wounds, one of them a grazing on the top of his head, a rare occasion when firing "too high" was no problem for the enemy. When not in his top hat, Thruston stood seven feet, seven and one-half inches, a genuine Texas tall tale.[28]

Whatever made them different or the same, most of the men North and South who answered the call were native-born Americans. Yet stepping forward with them, to lend their own special talents and accent to Civil War soldiering, were tens of thousands of foreigners of every caste and nationality. Company H of the 8th Michigan numbered among its men, 47 New Yorkers, 37 Michiganders, 26 other native Americans, 7 Canadians, 5 Englishmen, 4 Germans, 2 Irishmen, 1 Scotsman, 1 Dutchman, and one mysterious fellow who simply listed his nationality as "the ocean."[29]

It was hardly an unusual national mix in the Union army. Some camps were a virtual babel. In one Yankee regiment hosting fifteen different national origins, the colonel had to give orders in seven separate languages. Many of the immigrants spoke English indifferently at best, making communication often a nightmare. In Major General Franz Sigel's command in 1864, his orders given in German had to go through three successive translations from German to Hungarian to English, and back to German, before they filtered through his international staff to his German-born men in the ranks. He was never a great general, but given the party game nature of his chain of communications, it was a miracle that all of his men even marched in the same direction.

These immigrants had come rushing to America, refugees from the European upheavals of the 1850s and the Irish potato famines. Available land and work attracted the majority of them to the North so that by 1860, nearly a third of the North's male population were foreign born. The fact that Lincoln gave general's commissions to popular men like Franz Sigel, Carl Schurz, Thomas Meagher, and others, was a powerful inducement for their fellow immigrants to enlist enthusiastically under their banners.

Over 200,000 Germans served in the Northern armies, with several regiments composed entirely of them. The 9th Wisconsin did not number a single non-German in its ranks. New York furnished ten regiments that were predominantly composed of Germans, and Ohio did the same. "I fights mit Sigel," many of them sang as they marched off to war, only to learn that they were often despised by native-born soldiers, and that their beloved Sigel was an incompetent who got a good many of them killed. Fellow Yankees regarded them as "dumb Dutchmen." Worse, because they were often ill-led, as with the Union XI Corps, they suffered more than their share of defeats and panics. But the "Dutchmen" were technically skilled and suited by culture to military discipline, which, added to their impeccable devotion to the Union cause, made them valuable allies. Philip Smith of the 8th Missouri, a German immigrant, wrote in his diary on the day after the defeat at Bull Run that he had: "grasped the weapon of death for the purpose of doing my part in defending and upholding the integrity, laws and the preservation of my adopted country from a band of contemptible traitors who would if they can accomplish their hellish designs, destroy the best and noblest government on earth."[30]

Much the same sentiment would be heard from the Irishmen wearing the blue. But they were a different sort of soldier entirely. While many joined to save the Union, it has to be said that quite a few of the 150,000 who served the North were in it purely out of the Celtic love of a fight. "There is an elasticity in the Irish temperament which enables its possessor to boldly stare Fate in the face, and laugh at all the reverses of fortune," wrote Felix Brannigan of the 79th New York.[31] In the fight at Winchester, Virginia, in September 1864, an officer reported seeing one "wild looking Irishman" who was loading and firing his weapon as fast as he could, mumbling an occasional prayer, and shouting as he fired, "Now Jeff Davis, you son of a bitch, take that," giving his head a twist at the same time and his eyes looking wildly in front.[32]

At least twenty regiments, most notably Meagher's Irish Brigade of the 9th, 63rd, and 88th New York, were composed almost entirely of men from Ireland. These Irish soldiers were rowdy and insubordinate, but they were also fierce fighters, especially on the offensive. As one of their generals said, "I would prefer Irish soldiers to any other." They had more dash, more élan, were more cheerful, and more enduring than other soldiers. "They make the finest soldiers that ever shouldered a musket."[33] And they never lost their good humor. At the Battle of Ocean Pond, Florida, in 1864, Brigadier General Joseph Finnegan, himself an Irishman, yelled to his son and aide, "Go to the rear, Finnegan, me b'ye, go to the rear! Ye know ye are yer mither's darlin'!"

Over 60,000 Englishmen and Canadians served the Union, as well as a varied selection of Frenchmen, Scandinavians, Hungarians, and even a very few Orientals. The 79th New York was made up mostly of Scotsmen who wore kilts early in the war, until the derisive laughter of fellow soldiers every time they climbed over a fence drove them to adopt trousers.[34]

In 1864 Colonel Theodore Lyman, of General George G. Meade's headquarters, sneered: "By the Lord! I wish these gentlemen who would overwhelm us with Germans, negroes, and the offscourings of great cities, could only see – only *see* – a Rebel regiment, in all their rags and squalor. If they had eyes they would know that these men are like wolf-hounds, and not to be beaten by turnspits."[35] Foreign-born soldiers were never popular with their native-born counterparts.

Yet some of those Rebel "wolf-hounds" were themselves immigrants, though in far smaller numbers. There was one brigade of Irishmen, several German regiments, as well as a Polish "legion." A European brigade of mixed nationalities came from Louisiana, and was commanded by the resplendent French Count Camille Armand Jules Marie, Prince de Polignac. His men abbreviated that considerably, and simply called him "Polecat." A company of Georgia mountaineers listened in utter marvel as the Prince gave his orders in French. "That-thur furriner he calls out er lot er gibberish," drawled one, "an thum-thur Dagoes jes maneuvers-up like Hell-beatin'-tanbark! Jes like he was talking sense!"[36]

Often overlooked in both armies were the much smaller numbers of native minorities who wore blue and gray. Perhaps as many as 12,000 Indians served the Confederacy, most of them members of the Five Civilized Tribes living out in the Indian Territory. In all, the Confederates would raise some eleven regiments and seven battalions of Indian cavalry out there, not to mention a few hundred other red men scattered through some of the white Confederate regiments from North Carolina, Tennessee, and Kentucky. They did not exactly look the picture of the Rebel soldier. "Their faces were painted, and their long straight hair, tied in a queue, hung down behind," wrote a Missouri Confederate. "Their dress was chiefly in the Indian costume – buckskin hunting-shirts, dyed of almost every color, leggings, and moccasins of the same material, with little bells, rattles, ear-rings, and similar paraphernalia. Many of them were bareheaded and about half carried only bows and arrows, tomahawks, and war-clubs."[37]

Ill-treated and ignored even by their own superiors, the Indian soldiers had only half a heart in the cause, and much the same could be said of the 6,000 or more who wore the blue. All too often they were enlisted only to take advantage of old tribal hatreds, pitting Union Indian against Confederate Indian, and all too often they ignored army regulations and fought in the old ways. But they certainly lent color to the muster rolls of North and South. Spring Frog, John Bearmeat, Alex Scarce Water, Big Mush Dirt Eater, Warkiller Hogshooter, George Hogtoter, and Jumper Duck, were all soldiers of the Union, and these were simply anglicizations of Indian names probably impossible to pronounce.[38] In the Confederate First Kentucky Brigade there served a Mohawk sachem named Konshattountzchette, whose name was spelled in so many different ways that his official record could never agree with itself. His fellow soldiers simply preferred to call him Flying Cloud.[39]

Native born, too, were the few thousand Mexican-Americans who took up arms. The 1st New Mexico was known as Martinez' Militia during its Union service, and two Colorado regiments contained far more Sanchez' than Smiths.[40] On the other side sat the 33rd Texas, led in part by Refugio Benevides and manned mostly by Mexicans. They, like the Indians, would receive little attention from their government.

But not so the continent's largest minority. Out in Kansas in 1863, Major General James G. Blunt spoke of the non-white soldiers in his command, and declared emphatically that, "I would not exchange one regiment of negro troops for ten regiments of Indians."[41] Blacks, too, would step forward to the recruiter, though not without the trials and setback that ever accompanied their progress in America. Yet they would fight and prove themselves.

Many openly argued against enrolling blacks, both among civilians and white soldiers. "Thair is a great Controversy out hear about the niggar Question at present," wrote an enlisted man of the 110th Pennsylvania. "If they go to Sending them out hear to fight they will get Enough of it for it Will raise a rebelion in the army that all the abolisionist this Side of hell Could not Stop. the Southern peopel are rebels to the government but thay are White and God never intended a nigger to put white peopel down."[42] Besides fears that arming Negroes would degrade the army, and even risk rebellion among them, most asserted that it would be a threat to white rule. "They are good for such purposes as throwing up breastworks and digging canals," said an Illinois private, "but I cannot think they are a class that should be armed."[43]

By late 1861 abolitionists and poiliticians began to argue that the Union Army could use black numbers to bring a speedy conclusion to the war, and at the same time the army would teach them discipline and prepare them for their place in postwar society – whatever that place was to be. But the issue was politically explosive, especially in the still loyal slave states like Missouri and Kentucky, and Lincoln had to be wary. Not until September 1862, after a string of humiliating defeats, was Lincoln ready to risk his Emancipation Proclamation. The border states were at least secure to the Union now, and redirecting the war into a crusade for black freedom would strengthen the North with European powers wavering between Union and Confederacy. Lincoln declared the Proclamation as a military necessity which craftily opened the way for him to authorize enlistment of black soldiers in January 1863.

Gradually most Northerners came around to the notion. As the sight of Negroes in uniform became more and more commonplace, they were slowly accepted, though not as equals. White soldiers welcomed them to do menial tasks like digging ditches and latrines, thus saving the whites those duties, while ambitious young officers saw opportunities for advancement by taking higher commissions in black regiments. Not until the war's end would there be a very few Negro officers in their own outfits, and not until 1864 would be the black soldier finally receive the same pay as his white comrade. There was open discrimination of every kind, but they endured.

The worst hostility came from white soldiers, some of whom believed that authorities favored the blacks. After a day of shoveling mud in December 1864, a New Hampshire soldier grumbled that, "Some of the Boys say that Army Moto is First the Negro, then the mule, then the white man."[44] Most thought blacks were lazy and insolent, and many resented the Negro as the primary reason that they were all fighting in the first place. "I have slept on the soft side of a board, in the mud, and every other place that was lousey and dirty," grumbled Private Richard Puffer of the 8th Illinois. "I have drank out of goose ponds, horse tracks, etc., for the last eighteen months, all for the poor nigger; and I have yet to see the first one that I think has been benifitted by it."[45]

Blacks and whites were often in fights when they met outside their encampments, and not a few Billy Yanks were just as ready to shoot a Negro as a Confederate. In the battle at Ocean Pond, or Olustee, in February 1864, a Virginia Rebel wrote that, "The negroes saw a hard time; those who stood were shot by our men, those who ran by the Yankees."[46]

In the end, some spirit of comradeship arose with a few white soldiers. What changed white soldiers' – and civilians' – minds the most was the black man's performance in battle.

General Blunt's declaration about the worth of a Negro regiment came from first-hand knowledge. During the last three years of the war, black Yankee regiments participated in 39 major battles and over 400 skirmishes, and Blunt himself led them in battle at Honey Springs, in the Indian Territory, on July 17, 1863. Opposing Confederates had brought slave shackles with them, expecting to take the blacks. Instead, Blunt's 1st Kansas Colored Volunteers routed them. While abolitionists constantly overrated black solders' qualities, and opponents underrated them, nevertheless much of their subsequent behavior on the battlefield was outstanding. Particularly at Port Hudson, Louisiana, in May 1863, and at Fort Wagner, South Carolina, two months later, Negro regiments distinguished themselves.

They did so at considerable extra risk not faced by whites, for the Confederate government never countenanced blacks as legitimate solders. Enraged Southern soldiers sometimes murdered those that fell into their hands, and later in the war a few "massacres" occurred. Even when the politically motivated rhetoric is sifted for exaggeration, still it is certain that most especially at Saltville, Virginia and Fort Pillow, Tennessee – both in 1864 – hundreds of defenseless blacks were murdered.

Nevertheless black troops did win acceptance and even a measure of respect. A total of 176,895 of them served the Union, and 68,100 – more than a third – died in uniform, mostly from disease. Yet nearly 3,000 of them fell in battle, and the Yankee government acknowledged their bravery by awarding at least twenty-one of them its newly created Medal of Honor. Just after the Battle of Nashville in December 1864, Major General George H. Thomas rode over the bloody field where blacks lay in death beside whites. "Gentlemen, the question is settled," he said to his staff. "Negroes will fight."[47]

It was a question, however, that would never be answered in the Confederacy, and was dangerous even to ask. With 3 million slaves and 135,000 free blacks in the South in 1861, Rebels had an enormous manpower reserve if they had chosen to mobilize it. Many of the slaves felt great loyalty to their masters. Several hundred asked to be allowed to take arms to defend a Southern homeland that was *theirs,* too, when war broke out. And many did go to war as cooks and servants, occasionally even performing picket duty.

In a few cases, blacks informally served Confederate soldiers. The 9th Virginia listed Jacob Jones as a musician, and another black known only as "Joe" served as a teamster with the 13th Virginia Cavalry. Occasionally in battle one of these blacks, caught up in it all, would grasp a fallen weapon and go into fight himself. But Confederates had a deep-felt conviction that giving Negroes any sort of chance for equality posed a mortal threat to Southern culture. "The day you make soldiers of them," said Georgia statesman Howell Cobb, "is the beginning of the end of the revolution. If slaves will make good soldiers, our whole theory of slavery is wrong."[48]

Only as the war was coming to a close, in March 1865, in response to foreign pressure, and by the slimmest of votes, did the Confederate Congress approve legislation authorizing black enlistments. One such unit did appear in Richmond, only days before the city fell. Whites standing by threw mud at them when they marched past.

White or black, red or brown, native or immigrant, once enrolled all of these Johnny Rebs and Billy Yanks were much the same – raw, untrained, unready new recruits, with no resemblance to real soldiers. Sometimes they banded together in informal companies before setting off for the camps of instruction. "There was nothing very martial in the appearance of the company," recalled a Virginian of Lee's Light Horse of Westmoreland County. "The officers and men were clad in their citizen's dress, and their horses caparisoned with saddles and bridles of every description used in the country. Their only arms were sabres and double-barrelled shotguns collected from the homes of the people."[49]

The mandatory physical examination they received on arrival at the rendezvous camp was barely cursory at best, often nothing more than a few questions. "You have pretty good health, don't you?" a surgeon asked Charles Barker of the 23rd Massachusetts. When Barker allowed that he did, the surgeon felt his collarbone, asked if he suffered from fits or piles, and promptly pronounced him fit for duty.[50] No small wonder then that as many as 400 women actually managed to pose as men, enlist, and serve in the ranks. One of them, Jennie Hodgers, enlisted in the 95th Illinois as Albert Cashier, served entirely through the war without discovery, and continued her pose until struck by an automobile in 1911. When that revealed her sex, one of her old messmates recalled of their enlistment that, "when we were examined we were not stripped. All that we showed were our hands and feet."[51]

Once past the surgeons, the men – and women – formally swore to "bear true allegiance" to their government and its flag and "to serve them honestly and faithfully against all their enemies or opposers whatsoever, and observe and obey the rules of the President," and so forth. It was their final act as civilians.

REFERENCES

1 Arthur A. Kent, Three Years with Company K (Cranbury, N.J., 1976), pp.15-16.

2 Bell I. Wiley, *The Life of Johnny Reb* (Indianapolis, Ind., 1943), p.13.

3 Bell I. Wiley, "A Time of Greatness," *Journal of Southern History*, XXII (February 1956), p.23.

4 Frederick S. Daniel, *The Richmond Examiner During the War* (New York, 1868), p.13.

5 William Howard Russell, *My Diary North and South* (Boston, 1863), p.92.

6 Allan Nevins, *The War for the Union* (New York, 1959-71), I, p.88.

7 James M. McPherson, *Ordeal by Fire* (New York, 1982), pp.149-50.

8 Wiley, *Johnny Reb*, pp.16-17.

9 Howard C. Perkins (ed.), *Northern Editorials on Secession* (New York, 1942), II, p.731.

10 Bell I. Wiley, *The Life of Billy Yank* (Indianapolis, Ind., 1951), p.18.

11 *Ibid.*, p.18.

12 *Ibid.*, p.21.

13 Bell I. Wiley, *Confederate Women* (Westport, Conn., 1975), p.142.

14 Walter P. Lane, *Adventures and Recollections of. . .* (Austin, Tex., 1970), p.83.

15 Wiley, *Billy Yank*, p.38.

16 *Ibid.,* pp.40-1.

17 *Ibid.,* p.42.

18 *Ibid.,* p.43.

19 B.W. Jones, *Under the Stars and Bars* (Richmond, 1909), p.1.

20 Wiley, "Time of Greatness," p.22.

21 *Ibid.,* p.23.

22 *Ibid.,* p.23.

23 Wiley, *Johnny Reb,* p.332.

24 William M. Dame, *From the Rapidan to Richmond and the Spotsylvania Campaign* (Baltimore, 1920), pp.2-3.

25 Weymouth T. Jordan (comp.), *North Carolina Troops, 1861-1865: A Roster* (Raleigh, N.C., 1966), V, p.180.

26 Susan L. Blackford (comp.), *Letters from Lee's Army* (New York, 1947), pp.48-9.

27 Roger S. Durham, "The Biggest Yankee in the World," *Civil War Times Illustrated,* XIII (May 1974), pp.29, 31.

28 "The Tallest Confederate," *Civil War Times Illustrated,* XIII (November 1974), p.42

29 Wiley, *Billy Yank,* p.311

30 Bell, I. Wiley, *The Common Soldier of the Civil War* (New York, 1975), p.79.

31 *Ibid.,* p.102.

32 *Ibid.,* p.103.

33 *Ibid.,* p.106.

34 Bell I. Wiley, and Hirst D. Millhollen, *They Who Fought Here* (New York, 1959), pp.8-9.

35 Theodore Lyman, *Meade's Headquarters, 1863-1865* (Boston, 1922), p.208.

36 James C. Nisbet, *Four Years on the Firing Line* (Chattanooga, 1915), p.46.

37 Wiley, *Johnny Reb,* p.325.

38 Wiley, *Billy Yank,* pp.316-17.

39 William C. Davis, *The Orphan Brigade* (New York, 1980), p.102.

40 Wiley, *Billy Yank,* p.310.

41 *Ibid.,* p.319.

42 Bell I. Wiley, "Billy Yank and the Black Folk," *Journal of Negro History,* XXXVI (Spring 1951), p.48.

43 "War Diary of Thaddeus H. Capron, 1861-1865," *Journal of the Illinois State Historical Society,* XII (1919), p.358.

44 Wiley, *Billy Yank,* p.109.

45 Leo M. Kaiser, ed., "Letters from the Front," *Journal of the Illinois State Historical Society,* LVI (Summer, 1963), p.154

46 Robert U. Johnson and C.C. Buel (eds.), *Battles and Leaders of the Civil War* (New York, 1884-88), IV, p.418.

47 Dudley T. Cornish, *The Sable Arm* (New York, 1956), p.261.

48 U.S. War Department, *War of the Rebellion: Official Records of the Union and Confederate Armies* (Washington, 1880-1901), Series IV, Volume III, pp.1009-10.

49 R.L.T. Beale, *History of the Ninth Virginia Cavalry in the War Between the States* (Richmond, 1899), p.9.

50 Wiley, *Billy Yank,* p.23

51 *Ibid.,* pp.337-8.

II

DRILL, DRILL & MORE DRILL

The first basic training the new recruits received frequently took place at the regimental rendezvous, well before the men marched away to join the armies. A little drill, some exposure to weapons, informal organization into companies, and perhaps the issuing of uniforms, was all they did. In many regiments, an additional ritual was the election of their officers.

These were volunteer outfits, and the custom in the old Union for decades had been for volunteers to select their own commanders. There were good reasons for such a seemingly unmilitary practice. For one thing, many regiments were raised by the personal magnetism and local reputation of one or two individuals, and men who enlisted because of their regard for the man who recruited them would naturally want him to command. Also, independent as always, the American citizen-soldier would resent having some outsider imposed upon him by the War Department. The policy inevitably led to all manner of excesses, with venal men bribing others to vote for them. The system, unfortunately, led to a host of inexperienced and incompetent men being put in command of regiments, where only time would weed them out.

Inevitably a delegation of ladies from hometowns came to the public square on departure day to bestow an ornate flag, frequently sewn from their wedding dresses, upon the regiment. Flowery fustian speeches invariably accompanied the proceeding. "This eve we were presented with a flag by the Ladies of this town," a Bay State officer wrote on July 22, 1861. "A very homely young lady (though she was the best looking one in town) made a speech which she learned (at least she thought so, but I did not for she went through with [it] about as smooth as one might come down a rocky hill in the dark)."[1] Then an officer accepted the proffered banner in glowing words of thanks and promised never to disgrace the cloth.

Sometimes the ceremony did not go too well. In Fayetteville, North Carolina, the ladies of that town came up with the flag well enough, but all were too shy to attempt to make the obligatory speech. Instead, they asked a local orator of some small repute to do it for them. Alas, he appeared on the stand apparently much the worse for drink, wavered on his feet and plunged through his speech by fits and starts, then proceeded to repeat most of it over a second time. That done, overcome, he sank into his chair and wept.[2]

Stirring as such festivities could be, and often were, the big moment in the recruit's life came when he and his regiment left for the field. It was a time of mixed feelings: elation at the glorious prospect ahead, and sadness in parting from family and friends. A reporter found a company of students from the University of Iowa "in first rate spirits" and "rightly impressed with the patriotic duty confided to their hearts and muskets." Yet many a soldier suffered last-minute second thoughts about leaving. "One of the men whilst bidding his wife good buy Whimpered a little and Showed Signs of backout," wrote William Shaw. "His Wife told him if he was agoing to Cry about it to pull off his Breeches and she would put them on and go in his place and he might go home and tend the Farm."[3]

It was a host of average and unusual units that said those farewells and marched or sailed or steamed off to war. Four out of five of them were infantry, the backbone of the army. Artillery comprised only six percent of both armies, and cavalry made up the rest. On either side, these units reflected the colorful diversity of Americans in culture, education, and taste. The Richmond Howitzers, the Washington Artillery of New Orleans, South Carolina's Hampton Legion, and the Oglethorpe Light Infantry of Savannah, boasted the affluent and educated flower of Confederate society. Lexington, Virginia's Washington College furnished seventy-three students for the Liberty Hall Volunteers – fully a quarter of them studying for the ministry. At the opposite extreme were companies of farmboys so raw and unschooled that over a quarter of the men in the 11th North Carolina's Company A, for example, could not sign their names, and exactly half of the recruits for another company could only make their mark on the muster roll when they enlisted.

They marched out of their hometowns garbed not only in righteousness, but also cloaked in nicknames calculated to terrify the enemy. Out of the woods and hills of the Confederacy came the "Tallapoosa Thrashers," the "Bartow Yankee Killers," the "Dixie Heroes," "Hornet's Nest Riflemen," "Clinch Mountain Boomers," "Franklin Fire Eaters," and the "Tyranny Unmasked Artillery." It would be hard to decide just who was to be intimidated, however, by the one East Tennessee company enigmatically known as "Bell's Babies."[4]

The North, too, had its share of unusual outfits. The 7th New York, composed of the fashionable elite of Grammarcy Park, went to war with 1,000 velvet-covered footstools among its equippage. "Birney's Zouaves," the 23rd Pennsylvania, averaged just nineteen years of age in the ranks, while the 37th Iowa was restricted to men over forty-five and, not surprisingly, was known as the "Graybeard Regiment." To enlist in "Ellsworth's Avengers," the 44th New York, a recruit had to be unmarried, thirty, at least five feet eight inches tall, and of demonstrably good moral character. The officers of the 48th New York were all ministers of the gospel, and in honor of their colonel called themselves "Perry's Saints." The 33rd Illinois contained so many college professors that it became known as the "Teacher's Regiment." Its officers were frequently accused of ignoring any order that was not framed in precisely the correct spelling and syntax. A vow to "touch not, taste not, handle not spiritous or malt liquor, wine or cider," led a band of Iowans to be dubbed the "Temperance Regiment."[5]

By the second half of the war, however, the men marching off to the regiments were not to be so high-toned. The battlefield was a voracious consumer of men, and as the war dragged onward without conclusion, the first enthusiastic and patriotic rush of enlistments settled down to a trickle. The most motivated men had signed on early. What remained were the under- and over-age, the uninterested, the infirm and the cowardly. Inevitably the need to fill the vacancies in the ranks forced both the governments of Washington and Richmond to resort to conscription, the military draft. It was never popular with anyone, and unfortunately it tended to bring into service many of the least desirable, with the result that the overall quality of soldier in the regiments declined steadily after 1863.

Ironically, the threat of the draft actually inspired many men to join of their own volition. Better that than be branded as a conscript, and at least an enlistee usually got a cash bonus. "God knows that the country needs men and I regard it as the duty of every able bodied man who can possibly do so to enlist at once, the sooner the better," wrote W.H. Jackson of Vermont, adding "and it is better by far to enlist voluntarily than to be dragged into the army a conscript. Nothing to me would appear more degrading."[6]

Conscripts, substitutes – those whom wealthy men paid to go to war in their place – and naive youths flooded into the Northern and Southern armies after 1863. The lines drawn along wealth and class by the substitute system rankled the poor especially. "All they want is to get you pupt up and go to fight for their infurnal negroes," complained an Alabama hill farmer, "and after you do there fighting you may kiss there hine parts fur all they care."[7] The lament of it being a "rich man's war and a poor man's fight" was heard on both sides of Mason and Dixon's line.

Another problem with these later recruits was the condition they were in when they reached the camps. Doctors, themselves often not too competent, were shocked at what they saw. Some recruitment "brokers," who received a commission for every man they induced to enlist, actually persuaded inmates of a New York insane asylum to sign up as substitutes, leaving it to the army physicians to worry over what to do with them. A New York artillery unit had to eliminate more than a third of its new replacements in 1864, all for unsound health. Men commonly showed up with missing or impaired limbs, failed eyesight and hearing, and often communicable diseases. As a result, the veterans in the ranks felt a natural skepticism toward the new recruits in later years, sometimes approaching loathing.

"They were moral lepers," complained one Yankee. "They were conscienceless, cowardly scoundrels, and the clean-minded American and Irish and German volunteers would not associate with them." They were, he protested, "the weak, the diseased, the feeble-minded, the scum of the slums of the great European and American cities." Many were blackguards, and others "the rakings of rural almshouses and the never-do-wells of villages." Such strong words about "the worthless character of the recruits who were supplied to the army" were commonplace, and few veterans would have offered a dissent.[8] Sergeant Charles Loehr of the 1st Virginia Cavalry looked at a number of replacements received late in 1864 and complained that "some of them looked like they had been resurrected from the grave, after laying therein for twenty years or more."[9] A New Englander was even more emphatic when he declared that "such another depraved, vice-hardened and desperate set of human beings never before disgraced an army."[10]

Undoubtedly much of this disdain stemmed from the widely known fact that a huge proportion of these later recruits would desert, many of them men who enlisted under false names to get a bounty, fully intending to run away at the first opportunity to enlist again and again under different names. The only salutary effect of the sorry business was that the men who stayed in the ranks were the better soldiers, and seasoned veterans. "If new men won't finish the job," said one man from Massachusetts, "old men must, and as long as Uncle Sam wants a man," he was ready and willing to stay in the service.[11] Thus it would be left chiefly to the real Johnny Rebs and Billy Yanks to finish off what they had begun. The original volunteers of 1861 and 1862 re-enlisted in vast numbers when their first hitches expired, evidence that though their enthusiasm might have been tempered, yet their conviction to the cause and sense of duty remained high.

Perhaps it was also in part due to the fact that the old veterans knew the life of the soldier intimately, and had grown accustomed to it, however much they might resent and resist its regimentation. Certainly they knew all too well the endless lot of the private soldier, and that was drill. The first taste they had seen of marching in time and step in their recruiting camps hardly prepared them for the incessant bondage to drum and bugle to follow. Private Oliver Norton of the 83rd Pennsylvania aptly captured the essence of the military's preoccupation with evolutions. "The first thing in the morning is drill," he wrote home, "then drill, then drill again. Then drill, drill, a little more drill. Then drill, and lastly drill. Between drills, we drill and sometimes stop to eat a little and have roll-call."[12]

Those first days in training camp were hectic and confused. At 5 a.m. the reveille calls of the bugles jarred sleep-fuddled men out of their blankets more rudely than the wakening calls of the mothers and wives they had left behind. For the farmboys, the early rising was little problem, but for the city-bred and the sons of wealthy planters and businessmen, being aroused before dawn took more than a little getting used to. Almost drunkenly they shambled out onto the company street or parade ground and stumbled to find their places in the line, pulling on what clothes they had remembered or were able to find in the dark. "Some wore one shoe, and others appeared shivering in their line," newspaperman George Townsend wrote. "They stood ludicrously in rank, and a succession of short, dry coughs ran up and down the line."[13]

Even at this early hour there could be some drilling in store for them before they were sent to their breakfast. Then came guard posting and sick call, followed by the host of chores necessary to keep the camp neat and – when possible – clean. Then came "dinner," the noonday meal, several hours of fatigue duty, and two or three more hours of regimental drill. Around 5 p.m., when they had already been actively engaged for a full twelve hours, the men returned to their tents with an hour to prepare themselves and their weapons and equipment for the 6 o'clock dress parade. That done, supper was waiting for them in the huge boiling cauldrons at the mess tents, and then, finally, they had a couple of precious hours to themselves before the 9 o'clock "lights out." It has been a packed day for the new men, and each day was just like the one before it, with only some respite on Sundays with church services and perhaps a few extra afternoon hours of free time.

Much of this unrelenting activity was designed to keep the soldiers too busy to get into trouble, as well as to accustom them to following orders automatically and without question. Neither goal was ever achieved entirely. "We had good organization, good men, but no cohesion," William T. Sherman lamented after the Federal defeat at First Manassas or Bull Run in July 1861; "no respect for authority, no real knowledge of war."[14] The soldier hated taking orders, and many officers shrank from giving them. Men obeyed those directives which seemed sensible and sound to them, but often only because they saw the use of such orders. If a man, a volunteer, doubted the wisdom of an order, he was very likely to question it at least, and refuse to obey at worst. Additionally the close personal familiarity between officers and men worked against discipline. Men in the ranks could find their brothers and childhood playmates put in positions of authority and it was hard to stand quietly and stoically take orders from someone they had grown up with. It was hard to salute and stand at attention before one whom the private saw not as his officer but as a neighboring farmer, the village blacksmith, or perhaps his old school teacher.

It was to break down all these impediments to discipline that the war departments of North and South imposed a regimen of drill and training upon their soldiers. In fact, since both Union and Confederate armies were largely officered in the early days by men who had served in the pre-1861 military service, the "Old Army" as it was called, and since many had shared military education at the United States Military Academy at West Point, the manuals and methods they used to train the new regiments were virtually identical North and South.

There were a number of drill manuals available, including one penned by General Winfield Scott in 1835, a translation of a French work. By 1860, however, most of his work had been revised and updated by William J. Hardee, soon to become a Confederate lieutenant general. *Hardee's Tactics*, as it became known, was the most influential manual in the first two years of the war, especially since it included maneuvers designed to incorporate the influence of the relatively new rifled musket upon the movement of men. Indeed, so versatile was *Hardee's* that it came out in several editions "tailored" for its users, including one for black troops, another for the fancy French-inspired zouave regiments, another for the use of militia, several Southern editions, and one Northern edition which omitted Hardee's name from the title page.

Hardee exerted a lot of influence on the Civil War battlefield. He prescribed that the line of battle move in two ranks, one behind the other. Skirmishers who moved in advance of the main lines were to operate in four-man squads, and the time-step at which men moved was updated to allow for a "double quick" speed of up to 180 steps a minute. With a rifled musket able to fire two or three rounds per minute in the hands of skilled infantrymen, soldiers had to move faster than ever. Hardee decreed that markmanship had to be improved through target practice, and that some units be designated to move at a rate of five miles per hour while still keeping order. In the main, however, it was still a manual in the Napoleonic tradition, assuming that battles would be fought between armies standing upright in the open, and firing by volley.

Even Hardee was soon superseded, however, with the 1862 publication of Silas Casey's *Infantry Tactics*. Casey was a Union brigadier himself, and at fifty-five one of the oldest and most experienced officers in the service. He issued his work in three volumes covering individual and company drill, battalion drill, and evolutions for brigade and corps units. It was the first comprehensive manual adapted and designed for the kind of military organizations then in service, and it was quickly adopted by both sides. Unlike its predecessors, however, it benefited from its author's year and more of field experience on the battlefields of Virginia. Casey knew that raw American volunteers were easily baffled by all the obscure jargon of most manuals, much of it in French or German. He greatly simplified his descriptions of maneuvers, using everyday language that was clear and concise. Inexperienced officers could intelligibly work out where they were supposed to be in brigade drill, and simple country boys could understand what was expected of them. "If the system here set forth shall in any manner cause our armies to act with more efficiency on the field of battle," wrote Casey, "and thus subserve the cause of our beloved country in this her hour of trial, my most heartfelt wishes will have been attained."[15]

Whichever manual they were trained from, the daily exercises of the soldiers, North and South, were much the same. Most regiments, especially at the war's outset, plunged into their drilling with an enthusiasm which only waned as the days of practice seemed to go on interminably. "It is drill, drill, battalion drill, and dress parade," wrote one soldier of his daily regime.[16]

The officers were out to achieve two specific tactical goals with their drill. One was morale, *esprit de corps*. A regiment or brigade which looked smart at its evolutions took pride in itself, and unit pride was a powerful motivator once the men went into battle. The other goal was what they described as "tactical articulation" in the moments prior to combat. Simply put, it meant the speedy and precise movement of large numbers of men from one point to another. A commander needed to be armed with a whole set of commands to move men down a road in ranks of four, or to march them across country, over fences, through woods, across streams, to turn them left or right, or about-face, with all manner of natural and manmade obstacles to impede their progress. Getting them from a column into a battleline several hundred yards wide in just a few moments would have taken forever if a commander simply told the men to break ranks and make a line. By having a succession of specific commands, however, he could tell a thousand men how to do so almost instantly, with no confusion. This was especially important when some generals had to move not just companies or regiments, but brigades of three thousand or more, and even divisions and corps which could number up to five times that number.

Contrary to the impression they had at the time, Civil War soldiers probably suffered less drilling than did their counterparts in later wars. They exercised by squads, companies, and regiments, practiced the manual of arms, and learned to perform the requisite turns and facings. They learned their formations in order of battle, how to stand at attention and rest, how to march both in common time – ninety steps per minute – and at the several faster paces. They learned these things individually, and by the company and regiment, and so forth. Those assigned as skirmishers – and it could be anyone, so everyone learned the routine – had to learn how to move in advance of the main line in any direction, how to withdraw, how to fire from the ground or prone position, and how to fire while moving.

Since all of the essential orders could not be heard from a single voice by hundreds or thousands of men on the parade ground, much less in the din of battle, the men had to learn a host of drum rolls and bugle calls which specifically transmitted certain orders. There were fifteen general drum and twenty-six bugle "calls" for the men in the ranks, and twenty-three more bugle and drum calls for skirmishers. In battalion drill, the men had to learn to open and close ranks, to shift from line of battle to a column and back again, changing front in battle formations to meet a cavalry attack, and so forth. In regimental and brigade drill, it was very much the same.

No wonder that, even with Casey's simplified tactics, many officers and men were bewildered by it all as they began their turns on the drilling field. Frequently, even the simplest exercises left green young officers at a loss. When Captain Daniel Candler of Georgia found that he was marching his company directly toward a fence, he was at a loss over what to do. At the last instant he ordered the men to halt. "Gentlemen," he then announced, "we will now take a recess of ten minutes. Break ranks! And when you fall in, will you please re-form on the other side of the fence."[17]

When ambitious leaders tried to impose the more intricate drill practiced by some of the Zouave and other parade ground units on these raw new recruits, the result was all too predictable. Virginia artilleryman George Eggleston lamented that in some regiments "maneuvers of the most utterly impossible sort were taught to the men, every amateur officer had his own pet system of tactics," he went on, "and the effect of the incongruous teachings, when brought out in battalion drill, closely resembled that of the music at Mr. Bob Sawyer's party, where each guest sang the chorus to the tune he knew best."[18] Welcome, indeed, was the down-to-earth officer who could cut through jargon and simply make his point with the men. When Captain John Trice of the 4th Kentucky Infantry was asked what he would do to meet the Yankee foe, he answered, "Well, Major, I can't answer that according to the books, but I would risk myself and the Trigg County boys, and go in on main strength and awkwardness." Another backwoods officer, quizzed on the orders he would give to move his unit obliquely to one side, responded that the proper jargon evaded him, but he would "move the reegiment *stauchendicilar* to the right."[19]

Even when they understood their officers and their drill, all too many men were unfamiliar with their new weapons. In the first few weeks of training, and in the months of drill that followed, accidents were inevitable. Cavalrymen drilling with sabers in their hands for the first time frequently drew blood from their horses and themselves as they tried to master the heavy and clumsy weapons. Artillerymen new to their positions could be even more dangerous. For practice one day, members of one Massachusetts battery took aim on a tree atop a hill some 1,000 yards distant. Yet they carelessly set the elevation screws on their guns for 1,600 yards instead, and then calmly lobbed their shells completely over the tree, and the hill, and into a village on the other side.

As for the infantrymen, they would spend most of their time with their rifles, but they also had to master the use of a terrible, much-feared weapon at its muzzle, the bayonet. Thanks to legends from earlier wars, and the initially accepted tactics of this one, nothing held more terror for a soldier than the thought of facing a bayonet charge. The sharpened triangular blade, eighteen inches or more in length, with deep grooves presumed to allow a victim's blood to drain effectively, had won battles in past conflicts thanks merely to the frightening aspect of a line of brightly polished blades advancing across the field. In this war, however, their role would prove to be less than minor. Only four out of every thousand wounds treated by Union surgeons would come from the bayonet and saber combined. Most men would use them as candlesticks and fire spits. In fact, they inflicted far more wounds on the practice field as recruits tried to wield them in the complex bayonet drill. When one Green Mountain boy watched his regiment at practice, he found that they looked like "a line of beings made up about equally of the frog, the sand-hill crane, the sentinel crab, and the grasshopper; all of them rapidly jumping, thrusting, swinging, striking, jerking every which way, and all gone stark mad."[20] Ironically, many of these weapons were turned to more peaceful use after the end of the war. Farmers in the impoverished South often converted them into scyths, sickles and hoes.

Yet in time they all learned enough to get where they had to be, and do what they had to do. Despite a few outfits which became so proficient at their evolutions that they engaged in and won drill competitions, most regiments simply followed their orders out of habit. They became soldiers, of a sort; they never became drill-perfect performers.

REFERENCES

1 Wiley, *Billy Yank*, p.30.
2 Wiley, *Johnny Reb*, pp.21-2.
3 Wiley and Milhollen, *They Who Fought Here*, p.28.
4 Wiley, *Johnny Reb*, p.20.
5 Lurton D. Ingersoll, *Iowa and the Rebellion* (Philadelphia, 1867), pp.501, 513.
6 Wiley, *Billy Yank*, p.38.
7 *Journal of Southern History*, XXIII (December 1957), p.525.
8 Wiley, *Billy Yank*, p.284.
9 Charles T. Loehr, *War History of the Old First Virginia Infantry Regiment* (Richmond, 1884), p.53.
10 McPherson, *Ordeal*, p.410.
11 John G.B. Adams, *Reminiscenses of the Nineteenth Massachusetts Regiment* (Boston, 1899), pp.79, 89.
12 Oliver W. Norton, *Army Letters, 1861-1865* (Chicago, 1903), p.28.
13 Wiley, *Billy Yank*, p.45.
14 William T. Sherman, *Memoirs* (New York, 1890), I, pp.209-10.
15 Silas Casey, *U.S. Infantry Tactics. . .* (Philadelphia, 1862), I, p.7.
16 Paddy Griffith, *Rally Once Again* (Ramsbury, U.K., 1987), p.105
17 Wiley and Milhollen, *They Who Fought Here*, pp.41-2.
18 George C. Eggleston, *A Rebel's Recollections* (New York, 1875), p.20.
19 Davis, *The Orphan Brigade*, p.50.
20 S. Millett Thompson, *Thirteenth Regiment of New Hampshire Volunteer Infantry* (Boston, 1888), p.221.

III
LOAD & FIRE

When the war commenced, boastful Confederates proclaimed that, "We can lick 'em with cornstalks." Four years later, the war and their Southern nation a memory, they had to add, "But, d–m 'em, they wouldn't fight us that way!"[1] Of course, neither side would fight that way. If they had, it would have made for a very peculiar, and mercifully bloodless sort of war. But cornstalks would have to wait for another time, for in 1861 the plowshares were beaten into swords, and North America became an armed continent.

Nothing could have been more fortuitous than the timing of the war's coming, at least so far as the makers of weapons were concerned. For the men who had to use and suffer by those arms, of course, it was a different story. Because only now was the nation technologically "ready" for a civil war. Had the two sides come to blows thirty or even twenty years earlier, there would have been little contest. In 1840, with almost all small arms in the country still smoothbores, the sections simply could not have fought a war that was either very costly in human lives, or very effective on the battlefields. In 1861, however, the technological development of the country ensured that when brother fired upon brother, he could do so with terrible force, and with a steady supply of weapons to equip the millions of men of military age north and south of the Mason-Dixon line.

In the previous decade especially, there had come to fruition a manufacturing revolution called, for want of a better name, the American System. It was, in essence, the forerunner of modern mass production. Weapons and machinery of war which formerly had to be made slowly and largely by hand, were now made almost entirely by machine, by something approaching assembly line techniques. As well as these "advantages," advances in ballistics now gave the gun, through rifling, a major advance in range and accuracy. Thus, consciously, North and South had waited until they had the capability to wage a real and bloody war, before they actually began one.

A generation before the firing on Fort Sumter, American soldiers were still carrying old-style flintlock muskets, which were smoothbores with a limited range and, within that range, indifferent accuracy. A series of inventions, however, gradually put in motion a rapid technological evolution during the first half of the 19th century. Among these in particular was the development of the percussion lock.

No more did the soldier have to pour powder into a flash pan, and hope that the flint striking the frizzen would send sparks into the pan, ignite the powder, send a flame through a vent into the barrel, and finally discharge the piece – he hoped without putting out his eye with sparks or flint chips in the process. Now a copper percussion cap simply fitted over a nipple affixed to the weapon's breech. The hammer striking the cap sent a spark into the barrel. Barring a defective cap, a clogged nipple, or a weak hammer spring, the lock would fire every time, and in all weather, and with a faster rate of fire. Research into ballistics established marginally more accurate sights, and even more important strides were made in the general acceptance of rifling for improving accuracy and range. Probably most significant was the introduction of the cylindroconoidal Minié bullet, generally if inaptly called the "minnie ball." Where spherical bullets or balls had been used before, the new Minié was more stable in its flight, greatly improving accuracy, while its hollow base, which expanded into the barrel's grooves at firing, ensured that it took full advantage of the benefits of rifling.[2]

All of these improvements foresaw the change in attitude toward the infantryman which the Civil War would help bring about. Older and less effective weapons had constrained the foot-soldier's functions to those of massed fire by volley, the hope being that at least some of the ill-aimed balls would find a mark. But by 1860 technology had a weapon ready that did not need to rely upon numbers. In the hands of a sufficiently skilled marksman, the rifle-musket could be deadly at ranges up to 500 yards. The war would actually play a large role in the evolution of the infantryman, but when it began the old mass tactics were still the accepted military wisdom, with the odd result that in the first years of the conflict, many of the weapons carried into battle were superior to their users' abilities.

The weapon that almost all soldiers had to try to master was, of course, the shoulder arm. A hint of what such weapons could do was given in the war with Mexico several years before, when the Model 1841 United States Rifle was used with deadly effect by a Mississippi regiment commanded by then Colonel Jefferson Davis. Dubbed thereafter the Mississippi Rifle, it was the first officially designed and issued military percussion rifle in America, and fathered a succession of refined models which appeared prior to and during the Civil War itself.

Yet when war broke out in 1861, and the men mustered from Maine to Texas, they brought with them not only the Model 1841s left over from the Mexican War, but also a bewildering variety of other weapons, some dating from even earlier conflicts. As state and national governments struggled to equip their regiments, double-barreled shotguns, hunting rifles and fowling pieces, flintlocks, caplocks, muzzleloaders and new breechloaders, single-shot and repeaters, pop-guns barely big enough to kill a squirrel, and mammoth .69 and .75 caliber "smoke poles," all came into the camps in the hands of the new recruits.

Observers often wondered just who stood to suffer the greater damage from them. "I think it would be a master stroke of policy to allow the secessionists to steal them," wrote Yankee journalist Frank Wilkie after seeing one such shipment of arms. "They are the old-fashioned-brassmounted-and-of-such-is-the-kingdom-of-Heaven kind that are infinitely more dangerous to friend than enemy." Thinking of the tender shoulders of the young soldiers, Wilkie added they "will kick further than they will shoot."[3] And when they did fire, they often proved dreadfully inaccurate. At one practice shoot with .69 muskets, only three out of 160 balls hit a barrel at 180 yards. General U.S. Grant later declared that a soldier armed with one of these antique "pumpkin slingers" might "fire at you all day without you ever finding it out."[4]

Despite their variety, almost all of the muzzle-loading weapons required precisely the same routine from the soldier, a routine which Casey in his *Tactics* reduced to a dozen commands and twenty specific motions. At the command, "Load," the soldier stood his rifle upright between his feet, the muzzle in his left hand and held eight inches from his body, at the same time moving the right hand to his cartridge box on his belt. At "Handle Cartridge," the paper-wrapped powder and bullet were brought from the box and the powder end placed between the teeth. The next two commands brought the cartridge to the muzzle, poured the powder into it, and seated the Minié in the bore. "Draw rammer" elicited the appropriate action, and "Ram" send the bullet driving down the bore to sit on the powder charge. Another command replaced the rammer, then came "Prime." The soldier brought the weapon up and extending outward from his body with his left hand, while with his right he pulled back the hammer to the half-cock position and reached into his cap pouch, removed a cap, and placed it on the nipple. Now came the real business. "Shoulder;" he put the rifle to his right shoulder. "Ready;" he took the proper foot stance and returned the piece to a verticle position at his right side, his right hand on the lock, his thumb pulling the hammer back to full-cock. "Aim;" up went the rifle to his right shoulder, his head to the butt so that his eye could sight between the opened "V" notch at the rear and over the blade sight at the muzzle. His finger sat ready on the trigger. "Fire;" and he did.[5]

In the hands of a careful, practiced marksman, these weapons, especially the rifles, were capable of substantial distance and accuracy, but, even with months of practice and new and improved weapons, the fact is that the marksmanship of the average Civil War soldier never proved to be exceptional. In the hands of Johnny Reb and Billy Yank, these guns were more often than not just a lot of smoke and noise. Some officers actually declined to issue to their men live cartridges during skirmish drill, for fear of the mishaps that almost inevitably followed. A British observer viewing the training camps around Washington during the first months of the war wrote that: "the number of accidents from the carelessness of the men is astonishing."[6] Almost every day the Capital's press carried reports of men killed or wounded by the accidental discharge of weapons in the camps, even in the soldiers' tents. And when the men were allowed to practice with real charges, as well as in the actual heat of battle, they invariably aimed too high.

No wonder that years after the war it was calculated that, on average, a Civil War soldier on either side burned 240 pounds of powder and hurled 900 pounds of lead bullets, for every single man actually hit.

At first, the governments North and South looked to arms purchased from Europe to fill their needs, for American armories needed time to gear up for war production. Most of them came from Austria and Belgium, and they almost uniformly won nothing but loathing from the soldiers. They usually either turned out to be so flimsy and ineffectual that soldiers dubbed them "European stovepipes," or else so heavy and clumsy that they were called "mules." When Dresden-made rifles were issued to a Wisconsin regiment, one private decried the "miserable old things" as liable to "do about as much execution to the shooter as the shootee."[8]

Rifles from Belgium and Austria came in .70 and .54 calibers. The Belgian guns were notorious for their terrible kick, no doubt enhancing their "mule" sobriquet. Worse, they proved to be so shabbily made that some came with crooked barrels, and others simply fell apart after limited service. One Indiana boy declared his Belgian rifle to be the "poorest excuse of a gun I ever saw."[9]

The Austrian model was no better. Its mass and weight made it the terror of any soldier issued one. General Grant testified before a Congressional committee that the weapon so terrified his men that in battle they would simply hold on to it like grim death, "shut their eyes and brace themselves for the shock."[10] One Confederate who found himself burdened with a "mule" speculated that the Austrians for whom it was originally made, "must be hard, large-fisted fellows." The weapon "is certainly the most ungainly rifle mortal ever used, being furnished with a heavy oak stock, and trappings of iron and brass, sufficient to decorate a howitzer."[11] Nevertheless, until they were able to make or purchase better arms, both sides bought many thousands of these "mules" and "pumpkin slingers" and "stovepipes." Estimates suggest that Union and Confederacy forces combined acquired more than half a million such execrable weapons.

Rather quickly, however, both governments settled down to two basic and favored shoulder arms, the U.S. Springfield Rifle – in one of several variants – and the British-made Enfield. The Springfield especially became the workhorse weapon of the Union Army, with 1,472,614 of them purchased on contract by the War Department in Washington, along with 428,292 Enfields. Together they tallied almost three times the combined numbers of all other shoulder arms purchased by Washington, ample evidence that the army recognized the truth of what one of its foes, a boy in the 16th

Mississippi, declared when he wrote that: "Springfield and Enfield Rifles generally do best."[12]

The origins of the Springfield can be traced back to the old US Rifle Model 1841, which saw its first active service in the 1846-8 war with Mexico. A short, two-banded weapon just four feet long and weighing a little over nine pounds, it combined the percussion system with the new Minié bullet in powerful .54 caliber. The 1841 model was adapted in a new version in 1855, and then, the bore enlarged to .58 caliber, it evolved into the Model 1861 rifle-musket which, with modifications, dominated the field of Union longarms for the duration of the war. The armory at Springfield, Massachusetts, produced over 800,000 of them, hence its more popular designation as the Springfield Rifle. Springfield was unable to keep up with the demand and the War Department was forced to manufacture another 900,000 with private firms.

The Springfield was, and remains, probably the simplest, sturdiest, most dependable and effective percussion military longarm ever designed. Its 40-inch bright steel barrel was held to a walnut stock by three bands spaced along the tube, making the gun four feet eight inches in length overall, and just over nine pounds in weight. Before being adopted officially in 1861, it had undergone extensive testing the year before. The results were everything the designers could have wished. A single man was able to load and fire the weapon ten times in five minutes, and in that test he put six of his bullets into a two-square-foot target 100 yards distant. Allowed to take his time, the same man put all ten bullets into a target less than one foot square at the same distance; at 300 yards he got them all inside two and a-half square feet; and at 500 yards he put one into a target of four square feet.

At the same time, it demonstrated awesome penetrating power with that big bullet and sixty grains of black powder. It could punch through eleven inches of pine boards at 100 yards, and almost six inches at 500 yards. "The rifled musket, of the calibre of .58 of an inch is a decided and important improvement," concluded the examining board, "and considering the compactness, lightness, accuracy at long ranges and the use of the bayonet, the arm is in every respect well-adapted to the general service of Infantry."[13] Indeed, in some tests, a trained man could load and fire up to six times per minute though, significantly, that allowed no time for taking steady aim. Tests that looked toward such rapidity revealed the still prevailing preoccupation with volume, rather than accuracy, of fire.

Two other models followed the 1861 Springfield. Both were introduced in 1863, but neither made much more than subtle, cosmetic changes to the 1861 design. Seeming to understand that it had created a classic, the War Department did not tamper with it. Indeed, it would be the very last muzzle-loading model ever adopted by the United States Army. The men who carried it regarded the sleek, graceful marriage of walnut and steel with general admiration. A New Hampshire private boasted that, "We have not got the enfield rifles but the spring field. They are just as good and a good deel lighter." When he and his comrades test fired them, they set up a target that rudely impersonated Jefferson Davis, and then blazed away at it until they had expended 600 rounds. "We put 360 balls into a mark the size of old Jeff," he boasted, adding with relief that "They do not carry so big a slug as our old [Belgian] rifles and are not as heavy by 6 lbs which is considerable on a long march."[14] Each Springfield cost the Treasury between $18 and $25 depending upon the manufacturer. When Lincoln sent his soldiers forth, armed with a Springfield, a bayonet, and forty rounds of ammunition, he sent them well-girded for war.

The Enfield was somewhat less favored by Billy Yank, even though it was two inches shorter, and overall nearly a pound lighter. One of its best features was that the British .577 caliber bore could accommodate the .58 bullet then in use for the Springfields and some other makes, thus making the ordnance officer's job a little bit easier. Some maintained that it enjoyed a slight edge in accuracy, but that was always a very subjective judgment, depending far more upon the marksman than the rifle. Still, it was an excellent weapon which thousands of Federals found more than satisfactory. "Our Co. and Co. A get beautiful Enfield rifle," a Billy Yank wrote in his diary in 1862. "We are all right now."[15] And across the lines in the Confederacy, the Enfield quickly became the predominant shoulder arm, so much so that in June 1862 the Richmond government made .577 the official caliber for all Confederate arms, thus patterning them after the bore size of the Enfield. The Rebels bought more than 120,000 of them during the war.

Lest the seeming uniformity of Springfield and Enfield give the impression that the Civil War soldiers' weaponry was rather one-dimensional, it needs to be pointed out that this was, in fact, an aberration. All the Springfields and Enfields combined amounted to no more than forty percent of all the shoulder arms used by the two governments. In fact, there was a virtual jumble of differing weapons in use throughout the war. In 1863 the Union Army officially recognized seventy-nine different models of shoulder arm, both rifles and muskets, another twenty-three models of carbines, and nineteen different pistols and revolvers. The Confederacy "recognized" any weapon it could get, but for both governments the proliferation of models meant that hard-pressed ordnance chiefs had to procure a bewildering variety of ammunition. In the Confederate Army of Tennessee in August 1863, just forty-five percent of the men carried Enfields or captured Springfields in compatible calibers. Another seven percent fought with older .54 Mississippi Rifles and other models. More than a third of the army, thirty-six percent, still lugged old Model 1817 and later .69 smoothbores. Nearly ten percent had .52 and .53 caliber Hall Rifles, and 900 men, three percent of the army, were still cursed with the massive .70 Belgian "mules."

Indeed, for the Confederates, arms procurement would always be a haphazard affair, and at one time or another almost every Johnny Reb took care of the matter for himself by picking up a lost or abandoned Yankee rifle from a battlefield. Indeed, this accounted for Lee's Army of Northern Virginia being the best equipped of all the Confederate armies, for the simple reason that in all its battles it faced – and for two years defeated – the best equipped of the Federal forces, the Army of the Potomac.

In June and July of 1862, Lee's men captured 35,000 stands of arms; in August another 20,000; 11,000 more in September; and yet another 9,000 in December. Late that same year the Army of Tennessee, by contrast, took only a total of 27,500 mixed muskets and rifles. Yet these were still a welcome relief to men, many of whom were actually carrying shotguns and old British Tower muskets left over from the War of 1812.

What the Rebels captured, however, hardly ended their armament woes, for the variety of what they took only increased the burden of supply they already felt. After the Battle of Fredericksburg, Virginia, in December 1862, the 9,000 weapons captured by Lee came in every size and description: 250 Springfields; 3,148 Model 1841 muskets in .69 caliber; 1,136 older muskets of varying dimensions; 772 of the .54 Austrian guns; another 78 of the .70 Belgian "mules;" 478 of the .54 Mississippi Rifles; and a scattering of other calibers, including even 13 flintlocks.

It could be a frustrating experience for a man in blue or gray to find himself in a regiment that was inadequately or incompletely equipped. As late as Fredericksburg there were still several dozen men in one Rebel Texas brigade with no guns at all. In most Confederate outfits, and not a few Yankee units as well, the process of re-arming was a constant effort. Rebels especially often brought their own guns to war with them, some of them old muskets and shotguns even dating back to the previous century.

The smoothbores were wildly inaccurate at anything more than close range, and to counter this the Southerners often turned them into ersatz shotguns by firing a load they called "buck and ball," three smaller buckshot loaded behind the full-sized ball. As soon as they could trade with a dead or captured Yankee, they did. At Shiloh the 9th Kentucky Infantry dropped its old smoothbores for hundreds of captured Enfields. In the East, the 21st Virginia went into the Battle of Gaines' Mill with a hodge-podge of captured Springfields, Enfields, Mississippi Rifles, and smoothbores, but soon took enough from the enemy to uniformly equip the entire regiment.

With all this variety of weaponry even within a regiment, commanders had to be careful how they apportioned the guns they had. As a rule, the rifles – if there were any – went to two companies which in battle occupied the extreme left and right flanks. It was believed that this would help them act as a stabilizing influence over the less adequately armed line companies. It may also have been a way to combat the frustrating taunting that many Yankees threw across the lines at regiments they discovered to be equipped with smoothbores. A few well-placed shots from those flank companies could discourage an insulting enemy who purposely exposed himself in order to mock the inadequacy of his opponents' guns.

Even as late as 1863, more than a third of the regiments in the Union Army of the Potomac were armed with two or more differing shoulder arms requiring differing ammunition, and the 1st Minnesota had no less than four. Like their Southern counterparts, they did the best for themselves that they could when their own ordnance officers could not supply them adequately. A kind of hierarchy of preference took informal effect in both armies when it came to battlefield captures, and soldiers repeatedly "traded up" until they had what they wanted. The weapons preferred, of course, were the Springfield and Enfield. Next most admired was the still reliable Mississippi Rifle. "Our choice was the Mississippi Rifles," a North Carolinian wrote in 1861.[16] A sharpshooter tried to get a British Whitworth rifle if he could find one, for its unrivaled accuracy, and any private soldier who happened upon a pistol usually kept it to augment his private arsenal, even though regulations did not allow the infantryman a sidearm.

The Civil War, however, did not just come along on a wave of technological advance in weaponry. At the same time, it fed the wave and pushed it forward, giving rise to a seemingly incalculable number of new innovations in weaponry, and the development of new weapons themselves. Consequently, the soldier who scoured the battlefield for something better than his current longarm might find himself choosing from a variety of often exotic guns. Many were little more than copies. From the outset of the war, while Confederate agents sought to buy weapons overseas, Southern industry struggled to convert itself to the wartime production of its own ordnance, and to a surprising degree succeeded. Two major armories at Richmond and at Fayetteville, North Carolina, were established for the manufacture of rifles, most of them essentially imitations of the Springfield or Enfield. At the same time a number of private manufacturers converted their machinery to gunmaking, and under contracts from Richmond produced their own weapons, again chiefly copies. As time went on, however, the armorers, public and private, became more inventive. First they made conversions, such as turning shotguns into cavalry carbines, or adapting flintlocks to the percussion mechanism.

But then the wave of interest in breechloaders that was sweeping the North, crossed the lines and passed through the South. A breechloader offered several distinct advantages, assuming it worked efficiently. It was especially good for the cavalry service. Reloading a muzzle-loading carbine while astride a horse and in motion was a tiring challenge for even the best cavalryman, and simply too awkward for most to attempt in battle. A breechloader, however, did not require the time-consuming and clumsy ramrod operation and could be reloaded with the piece held close to the rider instead of at arms' length, which galloping could make impossible. It could also be accomplished much faster, whether riding or standing. That was part of the problem it faced with officialdom, for old-line army officers, distrustful of the infantryman's marksmanship and profligacy with ammunition, feared that a man armed with a breechloader would simply squander away his ammunition that much faster without using it to effect.

Nevertheless, a host of breechloading designs came from Confederate manufacturers, though most were little more than experimental, and few saw even limited production thanks to insufficient machinery and raw materials. George Morse of Greenville, South Carolina, even manufactured a few score breechloaders that accepted the relatively new self-contained metallic cartridges which held the bullet in a brass or copper casing along with the powder, and which was discharged by striking the base of the casing with the gun's hammer, the precursor to all modern cartridges. Confederates even made their own fairly successful copy of the most popular of all Yankee breechloaders, the Sharps Rifle, but as with all of these new weapons, quantities produced were few.

This was not so in the Union though. The proliferation of new varieties was dazzling, and thousands were produced. There came the Burnside carbine, actually the pre-war invention of Ambrose Burnside, by 1862 a major general and commander of the Army of the Potomac. Other carbines – breechloaders – came off the assembly lines with names like Star, Maynard, Remington, Merrill, Terry, and Gibbs. The best of them all, however, was surely the one invented by Christian Sharps. It was a simple, yet invariably reliable weapon. A lever which also acted as trigger guard was pulled down, which also lowered a block at the breech, exposing the open barrel. The soldier simply inserted a linen-wrapped cartridge into the barrel, and the act of raising the lever and block once more clipped off the back of the linen, exposing the powder. A cap placed on the nipple readied it for firing. Sharps manufactured them in carbine and rifle models, and Washington purchased nearly 90,000 of them during the war, making it the most prevalent percussion breechloader of the war. Lincoln himself placed the first order after seeing a demonstration of the weapon's ease and accuracy.

Indeed, it was Lincoln's personal interest which put an even more inventive weapon in the hands of several thousand Billy Yanks. Ironically it was the invention of a man of peace, a Quaker named Christopher M. Spencer, yet his brainchild came to be regarded by many as the best single rifle of the war. He patented it just a year before the war began.

A tube that inserted into the butt of the gun held seven metallic self-contained cartridges. Pushing the trigger guard-lever down opened the breech, allowing the spring in the tube to shove a cartridge forward into the barrel. Pulling the lever back readied the gun for fire. All the operator had to do otherwise was cock the hammer before he lowered the lever. After firing, the lever also served to eject the spent casing. "Mr. Lincoln's gun," it was called after the President himself test fired it and took a hand in having it issued to some of his regiments. After some refinements as the war progressed, it could pump out fifteen shots in a minute, with both telling accuracy and a deadly punch.

In all, about 106,000 Spencer carbines and rifles were bought by the Lincoln government, and they saw service in nearly every theater of the war. Men armed with them felt almost invincible at Gettysburg, Chickamauga, Atlanta, Petersburg, and elsewhere. After fighting at Bermuda Hundred, Virginia, in 1864, one Connecticut Yankee declared that, "the Rebs made three charges on us but we stood up to the rack with our seven shooters. The Rebs hate our guns," he continued; "they call them the Yanks 7 Devils; they say the G.D. Yankeys stand up there with their G.D. coffy mills wind em up in the morning, run all day shoot a thousand times." Exaggeration aside, he and thousands of others agreed that, "well they are a good rifel."[17]

Spencer's was not the only repeater either. The Colt Patent Firearms Company adapted its popular Colt revolver pattern into a longarm with the Model 1855 Colt Revolving Rifle. The .58 caliber weapon was the first repeater ever adopted by the US Army, but its experience with it was such that it prejudiced attitudes toward repeaters until the Spencer came along. The Colt's revolving six-shot barrel had a problem with accidentally discharging several chambers at once which, for the soldier whose left hand was out in front of the barrel supporting the rifle, could be costly, even fatal. Though some saw continued use during the war, most were sold off by Washington for a mere 42 cents each to get rid of them.

Most revolutionary of all was the rifle that came from the New Haven Arms Company, the Model 1860 Henry Rifle. This was the military firearm of the future. A simple lever-action repeater that could fire sixteen .44 caliber bullets as fast as the operator could work the lever, it made a single soldier almost an entire company. Whole regiments such as the 7th Illinois were armed with it, and the enemy soon learned to fear and envy them. When a Reb of the 24th Virginia captured a Henry late in the war, he proclaimed himself "the best equipped man in the army."[18] Yanks felt the same way. An Indiana boy paid $35 – "all the money I had" – to buy one in 1864. "They are good shooters and I like to think I have so many shots in reserve." Certainly it disconcerted the enemy. "I think the Johnnies are getting rattled," he wrote some months later after using the Henry; "they are afraid of our repeating rifles. They say we are not fair, that we have guns that we load up on Sunday and shoot all the rest of the week. This I know, I feel a good deal more confidence in myself with a 16 shooter in my hands than I used to with a single shot rifle."[19]

It is altogether fitting that the repeaters, the weapons of the future, were not man-ufactured to be used with the weapon of the past. The Henry Rifle could not accom-modate a bayonet, and it is just as well, for of the millions of other Civil War weapons which did allow the attachment of the bayonet to the end of the barrel, only the barest fraction ever drew blood. Like the sabers carried by cavalrymen, they came to be regarded largely as encumbrances left over from some earlier notion of warfare. In America in 1861 faced with a greater kind of firepower, they did not fit.

Beyond his rifle and his bayonet, Johnny Reb and Billy Yank had no other stan-dard issue weapons. A few carried pistols, though many threw them away when they found little use for them. Many, especially Confederates, brought large bowie knives with them, and these they kept, though again they did little damage to the foe.

No one "licked" anybody with cornstalks in this war, nor did another Confederate live up to his optimistic boast that, "we can whip the Yankees with popguns." It took rifles, millions of them, carried by men who came to learn soon enough in the face of combat, that in battle a man's weapon and his understanding of it was his strength, and sometimes his salvation.

REFERENCES

1 William A. Albaugh and Edward N. Simmons, *Confederate Arms* (Harrisburg, Pa., 1957), p.47.

2 Wiley, *Billy Yank*, pp.62-3.

3 Cyril B. Upsham, "Arms and Equipment for the Iowa Troops in the Civil War," *Iowa Journal of History and Politics*, XVI (1918), p.18.

4 "Diary of Colonel William Camm, 1861 to 1865," *Journal of the Illinois State Historical Society*, XVII (1926), pp.802, 813; U.S. Grant, *Personal Memoirs* (New York, 1885), I, p.95.

5 Casey, *Infantry Tactics*, I, pp.42-8.

6 Russell, *My Diary*, p.396.

7 Casey, *Infantry Tactics*, I, p.48.

8 Fred A. Shannon, *The Organisation and Administration of the Union Army, 1861-1865* (Cleveland, 1928), I, p.139; Francis A. Lord, *They Fought for the Union* (Harrisburg, Pa., 1960), p.141.

9 Wiley and Milhollen, *They Who Fought Here*, p.112.

10 *Ibid.*, p.112.

11 Wiley, *Johnny Reb*, p.290.

12 Wiley and Milhollen, *They Who Fought Here*, p.106.

13 *Ibid.*, p.105.

14 Bell I. Wiley, "The Common Soldier of the Civil War," *Civil War Times Illustrated*, XII (July 1973), p.41.

15 Wiley and Milhollen, *They Who Fought Here*, p.107.

16 Wiley and Milhollen, *They Who Fought Here*, p.107.

17 Wiley, "Common Soldier," p.42.

18 Wiley, *Johnny Reb*, p.289.

19 Wiley, *Billy Yank*, p.63.

IV

JOIN THE CAVALRY

O ut of those tens of thousands of young men who flocked to the recruitment centers in the first days of the war, many went with a special branch of the service in mind. Lured by the romantic notions of gay cavaliers, bedecked with plumes and flashing sabers, riding merrily through the countryside, and cutting a dashing picture before the ladies, a host of enlistees chose the newly forming cavalry regiments for their service. Inevitably these and other preconceived notions about cavalry service would be proven false, as they would be in every aspect of the war. Indeed, in the spring of 1861, the role, if any, of the mounted arm in the coming fray was entirely uncertain. If any of those confused and faintly frightened young men could have looked ahead, however, they would have seen that the cavalry as it was at the war's outset, and as it would become by war's close, was destined to play an integral part in the national tragedy.

Nowhere could this be seen more clearly than in two events almost four years apart. On June 1, 1861, in a minor skirmish at Fairfax Courthouse, Virginia, the first Virginia Confederate to die in battle was a cavalryman. On April 9, 1865, when Robert E. Lee, general-in-chief of the Confederate armies, surrendered the Army of Northern Virginia at another courthouse town, Appomattox, it was because Federal cavalry had cut off his last avenue of escape and trapped him between it and Grant's legions.

As 1861 dawned, even with the nation in crisis, few seemed yet to appreciate the need that would be felt for substantial numbers of horsemen. Indeed, with the peacetime neglect that afflicted every branch of the service, the United States Army on December 31, 1860, counted just five regiments of mounted men: the 1st and 2nd Dragoons, the 1st and 2nd Cavalries, and the Regiment of Mounted Riflemen.

Worse, these regiments lay scattered all across the western expanse beyond the Mississippi River, protecting frontier posts against hostile Indians. Not a single company of organized cavalry was within a thousand miles of Washington and the scene of impending action.

Of the five colonels commanding the regiments, four would go to the new Confederacy, including Lee and Albert Sidney Johnston. Many officers of lesser rank, men like William J. Hardee, James Ewell Brown Stuart, John Bell Hood, Richard Ewell, Earl Van Dorn, Joseph Wheeler, and more, would also resign to "go south," many of them to become Rebel cavalrymen. In the 2nd Cavalry alone, seventeen of its twenty-five officers resigned to don the gray.[1] Worst of all, almost none of the officers, regardless of their loyalties, had any real experience or understanding of the role of cavalry in major military operations. They had spent their careers engaged in small actions and outpost duty, confronting at best only modest parties of Indian irregulars.

In fact, in 1861, cavalry doctrine North and South, as preached at the military academies and in the tactical manuals widely circulated, showed little development since the days of Napoleon. The Army's standard text, *System of Cavalry Tactics*, was twenty years old, and was borrowed almost in its entirety from a French book. It still reflected the Napoleonic ideal of using cavalry in masses – up to 12,000 in some of the Emperor's battles – to thunder down upon, intimidate, and plunge through enemy infantry lines. The value of cavalry, read a West Point text, "resides in its shock."[3] Furthermore, despite some Napoleonic examples of horseman riding to battle, then fighting dismounted very effectively, the prevailing notion remained that, in the words of Captain George B. McClellan, "The strength of cavalry is in the spurs and sabre." And this is what he wrote in an all new cavalry manual published in 1861, just as war was commencing.

In other words, cavalrymen in this new war were expected to behave as in wars more than a century before – to ride to battle, then dash into the fray in the overwhelming mounted saber charge. Very few, though McClellan and General Winfield Scott were among them, seemed to suspect that the wooded ground and narrow roads of America might make inoperable the cavalry tactics used in Europe decades before, and that new ideas would be needed.

Lincoln and his administration blundered badly at first by entirely ignoring the mounted arm, probably because, like most, he failed to grasp its necessity in the war to come. Incredibly, only a few more immediately available companies of the existing regiments were called east in the days after Fort Sumter, and no plans went forward to raise new regiments. In his first call for volunteers, Lincoln said nothing about cavalry, and when Northern governors offered to send mounted units, the War Department issued orders to accept no cavalry.[3] Expecting a short summer's campaign before the rebellion was put down, Washington continued under the influence which had always kept the cavalry small – economy. Horses were expensive to maintain.

Then came the disaster at First Manassas or Bull Run. General Irvin McDowell, with an army numbering close to 37,000, marched into Virginia with just seven companies, fewer than 700 horsemen, riding along. As a result, he moved almost completely in the dark, with no useful reconnaissance, no scouting reports, and in the battle itself, no substantial mobile force to exploit a breakthrough or guard his flanks. Worst of all, he had nothing with which to neutralize the enemy cavalry, which itself consisted only of the 1st Virginia Cavalry commanded by Colonel Jeb Stuart. Filled in advance with dread of the so-called "Black Horse Cavalry," Federal infantrymen panicked when Stuart rode out of some woods against them. Later, at the critical moment of the battle when McDowell's shaky flank was wavering, Stuart with infantry support put that flank into a flight which soon became a general rout.[4] McDowell's lack of cavalry, and Stuart's presence, did not alone account for the Yankee disaster, but they did reveal that cavalry could not be overlooked. Furthermore, as McDowell himself would point out after the fact, cavalry was most needed for gathering information while operating in an enemy's country, and for shielding from an enemy one's own movements. Already, from bitter experience, men were beginning to sense glimmers of change.

But learning remained slow, especially in the Union, and old habits of economy at the price of innovation died hard. It cost nearly a half million dollars to raise and fully equip a mounted regiment, and many professional soldiers doubted the point of it. Old General Scott, for instance, shared the disdain and suspicion of many infantrymen for their mounted compatriots.

It was also a question of time. Current military wisdom maintained that it took three full years to adequately train a cavalry officer, and nearly as long for the men in the ranks to be trained and disciplined. Since this would be a short war, there was little point in raising such outfits. The conflict would end before they could render any useful service. Besides – and here came the early expressions of a prejudice against volunteers that almost all professional soldiers repeated again and again – such work as the cavalry would be required to do was best left to the Regulars, and the five regiments in service would be enough. Small wonder, then, that in Lincoln's call for forty regiments for three years' service that spring, only one of these regiments was to be of cavalry.[5]

In the end, political pressure placed on Lincoln by his governors induced him, in turn, to move the War Department into accepting the first volunteer cavalry regiments. And after the disaster at Bull Run, Washington's attitude changed dramatically. Within six weeks of the defeat, there were thirty-one mounted volunteer regiments in service, and eighty-two by December 31, more than 90,000 cavalrymen.[6]

Across the lines, in the new Confederacy, the story was much different. It helped that President Jefferson Davis himself once served as a lieutenant in the 1st US Dragoons, and later as secretary of war for President Franklin Pierce he showed considerable interest in studying French cavalry technique. Even more important was the emotional attraction which the dashing mounted service had for the more high-spirited young men of the South. Accustomed since youth to riding, and inspired from childhood by stories of Revolutionary forebears like the "Swamp Fox" Francis Marion, "Light Horse" Harry Lee, and other cavalry heroes, sons of high-born and wealthy families were anxious to lead new regiments of heroes. Many a farmboy eagerly enlisted to serve them, especially after the exaggerated stories of Stuart's "Black Horse Cavalry" at Manassas assured them that all the real glory would be had in the saddle.

North or South, the story of raising the volunteer regiments proved much the same. Once a governor authorized a new regiment, an appointment to its colonelcy went to the man who would raise it. He might be an officer from another branch of the service, a prominent politician whose popularity could lure 1,200 or so to enlist, someone to whom the governor owed a favor, or from whom he sought one. There were as many considerations for appointment as there were men to commission; Presidents and secretaries of war also often got involved in designating new colonels. In short, it was American political democracy in action. However he got his appointment, once the colonel enlisted his men – later General Philip H. Sheridan would declare that the ideal cavalryman was between 18 and 22 years old, and about 130 pounds – he equipped them with whatever the governor, or the Capital, provided. Few regiments on either side went off to war with everything their army regulations required, but almost every trooper had the basics – revolver, saber, carbine, saddle, and horse. Beyond that, equipment depended upon good fortune, and the whim of the quartermasters.[7]

Not only did the Confederacy begin the war with the first victories – Fort Sumter, Big Bethel, and Bull Run – but from the first it enjoyed almost undisputed pre-eminence in the mounted arm. That came in part from having a head start in enlistments, and a more enlightened attitude towards cavalry. After all, Confederates knew the war would be fought on their own territory, and they knew best from riding all those fields and roads just how cavalry could use them. Moreover, it cannot be doubted that Southerners were by and large better horsemen thanks to having more experience in a predominantly rural society. The Southern policy of men providing their own horses meant that a cavalryman did not need weeks or months to get accustomed to his mount. North of the Potomac, where all horses were issued by the government, a mount and rider met for the very first time when they started training together. Additionally, a Rebel rider went to war knowing he had a sound, healthy horse. In the Union, already suffering the abuses of contract frauds and dishonest traders, tens of thousands of unsound animals were bought and, through faulty inspection procedure, allowed to get into the hands of green recruits.

It hardly afforded cause for wonder, then, that for two years after the commencement of the war, the Confederate cavalry reigned supreme in every theater of the war, and Southern mounted leaders quickly became national heroes. Even one of their foes, General William T. Sherman, would declare that Confederates were "splendid riders, first-rate shots, and utterly reckless." He frankly termed them "the best cavalry in the world."[8]

One of the first of them to achieve prominence was a 33-year-old Virginia farmer named Turner Ashby. Adjudged by many to be a born leader, and a horseman of unquestioned skill, young Ashby went from command of a company of horsemen at the war's start, to a leadership of all the cavalry in General Stonewall Jackson's army in the Shenandoah Valley in 1862. He used his men as Jackson's eyes, watching enemy movements, and masking Jackson's own movements, behind a screen of cavalry. He harassed enemy communications, gathered intelligence, and moved quickly wherever needed. It was the traditional role of the cavalryman, and only Ashby's death on June 6 kept him from rising even higher.

His role as premier cavalryman was quickly assumed, however, by Stuart. Manassas made him a hero overnight. Handsome, a born leader, daring to the point of rashness, and prone like many to get carried away with the sheer joy of being bold, Stuart would be *the* cavalryman east of the Alleghenies for the next two years. And in the spring of 1862, as commander of the cavalry corps of the Army of Northern Virginia, he would quickly show how a horseman could best – and worst – be employed. Lee sent him on a bold expedition to find the enemy's exposed right flank and to hit his supply lines if they were vulnerable to attack. Stuart turned what was to have been a reconnaissance into a stunning ride completely around General George B. McClellan's army. They rode all day June 12, 1862, without stopping. The next day they pressed on, Yankee horsemen nipping at their heels. Skirmishing went on all day. "Friend and foe alike were soon enveloped in bellowing clouds of dust, through which pistol and carbine shots were seen darting to and fro like flashes of lightning," wrote a Rebel trooper.[9] Surprising and capturing enemy camps, the Confederates took what they could and destroyed the rest. In the end, Stuart took 165 prisoners and 260 horses and mules, and revealed what the mounted arm could do. He had spread consternation in the enemy rear, done considerable damage, gathered useful intelligence, and brought away much-needed captures. Yet there had been no saber slashing charges, no grand and glorious battles. It was, rather, hit and run with pitched battle something to be avoided; the prototype of a host of raids to follow in this war, both for better and for worse.

Stuart's ride also revealed something else about the cavalry service as it began its evolution. He went above and beyond his orders. The information Lee wanted could have been obtained with far less dash and risk. Because he was successful, few gainsaid Stuart's feat, even Lee calling it a "brilliant exploit." But by its very flamboyance, it also alerted McClellan to the danger of vulnerability which Lee was seeking. The Federal leader soon shifted his army, denying Lee the chance of a crushing blow. In short, Stuart's zeal may have ruined the very opportunity that he had discovered for Lee. That zeal, that enchantment with the romance and dash of the cavalry service, would plague both sides time and again, especially with the example of the gallant

Stuart urging others to emulate his flair. The potential for disaster with this type of attitude was great indeed.

Of course there was far more to it than that. North and South, the life of the average mounted soldier was not markedly different, nor was it greatly varied from that of the other branches of the service. For all the glamor of youthful expectations, real soldiering turned out to be weeks of inactive camp life for every day of glorious battle. Drill, foraging for food, tending to animals and equipment, occupied an inordinate amount of time, and what time was left, the troopers took care of with gambling, prank-playing, and simply lolling about camp. Yet for the cavalryman there was, at least, an added dimension of mobility thanks to his horse. The need for frequent scouts and reconnaissance, even when the armies sat in winter quarters, allowed the troopers to break the monotony of camp life.

Better yet, from the point of view of the cavalryman, that mobility allowed him a far greater opportunity to scavenge and, occasionally, to plunder. This, and the natural interservice rivalry that arises in all armies, rather quickly led to the mounted arm being the most resented of all, in and out of the military. A Federal officer in Arkansas in 1862 complained that, "Cavalry are plenty among us, and go in any direction you may for miles you will find their horses hitched near every dwelling." They scoured the country, he lamented, "and generally help themselves to anything they wish." Creating the most resentment of all was the almost universal experience of the weary and footsore infantryman asking at a house for something to eat, only to be told that, "the cavalry has been here and there is nothing left."[10]

Adding to the hostility was the fact that, with the evolution of cavalry doctrine slowly taking it away from participation in pitched battles, the big fights were almost exclusively the realm of infantry and artillery. As a result, men in those branches rarely saw horse soldiers actually engaged in combat, Inevitably this led to the taunt of "whoever saw a dead cavalryman." When a mounted unit passed a marching column, the foot soldiers invariably hurled insults, and one soldier even declared that cavalrymen went so far out of their way to avoid danger that, instead of being part of the army, they should be termed a life insurance company. The cavalry "will never fight," complained a Rebel soldier. "I think it is useless to have them in the army eating rations."[11] They were, in the words of an equally cynical Yankee, "mere vampyres hanging on the infantry – doing but little fighting but first in for the spoils."[12]

Many a trooper carried a shotgun instead of a hard-to-get carbine. Hand guns came in all descriptions, from the multi-shot Le Mat revolver with shotgun barrel affixed that Stuart carried, to old Mexican War single-shot horse pistols. While all cavalrymen probably acquired a saber at the outset, many later gave it up in favor of a dirk or bowie knife, and many more Rebels carried no cutlery at all, which shows how quickly the notion of saber charges died away. In General John Hunt Morgan's Kentucky cavalry, by the middle of the war any man who carried a sword "would be forever after a laughing stock for the entire command," one of his scouts recalled.[13]

And the partisan raider John Singleton Mosby, "Gray Ghost of the Confederacy," declared of sabers that "the only real use I ever heard of their being put to was to hold a piece of meat over the fire for frying."[14]

Ironically, it was in the Union Army, which seemed for so long to lag behind the Confederates in leadership, experience, and everything else except manpower and supply, that the ideal role of Civil War cavalry first evolved. Perhaps it came thanks to Northerners being less hidebound by a mounted tradition, less wedded to classical notions of cavalry doctrine. Whatever the case, Federal horsemen, though they started the war substantially behind their foes in experience and competence, gradually erased the difference.

Only better leadership, more efficient organization, and actual field experience would raise the Federal cavalry to the level of the Confederates, but it was slow in coming. That summer a significant change did come when General John Pope, taking command of the Army of Virginia, directed that all cavalry units within each army corps be consolidated, to serve under a corps chief of cavalry. At least after this the horsemen would not be inefficiently dispersed among infantry brigades, and it paved the way for a time not far off when, like the Confederate horse, they would all be consolidated into a single cavalry corps. Pope, himself a former cavalryman, also ended the policy of encumbering cavalry operations with baggage and supply wagons, effectively slowing horsemen down to the speed of their wagons. In future, troopers were to carry with them what they needed and take anything else from the countryside, thus achieving the dual benefit of speeding their expeditions and visiting a bit of hardship on the disloyal population of Virginia.[15]

The summer, however, still did not go well for them. In Pope's failed Second Bull Run Campaign, he again had too few cavalry and, though they did good work at picket and outpost duty, extended marching and counter-marching exhausted them. After his defeat, his cavalry went back to Washington to refit and rest. Though beaten once more they had at least learned self-reliance; how to move quickly in all weather; how to stretch three days' rations to six; how to forage in a land already scoured; and even how to start a blazing fire in the rain with wet wood if necessary. Further, they had learned that they did have a few good leaders, men like William Averell, Alfred Pleasonton, and John Buford – not perfect men, but good up to their limitations. With the experience that leaders and led were acquiring together, especially in the host of small skirmishes that summer and fall of 1862, they also learned that they could fight. And the style they evolved was a new one. While the mounted saber charge was still the most dramatic part of their repertoire, most often for a small action, especially against infantry, the cavalrymen used their horses only for mobility. Riding quickly to the point where they were needed, they dismounted, and while one man in four held the horses, the other three went into the action with their carbines, fighting on foot. By war's end it would be the dominant form of cavalry fighting.[16]

But they would do little of that in the next campaign. During Lee's invasion of

Maryland in September, Federal cavalry played almost no role. Stuart, however, made yet another brilliant raid, adding to his luster. Only in its organization, as it looked for the right commander, did the Yankee horse slowly progress. "Our cavalry can be made superior to any now in the field by organization," declared General Alfred Pleasonton. "The rebel cavalry owe their success to their organization, which permits great freedom and responsibility to its commanders, subject to the commanding general."[17] By 1863 there was a single cavalry corps in the Army of the Potomac, following Pleasonton's suggestion. Soon thereafter, in March, the Yankee horsemen first stood their ground with their mounted foe and showed what they might do. At Kelly's Ford, on Virginia's Rappahannock River, a Union brigade commanded by William Averell forced a crossing of the river and then advanced toward a smaller body of Confederate troopers on the other side. Pistols blazing, the Rebels charged, and before they reached the Yankee line Averell's own men drew sabers and rushed forward. Back and forth they went. The men in blue stood their ground well, behaved like seasoned veterans, and for the first time showed the enemy that they had learned about war in the saddle now, and were ready to win their spurs. Though the battle was inconclusive, Averell's men had demonstrated that in an all-cavalry battle, almost all of it fought from the saddle, Blue could stand toe-to-toe with Gray.

Thus was the stage set for one great, and inevitable test between horsemen North and South, and it waited only three months to come. With Pleasonton now in command of the cavalry corps of the Army of the Potomac, his commander sent him on a raid toward Culpeper to "disperse and destroy the rebel force" believed to be there. That force was Stuart. In short, Pleasonton was ordered to bring on a major cavalry battle between his own 8,000 troopers and Stuart's 10,000.

He took Stuart almost completely by surprise in the early hours of June 9, and pushed his forward units back to the vicinity of Fleetwood Hill, near Brandy Station. Only a plucky defense by H.B. McClellan held the hill long enough for Stuart to reach the scene, and already charge and counter-charge had swept across its slopes before Stuart arrived. The greatest cavalry battle of the war had begun, and what followed was never to be forgotten by any who lived through it. "There now followed a passage of arms filled with romantic interest and splendor to a degree unequalled by anything our war produced," wrote one Confederate. Not a single trooper dismounted to fight, nor, he said, could he hear more than an occasional pistol and carbine shot. "It was what we read of in the days of chivalry, acres and acres of horsemen sparkling with sabers, and dotted with brilliant bits of color where their flags danced above them,"[18] It was the dying gasp of an old mode of warfare.

In the next several hours, Fleetwood Hill was taken and lost repeatedly. Charge and counter-charge went on through the grim afternoon, yet some of the troopers, especially Yankees, found it all somehow exhilarating. Edward Tobie of the 1st Maine Cavalry never forgot the feel of his very first saber charge. "On they go, faster and faster," he remembered, "over fences and ditches, driving the enemy a mile or more.

Oh, it was grand!" A man in the 6th New York rhapsodized over the "wild intoxication" of the mounted charge, "the most inspiriting, romantic, and thoroughly delightful kind."[19]

Though Pleasonton finally retired from the field, he left unbeaten, having achieved something of a moral victory by showing that Yankee horsemen could take the offensive against Rebel horse, give blow for blow, and stand their ground. One New Yorker called it "a glorious fight, in which the men of the North had proved themselves more than a match for the boasted Southern chivalry."[20] Even the enemy agreed, Stuart's adjutant McClellan declaring that Brandy Station "*made* the Federal cavalry."[21]

Thereafter, Pleasonton's men performed as well as Stuart's, and the somewhat embarrassed Rebel chieftain resorted to yet another raid to redeem his reputation. Unfortunately, he did it when Lee needed him with the army fighting for its life at Gettysburg in July, and Stuart's reputation never completely recovered. The cavalryman's inherent desire for flash and dash lured him away from his real role of reconnaissance, screening, and protection for the main army.

It was the same west of the Appalachians, yet there were differences out there, not the least being that from the war's outset the Federals were every bit the equals of their foes. All of these western troopers were accustomed to riding and shooting, and all, as it developed, were more given to irregular warfare, even to plunder and pillage. Initially, the cavalry's role was small and organization varied. John Hunt Morgan, by 1862 the premier cavalry raider for the western Confederates, began the war commanding a squadron of Kentucky cavalry attached to the 1st Kentucky Infantry Brigade. Only by mid-1862 did North and South begin to expand their mounted commitments in the region, and then almost from the first they did so in a way different from their armies in Virginia. Difficult as the Old Dominion's landscape was for the traditional operations of cavalry, Mississippi, Tennessee, and Alabama were even worse, far too broken by woods and hills and rivers for the Napoleonic style. On the other hand, the myriad hidden back roads, the dense woods, the innumerable places for ambush, and the tenuous routes for maintaining supply lines and communications, all made this territory ideal for raids, though raids of a different sort than those of Stuart's. Out here they would be lightning quick, deep penetrations, speedy destruction, and hasty withdrawal. And out here they would, in the end, do far more real damage to the Federal war effort than all of Stuart's bold strokes combined.

Both sides turned raider early on. Morgan achieved a quick rise and maintained it through the war until his death in 1864. Nathan Bedford Forrest assumed prominence for a certain natural gift as a leader. Joseph Wheeler became, at 26, chief of cavalry of the Confederate Army of Mississippi, and a noteworthy – if often ineffective – raider behind Yankee lines. In the Blue, Yankee generals turned to men like Albert Lee, David Stanley, and John T. Wilder. All of them operated on the same terms and with the same goals: get in the enemy's rear; burn railroad bridges and tear up track; hit supply bases and attack wagon trains; cut telegraph wires or, like Morgan, "tap" into them to learn the foe's intentions; force the enemy to weaken his main army to deal with the raiders; gather information, and avoid a pitched battle unless certain of victory. Not every raid went this way, but every raid in the West began in whole or part for these reasons.

So it was in the spring of 1863 that General U.S. Grant, commanding the forces advancing toward Vicksburg on the Mississippi, sent Colonel Benjamin Grierson and 1,700 troopers on a 600-mile ride in sixteen days, from La Grange, Tennessee, to Baton Rouge, Louisiana. "We are going on a big scout," wrote one of Grierson's men, "and play smash with the railroads."[22] So they were. Grant wanted them to cut rail lines, disrupt communications, and divert Confederates away from the defense of Vicksburg. It was a brilliant raid, perhaps the best of the war. With just two dozen casualties, the Yankee raiders inflicted about 600, tore up 60 miles of track and telegraph wire, destroyed 12,000 or more rifles and other Confederate supplies, and captured 1,000 horses and mules. William T. Sherman called it "the most brilliant expedition of the war."[23] More to the point, said Grant, "it was Grierson who first set the example of what might be done in the interior of the enemy's country."[24]

Grant would follow that example for the rest of the war. Meanwhile, farther west, beyond the Mississippi, lay an entirely different sort of war. The prairies and plains had been a nation of men on horseback, already experienced at Indian fighting and handling firearms. As a result, the region was a spawning ground for legions of cavalrymen, North and South, and the wide and open landscape allowed for mounted operations on a grand scale. Indeed, the mounted arm rose to the greatest extent of its offensive potential out there. In the Rebel army commanded by General E. Kirby Smith in 1864, 22,800 of his 40,000 men were horsemen, making up fifty-seven percent. By contrast, in Lee's army the number was rarely more than ten percent. Indeed, cavalrymen were too numerous, and Smith actually strove to reduce his mounted arm.

These cavalrymen often went into battle mounted alongside infantry, reins in their teeth, pistols blazing from both hands. In that expanse only a very brave man, or a very great fool, risked being separated from his horse. Friendly lines could be a hundred miles away, and a merciless foe only too near.[25]

It was that merciless character for which the mounted fighting west of the Mississippi became most notorious. Both sides enlisted Indians, mostly Cherokee, and that alone introduced an element of occasional savagery into the fighting. While stories of scalpings were greatly exaggerated, still it did occur, though it fell to whites to raise brutality on horseback to a science. Men like William C. Quantrill, George Todd, and William "Bloody Bill" Anderson, were nothing more than mounted Confederate terrorists, an embarrassment and sometimes a danger even to their own side. Across the lines, men like John Chivington and Charles Jennison were little better.

These men did do some good work, but most were in the war for themselves, using the civil dispute as a mere excuse for sanctioned pillage. Executions, tortures, scalpings and mutilations, all in the name of "the cause," revealed the guerrillas west of the Mississippi to be little else than criminals. If there was any doubt of that, then Anderson's Centralia massacre of September 27, 1864, offered the proof. In Centralia, Missouri, having captured a trainload of twenty-four unarmed Union soldiers on furlough, Anderson and his men shot them in the head one by one. Later the same day they rode over a dismounted detachment of 147 Yankees, killing 124, most of them as they surrendered or begged for their lives. Anderson's men took heads and scalps as trophies and decorations for their saddles.[26]

There were plenty of other excesses, not least the Lawrence, Kansas, "massacre" perpetrated by Quantrill in August 1863. While these cut-throats in uniform were by far the minority of the cavalry in the so-called trans-Mississippi region, their depredations assumed such proportion in the public mind that they came to represent the cavalry service in general beyond the great river. By the end of the war, both sides were weeding out these elements in their own forces, though most would escape justice or punishment, and go on after the war to become local heroes or to ride the outlaw trail. Indeed, the so-called "Wild West" of the 1870s and beyond was largely the offspring of Civil War irregular cavalry service of the 1860s.

Fortunately, the mounted service east of the Mississippi River never took on the level of brutality that emerged west of the river, but as the spring campaigns of 1864 commenced, it was clear that the air of dash and derring-do was about spent, as the grim relentlessness of the war made itself felt more and more. Men like Forrest, who cared little for the pomp or flair of war, came increasingly to command. Pleasonton was replaced by Major General Philip H. Sheridan, a ruthless man with a killer instinct, and in his first battle, at Yellow Tavern, Virginia, on May 11, he won the day. During the same battle, Stuart received a mortal wound, his death and the demise of the dashing kind of service he had symbolized being almost simultaneous.

The Rebels were routed from the field, and finally Yankee horsemen had an undisputed victory. "From that time until the close of the war," wrote one, the Confederate cavalry "ceased to be distinguished for the enterprise and boldness in aggressive movement for which it was formerly remarkable."[27] For the rest of the war, the horsemen in blue relentlessly wore down their opponents, keeping them almost entirely on the defensive. The only brief glimmer of the old Cavalry Corps of the Army of Northern Virginia came in September 1864 when, led by General Wade Hampton, Rebel troopers rode out of their lines and in a wide swinging arc behind Yankee lines, captured a cattle herd of 3,000 beeves and brought it back to Lee's hungry men.

By contrast, the Confederate horse in the West remained active, mobile, and dangerous almost to the end of the war. Those who fought with Forrest used horses to get to battle, not to fight in them. They rode quick, struck hard, then left just as fast. No one used sabers. Pistols were their weapons; pistols and carbines, and unflinching courage. And a willingness to kill. In the open spaces west of the Mississippi the

Confederates carried on even more ambitious operations almost until the end. Given the expanse of territory to be covered when Rebels tried to raid or invade Arkansas and Missouri, only cavalry were practical for the task. Major General Sterling Price's raid into Missouri in October 1864, however, dwarfed all other such operations. He left Arkansas with 12,000 mounted men, the greatest assemblage of cavalry in Confederate history, hoping to drive the enemy out of Missouri. An army of 20,000 Yankees, 8,000 of them horsemen, assembled to meet him, and on October 23 at Westport, near Kansas City, the two forces met. Price's numbers by that time had dwindled to about 9,000, but still the resulting battle engaged about 17,000 horsemen on both sides, second only to Brandy Station among cavalry battles of the war.[28]

Price was defeated, largely due to his own poor leadership. Yet his loss also revealed the limitations of cavalry's usefulness on major campaigns over wide territory. Even after years of experience, many men still would not treat their animals properly. It was menial, dirty, smelly, and tedious work, the more so since a cavalryman had to care for his horse before himself. Many men simply could not adopt the proper attitude. As a result, they broke down their mounts, and when a horse was out of the campaign, so was its rider. Furthermore, even if well cared for, after traveling several hundred miles a horse was tired and unequal to the demands of charge and counter-charge if a fight took place on horseback.

By this stage of the war, everything was different, and the men who had been in the mounted service since the beginning hardly recognized what it had become. If anyone on either side needed further demonstration that the role of the cavalry had changed in this war, and that its best use was for quick mounted raids, and for fighting afoot, then the last campaigns erased all doubt. On March 22, 1865, James Wilson, now a major general, led three divisions of cavalry across the Tennessee and into the heart of Georgia and Alabama. During the ensuing month, he moved swiftly to Tuscaloosa, and then on to the manufacturing center at Selma. Dogged and resisted by Forrest, Wilson and his 13,480 cavalrymen were simply too much for him. Wilson beat Forrest aside, destroyed Selma, and then moved on to Montgomery and the capital. By late April he had taken Columbus and Macon, Georgia.

In his wake he left a 525-mile march in which the bluecoat cavalry had beaten Forrest twice, captured more than half their numbers in prisoners and killed or wounded 1,000 more. Wilson destroyed seven iron works, seven foundries, seven machine shops, two steel-rolling mills, five collieries, thirteen factories, three arsenals, a powder works, a navy yard, and five steamboats, not to mention thirty-five locomotives, 565 rail cars, and a host of other equipment. For sheer destructive force, it was the greatest raid of its kind, the new mandate of American cavalry. It destroyed the industrial ability of the Confederacy to continue. Though American cavalry would never again fight in a war like this one, it is certain that Wilson helped provide the model for mounted doctrine in the future.[29]

Though resistance continued for a few weeks after April 9, 1865, symbolically

Appomattox meant the defeat of the Confederacy. It reflected all the changes that had come about for the horseman in arms. It was the failure of Lee's cavalry at the Battle of Five Forks on April 1 which in part helped make the Confederate position around Petersburg and Richmond untenable. Forced out into the open, Lee and his army had nowhere to go but a retreat to the southwest. Sheridan and his cavalry, already victorious at Five Forks, pursued Lee relentlessly while Grant and the infantry followed. At every point Sheridan cut off possible lines of march for the beleagured Lee. When Lee reached Amelia Courthouse, expecting to find vitally needed supplies sent ahead, he found nothing awaiting him. Sheridan had intercepted them. Marching on, hungry and exhausted, the Confederates were almost overwhelmed on April 6 by Sheridan's whole cavalry corps and elements of Union infantry. In fighting along Sayler's Creek, Lee lost a third of his army, including many of his generals, captured or dispersed.

From this triumph, Sheridan raced on to get ahead of the last remaining route open to Lee. On April 8, at Appomattox Station, Custer's division captured the only other supply train that might have helped Lee keep going, and then moved northeast to Appomattox Court House to find the remnant of Lee's army in position. Lee was virtually surrounded. A spirited but doomed attempt to break out the next morning convinced Lee that there was nothing left for him but to surrender.[30]

Union cavalry did not win the war, and Rebel cavalry did not lose it. They played their part along with the other services, and to the degree that their efforts integrated systematically into the entire scope of their nations' war efforts, they made their contribution. But one thing is certain. The evolution of the cavalryman from idealized poseur and parade-ground gallant, to swift, lightly equipped, and unchivalrously destructive raider helped ensure that the war would end in the way it did. But for Wilson's havoc in Alabama and Mississippi, and Sheridan's in Virginia, the Confederacy might have had the ability to continue the war for months more.

As for the cavalrymen they led, the volunteers took home with them at war's end a powerful sense of pride. Indeed, men North and South would look back upon their days in the saddle as the best of their lives, forgetting in time the hardship, the heat and dust and hunger. They had been the last of the old and the first of the new, and fought a war on horseback entirely of their own making. No other cavalry service, anywhere, in any war to come, would be quite like theirs.

REFERENCES

1 Stephen Z. Starr, *The Union Cavalry in the Civil War* (Baton Rouge, 1979), I, pp.48, 58.
2 *Ibid.*, pp.50-3.
3 *Official Records*, Series III, Vol.I, p.77.
4 William C. Davis, *Battle at Bull Run* (New York, 1978), pp.207-8.
5 Starr, *Union Cavalry*, I, p.66.
6 *Ibid.*, p.78.
7 *Ibid.*, pp.104-5.

8 Richard Berringer, Herman Hattaway, Archer Jones and William Still, *Why the South Lost the Civil War* (Athens, Ga., 1986), p.170.
9 Heros Von Borke, *Memoirs of the Confederate War for Independence* (New York, 1938), I, p.39.
10 Nannie Tiley, (ed.), *Federals on the Frontier* (Austin, Tex., 1962), pp.75-6.
11 Wiley, *Johnny Reb*, p.341.
12 Tilley, *Federals*, p.76.
13 India Logan, *Kelian Franklin Pedicord* (New York, 1908), p.114.
14 John S. Mosby, *Mosby's War Reminiscences* (New York, 1958), p.30.
15 *Official Records*, Series I, Vol. XII, Part 3, p.581; Part 2, p.50.
16 Starr, *Union Cavalry*, I, p.303.
17 *Official Records*, Series I, Vol. XXI, pp.785-6.
18 William W. Blackford, *War Years with Jeb Stuart* (New York, 1945), pp.215-17.
19 Starr, *Union Cavalry*, I, p.395.
20 Willard Glazier, *Three Years in the Federal Cavalry* (New York, 1874), p.223.
21 H.B. McClellan, *The Life and Campaigns of Major General J.E.B. Stuart* (Boston, 1885), p.294.
22 Dee Brown, *Grierson's Raid* (Urbana, Ill., 1954), p.5.
23 *Ibid.*, p.223.
24 *Official Records*, Series I, Vol. XXIV, Part 1, p.58.
25 Albert Castel, "They Called Him 'Bloody Bill'," *Journal of the West*, III (April 1964), p.238.
26 Stephen B. Oates, *Confederate Cavalry West of the River* (Austin, Tex., 1961), pp.167-9; Castel, "Bloody Bill," pp.237ff.
27 Starr, *Union Cavalry*, II, pp.108-9.
28 Fred L. Lee, *The Battle of Westport* (Kansas City, 1976), pp.22-3.
29 James P. Jones, *Yankee Blitzkrieg: Wilson's Raid Through Alabama and Georgia* (Athens, Ga., 1976), pp.9, 28, 185-6.
30 Douglas S. Freeman, *Lee's Lieutenants* (New York, 1944), III, p.723.

V

ROLLING THUNDER

In December of 1861 the Surry Light Artillery of Virginia was encamped near the James River, waiting out the winter, and waiting still to see some active service. Colonel Roger A. Pryor, its commander, really wanted the unit to serve as infantry, and apparently put quite a few roadblocks of his own in the way of his men receiving either serviceable cannon or training with the old pieces they had. But in the first week of December he finally decided to give the command "some sure enough practice at loading and firing," as Private Benjamin Jones put it. After six months in service, it was about time. "The Colonel wanted to see if our gunners could hit the broad side of a house," wrote Jones, and it turned out that that was literally what Pryor meant. Pointing to a farmhouse half a mile distant, the colonel challenged the battery to hit it, declaring that "he would be bound every one of them would miss it, clear and clean." In fact, there were soon four fine drafty holes in the side of the house, without anyone bothering to determine whether or not the building had occupants. For one of the Confederacy's premier batteries of artillery, it was hardly an auspicious beginning.[1]

In fact, rather few artillery units on either side began with much fanfare or good auspices. It was the forgotten branch of the service. In the first flush of enthusiasm, North and South, everyone rushed to get into the infantry. The foot soldier, carrying his mighty rifle with its gleaming bayonet, marching rank upon rank to war, was the image that captured the American imagination. For those with an extra quotient of dash, the cavalry beckoned, all leather and jingling harnesses, feathered caps and flashing sabers. The artillery, on the other hand, simply was not a romantic arm of the service, especially for volunteers. Hence the Virginia volunteer Colonel Pryor's anxiety to have the Surry Light become infantry instead.

Notwithstanding, there had been a number of private artillery companies before the war, some state militia, and other well-funded and organized "fraternal" outfits both North and South. The most famous was undoubtedly the Washington Artillery of New Orleans, formed in 1838, and already blooded by service in the war with Mexico. It enlisted the flower of New Orleans society into its ranks, and at times membership was almost mandatory if a young man wanted to rise. Yet by 1857 its strength had dwindled to a mere thirteen names on the rolls. Clearly, the rise of the infantry militia companies in the city had eroded its membership away to more popular forms of service. After all, cannon were dirty, noisy, heavy to manhandle around, and required almost constant maintenance.

Elsewhere in the nation before 1861 there were other such organizations as the Richmond Howitzers, the Washington Light Artillery of Charleston, the Norfolk Light Artillery Blues, and more. Yet compared to the burgeoning number of infantry and cavalry companies in pre-war America, their ranks were few. The fact is, there was no sort of artillery tradition in America, North or South. At West Point's Military Academy, every cadet studied the big guns, but artillery service was not one of the most favored postings for graduates, and much the same was the case at the several state and private military schools.

Consequently, when 1861 and war came there was no rush on either side to don the red stripes and facings of the artilleryman's uniform. Additional obstacles existed as well. Artillery service required of its enlisted men a greater degree of technical skill, frequently some mathematics, and no small degree of brawn. On top of that, it offered seemingly greater dangers than the other services. After all, cannon were the targets for other cannon, and it took a serene indifference to death for a man to stand at his gun impervious to the fact that the other side was hurling 12.3-pound iron balls at him at 1,440 feet per second. Furthermore, while infantry and cavalry regiments could be raised and even equipped within a small area, artillery batteries had to rely upon the state or Federal government for equipment, and many simply could not be raised locally.

From these and other causes, the artillery was always the smallest branch of the service North and South. By war's end, the Union would enlist 432 batteries, accounting for just twelve percent of all units that served. In the Confederacy, 268 batteries, battalions, and regiments numbered somewhat more, almost eighteen percent, but clearly neither army nor people were enthralled with serving the big guns.[2]

It is ironic, then, that once the new artillerymen were in their units, they often resisted strenuously the efforts of others to convert them to another branch. When the Washington Artillery of Augusta, Georgia, entered Confederate service and went to Pensacola, Florida, the commander, General Braxton Bragg, tried to switch them to infantry. The Georgians promptly arose in protest and requested transfer to another theater of the war before Bragg backed down. Similarly, Roger Pryor had to give up his designs on turning the Surry Light Artillery into infantry. The men would not have it. "We are born artillerymen," proclaimed Jones in September, 1861, "we are!" In fact, Pryor did not at first announce his intention, but the men soon divined it. In August they were "temporarily" assigned to the 3rd Virginia Infantry since no cannon had been assigned to them as yet. Consequently, they drilled with the infantry. The men grumbled, while officers assured them that their cannon would arrive before long. "The men shake their heads, and declare it is only a ruse to lure us piecemeal into the net, and fasten us to the infantry service for the war," wrote Private Jones. A month later they were finally given two old cannons for practice, which meant that while continuing their infantry training and drill, the men had to do double duty by commencing their artillerymen's routine. Pryor put Sergeant William Bloxam in charge, and he did even more to discourage their enthusiasm for the guns by making the men manhandle the ancient smoothbore six-pounders. "We are required to move the guns about by hand," wrote Jones, "over the field, to front and to rear, in echelon and in line, to sponge and load and fire in mimic warfare, until our arms ache, and we long for rest." But the men did not give up, so fixed had their determination become about being gunners. However much Bloxam and Pryor pushed them, they did not complain. The Surry boys, Jones proclaimed, "will never cry out, 'Hold! enough of artillery for us.'" And they never did.[3]

Batteries in the Union Army were, as a rule, issued their guns, teams, and attendant equipment soon after their initial training and indoctrination into the military were complete. Across the lines, on the other hand, equipping a battery was all too often a gradual process, accomplished in unplanned stages. After receiving those two old smoothbores in September, the Surry Light Artillery waited until December before receiving another brace of guns, and sufficient horses to pull all four pieces. A Mississippi outfit left home with sixty-five horses, but only one cannon, and had to wait many months before another three field pieces arrived. It was March 1862 before the final guns arrived, making up its full six-gun battery complement, along with caissons, limbers, traveling forge, and battery wagon. Horses were in equally uncertain supply, with so many of the best being sold to the cavalry. "Our church bells even are being cast into field pieces," wrote an Alabama lieutenant, "but they are useless without horses. Can any one prefer the luxury or comfort even of keeping horses, to the preservation of our homes and lives?"[4]

"What a time we had!" remembered Jones in later years. "What lessons we learned! What old Veteran does not recall the hard training of his early camp life, often under the command of men who were but little better than pig-headed martinets, regarding the private soldier as but a piece of putty, to be shaped into any form that might please them."[5] Yet there was purpose to the grinding repetition, and especially for the artillerymen. In the din of battle verbal commands could be garbled and could go unheard. Instead, they had to learn their tasks in a specific order, and do so by numbers so that even without orders the men would be able to function. The men were assigned numbers that designated their duties and functions, and in little or no time the men themselves came to be referred to by their numbers and not their names, even among comrades.

North and South, most artillerymen could have been interchanged, and they would have been able to function without flaw. The routine was unvaried, unless the special nature of the gun required it. Gunner Number 2 was handed a "cartridge" of ball and powder, which he set inside the muzzle of the cannon. Gunner Number 1, who never let go his rammer, shoved the cartridge down the tube until it reached the bottom. Meanwhile Gunner Number 3 kept his thumb – sometimes protected by a leather sleeve – over the vent hole at the breech. Once the cartridge was in place, he jabbed a wire pick through the vent to open the cloth bag at the base of the cartridge, exposing the black powder within. Gunner Number 4, who sometimes wore a pouch on his belt which contained friction primers, rather like blasting caps, now placed a primer into the vent hole. A lanyard, several feet of braided cord, was attached to the primer and, at the proper command, a jerk at the lanyard ignited the primer which, in turn, sent a blast of flame into the cartridge, discharging the piece. Immediately Number 1 reappeared, this time with a soaked sponge which he rammed down the barrel to put out any remaining embers or glowing fragments of the cartridge which might accidentally set off the next round prematurely. Gunner Number 5 ran forward with another cartridge and handed it to Number 2, and the whole process repeated itself. If the round happened to be an exploding shot, or shell, then Gunners 6 and 7 who manned the ammunition chest and handed cartridges to Number 5, cut the fuses according to the anticipated time of flight to the target.[6]

If it all went according to the numbers, a practiced gun crew could get through the whole process twice in a minute, even given that many batteries had gun crews of only five or six men. A sergeant or corporal stood at the rear of the piece, in overall charge of the operation, including using the variety of generally inadequate tools then available to sight the gun on its target. "Indirect" fire, the technique of shooting over a hilltop or obstruction toward some unseen objective, was still almost unknown. Men could only shoot at what they could see. That, and the limits of range of most cannon, meant that the sergeant had to sight on a target no more than a mile distant. Much of it was intuition and guesswork, and after every shot the process had to be done over again because the recoil of a firing field piece could send the gun rolling backward several feet.

While all of this took place, the other half of the battery, the drivers, were concerned with other duties. Ideally there were six horses drawing every cannon and its attached limber, or two-wheeled ammunition chest. One driver managed each of the three pairs of horses, called lead, swing, and wheel teams. Similarly managed six-horse teams pulled each of the four-wheeled caissons, carrying more ammunition chests. Thus a fully equipped six-gun battery could require 72 horses at least, not counting those needed to draw the forge and battery wagon, carry the officers and act as replacements. It is no wonder that of a battery's full complement of 155 men including officers and non-commissioned officers, 52 were drivers. Another 70 served as gunners.[7]

It required good officers to make it all work, for the artillery was easily the most technically demanding of the combat arms. Like soldiers of all times, the Civil War artilleryman often thought all too little of his leaders. "The company drill was a profound enigma to him," one Rebel wrote of his lieutenant. "He could not give commands for the most simple movements. With the company on the drill ground he was completely befogged."[8] Yet others were happier with their leaders, and even the initially despised Bloxam won credit for his untiring efforts with Jones' own boast that "we are becoming quite expert in the artillery tactics."[9]

That considerable élan and self-confidence characterized many of the artillery batteries in the war, no doubt aided by the fact that, on average, the more intelligent enlisted men seemed to serve the artillery branch. The Richmond Howitzers, for instance, contained quite a number of college graduates, and many of the rest were businessmen, clerks, and the like, for "the flower of our educated youth gravitated toward the artillery," confessed Robert Stiles.

Four prime attributes were necessary in a good gunner – intelligence, self-possession, comradeship, and loyalty to the gun. Of the first, little more need be said. As for self-possession, one need only consider the potentially terrifying effects of deafening explosions, torrents of flame shooting from the guns, and clouds of choking white smoke. A battery in action looked and felt like a scene from Dante's *Inferno*, and only men who could remain calm in the midst of that chaos could work the guns effectively. Comradeship was essential, for such a small group of men, six or seven on a gun crew at most, working tightly knit and vitally interdependent, had to get along with one another. A grudge, a hostile feeling between any two which might interfere with the efficiency of the battery as a whole, could endanger all their lives and lessen their effectiveness. Above all else loyalty to the gun was life to the gunner. Without his guns, an artilleryman was nothing, and nothing in the war would so wound the pride of a battery as the loss to the enemy of one or more of its cannon. Men would give up their lives to save their guns, and others seemed momentarily to forget even issues of loyalty and uniform in their devotion to a field piece.

There was considerable variety in the weapons that artillerymen both North and South were so devoted toward. The most widely used and respected gun of the war was the twelve-pounder gun-howitzer Model 1857, commonly known simply as the "Napoleon." It was a smoothbore whose tube alone weighed 1,227 pounds and measured five feet six inches in length. With a bore diameter of 4.62 inches, it took a cartridge consisting of a bag holding 2.5 pounds of black powder, attached to a 12.3-pound iron ball. Its effective range was up to 1,500 yards, though it was capable of firing well over a mile. It was named after Emperor Napoleon III of France, who adopted it for use in his army. When the Civil War began, the Union Army had only four of them. By the end of the war it had ordered the manufacture by private foundries of 1,157, making it far and away the most prevalent field piece in the

Federal forces. A very few were rifled, at least one was made of wrought iron, but virtually all others were of cast bronze. Almost indestructable, they were the easy favorite of almost all gunners. They all could fire solid shot, round or conical hollow shells filled with powder for exploding, grapeshot – loads of round iron balls an inch or more in diameter – and canister, a virtual scatter-load intended to fire into oncoming ranks of infantry.[10]

The Confederates, too, made extensive use of the Napoleon, though with far more variations, due often as not to necessity. The best estimate suggests that Confederates manufactured around 535 Napoleons, some in bronze, some in brass, and nearly a quarter in cast iron. Many more came into Confederate service through the expedient of battlefield captures, and the Rebels were delighted to get them. The Union War Department in Washington valued a Napoleon at just over $600, but it was worth far more than that in a South whose industrial output was so overburdened as to be near exhaustion.

There were also a host of six-pounder field pieces used North and South, as well as field howitzers in six- and twelve-pounder calibers, intended primarily for the high trajectory flight of exploding shells into an enemy line or position. Far more popular and dramatic, however, was the new generation of rifled artillery. The Civil War was the first active testing ground for such weapons. They came in many sizes and under a host of names, mostly derived from their inventors, but quickly the armies seized particularly upon the Parrott and Ordnance rifles.

Rifling presented immediate problems. Bronze and brass were too soft. An iron shell driving its way down the tube would quickly wear away the rifling grooves which gave it its name and its accuracy. Cast iron was harder, but also brittle. The concussion could crack or even explode such a cannon. Robert Parrott of the West Point Foundry in New York achieved an ersatz solution to the problem by taking a cast-iron gun tube, then wrapping a red-hot band of iron around its breech. As the band cooled, it contracted, forging itself to the tube and providing considerable extra support. Parrott manufactured up to 255 of them in a 2.9-inch ten-pounder bore, and another 279 in a full 3-inch diameter, also ten-pounders. He also turned out nearly 300 3.67-inch twenty-pounder Parrotts, and even a few monsters for seacoast fortifications, including 300-pounder rifles with ten-inch bores that used twenty-five pounds of powder to fire a single projectile that weighed 250 pounds well over a mile.[11]

Confederates quickly copied the Parrott design, and in the same calibers, thus allowing the use of captured ammunition in their own guns. Like their Federal counterparts, they were trouble-prone, and frequently blew up at the breech, even with the iron reinforcing band. Much more reliable was the 3-inch Ordnance rifle, the beneficiary of a new innovation in manufacture. Wrought iron was stronger than cast, but by its very means of formation it could not be poured into a gun mold. Instead, wrought iron rods were welded together to form a mandrel, and then four layers of wrought iron bars were wrapped diagonally around the mandrel, each in an opposite direction. A last layer of iron staves was welded to the outside, and the the whole was subjected to welding heat in a furnace. When the mandrel was then bored out and the tube rifled, a gun tube of incredible strength was the result. Experimental models could not be exploded until or unless loaded with powder and shell right up to the muzzle of the gun.

Almost 1,000 3-inch Ordnance rifles went to the Union armies during the war, and testimony to their accuracy came from all parties, including their targets. "The Yankee three-inch rifle was a dead shot at any distance under a mile," proclaimed a Rebel artilleryman.[12] No wonder that the Southerners emulated the weapon as best they could, but more often than not made use of captured guns and ammunition.

The weak point of all rifles was their ammunition, for time fuses were quirky, and often shells exploded in the air instead of on impact, and sometimes even before they had escaped the gun tube. As a result, experienced artillerymen generally preferred the simpler, more predictable, and dependable, Napoleon, which well accounts for their ubiquitous presence on every battlefield of the war.

A few gunners even had to deal with the leading edge of technology by adapting themselves to the new breechloading cannon. A number of inventors, chiefly British, experimented with guns which opened at the breech to accept their loads. The advantages could be many. More rapid fire, less time lost in forcing rifled shot down the tube, and the ability to place the projectile directly into the rifling grooves. A few 3-inch Armstrong rifles were shipped to the Confederacy, but not with great field success. Far more successful, though still limited in its field use, were the Whitworth rifles, in six- and twelve-pounder bores. There were several variants, but common to all was a hinged breech which unscrewed and swung to the side to allow loading. The Whitworths developed the highest muzzle velocity of all field pieces used during the Civil War, and could fire with telling accuracy farther than the gunner could see to aim. But they were easily disabled, and even General E.P. Alexander, Robert E. Lee's great artillery chief, confessed that "the United States three-inch rifle is much more generally serviceable."[13]

Whatever guns they served, the artillerymen North and South went through some of the same evolution of organization that their comrades in the saddle endured. At the war's outset, the Confederate artillery batteries were attached to individual brigades, usually in one or two batteries each. It was a cumbersome arrangement, for one general could jealously hold on to his artillery even though a fellow brigade commander elsewhere might desperately need it. By the end of 1862, the batteries were reassigned to the supervision of division commanders, who would order them about as needed among their brigades. It was a step in the right direction, and by 1864 they were all at the direction of the army corps commanders under chiefs of artillery. In the Union forces the batteries came to be brigaded together under the corps commanders as well, though with corps and army chiefs of artillery. Since the artillery, unlike the cavalry, was clearly and exclusively a support arm for the infantry, such formal organization, better than simply parceling it out among the several brigades, was imperative.

There was another sort of artilleryman in the armies, one whose service and weapons differed considerably from the men with the field batteries. All along the Atlantic seaboard stood masonry fortifications, some dating back to the turn of the century, built to guard river outlets, bays and harbors, and major cities like Charleston, Baltimore, and New Orleans. Several also guarded Boston, New York, and other Northern cities, and manning them was usually the task of "heavy artillery." These oversized regiments were intended to operate siege and seacoast guns, but often in the Union Army were rearmed with rifles and used as infantry. In the Confederacy, its forts were more frequently manned by displaced infantrymen or members of mobile siege and garrison units called siege trains. In the North it was a soft life, for no Yankee fort ever came under attack, or even threat. The men spent their war in garrison, practicing at their guns, decorating their barracks, making gravel pathways around the parade grounds, and polishing their gear for the frequent inspection visits of dignitaries.

It was a different matter in the Confederacy, and especially at hot spots like Fort Sumter in Charleston Harbor, or Fort Pulaski near the mouth of Georgia's Savannah River. The constant object of Union attacks, these places afforded little enough rest to their occupants. Indeed, Pulaski was taken from the Confederates in 1862 when Union siege artillery simply battered a huge hole in one side of its massive masonry walls, and infantry prepared to swarm through. Other forts, like Jackson and St. Philip guarding New Orleans, came under the bombardment of heavy naval guns from the Yankee fleets.

No fort and its occupants, however, endured what Fort Sumter did. Sitting almost in the middle of Charleston Harbor, it was an obstacle no invader could go around. To take Charleston, the Union had first to take Sumter. It had fallen easily enough when the Rebels took it in April of 1861, but then its defenders were undermanned, and hardly put up even a show of resistance. By the time the Federals returned to attempt to retake it, the story was altogether different. Confederates had strengthened the fort, added to its firepower, and ringed the rest of the harbor with even more guns and fortifications. Thus when April 1863 arrived, and with it a fleet of conventional warships and several of the new ironclad "monitors," the Confederates in Fort Sumter were ready. On April 7 the Yankee fleet attacked, steaming straight into the harbor. The Confederates held their fire at first, and at the same time the sailors aboard the leading ships began to see peculiar bouys ahead of them in the water. The Rebels had previously placed these bouys as range-markers, and carefully sighted their cannon on them. As a result, once the Confederates opened fire, it was with telling accuracy. Before long there were at least 76 Southern guns concentrating their fire on the slender line of nine Yankee ships, mounting among them just 32 cannon. In the two-hour fight that followed, the Confederates fired some 2,209 shots, of which fully one-fourth found their marks. The monitor *Passaic* took a hit once per minute for thirty-five minutes, firing only four times in response. Within a few minutes the ironclad *Keokuk* took 19 hits that penetrated her waterline, and suffered 90 hits all told. She sank the next day. Other Federal ships collided with each other, and in the confusion the entire fleet managed to fire only 154 shots. Five of the nine ships were disabled, and the forts and their intrepid gunners stood secure.[14]

The defenders came in for even more gruelling experience later that year when the man who took Fort Pulaski came to try a hand at Fort Sumter. General Quincy Gillmore brought his siege guns with him, and for fifteen days in August bombarded Fort Sumter, hurling tens of tons of iron at it from long-range guns. Twice more he repeated the bombardment, largely reducing it to a pile of rubble. Yet, incredibly, the gunners inside the fort held out. Indeed, not until Gallipoli in 1915 would warfare witness such a defense against combined military and naval attack. Bombarded by an ironclad fleet, by scores of enormous siege guns, attacked by amphibious parties, battered into a shapeless pile of brick and rubble, at times with every cannon in the place dismounted or out of commission, and sometimes with fevers and disease doing more damage to the garrison than the enemy, still it held out. At one time in 1864 the entire functioning defensive armament of Fort Sumter consisted of four shoulder rifles. Yet still it resisted.

The gunners burrowed inside the rubble, finding that it provided a wonderful defense. The loose mortar and brick absorbed the enemy shells better, more harmlessly, than had the standing walls. Deep within their tunnels, the defenders could sit out the bombardments in comparative safety. Indeed, the greatest loss of life in the fort in any single day came not from enemy shelling but, of all things, from whiskey. The gunners kept a barrel of it stored deep within the fort, and a candle flame – or perhaps a spark – came too near. The cask of spirits ignited, perhaps exploded, and soon set off a powder magazine nearby. The resulting blaze turned the underground passages into an inferno, killing or injuring 62 men, and forcing the rest to abandon the interior of the fort. It was ten days before the massive brick oven cooled enough for the gunners to re-enter. And Fort Sumter kept right on holding out until February 1865, after every other major Confederate city and fort had been taken.[15]

Wherever they served, whether in field or fort, the artillerymen of the Civil War were always in the thick of the action. It is no surprise that the very first shot of the war was an artilleryman's signal shell fired over Fort Sumter to commence the Confederate bombardment. If the account of one of Lee's officers may be accepted, the final shots fired by the Army of Northern Virginia came at Appomattox from the guns of Captain Valentine C. Clutter's Virginia battery. Two days later, with the war in Virginia over, an old colonel and his battery were guarding a pass in the Blue Ridge mountains when approaching Federals first tried to drive them out, and then passed on the news of Lee's surrender. When confirmation of the fact came to him, the old colonel formed his battery as if on parade, and ordered the men to run the guns up on to the bluff overlooking the Shenandoah River. The sun was setting in the west, the embers of their campfires dying out, as the colonel gave the order to fire. There was no target. It was simply a parting shot to the way of life they had known for four years. When the roar had ceased to echo in the surrounding mountains, he gave another command. "Let them go, and God be our helper. Amen!" Over the edge they all went. the guns splashing into the river's waters below.[16] All that remained were the men and the horses, and it is a fitting irony that, just as they had made war together, so now they would make peace. Federal terms allowed the men to take their horses home with them, and soon the animals that for four years had rushed their pieces to and fro in battle, were harnessed to the plow to turn soil for the rebuilding of the nation.

REFERENCES

1 Benjamin W. Jones, *Under the Stars and Bars* (Dayton, Ohio, 1975), p.20.

2 E.B. Long, *The Civil War Day by Day* (New York, 1971), pp.716-18.

3 Jones, *Stars and Bars*, pp.15-17.

4 Larry J. Daniel, *Cannoneers in Gray* (University, Ala., 1984), p.12.

5 Jones, *Stars and Bars*, p.17.

6 Daniel, *Cannoneers*, pp.12-13.

7 *Ibid.*, p.13.

8 *Ibid.*, pp.13-14.

9 Jones, *Stars and Bars*, pp.19-20

10 Harold L. Peterson, *Notes on Ordnance of the American Civil War* (Washington, 1959), pp.9-12.

11 *Ibid.*

12 Warren Ripley, *Artillery and Ammunition of the Civil War* (Englewood, N.J., 1970), passim.

13 *Ibid.*

14 Superintendent Naval War Records, *Official Records of the Union and Confederate Navies in the War of the Rebellion* (Washington, 1902), Series I, Volume 14, pp.4ff.

15 E. Milby Burton, *The Siege of Charleston* (Columbia, S.C., 1971), passim.

16 Jennings C. Wise, *The Long Arm of Lee* (New York, 1959), pp.956-7.

VI

LIFE AT SEA

Not surprisingly in a continent bounded by the seas, there were not a few Americans North and South who chose another kind of service in the rush to arms. The old Union, to a large extent, had always been a maritime nation. Yet, as was the case with its army, years of peacetime had allowed the United States Navy to dwindle dramatically. In 1861, out of a commissioned fleet of 90 vessels, some still uncompleted, the Union could count on just 35 modern vessels, with only three steamships readily at hand and not on some foreign station. That was not much of a force to cover some 3,500 miles of Confederate coastline, resupply isolated Federal outposts at Fort Pickens, Florida, and elsewhere, and maintain effectively the blockade of Southern ports proclaimed by Lincoln. Equally understrength was the manpower of the service, with just 7,600 seamen in uniform.[1] Of course, the Confederacy had no navy whatsoever at the outset, whereas the existence of a host of local militia units did give it an impressive headstart for its army. Thus for both North and South, there was a massive task ahead of the respective Navy departments in acquiring ships and men to crew them.

Finding ships was, for both sides, a matter of building some, converting others to war purposes, and buying the rest. The South put into service perhaps as many as 500 vessels before the end of the war, though most were small, ersatz boats hardly equal to the demands made upon them. A few Rebel ships, however, achieved well-deserved notoriety, most notably the commerce raiders *Florida*, *Alabama*, *Tallahassee*, and others, and the river and harbor ironclads like the *Virginia* (*Merrimack*), *Arkansas*, and *Albemarle*. As for the Union, by 1865 its Navy had seen service from 716 vessels, all but a few newly constructed specially for war.[2]

Finding the men to run those ships remained a constant challenge. A big problem, ironically, was the army. In the first rush of enthusiasm, everyone hurried to take up a rifle. No one even thought of the war lasting long enough for the navy to play a big role, nor did they really anticipate that there would be much need for naval engagement, even if the war did extend beyond the summer of 1861. Worse, the bounties offered to induce men to enlist in newly forming regiments usually lured the few experienced seamen to try their hand at land service instead. So great did the shortage become that colonels of many regiments were urged to comb their ranks for men who had the skiils to serve on boats, and to transfer them to the navy instead. Unfortunately, many officers used the opportunity not to transfer good men, but to get rid of undesirables. "Our Captain did some weeding out today," wrote a trooper of the 4th Illinois Cavalry in January 1862. A fleet of gunboats had asked for volunteers, "But the Captain took it upon himself to detail such men that he would rather spare and told them they had to go." One of the men so assigned was even then under arrest for drunkenness and attempting to kill his lieutenant.[3]

Before long, Congress authorized the payment of bounties for naval enlistments, though they were never as effective as with army enrollments, and by 1864 some volunteers were being paid as much as $1,000 per man to sign on. Though it never became a flood, Union naval enlistments rose sufficiently to crew every ship put into service, and during the course of the war some 132,554 eventually wore the blue. Across the lines, with far fewer ships of any size, and a fleet – such as it was – that was almost entirely confined to rivers and bays, the Confederate Navy had substantially smaller manpower needs. Even then, it was always hard-pressed for crewmen, and frequently had to borrow them from nearby army units when action approached. Probably not much over 5,000 men enlisted in the Southern navy during the war. [4]

However they came into the navy service, seamen North and South encountered much the same initial experiences as the youthful Alvah Hunter of New Hampshire. Unlike many young men, he actually wanted to get into the navy from the first, but when he appeared at a Boston recruiting office, he was repeatedly turned away. Just sixteen years old, he wanted to sign on as a "ship's boy," the lowliest of the enlisted grades, and essentially a fetch-all position for completely inexperienced young men. The navy already had too many boys, he was told, and only his persistence won out in the end, when the intercession of an officer assigned to the new ironclad monitor *Nahant* got him his shipping orders.

Hunter appeared on the appointed day before the old commodore in charge of the assignment office and presented his instructions. Despite some grumbling about there being already too many ship's boys in the service, the commodore nevertheless enrolled Hunter as a "First-Class Boy" and sent him off to the surgeon for inspection. Apparently, it was not much different from the cursory lookover given to most army enlistees at the time, and Hunter concluded that "a 'boy' wasn't of sufficient importance to require a close examination." From the doctor he went to the outfitter's, and there drew his new uniform – two blue flannel shirts, trousers, socks and shoes, a clothes bag to hold them, two blankets, a crude mattress, and a hammock. He might also have drawn white cotton duck clothing, depending upon the officer commanding his ship. Thus outfitted, Hunter and others were taken out to the receiving ship for the initial training.[5]

The United States Navy had several old sailing ships-of-the-line still in commission in 1861, though clearly obsolete for the war at hand. Washington consequently turned them into receiving ships, virtually wharf-bound barracks and schools. Hunter went aboard the old *Ohio*, and there he changed into his new uniform, stowed his hammock and gear, and first heard the shrill whistle of the boatswain's pipe that would order his days for the rest of his service. That first call, incidentally, was the one most welcome – the call for supper. "With the eating of that first meal aboard ship," he recalled, "I began to feel that at last I was really shipped into the navy."[6]

Hunter spent three weeks on the old *Ohio*, though many new seamen spent longer periods of time before their posting orders arrived. To a landsman like him, one with no experience of the sea, it was all wonder at first. "I was so well content with having at last found a way into the navy I was quite satisfied to remain on board." Like thousands of other farmboys and clerks, he marveled at the massive wooden ship, with its "countless portholes for guns" and "her vast bulk." Crammed aboard with between 300 and 400 others, most of them his own age or a little older, he found no lack of fun and frolic. Hunter spent hours studying the ship's fittings and hidden places, looking at the smartly dressed marines who guarded the gangways and officers' quarters. Not a few of his fellow ship's boys were black, for the Union Navy was ahead of the army in enlisting Negroes. A ready camaraderie seems to have grown up between white and black in most instances, not the least because a ship could be a very small world to live in, and men inevitably had to set aside or unlearn prejudices in the interest of working and living together. However, this spirit did not always apply to the marines and many Civil War seamen adopted the age-old antipathy for the "lobster backs" whose duty it was to perform none of the ship's drudgery, but simply act as ship's police and – in the event of battle – take posts as marksmen or boarders.

The common seaman's day, North or South, was much the same – one continuing routine, varied little except by the type of ship the man served, and the duty assignment of the vessel itself. Sometimes, if special duties like refueling or cleaning the ship were due prior to departure, the boatswain awakened the men well before dawn. More often, however, a bugler – a marine if the ship was large enough to carry a marine contingent – sounded reveille at 5 o'clock in the morning. While the bleary-eyed tried to clear their heads, the boatswain and others from the watch coming to an end ran along the berth deck shouting at the men and adding incentive by shaking or jarring their hammocks.

The first duty of the sailor was to stow his sleeping gear, wrap his blankets if any inside his hammock, roll it into a tight little ball, and stow it on the main deck in a special hammock netting behind the ship's bulwarks. There it served a dual purpose, for the netting and hammocks so placed could catch dangerous splinters sent flying about the deck by enemy cannon fire, and at the same time provide an obstacle to boarders in a close action. A seaman was expected to take only seven minutes from the sounding of reveille to the placement of his bedding in the netting, but depending upon the punctiliousness of his captain, and how much long, monotonous duty may have loosened discipline, he more often than not took longer.

With his bedding stowed, the sailor had more chores ahead of him before he was served his morning meal. He had to scrub his berth deck with seawater, and then use holystones to clean the main deck. That done, there were the guns to clean, with all exposed iron to be burnished to keep off rust. A ship carried lots of brass – bells, fittings, even ornamental hardware – and all of it had to be polished. Sails and rigging – if any – needed to be checked for mildew and wear, and the ship's ropes and tackle put in order. Only when his vessel glistened bright and clean in the morning sun did the sailor receive orders allowing him to wash and brighten himself.

By 7.30, all this behind him, the seamen dressed and waited for the sound of the boatswain's pipe calling them to breakfast. The men ate in "messes" of eight or more to a table, usually eating with others who shared their specific duty posts, such as gun crews, topmen on sailing ships, engineers, and the like. What they actually ate varied with the season and the climate of their station, as well as what might be locally available, but in the main every seaman was supposed to have a pint of strong coffee and a sizeable piece of hard, salted beef, called "junk" – and not without reason. Ordinarily the men took turns at acting as cook for their messes. The meal done, each man kept his cutlery and mug, while the mess orderly of the day stowed the cooking utensils and plates in the mess chest.

Happily, after a busy early morning, the sailor generally enjoyed a few hours of leisure after his breakfast, excepting perhaps a general call to quarters for inspection. Otherwise, he wrote his letters – if he could write – mended his clothing, played cards or backgammon with his mates, and tried any other means available to escape what could be an endless round of tedium, especially for the Yankee sailors on blockade duty.

Noon brought yet another meal, this one more substantial, with salt pork or beef, vegetables, coffee, and whatever local produce might be available, especially eggs or cheese. Victuals varied greatly, with Union sailors enjoying a much more standard bill of fare, while Rebels ate in much the same ersatz fashion as their compatriots in the armies. Only the men aboard the commerce raiders like the *Shenandoah* or *Florida* enjoyed really ample tables, thanks to what they captured from the prizes they took. As the war wore on, many Confederate seamen received issues of meat rations only two or three times a week.

Training and drill occupied some of the afternoon, though there was little actual schedule or regularity about it. Indeed, one ship's boy on a Federal blockader in 1863 wrote that "the life of a sailor is not one of a real and regular work, his hours of rest may not be uniform but they are more or less regulated." The details of ship's routine might vary considerably from day to day, he observed, "yet its original outlines are the same day after day."

The one immutable factor, other than reveille and the early morning duties, was mealtime, and thus many sailors came to measure their days not by hours but by when they ate. Like all other meals, the 4 p.m. light supper came at the end of a four-hour watch, and here there could be a problem, for this was the final meal of the day, and it would be sixteen hours before the next day's breakfast. Men with late night watches could become painfully hungry.

Following supper, the crews had one more call to quarters for inspection at 5.30 before the ship essentially finished with its active day – excepting, of course, vessels engaged in open-sea steaming or on active blockade duty where most of the real action took place at dusk and after. Once their inspection was done, the crewmen had the rest of the evening to themselves. They retrieved their hammocks and slung them on the berth deck, and then lounged, slept, read, and secretly engaged in a variety of forms of gambling, though officially it was against regulations and offenders could be disciplined or fined. They threw dice, bet on dominoes and cards, tossed coins, and even bet on times and distances involved in their vessel's travels.[7]

But much more was available for those who craved recreation and entertainment. Banjos, guitars, fiddles, fifes, and more, came out on deck in the evenings, with some ships actually forming ensembles from their company. Even amateur theatricals were performed on the upper decks of men of war. Sporting contests, boxing, footraces, acrobatics, all played the same stage on many ships, depending largely upon the attitude of the captain as to what was acceptable. Until the grog ration was prohibited in 1862, Union seamen could have one gill – about four ounces – of whiskey mixed with water, while his Confederate counterpart received his ration only when it was available.

Once a week the men washed their clothes, hanging them to dry on lines stretched between the masts. Sometimes the ship's pumps were hooked up to hoses, and seawater was sprayed over the decks, which inevitably led to "much skylarking on the part of the boys and distress of the old sailors who directed the performance," wrote Hunter.[8]

It was partly because of the frolicsome nature of youth that the Union Navy in 1864 adopted regulations to govern enlistments, stipulating that no one under the age of eighteen was to be enrolled. It defeated itself, however, in that the only proof required of a young man was his own sworn oath as to his age. Further, for positions such as ship's boys, youths as tender as thirteen could be accepted providing they stood at least four feet eight inches tall. At the other extreme, no one over the age of 38 was to be enlisted under any circumstances unless specifically endorsed by the Navy Department. There were a host of enlisted grades in both navies, ranging from the lowest, ship's boy, up to the yeomen and boatswains. Hunter received $8 a month;

a boatswain might receive $120 when at sea; and all the grades in between – landsmen, musicians, cooks, nurses, coopers, painters, stewards, quartermasters, and more – received varying amounts prescribed by their length of service.

There was quite a mixture of men filling those grades. Negroes were enlisted into the Union Navy officially commencing in September 1861, and were given equal pay even while their counterparts in the army had to endure receiving smaller salaries than white soldiers. A host of other nationalities also went into the naval service, most of them northern Europeans who came from seafaring nations such as Norway and Sweden. In some cases, nearly one-half of a ship's crew were foreign born. In the Confederacy, by contrast, no blacks were officially enlisted, though many served as servants and cooks, and the bulk of the seamen were native born, most of them with little or no nautical experience since the South did not have much of a maritime tradition.

The provisions for food in the navies were specified by naval regulations, and in the North they were almost always met or exceeded, while the Rebel navy suffered some of the same shortages of its army counterparts, though rarely to the same extent thanks to proximity to seaports, and easier access to produce from blockade runners and captured Yankee vessels. In Lincoln's navy, official rations per man per day were to consist of a pound of salt pork and half a pint of peas or beans; or else a pound of salt beef with half a pound of flour and a quarter pound of raisins, apples, or other dried fruit; or one pound of salt beef with half a pound of rice and two ounces each of butter and cheese, along with tea and nearly a pound of hardtack or baked biscuits. Additionally, each week the men were to receive a half-pound of cranberries or pickles, half a pint of molasses, and half a pint of vinegar. A number of substitutions were allowed by law, depending upon the availability of foodstuffs, but the basic quantities and proportions among the food groups remained the same.

It was a diet heavy in salt and starch, with an absence of citrus or fresh green vegetables to help prevent scurvy. Recognizing that it was not sufficient to sustain the stamina and health of the seamen on long blockade duty, Union Secretary of the Navy Gideon Welles early authorized supplementation of the ration where possible. In practice, the cooks at sea managed to prepare a number of variations out of the stocks in their larder, though the daily menu hardly varied enough to make the men relish their meals. Pork and beans became a staple, and a very popular dish, called "duff," was a simple boiled pudding of flour and water sweetened with molasses and given variety by mixing with it dried fruit or nuts. But this diet could be overdone. Charles Brother, serving aboard the USS *Hartford*, recorded in his diary his daily dinner ration, and just the month from March 14 to April 14, 1864, shows that he had pork and beans on twelve days for dinner, duff on seven days, and what he called "bullion beef" and coffee on six other occasions. At least the cooks refrained from serving the same dish more than two days consecutively. And on only two days did he note a special occasion when "fresh grub" – whatever that was – was presented to his mess.

Sometimes special concoctions of the cook's came out of the pots, a few of which still defy description, such as "dandyfunk," a stew of hardtack soaked in water and baked with salt pork and molasses. Sometimes there was 'sea pie," a multi-layered dish of meat and crust. It is no wonder that being served the same usually bland dishes over and over, the sailors developed a host of not very complimentary sobriquets for them. In both navies, for example, salted or pickled beef was invariably known as "salt horse", denoting not only its lack of savor and tenderness, but also the sailors' wry suspicions as to its source.[9]

The seaman's monotonous daily diet was only part of what proved to be an almost ceaselessly tedious existence. It is a fact that the average sailor saw substantially less real action than most soldiers, and many seamen never actually went into battle at all.

It is no wonder, then, that just as in the army, drinking became a major release, and a major disciplinary problem. For decades, the regulations had provided for a spirit ration, just enough to give a man a little ease, but not enough to get him intoxicated. The problem was that many men did not drink and either gave or sold their ration to others. Some men also hoarded their rations, saving it for one big evening, and now and then managed to smuggle a few bottles aboard after a shore leave. And when they drank too heavily, the men would misbehave. Aboard the CSS *Alabama* in November 1862, a troublemaker escaped the ship, swam to a nearby vessel in the harbor of Martinique, and returned with "a great quantity of spirits," which he passed out among the crewmen. They became so drunk that one threw a belaying pin at an officer who tried to control them, and soon Captain Raphael Semmes had a small-scale mutiny on his hands. Because of instances like this, the Union Navy Department, acting on Congressional mandate, abolished the grog ration entirely on July 14, 1862, substituting an additional five cents per day per man as compensation. Never popular, this act itself nearly led to mutiny, especially when the Bureau of Medicine and Surgery suggested that the men might like iced tea instead, or even oatmeal![10]

Obviously, because men would misbehave, there had to be means of punishment for offenders, though this presented special problems in the confines of a ship at sea or on station in a river in enemy territory. Serious offenses like mutiny, disobeying orders, desertion, treason, and the like, were to be dealt with by courts-martial. Even seemingly minor infractions like swearing, drunkenness and gambling could be thus tried, as could dueling.

Other than flogging, which was outlawed entirely, almost any penalty an officer could devise was allowable. A man could be demoted, his pay reduced accordingly. He could be confined in the brig – or the ship's hold or coal bunkers if there was no brig – for as many days as needed, with or without hand and leg irons, and on bread and water if the captain chose. He could be denied shore leave or punished with extra duty. And if he committed a more summary offense, he could be confined for up to two months, one month of it in irons and on bread and water, or even dismissed from the service. Lesser offenses were disciplined at the will of the captain or his officers, and serious crimes could be punished by death.

Generally, the seamen encountered less formalized punishments for their misbehavior, as officers suited the penalties to the crimes. When Semmes's mutineers were under control on the *Alabama*, he had them taken one by one to the gangway and ordered shipmates to douse them with buckets of water. At first the inebriates howled in derision at the paltry punishment, yelling at the quartermasters to "come on with their water." But the water came faster and faster, incessantly, leaving a man no time to catch his breath between one dousing and another. After a time, choking, sick, near to fainting, they begged to be forgiven. Then Semmes released them and sent them to their hammocks. He never experienced another mutiny.[11]

There was a considerable variety in the conditions experienced by seamen, depending upon their posting. Yankees stuck on blockade service endured, arguably, the most tedious life of all, spending months at a time patrolling back and forth a few miles outside a harbor or river mouth, waiting to catch an occasional runner. If the seas were down and the winds were low, it could be hot and sticky. When the weather rose, the churning seas battered ships and men alike, leaving the latter sea-sick and debilitated. It was somewhat better for the sea-going cruisers that plied the oceans in search of the Rebel commerce raiders. Though they spent months at a time on cruise, at least they encountered unusual or exotic ports, and more shore leave when available. The same was true of the men aboard the ships they hunted.

Sailor-for-sailor, there was far more real action, and much more relief from the tedium, for the men stationed aboard the river gunboats. Hundreds of these plied the Mississippi and its tributaries, as well as all the major navigable rivers along the eastern seacoast. Smaller, shallow-draft vessels, they usually operated out of bases in the interior, or else in a harbor, and returned frequently to refill their small coal bunkers. That meant many more opportunities for the men to get leave to go ashore. Additionally, water, wood, and foraging parties often left the vessel while on patrol, spending a few hours or even days on the riverbank and in the interior. It was still hot service, and muggy along the Southern waterways, but foul weather presented much less of a hazard.

The tedium was further relieved by the very real hazard of action, for a river gunboat might frequently encounter enemy shore batteries, an attack from shore-based boarders, even an occasional raid by cavalry. And now and then, especially on the Mississippi, there could be a major fleet battle or attack upon some fortified city like New Orleans or Vicksburg. For every blockade sailor who died of sea-sickness or scurvy, a river seaman died in action.

Ironically, the safest service of all was also the most uncomfortable. The rush of building of ironclads – called "monitor fever" in the North – led to the commissioning of scores of the ungainly monsters. The Confederate *Virginia*, converted from the old *Merrimack*, was not the world's first ironclad as is often supposed, but it was the virtual prototype for almost every other Rebel ironclad of the war. Its foe the USS *Monitor* was likewise the precursor of a host of others, most with one turret, some with two, and even one with three gun towers. The Union also built several other river gunboats that were iron-sheathed to protect the crew and machinery from shore batteries. Most were effective, a few were not. But all of them were absolutely miserable to serve aboard. Ventilation was almost non-existent, and in the hot and humid Southern summers, temperatures beneath the iron sheathing on decks and turrets could rise well over 120[deg]F during the day. With no windows to cool the interior, or to let in light, the men lived in a damp, dark, fetid, nightmarish underworld. "I began to think that in our Navy [comfort] does not exist," wrote a man aboard the CSS *Baltic*. Even worse was the Rebel ironclad *Atlanta*, serving in the sounds of Georgia. "I would defy anyone in the world to tell when it is day or night if he is confined below without any way of marking time," wrote a man aboard the ship. "If a person were blindfolded and carried below and then turned loose he would imagine himself in a swamp."[12] The only remedy the Confederates found was to berth their ironclad crews ashore at night when possible, and almost all ironclad sailors soon learned to abandon the steamy berthdeck for the top deck at night. "Hot, hotter, hottest," wrote a man aboard the *Monitor* in Virginia's James River in August 1862. "Could stand it no longer, so last night I wrapped my blanket 'round me & took to our iron deck – if the bed was not soft it was not so insufferably hot as my *pen*."[13]

No wonder every shipboard surgeon had to worry about a host of ills, from diarrhea and dysentery, to typhoid, malaria, and simple exhaustion. Quinine was liberally dosed when available, and canned tomatoes were the only answer for scurvy when fresh vegetables and fruit were unavailable. As for sea-sickness, the sailors had their own remedies. When Alvah Hunter first fell ill with it on the *Nahant's* initial voyage, an old salt persuaded him to drink sea water and, incredibly, he immediately felt better.

If the burden of boredom was greater for the sailor than for his counterpart in the armies, at least he carried a lighter load. The footsoldier lugged nine or ten pounds of rifle and another twenty or more of other impedimenta wherever he marched. Happily, the seamen had no knapsacks, nor any assigned rifles or other weapons to husband. Every vessel in the Union Navy carried arms racks of muskets or carbines, pistols, and the traditional cutlasses. While every man at one time or another spent his share of duty at cleaning and caring for the weapons stores, still he did not have a specifically assigned weapon that was regarded as his own, other than pocket or clasp knives which the Navy Department issued to every man.

What fighting the seaman did engage in was usually ship-to-ship or ship-to-shore manning the cannon of his vessel. He worked a variety of guns almost as great as that of the artillerymen in the army, though generally the ship's guns came in more awesome sizes. There were rifles that fired projectiles ranging from twelve up to 150 pounds, most of them Parrott's, though also a number of the newly designed

Dahlgren rifles, often called "soda pop" guns thanks to their shape resembling that of a bottle. Aboard some of the biggest vessels, and especially on ironclads expected to combat forts or other ironclads, massive smoothbores firing projectiles up to fifteen inches in diameter and weighing 440 pounds or more, were also served by the gun crews. And there were a lot of them. By the last year of the war, the Union Navy alone carried over 4,600 guns aboard its ships. Numbers for Confederate vessels are far less precise, but certainly more than 2,500 saw service. Regulations differed according to the gun and the availability of men, but in general it took sixteen seamen to operate one muzzle-loader, most of them performing functions that corresponded closely to the duties of the artillerymen with the army forces. In addition, the massive guns had to be manhandled forward by rope and tackle after every recoil, and that task alone could occupy nine seamen.

The experiences of sailors both North and South were quite apart from those of the soldiers, and distinct to the kinds of ships they manned. Rarely did any man ever have to face the ultimate test of a hand-to-hand, face-to-face encounter with an enemy. Most of the water-borne action of the war took place on the rivers and harbors of the South, between gunboats and ironclads, or such vessels and Confederate forts. In either case, most of the time the gun crews enjoyed the protection of an iron casemate or turret in the case of the ironclads, and at least some kind of iron reinforced wood, or even cotton, bulwarks aboard the gunboats and converted river steamers.

Of course, the protective bulwarks of iron or whatever else surrounded the ship above the water-line, varied greatly in effectiveness. A really accurate shot from one of those massive 15-inch smoothbores, or a heavy solid "bolt" or projectile fired from a big rifled cannon, might penetrate any but the strongest armor, and then a ship's crew was in trouble. Flying splinters of wood and iron could become deadly missiles inside a gun deck. And if an enemy shot penetrated through the protective hull and punctured the steam engines' boilers, then the ship's interior could become a scalding inferno.

Nevertheless, while advancements in warfare had made fighting increasingly more dangerous for the footsoldier, for the seaman the Civil War was comparatively the safest conflict to date. Consequently, of more than 132,000 Yankee sailors, just 1,804 were killed in action or died as a result of wounds, and of them nearly one-fifth were scalded to death by burst boilers. Perhaps another 3,000 died of other causes, but total deaths still amount to less than four percent. Confederate naval casualties are difficult to ascertain, though their overall percentage was likely greater, since Southern protective armor was less effective than that of the North, and considerably more Rebel vessels were battered into submission.[14]

Still, when compared to a better than one-in-five chance of meeting death in some form or another for the soldiers, the sailors' hopes of survival were immeasurably greater. As for the men aboard the Confederate commerce raiders, the few naval blockade runners, or the Yankee ships that chased both, injuries in action from enemy fire were almost non-existent. The commerce raiders took on only unarmed merchant vessels, and the blockaders the same. And when they did fire, often as not their target was only a dim smudge of sail or a column of smoke on the horizon.

Indeed, for most sailors, Blue and Gray alike, the real action of the war was invariably a dot on the horizon – an event dimly seen, indistinctly heard, and peripherally experienced. That they did their part cannot be denied, nor is it arguable that the control of the rivers, harbors, and coastlines for which they vied, was not ultimately crucial to success or failure. Yet for the men who often endured a year of inaction for every day of battle in those ships and boats, theirs was a war on the margins of the greater conflict.

REFERENCES

1 Long, *Day by Day*, p.719.

2 *Ibid.*

3 Francis Lord, *They Fought for the Union* (Harrisburg, Pa., 1960), p.286.

4 Long, *Day by Day*, p.720.

5 Alvah Hunter, *A Year on a Monitor and the Destruction of Fort Sumter* (Columbia, S.C., 1987), pp.7-8.

6 *Ibid.*, p.8.

7 William C. Davis (ed.), *Fighting for Time* (New York, 1983), pp.366-71.

8 Hunter, *Monitor*, p.8.

9 Lord, *They Fought for the Union*, p.287; C. Carter Smith, Jr. (ed.), *Two Naval Journals: 1864* (Birmingham, Ala., 1964), pp.19ff.

10 Davis, *Fighting for Time*, p.373.

11 Raphael Semmes, *The Confederate Raider "Alabama"* (Greenwich, Conn., 1962), pp.138-40.

12 William N. Still, *Iron Afloat* (Nashville, 1971), p.100.

13 Robert W. Daly (ed.), *Aboard the USS Monitor: 1862* (Annapolis, Md., 1964), p.205.

14 Long, *Day by Day*, pp.710-11.

VII

TENTING TONIGHT

There was, said an old Confederate Carlton McCarthy, a "fancy idea [that] the principal occupation of a soldier should be actual conflict with the enemy." The recruits of 1861 "didn't dream of such a thing as camping for six months at a time without firing a gun, or marching and countermarching," not to mention "the thousand commonplace duties of the soldier."[1] There, however, lay the true essence of Civil War soldiering. For every day spent in battle, Yank and Reb passed weeks – even months – fighting other enemies: heat and cold, hunger, deprivation, bad sanitation, foolish officers, the allurements of the devil, and worst of all boredom.

Out of it all came their most enduring memories of the days of their youth. "Let us together recall with pleasure the past!" exclaimed McCarthy years later; "once more be hungry, and eat; once more tired, and rest; once more thirsty, and drink; once more cold and wet, let us sit by the roaring fire and feel comfort creep over us."[2] They were simple pleasures all, but to the men in blue and gray they were triumphs in themselves, adversities conquered in the unending battle to make the campgrounds of North and South homes away from home.

The new soldiers came ill-prepared for their lives in camp. Hometown oratory charged their emotions to expect an immediate rush headlong into glorious battle, fight day in and day out, and then, the war won, return home again in triumph. Their first scanty drill and training in the rendezvous camps gave little hint of what would really come once they joined the armies in the field. No one taught them to cook, or pitch tents, or not to dig their latrines upstream of their camps. No one told them what to expect – because no one *knew* what to expect – when suddenly thousands of men from all stations of life were thrown together – saints and sinners, bullies and milktoasts. Sometimes those who had gone before sent back warnings of what lay ahead for the new recruit in camp, but in the end every man had to learn for himself.

The new soldier learned rather quickly that his only real place of refuge from the parade ground was his tent, his home for three seasons of the year. As with his weapons, a considerable variety of shelters first appeared in the summer of 1861. Some units like the Washington Artillery of New Orleans came with candy-striped tents. Others showed up with nothing at all, and the governments had to cast about for what would suit their regiments the best. Wall tents were initially popular, canvas dwellings shaped exactly like a small house. But they proved too expensive to manufacture, too cumbersome to pitch and carry, and eventually found themselves inhabited only by those too weak or too exalted to do the work of erecting them – hospital patients and officers.

Much more popular and efficient was the Sibley tent, named for its inventor Henry H. Sibley, now a brigadier general in the Confederate service. One Reb likened it to "a large hoop skirt standing by itself on the ground."[3] Indeed, it resembled nothing so much as an Indian tepee, a tall cone of canvas supported by a center pole. Flaps on the sides could be opened for ventilation, and an iron replica of the tent cone called a Sibley stove heated the interior – sort of. Often more than twenty men inhabited a single tent, spread out like the spokes of a wheel, their heads at the outer rim and their feet at the center pole. Yet regulations called for no more than a dozen inhabitants, and while some soldiers found the Sibleys more healthy and comfortable than a regular barracks, that only applied on days when the weather was fair. When the cold or rain forced the men to keep the tent flaps closed overnight, the air inside became unbearable. John D. Billings, a Massachusetts artilleryman, never forgot what it was like to enter a Sibley after such a night "and encounter the night's accumulation of nauseating exhalations from the bodies of twelve men (differing widely in their habits of personal cleanliness)." It was "an experience which no old soldier has ever been known to recall with great enthusiasm."[4] Eventually, Sibleys also proved too cumbersome for extensive field operations.

Rapidly the tents became simpler, lighter, and as a rule less comfortable. For a time Billy Yank tried sleeping in the wedge tent. Exceedingly simple, it was little more than a six-foot length of canvas that its four to six occupants draped over a center pole. Stakes held its sides to the ground, and end flaps closed the openings, allowing some privacy, but absolutely no comfort. With only about seven square feet of space per man on the ground, the men had to sleep "spoon" fashion. When one turned in his sleep, all the others had to do the same. And with the ridge pole only five feet off the ground, even the shorter soldiers were forced to stoop to enter.

If that were not bad enough, by the latter part of 1862, and for the balance of the war to follow, an even smaller soldier shelter came into use. "It would only comfortably accommodate a dog, and a small one at that," said Billings. So that is what they called it – the dog tent.[5] It differed little in nature or name from the pup tent of later wars. Two men shared it, and it took two to make it, each one carrying with him a half of the canvas. They buttoned their halves together, slung it over a center pole, and then lay down side-by-side in the cramped interior to contemplate what little impediment, if any, their shelter offered to the elements since it had no end flaps to hinder cold and wind. In 1862 the Yankee Asa Brindle told his family that the dog tent reminded him "forceable of a hog pen." He deeply lamented that its inventor had not been "hung before the invention had been completed."

Confederates suffered continually from want of proper shelters, as they suffered with a shortage of just about everything else. Captured Yankee tents were often all they had, for wartime shortages affected canvas as well as weapons and ammunition. Lacking tents, the Southerners improvised crude shelters as best they could, often piling brush or stretching oil clothes over fence-rail frameworks to make so-called "she-bangs." However crude, still inhabitants pronounced them "very comfortable in warm weather."

However it was that fourth season of the year, the winter's chill, that most challenged the Reb's and Yank's ability and imagination. When the leaves began to turn and the north winds freshened, the men in the tents took their axes and saws out into the neighboring woods and virtually mowed them down. If timber was in sufficient abundance, whole log cabins rose up. More often, however, the soldiers blended earth and trees, their tents, even scavenged portions of local buildings, to produce their winter quarters. Before the ground froze, they dug into the earth a foot or so, then they built their log walls another four or five above the pit, capping them with flat roofs of brush or boards, or even tents slung over a center pole. They waterproofed their roofs by spreading their own ponchos or rubberized blankets over the canvas, and kept the wind and rain from whistling through the walls by packing the chinks between the logs with mud. For many of the upper-crust soldiers from the affluent cities, it was like a return to the pioneer homes of their forebears. For the boys from the wooded hills and mountains of Appalachia, it was often just like home.

Every winter hut was as individual as the men who built it. They made fireplaces of sticks and mud, with an old barrel for a chimney. More ambitious men foraged brick to erect true masonry masterpieces. Furnishings came from whatever might be found – and more often liberated when in enemy country. No farmer's barn was safe, and any abandoned house presented a true emporium of domestic possibilities. Straw and pine needle mattresses covered bunks along the walls. Boxes and log ends made serviceable stools to set before their rough wood or crate tables. Bayonets thrust into the logs became candlesticks, and more straw spread upon the floor absorbed the mud from outside tracked in by visitors.

Nothing in the Civil War could escape the soldiers' penchant for nicknames, and certainly not their winter dwellings. A Louisiana unit dubbed two of its houses "Sans Souci" and "Buzzard's Roost." Some New Englanders called their's the "Swine Hotel," "Hole in the Wall," and "We're Out," while a Bostonian recalled the glories of home naming his domicile the "Parker House." Even the streets bore names, and not always just patriotic titles like "Lincoln Avenue" or "Lee Boulevard." Many an encampment had its "Mud Lane" and "Starvation Alley." Some, like one admiring Indianian, might declare that "Instead of appearing like a camp of rusty soldiers, it looks like a city of magnificent splendor," but few found winter quarters so delightful. The huts were not that much better than tents, and whether freezing in the snow or drowning in the rain, the whole camps were generally a mess. "This plain became a wallow-hole," complained one Bay State soldier; "the clay surface freezing at night and thawing by day, trampled by thousands of men, made a vast sea of mud."[9]

Confederates fared no better. In the first winter of the war, a Reb at Manassas spoke of the place as "literally a lake of mud. Wherever you go the ground is so soft that you have to hold your breath to keep from sinking. Men and horses are often completely buried in driving over roads, and you see their heads protruding above the mire." Perhaps he exaggerated just a bit, but it was no stretch of the imagination to look on the filth and inconvenience, the fleas in the mattresses, the lice in their clothes, and the mud caked everywhere, and see why he would "be perplexed whether to laugh or sympathize."[10]

While they were required to remain in camp, almost like prisoners, the soldiers had to contend with the ever-present mud in winter and dust in summer. In the latter season of 1864 one Connecticut soldier likened a walk through camp to a stroll through an ash heap. "One's mouth will be so full of dust that you do not want your teeth to touch one another."[11] A Yankee cannoneer wryly remarked that whenever a grasshopper jumped up, it raised such a cloud of dust that Confederate lookouts reported the Union army was on the move again. The dust blew through the holes in their worn clothing and caked to the sweat on their bodies. "I have no seat in my pants," lamented a Virginian, "the legs are worn out, have had but one pair of socks which are worn out completely, my shirt is literally rotted off me."[12] A new issue shirt proved to be so louse-ridden that he could not bear to wear it. Relief societies like the United States Christian Commission and several state societies, North and South, did what they could to bring a little comfort to the soldiers' lot, but it was ever a losing battle.

Filling all those countless thousands of hours of unoccupied time proved to be the greatest challenge facing Yank and Reb alike. Not surprisingly, so many men being away from home for prolonged periods for the first time in their lives, it was the common soldiers' preoccupation with the folks at home which afforded the most popular camp pastime. "Everybody is writing who can raise a pencil or sheet of paper," one Virginian wrote to his own dear loved ones in July 1861. Never before had such massive numbers of Americans been away from home for a prolonged period. Instinctively, they sensed that they were living through something unusual, an epoch worth remembering and reporting to their families. Letter writing, too, was the only contact that many could have with their loved ones, given the restrictions on furloughs. As a result, they sent letters back and forth that taxed the Postal Department as never before. In some regiments of 1,000 or more men, it was estimated that 600 letters a day were written and posted.[13]

There was a remarkable sameness to what men in blue and gray wrote home about. They talked of their battles, to be sure, but those were few and infrequent. More often they told of their friends, their day in camp, the marches, the heat, the weather, sickness – virtually anything that came to mind – as if the very act of writing was the bond with their loved ones, and not what was written. They used ink and pencil, even crayons. They wrote on foolscap and parchment, in the margins of newspapers and on the back of wallpaper. When a precious sheet of paper was filled, if there was more to say they gave the sheet a quarter turn and cross-wrote over what they had already written. "They is a fly on my pen," wrote John Shank of Illinois: "I just rights What ever Comes in my head."[14]

They wrote as they spoke, and those who could not write dictated letters for their friends to scrawl for them. Quaint as their spelling and grammar appear today, it is testimony not so much to the limits of model literary skill then prevailing, but rather to the surprising degree of at least communicable literacy among a host of men, many of whom had barely the rudiments of schooling. They were earthy, as in their speech, and they had their share of slang terms, many of which took on lasting meaning. "Snug as a bug in a rug," they wrote of their quarters. "Let 'er rip," "scarce as hen's teeth," "red tape," and a host of other idioms went through the mails. Just as a later world conflict would spawn such expressions as "snafu" for an operation gone awry, the Civil War soldier said that something bungled had "gone up." There was a certain homespun eloquence to their metaphors. One Ohio boy called a recent letter from home "Short and Sweet just like a rosted maget," and when another soldier complained to his wife about his spartan camp, he said "To tell the truth we are between sh-t and a sweat out here."[15]

But the most common element in all letters sent home by the boys in the field was the earnest desire for their family and friends to respond in kind. Nothing livened a day like mail call. "Those who received letters went off with radiant countenances," said Confederate John Worsham. "If it was night, each built a fire for light and, sitting down on the ground, read his letter over and over. Those unfortunates who got none went off looking as if they had not a friend on earth."[16] Private E.K. Flournoy lamented to his wife that he "was almost down with histericks" to hear from home.[17] When a Minnesota boy got a letter after a long silence, he confessed that "I can never remember of having been so glad before. I cried with joy and thankfulness."[18]

They saved their letters and read them again and again. And when there were no letters to peruse, the literate men consumed anything else they could find in print. "Everybody has taken to reading," wrote a Yank.[19] Some better-funded regiments actually established camp libraries. The 13th Massachusetts had its own library at Williamsport, Maryland, in 1862. In 1864 Colonel John C. Wickliffe of the Confederate 9th Kentucky even detailed one of his orderlies to forage for books in

Georgia, and built a camp library with rather eclectic holdings. They included Hugo's *Les Misérables*, Dumas' *Three Musketeers*, an encyclopedia of geography, a French reader and grammar, and even a volume of the 1859 *Patent Office Report*. The orderly also produced what he styled a "purty good book," though apologizing for the "damned *bad print*," that happened to be a volume of Cicero's works. "I don't know whether you can read it or not," he told Wickliffe. It was in Latin.[20]

Surprisingly, there were a few soldiers who could read Latin and Greek, and the classics were not at all unknown in the camps. The works of Shakespeare and Milton were read around many campfires as well, though Sir Walter Scott was far more popular. Popular novels of the day, as well as patriotic literature, were consumed with equal relish, not to mention the rapidly growing genre of works actually inspired by the war they were fighting. By 1862 the first memoirs of service began to appear, highly dramatized and often more than a bit fictional, still they enjoyed considerable popularity. Also popular was more serious fiction, like Edward Everett Hale's *The Man Without a Country* which appeared in 1863, and was widely believed to have been inspired by the story of Ohio Democrat Clement Vallandigham, who was expelled from the North for treason. Most popular of all, however, was the Bible. The US Christian Commission distributed tens of thousands of copies in the Union camps, and even more found their way to soldier hands North and South through private means.

Newspapers proved ever in demand, especially the illustrated press of the day. The *New York Illustrated News*, *Frank Leslie's Illustrated Newspaper*, *Harper's Weekly*, and for a brief time the Confederate *Southern Illustrated News*, provided the men with weekly accounts of the course of the war and events at home, illustrated with crude and often very inaccurate woodcuts. Literary magazines like *Harper's Monthly* and the *American Review* also came to the camps, but far more popular were booklets created especially for soldier consumption, the "dime" novels and paperback "penny dreadfuls" that the sutlers sold. Thousands of copies circulated among the soldiers. There were even a few copies of what a chaplain termed "licentious books" and "obscene pictures" to be had, most of them imported from Europe.[21] Entrepreneurs distributed flyers in the camps advertising their "spirited and spicy scenes," usually showing scantily clad maidens and captioned with heavy-handed puns about "storming the breastworks."[22] In the end, the men simply read or looked at whatever they could find, and if that was not sufficient, they sometimes created their own reading material. Scores of regiments edited and printed their own newspapers. General John Hunt Morgan's renowned Confederate cavalry issued the *Vidette* sporadically for two years, as much to badger the Yankees as to entertain the men.[23]

Music quickly came to occupy a special place of importance in the soldiers' life. It was a musical era. In the absence of other entertainments, family song fests around the piano were a cultural norm in the middle class of both North and South, augmented by public concerts and participation in church hymns available to everyone. Their songs, like their times, were highly sentimental, maudlin, demonstrating extremes of emotion, but especially concerning romantic love, the sorrow of loss, and patriotism. Stirring national songs helped rally men to enlist all through the war, especially at its outset. Often they learned their march steps to the tune of snappy martial airs, and later moved off to battle with songs in their ears. Sales of sheet music and song books were at their highest level in American history, and except in the bitterest of weather or the depths of depression after defeat, every camp North and South gave rise to hummed and sung melodies every night.

Most regiments, especially from the North, brought some kind of band with them to the war. The instruments were often indifferent in quality, and their players little better, though time and practice made some quite proficient. Many regimental and brigade ensembles, however, simply made a lot of noise. One Texas band was described by a dismayed auditor as "braying," while another listener described Confederate bands in general as so wretched that "their dismal noises are an intolerable nuisance."[24] Discordance was hardly the exclusive realm of Rebel brass, however, for many would have argued that the 6th Wisconsin band was the worst of the war. It knew only one song, "The Village Quickstep," and even hearers who knew the song could never recognize it when the Wolverines played. It did not help that the regiment's colonel looked on his band as a punishment assignment.[25]

Good or bad, still these bands were welcome in the camp as they brought relief from the tedium of daily life. Thousands did not wait to depend upon the bands however, and instead made their own music. Every company, and indeed many messes, had one or more men who could saw out a few tunes on the fiddle, strum a guitar, play a flute, or even just twang a Jew's harp. Singly or in ensemble, they entertained themselves with "Hell Broke Loose in Georgia," or the "Arkansas Traveler," or "Billy in the Low Grounds." Even more festive than this was the occasional banjo-picker, whose ringing strings could join with a good fiddler to provide a genuine hoedown for the men to dance.

Cheerful instruments were necessary, too, because the natural bent of the individual was toward more sad and sentimental songs, reflecting his longing for home. They sang songs like "The Empty Chair," "All Quiet Along the Potomac," "When This Cruel War is Over," and "Just Before the Battle Mother." Ironically, a favorite on both sides was "Auld Lang Syne." "My Old Kentucky Home" and other Stephen Foster tunes brought tears to blue eyes and gray, and looking forward to the day when peace would come, Yanks and Rebs alike sang of "When Johnny Comes Marching Home Again." Just as their songs could serve to stir their martial ardor, so could the mournful melodies depress low spirits even further. "Home, Sweet Home" was banned from the camps by commanders in the winter of 1862-3 after the Army of the Potomac had suffered the demoralizing defeat at Fredericksburg on December 13.[26]

Chaplains tried to boost morale with stirring hymns instead. They led the men in choruses of "Rock of Ages" and "All Hail the Power of Jesus' Name." "Amazing

Grace" even then had a special appeal to the military. Moreover, there were a host of happy secular tunes available when someone could start the tune going. The old song "John Brown's Body," already a favorite in the North before the war, became an informal anthem, with a host of different lyrics invented by the men, including the popular "We'll Hang Jeff Davis from a Sour Apple Tree." "The John Brown song was always a favorite, at all times and seasons," wrote the commander of a black regiment, and its stirring, moving melody became even more inspiring when Julia Ward Howe wrote yet another new lyric for it, and called her version the "Battle Hymn of the Republic."[27]

They sang "Yankee Doodle" and "The Girl I Left Behind Me," "The Star Spangled Banner," and in the South were heard "The Yellow Rose of Texas," "The Bonnie Blue Flag," and of course "Dixie." The Rebels teased their peanut-eating soldiers from Georgia with a song that told how, just prior to battle, the general heard an awful racket of popping and cracking, and believed it was the Yankees attacking, only to see that it was "the Georgia militia, eating goober peas."

Some men sang in battle, probably more to steady their own nerves than to inspire their comrades. They sang their old marching songs, or rousing patriotic airs like "Rally Round the Flag." During the fighting in the Virginia Wilderness on May 6, 1864, one solitary Yank began shouting the tune as his brigade struggled to regain its formation after a brutal Rebel attack. In a few minutes there were a hundred or more joining in with him, "Shouting the Battle-cry of Freedom!"

The most enduring musical contribution of the Civil War, however, was a bugle call. The soldiers' lives were ordered by the sounds of the bugle. The one that signaled an end to the day, the order to "extinguish lights" and go to bed, had been the "Tattoo," a call in constant use in the United States Army since at least 1835. One evening in July 1862, however, while General McClellan's army lay in bivouac at Harrison's Landing, Virginia, Brigadier General Daniel Butterfield called a bugler to his tent. He had heard the "Tattoo" that night, as on innumerable evenings before. As he later recalled, "it did not seem to be as smooth, melodious and musical as it should be." With the bugler before him to test his alterations, Butterfield slowed the tempo of the call, changed its rhythym, and extended a few of the notes. The only note that he actually changed in pitch was the first one. Once Butterfield had "got it to my taste," the new call was quickly adopted through most of the army, and eventually all of it. He would later receive erroneous credit for composing the piece, when he merely tampered a bit with an old call, but the resulting version of "Taps" became one of the most haunting, evocative melodies ever played, one that touches the souls of Americans of all times.[28]

As sobering as many of their songs were, the common soldiers were not the maudlin, doleful characters that their verses implied. They were raw, earthy, fun-loving men who valued a laugh above all else. Fun and pranks helped many a dull day in camp pass by. If a gullible civilian came into the bivouac and asked for Company B, somewhere down the line would arise the cry "Here's Company B," to be repeated all over the field. Just as often, some bored soldier decided to mimic a cow or a chicken. Within minutes, men all over the camp joined in a barnyard chorus that set officers on their ears.

Teasing was a chronic release, with practical jokes as commonplace as drill. In winter quarters someone could always count on a soldier dropping a handful of gunpowder down a chimney for some explosive fun, or else covering the chimney over with a blanket or boards to smoke the inhabitants out into the cold. If a new recruit went out on his first sentry duty, veterans would sneak up upon him in the dark. When he challenged their approach with "Who goes there?" the reply could prove to be anything from a blue streak of oaths, to "A flock of sheep." And when a new boy came to camp and was issued his first uniform, the old timers liked to tell him that he had been cheated by the quartermaster, sending the young Horatio scrambling back to the supply tent to demand that he be issued his regulation umbrella, too.[29]

Soldier fun took a more stately, ceremonious turn in some of the camps, especially those which were more permanently established. Fraternal orders and secret societies enjoyed a popular wave in the 1850s before the war, and many of their members brought their lodge ritual and dogma with them to the army. Masonic lodges thrived in many of the camps, North and South, with more than one recorded case of combatants ceasing hostilities temporarily in order to join in some fraternal ceremony. Several Yankee Masons who died in camp or combat were buried in Southern cemeteries with Confederate Masons presiding. Several camps were entertained by literary and debating societies. The 50th New York Engineers built their own theater out of timbers at Petersburg in 1864, in order that their dramatic club , the "Essayons," might perform. South of the lines, in the winter of 1862-3 a handful of well-educated men and officers of the 9th Kentucky Infantry staged their own production of *Bombasties Furioso*. The battle-hardened veterans who took the female roles had to go around Manchester, Tennessee, borrowing dresses from the local belles.[30]

The 48th New York and 45th Massachusetts were admired for their stage plays as well, and minstrel shows and burlesques were much in demand from anyone who could perform them. A mock court-martial provided good fun, and any opportunity to parody officers drew huge crowds, especially the dress parade with officers marching in the ranks while enlisted men, wearing huge comic opera epaulettes and medals the size of canteens, strutted and barked orders.[31]

Perhaps the soldiers' ways of finding fun were the more inventive because more conventional entertainments cost money, and the boys of 1861-5 were not very well financed. Indeed, even pay day itself was one of the happier diversions in camp, though rarely for long. When a paymaster was on the way, said one Illinois Yank, "a thousand pairs of eyes anxiously watched the road for the approach of the man who carried the panacea for all ills."[32] Even more emphatic was the Massachusetts private who declared that "A paymaster's arrival will produce more joy in camp than is said to have been produced in heaven over the one sinner that repenteth."[33]

They were not paid much. Privates on both sides at first received $11 monthly. North and South increased the pay somewhat, but especially in the Confederacy, uncontrolled inflation more than eradicated any benefit from the raise. By 1864 in the South, a pair of shoes could cost $125, seven months' pay. Worse yet, payday on both sides came with alarming irregularity. General John B. Floyd complained in 1862 that half of the men in his 51st Virginia Infantry had not been paid in six months. "They have not a single dollar to purchase the least little comfort, even for the sick."[34] Later in the war some Confederates would go a year and more without receiving a dollar. Families back home that needed a share of a soldier's pay became desperate, and thousands of disillusioned and bitter men deserted to return and care for their wives and children.

It is no wonder that the frustration of poor pay and harsh living environments often produced a ruggedness in soldier fun that sometimes had its roots in anger and frustration. Every winter saw snowball fights, usually on a small interpersonal scale. Most famous of all was the Great Snowball Battle of March 1864, when the Confederate Army of Tennessee in winter quarters at Dalton, Georgia, began an impromptu contest that eventually turned into a full-scale battle. Even generals joined in, personally leading whole regiments in charges, taking prisoners and giving no quarter. Among the spoils of battle were hats and frying pans "and 4 or 5 pones of corn bread."[35]

At Vicksburg, Mississippi, in 1862, Rebels staged a hog race between two such noble steeds. Unfortunately, one of them ran off a bluff carrying its rider on its back. The hog survived, the "jockey" did not, and his bereaved friends mourned him that night by cooking and eating his porcine charger with a grim sort of humor.

Soldiers raced with wheelbarrows, wrestled, boxed, leaped hurdles, and more, but probably their favorite sport proved to be the infant game of baseball. Contrary to later myth, it was not the invention of Abner Doubleday, then a Yankee general. The game used a soft ball then, and the base runner was only put out when actually hit by a batted or thrown ball. Consequently, high scores were the rule, the 13th Massachusetts once beating the 104th New York by 62 to 20. Some put too much gusto into throwing a man out. "He came very near knocking the stuffing out of three or four of the boys," a Texan wrote of a team-mate. "He could throw harder and straighter than any man in the company . . . and the boys swore they would not play with him."[36] Even cricket was played, and now and then, with ironic humor, the men would try bowling, knocking down the pins with rolling cannon balls.

As much as anything, the men, as soldiers of all times and places, simply sat and talked. Politics, philosophy, the progress of the war, reminiscences of home and family, any topic could draw a conversation to pass an afternoon or evening. Camp gossip filled most of their talk; what officer was a coward, which one was overlooked because he did not have the right connections, where the next battle would be fought, when the war would end. Rumors flew like flies in such an environment. "Every one tries to see what kind of rumor he can start," confessed a Virginia private, "so when our bodies are still we have our minds puzzled and harrassed."[37]

That last man was emblematic of all of the common soldiers of the war. Somehow amid the privations and disruption in their young lives, they made do and got along "as well as usual." A surgeon of the 5th New Hampshire might come to the field in Virginia in 1862 and recoil at "the bare-faced boys, the sallow men, the threadbare officers and seedy generals, the diarrhea and dysentery, the yellow eyes and malarious faces, the beds upon the bare earth in the mud, mist and the rain," and confess that the sight destroyed his "pre-conceived ideas of knight-errantry."[38] But through it all, the men got along with humor, open generosity, and the adaptability that became their trademark.

Of course they all wanted to go home. All of their games and pranks and pastimes were but ways of making the days go by until, the victory achieved, they could become civilians again. It showed itself most of all in their songs. "Many are the hearts that are weary tonight, waiting for the war to cease," went one air. "Many are the hearts that are looking for the right, to see the dawn of peace."

As in that song, they all, North and South, had their share of "Tenting Tonight on the Old Camp Ground." They all spent many an evening, telling the old stories, playing their fiddles, carving at a bit of wood, or merely staring into the glowing embers of their fires, watching them

Dying tonight, dying tonight,
Dying on the old camp ground.

But for all the sadness and melancholy, in afteryears, with the forgiving memories of age, they all took genuine pleasure in their days in the field. Even earlier, after four years of hard campaigning, many of the boys had to confess that they reveled in the soldier experience. Like Charlie Wills of Illinois, they could say in their hundreds of thousands that "I never enjoyed anything in the world as I do this life."[39]

REFERENCES

1 Philip Van Doren Stern (ed.), *Soldier Life in the Union and Confederate Armies* (Bloomington, Ind., 1961), p.301.
2 *Ibid.*, p.325.
3 Bell I. Wiley, *They Who Fought Here* (New York, 1959), p.84.
4 John D. Billings, *Hardtack and Coffee* (Boston, 1888), p.47.
5 *Ibid.*, p.49.
6 Bell I. Wiley, *The Life of Billy Yank* (Indianapolis, 1951), p.56.
7 John Worsham, *One of Jackson's Foot Cavalry* (New York, 1912), p.91.
8 James I. Robertson, Jr. (ed.), "An Indiana Soldier in Love and War," *Indiana Magazine of History,* LIX (1963), p.253.

9 John L. Parker, *Henry Wilson's Regiment* (Boston, 1887), p.219.

10 Stephen A. Repass to Mrs. Peter Shirley, February 16, 1862, in private collection.

11 Bruce Catton, *A Stillness at Appomattox* (New York, 1953), p.201.

12 W.G. Bean, *The Liberty Hall Volunteers* (Charlottesville, 1964), p.155.

13 Wiley, *Billy Yank*, p.187.

14 Edna Hunter, *One Flag, One Country, and Thirteen Greenbacks a Month* (San Diego, Calif., 1980), p.97.

15 Wiley, *Billy Yank*, p.187.

16 Worsham, *Foot Cavalry*, p.98.

17 Bell I. Wiley, *The Life of Johnny Reb* (Indianapolis, 1943), p.193.

18 Wiley, *Billy Yank*, p.190.

19 *Ibid*, p.153.

20 William C. Davis, *The Orphan Brigade* (New York), 1980), pp.202-3.

21 "Diary of Charles Ross," *Vermont History*, XXX (1962), p.135.

22 "Spirited and Spicy Scenes," *Civil War Times Illustrated*, XI (January 1973), pp.26-7.

23 Wiley, *Johnny Reb*, p.170.

24 Arthur Fremantle, *Three Months in the Confederate States* (London, 1863), p.71; *Battlefields of the South* (London, 1863), II, p.101.

25 Bruce Catton, *Mr. Lincoln's Army* (New York, 1951), p.19.

26 S. Millett Thompson, *Thirteenth Regiment of New Hampshire Volunteer Infantry* (Boston, 1888), p.104.

27 Wiley, *They Who Fought Here*, p.150.

28 Russell H. Booth, "Butterfield and 'Taps'," *Civil War Times Illustrated*, XVI (December 1977), pp.35-9.

29 Wiley, *Billy Yank*, pp.171-2.

30 Davis, *Orphan Brigade*, pp.168-9.

31 Wiley, *Billy Yank*, pp.163-74.

32 George Parks, "One Story of the 109th Illinois," *Journal of the Illinois State Historical Society*, LVI (1963), p.286.

33 Charles E. Davis, *Three Years in the Army* (Boston, 1894), p.15.

34 O.R. Series I, 52, Part 2, p.252.

35 Wiley, *Johnny Reb*, pp.64-5.

36 *Ibid.*, p.159.

37 Worsham, *Foot Cavalry*, pp. xxi-xxii.

38 William Child, *A History of the Fifth Regiment New Hampshire Volunteers* (Bristol, N.H., 1893), p.99.

39 Charles W. Wills, *Army Life of an Illinois Soldier* (Washington, 1906), p.14.

VIII

WILLING SPIRITS & WEAK FLESH

"There is some of the onerest men here that I ever saw," Virginian Adam Rader wrote home, "and the most swearing and card playing and fitin and drunkenness that I ever saw at any place." An Alabama boy invited his brother to visit his camp, but advised him to bring with him a shotgun for his own protection. In general, few who lived with the armies North or South would have disagreed with the Louisiana Confederate who counseled others not to follow him into the army, "for you will smell hell here."[1]

"They have every temptation to do wrong," wrote an Iowan, "and if a man has not firmness enough to keep from the excesses common to soldiers he will soon be as bad as the worst." With all that time on their hands in the camps and on the march, the men made their own diversions to take their minds from their condition, and it is no surprise that many of their pastimes ran toward the seamy and insubordinate. "There is no mistake," said the Yank from Iowa, "but the majority of soldiers are a hard set."[2]

A number of leaders on both sides tried to do something about the language in the ranks, and the Washington War Department even made it a punishable offense at one point, valuing one infraction as worth a dollar, more than two days' pay. It was a pointless attempt. "Oaths, blasphemies, imprecations, obscenity, are hourly heard ringing in your ears until your mind is almost filled with them," a Mississippi recruit complained, and a fellow Confederate chaplain lamented that in camp he "heard more cursing and swearing in twenty-four hours than in all my life before."[3] It was a soldier's form of release. He could not talk back to an officer, but he could curse him back in the semi-privacy of his tent. It did not make the mud any thinner, the cold any less chilling, the food any better or the lice any the less numerous, but somehow it helped. As a result, wherever and whenever soldiers gathered, the air rang with "profanity of the worst form from morning till night."[4]

A good reason for a soldier's profanity might have been his losses at wagers, for gambling of every kind was as common among the men as their colorful language. Every army camp was a virtual casino, with games of faro and "chuck-a-luck," "sweet blanket" and poker of all sorts in near constant operation. Many liked to roll dice, but far and away the men preferred card games. The sutlers did a good business in card decks, in part because of the popularity of the games, but also because before battle many a suddenly fearful and pious soldier threw away his deck, not wanting it on his person should he be killed and have to face an angry Maker. Officers as well as enlisted men joined in the games, "taking a twist at the tiger" as they called it, and even a few chaplains dealt the cards, though most of the latter complained of the Sunday morning games that drew men away from their services.[5]

Both sides attempted to put a stop to it, but they might as well have tried to make the soldiers drink pink tea instead of coffee. "Open gambling has been prohibited," a Confederate noted in 1862, "but that amounts to nothing."[6] And once a battle was done, the survivors, suddenly forgetting their earlier resolutions to reform their ways, could be seen scouring the countryside for the dice and cards they had so readily thrown away before the fight.

For all too many, the next stop down the ladder of degradation became an easy one. Theft in the camps was a common occurrence, and not too surprisingly, since it was an almost natural outgrowth of the "foraging" – essentially condoned theft – which they were encouraged to participate in along the march. A few individuals exhibited a natural talent at the craft of foraging. Sam Nunnally of the 21st Virginia would just vanish from camp for a few days, to reappear laden with booty. He was especially skilled at playing dead on the battlefield, and then rifling the pockets of the real slain after the fight. Perhaps the most accomplished plunderer in any army was Billy Crump of the 23rd Ohio. As orderly to Colonel Rutherford B. Hayes – future 19th President – he borrowed the colonel's horse, spent two days looting in West Virginia, and came back carrying fifty chickens, two turkeys, one goose, over twenty dozen eggs, and upwards of thirty pounds of butter.[7]

When not plundering the countryside, or their own messmates, many soldiers found sport in robbing the sutlers who followed the armies. Many regarded it as simply tit for tat, assuming that the sutlers were gouging them heavily by selling shoddy products at inflated prices. "He is always on hand promptly when his financial interest is benefitted thereby," an Iowa boy said of the army sutler, "and never to be found when most needed." When soldiers looted a sutler's stores, they might confess that it was, indeed, undisguised theft, but averred that "the sutler's business in many cases is not much better."[8]

Frequently bored or frustrated soldiers turned their misbehavior on each other. Fighting was commonplace in the camps, stemming from causes as simple as a personal insult, to resentment of being bivouacked next to despised immigrant regiments of Germans or blacks. Some outfits, especially the Irish units, became famed for their combativeness, and the 7th Missouri once had 900 fights break out on a single day, among just 800 men in the regiment.

Every kind of bad conduct had causes that were legion, but the most common of all was simple drunkenness. The stuff the soldiers drank was called "mean" whiskey, and not without reason. It was vile by any standard, and the attitude of the men who drank it is evidenced by what they called the stuff. "Rock Me to Sleep Mother," "Old Red Eye," "Rifle Knock-Knee," "Bust Skull," "Rot of Pop Skull," and "Oh, Be Joyful," are but a few of its sobriquets. A boy from Indiana described it as "bark juice, tar-water, turpentine, brown sugar, lamp-oil and alcohol." To consume it, many advised first warming it over the fire, while others put a match to it and let some of the alcohol burn off first. They could all agree that "it was new and fiery, rough and nasty to take."[9]

Given the opportunity, the men sometimes made their own drink, fermenting anything they could find, even pine boughs. Its effects were deadly. One Vermont boy remembered that he "saw snakes and devils and howled in terror" after an evening at the jug. The colonel of the 126th Ohio and most of his officers became completely incapacitated after several buckets of egg nog and whiskey, and the colonel of the 48th New York was actually found dead in his tent the morning after a bender. No wonder that General George B. McClellan charged in 1862 that "no one evil so much obstructs this army as the degrading vice of drunkenness." Could he but keep the liquor out of his bivouac, "it would be worth 50,000 men to the armies of the United States."[10] His more sober officers would have agreed, for drink caused more insubordination than all other influences combined. When he had had enough of "the creature," a soldier thought little at all of talking back to a superior. Men were on record as calling their officers "damned puppy," "whorehouse pimp," "skunk," "bugger," and "sh-t-house adjutant." "You kiss my arse, you God damned louse," one Yankee told his captain, while another confronted his commander with "You ain't worth a pinch of sh-t." Most often of all, they bought themselves time in the guard house by calling someone in authority a "son of a bitch."[11]

Drinking, swearing, and all the attendant vices, would be constant companions of the Civil War soldier, despite all efforts to the contrary – despite the influences of frequent revivals and temperance movements. These were red-blooded men who needed to give vent to their boredom and anxieties. There was an additional frustration that led to yet another kind of misconduct. The men were far from wives and sweethearts, and this in an era of exaggerated sentimentalities, when the courting ritual was almost medieval, and outward expressions of love and sexuality strictly confined. More than anything else, Civil War soldiers' letters were filled with protestations of love and fidelity and anxious promises of the reception to be met when "Johnny came marching home again."

442

Many women had actually been the catalysts in getting their men to enlist in the first place, and thereafter their role was to sustain their men's patriotism and morale by mail. As for the men who went to war without a girl waiting back home, the competition to find a lady friend became keen. Indeed, when women were in short supply, one girl might often give her attentions to more than one suitor. And when a boy did find a girlfriend, he could become ecstatic, if not poetic. "My girl is none of your one-horse girls," proclaimed a jubilant Yankee. "She is a regular stub and twister. She is well-educated and refined, all wildcat and fur, and union from the muzzle to the crupper."[12]

Some wrote simple home or camp news, while others penned poetry, some if it of no mean caliber. But generally the men's minds were on more elemental matters. "I aint hugged a gal for so long I am out of practice," complained one soldier, and most men and women managed to turn the subject to fidelity sooner or later. Some joked. "I don't feel much like a maryed man," Leander Stilwell wrote to his wife, "but I never forget it sofar as to court enny other lady," adding that "if I should you must forgive me as I am so forgitful." When a Reb from Tennessee chided his wife on giving birth to a girl nine months after a furlough, she teased him that "I think you give your boys to some body else."[13]

Occasionally, despite the mores of the time, the letters from home were positively inflammatory. "Remember me when you lay on your hard bed," one wife wrote her man, and another warned her husband to store up his sleep, for "you would not sleep in a weeak when I got my arms around you."[14] When James Goodwin received a letter from his wife around Christmas on 1862, he must have squirmed on his camp stool when she described in detail their recent honeymoon and "the night when first we retired to the mid night couch, one by one to enjoy the highest streams of pleasure that the soul and body ever knows."[15] This was no cringing violet. And with the pleasures of the flesh on the minds of the women at home, and with them writing about it to their husbands and sweethearts, how much more so did the men in the field feel their enforced abstinence. "I have not seen a gal in so long a time that I would not know what to do with myself if I were to meet up with one," wrote a Rebel from Virginia, "though I recon I would learn before I left her."[16]

It should hardly come as a surprise, then, that many men sought the companionship of local ladies of rather casual acquaintance to relieve their loneliness. "I had a gay old time I tell you," one Massachusetts soldier wrote from Virginia in 1863. He drank during the day, and "in the evening Horizontal Refreshments or in Plainer words Riding a Dutch gal."[17] Alluring opportunities were everywhere. Washington alone had more than 450 bordellos in 1863, employing 7,000 or more prostitutes. Pennsylvania Avenue teemed with whole blocks of fancy houses, many with names like "Hooker's Headquarters," "the Ironclad," "Madam Russell's Bake Oven," and more. "It is said that one house out of ten in the city is a bawdy house," an Indiana boy wrote of Alexandria, Virginia, just over the Potomac from Washington; "it is a perfect Sodom."[18]

Similar temptations waited for the boys in gray. After the war the old veterans tried to deny any such behavior, claiming that "Confederate soldiers were too much gentlemen to stoop to such things," but the fact is they felt the same needs as their enemies in blue. Richmond fairly teemed with prostitutes, openly walking the streets and sometimes soliciting customers on the park around the Capitol itself. Prices became competitive. "I have not got but three tast[e]s since I have been in Va.," a Johnny Reb wrote home, "and I got that from two fine looking women. I tell you the three goes cost me but eleven dollars."[19]

For the soldier who did not or could not get to the city, there were more than enough camp followers near the armies. Some even donned uniforms and got away with pretending to be solders, their comrades helping with the charade in order to keep the ladies handy. Of course a man took a chance with a prostitute, and many found themselves the losers. "You can get plenty of Grous here," one Confederate wrote from Petersburg in 1864, "but you will get wounded nine times out of ten."[20] Venereal disease was always a hazard, and occasionally an epidemic. The problem began at the very beginning of the war. In 1861 one out of every dozen Yanks was diagnosed with some variant, a percentage that held up throughout the conflict. Confederates fared no better, and some regiments were particularly prone, like the 10th Alabama, which contracted no fewer than 68 cases in a single month.

Cures varied widely, and were almost all completely ineffectual in those days before antibiotics. A Confederate surgeon west of the Alleghenies gave his patients whiskey-soaked silk weed root, along with pills derived from pine resin. Others dispensed silver nitrate, zinc sulfate, mercury, and a host of herbal remedies. None of it worked, of course, and the more strait-laced came to regard the afflictions as divine punishment for their comrades' conduct. "If there is any place on God's fair earth where wickedness 'stalketh abroad in daylight'," wrote an Illinois private in 1862, "it is in the army."[21]

In the end, many officers would have agreed with Lieutenant Colonel H.E. Peyton, when he reported to the Richmond authorities in September 1864 that "the source of almost every evil existing in the army is due to the difficulty of having orders properly and promptly executed."[22] The fact is that neither side in this war ever completely accomplished the task of turning raw civilians into soldiers. "There is not that spirit of respect for and obedience to general orders which should pervade a military organization," concluded Peyton. "We had enlisted to put down the rebellion," wrote an Indiana private, "and had not patience with the red-tape tomfoolery of the regular service. Furthermore the boys recognized no superiors, except in the line of legitimate duty."[23] In battle, the men looked to their officers for leadership, but when it came to the ways they used – and misused – their leisure time, it was no one's business but their own. These men were products of the days of Jacksonian America, highly individualistic, independent, deeply imbued with the American ideal that one man was as good as another. They would not be ordered about like cattle, and such discipline as officers were able to maintain came at the enlisted men's sufferance, and only after the officers earned their respect. No wonder that at the war's outset, foreseeing the problems ahead, Confederate General Joseph E. Johnston lamented that "I would not give one company of regulars for a whole regiment" of volunteers.[24]

As a consequence, discipline in this war would never reach a point at which it could predictably deter the men from doing what they pleased. whether it be gambling, drinking, thievery, or whoring. They had no use for the pomp and ceremony of soldiering, nor for its artificial etiquette.

There were good leaders, to be sure, and the men in the ranks were not sparing in paying tribute to those whom they respected. An Alabama soldier wrote with pride when he boasted of his regiment's leaders that "a more impartial set of officers . . . cannot be found in any company in the army." His captain was so loved that hundreds "would defend him to the last, and follow him into the most imminent danger."[25] Good officers could elicit that kind of admiration and devotion from their men, and with it they had little difficulty in maintaining discipline and keeping them out of trouble.

Yet there were all too many wearing shoulder straps who did not enjoy such respect. Thousands of officers on both sides used political or family influence to obtain commissions, or else won election to their posts by buying votes or bribing the men with liquor. Others received commissions thanks to earlier service in Mexico or against the Indians on the Plains, but that experience was no guarantee of ability. At the same time, while these often incompetent seniors tried to impose some discipline on their men, there were many more fresh, inexperienced young men with commissions who were hardly older than their enlisted subordinates. An Iowa Yank bemoaned that "I never saw so many green officers as are in some of the new Reg[iment]s. There is fun for us to see them go through their maneuvers. It is rather a funny operation for one man to teach another what he don't know himself."[26]

Fortunately, the most extreme form of insubordination was very limited. Nevertheless, it is one of the ironies of the Civil War that the common soldier often thought a good deal better of his enemies than he did of his own officers. From the beginning of the war to its end, the most prevalent form of insubordination of all was fraternization with the foe, which is hardly surprising. Bonds of language, friendship, sometimes even blood, linked thousands of Rebs and Yanks. "Although intercourse with the enemy was strictly forbidden," one Pennsylvanian wrote after the war, "the men were on the most friendly terms, amicably conversing and exchanging such commodities as coffee, sugar, tobacco, corn meal and newspapers."[27]

"It was a singular sight," wrote one Yank, "to see the soldiers of two great hostile armies walking about unconcernedly within a few yards of each other with their bayonets sticking in the ground, bantering and joking together, exchanging the compliments of the day and even saluting officers of the opposing forces with as much ceremony, decorum and respect as they did their own. The keenest sense of honor existed among the enlisted men of each side. It was no uncommon sight, when visiting the picket posts, to see an equal number of 'graybacks' and 'bluebellies' as they facetiously termed each other, enjoying a social game of euchre or seven-up and sometimes the great national game of draw poker, with army rations and sutler's delicacies as the stakes."[28]

The private soldiers were little concerned with the philosophical, economic, and other weighty issues that had brought about the war. For them it was simply something that seemed to drag on interminably. While they could muster their hatred of the enemy before and during a battle, it was difficult to sustain this emotion during the long lulls that generally followed an action. Instead, facing each other for weeks or months across a field or from opposite sides of a river, it was only natural that the men would start shouting a few epithets and jokes at each other. That led to familiarity, and familiarity bred fraternization. They traded scarcities for scarcities: Yankees always wanted good Virginia tobacco, the Rebs never had enough real coffee. When a river divided their lines, they made little sailboats and passed them back and forth with the precious cargoes. When only a field or wood lay between, the soldiers met in the middle. A certain kind of etiquette even evolved in such dealings, one of its strictest rules being the one "that forbade the shooting of men while attending to the imperative calls of nature."

When the prospect of a fight loomed, the men unconsciously began to work up their hatred once more. "All I want to do is to lick these Sons of B–ches across the river," one Yank private vowed before a battle.[29] Nevertheless, except for such times, acts of mercy and friendship across the lines – even during battle – became commonplace in every major conflict of the war. Despite all the efforts and threats of their officers, Johnny Reb and Billy Yank could not help liking one another now and then.

Faced with all these varying forms of insubordination and misbehavior, the best the officers on either side could do was to use punishment as an example and hope that it worked. It did not. The problem was the complete lack of uniformity in dealing with miscreants. Punishment was not specifically prescribed for most offenses by military code, and so the officers in charge used their own judgment in selecting appropriate atonement. As a result, glaring inequities existed from the outset. One poor fellow, possibly dull-witted, found himself sentenced to three years of hard labor just for being absent from camp without leave for five days. At the same time, six Rebels who actually deserted the service were caught and, instead of facing prison or worse, were simply stood before their colonel, given "a little fatherly advice," and returned to the ranks of their regiment.[30]

It is hardly a surprise, therefore, that when offenders of capital crimes got off with a lecture, while others guilty of minor infractions could find themselves treated like heinous criminals, most men in the ranks simply ceased to regard punishments as a deterrent. Worse, for the serious offenses that required courts-martial, the military justice system was overwhelmed with cases. Witnesses necessary for prosecution and defence could always fall in battle before testifying, and the officers needed to sit on the courts were more urgently required at the front. A trial could take months, even years, to take place, and to avoid the delays, many commanders simply did not resort to the regular system. Instead, they passed judgment and meted out punishment on their own.

This instantaneous form of justice could prove dangerous for the offender, for a ranking officer handing out his own sentences immediately after an offense was likely to be angry, and his sentencing thus influenced. When Union General Jefferson C. Davis had to sentence five soldiers just caught molesting a Tennessee girl, he first fumed and then as they were stripped and tied to a cannon wheel, he ordered the man who gave witness against the others to himself wield the whip and flog the other four fifty lashes each.

The guardhouse was the most common punishment, the number of days inside determined by the severity of the offense, from only a few hours to a month or more. Whatever the sentence, the guardhouse – often just an open field marked by ropes and watched by sentries – was hardly a hardship. Bread and water could make it less bearable, but in fact many offenders looked upon it as a respite from regular duty. In the 2nd Kentucky Infantry, Confederate Colonel Roger Hanson found infractions so frequent that on some days the guardhouse became more an informal bivouac for his regiment, and he began making daily visits to lecture the men sternly about their behavior.[31]

Commanders used their imaginations a bit more when it seemed necessary for the punishment to fit the crime. For several hours messmates saw one Federal cavalryman walking about their camp carrying a saddle on his back, only to learn that this was his sentence for stealing the saddle. A Rebel who sold whiskey in camp against regulations, spent the better part of the day straddling a fence rail and riding around the camp with bottles tied to his feet and a sign saying "Ten Cents a Glass" hanging from his neck. A Confederate who shot a stray dog was ordered to run around the camp with the dead animal in his arms as punishment, and another Southerner who fired his rifle in camp against orders had to carry a log for three hours.[32]

Insubordination could bring several hours of the ball and chain, usually a thirty-pound cannon ball on a few feet of heavy chain attached to the offender's leg. Wherever he went he had either to carry the ball or else drag it behind him, an exhausting exercise after a surprisingly short time, even for the most robust of offenders. For cowardice or unauthorized absence, soldiers tied the transgressor's hands in front of him, shoved his knees up and inside his arms, and thrust a stick over one elbow, under the knees, and over the other elbow. A gag placed in his mouth completed his being "bucked and gagged" and several hours in the hot sun in this very uncomfortable position was a punishment fit for all but the most serious of crimes.

Ironically, what most soldiers dreaded more than many other forms of punishment was being ordered to perform extra hours of guard duty, and yet it is the punishment that they most infrequently received. Many officers felt, as did General

Thomas C. Hindman, that "standing guard is the most honorable duty of a soldier, except fighting, and must not be degraded."[33] Yet this attitude did not mean that commanders were overly inclined toward mercy in judging their men. "There was a class of officers who felt that every violation of camp rules should be visited with the infliction of bodily pain in some form," John D. Billings of Massachusetts lamented.[34]

Certain special crimes such as cowardice, desertion, insubordination, rape, murder, treason, and the like, were regarded almost uniformly by all officers, and nearly all shared the same notions of proper punishment. The lucky man was simply discharged from the service dishonorably. His head shaved, his uniform stripped of its buttons and insignia, he was drummed out of camp in sight of his comrades while the regimental band played the "Rogue's March." All the while his former mates showered on him the vilest sort of verbal insults, and on these occasions, at least, no attempts to curtail profanity were made. When this punishment seemed insufficient for the offense, a man could be branded, to carry his shame with him for life. His cheek, or forehead, or hip, would feel the red-hot iron imprint the appropriate letter for his crime – "c" for cowardice, "d" for desertion, "t" for thievery, and so on from crime to crime.

In a few cases, even this was not adjudged to be enough, particularly for desertion. It was a crime that, left unpunished, could demoralize whole regiments and cripple an army. The inducements were many, and ever-present. "My dear Edward," a North Carolina wife wrote to her soldier husband with the army. "I would not have you do anything wrong for the world, but before God, Edward, unless you come home we must die. Last night I was aroused by little Eddie's crying. I called and said 'What is the matter, Eddie?' and he said 'O Mamma! I am so hungry.' and Lucy, Edward, your darling Lucy; she never complains, but she is growing thinner and thinner every day. And before God, Edward, unless you come home, we must die."[35]

Such appeals from home were many and persuasive, especially in the South where civilians felt the war as much as soldiers. The desertion rate stayed low at the war's outset thanks to patriotism, but as the conflict wore on, the number of absentees rose dramatically. One of every nine Rebels would desert during the war, and in the Union army one out of seven took "French leave," some soldiers deserting again and again after being returned to the army. During 1864 and beyond, the influx of draftees and men who enlisted to receive bounty payments introduced an undermotivated element into the Union forces, which further aggravated the desertion rate. And the seemingly interminable war itself put the severest tests upon the resolve of men and homefolk on both sides. "It is useless to conceal the truth any longer," a Confederate wrote from the Petersburg trenches in 1865. "Many of our people at home have become so demoralized that they write to their husbands, sons and brothers that desertion *now* is not *dishonorable*."[36] By the time he wrote those words, over 420,000 Rebs and Yanks combined were on the rolls as being absent without leave.

From the start, military law provided for the death sentence to deal with deserters when caught. However, commanders were reluctant to impose capital punishment early in the war, not realizing the necessity of the example, and still feeling the personal sympathy for the volunteer soldier which several years of war would eventually replace with a more strictly professional military attitude. When the sentence of death was imposed, it was often commuted to life imprisonment, or incarceration for the duration of the war. But finally, in cases of rape, murder, spying, severe theft and, of course, desertion, the death penalty was more and more frequently imposed. Edward Cooper of North Carolina, whose wife sent him that heart-wrenching letter, was saved from the death penalty by producing his wife's plea. Few hearts were hard enough not to sympathize in such a case. Indeed, in the Union Army fewer than ten percent of all desertion convictions eventually led to death sentences, and only a quarter of those so sentenced failed to receive a commutation. The rate of executions in the South ran somewhat higher.

But occasionally the sentence had to be carried out, publicly, usually by firing squad, though hanging was sometimes employed for specially unsavory offenses such as rape. The regiment – sometimes the entire brigade – was drawn up on three sides of a square, while the condemned man, to the tune of a funeral dirge, rode on top of his coffin or walked to the open side of the formation. Standing beside his own freshly-dug grave, he heard the sentence of the court read aloud one last time, spoke with a chaplain if he wished, and accepted or declined a handkerchief for his eyes.

Then the sentence was carried out. "It was hard to bear," wrote a witness to one execution. "Faces paled and hands shook which were not accustomed to show fear; and officers and men alike would have welcomed a call to battle in exchange for that terrible inaction in the sight of coming death."[37]

Adding to the apprehension were the stories which many of the men had heard, of muffed executions. The average soldier was not an able marksman, and when about to shoot a defenseless comrade his aim could be even more unsteady. When Frank McElhenny deserted in 1862, going over to the enemy, and then deserted them to go back to his own lines, he had the misfortune to run right into his own old regiment. Tried and convicted, he was set for execution on August 8, 1864. His hands bound, his eyes blindfolded, he stood before a firing party a scant few paces away. When they fired, he fell to the ground with five bullets in him. But still he lived. Another squad sent another eight slugs into his chest before he died.

Others fared even worse. In the Army of Tennessee in 1862, twenty Confederates stood twelve paces from a man and only slightly injured him. Four more soldiers came forward and fired and still he breathed. Finally all twenty-four reloaded and managed to kill him with a volley that might have mowed down a whole squad of the enemy. When a Pennsylvanian was being executed, he was still sitting upright on his coffin after the first volley. When a second squad fired, he fell, but then got up and gamely sat on his coffin again. Only the third firing party finally managed to kill him.

Perhaps worst of all was the execution of two "bounty jumpers," men who enlisted to be paid a few dollars, and then deserted, probably intending to enlist yet again under different names to collect yet more bounty money. George Elliot and Edward Latham of the 14th Connecticut were tried and convicted, September 18, 1863, being set for their execution. All the usual ritual, blindfold, prayers, reading of the sentence, passed without event. Pluckily the condemned men shook hands with each other and the officer in charge, and then sat down upon their coffins. When the smoke from the volley cleared, they could see that Elliot had fallen, apparently killed. Latham, however, still sat upright on his coffin, and feverishly ripped the blindfold from his eyes to see what had happened. At once two men were ordered forward to dispatch him as he sat there "wildly staring them in the face." Both rifles misfired, and Latham's old comrades back in the ranks began to wish that he would get up and simply run away. He had faced death twice, and that was enough. Apparently he was too consumed with fright to move. Finally the officer in charge ran to him and put his pistol against the man's temple. Again it misfired, and still Latham sat there like a panicked rabbit. At the next try, the officer finally put a bullet into his brain.

And all the while, George Elliot, far from being dead, was standing up watching the proceedings and bleeding from a painful wound in his abdomen. "Blow my brains out!" he begged the firing party, and the officer in charge tried to so do, but at point-blank range his pistol botched the job, and only two more rifle balls in Elliot's chest finished the job. Even then, so thoroughly shaken by the macabre events of the past few minutes that he could not be sure anyone was really dead, the officer ordered two more riflemen to continue firing. One slug took away half of Elliot's face, and the other was fired into his heart from such a close range "that his clothes took fire from the powder flame."[38] It was a disgusting exhibition for everyone involved, yet still they had to file past the dead men and look at the price of justice before the two were placed in their coffins, face downward so they could not look toward heaven, and then covered over with earth and no marker.

Capital punishment was meted out to about 500 Yanks and Rebs in the Civil War, more than in all other American wars combined, and two-thirds of them for desertion. Yet the fate of men such as Elliot and Latham never came close to curbing the volunteers' natural bent for insubordination, their rejection of military regimentation, and the urge to leave the army when they chose. "Shocking and solemn as such scenes were," concluded Billings, "I do not believe that the shooting of a deserter had any great deterring influence on the rank and file."[39] There were always those willing to risk getting away, just as there were always those who would not find any sort of punishment a hindrance for misconduct of any kind.

The offenses that led to these punishments, like the punishments themselves, attracted a great deal of attention then and later, but they were happily the exception in soldier life. Relatively few Yanks and Rebs were ever seriously insubordinate, and far fewer still suffered any rigorous retribution for their occasional antics. As for their attitude toward the military, and their grumbling and grousing about it, that would never change, and if disliking officers and wishing to be somewhere other than in the service were adjudged to be crimes, then every army in history has been populated with "criminals."

REFERENCES

1 Wiley, *Billy Yank*, p.26; James I. Robertson, Jr., *Tenting Tonight* (Alexandria, Va., 1984), p.56.

2 "Peter Wilson in the Civil War," *Iowa Journal of History and Politics*, XL (1942), pp.402-3.

3 Wiley and Milhollen, *They Who Fought Here*, pp.190-1.

4 D.E. Beem to . . ., May 20, 1861, David E. Beem Papers, Indiana Historical Society, Indianapolis.

5 Robertson, *Tenting Tonight*, p.62.

6 Wiley, *Johnny Reb*, p.39.

7 William C. Davis, ed., *The Guns of '62* (New York, 1982), p.216.

8 Mildred Thore, ed., "Reminiscences of Jacob Switzer," *Iowa Journal of History and Politics*, LV (1957), p.325; Charles D. Page, *History of the Fourteenth Regiment, Connecticut Volunteer Infantry* (Meriden, Conn., 1906), pp.131-2.

9 Robertson, *Tenting Tonight*, pp.59-60.

10 Wiley, *Billy Yank*, p.252.

11 *Ibid.*, pp.199-201.

12 Francis Lord, *They Fought for the Union* (Harrisburg, Pa., 1960), p.215.

13 Wiley, *Johnny Reb*, p.271; Bell I. Wiley, "A Time of Greatness," p.6.

14 Bell I. Wiley, *Confederate Women* (Westport, Conn., 1975), p.171.

15 Jane Goodwin to husband, n.d., *Civil War Times Illustrated* Collection.

16 Wiley, *Johnny Reb*, p.271.

17 Robertson, *Tenting Tonight*, p.60.

18 Wiley and Milhollen, *They Who Fought Here*, *passim.*

19 *Ibid.*

20 *Ibid.*

21 *Ibid.*

22 O.R., I, 42, Part 2, p.1276.

23 Bruce Catton, *America Goes to War* (Middletown, Conn., 1958), p.53.

24 Douglas S. Freeman, *Lee's Lieutenants* (New York, 1945), I. p.13.

25 James G. Hudson, "A Story of Company D, 4th Alabama Infantry Regiment," *Alabama Historical Quarterly*, XXIII (1961), pp.156-7.

26 "Peter Wilson," p.301.

27 Gilbert A. Hays, *Under the Red Patch* (Pittsburgh, 1908), pp.270-1.

28 *Ibid.*

29 Wiley, *Billy Yank*, pp.350-1.

30 *Ibid.*, p.213.

31 Davis, *Orphan Brigade*, p.53.

32 Wiley and Milhollen, *They Who Fought Here*, p.178.

33 O.R., I, 32, Part 2, p.654.

34 Billings, *Hardtack and Coffee*, p.146.

35 Ella Lonn, *Desertion During the Civil War* (New York, 1928), pp.12-13.

36 George D. Harmon, (ed.), "Letters of Luther Rice Mills," *North Carolina Historical Review*, IV (1927), p.307.

37 O.R., IV, 3, p.1182; A.S. Roe, *The Twenty-Fourth Regiment Massachusetts Volunteers* (Worcester, 1907), p.428.

38 John H. Silverman, "The Excitement had Begun!," *Manuscripts*, XXX (1978), pp.276-7.

39 Billings, *Hardtack and Coffee*, p.161.

IX

IRON BARS A PRISON MAKE

"Will no one send a little word to cheer us in our gloomy hours of activity?" bemoaned one Confederate. "Oh, God! how dreadful are these bitter feelings of hope deferred. Thus we linger, thus we drag the slow, tedious hours of prison life."[1]

That lonely Southerner spoke volumes for all the hundreds of thousands of men, Blue and Gray, who survived the rigors of camp life, the dangers of battle, even the horrors of illness and wounds, only to fall victim to an enemy just as insidious and deadly. Johnny Rebs and Billy Yanks went off to war with a host of naive hopes and genuine fears: new friends, novel sights, camp life, hard marches, battle, martial glory, perhaps even wounds and death. But none of them went expecting capture or the nightmarish lot of the prisoner-of-war. None who went through that experience would ever forget it.

As so often in this war which everyone had been predicting for years, North and South were entirely unprepared to deal with captured enemies. As was so often the case, that lack of foresight led to tragedy. When 1861 dawned, not a single military prison existed on the continent capable of holding more than a few ill-behaved enlisted men. Even when the guns spoke at Fort Sumter, both sides immediately expected the conflict to last barely through the summer, and thus no preparations for prisoners were made. The release of Major Robert Anderson and his entire garrison from Sumter, with all courtesy and honor, seemed a matter of course.

Yet even as the Federals left the smoldering fort amid an air almost of gaiety, there were hundreds of forgotten comrades in blue, over a thousand miles to the west, who had been virtual prisoners of war for two months, and still the Confederate authorities did not know what to do with them.

It was on February 18, 1861, that Major General David E. Twiggs surrendered his Department of Texas to the New Confederates. His command included 2,648 United States Regulars, all of whom, he was assured, would be allowed to keep their arms and equipment. Further, they were to be left to march out of the state free and unmolested. "They are our friends," declared a Confederate decree exhorting Texans to show courtesy to the Yankees; "they have heretofore afforded to our people all the protection in their power, and we owe them every consideration."[2]

Yet confusion set in immediately. Authorities became fearful of so large a body of armed Federals. Transport that was to take them from a Gulf coast port to the North was delayed. Then Confederate leaders decided that Twiggs' men should not be allowed to leave before an attempt was made to recruit them to Southern arms. Special recruiting officers were dispatched, among them Colonel Earl Van Dorn. When Van Dorn took command in Texas, the Confederacy reversed its policy completely. Going back on the agreement, they now decided that the roughly 1,600 Yankees remaining in the state constituted a hazard. "Officers and men must be regarded as prisoners of war," were Van Dorn's orders.[3] Those instructions went out on April 11, just as final orders were going to Charleston to open fire on Fort Sumter. With war coming at last, there must, at last, be prisoners of war. The Yankee officers were released on parole and sent home, but their men in the ranks would spend the next two years in Texan prison camps. The first to suffer from administrative shortsightedness, they were only the first of legions to follow.

It is indeed fortunate that the balance of 1861 saw so little action. With no major battles other than First Bull Run in the East and Wilson's Creek out in Missouri, Union and Confederate authorities did not immediately face massive numbers of prisoners. After the debacle at Manassas, Confederates found no more than 1,100 Yankees on their hands, and the Federals' captures were less than a dozen. Combined prisoners-of-war on both sides out in the Missouri battle barely exceeded 200. Numbers like these were manageable, placed little strain on resources, and afforded North and South both time to evolve some kind of policy for dealing with prisoners. Alas, even with this breathing space, neither side moved with dispatch or imagination.[4]

In fact, it took some time before Lincoln even recognized Confederates as prisoners. Since he maintained all along that the South never left the Union, and was instead in a state of insurrection, there was, therefore, no "war," and only in a war could there be prisoners to be accorded the standard treatment for captured enemies. Confederates were involved in a treasonous rebellion, subject to being dealt with as traitors, not as prisoners.[5]

As a result, in the months following Bull Run, when both sides might have been erecting prison camps and setting up the administration necessary to care for prisoners, they devoted more time instead to posturing and blustering. Lincoln intended to try captured Confederate privateers as traitors, for whom the punishment was well known. So Jefferson Davis declared that he would execute an equal number of Federal prisoners for every Southerner hanged. Only after heavy public and administrative pressure did Lincoln finally back down and agree to consider the privateers as legitimate prisoners. And all the while, as additional – though small – numbers of men were taken prisoner, they joined the hundred of others languishing in hastily improvised military prisons. In 1861, if the boys North and South had any awareness of the indecisiveness of their governments on the prisoner issue, and of the woefully inadequate means of caring for prisoners of war even at the most basic level, they might have marched off to battle with a little less spring in their step.

When they did go to battle and suffer capture, they soon found themselves standing for hours in holding pens, or in a gully surrounded by armed guards, while officers recorded their names and units. Provost marshals issued orders for sending the prisoners to established compounds far behind the lines, and then the prisoners were off. The lucky ones traveled by boat or rail, but as the war went on such transportation, especially in the South, was most needed for other proposes, and so more often than not the prisoners walked into captivity.

Those who rode found it less than pleasant. After Lieutenant Alonzo Cooper of the 12th New York Cavalry was captured at Plymouth, North Carolina, on April 20, 1864, he was marched in full uniform for several days before he and his men reached the railroad at Tarboro. There they were crowded into cattle cars, forty to the car, and the rolling stock had not been cleaned out since the last "beeves" departed. "It was, therefore, like lying in a cow stable," complained Cooper. Things got worse, however. "We now began to realize what short rations, or no rations, meant." While some of their guards and the local citizens performed acts of comfort and kindness, others sought immediately to profit by their adversity. Cooper had to pay ten dollars to buy nine sandwiches for himself and some comrades. Later on a pie cost him five dollars. "At this rate a millionaire could not long remain outside the poor house," he lamented. And when rations were issued, they were soft bread and spoiled bacon.[6]

Yet in the days ahead, most of the prisoners would look back on such fare as princely compared to what awaited them. After leaving the front, many arrived first at depot prisons like Point Lookout, Maryland, or Richmond's later infamous Libby Prison. From these points they were sent deep into the interior, where they were to spend the balance of their prison days. And once at their ultimate destinations, the men's names were once again checked against a list, like bills of lading.

Early in the war the captured Yanks and Rebs did not necessarily feel any great apprehension, even when they saw the old tobacco warehouses or the hastily erected tent compounds that were to be their prison homes. They did not expect to be there for long. Indeed, the practice up to Bull Run had been to release prisoners on their parole, that is, to send them home under an agreement not to take up arms once again until properly "exchanged." Prisoner exchange was an old practice in warfare. Paroled prisoners remained free at home, though still members of the military and subject to its orders. However, they could not fight again until formally traded – exchanged – for a like number of paroled prisoners on the other side. A paroled man who fought again before being exchanged was subject to harsh punishment if discovered, even death.

It came as a rude shock, then, when the Yankees taken at Manassas found themselves spending several months in prison after their capture. Lincoln's refusal to recognize that a real war existed precluded any prisoner exchanges. To negotiate with the Confederates would in effect, he feared, constitute recognition of the Richmond authorities as a legitimate government, which could have grave diplomatic implications. Only under considerable pressure did Lincoln finally designate General John Dix to arrange a formal exchange system with the enemy. The agreement allowed for the man-for-man trading of private soldiers as well as officers of equivalent rank. Within the hierarchy of officers, trading was to take place on the basis of a cartel with the British made back in 1813. A corporal was worth two privates. A captain was equal to two lieutenants. A major general required 30 enlisted men for exchange. If there were not enough men available for exchange on one side or the other, those remaining unexchanged were to be paroled pending exchange. "Friendly discussions" were to take care of any disputes, but in any case the process of exchange was to continue uninterrupted. If it had worked, there would have been no Civil War prisons.[7]

Unfortunately, it did not work. Neither side was ready for the overwhelming load of record-keeping required, nor for the scale and pace which the war would quickly assume. Worse, some generals believed that the system impaired morale, actually encouraging men to get themselves captured in order to be paroled home with slim prospect of exchange. The system only worked well for the first few months before it steadily broke down. Both sides launched accusations of bad faith, and when black soldiers entered the equation after 1863, the Confederates refused to treat them on an equal basis with whites in the exchange. That same year the whole agreement fell apart amid accusations and recriminations.

Even when the cartel was still in effect, North and South began to take halting steps toward dealing with the prisoner problem, though their solutions betrayed little genuine long-range planning. In October 1861, Colonel William H. Hoffman was appointed commissary general of prisoners in the Union Army, charged with keeping record of prisoners taken, managing any exchanges, transporting supplies to Union prisoners in the South under truce agreements, and, of course, maintaining and administering the camps established to hold captured Confederates. Hoffman proved to be admirably efficient. His initial task was to establish the first specially created prison on Johnson's Island on Lake Erie, near Sandusky, Ohio, and he did so with speed and skill. He also did it with something that characterized all his operations for the rest of the war – spartan thrift. Intended solely for the sake of wartime economy, Hoffman's stinginess would unintentionally lead to considerable hardship and suffering for many Rebel prisoners.[8]

That measures were short-sighted is all too clear in the fact that Hoffman's prison at Johnson's Island was originally designed for only 1,000 men, this in a war that would see hundreds of thousands captured. The fall of Fort Donelson alone, in February 1862, just two weeks after Johnson's Island opened, funneled 15,000 new prisoners into Hoffman's system. The captives from this one engagement forced the ersatz creation of four new camps in Indiana, Illinois, and Ohio, as well as swelling numbers in other established compounds. After the cartel gave way in May and July 1863, Hoffman was never entirely able to keep up with the rapid influx of prisoners.

The story was even worse south of the Potomac. Management of Confederate prisons was put in the hands of Brigadier General John H. Winder, a sixty-one-year-old Marylander who began the war as provost of Richmond. Gradually his authority spread until, on November 21, 1864, he was finally made commissary general of prisoners. Where Hoffman's economy was self-induced, Winder had no choice but to cut corners. He established a few new camps, notably Camp Sumter near Andersonville, Georgia, but most Yankee prisoners were stuffed wherever he could find room, whether on a barren island in the James River, or in Libby's tobacco warehouse in Richmond. Like Hoffman, Winder never intentionally set out to mistreat or harm the prisoners entrusted to him, but suffer they did.

Filthy, unsanitary, riddled with vermin, the prisons of the Civil War were all, in varying degrees, hells on earth. "It is useless to attempt a description of the place," declared an Alabamian incarcerated at Fort Delaware; "a respectable hog would have turned up his nose in disgust at it." Bedbugs inhabited every mattress and dark place. Confederates in Washington's Old Capitol Prison occasionally joined forces against the insects and had "a promiscuous slaughter, regardless of age or sex." Yet when it was all done, the bugs were back, and the Rebs had to conclude that "they must recruit from the other side, like the Yankee army, as we can notice no diminution in the forces."[10] A Rhode Islander held prisoner in the South declared that "the vermin was so plenty that the boys said they had regimental drill."[11]

Perhaps worst of all were the fleas. "The beasts crawled over the ground from body to body," wrote a New Yorker, "and their attacks seemed to become more aggravating as the men became more emaciated."[12] By daylight they could be found and killed, but in the dark of night the men had no choice but to suffer. "We hunted them three times each day but could not get the best of them," wrote John Adams of Massachusetts. "They are very prolific and great-grandchildren would be born in twenty-four hours after they struck us."[13]

The constant scratching helped make a shambles of the prisoners' already tattered clothing. Many, and particularly Confederates who were hardly well clad to start, often wore little more than rags when they first reached the prisons. A few months in a warm climate where the mildew could rot the fabric from their frames might leave the poor men virtually in threads, often reducing them to the humiliation of scavenging rags from the bodies of their dead comrades, vermin and all. Happily, if they had to wear rags, at least the prisoners held in the South faced winters less harsh than the Rebels incarcerated at Johnson's Island and the like. There the gales of winter tore through open stockades and drafty barracks. Hoffman recognized the problem, but dealt with it in his usual miserly fashion by acquiring ill-made or wrong-sized Federal uniforms which had been rejected for field service. With these he equipped such of his prisoners as he could, in the process also managing to find blankets for most of them.

On both sides of Mason and Dixon's line, with little else to occupy their day, prisoners spent much of their time thinking about their rations. Eating them, such as they were, provided the only break in the monotony of the day. What they ate matched their surroundings for miserliness and contamination. Meat rations came spoiled and fly-and-worm infested, while bread was moldy and full of maggots.[14]

Ration quantities were often such as merely to whet appetites, not satisfy them. A South Carolinian tallied his daily fare as a half-pint of "slop water" coffee for breakfast, a half-pint of "greasy water" soup for dinner, and with it a three or four ounce piece of meat. "The writer has known large, stout men to lay in their tents at night and cry like little babies from hunger," he said.[15]

The prisoners went after any source of meat, be it dog, cat, bird, or rat. "We traped for Rats and the Prisoners Eat Every one they Could get," wrote an Arkansan at Johnson's Island. He captured and ate a "mess of Fried Rats" himself, finding that they tasted like squirrels and "was all right to a hungry man."[16]

Before long rumors swept the camps that prison authorities actually intended to starve the men to death, and the accusations were often repeated after the war. There was no truth in it on either side. War demands simply limited what was available, especially in the South. As a rule the Yanks held there ate almost as well – or as badly – as Confederate soldiers in the field. Yet when he heard reports of starvation in Southern prisons, Colonel Hoffman ordered a cutback in rations to his own prisoners in retaliation. By the end of the war he could proudly return to the Federal Treasury nearly $2 million that he had saved by ration reduction. A move which no doubt made the plight of his prisoners worse.

Drinking water matched the food, coming from polluted wells, or camp streams fouled by prison waste.[17] In such a situation, sickness on a massive scale was inevitable. Immediately apparent was scurvy. First the skin discolored and lost its resiliency. Then hair and teeth fell out – then came weakness, lethargy and death. In the camp at Elmira, New York, in its first three months over 1,800 cases occurred, while at Fort Delaware more than ten percent contracted it. A terrible suffering made all the more horrible by the fact that the fresh vegetables that could have prevented the disease were readily available. But Colonel Hoffman regarded them all as luxuries, and after his retaliatory cutback in rations for Confederate prisoners, no "luxuries" were to be allowed. As a result, while thousands of men suffered from the disease, the $23,000 appropriated for vegetable purchase lay dormant in the Fort Delaware relief fund.

Conditions were just as bad in the South. Surgeon Joseph Jones at Andersonville reported that "from the crowded conditions, filthy habits, bad diet and dejected, depressed condition of the prisoners, their systems had become so disordered that the smallest abrasion of the skin, from the rubbing of a shoe, or from the effects of the sun, the prick of a splinter or the scratching of a mosquito bite, in some cases took on a rapid and frightful ulceration and gangrene."[18] All the prisons had hospitals, but Andersonville's was the worst. It comprised five acres of open ground outside the main stockade, and there stewards tended to men who languished under the sun on straw piles and boards. Even in Northern prisons like Camp Douglas in Illinois, the death rate in a hospital could be six a day. At Camp Sumter it was far worse. Stewards cleaned wounds with dirty water poured on them, forming pools on the ground where insects bred in the moist filth. Inevitably, millions of flies swarmed over the helpless patients, relentlessly laying eggs in their open wounds and sores. Scores of men went mad from the pain of maggots eating their way through their inflamed flesh.

Men who formerly had faced enemies with guns and bayonets, now had to contend with a new sort of foe, sometimes just as fatal: boredom. The hours of confinement crawled past, even more tedious, more empty, than the long days of winter quarters. No prisons provided any sort of organized occupation for their inmates; the men were left entirely to their own devices for recreation. Most of them wrote as often as they could, in part to pass the time, and in part in the hope that they would receive mail in response. Paper, especially in the Rebel prisons, was in short supply, with many men asking their loved ones to send them blank foolscap with their replies. Censorship by authorities was so rigid that often letters were barely decipherable after the censor's eye had passed over them. Offending words or passages were blacked with ink, or sometimes even cut out with scissors, leaving the missive in tatters. In time, some prison commanders even had to limit the quantity of outgoing mail because of the overloading of work for the censors. "I found it impossible to permit them to write to everybody as they please for the reason that four clerks in the post-office could not read 2,000 letters a day," wrote the commandant at Fort Delaware.[19]

Commandants could not deny the prisoners religion, however, and the Almighty found thousands of friends and converts in the camps. Like prisoners of all places and all times, Johnny Reb and Billy Yank could take some measure of succor in faith. "Often while walking the floor of the prison," wrote a Reb on Johnson's Island, "I repeat the Lord's Prayer, and I find my whole mind absorbed upon the subject of my future state of existence or my appearing before God." In the prison hells, meeting their Maker seemed all too imminent to the captives.[20]

For a few of the prisoners, nothing, not faith or singing or writing or games, could maintain their spirits. At Camp Sorghum, South Carolina, a New York prisoner looked upon men who sat "moping for hours with a look of utter dejection, their elbow upon their knee, and their chin resting upon their hand, their eyes having a vacant, far-away look."[21] After a time all of the miseries and hardships weighing them down simply became too heavy. Faced with their condition, short food and bad clothing, crowding, filth, the suffering of comrades, and the ever-present specter of death, some men simply gave up their grasp on reality or their will to live. "The sufferings of the body were not equal to the tortures of the mind," wrote a prisoner from New Hampshire. Uncertainty, isolation, ignorance and despair, "all had a depressing effect upon the mind, and finally many became insane."[22] Many more simply gave up and died.

For those who held on to their reality and their hope, it was endless talking that got them through the days, and they discoursed on everything. Newly arrived prisoners, "fresh fish" as they were called, were pumped mercilessly for what they knew of the war, of affairs at home, and most of all – the unceasing topic – of the prospect for an exchange. "There is considerable excitement this morning about Paroling," wrote a Minnesota private at Andersonville, "but it is all gass I reckon for there never was so ignorant a lot of men to gether since the World stood."[23] Yet for every hope dashed, another surfaced soon in its place. It was all they had.

When they tired of talking of the prospects for release, the prisoners turned their tongues toward the men who held them captive. Ironically, only two prison commandants of the war were later honored with memorials, though for very different causes. One was Colonel Richard Owen, in command of Indianapolis' Camp Morton. So well liked was he that after the war his former prisoners commissioned and paid for a bust of the colonel that still stands in the Indiana capitol. Equally admired was Colonel Charles Hill, commandant at Johnson's Island, a "good friend to the prisoners, all of whom esteemed him very highly for his kindness of heart."[24] Indeed, so kind of heart was Colonel Robert Smith, in charge of the Confederate prison at Danville, Virginia, that he is reputed to have become an alcoholic when he could not endure seeing the suffering of his ill-supplied charges.

Far more common, of course, were the commanders regarded as evil incarnate by their prisoners. It was a natural, if not always deserved, opinion, and the men delighted in telling sometimes exaggerated stories of Point Lookout's Major Allen Brady trampling prisoners under his horse's hooves, of Lieutenant Abraham Wolf at Fort Delaware exhibiting "all the mean, cowardly, and cruel instinct of the beast from which his name was taken," or of that "vulgar, coarse brute," Richard Turner of Richmond's Libby Prison, who kicked dying men for the fun of it.[25]

Much worse were the guards. "We are under the Malishia," an inmate wrote of his guards, "& they are the Dambst set of men I ever had the luck to fall in with yet." Prisoners did not fail to comment on the fact that most guards were either men too old to serve in the regular forces or else too young, and most were looked on as "the worst looking scallawags." In Camp Sumter, Captain Henry Wirz reported that the carelessness and inefficiency of his guards was "on the increase day by day."[26]

It is hardly surprising that, with all he faced from unintentional neglect to willful mistreatment, many a prisoner decided not to wait around for exchange. "Freeedom was more desired than salvation," wrote a Yankee, "more sought after than righteousness."[27] Many men escaped soon after their capture and before reaching prisons. Once in the pen, thousands more were not deterred from making the attempt. Every prison had its breakouts, and many were successful, though more were not.

By one's and two's, several hundred prisoners made good their departure, though often only to be recaptured. Attempts of larger proportions usually failed because of the enhanced risk of discovery. In December 1864 the war's largest attempted escape involving enlisted men took place at Danville, but it went wrong almost from the start. Led by General Alfred Duffie and Colonel William Raulston, the men intended to overpower their guards, rush out of their warehouse barracks, free the rest of the prison's inmates, and then destroy the Confederate supply base at Danville and disappear into the Shenandoah Valley to rejoin the Federals. Unfortunately, an outcry arose as soon as Duffie grabbed a guard, and the warehouse was quickly locked from the outside. A warning shot accidentally gave Raulston a mortal wound, and the rest of the would-be escapees flocked back to their bunks. That was all there was to it, and Danville never experienced another escape attempt. Some tries were more successful, most notably Confederate General John Hunt Morgan's break from the Ohio State Penitentiary with several of his cavalrymen, but these were basically exceptions to the rule, for most of those who walked through a prison gate, the only way they left again was by release – or death.

Most prisoners never attempted to escape. Their conditions simply wore them down mentally and physically to the point where they simply languished away in places little heard of before the war, but which rapidly became storied scenes of hardship and suffering. Probably the worst of all in the North was the prison camp located outside Elmira, New York, on the Chemung River. "If there was a hell on earth," wrote a Texan, "Elmira prison was that hell."[28] Badly located where the receding waters of the river left a stagnant pool in the compound after a flood, its condition was made the worse when the prisoners dumped their garbage and camp sewage into that pool. This "festering mass of corruption" went unremedied for months while Hoffman obtained careful estimates of the expense of draining it. When it was drained, he spent a modest sum to allow the prisoners to build their own sewer. Yet elsewhere the barracks were falling apart due to cheap green wood being used in their construction. Worse, Hoffman built a prison for half the numbers he was told to expect, with the overflow frequently having to sleep out in the open. When winter came, there was but one stove for every 100 prisoners. Morning roll call sometimes made 1,600 or more Rebels stand barefoot and ill-clad in the snow. As a result, one man in five had scurvy, and men died at the rate of ten a day. In October 1864, when the post surgeon almost boasted that deaths were down to forty per week, a guard lamented that prisoners were dying "as sheep with rot." Before it closed at war's end, a quarter of all of Elmira's prisoners died within its confines.[29]

Elmira and all the others could not match the infamy attached to a Confederate prison which was opened in Georgia early in 1864 to hold the overflow from

Virginia's camps. Camp Sumter it was called, but it quickly came to be known generally by its proximity to Andersonville. Poorly located and hastily built, it afforded to its inmates only such shelter as they could themselves built out of scanty materials. The South's transportation woes denied a sufficient supply of anything from reaching the camp. Its only water came from a sluggish stream which served as latrine, garbage dump, breeding ground for millions of insects, and drinking water for up to and exceeding 33,000 prisoners. It is no wonder that fully half of the prison population was on the sick list every month. Indeed, it was more a huge hospital than a prison, and its sheer size worked against the men it held. In population, it would have ranked as the fifth largest city in the Confederacy, behind New Orleans, Richmond, Charleston, and Montgomery, yet its 33,000 "citizens" were crammed into a 26-acre space that allowed each man a bare twenty-five square feet to live on.

All the anguish of Andersonville required someone to blame, someone to hate. And all the blame was laid upon its commander, Major Henry Wirz. He was an easy man to hate, a foreigner who spoke poor English, a man of quick temper and little patience. Unspeakable atrocities were laid at his feet. He paraded before his prisoners with a pistol threatening to shoot them at random. He intentionally withheld food and clothing and medicines. He lured men over the "dead line" inside the prison's stockade, a line beyond which no man was to step without being shot by guards. He was a fiend incarnate, they said. Few realized that he was nearly as much a victim as his prisoners. He had not built the prison. Winder, not Wirz, bore what responsibility there was for shortages, and he, worn down by the war and his responsibilities, died on February 7, 1865, before the conflict ended. As a result, many a prisoner in Camp Sumter turned all his hate upon Henry Wirz, and vowed vengeance if ever the war should end.

At last the suffering came to an end. Federal authorities recommenced the exchange system early in 1865, even while advancing Yankee armies were taking whole states from the Confederates and thereby freeing prisoners by the thousands. Finally the Rebel government stopped trying to hold on to their prisoners. Thousands were simply paroled where they were and released. After the surrenders of April and May, prison doors everywhere opened at last. For the returning Southerners, there was nothing to do but try to forget. But for the winners came the opportunity for justice against their tormentors. Hysteria and exaggeration of prison excesses in the South soon swept the Yankee press and pulpit. "I have seen prisoners knocked down by the guard with iron bars and clubs," asserted one New Englander, "and have seen Union men stripped of their clothing and ducked in the freezing cold water."[30] Tales of every sort of torture were told, many of them imagined, more greatly exaggerated, but the public listened and believed.

Inevitably someone had to pay for the horrors. Winder was dead, and that left Wirz. In May 1865 he was arrested and taken to Washington where he was subjected to a sham of a trial before a military tribunal. Admittedly an unsympathetic man, probably not an able administrator, Wirz became the classic victim of circumstances. Protesting that he had been simply a soldier following orders, he was convicted of "murder in violation of the laws and customs of war." There had never been any doubt of the verdict, or of the sentence. On November 10, 1865, in a carnival atmosphere, surrounded by soldiers chanting "Andersonville, Andersonville" over and over, he mounted a scaffold at Old Capitol Prison and became the last victim of Andersonville.

Unfair as it was, Wirz' death was symbolic of unbelievable restraint on the part of the North, for he was the only Confederate to be executed after the four years of bloody, bitter war. Forty years later he became the second Civil War prison commander – along with Richard Owen – to be memorialized. A simple marker went up to his memory just outside Andersonville, commemorating his innocence of the crimes charged against him. Ironically, today, over the spot where he died, symbolic of the justice which he was denied, stands the United States Supreme Court.

So many had died. Over 211,000 Billy Yanks were captured during the war, and of them at least 194,000 went into Southern prisons. Of their number, 30,218 never came home again: more than fifteen percent. About 214,000 Confederates were sent north to Union prisons, and there 25,976 were to die. Over 56,000 Americans, thus, had expired painfully, isolated, cut off from the comfort of friends and family, locked away in the cold and festering prison hells of North and South. "Abandon hope, all ye who enter here," was supposedly inscribed above the sallyport of the prison at Fort Jefferson in the Dry Tortugas. It might as well have applied everywhere that soldiers languished in captivity.[31]

When hope did spring forth, it came in strange guises and often so unlooked for that it gave to the poor unfortunates a rare glimmer of good in what must have seemed to them an evil world. At Andersonville, where there was the least cause for hope, the crowding and lax sanitation polluted most of the compound's water. But then in August 1864, after a heavy downpour, a spring suddenly bubbled up from the ground. It was pure, clear water, and its seemingly miraculous appearance was taken by the hapless inmates as a sign from the Almighty that they had not been forgotten. They called it Providence Spring, and it flows still, long after the stockades and huts and all the other vestiges of that squalid horror have long since disappeared.

REFERENCES

1 Walter Clark, ed.,*Histories of the Several Regiments and Battalions from North Carolina*... (Goldsboro, N.C., 1901), IV, p.677.
2 O.R., Series II, Vol, 1, p.6.
3 William B. Hesseltine, *Civil War Prisons* (Columbus, Ohio, 1930), pp.3-5.
4 William C. Davis, *Battle at Bull Run* (New York, 1977), pp.245, 253.
5 Hesseltine, *Prisons*, pp.7-14.
6 Alonzo Cooper, *In and Out of Rebel Prisons* (Oswego, N.Y., 1888), pp.39-40.

7 O.R., Series II, Vol. 4, pp.266-7.

8 Hesseltine, *Prisons*, pp.38-46.

9 Edmund D. Patterson, *Yankee Rebel* (Chapel Hill, N.C., 1966), p.120.

10 James J. Williamson, *Prison Life in the Old Capitol* (West Orange, N.J., 1911), p.68.

11 Frederic Denison, *Sabres and Spurs* (Central Falls, Iowa, 1876), p.196.

12 George Putnam, *A Prisoner of War in Virginia* (New York, 1912), pp.40-1.

13 John G.B. Adams, *Reminiscences of the 19th Massachusetts* (Boston, 1899), p.140.

14 *The Papers of Randolph Abbott Shotwell* (Raleigh, N.C., 1931), II, p.140.

15 James T. Wells, "Prison Experience," *Southern Historical Society Papers*, VII (July, 1879), pp.327-8.

16 Ted R. Worley, ed., *The Memoirs of Captain John W. Lavender* (Pine Bluff, Ar., 1956), p.132.

17 Anthony M. Keiley, *In Vinculus* (Petersburg, Va., 1866), pp.66-7.

18 O.R., Series II, Vol, 8, p.602.

19 *Ibid.*, Series II, Vol. 6, pp.809-10.

20 William N. Norman, *A Portion of My Life* (Winston-Salem, N.C., 1959), p.205.

21 Cooper, *Rebel Prisons*, p.267.

22 Leander Cogswell, *A History of the Eleventh New Hampshire* (Concord, N.H., 1891), p.531.

23 Ovid Futch, "Prison Life at Andersonville," *Civil War History*, VIII (June 1962), p.123.

24 Hattie L. Winslow and Joseph R.H. Moore, *Camp Morton, 1861-1865* (Indianapolis, 1940), p.262.

25 Military Historical Society of Massachusetts, *Civil War and Miscellaneous Papers* (Boston, 1913), p.181.

26 Futch, "Prison Life," pp.129-30; O.R., Series II, Vol. 7, p.708.

27 Abner Small, *The Road to Richmond* (Berkeley, Calif., 1939), p.175.

28 James I. Robertson, Jr., "The Scourge of Elmira," *Civil War History*, VIII (June 1962), p.184.

29 *Ibid.*, p.191.

30 Denison, *Sabres and Spurs,* p.317.

31 O.R., Series II, Vol. 8, pp.946-8.

X

THE DEADLIEST ENEMY OF THEM ALL

Lurking in the shadows behind the pomp and glory, beneath all the patriotic fervor, the thrill of the battle, and even the serene camaraderie of the campfire, awaited enemies more dread and sinister than all the bullets on the continent. Ignorance and disease lay in store for everyone. The common soldiers of the war faced each other only infrequently. Yet every day they risked their lives in battle with the unseen minions of corruption and decay, sometimes the result of their wounds, more often from the simple act of living through another day in camp. They entered the lists armed only with superstition, protected chiefly by neglect. So pitiful was their armor that the Union Army, which enlisted more than two million men during the course of the war, went out in 1861 to administer to sick and injured – who would number in hundreds of thousands – with no more than twenty thermometers. No wonder that poet and nurse Walt Whitman would cry out that "future years will never know the seething hell and black infernal background, and it is best they should not."[1]

The kind of medical examination given to new recruits was often their introduction to the kind of medical care they could expect in the army, and was itself the first inferior obstacle that disease frequently vaulted in making its way into the camps. All too often the examining physicians seemed to pay little more attention to the man in front of them than that necessary to ensure that he had both arms and legs. One physician, a "fat, jolly old doctor," told jokes to the men he examined, then gave them "two or three little sort of "love taps" on the chest," and squeezed their back, shoulders, and limbs. "I only wish you had a hundred such fine boys as this one!" he would say to the enrolling captain. "He's all right, and good for the service."[2]

In fact, thousands of soldiers entered the armies without ever seeing a doctor at all, while others were pronounced sound by men who knew nothing at all about medicine. If a man had been able-bodied enough to walk behind his plow or wield a shovel in civilian life, then so far as they were concerned, he could shoulder a rifle. Consequently, lax or ignorant examinations – or none at all – allowed thousands of ill and frail men to come into the military, many of them bringing their infections and infirmities with them to pass them along to their messmates.

No wonder that a short time after organization, the regiments began to suffer a high rate of attrition from sickness. Most units started the war around 1,000 strong. But by the time the 1st Connecticut went to its first battle, a few months later, it counted only 600 fit for duty. And the 128th New York suffered even more, numbering barely 350 men after only a year of active service. Some 200,000 men, over twenty percent of those enlisted in 1861 and 1862, had to be dismissed and sent home after their illnesses and handicaps manifested themselves in the field. Even then, the state of sophistication in dealing with unsound bodies was such that the best authorities hardly knew what to look for. In the South, always hard-pressed for manpower after the first year of the war, instructions governing who should serve and who should be rejected cautioned doctors to "exercise a sound and firm discretion and not yield your judgment in favor of every complaint of trivial disability."[3] Wisdom suggested that an active outdoor life in the army might even be a curative, and that many ailments were "strengthened and improved by the exposure incident to the life of the soldier." If a man had a short leg, a weak heart, bad eyesight, a stutter, bladder trouble, hemorrhoids, a hernia, even a missing eye or absent fingers, still however interesting his case might be to the doctor's "professional" curiosity, so far as the army was concerned he was fit for service.

Very few of these men had ever congregated with large numbers of others in their lives. Indeed, many had never even attended school, nor experienced sufficient exposure to others in childhood for them to contract and survive even the most rudimentary childhood diseases. Mumps, chicken pox, measles, whooping cough, scarlet fever, were entirely new to them, and what was usually a two-week inconvenience to a child, could prove to be fatal to an adult.

In three regiments from Mississippi in 1861, camp measles killed 204 men in just three months. A surgeon visiting the hospital found 100 or so men stuffed into a room with the patients lying on the hard floor, without mattresses or even straw, with nothing but blankets for comfort. Several were obviously close to death, vomiting, some with blood poisoning, while their condition was "something that astonished everyone, even the surgeons."[4] It was the same everywhere. In one Yankee outfit from Iowa, almost half its men fell out of duty with measles.

Sanitation was a foreign word to almost all soldiers, and the men paid for their ignorance. Indeed, their behavior made their naivety even more costly. In an era of often exaggerated modesty, many men objected to using the regimental latrines, which were usually located out in the open. Others were too lazy to walk to the "sinks" as they were called. Instead, thousands simply relieved themselves where they stood, even in their own camps, or else walked behind a tree. New men soon learned to watch where they walked, and even where they slept. One Virginian awoke one morning and rolled up his bedding only to discover that "I had been lying in – I won't say what – something that didn't smell like milk and peaches."[5] A Federal camp inspector in 1861 reported most Yankee bivouacks awash in litter, garbage, and decomposing trash of every description, "slops deposited in pits within the camp limits or thrown out broadcast; heaps of manure and offal close to the camp."[6] The excrement and castout garbage of hundreds of thousands of men turned the camps – especially in the heat of summer – into an olfactory nightmare. However tragic the war was for the human beings who had to endure it, for untold numbers of microbes and vermin it was a bonanza, a five-year feast with the soldiers themselves destined to be the dessert.

Army regulations did provide some instructions for covering the latrines and for camp cleanliness. But then, Union regulations also required men to wash their hands and feet daily, and to bath completely once a week, though in reality soldiers went months at a time without bathing. Consequently, Johnny Reb and Billy Yank simply learned to live with their unwelcome companions. They joked about the mosquitoes, claiming they could be heard to bray "like mules." Lice were reputedly found in clothing with the letters "I.F.W." ("In For the War") on their backs. Even in battle the men were sometimes seen using one hand for their weapon and the other busy swatting flies or scratching bites. "I get vexed at them and commence killing them," one Confederate said of the swarms of flies, "but as I believe 40 of them comes to every one's funeral, I have given it up as a bad job."[7]

Considering this world in which they lived, it is no wonder that the soldiers suffered staggering losses to the pestilences thriving in their midst. Malaria took a respectable toll, though the men knew it variably as "the shakes," the "ague," or "intermittent fever." "We are more afraid of the ague here than the enemy," an Illinois boy wrote home. Almost half of the 38th Iowa was hospitalized or killed by it, and over one million cases were diagnosed before the war was done.[8] At morning sick call, malaria on average accounted for twenty percent of those who fell out. No one suspected the pesky mosquitoes that bit them. Instead, doctors and men alike attributed the disease to the "poisonous vapors" arising from swamps and ponds.

Typhoid was an even greater threat. "We would rather die in battle than on a bed of fever," a Federal colonel protested, yet this was the fate of all too many.[9] The colonel could see them "jabbering and muttering insanities, till they lie down and die," but he could not find out why they died. They called it "camp fever," and never traced it to its origins in tainted water. In the Southern armies it may have claimed as many as a quarter of all who died in the war.

But of all diseases, the one the soldiers feared most, and the one to which their own habits most contributed, was the alvine flux. Typically they endowed it with a host of sobriquets – "diarrhea," "dysentery," "the debility," "the runs," "Virginia Quick Steps," "Tennessee Trots," and so forth. Most often they simply called it what it most demonstrably was: "the shits." More than one wag quipped that in this war "bowels are of more consequence than brains," and it was only part jest. Intestinal disorders killed more men than all the bullets fired in four years of combat. Soldiers lived in mortal fear of the diseases, and well they should have, for contracting one or more of them was a virtual certainty. One and three-quarter million cases were reported in the Union Army during the war, and that does not include the untold thousands that went unreported thanks to the soldiers' well-founded contempt for the remedies and doctors available to them.

It was no wonder. Often as not, the doctor did not make an examination, but rather left it to the patient to perform his own diagnosis by asking "what is the matter with you." For those who complained of dysentery, the standard prescription was a dose of "salts," a cathartic which, in fact, acted as a laxative, only making matters worse. Complaints that it had not been effective often produced nothing more than another, larger, dose of the same, and on top of that castor oil. The result was predictable. "You are realy now subject to disease," wrote one who went through the treatment, "and that is just the way that we had so many sick." Worn down by ineffectual treatment that reduced their resistance, many men only contracted other diseases. "Sick dogs are treated better than this," a bitter Yankee complained of such treatment.[10]

All of these maladies were aggravated by the want of proper clothing and equipment. The soldier had but one uniform, and replacements came infrequently. The result was worn garments, inhabited by all manner of insect guests, and not much inclination to bathe when a man was forced to put his dirty old clothes on once again.

Exposure out in the field, especially in the cold months, killed thousands. Many men simply froze to death. "It is really pitiful to see our boys at night sitting around their fires, nodding and almost asleep," wrote a Rebel officer. "The ground is too cold for them to lie down on, and their blanket is not warm enough for them to cover with."[11] Such exposure opened the door to infection even wider.

The soldiers' diet only added to the problem, for the concept of nutrition was as foreign as the commands in the French drill manuals. Reb and Yank alike received rations that were ill-balanced, ill-preserved, and ill-prepared. Surviving their own food was often a greater feat than escaping the enemy shot and shell. Most desirable was meat, but it was one of the least plentiful elements of the soldier fare. Perhaps that was a blessing, for whatever its form or manner of preservation, the meat came tough, old, and sometimes virtually rotting. So bad was it that one Yank declared, "one can throw a piece up against a tree and it will just stick there and quiver and twitch for all the world like one of those blue-bellied lizards at home will do when you knock him off a fence rail with a stick."[12]

Much of the beef came pickled, but the men called it "salt horse." It was so tough, briny, rank when cooked, that one bunch of Yanks reacted to a particularly ripe issue of pickled beef by parading it through camp on a bier, then giving it a funeral complete with a military salute and volley over the grave. A Confederate joked that his men needed an issue of files to sharpen their teeth if they were to eat the the petrified beef issued to them. In fact, many ate their beef raw, for it was less tough that way, and many feared that it was only a matter of time before they were fed hooves and horns.

Yanks ate their meat pretty much as it came, but Rebs seemed to prefer frying several chunks of it in the ubiquitous grease in which they cooked everything. They added water, and sometimes vegetables to make a stew, crumbling into it some cornbread and calling the resultant mush "cush." The grease content only further contributed to the stomach ailments already besetting them, but the Rebs liked it just the same. Besides, the mixture helped disguise another feature of the meat ration North and South: passengers. Men joked that they never had to carry their own meat, for the maggots infesting it made it travel on its own, adding that "we had to have an extra guard to keep them from packing it clear off."[13]

Vegetables provided just as much opportunity for derision, and just as many chances of disease and malnutrition. Shipment of raw vegetables to distant armies was impractical in most cases, and so Yankee commissaries supplemented the soldier diet with dehydrated shredded vegetables packed into tight hard cakes. Called "dessicated" by the issuing sergeants, the men in the ranks dubbed them "desecrated vegetables," and more often referred to the cakes as "baled hay," for many believed that not a little grass and straw found its way into them. Prescribed procedure was for the men to immerse the cakes in boiling water, but the rate of expansion was so great that tall tales inevitably arose of men who ate their cakes dry, then began writhing in agony on the ground, in imminent peril of explosion as the cakes expanded within them. Consequently the men took fresh produce whenever they could get it, and few farmers' fields were safe in the harvest season.

Most prevalent of all in the soldier diet was hardtack, a large, dense cracker made of shortening and flour. Too stale to eat whole, it was generally broken up with a rifle butt or soaked in water or fried in grease to soften it. The men called the crackers "sheet-iron crackers," "teeth-dullers," and "worm castles" in reference to the weevils and maggots all too often found in the cracker boxes. "All the fresh meat we had come in the hard bread," one wag quipped, "and I preferring my game cooked, used to toast my biscuits."[14] A few playfully fired bits of hardtack across the line at the enemy.

Confederates also ate hardtack crackers, though wheat flour was in shorter supply in the South, and most Rebs ate cornbread instead. Yet it, too arrived in the mess tents barely palatable, sometimes full of mold and cobwebs. When the men in either army got their hands on actual flour itself, they had a field day baking their own soft bread, although not all of them knew how to go about it. In the 101st Ohio an issue of a barrel of flour sent the men wild. Some added water to it and kneaded it on their rubber blankets while others balled the dough on to their bayonets and tried to roast it over the campfires. "Some pegged the stuff to trees near the fire and swore at it," and most of it wound up wasted, though "we had lots of fun if we did go hungry."[15]

All of these privations could be borne so long as the men had their coffee. Most men were issued the beans themselves, either raw or roasted. It was up to them to find a way to grind them down for brewing. Some crushed them on rocks, and a few regiments were even issued special Sharps rifles that had coffee grinders built into the stocks. However ground, the brew was a ubiquitous companion. Rarely did a column halt for more than a few minutes before someone started a fire and made a pot of coffee. Billy Yanks had by far the best of it, for their supply was unlimited during the war, while their foe had to make do much of the time with substitutes like chicory or parched corn. Both sides drank it strong and without sugar and milk.

The men enjoyed few opportunities to better their diet beyond what the commissary provided. Most permanent camps had sutlers, licensed civilian vendors whose rates were all too often usurious in the absence of competition. Enlisted men came quickly to notice that the sutlers arrived with their pies and cakes and other delicacies just about the same time as the paymaster. The goodies stayed in camp, but the soldiers' hard-earned pay disappeared overnight. Packages from home also augmented camp diet, though what arrived in the boxes was usually stale or beaten about from travel, and frequently raided by government "inspectors" along the way. Generous boys often shared these prizes from home with their tent mates.

Whatever the sutler or homefolk could not provide, the soldier found for himself, usually at the expense of the farmers in the vicinity of his camp or march. Foraging was a universal pastime in both armies, and though sometimes actually punished by officers, it was most often tacitly allowed, and sometimes even encouraged. Men would often ask a hog to take the oath of allegiance to the Union. When it naturally refused, or else simply did not answer, the loyal Yankees had little choice but to kill it and serve it at their mess. Confederates felt the same way about chickens, jesting that on the march "we would not allow a man's chickens to run out in the road and bite us."[16] Consequently, chicken bite was one form of malady rarely if ever reported to the surgeons. The thinking on both sides in the war was that if the government supplied the basic foodstuffs in sufficient quantity, the men would get by satisfactorily. However, such was rarely the case. On the march or in battle, food became rare and of suspect quality. Sometimes men even scavenged corn from the feeding sites of army animals, hoping the beasts' rations might be less tainted than their own.

Hope, of course, was not enough. The rate of disease from all causes was epidemic and the endless sick reports and the bulging hospitals were ample testimony to the persistent problem. Keeping in mind that a single soldier could step out at sick call several times for different maladies, still the Union Army's sick rate for the first full year of the war was well over 3,000 cases reported for every 1,000 men in service. By the end of the conflict it had declined somewhat to 2,273, still a staggering figure. The burden this placed upon the armies' medical departments would have been overwhelming even if they had been well prepared for it.

No one was prepared, and once again it was the common soldier who paid the price. Attitudes were so ill-informed that in 1861 the Union's chief doctor actually believed that some theaters of the war did not need hospitals at all – thanks to their healthful climates. The physicians who served under him were equally ignorant. In that era a man became a doctor by spending at most two years in medical school, and often as not the second year consisted of nothing more than repetition of the first. Furthermore, anyone who could pay qualified for attendance. As for the rest of the practicing doctors in the army, they had learned their trade by apprenticeship, learning the age-old myths and misapplications by watching older doctors who were just as ill-informed. Germs were yet unheard of, and understanding of asepsis lay years in the future. Most medications were useless, and some methods of treatment had not seen improvement since the days of Caesar. Surgeons looked upon bodily temperature as so unimportant that there was rarely a call for those twenty thermometers.

For a "violent Conjestion of the Stomach," poor Ben Pearson of the 36th Iowa endured "about all it was possible for me to suffer & live." The surgeons put hot bricks at his feet and oil cloths on his abdomen, thinking the heat would "draw out" the illness. "Cold clamy Sweat ran out at every poar cold as death," he remembered. "Oh such hours of suffering."[17] When pneumonia baffled physicians, they prescribed liquor and quinine, even laudanum, a tincture of opium. That failing, they might slash a patient's wrists to bleed him, or even pour burning alcohol on his chest. For intestinal disorders, in addition to the salts, calomel, turpentine, mercury, chalk, and even strychnine, were dosed. Watermelon juice helped a cold, so they thought, and tree bark and whiskey relieved malaria.

Army medicine could turn a man's stomach inside out. A New Hampshire boy sent a sample of a stomach powder administered to him home to his family. "It will cure any ails that flesh is heir to," he said, "from a sore toe to the brain fever."[18] So indiscriminately did surgeons administer opiates that they indirectly created a substantial post-war problem: the nation's first real bout with drug addiction.

Faced with these bogus remedies, many soldiers tried treating themselves, with about equal success. Morphine was available to anyone who could purchase it, and many men used it for a variety of ills. Whiskey and mustard plasters were even more popular. Miraculously, some hardy souls simply got better despite what they gave themselves, reinforcing the determination of thousands of sufferers to go "*anywhere else first*" before entering a camp hospital.[19]

In their defense, the surgeons, so heavily outnumbered by the sick and injured, were dreadfully overworked. In the North there was but one doctor for every 133 men in the ranks, and in the South it was worse – one for every 324. These massive case loads could be death-dealing, and it is no wonder that alcoholism was a common complaint lodged against the doctors.

470

No wonder the soldiers coined a host of epithets for their doctors, from "saw-bones" and "Old Quinine," to "Loose Bowels." Yet when a man felt that he needed his physician, when he was wounded and bleeding, in pain, he wanted whatever treatment was available, and quickly. It was a veritable bedlam. "The horrors of the war are best witnessed after a battle," said a Vermont sergeant, and he was right.[20] Every building and tent available became a hospital. Wounded and screaming men were lying everywhere in their own blood and filth. Doctors were in short supply, medicines and opiates often the same, and even water to cool the parched tongues of the wounded and dying might be contaminated and so offensive that men retched at the smell of it. "The foul air from the mass of human beings made me giddy and sick," wrote a resident of Corinth, Mississippi, after a battle in April 1862 turned the city into a Confederate hospital. "And when we give the men anything we kneel in blood and water."[21]

Rifle bullets caused more than ninety percent of all Civil War wounds, and artillery accounted for most of the rest. Whatever the agent of his injury, the soldier at first felt little pain on being struck – just a staggering impact that frequently sent him sprawling on the ground in a momentary daze. Then began an ordeal of one crisis after another.

Those fortunate enough not to fall between the lines, where they might lie for the duration of the battle or be overlooked in the confused aftermath, were carried from the field either by friends or litter-bearers. Their feeling was returning by then, and the pain could quickly escalate to agony. Clumsy bearers could make it worse as they jolted and often dropped their litters, on top of which all too many of the bearers were practiced thieves whose first interest was in rifling the pockets of the helpless wounded on their stretchers. Ambulances were little better, with inadequate springs and uncaring drivers; the excruciating pain exacted by a rough ride could itself send a soldier out of his pain and on his way to the next life.

At the field hospital itself, a sort of triage separated the slightly wounded from those needing immediate attention, and from those beyond help. The first and last were placed aside, the former to wait, the latter to be made as comfortable as possible as they died. They were given opium or whiskey if available, and then ignored while the surgeons went to work with their probes, their knives, and their saws.

The size of the bullets that struck men in the Civil War, ranging from .36 caliber all the way up to a massive .75, ironically made some of the surgeon's work simple, insuring that any abdominal or chest wound was almost invariably fatal. Men with head or serious body wounds were usually set aside. Amazingly, about a quarter of these men actually recovered, very likely a better result than if the physicians had actually tried to save them. For the rest, any limb wound that did not shatter the bone had probably done irreparable damage to the nerves, tendons, or arteries, leaving the surgeon only to find the bullet and stop the bleeding, and three times out of four, amputate the limb.

The lucky soldier received some anesthesia before the knife sliced into him. Doctors preferred chloroform when they could get it, putting a soaked sponge or cloth over the patient's nose until he went limp and limber. Ether, too, saw use, as well as laudanum. But all anesthetics, especially in the Confederacy, could suddenly fall into short supply if the surgeons were not prepared for a major battle and its attendant casualties. Stories of men being given a dose of whiskey and told to bite on a bullet or a stick were widely told and exaggerated, but it happened just the same. Meanwhile, outside the operating tent, those awaiting amputations of their own could only lie and listen to the screams of those not fully anesthetized, and watch the results of the knives' and saws' work accumulate. After Gettysburg some men told of seeing piles of severed limbs five feet high.

"The surgeons and their assistants, stripped to the waist and bespattered with blood, stood around, some holding the poor fellows while others, armed with long bloody knives and saws, cut and sawed away with frightful rapidity, throwing the mangled limbs on a pile nearby as soon as removed," wrote a Confederate cavalryman.[22] The sight was too much for many of his men, who vomited in their saddles when they passed by. The surgeons had little time, and often no inclination, to clean either their hands or their instruments, unknowingly spreading a host of diseases from one man to another. With hideously contaminated hands, they handled the raw flesh of new wounds, probing deep with their fingers. After the Battle of Perryville, Kentucky, in October 1862, one whole Yankee hospital was filled with cases of meningitis, osteomyelitis, and peritonitis, almost all certainly caused by the surgeons' filthy hands. Their diagnosis, however, was "poisonous vapors" once again, and their treatment was simply to open the hospital windows.

"Oh it is awful," a surgeon cried after the fighting in the Wilderness in Virginia in May 1864. "It does not seem as though I could take a knife in my hand to-day, yet there are a hundred cases of amputation awaiting for me. Poor fellows come and beg almost on their knees for the first chance to have an arm taken off. It is a scene of horror such as I never saw. God forbid that I should see another."[23] Most surgeons, despite their ignorance, tried their best for their men, and the pressure and the overwork took its toll on their own well-being. They could not rest so long as there were wounded, and after a battle like Gettysburg or the Wilderness, the men needing immediate attention could number in the tens of thousands. "We are almost worked to death," Surgeon George Stevens of the 77th New York wrote, "yet we cannot rest for there are so many poor fellows who are suffering." All too many they had to watch die. "They look to me for help, and I have to turn away heartsick at my want of ability to relieve their sufferings." "All my friends," he grieved, "and all thought that I could save them."[24] No wonder doctors took to the bottle.

Even if they survived the field hospitals, the wounded had another ordeal to endure as they were taken to the rear to the hundreds of general hospitals that grew up in most of the cities of North and South. Here, where the fatal infections and gangrene most often surfaced, they might spend months, even years, slowly recuperating. Richmond was a city of hospitals, with thirty-four of them in operation. One, Winder Hospital, held 4,300 beds, and Chimborazo was even bigger, with a capacity of up to 8,000, as well as a number of its own support operations including bakeries and factories, and even its own cattle and fields. Chimborazo alone treated some 76,000 wounded and ill during the war. Across the lines, Washington nurtured even more. There were twenty-five military hospitals in the Yankee capital, and even more in its environs.

The doctors running these established hospitals ranged from those too old for field service, to those too inexperienced. The nursing staffs were little better. Volunteer women helped, especially in the Confederacy, but in the North a gradually developing professional nursing corps took over those duties left to them. It was here that Whitman acquired his insight into the dark side of warfare's byproduct of suffering. "I go every day or night without fail to some of the great government hospitals," he told a friend. "O the sad scenes I witness – scenes of death, anguish, the fevers, amputations, friendlessness, hungering and thirsting young hearts, for some loving presence." He had to keep himself constantly busy to keep from weeping, though the kindness and comfort he could give to the suffering rewarded him for his turmoil. "I find I supply often to some of these dear suffering boys in my presence and magnetism that which nor doctors, nor medicines, nor skill, nor any routine assistance can give."[25]

With men in short supply, and needed in the armies, women came forward to help treat the wounded and ill. While most went through the war unnoticed, some like Dorothea Dix and Clara Barton achieved considerable fame, and began careers which led to great strides in health care after the war. Mostly, they were volunteers, though Barton organized a corps of nurses to her exacting standards, which included the stricture that no nurse should be too pretty.

The situation in Richmond remained less formal throughout the war, and the male opposition to female nurses was harder to overcome. A middle-aged Jewish widow named Phoebe Pember was not to be deterred, however. Refusing to take no for an answer, she was appointed Chimborazo Hospital's first female hospital matron and worked there for the rest of the war. She found herself, "in the midst of suffering and death, hoping with those almost beyond hope in this world; praying by the bedside of the lonely and heart-stricken; closing the eyes of boys hardly old enough to realize a man's sorrows." Faced with all that, she could not be bothered with nineteenth-century conventions of propriety in caring for a man's body. "A woman *must* soar beyond the conventional modesty considered correct under different circumstances," she said. The ordeal of a woman's experience would place her above these pedestrian considerations. "If the fire through which she passes does not draw from her nature the sweet fragrance of benevolence, charity, and love – then indeed, a hospital has no fit place for her!"[26]

Certainly Phoebe Pember earned her place at Chimborazo. Nothing so typifies the sacrifice and anguish of those treating the men, as a cold night in 1863 that she spent with a boy named Fisher. He was a special favorite on her ward, a boy badly wounded in the leg who had escaped amputation and, ten months later, was taking his walk up and down between the rows of beds. "He had remained through all his trials, stout, fresh and hearty, interesting in appearance, and so gentle-mannered and uncomplaining that we all loved him," she wrote. But this night she was called to his side to find a jet of blood spurting from his leg. The walk had unsettled a jagged bit of bone and severed an artery. At once she put her finger on the wound to stop the bleeding, then called for the surgeon on duty. He came, shook his head, and pronounced the artery too deeply encased in the fleshy part of the leg to be repaired. The boy must perish.

"Long I sat by the boy," she later wrote. At length she told him what the doctor had confided to her, that in the prime of life, young Fisher was going to die. He took the news with his usual equanimity, gave her instructions for informing his mother, then looked in her eyes.

"How long can I live?"

"Only as long as I keep my finger upon this artery," she replied.

For a long pause he was silent, while she wondered what passed through his mind. Finally he calmly spoke again.

"You can let go."

But she could not, "not if my own life had trembled in the balance." Her eyes filled with tears, her own blood rushed to her head and pounded in her ears, her lips went cold, but she could not make herself let go and condemn the boy. Finally "the pang of obeying him was spared me, and for the first and last time during the trials that surrounded me for four years, I fainted away."[27]

Phoebe Pember's story was typical of those who tried to care for the suffering and relieve their pain. Fisher's was the tale of hundreds of thousands who faced and met disease, wounds, and death manfully – and often cheerfully. Their numbers spoke for themselves. In the course of the war, 360,222 Union soldiers died, fully a quarter million of them from disease and infection of their wounds. Just over a quarter million Confederates perished in the conflict, three-quarters of them from sickness rather than from combat.

For all their suffering, little in the way of medical advancement came as a result to temper the cost paid. More efficient hospital organization, and the advent of female nursing did evolve, as did some rudimentary understanding of the role of cleanliness in preventing disease. Evacuation of the wounded took a giant leap forward in speed and efficiency thanks to a reorganized ambulance corps in the North. But these were modest gains when measured against the price. The real medical lessons of this war would not be learned for decades, long after it was too late for the hundreds of thousands who perished in the "seething hell and black infernal background" of this conflict.

REFERENCES

1 Walter Lowenfels, ed., *Walt Whitman's Civil War* (New York, 1961), pp.181-2.

2 Wiley, *Billy Yank*, p.23.

3 Wiley, *Johnny Reb*, p.245.

4 L.J. Wilson, *The Confederate Soldier* (Fayetteville, Ark., 1902), pp.19-20.

5 Wiley, *Johnny Reb*, p.248.

6 Wiley, *Billy Yank*, p.127.

7 Wiley, *Johnny Reb*, p.249.

8 Wiley, *Billy Yank*, p.133.

9 *Ibid.*, p.135.

10 Paul J. Engle, ed., "A Letter from the Front," *New York History*, XXXIV (1953), pp.206-7.

11 Wiley, *Johnny Reb*, p.247.

12 Wiley, *Billy Yank*, p.240.

13 *Ibid.*

14 *Ibid.*, p.238.

15 L.W. Day, *Story of the One Hundred and First Ohio Infantry* (Cleveland, 1894), pp.77-8.

16 John O. Casler, *Four Years in The Stonewall Brigade* (Guthrie, Okla., 1893), p.78.

17 "Benjamin P. Pearson's Civil War Diary," *Annals of Iowa*, XV (1926), p.520.

18 Wiley, *Billy Yank*, p.139.

19 Wiley, *Johnny Reb*, p.267.

20 George H. Scott, "Vermont at Gettysburg," *Proceedings of the Vermont Historical Society*, I (1930), p.73.

21 Wiley, *Johnny Reb*, p.263.

22 William W. Blackford, *War Years With Jeb Stuart* (New York, 1870), pp.27-8.

23 George T. Stevens, *Three years in the Sixth Corps* (New York, 1870), pp.343-4.

24 *Ibid.*, pp.344-5.

25 Lowenfels, *Whitman*, p.293.

26 Phoebe Y. Pember, *A Southern Woman's Story* (Jackson, Tenn., 1959), pp.45, 146.

27 *Ibid.*, pp.66-8.

XI

ON THE MARCH

Since the overwhelming majority of young men who entered the ranks, North or South, were farmboys who had rarely if ever left their home counties, the trip to the war zone had about it the air of a grand tour. The men's eyes were opened to a host of scenes they had never dreamed of seeing. Even the manner of their travel was a "wonderment" to them for many had not even seen locomotives or steamboats, much less thought ever of riding them. When one Wisconsin lad made the trip from Madison to La Crosse by train, he had to confess that "it was a new experience for me." He sat awake the whole time. "I was afraid we were off the track every time we crossed a switch or came to a river."[1] Others going by boat felt similar experiences at the strange sounds and belching engines of the paddlewheelers. By the time they reached their destinations, most boys already agreed with the Ohioian who wrote home that "since I seen you last I hav seen the elephant." After a day and a night on a steamboat, and another hair-raising day on a train, he confessed that "we past through some of the damdes plases ever saw by mortel eyes." Some "god dames hills" he found to be as "dark as the low regeons of hell." When passing through a long tunnel, the train hit a heavy boulder on the track and "if the engen had not bin so hevy we would hav all went to hell . . . or some other seaport."[2] That was a lot of experience for a plowboy who had never been away from home.

Even before their trips, the boys could not help but be impressed by the send-off their towns gave them. Bands, cheering citizens, endlessly droning politicians, and bevies of handkerchief waving girls, bid them fulsome patriotic farewells. And once on the trains and boats, they were often met at succeeding towns by more of the same. "At the towns the girls swarmed on the platforms to ask the boys for their pictures and to kiss the best looking ones," one Yankee remembered. A little French fellow got the most kisses, being held by his legs as he leaned out the train windows while other soldiers on the platforms lifted the ladies to his lips. "It was fun anyway," said a fellow soldier.[3]

Generally the young Yankees traveled farther, and saw a lot more of the country than did their foes-to-be, especially those boys from Ohio or Illinois who went to the front in Virginia early in the war. Chicago, Pittsburgh, Philadelphia, Baltimore, and Washington, were all sights for which farm life had not prepared them. In Philadelphia they were entertained at the Cooper's Shop, a volunteer hostelry that fed over 87,000 soldiers in its first year of operation. Pittsburgh became famous for the hot coffee that met the troop trains. All of the cities were overpowering in their sheer size and bustle. For many it was too much. A boy from rural New York complained that "Since I left Ninevah everything has been new, but I must say deliver me from citty life."[4]

Oddly enough, the nation's capital, the seat of the war and the burgeoning Union armies, disappointed many, though almost every soldier who came there could not help giving himself up to a bit of touring. Here were the great public buildings, the Capitol and the executive mansion. Here were the unfinished Washington Monument, the Navy Yard with its powerful warships. Here were tens of thousands of young men gathered to march against the Rebellion. And here a common soldier could even catch a glimpse of President Abraham Lincoln as he walked the Capital's streets or reviewed the new regiments. "We strolled from one end of the city to the other," wrote a Boston lad. Entering the Capitol, he wandered through its picture gallery, then climbed the steps to the dome and "had a fine view of Washington and the neighborhood, but I was struck with the mean appearance of the city of Washington with the exception of the Government Buildings." After all he had seen somewhat smugly he concluded that "there is not a building in the whole city which can be called a good one in comparison with the Stores and dwelling houses of Boston."[5]

The men this self-important brahmin was about to fight felt much the same in their way, and saw the same "elephant" for the most part. Given the South's limited transportation facilities, Confederates more often rode to the seat of war in boxcars, into which they irreverently knocked holes in order to provide ventilation, as well as a means of viewing the passing countryside. Civilians watching as the trains rolled by, thought the boxcars, with soldiers' heads sticking out of their holes, looked like poultry wagons loaded with chickens.

For the Southern boys, the great wonders were the Mississippi River and its cities like Memphis and New Orleans, or Atlanta, Charleston, and of course Richmond. The distances traveled were just as great as for Billy Yank, though more often than not the journey took much longer thanks to the inadequate rail and river transportation available. It took one Texas company a full month to get from San Augustine to Richmond. Rebels, too, met with enthusiastic crowds that cheered them on and showered them with gifts, pies and goodies, and not a few kisses. Like their foe to the north, they would also find that as the war ground onward, the enthusiasm grew less and less, and in time many civilians would meet their passing only with scowls, regarding the soldiers now as competitors for the limited resources of the hard-pressed Confederacy.

But in 1861 all was fresh and gay. "I have Saw a rite Smart of the world Sence I left home," a North Carolinian from Buncombe County wrote to his father in the first days of the war, "But I have not Saw any place like Buncomb and henderson yet."[6] Confederates, too, could be just a bit chauvinistic about the merits of their home towns compared with those of the outside world. Yet most were awed by what they saw, even urging their brothers and friends back home to enlist so that they, too, might see and experience this great new world opening before them. This business of going to war and seeing the world – or the "elephant" – was an experience of a lifetime not to be missed.

Rail travel was an adventure for everyone right up to the end of the war, and produced an unending string of memories of accidents and mishaps. When a division of Confederates was bound by rail from Jackson, Mississippi, to Meridian in September 1862, one car jumped the worn track. Convinced that the whole train was about to derail itself, Colonel Thomas Hunt, commander of the 9th Kentucky Infantry, though himself still recovering from a wound, leapt from his car to the ground. His staff officers, "not questioning rank," followed his lead, as did a considerable number of enlisted men. Shortly the train stopped to reposition the derailed car, and men still aboard the cars looked back to see their comrades strewn along several hundred yards of roadbed, lying down, sitting up dazed, feeling their heads and bones for breaks and scratches, and most of them laughing.[7]

The same command had to retrace its route the next summer, and not without similar mishap. As their train left Montgomery, Alabama, bystanders wondered that "all seemed in the highest spirits, cheering and yelling like demons." What the bystanders did not know was that the reason for all the cheering was that, on the train to Montgomery just the day before, two whole regiments had almost disappeared. While steaming down a steep seven-mile grade from Wartrace, Tennessee, their train had run out of control, careering downward even faster, barely holding on to the track on the turns. One man of the 9th Kentucky calculated that they covered the seven miles in just over four minutes. "We thought every moment the car would be dashed to pieces against the rocks or be pitched off some of the cliffs and be ground into dust," wrote one Reb. He actually looked overhead on the wild ride, occasionally catching glimpses of the moon as it appeared through breaks in the overhead crags, and thought seriously about saying goodbye to it. Worse yet, some of his comrades, as many soldiers tended to do, had actually started the ride perched on top of the cars, and now they were holding on for their very lives. The last car on the train actually disintegrated, showering the track with timber and iron. When it flew apart, one Kentuckian on top of it suddenly found himself catapulted through space, flying over a telegraph wire and into a bramble bush. "Receiving no other injury than being 'powerfully' scratched," he thankfully joined the others from his car as they bivouacked beside the track to await the arrival of the next train. Miraculously, no one was fatally injured.[8]

Difficult as rail travel was between campaigns, it could be even more exasperating when on the way to battle, especially for the Confederates. Even at the outset of the war, Rebel trains frequently covered no more than a few miles an hour, with frequent stops for broken track, derailed cars, or broken-down engines. When in July 1861, men of General Joseph E. Johnston's small Army of the Shenandoah were moving from that valley eastward to join with another Rebel army immediately before the First Battle of Bull Run, only one single train was available to handle the entire command, a brigade at a time. As a result, to prevent breakdown to the vital engine, its engineer pushed it at no more than four miles an hour. "We slowly jolted the entire day," wrote one Virginian, covering only thirty miles in eight hours. The next brigade took all night to convey, and the subsequent brigades moved faster. When the train stopped from time to time, the men invariably jumped out of their cars and started combing the the roadside for wild blackberries, often requiring their officers to spend half an hour or more getting them back on the train. As for the last of Johnston's army, when it boarded the by now overworked equipment, the poor old engine could take no more. Soon after departing it simply stopped. Some thought it had suffered a collision, but no one seemed ever to know what it had supposedly hit. Frustrated beyond reason by a delay that they feared would prevent them from reaching the battlefield in time, the men and officers decided that the train's conductor was a traitor who had intentionally slowed their progress. A military trial was immediately convened beside the tracks. Charging the hapless trainman with bribery and treason, it convicted him, and turned him over to a firing squad who promptly shot him.[9]

Steamboat travel could be just as hair-raising, and a lot of fun as well, especially for Rebs and Yanks who came from the western states in the Mississippi Valley, many of whom went to war with some experience of boats. In September of 1862 one Confederate brigade in Mobile, Alabama, boarded two old steamers, the *Waverly* and the *R.B. Taney*, for the trip to Montgomery. The *Waverly* was an old cotton boat, while the *Taney* turned out to be a much more finely appointed passenger or "packet" ship. Almost as soon as they embarked, the men on board the vessels began to shout jibes at each other, each ridiculing the other's boat, until taunts led to challenges. Inevitably, a steamboat race began.

The *Waverly* began the contest at a disadvantage, for her steam pressure was down, and the *Taney* handily passed her by, the men aboard the lead vessel cheering and shouting, their band playing, and even the *Taney's* steam calliope shrieking in victory. But most of the men in the regiment aboard the *Waverly* were old steamboatmen, and there was nothing that could raise their blood more than being beaten, especially by a fancy boat. They literally took control of the *Waverly*. Privates stripped to the waist and lined up in the boiler room, taking turns at furiously stoking the firebox with anything that would burn. Within a few minutes they had the old *Waverly* picking up steam, and speed, and driving over the waves "like a thing of life." Rapidly she caught up with the *Taney*. A mood of intense excitement took over on both vessels, so much so that no one even noticed when Sergeant Bartholomew Sullivan of the 4th Kentucky fell overboard from the *Taney* and was never seen again. All eyes were on the steam gauges and the vessels' bows. Finally, in an attempt to cut off the advancing *Waverly*, the *Taney* actually turned itself sideways in the narrow river to block passage, but the intrepid old cotton boat dashed past her just the same.[10]

Sometimes when traveling over the swampier Southern riverways, soldiers passed the time on their voyages by shooting local wildfowl, and even alligators, from the rails of their boats. Many other youthful soldiers spent the idle hours of travel with a good bottle. "Whiskey was freely used," a New York private wrote after a steamboat trip in 1863. "I 'piled in' down in the hole with a man half tight, while those that were wholly so made merry until a late hour."[11] Being drunk aboard ship accounted for many a man simply falling overboard, and may well explain for poor Sergeant Sullivan's disappearance from the *Taney*. Indeed, one Connecticut sergeant told of a night aboard ship when a private "was taken with the tremens and of all the Horride noises and actions I ever saw."[12] It took five men to subdue the delirious inebriate.

Some stiff drink may have been necessary to see a lot of young men through their travels, either by train or steamboat. With rare exceptions, the cars they rode were little more than boxcars with a few backless benches set on the flooring. These were cold in winter, stifling hot in summer, provided a bone-shatteringly rough ride, and were too tightly packed to allow for reclining, even assuming a man could get to sleep. No wonder that the men poured off of them at every opportunity, and at a journey's end it was not unusual to see whole regiments lay down on the station platform and drop into slumber. At the same time, while vessels like the *Taney* made river travel far more luxurious, there were all too many ships like the *Waverly*, many of them converted ferryboats, cotton transports, even livestock ships. One Maine Yankee boarded a boat for the trip south and found "men packed in a nasty hold so close that they could scarcely lie down," and many of them so drunk that they kept the rest awake. "We were huddled together more like a lot of pigs than human beings," a New Yorker said of his voyage. He had to sleep on the deck, and found his rations so nearly spoiled that he and others could hardly force them down. "The water was very dirty," he lamented, "yet we were glad to get enough of it."[13]

It could be even worse, especially for the Federals who had to travel on the ocean to reach Federal beachheads in South Carolina, Florida, or the Gulf coast. One Maine man recorded a nightmarish voyage to Ship Island, off the mouth of the Mississippi. "We have at least 300 men on board more than the ship can decently accommodate," he wrote, and "in the morning the air & filth between decks is enough to sicken a dog." The first day out he counted 300 men seasick, and "quite a number crazy drunk."[14] In a voyage lasting twenty-nine days, men could not sleep for the stifling heat in the overcrowded holds, they did not have room enough to prepare their rations properly, their water ran so low that they had to ration it, and men began to die of seasickness. Burials at sea became frequent ceremonies. "A sad sight this evening," wrote another Billy Yank; "a poor old father burying his son at sea." In time the illness hit almost everyone. "Sick myself," a soldier wrote in his diary while on the way to Ship Island. "O dear, sick enough; sea-sick and sick of the sea." The lice attacked the men in their sleep, the air was unbreathable day or night, and worse yet, many encountered storms and even hurricanes. "The squall struck us with terrible force," a Yankee wrote on March 4, 1862. "No one could walk or stand without holding on with both hands." When finally they reached their destination, "we rent the air with cheers."[15] After a similar experience en route to South Carolina, a Pennsylvania boy marveled at the scene of men sick all about him, "and ye gods what a time." Many men prayed, others swore, and at least a few simply gave up and "wanted to be throd overboard."[16]

However they reached the main armies, by rail or boat, eventually every soldier North and South had to make his way to the war by the one means common to them all. At the beginning of the war enthusiastic Yankees sang of John Brown's body moldering in the grave while his soul "goes marching on," and they sang it as they themselves marched. If any calculation of the total number of man-miles marched in the Civil War were possible, the figure would climb well into the hundreds of millions. While a number of regiments, most notably those assigned to post and permanent garrison duty, rarely moved at all during the war, others literally walked out several pairs of shoes. This was especially the case with the units operating west of the Alleghenies in the vastness of Kentucky, Tennessee, the Deep South, and the trans-Mississippi. In the course of a single year some of these regiments might cover in excess of 1,000 miles on their feet. In the eleven months from the commencement of the Atlanta Campaign in May 1864, until the conclusion of the famed March to the Sea, the overall ground covered by General William T. Sherman's armies measured a straight-line distance of over 700 miles. Add to that the almost constant flanking movements and side-trips for intermediate objectives, and the total must exceed well over 1,000 miles. And the Confederates he opposed were marching with him every step of the way, and farther.

From the beginning of the war to the last, marching was a tiresome, often exhausting, exercise. At the outset, few were really ready for it, and their trial was made the worse by the fact that the first major campaign, culminating in the First Battle of Bull Run, took place in July, in northern Virginia, in stifling heat and humidity. It all started for the Federals like storybook soldiering. Leaving their encampments near Washington, they made an easy day of it initially, and though tired that night after covering only a few miles, still they relished their first night spent sleeping in the field. "Beneath the clear sky, studded with the sentinel stars, that paced their ceaseless round," wrote one Yankee, "we slept the sleep of soldiers."[17] But the next day it wasn't so easy, and by the next they were tired, dirty, sore-footed and insubordinate. With remarkable alacrity the hot, dusty road took the glamour out of war. Sunstroke, a constant companion in the summer months, claimed its first victims here, and scores of men on both sides would actually die of it during the war, exacerbated as it was by thirst and exhaustion. Nor was the occasional rainstorm necessarily a relief, for the dirt roads of the South were quickly turned into mires that sucked the boots and shoes from the soldiers' feet and soaked their heavy woolen or cotton uniforms. Even lightning could be an enemy, as eleven men of the 22nd Virginia found out in May 1864 when a bolt struck them on the road.

Perhaps it was because the march held so much of tedium mixed with the constant presence of danger, that the men on both sides took every opportunity of momentary escape. Whenever their officers called a halt in the course of the day, the men broke ranks to pick berries, brew coffee, play cards, or run off for a little quick foraging. These were volunteer soldiers, men who would never completely accept military discipline, and try as they might, their officers could never entirely control them. This became evident early on the march to Bull Run, when Sherman, then a colonel and a brigade commander, had to ride constantly up and down the lines of his men shouting "You must close up, you must not chase the pigs and chickens." It did him little good. Sherman himself confronted one soldier carrying a joint of mutton over his shoulder. "Didn't you know the orders against foraging?" asked the Colonel. "Yes, but I was hungry," came the reply, "and it was rebel mutton, anyhow." Insubordinate men even shouted back at his officers to "tell Colonel Sherman we will get all the water, pigs and chickens we want."[18]

When they weren't foraging, the soldiers of both sides were often looting, and it frequently did not matter from whom. On the march to Bull Run, the 1st Massachusetts passed through Vienna, Virginia, and swarmed over a grocery store like locusts. Nothing was left, not even the grindstones and whole barrels of molasses. Out in the western theater of the war it was much the same. Men of John Hunt Morgan's Kentucky Confederate cavalry stole whiskey at every opportunity, sometimes even "officially" confiscating it from stores that they passed. When headquarters prohibited men of the Kentucky "Orphan Brigade" from using farmers' fence rails for firewood, someone found a loophole in the order where it specified only "whole" rails. Obeying the order to the letter, the men soon broke every nearby rail into small pieces. They burned the pieces, but no "whole" rails.[19] Some outfits became specially famed for their depredations while on the march, and word of their coming could lead even friendly civilians to hide their chickens and their silver and generally keep a low profile.

In fact, even the slaves were not free from the raiding of passing soldiers, North or South. One Confederate regiment had a Mohawk sachem named Konshattountzchette in its ranks, though the men called him Flying Cloud. A Yankee

482

bullet had removed much of his upper jaw, leaving him looking "rather hideous," an aspect not softened by his flashing dark eyes and swarthy complexion. For some reason, the slaves in South Carolina found him particularly terrifying, and his white comrades in arms soon learned to use his appearance to the best purpose. When foraging for food, they would send him to a slave cabin where he would give several war whoops and then shout what he wanted. "Beans," he cried before one cabin. While the women and children fled in terror, the men quickly produced the food they had been hiding. "Here, here, boss," they said meekly, whereupon Flying Cloud usually relaxed his appearance and reassured them: "Me no hurt you . . . cook beans quick."[21]

For all the similarities between the experiences of Yank and Reb on the march, still with only a few exceptions, there was one very basic difference that predetermined much of their opinion of what they saw and experienced. The Confederate soldier spent the entire war within the borders of the Confederacy. In effect, he was in his homeland, and however much special affinity he might feel for his native state, still he felt in varying degrees some measure of devotion to the South at large. As the war progressed, and more and more signs of the exhaustion and distress the burden of war placed on the Confederate heartland became evident, the more sorrowful became the Rebel soldier's trek from campaign to campaign. Burned or abandoned farmhouses, fields grown over with weeds, factories laid waste, bridges burned, and cities either deserted or else crowded to overflowing with refugees, all confronted his eyes. It saddened his heart, yet generally hardened his resolve as well, for the cause of all this hardship was in simple soldier logic, the enemy.

It could be especially heart-rending for the Confederates from states like Missouri, Kentucky, Maryland, and Tennessee, for their native soil lay, in whole or part, behind Yankee lines through much of the war. With no chance of visiting home on furlough, and often no news of friends and family coming across the lines, these soldiers felt an additional anxiety. Consequently they marched with a quicker, lighter step on those occasions when the campaign was destined to take them back into their native states.

In the fall of 1862, when an ill-fated Confederate offensive sought to retake Kentucky from the Federals, the Orphan Brigade was ordered up from Mississippi to join in the fight. Alas, one obstacle after another stood in their way. After seemingly surmounting every impediment possible, they finally started the last leg of their march that would take them home. "All marched with a buoyant step," wrote one; "our hearts beat high with hope." Finally they came in sight of the mountains around Cumberland Gap, the gateway to Kentucky, just twenty miles away. The next day they would re-enter the Bluegrass state at last. But their army in Kentucky had been defeated and was already in retreat, and the next morning, lined up on the road to start their last march, they got their orders to turn around instead and march once more away from their homeland. "The silence that prevailed in the ranks then was not the silence of restraint," wrote one of the Kentuckians; "it was the silence of stern manhood bowed down by bitter disappointment."[22] When finally they began to march, a spontaneous shout of frustration surged through the entire brigade, then they fell silent and marched on.

The Federals were not immune to moments of sadness and reflection on the march, either. Particularly in Virginia, where the armies moved back and forth over roughly the same ground for three years, the invading Yankees frequently had to pass places they had seen before on previous campaigns, and witness sad remembrances. Marching south in the Shenandoah valley in May 1864, one small Federal army saw all along the way the graves of men who had fallen there in earlier operations. There was, wrote one Billy Yank, "perhaps not a mile of the whole route over which we passed along which there could not be seen a soldier's grave."[23] Passing by the old battlefield at Winchester, they saw the dead from the battle there in June 1863, hastily buried by the Confederate victors, barely covered by earth, and many with arms and legs protruding from the soil.

All the scenes of destruction were just as unnerving to the more reflective Yankees as they were to the Confederates, though others took a kind of perverse pride both in the visibly demonstrated might of the Union war machine, and in the punishment thus being dealt to the South for firing on Fort Sumter and starting the war.

Yet the sights of sadness were few compared to the curiosities that men from the North experienced in marching across the South. Of course, Virginia could be just as strange a place to a boy from Arkansas as to one from Maine, but at least Arkansas was essentially a part of the same culture, and to a degree even the same social order. For Yankees, however, men who had mostly only heard about the South from newspapers or the fiery oratory of petty politicians, the tramp across the fields of the Confederacy was the adventure of a lifetime. Nearly two million Northerners marched into the Confederacy during the war, virtually every one of them a "tourist."

With the smugness characteristic of his region, one soldier from Maine declared of Virginia that "in the hands of New England people this country might be converted into a garden." In the hands of its current inhabitants, however, most Federals agreed that it was a poor place at best. "The country is behind the times 100 years," said one Yank, echoed by yet another who declared that "everything is a hundred years behind the times." One wag explained to folks back home that "there is a good deal of this part of the world that the Lord has not finished yet." Of Louisiana he declared that the Almighty "meant the snakes & aligators to hold possession for a thousand or two years more before man [came] to occupy it."[24]

By and large the Yankees were not impressed with what they saw of the South. The relative poverty, the wide areas with little or no development, the limited literacy of the people, and all the signs of the hated institution of slavery, gave them a poor impression of the region. "I dont like this country nor the people that live here at all," wrote a Minnesotan, "and wouldn't live here if they would give me the best farm in the State and the prettiest Girl in the State for a Wife throwd in."

Few Northerners were prepared for the Southern heat. While remarking that the countryside in Virginia reminded him of New England, one Billy Yank went on to say that "the climate reminds me more of that infernal place down below that I have not seen but often heard of." Many complained that the air scorched their throats on its way to their lungs. Having to march and actively campaign in such a climate left thousands listless and in a near-constant state of exhaustion.[25]

Wherever they marched, the soldiers were not much impressed with the inhabitants. The men they thought ignorant. "I dont believe the inhabitants even know the day of the week," wrote one Federal in Maryland. And the women they found generally to be crude and unattractive. "They are void of the roseate hue of health and beauty which so much adorns our Northern belles," declared one soldier. And the men found them too skinny by far. "They look more like polls than any thing else," one complained. "The women here generally are shaped like a lath, nasty, slab-sided, long haired specimens of humanity. I would as soon kiss a dried codfish as one of them."[26] The most ungallant description of all came from a Federal in Mississippi, who called the local girls "sharp-nosed, tobacco-chewing, snuff-rubbing, flax-headed, hatchet-faced, yellow-eyed, sallow-skinned, cotton-dressed, flat-breasted, bareheaded, long-waisted, hump-shouldered, stoop-necked, big-footed, straddle-toed, sharp-skinned, thin-lipped, pale-faced, lantern-jawed, silly-looking damsels."[27] Many Yanks believed that the women of the South had loose morals. They drank in barrooms, swore "like troopers," and seemed to breed ceaselessly. Of course, Billy Yank mostly came into contact with the lower classes, the middle- and upper-class Southerners having fled before the armies, or else associating exclusively with the officers.

All the same, for all their grumbling, as they marched across the Confederacy the Federals also had to admit that there was much to like. "This country is so beautiful I wish I had been born here," one wrote of Virginia, and several areas like coastal Florida and middle Tennessee were thought exceptionally attractive. So were at least a few of the women, despite all that "slab-sided" and "lantern-jawed" hyperbole. One private in Kentucky declared that "I fell in love with Paducah while I was there, and I think I will settle there when the war is over. I never saw so many pretty women in my life."[28] Not a few such meetings led to marriages that lasted through the war and for years after.

Billy Yank's foe had far fewer opportunities to see new sights as he moved to the sound of the guns. Only once, in the Gettysburg Campaign in 1863, did a Confederate army actually penetrate well into undisputed Union territory, though in 1863 and 1864 cavalry and sizeable infantry raids also swept briefly across Ohio, Indiana, and Pennsylvania. States claimed by both sides – Maryland, Kentucky, and Missouri – also hosted a few major invasions, but the territory there was not all that unfamiliar to many Rebels, especially those who enlisted from those states and who really looked on their invasion as a return home.

When in enemy country, as on the Gettysburg invasion, Confederate generals ordered their men not to forage or plunder, but of course to no avail. "I felt sorry for the farmers," wrote Robert Stiles, "some of whom actually concealed their horses in their dwelling houses, or, rather, attempted to conceal them, for we became veritable sleuth-hounds in running down a horse."[29] A few Confederates maintained that the farmers of Maryland and Pennsylvania freely gave their produce to the passing Rebels. "Many of them bade us help ourselves to poultry, milk, vegetables, fruit, honey, bread, whatever we wanted to eat," remembered John Caldwell of South Carolina.[30] Sometimes they paid in captured Northern greenbacks for their food, and more often with Confederate script which was, of course, worthless in the Union. But mostly they simply took what they needed.

That they did not threaten their unwilling hosts did not make the contributions any the less the fruit of intimidation. "Soldiers as hungry as were the Confederates could not be expected to refuse proffers of food," wrote one wag from a Texas brigade, "even when they suspected such proffers were made through unwarranted fear of ill-treatment." As a result, when one Texan came into camp near Chambersburg on the night of June 30, the eve of Gettysburg, he stared in wonder at what he saw. "Every square foot of an acre of ground not occupied by a sleeping or standing soldier, was covered with choice food for the hungry. Chickens, turkeys, ducks and geese squawked, gobbled, cackled and hissed in harmonious unison as deft and energetic hands seized them for slaughter, and scarcely waiting for them to die, sent their feathers flying in all directions; and scattered around in bewildering confusion and gratifying profusion appeared immense loaves of bread and chunks of corned beef, hams, and sides of bacon, cheeses, crocks of apple-butter, jelly, jam, pickles, and preserves, bowls of yellow butter, demijohns of buttermilk, and other eatables too numerous to mention."[31] Men slept with loaves of bread for pillows, their arms wrapped around hams as if they were wives.

The Confederate soldier never ate better during the war than he did in those few days of the invasion of Pennsylvania, and he enjoyed the sight of the plump and rosy-cheeked farm girls along the way, having much better things to say about them than his Yankee counterparts said of most Southern girls. Yet other than for those differences, men in blue and gray for the most part saw the same sights, heard the same sounds, smelled the same scents, as they moved across the landscape, marching to war. The ground of the battle-scarred continent was just as hard to sleep upon for Yank or Reb alike, and for all of them the countryside through which they walked bore witness to the hardship and pain in the wake of warfare's passing, and admonished them of what lay ahead as they tramped toward the sound of the guns.

REFERENCES

1 Wiley, *Billy Yank*, pp.36-7.
2 *Ibid.*, p.36.
3 *Ibid.*, p.37.
4 *Ibid.*
5 *Ibid.*
6 Wiley, *Johnny Reb*, p.26.
7 John S. Jackman Diary, September 23, 1862, Library of Congress,
8 *Ibid.*, May 25, 1863.
9 Davis, *Bull Run*, p.140.
10 Jackman Diary, September 27, 1862.
11 Wiley, *Billy Yank*, pp.31-2.
12 *Ibid.*, p.32.
13 *Ibid.*, p.33.
14 *Ibid.*
15 *Ibid.*, p.34.
16 *Ibid.*, p.33.
17 Davis, *Bull Run*, p.92.
18 *Ibid.*, p.96.
19 Davis, *Orphan Brigade*, p.188.
20 *Ibid.*, p.249.
21 *Ibid.*, p.247.
22 *Ibid.*, pp.135-6.
23 William C. Davis, *The Battle of New Market* (New York, 1975), p.34.
24 Wiley, *Billy Yank*, pp.96-7.
25 *Ibid.*, p.97.
26 *Ibid.*, p.100.
27 *Ibid.*, p.101.
28 *Ibid.*, pp.106-7.
29 Robert Stiles, *Four Years Under Marse Robert* (New York, 1903), p.199.
30 J.F.J. Caldwell, *The History of a Brigade of South Carolinians* (Philadelphia, 1886), p.133.
31 J.B. Polley, *Hood's Texas Brigade* (Dayton, Ohio, 1976), p.148.

XII
THIS FACE OF BATTLE

In the summer of 1863, the 33rd Illinois had reached the sound of the guns, and lay behind its earthworks facing Vicksburg, Mississippi, waiting for the word to rise up, rush forward, and attack the Rebel lines. Minute after agonizing minute passed by, and still no order came. James Wilcox grew increasingly restive. "Oh how my heart palpitated!" he confessed to his diary. "It seemed to thump the ground (I lay on my face) as hard as the enemy's bullets. The sweat from off my face run in a stream from the tip ends of my whiskers." He had been a soldier for a long time now. He knew that he was supposed to remain quiet. But for eight minutes he had lain there, with enemy bullets and shells flying over his head, while he and his companions were not allowed to return fire. Twice the waiting proved to be too much for him. Unable to control his anxiety, he cried out, "*My God, why dont they order us to charge!*"[1]

For Wilcox, as for three million other Yanks and Rebs, all their experience as soldiers prepared them for this one moment. Enlistment and training, the drudgery of drill and camp routine, the risk of illness or wounds, the hazards of falling into enemy hands, the separation from home and loved ones – all of this they endured and suffered, so that now at last they might go into battle and acquit themselves well. It was the final measure of what success their armies had achieved in turning raw men and boys into soldiers and fighting men. Of course, they never really became trained and professional *soldiers*, but when they set foot on the battlefield, these men behaved superbly. Though they frequently ignored or subverted every lesson of discipline designed to prepare them for the fight, when the final test of arms came, they passed with honors. And when two armies close in battle, all else in warfare becomes incidental.

Whether facing its first battle or its fiftieth, an army took on a progressively more sober and serious aspect in the two or three days prior to a fight. Even before being told what was coming, the men in the ranks quickly learned how to read the signs. The first campaigns of the year came in the spring, when the roads were firm enough for marching and the temperatures at least minimally warm enough for the men to function. They received orders to tear down, burn, or simply abandon their winter quarters. Large stockpiles of supplies – crates of hardtack, barrels of salt pork, mountains of hay and fodder for the animals – grew throughout the army's encampments. The activities of couriers, inspections, arrival of new regiments, and the flood of camp rumors, all increased daily, and with increasing rapidity. Since the opposing armies tended to winter only a few miles from each other, the men knew that any movement could lead to battle. When the order came to prepare three or more days' rations in advance, it meant only one thing: the army was about to march – and when that happened, battle could be only a day or two away.

A combination of frightened introspection and nervous chatter and forced hilarity swept the marching columns as they moved toward certain confrontation with the enemy. Soon the distant sounds of sporadic firing gave evidence that scouts or perhaps a cavalry screen had encountered the advance outposts of the foe. It was not fighting – not yet – but rather the occasional shooting incidental to small and often isolated clashes as Yank and Reb felt each other out, seeking some clues as to numbers and positions. But when the main van of the armies were close enough to one another to hear those shots, veterans and amateurs alike knew that the next day men would begin to fight and die.

At the beginning of the war, when alike they were all new to battle, the men in blue and gray faced the coming fray with solemnity approaching reverence. The day before the first Battle of Bull Run, on July 20, 1861, one commander assembled the regiments of his division together in a field, ordered hats off and heads bowed, and prayed with them. "The God of battles was entreated for guidance, for shielding in battle, and for care of those so precious in our far-away homes."[2] Later that evening, while the generals and officers bent over their lamp-lit maps and made final plans to test the Almighty's attention to their prayers, the men in the camps lay on the ground, resting as much as they could. Rumor after rumor passed through the camps. They would move at 2 a.m., said one. Others gave exaggerated reports of the foe's strength, or even that the enemy had retired.

Few slept that night, north or south of Bull Run. "This is one of the most beautiful nights that the imagination can conceive," one Yankee wrote. Tens of thousands lay awake looking up into the heavens. "The sky is perfectly clear, the moon is full and bright, and the air as still as if it were not within a few hours to be disturbed by the roar of cannon and the shouts of contending men." Perhaps confused by the quiet that he encountered, one newspaperman passed through the Federal camps and thought them "a picture of enchantment." Five thousand blazing campfires sent a host of ghostly shadows across the Virginia fields and woods. In the distance, one regiment sang the current version of "The Star-Spangled Banner." Another unit's band played romantic favorites, popular patriotic airs, and even a piece or two from an opera. "Everything here is quiet save the sounds of the music and the occasional shout of a soldier," wrote the newspaperman, "or the lowing of the cattle, whose dark forms spot the broad meadow in the rear." One Reb, on another campaign, awaiting his own baptism of fire, confessed that "often at the still hour of midnight I wish the next day will be the 'cross over,' and we will meet the 'grand army' on fair ground."[4]

However they passed that last night of innocence, most soldiers handled themselves well on the next morning, during the hours when most battles began. In fact, their pent-up anxiety and fears sometimes manifested themselves by an unaccountable rush to get into the fight. Often when the sporadic firing of pickets or cavalry skirmishers was first heard, the soldiers, without orders from their officers, spontaneously rushed from their bivouacks to their arms, lining up ready to march to the fight. Their officers usually told them to go back to their campsites and finish dressing, make their coffee and eat their rations, and not be in such an infernal hurry. When officers did give the order to form ranks and march, the men in the rear files often could not contain their anxiety and marched too quickly, causing congestion at the backs of regiments, and sometimes actually passing through the files in their front.

Finally, before every soldier's first battle there came a halt on the way to the action, as commanders reformed their ranks, dressed their lines, made certain that each infantryman stood about thirteen inches from the men on either side of him, and that the file closers on the flanks were in place to keep the lines straight and orderly in the last advance, a hopeless task. This final halt could take an hour or more – sometimes two – and those were the longest, most agonizingly slow minutes the men had ever experienced. Their throats and mouths went dry. The muscles in their chest and abdomen tensed and contracted, making them feel as if heavy weights pressed down upon them. The untried soldier took short, difficult breaths. Even in cool weather he often felt sweat on his forehead and perspiration in his palms. All but the most indifferent felt some quaking in their hands, while others became drowsy and yawned, not from fatigue but rather from the sapping of energy by the enormous amounts of anxiety.

All were very frightened. "If you see anyone that says they want any afraid," wrote a Maine boy after his first fight, "you may know that it want me."[5] Ironically, for most Yanks and Rebs alike, fear of being killed or wounded did not rest uppermost in their minds. Rather, they feared that they would not "stand the gaff," as they said; that they would panic, freeze, or turn coward at the last minute and disgrace themselves completely by running away. "I have a mortal dread of the battle field for I have never yet been nearer to one than to hear the cannon roar & have never seen a person die," one Yank wrote before his first battle. "I am afraid that the groans of the wounded & dying will make me shake, nevertheless I hope & trust that strength will be given me to stand up & do my duty."[6] Across the enemy lines a similarly concerned Reb wrote home to say that "I may run but if I do I wish that some of our own men would shoot me down."[7]

As a result, when finally the green boys went into battle and fired their first shots and heard for the first time the whine of the enemy bullets as they whizzed past, there was a sense of tremendous relief. "With your first shot you become a new man," wrote a Confederate after his first engagement at Bull Run. "Personal safety is your least concern. Fear has no existence in your bosom. Hesitation gives way to an uncontrollable desire to rush into the thickest of the fight. The dead and dying around you, if they receive a passing thought, only serve to stimulate you to revenge. You become cool and deliberate, and watch the efect of bullets, the showers of bursting shells, the passage of cannon balls as they rake their murderous channels through your ranks . . . with a feeling so callous . . . that your soul seems dead to every sympathizing and selfish thought."[8] A Yankee echoed his sentiments. "After the first round the fear left me & I was as cool as ever I was in my life," he wrote. "I think I have been a great deal more excited in attempting to speak a piece in school or to make remarks in an evening meeting."[9] A Federal who fought at Shiloh in April 1862 confessed that "strange as it may seam to you, but the more men I saw kiled the more reckless I became."[10] Men became disoriented, and at First Bull Run one Maryland Confederate outfit broke into halves. One dropped back, but the other, along with Private McHenry Howard, went onward, "and I with it," he wrote, "feeling as if in a dream, the whole thing was so sudden, unexpected and novel."[11]

The first-time experience could be the same, just as confusing, frightening, even humorous, whether the soldier met it as part of a great army, or with only a small group of companions. Youthful Private John H. Alexander was a new recruit to Company A of the 43rd Virginia Battalion of Cavalry, commanded by the famed Confederate raider John S. Mosby. Alexander's baptism of fire came in April 1864, during a raid on Yankee camps in Fairfax County, Virginia. In the darkness as they approached the enemy outposts, word came back along the line to be silent. "My heart jumped into my throat," Alexander recalled. "This began to look like business." He put his hand to his gun, only to be scolded by an old veteran, "Pshaw! we're just getting in hearing of 'em. Don't be scared." As they moved forward slowly, the sounds of the horses' hooves crushing leaves reminded him of a funeral march.

Seeing some dark forms approaching, Alexander shouted "There they are," and drew his revolver, only to be told scornfully that it was only their own scouts. An impatient veteran asked sarcastically, "What the devil did you leave your mammy for?" Hopelessly jumpy now, Alexander shivered at every mournful call of the whippoorwill, and almost leaped out of his saddle when an owl hooted above him. Finally they dismounted, close to their prey, and advanced on foot. "Stalking one's fellow-kind is a grisly sort of business," he confessed. Then they were upon the sleeping Federals, Mosby shouted for a charge, and in they went. "There were shots and yells and running men and snorting horses and the odor of much brimstone, and – well, that's pretty much all that I know about the fight. Out of a hazy uncertainty whether I was on my head or my heels, there comes to me the recollections that I started into the charge with the others; that I struck the limb of a tree and knocked my hat off; that I even stopped to pick it up (think of it!) and that as I started on a few straggling shots were winding up the affair." Realizing that the fight was done and he had not yet fired his revolver, he pointed it in the direction the Yankees had withdrawn and fired what proved to be the last shot of the "engagement." Later, taking stock of the affair, Mosby found that he had suffered no casualties except for one man who had briefly followed the retreating Yanks. After the fight was done, he said: "some d – d greenhorn behind him had let off his gun and shot him on the heel." A sheepish Alexander later recalled that "I did not say a word." So much for his first shot of the war.[12]

However they faced up to that first test in battle, once they were through it Johnny Reb and Billy Yank became "veterans," and generally thereafter they approached an impending fight rather differently. The fear and anxiety were still there, and certainly so was the danger. But they knew what to expect now, and except for some unusual circumstance, or the always unpredictable event when a veteran of a score of fights could suddenly lose his nerve, they knew how they were going to behave.

On the morning of a battle the non-commissioned officers roused the men out of their slumber at 2 or 3 a.m. with the "long roll" on the drums. There was much to be done. The soldiers dressed and assembled speedily for inspection, and then broke ranks to prepare rations. Ordinarily their officers ordered them to cook three days' worth, though to little purpose. Practical as always, Yank and Reb alike often cooked and ate it all right then, reasoning that what they ate they did not have to carry, and assuming that they would live off the land as they marched. Besides, it was better to march off to battle on a full stomach and risk hunger later, than to chance dying in battle with uneaten food still in their haversacks.

Meanwhile the ordnance officers issued ammunition. In both armies the standard pre-battle issue amounted to sixty rounds of Minié cartridges and percussion caps. They put the caps in the leather cap-box on their belts, and forty of the rounds fitted into a cartridge box also on the belt. The remaining rounds went in their shirt or trouser pockets. This procedure out of the way, they were ready to march off to fight.

Sometime before they went into action, and usually before they began their march, the assembled soldiers listened to their colonel exhort them to stirring deeds, or else heard a staff officer read aloud a written address from the brigade or army commander, all designed to arouse their martial ardor. Inevitably they heard references to the bravery they had shown in past fights, of the cowardice and barbarity of the foe, of those at home whose hearthsides the men were here to defend, and of the cause for which they would cheerfully lay down their lives if necessary. Often the speeches brimmed with the seemingly pompous posturing which men of that time took so very seriously. Before Shiloh, General Albert Sidney Johnston, commanding the

Confederates, told his men that "The eyes and hopes of eight millions of people rest upon you."

> You are expected to show yourselves worthy of your race and lineage; worthy of the women of the South, whose noble devotion in this war has never been exceeded at any time. With such incentives to brave deeds and with the trust that God is with us, your general will lead you confidantly to the combat, assured of success.[13]

Others could be less elevated. "Remember that the enemy has no feeling of mercy or kindness toward you," General Thomas C. Hindman told his army prior to its December 1862 battle with Federals at Prairie Grove, Arkansas.

> His ranks are made up of Pin Indians, free negroes, Southern tories, Kansas jayhawkers and hired Dutch cutthroats. These bloody ruffians have invaded your country, stolen and destroyed your property, murdered your neighbors, outraged your women, driven your children from their homes and defiled the graves of your kindred.[14]

However they exhorted their men, once the rhetoric was done the officers of both sides usually gave the same instructions. Aim for enemy officers. Kill artillery horses. Wait until within range before firing, and then only on order. Aim at the knees. Stay quiet except in the charge. Leave the wounded where they fall. Do not break ranks to plunder. "If we whip the enemy," said Hindman, "all he has will be ours."[15]

A few of these pre-battle speeches proved positively depressing. The colonel of a midwestern regiment told his Billy Yanks that "The secessionists have ten thousand men and forty rifled cannon. They are strongly fortified. They have more men and more cannon than we have. They will cut us to pieces. Marching to attack such an enemy, so entrenched and so armed, is marching to a butcher shop rather than to a battle. There is bloody work ahead. Many of you boys will go out who will never come back again."[16] It was hardly a performance calculated to encourage the timid, and no doubt few in his regiment were saddened when the colonel shortly resigned.

Now and then some unexpected mirth lightened the tension during an officer's exhortation, and it was all too welcome, though usually at the expense of someone's dignity. At the Battle of Stones River, in Tennessee in December 1862, Colonel Granville Moody addressed his 12th Ohio before they launched into the fearful battle against the enemy. He had been a minister before the war, and now he led them in solemn prayer. "Now, boys, fight for your country and your God," he said, "and . . ." Just at that moment the first volley from the enemy came speeding past them. Forgetting all about the obligatory "amen" to close, he shouted ." . . and aim low!" Thereafter his men nicknamed him "Aim Low."[17]

This done, the regiments began their march to the fighting. At almost the same time, many of the men began lightening their personal loads, casting aside their blanket rolls, knapsacks, haversacks, even jackets and hats – anything that would possibly get in their way in the fight. Suddenly concerned about their mortality, and the possibility that they would see their maker by nightfall, many men also threw away decks of cards, dice, lurid novels and photographs, whiskey, and more. Though the veterans marched with a surer step, they were more quiet in the advance, in part because they did not feel the same nervousness which impelled so many first-timers to chatter incessantly, but also because many believed in a certain law of averages. Every time a veteran survived one battle, so the logic went, it increased his chances of being hit in the next one. Noticing that one veteran regiment did not show the same alacrity to "see the elephant" as some new and untested units at Shiloh, one colonel explained that the old-timers "had seen the elephant several times, and did not care about seeing him again unless necessary."

In fact, before almost every battle of the war, many soldiers felt premonitions of their own death, wounding or capture. Most were proved wrong, but many were right, and thousands took precautions that they would be identified and taken care of after their deaths. They wrote their names and regiments and the addresses of their families on slips of paper, stuffing them into trouser pockets or pinning them on their shirts. Many made their messmates swear vows to search them out after the fight and, if slain, to see that their remains were returned to home and family. Hundreds of miles from home, in a strange country, Johnny Reb and Billy Yank did not want to lie for eternity among strangers in an unmarked grave. Thousands were not granted their last wish.

With the sounds of firing before them, the men moved steadily toward the fighting line. Soon they were confronted by signs of the carnage as wounded and dying men were carried to the rear by the stretcher-bearers and musicians. All too often, the veterans noted sardonically that it required two or three able-bodied soldiers to help to the rear a wounded comrade with nothing more than an injured hand or finger. Most of those they passed, whether shirkers or seriously wounded, cheered the fresh soldiers on, telling them to "give it" to the enemy. Frightened animals raced in panic away from the fighting and noise. Equally scared men who could not stand the fire rushed to the rear, sometimes disrupting the orderly formations of the advancing units they ran through. The scene was well calculated to unnerve even the most experienced and steadiest of veterans, and it could set to panic fresh troops awaiting their first taste of battle.

Finally they came to the staging area, either directly in a front line that was preparing for an attack or defense, or immediately behind it to serve as support. Civil War battles were not affairs of one continuous fight, but rather a series of localized actions between units in the immediate area. Rarely if ever was an entire army engaged in combat simultaneously. Men just arrived at the front watched or listened to the sound of battle from one of their flanks while waiting for their own assault to commence.

These were perhaps the most trying moments of all. The coolest of the men rested on their arms or on the ground, read a letter from home or smoked a pipe. The rest felt all the sensations that fear could induce. There was a tremendous feeling of solitude, of being alone amid thousands. Many silently repented their wicked ways, promising their god to reform if only he saw them through this fight – promises rarely kept. Some prayed, others sang, and many found all their senses heightened, taking in through eye, nose, and ear every aspect of the scene before them. These were the moments when, now under some fire from the enemy, the men felt a building tension and frustration, fear being gradually replaced by an anxiety to get moving, to fire back, to do *something, anything,* to put an end to the waiting. It was in this pre-battle silence, with all of these tremors running through the men, that the line finally grew silent as each man wrestled with his emotions and steeled his nerves. It was in such a deadly tense time of waiting that James Wilcox had been unable to stand it any longer, shouting, *"My God, why dont they order us to charge!"* And finally they did.

The orders were carried either by word of mouth or by bugles or drums. The colonels had their regiments fall in and sent them forward. Constantly they shouted at the men to maintain that thirteen-inch distance between each other, to keep their line straight. They were not themselves allowed to fire, saving that for the final charge, but the enemy was certainly sending a hail of bullets and shells towards them. The men could hear the bumble-bee-like sound of the Minié bullets whizzing past, and now and then the thump of one hitting flesh and bone. Shells began to explode overhead and near their line, bringing more men down. And still the attackers' rifles remained silent. The tension mounted until it became intolerable. "Oh, dear!" one Yankee corporal cried; "when shall *we* fire?"[18] Finally, the order to fire came as an enormous relief.

There was little that was subtle about Civil War combat. One line advanced against another in its entrenched or hastily fortified position, usually atop some rise of ground. The advance itself was almost always across open ground. The soldiers charging could see their enemies in the distance, and their enemies had them in full view. The closer they got, the less the foe seemed like some propagandized abstraction, and more like just other Americans.

For all the slaughter they promoted, such unsophisticated tactics inevitably led to incredible heroism as well. "To mass troops against the fire of a covered line is simply to devote them to destruction," a Yankee general declared. "The greater the mass, the greater the loss – that is all."[19] Facing a fight like that, it took raw nerve to charge into the mouth of a cannon and a line of guns bristling with gleaming bayonets.

A day or so after the fight, as they wrote their letters home, the men in the ranks would often recollect that a great sense of calm came over them once the fight commenced, and that time passed away rapidly. "Time rolls off very fast in time of battle," one Rebel wrote in 1861, "when we had been in 3½ hours it appeared to me that it hadent been two."[20] In fact, the pace of activity during the fight was every bit as confused and exhausting as had been the hours leading up to it, only the men simply had no opportunity to reflect upon the chaos all around them. In the final rush to the enemy's line, many frequently broke away from their own ranks and rushed on too quickly, losing all track of where they were. They often exhausted themselves in their eagerness, and officers who ordered them to double-time in the assault – 165 steps per minute – sometimes wore out a regiment before it reached the foe. "We started in double quick from our entrenchments and went untill we were near broke down," a Reb of the 19th Virginia wrote of its charge at First Bull Run.[21]

The excitement was almost too much for some. "I with a number of others were sufferers from camp diarrhea, and up to that time we had found no cure," wrote William A. Fletcher of the 8th Texas Cavalry of his first action, "so, entering the battle, I had quite a great fear that something disgraceful might happen and it was somewhat uppermost in my mind; but to my surprise the excitement or something else had effected a cure."[22]

In the first flush of battle fever, very few men ever fired their rifles effectively. Often, especially among new, fresh troops, the initial bullets were aimed more at the stars than at the foe. "I recollect their first volley," one Reb wrote of a Virginia unit, "and how unfavorably it affected me. It was apparently made with the guns raised at an angle of forty-five degrees, and I was fully assured that their bullets would not hit the Yankees, unless they were nearer heaven than they were generally located by our people."[23]

A common problem among men of both sides came with their second shot. Amid the shouting and firing, most men were not conscious of the sound of their own rifle firing, nor of the kick against their shoulders when they did. Consequently, thousands improperly reloaded their weapons – forgetting to bite off the end of the paper cartridge before ramming it home, or else neglecting to place a percussion cap on the firing nipple – but when they pulled the trigger they did not notice that their gun had failed to discharge. Occasionally this oversight led to a situation in which the rifle could be more dangerous to friend than foe. After the three-day Battle of Gettysburg in July 1863, the victorious Federals retrieved 27,500 rifles from the battlelines, most if not all of them dropped by the wounded and killed. Nearly half of them were found to hold two unfired rounds in their barrels. Between three and ten loads crammed the breeches of another 6,000. And one rifle was filled almost to the muzzle with twenty-three cartridges.

Untold numbers of Yanks and Rebs lost their control and fired away wildly at anyone in sight, even their own men, a problem made the more prevalent early in the war thanks to the number of Union regiments clothed in gray and an equal number of Confederate outfits that wore blue. Only with experience did the soldiers learn to curb their nervous activity, none ever succeeding completely. Those in the advance either stood in the midst of the firing to reload, or else lay down on the ground, rolled over on their backs, and rammed their fresh cartridges home before rising once more and continuing the advance.

By this time the confusion was growing, the sense of detachment, of being alone amid chaos, increasing. Men and officers alike were swearing constantly, and in ways and with words they did not ordinarily use. Even chaplains or former ministers in the ranks were heard to utter most unclerical oaths. "The air was filled with a medley of sounds," a boy from Maine recalled, "shouts, cheers, commands, oaths, the sharp reports of rifles, the hissing shot, dull heavy thuds of clubbed muskets, the swish of swords and sabers, groans and prayers."[24]

Men began to act without thought of who or where they were. Some, despite all pre-battle resolutions and fears about cowardice, simply turned and ran. Most were sworn or spanked back into line by officers and file closers waving their swords. Others assumed a bloodlust they had never before experienced. "I acted like a madman," remembered one Pennsylvanian, "a kind of desperation seized me. I snatched a gun from the hands of a man who was shot through the head, as he staggered and fell. At other times I would have been horror-struck, and could not have moved, but then I jumped over dead men with as little feeling as I would over a log. The feeling that was uppermost in my mind was a desire to kill as many rebels as I could."[25]

After covering a good bit of ground, the officers generally felt it necessary to call a halt to the advance to reform their by now thinned and disorganized ranks, prior to making the final push to the enemy's line or works. At this moment the fighting men were the most difficult to control. Their blood up, some simply could not be stopped from rushing headlong alone. Others, having stood the fire until this point, felt their courage ebb as they stood under fire, close enough now to see the face of the foe. "If I hadent seen the fix I was in, and run like blazes, I would have been a goner by this time," one Yank wrote in 1864, and thousands of others like him discovered at this penultimate moment in the attack that their feet seemed to have a will of their own.[26] "I limbered up for the rear as fast as legs cood carry," another Federal wrote after a battle, "and that was prety fast."[27]

With the men reformed, and as many of the shirkers and faint-hearted forced back into line as possible, the order for the final push went out. Forward they went, almost at a run, and now, thankfully, it all happened too fast for a man to think about where he was or what he was doing. Unable to reload their guns, or too confused to remember to do so, some men picked up others from the fallen, or else grabbed their own rifles by the muzzles and used them as clubs as they reached the enemy line.

Hand-to-hand combat was not commonplace in the Civil War – despite the "evidence" of the stilted old Currier and Ives lithographs. By this point in the battle, nine times out of ten either the advancing lines were beaten back by massed fire before reaching the defending line, or else the defenders, seeing themselves outnumbered or else losing their own resolve, had pulled back. This is one of the reasons why there were so very few bayonet wounds in the war, for the men simply did not get close enough to each other to use them. However, now and then, as in the bloody fighting at Gettysburg on July 3, 1863, at the height of the great Confederate assault, the opposing troops did come eye to eye and blow to blow. Never was the fighting more personal: not a battle, but hundreds of single combats. "Occasionally, when too sorely pressed, they would drop their rifles and clinch the enemy," wrote a Yankee from Maine, "until Federal and Confederate would roll upon the ground in the death struggle."[28]

In those last moments of the attack, and in the hand-to-hand fighting that might follow, the men on both sides filled the air with their own distinctive cries. The so-called "Rebel Yell" became world famous even before the war was done, though many would not agree in later years upon its exact nature or origin. First heard at Bull Run in July 1861, it appeared on nearly every other battlefield of the war, and most likely grew out of some pre-war sporting or hunting shout when the game was being pursued, or else from the so-called "hollering" used in the Southern Appalachian region where neighbors communicated with each other by a high-pitched yell from one hilltop to another. It varied from one theater of the war to another, and even took on a particularly savage air west of the Mississippi where Confederate Indian soldiers added their own war whoops to it. Wherever heard, it could demoralize a fainthearted Federal. Indeed, in 1864, when General Jubal Early was told that a regiment could not attack the Yankees because there was no ammunition, he replied, "Damn it, holler them across."[29] And that is what they did. By contrast, the battle yell of Billy Yank was a much more disciplined "hurrah," and generally more in unison than the uncoordinated Rebel shouts. Deep-throated and lusty, still it sometimes adopted the more savage air of the Rebel cry as men became carried away in battle. On either side, ironically, these spontaneous yells grew not so much out of a desire to intimidate the foe, as to release pent-up tension for the yellers.

The shouting, the stabbing, the clubbing and firing, were quickly over. Few hand-to-hand combats lasted more than a few minutes before one side or the other – though most often the attacker – withdrew. Then there was the problem of keeping men from turning and simply running back to their own lines. No man wanted to be the last one killed in a failed assault, yet if some order were not maintained in a withdrawal, then the always-expected counter-assault could be disastrous. If such an attack did come, then all that Yank and Reb had just gone through was repeated, only with the roles reversed.

And thus the battle was fought. The more sophisticated matters of tactics, or seeking an exposed flank or a gap in the foe's line were all the province of the officers. The men in the ranks went where they were told and fought as they were ordered. If they won, the leaders got the credit, but win or lose, more often than not the blood on the soil came from the men in the ranks.

Inevitably there came lulls in the battle, and then – and only then – did the men realize the bone-crushing exhaustion they felt. The nervous tension before and during the fight was masked by the excitement of it all, but immediately after a fight was finished the men could find themselves so worn out that many fell asleep with the shot and shell still flying overhead. Now, too, the thirst and hunger set in, and with it often a post-battle depression, this last intense feeling especially heightened by what the soldier could see of his recent bloody work out on the battlefield. "When the fight was over & I saw what was done the tears came free," one soldier confessed later to his wife. "To think of civilized people killing one another like beasts. One would think that the supreme ruler would put a stop to it."[30]

Men – the victors – walked over the field once the foe had withdrawn. Most plundered at least a little, picking up a better rifle, swapping boots or shoes with one less fortunate who would no longer need them. A few rifled pockets for money and valuables. But most observed some reverence for their fallen comrades and enemies, and most – no matter how many battles they saw – felt some shock and shame for the awful work. "The stiffened bodies lie, grasping in death, the arms they bravely bore, with glazed eyes, and features blackened by rapid decay," wrote a Georgian. "Here sits one against a tree in motionless stare. Another has his head leaning against a stump, his hands over his head. They have paid the last penalty. They have fought their last battle. The air is putrid with decaying bodies of men & horses. My God, My God, what a scourge is war."[31]

A scourge it certainly was, yet it produced from these men some incredible acts of heroism, examples of rising above themselves for their cause or their fellow soldiers. Despite its being the most dangerous post in the line, men would vie with one another to carry the regimental banners into the fight, and as soon as one color-bearer fell, another rushed to take his place. In some regiments, as many as a dozen or more men would fall carrying the colors in a single battle. When an officer called for volunteers for a dangerous task, he seldom was wanting for men to do it. At the Second Battle of Bull Run, in 1862, several score Georgians went into the fight barefoot, even rushing headlong through briars and thorns, and leaving bloody footprints in their wake as they advanced to fight. So pronounced was the heroism of the men in blue and gray, that the Confederacy authorized a published Roll of Honor after every fight, to memorialize the names of the men who stood out for bravery. In the Union, Congress created the Medal of Honor, which would remain thereafter the nation's highest military award for valor.

Even in their death throes, the men could display magnificent courage and patriotism. "I can die contented," said an Iowa man after the Battle of Tupelo, Mississippi, in 1862. His abdomen was nearly ripped away by a Rebel shell, yet his only thought was for victory, and when told of the Union success he relaxed, expressed his happiness at the outcome, and died.[32]

"I see no reason to dread the future," wrote an Iowa soldier in January 1863, and both those who lived and those who faced their own death would have agreed with him. "If it is God's will that I find my grave," he wrote, "I hope to be ready."

Hundreds of thousands faced that possibility with the same equanimity. "Let it come when it may," he said, "I am determined to do my duty and come home honorably or never."[32] For all of them, whether they went home again or remained in the ground for which they fought, the men of North and South who looked into the face of battle and did not turn away, emerged from the fiery trial with honor unbounded.

REFERENCES

1 Wiley, *Billy Yank*, p.70.
2 Davis, *Bull Run*, p.157.
3 *Ibid.*
4 Wiley, *Johnny Reb*, p.28.
5 Wiley and Milhollen, *They Who Fought Here*, p.252.
6 Wiley, *Billy Yank*, p.69.
7 Wiley, *Johnny Reb*, p.29.
8 *Ibid.*
9 Wiley and Milhollen, *They Who Fought Here*, p.252.
10 Wiley, *Billy Yank*, p.71.
11 McHenry Howard, *Recollections of a Maryland Confederate Soldier* (Baltimore, 1914), p.37.
12 John H. Alexander, *Mosby's Men* (New York, 1907), pp.46-50.
13 O.R., Series I, Vol. 10, Part 2, p.389.
14 *Ibid*, Vol. 22, Part I, p.83.
15 *Ibid.*
16 John Beatty, *Memoirs of a Volunteer* (New York, 1946), pp.25-6.
17 Wiley, *Billy Yank*, p.68.
18 *Ibid.*, p.71.
19 John M. Schofield, *Forty-six Years in the Army* (New York, 1897), p.146.
20 Wiley, *Johnny Reb*, p.30.
21 Joseph Higginbotham Diary, July 21, 1861, University of Virginia Library, Charlottesville.
22 Wiley, *Johnny Reb*, pp.31-2.
23 *Ibid.*, p.30.
24 Theodore Gerrish, *Army Life* (Portland, Me., 1882), p.177.
25 Oliver Norton, *Army Letters, 1861-1865* (Chicago, 1903), pp.106-9.
26 Wiley, *Billy Yank*, p.84.
27 *Ibid.*
28 Gerrish, *Army Life*, p.177.
29 Wiley, *Johnny Reb*, p.71.
30 *Ibid.*, p.33.
31 S. Joseph Lewis, Jr., ed., "Letters of William Fisher Plane, C.S.A.," *Collections of the Georgia Historical Society*, XLVIII (1964), p.223.
32 Joseph Sweney, "Nursed a Wounded Brother," *Annals of Iowa*, XXXI (1952), p.142.

XIII

VICTORY & DEFEAT

T here is little that can be said that is good about any wars, except that inevitably they have to come to an end. Like all of the pestilences that afflict humankind, war cannot sustain itself indefinitely. And civil wars tend to consume themselves more rapidly than most others. The Civil War in America raged for 1,489 days, from the firing on Fort Sumter on April 12, 1861, to the last land engagement at Palmito Ranch, Texas, on May 12, 1865. During those forty-nine months of warfare, at least 10,455 shooting engagements of varying sizes took place, which meant that, on average, Blue met Gray somewhere on the continent seven times every day. Virginia was ravaged, one fifth of all engagements taking place in the Old Dominion. Not surprisingly, Tennessee ranked next, with almost 1,500 engagements within its troubled borders. Symbolic of the ferocity of the much-forgotten warfare west of the Mississippi, the state with the third greatest number of fights was Missouri. The conflict was truly continental in scope, with even California and the territory that would become New Mexico and Arizona totaling 163 engagements.[1]

Warfare on such a scale could not sustain itself forever. Indeed, as early as the summer of 1863, with the twin Union victories at Gettysburg and Vicksburg, leaving Lee with a shattered army and the Confederacy split in two by a Yankee-controlled Mississippi River, it was evident that only foreign intervention for the South, or a loss of will to win by the North, could prevent a Federal victory. Incredible resolve and sacrifice by Confederate soldiers and civilians prolonged the conflict perhaps as much as a full year longer than would have been thought possible.

When it came, it came almost all at once. On April 9, 1865, having forced Lee out of the defenses of Petersburg and Richmond and his tattered army out in the open, General Ulysses S. Grant speedily surrounded his old foe near Appomattox Court

House, Virginia. Hopelessly outnumbered, and with nowhere to escape, Lee had to capitulate. The once-mighty Army of Northern Virginia would fight no more. A few days later, on April 26, near Durham Station, North Carolina, the other major Confederate force in the east, the Army of Tennessee, surrendered to William T. Sherman. A week and a day later, General Richard Taylor surrendered remaining Rebel troops in Mississippi, Alabama, and part of Louisiana, and on May 26 the Army of the Trans-Mississippi gave up as well. All organized resistance had finally ceased.

For the winners, victory was a heady feeling, indeed. "We are through with our work," exulted Thomas Osborn with Sherman's army.[2] When the news of Lee's surrender reached the camps of the Army of the Potomac, a few men cheered, and at least one black regiment fired its rifles in the air in celebration. Yet most men met the news with quiet, and a surprising measure of compassion for the feelings of their defeated foes. There were no scenes of wild cheering, of endless salutes and volleys. The victors were simply glad that they had won, and more pleased that at last it was all over. "Never shall I forget the feeling that passed over my soul just before retiring," cavalryman Roger Hannaford of the 2nd Ohio wrote of April 9; "the knowledge that *now* we could go to bed & *feel sure* of enjoying a full night's rest." For the first time in four years he knew that he would not be aroused by an alarm in the night. "The thought that I was certain, yes, certain of having a quiet night, the idea of security, was ineffable."[3]

Other Federals expressed surprise at the absence of exultant feelings when the first news of the surrenders reached them. "I remember how we sat there and pitied and sympathized with these courageous Southern men who had fought for four long and dreary years all so stubbornly, so bravely and so well," wrote a New Hampshire volunteer, "and now, whipped, beaten, completely used up, were fully at our mercy – it was pitiful, sad, hard, and seemed to us altogether too bad."[4]

It was not so easy across the lines. No Americans had ever been defeated in a war. Worse, Southerners had always entertained a substantial martial tradition. Now they were beaten. It was almost more than some could bear. "I would like to go out in the woods and die drunk and bury all my sorrows," one Kentucky Rebel cried after Johnston's surrender to Sherman. "This was the blackest day of our lives," declared another. "All was lost and there seemed to be no hope for the future."[5] When Lee's men learned that he had surrendered them to Grant, some became highly emotional. "Blow, Gabriel! Blow!" one North Carolinian shouted as he threw his rifle. "My God, let him blow, I am ready to die." Some could not accept defeat as final. "We will go home, make three more crops, and try them again," one soldier suggested to his commander. "My God, that I should have lived to see this day!" a South Carolinian with Lee exclaimed. "I hoped I should die before this day!" A cavalryman shook his fist heavenward and cried, "If General Lee has had to surrender his Army, there is not a just God in Heaven!"[6]

After the first shock, though, most of these men's feelings subsided to match those of the overwhelming number of their comrades. A North Carolinian observed of the army that "a feeling of collapse, mental and physical, succeeded for some hours" after the first news of their surrender. Neither men nor officers spoke much. "They sat, or lay on the ground in reflective mood, overcome by a flood of sad recollections." When they did speak, it was to comfort one another with reassurances that "they had discharged their duty, and therefore that they bore no share of the national disgrace."[7]

Of those who could not face defeat, a few hundred simply melted into the countryside rather than face the inevitable formal surrender ceremony. A handful even committed suicide. But for most, the extent of final resistance came when they buried their flags or tore them to shreds rather than give them up, and not a few preferred bashing their rifles to bits against a tree to handing them over. They were too tired and hungry and saddened to do anything more overt. In fact, their former foes now fed them, hundreds of Yankee supply wagons coming into the Confederate camps with hardtack and bacon and beef.

A relief at war's end, even if it did come in defeat, also played its part in calming the Southerners. Before long, with the guns silent and the formal surrender ceremonies being planned by the officers, the enlisted Union men began crossing the lines of their own accord, renewing old friendships, inquiring about relatives who had served on the other side, and simply sharing their comradeship and delicacies with men whom, though beaten, they admired and respected the more. A Pennsylvanian at Appomattox strolled into the depressed camps of the former foe after the surrender had been signed and found that "as soon as I got among these boys I felt and was treated as well as if I had been among our own boys, and a person would of thought we were of the same Army and had been Fighting under the Same Flag."[8]

According to the terms worked out by the generals in command, each of the surrendered Confederate armies had to endure some form of formal ceremony, not so much as a humiliation – though many felt it so – as simply an organized means of turning over weapons and equipment and signing formal paroles not to take up arms again against the United States government. All were conducted with an eye to the dignity and feelings of the beaten Confederates. When the Kentucky "Orphan Brigade" marched into Washington, Georgia, to surrender on May 4, they rode down the main street with flags flying. "Steadily they marched, the very horses seeming to vie with the riders in keeping up the military to the last," wrote John Jackman of the 9th Kentucky. "The Spring breezes gently waved the banners – banners that bore the marks of the contest, and that had the names of many fields written upon their folds – and the evening's sunlight, on the eve of fading from the hills, danced and quivered upon the long trusty Enfields, thus smiling pleasantly upon one of the last scenes of Southern pageantry."[9]

At Appomattox, the ceremony came on April 12. The Confederates were to march out of their camps and up the road leading to the small courthouse town. They would pass between ranks of Federal soldiers and officers until they reached the appointed spot, where they were to stack arms and lay down their furled colors. The Second Corps led the mournful procession, at its head the old Stonewall Brigade, formed and first led by the mighty Stonewall Jackson. As the first Confederates approached General Joshua Chamberlain of Maine, who was designated to formally receive the surrender, he ordered a bugler to sound a call for the Federal troops to move their rifles to "carry arms," a salute to the passing Rebels. The Confederate commander, General John B. Gordon, responded in kind, the proud old Second Corps springing to carry arms in response to the compliment of their former foes. Chamberlain was deeply moved. "On our part not a sound of trumpet more, nor roll of drum; not a cheer nor word nor whisper of vain-glorying." Instead, he found "an awed silence rather, and breath-holding, as if it were the passing of the dead."[10] "It was a trying scene," wrote another Federal present. "And then, disarmed and colorless, they again broke into column and marched off, disappearing forever as soldiers of the Southern Confederacy." And for the past three days, here and there among the camps, regimental bands had already been heard playing "Auld Lang Syne."[11]

At the time of the surrenders in April and May of 1865, the Union Army had at least 1,034,000 men in uniform, spread from the Atlantic to the Pacific, and from the Gulf of Mexico to the Ohio River and beyond. Worse, units from any one state might be found in several armies hundreds of miles apart. Sherman's army alone had men from seventeen different states scattered throughout its corps. Consequently, an army could not simply return to its region as a unit and disband there. Instead, each army corps had to be broken regiment by regiment, and the men sent home in that fashion.

An even greater challenge faced the Union War Department. For potential pension purposes, Washington needed to be sure that it had a service record of each man. Then there was the matter of calculating and delivering to each man his final soldier pay up to his date of discharge. Republican leaders in Washington, looking to their political future, wanted to be certain that each soldier returned home with money in his pocket and no complaints on his lips.

The plan finally arrived at succeeded admirably, no doubt because it approached a complex task with an uncomplicated solution. Simply stated, it reversed the means by which men had been brought into the army, employing the very same apparatus. Without altering individual army organization, the men were to be gathered at rendezvous points where muster and pay rolls would be created. Then the same rail and shipping lines which had brought them to the war in the first place would be used to return the individual regiments to their home states, generally to the cities where the regiments had originally mustered. There the men would be given their final discharges and their last pay issue. The scheme allowed for a staged discharge, starting with new recruits, hospital patients, and men whose enlistments were due to expire by May 31, 1865. Even before the last Confederate forces had surrendered, the first of the recall orders had gone out summoning men home.[12]

The armies that had defeated Lee and Johnston were to come to Washington; the army that subdued Taylor would go to New Orleans, Vicksburg, or Mobile; Federals in Tennessee rendezvoused in Nashville, and so on. Soon the trains and boats and roads of the South teemed with tens of thousands of blue-clad soldiers on their way home. They went with joy at first, then uncertainty over what lay ahead of them, a sense of insecurity at leaving a way of life which many had known for four years, and then again with happiness as the full realization of peace came over them. It was a joy that lightened their steps, so much so that Sherman's army covered the 156 miles to Richmond in just five and a half days, a rate of twenty-eight miles a day, much better than they usually made on active campaign.

Once at the rendezvous, the men encountered once more the age-old army game of "hurry up and wait." It took time to print all the needed forms, and more time for a small army of clerks to make out all the necessary rolls. Some volunteers, unable to contain themselves any longer, simply tried to skip all the formality and go home. As a result, that summer prisons in Washington and Richmond were full of men who could not wait and had to be brought back. To keep the men occupied, drills and reviews continued, none so impressive as the Grand Review in Washington, when on May 23 the Army of the Potomac passed in review down Pennsylvania Avenue, and the next day Sherman's veterans did the same. This done, on May 29 the first regiments from the two armies embarked at the Capital's railroad station for the journey home. It took forty days before the last of the two armies was on its way.

The entire transportation system of the North was pressed into service to get the men home, and it demonstrated what an impressive rail and river communications network America had, much of it stimulated originally by the needs of the war. Major cities like New York and Cincinnati were primary destinations, from which troops for individual states in the region were embarked. Once in their home states, the regiments were broken into companies and returned to their original mustering-in locations. Once there, as the companies assembled the men experienced touching scenes of reunion with old friends not seen for years. Brothers were reunited, families rejoined, and all amid the familiar scenes of boyhood.

The last day of service was bitter-sweet: parting from the friends made in the maelstrom of war, going off to home a civilian once more. The War Department purposely withheld final pay until this last day, and in all more than $270,000,000 was disbursed to the 800,000 soldiers mustered out by November 15, 1865. By February 1866 another 150,000 men were sent home, leaving the United States Army reduced to fewer than 80,000 men scattered among a number of garrisons in the South and far west.[13]

How different it was for their one-time foes. Once a Confederate soldier turned in his weapons and signed his parole, he was no one's responsibility. He had no government of his own any longer, and the government to which he had surrendered certainly felt no obligation to help him out. There would be no issue of pay, no provision of transportation home. Generous victors like Grant and Sherman did open their commissaries to the beaten Rebels, and men who claimed to own horses in Confederate batteries and cavalry outfits were allowed to keep the animals. But when or how a Confederate soldier returned home again was exclusively his own concern. In Johnston's army, men who lived west of the Mississippi were given water transportation to New Orleans or Galveston, but all the rest had to rely upon their feet to get them home. Within a few weeks, the roads of the South were crammed with former Confederates moving singly and in groups, walking and working their way home, passing through a land which had strained to the breaking point to support them during the war, and which was in no better condition to sustain them on this last march. A correspondent for the New York *Tribune* wrote with dismay of the scene he found "by seeing these poor homesick boys and exhausted men wandering about in threadbare uniforms, with scanty outfit of slender haversack and blanket roll hung over their shoulders, seeking the nearest route home; they have a care-worn and anxious look, a played-out manner."[14]

Their journey was made the worse by having to pass through a ravaged South whose every mile reinforced again and again the depth of their defeat. Reaching home could be even worse, as men found homesteads either destroyed by the armies, or else run down from neglect. Cities lay in ruins, whole forests were cut down, the transportation system – such as it had been – was destroyed. Ironically, those who were the poorest at the outset fared best, for the simple man's home and meager crop land rarely caught the eye of Federal raiders or Confederate renegades. For both high-born and low, there was little to come back to but a scramble to get in a crop, find a job if possible, and start rebuilding.

For some this was too much to face. Indeed, several thousand Confederates simply melted into the darkness the night before their surrender. At first they intended to band together and continue the war as guerrillas, but most soon abandoned that plan as clearly impractical. Others, too proud to concede defeat, headed toward the Rio Grande where they joined with a few generals who led their commands across the river into Mexico. Perhaps as many as 5,000 ex-Confederates crossed the border, offering their services to both sides involved in the civil war going on there, and settling down to start small colonies. Others went even farther, to Central and South America, to Europe and England and the Far East, to Canada, and a few even to the Orient. In all, about 10,000 Southerners took part in what became the largest expatriation movement in American history. Most eventually returned within a few years, disillusioned with their new homes, and longing for their old ones.

Because of the continued resistance in some backward areas, especially Texas and Missouri, Washington did not declare an official termination of the "insurrection" until August 20, 1866. Scores of small bands of ex-Confederates, mingled with renegade Federals, and men who had never worn any uniform, operated simply as outlaws. Many were hunted down, and more simply disbanded, some to make careers putting the "wild" in the so-called Wild West.

Confederate leaders like Lee counseled all who asked, to accept the verdict of the war, go home, and start building the South anew. From the first, too, these leaders tried to instill in the men who had followed them a strong sense of pride in what they had done, what they had stood and fought, and died, for. That their cause failed somehow only more ennobled their sacrifice, with the result that it was a rare Confederate indeed who held his head low in later years. Defeat did not mean dishonor, and with that soldier wit which even the hardest of circumstances could not dampen, some former Rebels even took to denying that they were in fact defeated at all. "We just wore ourselves out whipping the Yanks," they japed. For many, humor was all they had with which to face a hard future.

For all of the Johnny Rebs and Billy Yanks who went home after the end of the war, there lay ahead a new life unlike that known by their forefathers, and which would not have come about had it not been for the war. The conflict had made the United States a power on the world stage, and for the first time even simple farmboys became in some degree aware of the interrelationship of nations, since every one of them came to know that foreign intervention in their war was a theoretical possibility. They knew that just across their border France was adventuring in Mexico, and many regiments that might otherwise have gone to the Grand Review in Washington were instead rushed to the Mexican border to prepare to meet the Emperor Maximilian's French forces if need be.

More immediately apparent to the men who served was what they had seen and learned of their own country. Boys who ordinarily might never have set foot outside their home counties had seen more than "the elephant" or the "monkey show," as they called the war. They had seen America, some traveling thousands of miles, exploring cities undreamed of in their youth, and others literally saw the world aboard ships that called at every major foreign port. Moreover, these men had seen deeper within themselves than most men are called upon to delve, tested by trial and fire, and most were not found wanting. They were in a degree changed men, a generation who had paid with their blood and received in exchange a greater awareness, self-confidence, and assertion. For the next half-century, the course of the growing American nation, the conquest of the West by gun and rail and plow, and the beginnings of empire outside its borders, lay in the hands of this generation of battle-tested young men. And not just men who had worn the blue, either, for former Confederates as well took part. A host of them settled the new lands west of the Arkansas. Not a few donned the blue to serve in the United States Army out west. Some even fought in the war with Spain in 1898. They sat in Congress and legislatures, began industries and corporations, and in time came to stand side-by-side with their old foes – even in commemorating the war they had fought together.

Men of both sides formed veterans organizations, both to gather for fraternal reasons, and to lobby for pensions. Washington granted increasingly attractive benefits to Union veterans, including land grants in the western territories for many, and the

Grand Army of the Republic, as Union veterans styled their organization, became the most powerful political and social lobbying force of the era. Confederates, having no surviving government, could look only to their impoverished states for any sort of service pensions. A few were forthcoming from Virginia and other states, and in the end, ironically, Washington even began paying pensions to former Rebels and their widows. Where else in the world would a victorious government pay benefits to the men who had fought to disrupt it?

As the years went on, the aging veterans' ranks grew thinner and thinner. Still there were thousands of them able to attend the massive fiftieth anniversary reunion held in Gettysburg in 1913, and a few thousand still remained to come to Pennsylvania again in 1938 for a seventy-fifth anniversary. But from then on their numbers dwindled fast, and the last of them died in the 1950s, just as America prepared for the centennial of the war they had fought. All are gone now – but they are remembered for what they did. Rowdy, undisciplined, raucous, sentimental, anxious to share what they had as well as to steal from one another, incorrigible in camp and unconquerable in battle, they were Americans of their time.

To study and understand what it is that makes the American Civil War so distinctive among domestic conflicts, so gripping on the imagination not only of Americans, but also of the world, one must inevitably step down to the level of the common soldier and understand him. Indeed, the term is something of a misnomer, for Johnny Reb and Billy Yank were hardly "common." As a group they proved remarkable. "No encomium is too high, no honor too great for such a soldiery," declared Confederate General Braxton Bragg (a man roundly hated by most of the men to whom he paid tribute!). "In the absence of the instruction and discipline of old armies," he continued, "we have had in a great measure to trust to the individuality and self-reliance of the private soldier." Unable to hope for the glory reserved for officers, and with no other reward to look to, "he has, in the contest, justly judged that the cause was his own, and gone into it with a determination to conquer or die." Leaders would receive the credit for winning or losing in the short term, he declared, but "history will yet award the main honor where it is due – to the private soldier."[15]

None could argue. For the hundreds of thousands of the dead, however they gave their lives, they would be recalled with honor, as General William B. Bate wrote of the dead after the Battle of Chickamauga: "While the 'River of Death' shall float its sluggish current to the beautiful Tennessee, and the night wind chant its solemn dirges over their soldier graves, their names, enshrined in the hearts of their countrymen, will be held in grateful remembrance."[16] For the millions who lived, the task before them with the coming of peace was almost as daunting as the trial through which they had passed, yet they faced it with the same simple bravery that they displayed on ten thousand battlefields of the war.

Late in April 1865, after Lee's surrender, Union Brigadier General Robert McAllister and a friend took a walk along a country road leading to Farmville,

Virginia. Along the way they met a young Confederate resting beneath a tree. Barely nineteen, careworn, exhausted, malnourished, the Federals found him "very despondent." Yet he rose to talk with them and after a while joined them in their walk. In a few short minutes reserve grew into warmth, the boy forgot any animosity toward the former foe or pain at being defeated, and joined in free and lively discussion. Finally, when McAllister and his friend reached their camp, he found that the boy "seemed very reluctant to part with us." Yet part he must, for the Federals' road lay in one direction, and his, now solitary, path lay in another. Much lay ahead of them all.

"Well, sir, where are you going?" McAllister had asked him.

"Home, sir," the boy replied.

"Home."[17]

REFERENCES

1 E.B. Long, *Day by Day*, pp.718-19.
2 Richard Harwell and Philip Racine, eds., *The Fiery Trail* (Knoxville, 1896), p.217.
3 Stephen Starr, *The Union Cavalry in the Civil War* (Baton Rouge, 1981), II, p.488.
4 Bruce Catton, *A Stillness at Appomattox* (New York, 1953), p.380.
5 Davis, *Orphan Brigade*, p.251.
6 Freeman, *Lees' Lieutenants*, III, p.740.
7 *Ibid.*, III, pp.740-1.
8 Catton, *Stillness*, p.380.
9 Undated clipping in Jackman Diary, Library of Congress.
10 Joshua Chamberlain, *The Passing of the Armies* (New York, 1915), pp.260-1.
11 Ida Tarbell, "Disbanding the Confederate Army," *Civil War Times Illustrated*, VI (January 1968), p.10.
12 Ida Tarbell, "How the Union Army was Disbanded," *Civil War Times Illustrated*, VI (December 1967), pp.4-5.
13 *Ibid.*
14 Tarbell, "Disbanding the Confederate Army," p.14.
15 Wiley and Milhollen, *They Who Fought Here*, p.268.
16 *Ibid.*
17 James I. Robertson, Jr., ed., *The Civil War Letters of General Robert McAllister* (New Brunswick, N.J., 1965), p.614.

INDEX